THOMAS MANN
EROS AND LITERATURE

THOMAS MANN

EROS AND LITERATURE

ANTHONY HEILBUT

ALFRED A. KNOPF NEW YORK 1996

THIS IS A BORZOI BOOK
PUBLISHED BY ALFRED A. KNOPF, INC.

Copyright © 1995 by Anthony Heilbut

Library of Congress Cataloging-in-Publication Data
Heilbut, Anthony.
Thomas Mann : eros and literature / by Anthony Heilbut. — 1st ed.
p.   cm.
Includes bibliographical references and index.
ISBN 0-394-55633-X
1. Mann, Thomas, 1875–1955—Biography.
2. Novelists, German—20th century—Biography.   I. Title.
PT2625.A44Z54415   1995
833'.912—dc20
[B]   94-37034
CIP

Manufactured in the United States of America
First Edition

In no other poet in the world, perhaps, can we so well and rewardingly study the personal mystery of conception, the inward spur compelling production. . . . As we can see, it was a psychological spur, for it was always the personal and the intimate that made [him] produce.

THOMAS MANN, "Goethe's Career
As a Man of Letters," 1932

As it is, in three days I won't see the boy anymore, will forget his face. But not the experience of my heart. He will join that gallery about which no literary history will speak.

THOMAS MANN, *Diary*, July 11, 1950

CONTENTS

INTRODUCTION

S hortly after arriving in Hollywood, Bertolt Brecht wrote these words:

> Wherever I go, they ask me "Spell your name!"
> And oh that name was once considered great.

At that time the émigré writer known everywhere was Thomas Mann. He seemed to have achieved every kind of success. His novels were bestsellers, acclaimed by critics and academics alike, and he dined with the President: indeed, Roosevelt briefly considered naming him the head of postwar Germany. To disgruntled émigrés like Brecht, Mann had it all and deserved none of it.

Literary taste can be as ephemeral as fashion. While preparing this biography, I was astonished to find how low Mann's stock had fallen. During the 1960s, when I was in college, it was received wisdom that he ranked among the century's great authors. By the 1980s, however, it seemed that he had been dropped from the canon, at least among English and American readers. This was a turn he had predicted. "We don't see ourselves," he liked to say, and he depended on time and chance to fix his place in history.

But what accounted for so remarkable a change of fortune? Mann himself admitted that he belonged to no "school." While there never were disciples ready to defend his reputation, there were, right from the start, many who wished him ill. They despised him as the symbol of a blasted tradition. Brecht quipped that when "the Starched Collar" spoke, he felt the weight of German history looming, cathedral-like, above him. George

Grosz, excusing his erratic behavior, complained that artists were too quickly labeled: "One is either a Mephisto and a clown—or one is Thomas Mann."

Famous as the proud father of six prodigiously gifted children, Mann was also the impeccably groomed public man. When in his diaries he removes his shirt to sunbathe, the disrobing seems almost scandalous, as if Kaiser Wilhelm had been caught stripping. With his refined image and aggressively nonbohemian habits, he appeared unreachable, an onerous parent, the Establishment figure German writers loved to hate.

Americans were often friendlier. But for opposing political reasons they abandoned him as well. In the late 1930s, *Time* and *Life* welcomed to this country "the greatest living author." By the early 1950s, they regarded him as a left-wing patsy; both magazines described his behavior as "The Way of the Dupe."

He may not have been well served by his translator. H. T. Lowe-Porter had the thankless task of making readable English of a highly stylized German, dense with literary and historical allusions. In recent years her gaffes have been well documented, and superior translations have begun to appear. But the failure is not hers alone. Young Germans frequently complain about reading Mann in the original; they too find the sentences oppressive and the vast design impenetrable.

Matters have changed, at least in Germany, since the publication of his diaries, the most recent appearing in October 1995. They enable us to see him more precisely as a great erotic writer, a man whose language was saturated by his sexuality. In 1918, he admitted to himself that "everything I have written expresses my inversion"; and he made no distinction between his fiction and essays, poetry and polemic. Liberated by his diaries, he becomes no longer the magisterial titan but a troubled, self-doubting artist attempting a spectacular form of literary transcendence.

Mann's family affairs were always problematic. His brother Heinrich was, for years, his rival, briefly outselling him and, to this day, promoted by left-wingers as the superior Mann. His relations with his six children, each of them a writer, were similarly charged, further complicated by the fact that his three oldest children, two sons and a daughter, were homosexual. Their father could see them living out his own desires.

After *Death in Venice*, he became identified with the notion that sex and disease are coterminous. For his conservative admirers, he became a prophet of renunciation, advising men that the wages of love are death. But the diaries reveal the story to be less definitive, and that, while its hero Aschenbach dies, someone very much like him will be resurrected in each subsequent work of fiction. In an era cursed by AIDS, when millions of people must divert their desires for the body from the body, Mann's situation has become emblematic. We can read him now as someone almost overwhelmed by longing. His idea of love involves a psychological imbalance between a lover, consumed by passion, and the elusive object of his desires. There are no happy endings; the pursuit is all. Worship of beauty is its only reward; in his old age he seconded Michelangelo's lyric, "love has ravished me, beauty has me spellbound."

In the 1990s, Mann's political dilemmas have also acquired a frightening resonance. During World War I, his sibling rivalry with Heinrich turned into a displaced civil war over Germany's soul. At that time he was a conservative nationalist. (His views changed so radically that, within ten years, the Nazis had invented a new term for their enemies: *"die Thomas-männer,"* the Thomas Mannians.) But he lived in Munich where the Nazis arose, and he first attacked them in 1921 when they were still an incipient local nuisance. Together with his children Mann participated in several forms of political warfare, including cultural and sexual. Today when the issues of 1918, not to mention 1938, have revived, his battles seem ripped out of this morning's newspaper.

For years he suffered from the disdain of modernist critics. But now his literary ambitions appear most daring, precisely because they evade categorization. His artistry resides less in the ringing humanism that made him famous and that predictably also made him appear sententious and irrelevant; instead he can be seen as a literary adventurer, seeking to accommodate in literary form experience intractable to verbal expression, from irrational desires to the symptoms of physical illness and the shadow world of the occult.

He is the supreme observer of that nexus of cultural, political, and erotic response, the area where historical change is most vividly engaged. Only his acolyte Franz Kafka registered with comparable immediacy the terrors of modern life inflicted on those who stand on the margins of society, half bourgeois, half outlaw. One of his most revealing stories is called "The Hungry," a physical condition recalled in Kafka's "The Hunger Artist." Kafka's prose is more distilled and metaphorical. But with his voracious appetite for physical detail, Mann fills his books with cultural information. To paraphrase Goethe's remark about Schiller and himself, we should be glad to have two such boys.

This biography covers Mann's life and work up to his late fifties, the period succeeding *The Magic Mountain* when his success reached its zenith, crowned by a Nobel Prize, followed by the first years of exile.

A postscript covers his years in America and his final return to Europe.

Throughout, there are "fast forwards"—a cinematic term appropriate to so fervent a movie lover. These leaps draw attention to the diaries of his midseventies. For it was then, when he had the least to lose, that he proclaimed his desires, the enduring frustrations, and the pitifully few, but all the more cherished, moments of satisfaction.

The diaries show that fundamentally he never changed. In his late sixties he imagined a seventy-five-year-old Judah, Joseph's brother, lamenting that he remains sexually vulnerable. The narrator consoles the venerable lecher, "Slavery to desire . . . lasts to the last breath." As if predetermined, when Mann hit seventy-five he fell in love again and compared the paroxysms to adolescence: "In that respect, nothing has changed." And it lasted to the end, to his final work, a tribute to *Billy Budd* composed on a Dutch beach.

Mann hoped that his own story would evoke sympathy, illumination, and—this was crucial—amusement. "I only wish to entertain," he often declared, and he meant it. This greatly gifted, greatly wounded man put his feelings into Goethe's mouth, "If you don't have a sense of humor, I'm not the man for you."

This book was originally planned as a study of Mann's old age, following a line I had developed in *Exiled in Paradise: German Refugee Artists and Intellectuals in America from the 1930s to the Present.* As it became clear that the late Mann was still engaging the obsessions of his youth, the focus changed. Victoria Wilson, my editor, encouraged this development, and displayed a keen attention to questions of form and balance. Any excesses must be blamed on the author. William Koshland offered the advantage of his critical wisdom and unmatched experience. His close working relationships with both Mann and Alfred A. Knopf make him an invaluable witness. Elisabeth Mann Borgese gave me details about her family; and, better yet, a sense of their tone. Not surprisingly, it was the brisk, pitiless tone that survived emigration and, indeed, enabled it. I also learned from Fritz Landshoff, a veteran publisher who boasted of being Heinrich Mann's advocate and Klaus Mann's friend. It was a particular pleasure to interview Franz Westermeier, Mann's last muse, and his wife, Brigitte. Other émigrés who offered their views of Mann and his family included Christiane Zimmer, Lotte Jacobi, Douglas Sirk, Paul Falkenberg, Wieland Herzfelde, Helen Wolff, Hans Staudinger, Henry Pachter, Gertrude Urzidil, Hans Reissner, and Rabbi Joachim Prinz.

Several scholars of German literature assisted me. Richard Exner and

Frederick Lubich, who share my interest in Mann's sexual politics, and Shelley L. Frisch, the biographer of Erika Mann, were particularly helpful. Albrecht Betz clarified the nature of Mann's erotic sympathy with Goethe, and Michael Morley provided an elegant translation of the gay poem Brecht wrote under Mann's name. I also thank Frederic Kroll, a leading Klaus Mann scholar; Richard Plant, a much-published critic of German literature and Klaus Mann's former secretary; Volkmar Sander, who filled in details about the Low German novels Mann enjoyed; and Mark Anderson, who directed me to the Mannian homoeroticism in Kafka's diaries. I am grateful to the Thomas Mann Archives in Zurich (particular thanks to Yvonne Schmidlin), Harvard University, Yale University, Columbia University, and Goethe House for letting me use their libraries and research facilities. The New York Public Library was an invaluable resource.

I had two superb copy editors, Patrick Dillon, who brought to my attention some of the predictably Wagnerian puns in Mann, and Kevin Bourke. Special thanks to Lee Alan Buttala of Knopf.

Friends and relatives were crucial allies over the years. I received priceless guidance from Edwin Kennebeck, the close reader a writer dreams of. Stephan Stachorski, Margo Jefferson, Leonard Lopate, Richard Kaye, Vivian Gornick, Irma Commanday, Mordecai Bauman, Helen Merrill, Leslie Karsten, Philip Pochoda, Susan Lhota, and Donald Wesling all saw the book in various stages of composition. As someone whom Mann greatly admired, Marguerite Yourcenar provided a unique perspective. Her vision rounded the circle. I thank them all.

ANTHONY HEILBUT

I

A PRODIGAL SON
OF HIS CLASS

1

SENATOR MANN'S SON

Don't expect scholarly rigor from me, Thomas Mann wrote at fifty. His talent lay elsewhere, in "telling tales out of school." His pleasure was to find random events cohering in an orderly pattern, linked in an exquisite narrative design. Occasionally he accelerated the process. He was born June 6, 1875; his father recorded the time as 10:15 a.m. But in 1936, at a time when Mann was composing his great novel about Goethe, *The Beloved Returns*, he declared the hour was noon, and that "the planets were favorable." Goethe had stated that he was born at noon and that "the constellations were fortunate."

Mann placed great credence in numbers. He was born in the middle of a decade, and his life appeared to be a series of mediations, echoes, and cycles. He benefited from a family history that could be precisely measured. The Mann business was established in 1794; its hundredth anniversary coincided with his decision to abandon commerce for art. He finished his first masterpiece, *Buddenbrooks*, when he was twenty-five, and his second, *The Magic Mountain*, nearly twenty-five years later. Biographical parallels flashed before his eyes. A sister who had represented his "female self" became a morphine addict and committed suicide. A son who lived out his own homosexual desires resembled that sister and suffered her fate. Mann believed that his mother had died at seventy (he later learned that she was almost two years older); he expected to do the same, and in 1945 he nearly did so.

Five years later he observed that "the man whose life spans two epochs learns at first hand about the continuity and transitional character of history." He regarded this divided consciousness as a "cultural advantage." He could have added "psychological": events forced him to take political and historical matters personally.

He was born in the old Hanseatic city of Lübeck, four years after Bismarck created the modern German nation. Before 1803 there had been as many as three hundred sovereign states; and the sense of local identity endured as late as 1923, when Mann depicted Germany as inherently anarchic, with each metropolis virtually a discrete culture. Lübeck's history as a free city, facing outward to its neighbors and trading partners in the Netherlands, Denmark, Sweden, and the Baltic countries, resulted in an attitude both cosmopolitan and provincial. Not until 1937 did Lübeck become absorbed in Schleswig-Holstein. The city's spirit was practical and forthright. A kinder, gentler Calvinism obtained: the Royal Merchant motto, "Enjoy your business during the day, but do it so you can sleep well at night," was posted over the Manns' office doors.

The town itself provided continual images of transition. Physically, it was a city dependent on wilderness (lumber) and ocean (herring, salt) for its products. High-steepled churches and gingerbread mansions abutted the canals: the fabricated and the natural in fitful resolution. The port sections broadcast a "reeking air, compact of good living and a retail trade that embraced the four corners of the earth." The salt air mixed with the smells of coal and tar, and the "sharp tang" of "heaped-up stacks of colonial produce." A good breath of air had imperial pretensions. Its benign exports were saltwater taffy and marzipan.

The architecture was centuries old, medieval Gothic in tendency with Dutch and Italianate elements. Incorporated as a free imperial city in 1226, Lübeck built its city hall between the thirteenth and fifteenth centuries, and several grand churches in the fourteenth. To this day, the city gate is flanked by round, slate-gray towers, icons of insularity and protection. Its streets remain narrow and intimate. Behind the stately homes are large gardens: it is a famously comfortable place to live.

The town leaders comprised a merchant aristocracy, known as the *Bürgertum*, in sharp distinction to the bourgeoisie, who threatened to succeed them supposedly at the cost of all traditional standards. The older class represented productive forces of commerce and manufacture; the newer bourgeoisie were disposed to trade and journalism. While the *Bürgertum* were sturdy and accomplished, the new class was regarded as frivolous and second-rate. The *Bürgertum* incarnated sober Nordic authority; the bourgeoisie were arrivistes, a conspicuous portion of them Jewish. These distinctions were duly noted by Thomas Mann and his brother Heinrich. Their

Lübeck around 1870

father was a late representative of the *Bürgertum*, a social rank whose decline they both mourned in their early works.

Yet Thomas's attitude toward Lübeck was ambivalent. In his forties he wrote that the city was his "Faubourg Saint Germain," the public whose approval still concerned him most. How do things play in Lübeck? is the anxious query of his early letters. But he would also claim that nobody there understood him, that it was a benighted territory where nobody knew how to read. In 1931 he wrote in a public memoir, addressed to Heinrich, that despite its political evolution—by then the mayor was a Social Democrat; Communists worked in the harbor—he still discerned a whiff of Gothic horrors. In *Buddenbrooks* he describes the various eccentrics and madwomen parading through the city; and even in 1931 he could imagine a St. Vitus's dance conflagrating the streets.

Because his birthplace was a seaport, his local identity was always turned, at least partially, outward. As a young man, he wrote that Goethe's concept of "world literature" meant simply the French version—"What else is there?" He understood, as all Germans did, that they lacked the refinements of older cultures. At twenty he quoted the French belief that a German's idea of grace is a nosedive through a window. Yet he also honored the familiar German virtues of discipline and endurance. For him Lübeck's heritage exemplified a virile power that he identified with Dürer and Goethe, cultural heroes to match any Frenchman. Yet even their achievements had been incomplete. Dürer's graphic skills required an infusion of color; Goethe's magisterial posture lacked warmth. Both traveled abroad in order to satisfy personal and aesthetic needs; both wound up in Venice. Long before Mann's Aschenbach died there, German artists had recognized the south's allure as potentially fatal. To the boy Mann, strolling by the city's docks, that lure was as pungent as the aroma of tropical fruit and melting tar.

Thomas Mann claimed that he was blessed by chance to live when he did. While he often described himself as "belated," the last offspring of his class, the last of his generation to discover Nietzsche and Wagner, he was also immersed in beginnings. Four years before his birth, the German nation was virtually invented. In that year Jewish emancipation was sealed; two years earlier the word "homosexual" entered common usage. Mann witnessed and lived out the complicated and imbricated growth of consciousness of modern Germans, Jews, and homosexuals. His life can be read as an attempt to register all three in a prose grounded in a tradition that had once excluded them all.

As a boy Thomas explored the city streets: "It was old, and age is past as present, a past merely overlaid by the present," a palimpsest of impressions. He saw himself as the descendant of Lübeck's "noble pirates"—he relished the contradiction—and Nuremberg craftsmen. The civic-minded outlaw and the steadfast laborer became twinned in his imagination, although both would leave their homes to conquer the "world." Mann's past was synonymous with commerce—he admitted that he was raised in an atmosphere of "gilt-edged securities." More than gilt-edged: "Gold was actually in circulation. Those who have never fingered gold coins cannot possibly have known the golden age of the bourgeoisie."

His father, Thomas Johann Heinrich Mann (known as Heinrich), was a town leader. He was born at Mengstrasse 4, later known as "the Buddenbrook house," in 1840. As an adult, he assumed ownership of the Johann Siegmund Mann firm, a granary and shipping business dating back to the previous century. At its peak in 1879, the business dominated Lübeck, with warehouses spread over more than a hundred floors in thirty buildings; in 1883, Johann Siegmund Mann Corn Merchants and Transportation Agents bought a steamship. But T. J. H. Mann was disappointed in his relatives. His mother withdrew family funds to aid her brother; his niece married a crook; and neither of his sons showed interest in the business. The firm's decline occurred on his watch: "For some time it had not gone very well, and the hundred-year-old grain firm went into liquidation not long after his funeral, which in size and pomp surpassed anything that had been seen in Lübeck for many years." This discrepancy between apparent success and incipient failure preoccupied several generations of the Mann family.

Three of T. J. H. Mann's four siblings reached adulthood: Elisabeth, born in 1838; Olga, born in 1845; and Friedrich (Friedel), born in 1847. His role as family head came with a price; he would die at age fifty-one, while Elisabeth and Friedel both lived till they were seventy-eight (Olga died at forty-one). All four were beholden to a family tradition of self-display. Thomas Mann's second son, Golo, writes, "A whole series of members of the Mann family had the gift of playing a public role, but in the most varied guises or nuances." Golo imagines his grandfather's manner as resembling his uncle Heinrich's: aristocratic reticence and impenetrable decorum.

From this we can deduce that the senior Mann was neither lively nor outgoing. His photos show a stylish man with a perfectly sculpted goatee and mustache, more regular-featured than Thomas, who inherited his mother's close-set eyes. He considered himself advanced, worshiping Bismarck and the Kaiser, a sign that he had transferred his loyalties from the city to the nation. Yet he was doomed to preside over the expansion and precipitate decline of the family's trade. The melancholy that Thomas captures in *Buddenbrooks* suffused his father's household and would be played out for generations. Both of T. J. H. Mann's daughters would commit suicide, as would one of his nephews and two of his grandsons. Friedel, the family misfit, lives on in family documents as a fey curmudgeon, a source of harmless quips and gratuitous complaints. He became his nephew Heinrich's godfather and may have escorted him to his first brothels, when Heinrich was seventeen and Friedel forty-three.

Thomas Johann Heinrich Mann served as Lübeck's consul to the Netherlands in 1864 and later as senator. He was politically conservative; when sixty socialists were elected to the Reichstag, he wrote his eldest son, "God preserve the Kaiser and Bismarck." His attitude toward his employees was that of a benevolent parent. Thomas remembered his father's "dignity and common sense, his energy and industry, his personal and spiritual elegance, his social grace and humor, and the bonhomie with which he could talk to the common folk, who depended on him in a genuinely filial way."

In his memoir, Thomas elaborates—and deflates—his father's public image. The senator was "not a simple man, not strong, but rather nervous and sensitive." Thomas inherited the frazzled nerves and self-doubt, but also the sharp humor and lack of sentimentality. As he lay dying, "a relatively young man, of blood poisoning," the elder Mann had no tolerance for kitsch. While the minister intoned his pieties, the moribund barked out "Amen," as if to say, "Stop this nonsense, I'm a dead man."

Thomas Buddenbrook shares Senator Mann's problematical nature. He is the self-appointed custodian—and visible embodiment—of good manners and noble thoughts. He is also a man shaken by doubt, perpetually questioning his own integrity. At forty, Mann referred to Thomas Buddenbrook as "my father, my brother, my double." Thomas Johann Heinrich Mann might not have expected this assertion. His second son was a poor student: young Mann was convinced that his father saw him as a dreamer, vastly inferior to Heinrich.

Similarly, in *Buddenbrooks* the pathetic Hanno is the only witness to his father's anguish. Buddenbrook has no confidence whatsoever in his morbid son; but, as Mann brilliantly observed, nervous exceptions like Hanno are granted a precocious insight. Throughout his career, when he considers his forerunners, Mann focuses on their displays of emotional strain. Like young Hanno spying on his father, Mann trusts a sympathetic leap to reveal his literary ancestors.

On June 4, 1869, a twenty-nine-year-old Consul Mann married Julia da Silva Bruhns. She was his junior by eleven years, having been born on August 14, 1851, near Rio de Janeiro. The daughter of a Lübeck-born plantation owner and his Portuguese-Creole-Brazilian wife, Julia moved to Germany when she was seven, following her mother's premature death. She attended boarding school in Lübeck, where she was trained by a French-born hunchback, Thérèse Bousset, whose combination of formality and insight Mann immortalized as Sesemi Weichbrodt in *Buddenbrooks*. Chez Bousset, Julia acquired the traditional graces, as would her daughters. But in *Doctor Faustus*, where he thinly disguises the misfortunes of his mother and sisters, Mann says they were trained for a style that was already outmoded in Julia's youth. As a dramatic contrast, in the years Julia was learning to be a lady, Thomas's wife's grandmother Hedwig Dohm became known as Germany's leading feminist writer.

Julia's father, a famous flirt and ladies' man, would marry his brother's widow and proceed to dominate his daughter's imagination. He remained an active figure in her life, outliving her husband by a year and a half. As a young woman, she fell in love with a Latvian merchant. Her father objected, but after her widowhood she boasted that she continued to receive

Thomas Mann's father,
Thomas Johann Heinrich Mann,
known as Heinrich

Thomas Mann's mother, Julia,
née da Silva Bruhns

messages from Riga. Her marriage does not seem to have been a love match. In his sketches Heinrich depicts Julia as ramrod straight, with deep, emotive eyes and imposing cheekbones. He presents an imperious temperament in a steel-lined corset, with the unforgiving gaze of a nineteenth-century Joan Crawford.

But Heinrich's glances may have been invidious. Thomas was his mother's favorite. Where Golo found his grandfather in his uncle Heinrich, Klaus, Mann's oldest son, thought his father resembled his grandmother, particularly when she told her "didactic atrocities," moralistic fables she enacted with a darkened expression and a full array of melodramatic technique.

In his brief "Sketch of My Life," Mann described his mother as "a much admired beauty and extraordinarily musical." He diplomatically salutes the contribution of both parents: "When I ask myself the hereditary origin of my characteristics, I am fain to recall Goethe's famous little verse ["Den Originalen"] and say that I too have from my father 'des Lebens ernstes Führen' [most serious bearing], but from my mother, the 'Frohnatur' [joyous nature]—the sensuous, artistic side, and in the widest sense, the 'Lust zu fabulieren' [the desire to tell tales]." By 1929, the chutzpah of his comparison to Goethe had become habitual; like the earlier German, Mann claimed a sexual distribution of qualities: his father's application, his mother's verve and impulse to fable. With some coyness, he identified an androgynous temperament, doubly hallowed by genetics and Goethe's example.

Thomas believed that "I, her second child, was dearest to her heart." But Julia Mann had four other children: Heinrich (born 1871); two daughters, Julia, known as Lula (born 1877), and Carla (born 1881); and the late child, Victor, known as Vico (born 1890, a year before his father's death). She enjoyed reading aloud to her children, particularly the fairy tales of Hans Christian Andersen. In his last years Thomas would invoke Andersen's Steadfast Tin Soldier as the symbol of his life, an admission rich in sexual honesty. The best of sons denies himself but never quits his task.

He preferred his mother's music to her words. She played Chopin on the piano—sometimes accompanied by him on violin—and sang the lieder of Schubert and Schumann. Hers was a domestic temperament; these were the artistic graces of the parlor. She was also a modestly gifted writer, as evidenced by her memoir *Aus Dodos Kindheit* (*From Dodo's Childhood*) and the letters in which she laments family tragedies or echoes her husband's conservatism.

Among her children, Heinrich set the pace for his siblings. He was his father's favorite, the best scholar, clearly the most promising. He wrote the earliest plays and cast all the parts. By comparison, Thomas was the family dreamer; and while he claims that Vico grew into a perfectly splendid fellow, for all intents Heinrich was his only brother. Yet Heinrich may have been even more hermetic than Thomas. Katia Mann considered him the strangest person she ever met. While knowing him for fifty years— frequently nursing him and even cleaning his soiled underwear—she never addressed him by his first name. He also had a lisp (his niece Elisabeth Mann Borgese recalls his summons "Kommen Thee her, Elithabet"), which further hindered communication.

As girls, the daughters were pretty, well-trained acolytes of the Julia Mann–Thérèse Bousset charm school. But in his will Senator Mann warns that Lula, then only thirteen, needs to be "closely watched. Her passionate nature must be controlled." In the subsequent family politics Heinrich and Carla would be allied, bohemian rebels against the bourgeois siblings Thomas and Lula. Indeed, Thomas would refer to Lula as his "female self." As he recreates her in *Doctor Faustus*, she appears a caricature of Mann himself, torn between a self-imposed noblesse oblige and a hysterical eroticism.

The Mann children's games were theatrical ones. The boys were not good at sports; Klaus claims both were shunned by their schoolmates for this incompetence. Friendless or not, raised more by servants than by their parents, the four youngsters were bound together. A concern with representation came early, first in the politesse required of Senator Mann's children, but more so in the plays and stories about each other that they composed.

No matter how aloof the Manns appeared away from home, so conventionally proper and cultivated, their private theater careered from burlesque to melodrama. This was a family that could not keep secrets. The ease with which Christian and Thomas Buddenbrook torment each other suggests a tradition of richly vocalized exchanges, operatic arias with texts by Freud and scores by Wagner.

Thomas Mann's biological parents were Thomas and Julia, but since his instinct was always to generalize or mythicize his personal fate, he saw himself as the descendant of larger forces. This grandiose view was perhaps inevitable. Mythology surrounded him, was literally domesticated, from the statues hovering on the town bridge to the Olympians gamboling on the Manns' drawing-room wallpaper. A more concrete force was his physical environment. He was plainly a child of Lübeck, a city boy who would become a master of the urban imagination.

Yet, much as he was born not in the Buddenbrook house but in a suburban villa, Mann combined the city's kinesis with an oceanic indolence. His urban landscape expanded the city limits to include the nearby seaside community Travemünde. This was a place humid with possibilities where he whiled away vacation days, "wishing for nothing at all." Mann paints his summer dreams in northern colors, "subdued and luminous" beneath a "pastel sea and pallid sky." He loved equally the afternoons "by the steps of the bandstand" almost as much as the mornings spent idling on the beach. Either form of indolence, natural or manmade, was alluring.

A subdued landscape was the appropriate setting for a writer who admitted rather proudly that his temperament was circumspect. His disposition also reflected his city's verbal tone: "irony, mockery, pedantic thoroughness, absence of passion and grandiloquence." Among Germany's several urban idioms, Lübeck's is wrier and drier than Munich's, less biting and nihilistic than Berlin's.

Unlike Heinrich, Thomas was admittedly deficient in visual aptitude; when he sketched cartoon figures, they all tended to resemble himself. Instead he regarded atmosphere as an "acoustic" phenomenon, a matter of language. The lure of home was aural; "a writer's style is the sublimation of his father's dialect." Mann's Lübeck German incorporated Low German [Plattdeutsch] and he frequently gave his characters outlandish idiomatic names or had them break into dialect. He remembered his mother reading Plattdeutsch tales with a Creole accent. As an adult he would regale his children with imitations of Plattdeutsch or Yiddish patois, the filter being more a question of class than of accent.

Living so deeply in language, marking it as the very essence of home, is paradoxically a traditional preparation for exile. Much like his beloved Heinrich Heine, as an émigré Mann could utter in 1938, "Where I am is Germany," because the acoustic essence was geographically boundless. Consider the many places where he wrote the language, among them Lübeck, the city of his youth, and Munich, where he lived and suffered most fervently. Or, after 1933, Zurich, where twice an émigré—in the 1930s from Germany, in the 1950s from America—he composed novels of exile and alienation; and Los Angeles, where he concluded the story of Joseph, the wiliest émigré of them all, within driving distance of the movie studios. Each city informed his sense of idiom and tone; where once he employed Plattdeutsch and Bavarian dialect, he would later Germanize American slang.

But the idiom of a private country was also a patrimony he shared with other Germans. In the eighteenth and nineteenth centuries, when language and culture were all that united the German-speaking communities, nationalist writers like Fichte and Herder boasted that while other nations had a superficial understanding (*"Verstand"*), Germans alone could achieve *"Vernunft,"* a profound awareness of the implications and divagations of thought. Mann sometimes claimed that "I don't need to see anything," although his work can be overloaded with details and the beholding of male beauty was the one constant pleasure of his life. He meant that by delving inside himself, he could see it all. Such assurance might have been more difficult in another language, *"Innerlichkeit"* being a uniquely German concept.

Likewise, if Mann is a genius at disassembling icons of history and myth, it may be because German showed him the possibilities: he once told his brother-in-law that it was far subtler than English. Consider, as one of a dictionary full of examples, the word *Mitschuld*. It means "complicity," literally "with guilt," a shared failing much plainer in German than in the Latinate English. German vocabulary and grammar encourage forms of verbal play that reflected Mann's fiercely inquisitive and visceral temperament. He grew up to be a restless, thought-provoked stepchild of language.

As Lübeck marzipan evoked the Venetian cathedral, Mann's youth was saturated by foreign influences. From an early age he loved Russian ("Holy Russia") and Scandinavian writers; as an adult he embraced French literature. (For his siblings, the idiom of love was always French. Both sisters made florid declarations of passion in that language; while Heinrich would become the most Gallicized German writer of his time.) But the dominant cultural influence was English. In 1950 he recalled the previous generation's pursuit of safety. "Safety—that was the British watchword of the times. Indeed, bourgeois society and its liberalism were English to the core. The Continent rested in the shadow and under the protection of the British empire." If the young Mann lacked this political consciousness, he unwittingly endorsed British values as the ideology of his class.

Since the Germany of 1875 was so recent a nation, virtually every attribute was newly formed. Its motifs were romantic inventions, whether they involved medieval legend or socialist revolution. Newcomers in politics always honor the ascendant power. British culture specially appealed to northern Germans, like the citizens of Lübeck and Hamburg, with their comparative proximity to England. Similarly, German Jews, new leaders in the youthful nation, also regarded Great Britain as the arbiter of cultural standards. Mann's crush on the British extended to a (putative) flirtation with a young Englishwoman.

The greatest British influence on Mann was literary. In 1926, ostensibly commenting on Joseph Conrad, he wrote, "The grotesque is the genuine anti-bourgeois style; and however bourgeois Anglo-Saxondom may otherwise be or appear, it is a fact that in art the comic grotesque has always been its strong point." It is precisely the comic /grotesque that characterizes his own literary treatment of the bourgeoisie, anti-bourgeois with a vengeance, demolishing German pretense with English wit. But the comic / grotesque is also the familiar tone of Jewish humor, of the *Berliner Schnauze*, (smart-talking, "Berlin lip") and of sexual renegades. It is a tone German aesthetes regarded as journalistic, insufficiently high-minded, unworthy of a real artist. But this tone allowed Thomas Mann to get through a hard life. It enabled him to, in a favorite word, *durchzuhalten* (hold out).

Mann customarily parsed his childhood as unmitigated bliss: "My childhood was sheltered and happy. We five children, three boys and two girls, grew up in a spacious and dignified house built by my father, but we had a second home in the old family dwelling beside St. Mary's, where my paternal grandmother lived alone, and which today is shown to the curious as 'the Buddenbrook house.'" Two residences; vacations by the seashore; books and music; a heroic father and a glamorous mother—what could be missing?

Apparently a great deal. In 1950, after Heinrich's death, upon learning of the pornographic drawings stashed under his brother's bed, Mann wrote in his diary that sex had been a problem for "all of us." While outsiders mocked their coldness, they craved the simplest expressions of warmth. It is deeply sad to track the reigning despair from Thomas at twenty-five advising, "Little children, love one another," to Heinrich in his mid-fifties beseeching his readers (and himself), "Learn to be happy . . . help one another, don't be so aloof," to Klaus writing at fifteen, "I will be an outsider always and everywhere," and Golo writing in his seventies, "I wish I were happier."

(One time Thomas revealed a possible source of their dilemma. In 1935 he met an old friend who was disappointed by Mann's overly formal reception: "The stiffness and coolness with which I reacted made me think of Mama, who used to treat unwelcome demonstrations of love in the same way.")

Mann's two oldest sons shared his sexual preference, though both acted on it more happily than he did. His diaries make clear that his desires were primarily, if not exclusively, homosexual, despite his fifty-year marriage and the births of his six children. At seventy-five, in love again, he wrote, "That the adoration of 'godlike youths' surpasses that for everything feminine and arouses a desire comparable to *nothing* in the world is my axiom." His sexuality animates his fiction. Readers of Charles Dickens know that he is never so comfortable as when he observes a defenseless child. Similarly,

Mann is most imaginatively engaged when he can dramatize a problematic, sexually inflected relation between two men.

At least once, to be sure, he became infatuated with a girl. In 1945, while vacationing in the Catskill Mountains, he met an American teenager, Cynthia Sperry, who charmed him, perhaps because she was carrying a copy of *The Magic Mountain*. He records having a dream of her, more romantic than erotic, which he interprets as a sign of his advanced age. Even that dream, he concludes, was inspired not by her alone but as well by a handsome young man and a compelling, if unattractive, movie actor.

Though his love objects were often adolescent, he also eroticized older men. The great love of his seventy-sixth year was a nineteen-year-old waiter, Franz Westermeier, who, of course, had no idea of Mann's interest. Drawing on Michelangelo's imagery, Mann even allows Moses a sexual charisma in the figure of the Sistine Chapel's God, a spectacularly muscled embodiment of old age at its most potent. Throughout his life, Mann assumed he would be rejected. "Impossible," he wrote in his late seventies, "that any young man could love me." He had a point then, but his pessimism dated from adolescence.

When he was fourteen, Thomas fell in love with a classmate, Armin Martens. His feelings persisted for at least two years. In *Tonio Kröger* the infatuation is outgrown; after daringly depicting one boy's love for another, Mann dismisses it as a phase, something Tonio will not recall for years. In his autobiographical sketch, Mann downplayed Martens's significance: "In real life he took to drink and made a bad end in Africa." It sounds like a negligible schoolboy crush. The truth is that his first love superseded all later ones. When he was in his seventies, he could recall it as the most "delicate, blissfully painful" time of his life. "Something like this is not forgotten, even if seventy eventful years pass by."

Thanks to Mann's indefatigable biographer Peter de Mendelssohn, we now know that Armin was courting Lula, the older of Mann's two sisters.

In 1931, when asked to describe his first love, Mann replied briefly that all the details could be found in *Tonio Kröger*, wherein he recalls his infatuation with Armin, albeit without any reference to a female rival for the affections of the "Armin" character.

Like all well-bred children of their time, the Manns attended dancing class. Here Armin would dance with Julia while Thomas danced with Armin's sister, Ilse Martens. The dancing instructor was Rudolf Knoll, ballet master of the Hamburg theater. In *Tonio Kröger*, Mann depicts him as an effeminate martinet, the first of Mann's courtiers, lower-class men who show the upper classes how to perform their roles. For the precociously vigilant Thomas, dancing class was an excruciating experience. He was obliged to dance with Ilse and watch the one he desired, Armin, dance with his own sister. Meanwhile a screaming queen of an instructor embarrassed him doubly: first for his physical gaucherie, the mistakes that lead the fictional Herr Knaak to call Tonio "Miss Kröger," and then for his display of the mannerisms commonly associated with what the sexologist Magnus Hirschfeld would shortly call "the third sex."

Throughout his career Mann dramatizes the social constraints that inhibit an honest expression of desire. He specializes in failed lovers, but he always gives them a context. Tonio / Thomas's heart may bleed as he dances, but Mann gives us every surrounding detail: gas chandelier; the talc-covered floor and upholstered chairs; the grandiose, plushly hipped dancing instructor; and—surely not least—the bored piano accompanist, recruited from the local opera house. The young Thomas Mann saw it all, even if his eyes kept gazing, surreptitiously, at Armin.

Somehow Thomas made his feelings known to those around him. But Heinrich, already locked into an obsession with buxom women that accompanied him to his deathbed was unsympathetic. On November 21, 1890, he wrote a friend, Ludwig Ewers:

> Let my poor brother Tommy reach the age when he is unsupervised and has enough money to express his puberty. A real sleeping cure with a passionate, not yet overly experienced girl will cure him. But don't tell him that; ridicule the story. That will help. Don't make anything tragic of it. He wants me to convey my opinion through you. Give him that immortal word "Nonsense." That will suffice.

Relations between the two brothers were often tenuous. For a whole year, when Heinrich was fifteen and Thomas eleven, they shared a bedroom without speaking to each other. In later years they quarreled frequently. Invariably, Heinrich would portray Thomas as a self-obsessed hysteric. Thomas would reply that Heinrich was arbitrary and inhumane. During World War I, the sibling quarrel assumed a political cast.

The critic Hermann Kesten knew them well. He considered the late bloomer Thomas more complicated, vain, easily hurt—and also far more ambitious: "threatening in his innocence." This apparent conflict points to a salient quality of Thomas Mann. It is not the much-vaunted "irony" with all the chilly abstention that implies. Rather, one always finds in him a balance of ingenuous and disingenuous responses. The ingenuous Thomas is easily wounded; the disingenuous Mann avenges himself in art. His panoply of responses is more prodigious than dialectical; reconciling two forces would have been comparatively easy, and he liked to make things hard for himself.

Yet something very simple underlies the fraternal conflict. It was rooted in their different sexual natures. Thomas's sensuality embraced his family; in his diaries he confesses a brief infatuation with his adolescent son Klaus. There are no recorded confidences about Heinrich; their enmity may have precluded sexual feelings. But it may signify that Thomas used Heinrich's episodes with actresses as the basis for an early story, "Fallen," that betrayed his inadequacy in matters heterosexual. Or, perhaps more telling, that in *Doctor Faustus* Mann used the same lodgings in Palestrina where he and Heinrich spent a hugely creative summer as the setting for a brief homosexual affair. (To further complicate matters, this episode was based on Thomas's passionate friendship with another man.) Given his appetency, it seems psychologically inevitable that sexuality would color his competition with Heinrich. In Palestrina he reportedly first saw the diabolical, red-bearded fellow who recurs in his work as an icon of death-in-life. Later he would call this aging roué "my brother."

In 1906, Heinrich published a story, "Abdication," about adolescent homosexuality in a boarding school. The hero, Felix, is a pubescent Superman brought low by an overweight ephebe, ignominiously named Hans Butt. Later Thomas realized that Felix's roiling sadomasochism was possibly a joke, made at his expense. But his initial response was to declare "Abdication" the best thing Heinrich had done. "I almost feel as if it were by me" . . . i.e., *about* me—this a good year after his marriage to Katia Pringsheim.

Three decades later, in a much gentler though equally recondite manner, Heinrich expressed his sympathy for Thomas's form of love. In his masterpiece, the two-part novel about Henri IV of France, Heinrich depicts his hero in his youth as the last unabashedly heterosexual courtier during the reign of a gay dauphin. The ruler summons Henri and in an outburst of self-hatred wishes he were free of homosexual desires. Henri will not hear the dauphin's apology. Having been stupefied by love, he envies a massive area of response forever inaccessible to him. If this seems a spectacularly orotund way of gesturing fraternal awareness, it should be noted that by 1936, the Mann brothers had made public ceremonies out of birthday greetings, and that the "Du" in their utterances was more like a "Sie." No kinder or more literary way existed for Heinrich to tell his brother that love cannot be dismissed as "nonsense."

2

A PRINCE IN DISGUISE

Thomas Mann was a city boy of a particular type. His youngsters are no good at games; they are not Huck Finns or Lord Fauntleroys but little Lord Percys, those intense, piano-playing children whom other boys despise. An American neoconservative has written that he finds something "humanly deficient" in people who do not love sports. Mann would throw this "deficiency" back at him. His worst early memories were of a gym class—the bullying instructor and the overall stench and filth. At twenty he railed against the mindless obsession with gymnastics that had swept Munich. Thirty years later he ridiculed the Nazis' infatuation with athletes. In all three instances, his fears were prophetic. The classroom bullies would hound him out of Germany.

Gym class was the worst, pedantry crossed with sadism. He never forgot the "distressing gymnastics in dreary *Turnhallen*, using gear that dated back to the days of Father Jahn and the program of hardening youth for the war against Napoleon." Johann Carl Schramm, the instructor, cut a ludicrous figure, his sleeves rolled up though his shirt and collar were starched. Sweating in his carapace, he became an image of the insane excesses of physical training, Junker-style. While Schramm barked out his drills, Thomas could only suffer the bullies, play-act, and dream of another student, Willri Timpe.

At twenty he wrote, "How I hate 'healthy' men." Physical life, as he understood it, is defined by Baldassare Castiglione in *The Courtier*, "studied elegance and effortless grace." The courtier's grace is calculated and unnatural, his manner not a reflex. "Studied elegance" characterizes Mann's courtiers Joseph and Felix Krull. Their physical charm is learned behavior, the product of applied research and long hours of rehearsal. Charm carries these boys far, from ghetto and demimonde into the hearts of the aristocracy. (It also lands them both in jail.) Elsewhere in his stories Mann allows a similar ambition to a dancing-school instructor and a chauffeur bent on breaking into the movies. They all await their close-ups, their chance to say—as the dancing instructor puts it—"Je me représente."

I

In his essay "The Beautiful Room," Mann describes his need for creature comforts. Nature is cruel, he argues, and the well-furnished room provides a necessary refuge. The house he lived in until 1883 was a three-story affair exhibiting a classic, neo-French decorum. The house at Beckergrube 52, built between 1881 and 1883, situated directly opposite the Marienkirche (St. Mary's Church), was much grander. It also had three stories, but was nearly twice as wide, with contrasting friezes on each level. (Pediments were applied above the top floor, surmounted first by a bulky cornice, and then by an iron grill that linked finials in a delicate pattern.) The intended effect was of palatial confidence, a moment in architectural history reflecting politics more than aesthetics. The home was sold in 1891, after Senator Mann's death. For the next several years, Thomas lived in a series of flats, content with a few rooms, albeit ones he made "beautiful."

As an adult, he recalled the pleasure of "small boys in a dignifiedly provincial corner of the Fatherland . . . making fun of that dignified corner . . . the freedom, irreality, purity of living, the absolute bohemianism of youth." This irreverence was a function of class, vouchsafed only to the offspring of high society. It was not a bohemianism of the streets, much less of any clique. Instead it was a private abandon, manifest in the theatrical games played at Beckergrube 52 and during the Travemünde vacations. As such, it anticipated the "highly dubious" satisfactions of Mann's career.

Within the area he mapped out for himself—to be a bourgeois was to be both "ascetic" and "a lover of luxury"—Mann was a lifetime hedonist. During his exile, he often noted in his diary when his lodgings didn't meet his usual "standard." To be sure, he was accustomed to comfort. But a more telling explanation occurs in *Tonio Kröger* when he observes that the ambivalent should live very well, cosseted in their neurasthenia. He took a "childlike" pleasure in jewelry, sketched in detail perfectly delightful meals, traveled well and publicly. He was also a chronic smoker.

Beckergrube 52, Thomas Mann's home from 1883 to 1891

Yet, typically, while his juvenilia includes druglike reveries induced by tobacco, he was horrified by Aldous Huxley's advertisements for psychedelia; these endorsements violated the compact between author and reader. In truth, Mann is that rare figure, a man lamenting the loss of Yeats's ceremony of innocence, but from the left. One lives well as a reward for hard work and as a reminder of one's duties. He condemned vulgar display—decorum was obligatory. During World War I, he cited the way his father was honored by his employees as evidence that if the burghers were elitists, they were never snobs.

The adult Mann lived to work. He confessed that "I really feel like myself and know something about myself only when I am doing something; the intervals are gruesome." No doubt many overachievers keep busy because they fear the temptations of inertia: like dieters shunning a feast, they don't trust themselves to abstain. But Mann found hidden charms in indolence. When he was thirty-three, he published a short sketch, "Sleep, Sweet Sleep." It is easily his most sensuous essay, far more visceral—despite its encomiums of quietude—than anything in *Royal Highness*, the novel about his marriage published the same year.

In the essay, Mann reveals that he is a passionate sleeper. Unlike Proust in the first pages of his great novel, Mann claims that he is a stranger to insomnia (matters changed later, particularly in exile). Having it both ways, Mann possesses the world even as he loses it; he remembers every bed he has slept in. He recalls "loving sleep when I still had nothing to forget." No longer so fortunate, he is restored by simple means—language, humor, the chance to rest.

Sleep is for him the most poignant of human facts. Mann echoes this almost biblical notion when he has Joseph console an insomniac with the gentle distinction between "you must sleep" and "you shall sleep." Sleep dissolves the juggernaut of "egoistic concentration, the will to form, to limit, to shape, to embody." What sleep overpowers is "cold, calculated resolve." That is precisely the posture his enemies associate with Mann. But he prefers a morality of "abandonment, devotion, surrender and error," all wondrously realized in the fact that after men work, they sleep.

Yet he knows that this agreeable cycle is not quite natural for him. Sleep prepares him for dissolution, death. He discloses a "highly inartistic inclination toward Eternity, expressing itself in a disinclination toward structure and standards."

His erotic bliss is actually suspended animation, an aria performed solo. With the psychic logic of a syllogism, he concludes by declaring that he loves *Tristan and Isolde* above all works of art because of its "yearning after the holy night." The lullaby of this sweet sleeper is a *Liebestod*.

Mann also evoked his earliest satisfactions in the essay "Children's Games." Like a true little burgher, he took pleasure in his accumulated goods. He kept a toy delicatessen complete with its own sales table and scale, its drawers crammed with merchandise. These mundane objects acquired mythic significance. While other German boys read the Wild West epics of Karl May, he fantasized about Achilles and Hermes. Garbed as Helion, he wore a golden crown; disguised as Achilles, he carried his sister about, "whether she wanted it or not," then threw her "clumsily" three times from the walls of Ilion.

Heinrich directed his siblings in various dramas, performed in a doll theater. Early photos show Thomas dressed as a hussar; and he owned a toy horse, on which he masqueraded as a knight. (As a small boy, he had instructed his baby nurse to tell everyone she was taking the Kaiser for a stroll.) He was most drawn to his horse out of a sympathy with the creature's hair, muzzle, and hooves. A sensuous identity was paramount. Acting became the measure of his development. "With joy" he anticipated the time when his voice would change and his bass-baritone perform "at the service of music drama." Heinrich quickly disabused him of his fancy: the doll theater was reserved for sopranos.

The young Mann didn't need stage "machinery." He learned to rely on his "imaginative independence." Heinrich could no longer assign his images. One morning he walked through the town pretending to be the eighteen-year-old Prince Karl. His novel about court life, *Royal Highness*, makes clear that the prince's role is "to be seen." But Thomas Mann as Prince Karl was not truly seen by a soul.

This charming sketch does more than entertain. It is another discreet admission that his representative posture is studied, artificial, not to be trusted. While observing his father's febrile impersonations of a public figure, the young Mann conceived for an audience of one a regal fantasy. From his youth, he was manipulating his identity for both public approval and private amusement.

His schoolmates at the Katharineum Gymnasium weren't tipped off. Striving not to appear arrogant, Mann claims that his figures were not exclusively regal, though he kept that fantasy going well into his thirties. He wooed the plebs with other devices: "I knew a thousand little play-acting tricks and had a quite superior use of language." The verbal facility strengthened the performance; he began to mimic his professors with their pompous delivery.

The four Mann children, LEFT TO RIGHT:
Lula, age four; Thomas (in Hussar's cap), age seven;
Heinrich, age eleven; and baby Carla, age one

How theatrical was he? The first letter we have, written on October 14, 1889, is addressed to his nurse, Frieda Hartenstein, who was fifteen years his senior. He salutes her "Dear Fried," and immediately comments on his own language, "(The old name for you)," a literary gesture more for his benefit than for hers. Displaying an adolescent penchant for self-promotion, he quotes an unremarkable phrase, "Still no news," from one of his dramas. The most telling detail is his reference to a "farewell scene at the railroad station. . . . Touching, wasn't it?" (Three months later he described Heinrich's departure as a "dramatically touching scene" and appended a message from Schiller.) In his earliest extant letter, Mann focuses on the roles people play and the impressions they make; to use his terms, how they are "seen and seem."

He concludes: "Write very soon to your friend, admirer and adorer, Th. Mann, Lyric-dramatic author." Even then he was play-acting, since the real object of his adoration was Armin Martens, who had inspired his first "lyric poetry." Clearly this boy knew how to deceive a public with showmanship.

He had also become a scholar of the affections. That can be inferred both from his recollections of Martens and from *Tonio Kröger*, in which he transforms the boy into a warm-hearted athlete, Hans Hansen. Already at fourteen, the story tells us, Mann was exquisitely attuned to each shift in his beloved's nature. Tonio/Thomas is a boy whose happiness depends on the evanescent—an involuntary smile, a chance brush of hands, a momentary indulgence of fellow-feeling.

While his teachers droned away, Mann would tease out the "implications" of his passion. In other words, a precocious intelligence was applied to self-interpretation, not Greek mythology or German poetry. Instead of learning military history, he became a strategist at placing himself in Armin's path after school. He was immune to Bismarckian chauvinism, having pledged himself to a more benign idol.

Mann decided that thinking about Armin was comparable to playing the violin or writing poetry. So, in a familiar progression, he barely attended to his studies, and used his infatuation as the source of his first poems. Although his novels were to demand intensive research, Mann initially conceived the act of writing as exclusively self-referential. He remembered that his classmates ridiculed his efforts; everyone knew that poetry was not a proper job. But, knowing himself improper, he wouldn't give it up. In his intermittent acceptance of bourgeois standards, and his affirmation of a desire that could be lived out only on the page, Thomas Mann had discovered at fourteen the themes of his career.

And why not? If musical or mathematical genius can assert itself in adolescence, why not the genius of a certain kind of lover? Everything Thomas Mann would understand or dramatize about love can be traced to his first infatuation.

II

Under the spell of their British mentors, bourgeois Germans reveled in a claustrophobic comfort. They imagined something magical, that their glittering prizes were protective weapons. If the culture's watchword was "safety," its citadel was the parlor. Even the deeply alienated Walter Benjamin loved snuggling up in his grandmother's overstuffed chairs, "the immemorial security of bourgeois furniture sealed off from death or change." Leaving these rooms was tantamount to a cultural rebellion; at seventy-five, Mann applauded the gypsies of his generation for their revolt against the parlor.

His youthful rebellion simply entailed his quitting the family home and walking the Lübeck streets, exchanging the homegrown myths for the fantastic display of city life. By virtue of his irrepressible urge to gaze adoringly, he became an observer of urban culture, for surely cruising— the transparent motivation for his *Spaziergang*—is an urban specialty. Benjamin's ideal *flâneur* strolls through the town with an aesthetic lack of purpose. But the Mannian figure remains focused when he dallies. Mann's eyes noticed the same elements—social configurations and male appearances—throughout his life. In a Zurich auditorium or along California's Muscle Beach, his stroll had an aim.

What the young Mann saw in the streets of Lübeck, or Munich, Venice, or Naples, was a crowd of actors. Everywhere he saw types—a half-mad crone, itinerant musicians, beggars, pimps, and prostitutes, as well as respectable burghers. But even these solid citizens were actors, performing their rituals on the stage of public opinion. (Heinrich eventually wrote that the actor had become the archetypal modern. Today, of course, everyone seems ready for the camera.) Self-display involved politics and economics; the most casual glance was historically vested.

Mann's theatrical tendencies were observed by an American scholar. Hermann Weigand had explicated *The Magic Mountain* shortly after its publication, as if it were already a landmark of world literature. But upon meeting its author, he exclaimed, "Herr Mann, you are [nothing but] an actor!" Mann didn't deny it.

While he cultivated a knack for "representation" in its specifically German sense, he was equally alert to the other kinds. He once claimed that as a city boy he was uninterested in landscape. But the reality of his glass-enclosed store goods is as vital as any naturalist's outdoors. He is wonderful on the new department stores with their seductive representations of the good life. Not merely is love for sale. The store windows also advertise youth, beauty, taste, and breeding.

From the children's plays, he had acquired a cultural historian's appreciation for theatrical games. As he moved outdoors, he extended this awareness to musical festivals and, later, political rallies. He was both anthropologist and psychologist. Without any theoretical underpinning, he figured out the cadences of symbolic exchange and commodity fetishism. He knew from within—"it's all mine"—the insidious lure of aesthetic and sexual bliss. He also knew that the price was higher than advertised. His tip to consumers, readers, *l'homme moyen sensuel* could be distilled as "caveat emptor."

III

Mann's revelations were always qualified, double-edged. The Berlin scribe Kurt Tucholsky said of those who patronized his town's cafés, "We say no to everything." Mann would amend that; he says "Yes/no, a bit more yes," but only a bit, and that provisionally. Nothing was permanent except the lingering, unsatisfied hungers of his youth. He might pose as a representative of tradition, but he was drawn—in spite of himself, often in *active* spite of his protean self—to marginal figures. The first outsiders he encountered were the Jews of Lübeck. After his father's death and his move to Munich, he confronted others.

Sixty years later, he remembered how a "gypsy spirit" swept through Munich. Its first manifestation was casual dress. But the word "gypsy" fitted uncomfortably in his soul. He felt threatened by "another kind of gypsydom, creative and literary, that had more to do with hashish and perfumed cigarettes than with health." When Tonio Kröger says, "After all, I am not a Gypsy in a green wagon," it means he is neither kind of gypsy, the relaxed ambler or the wasted bohemian.

Yet he remained obsessed with mavericks and pariahs. His types would include nomads, child prodigies, and confidence men. The most enduring image of the outsider was provided by Jews. Mann declared himself "a confirmed philo-Semite." As a "son of a mixed people . . . mixed himself," he celebrated the Jews' cosmopolitan nature. But he also saw that their chameleon quality was assigned them, a social coloration. They were everywhere perceived, everywhere misunderstood; princes of society one moment, laughingstocks the next. They were, in two words, like himself.*

Mann never exhibited religious tendencies; with Goethe and Nietzsche as his mentors, it was impossible to be "overly pious." Therefore, no religious compunction prevented his association with the few Jews in his school. But anti-Semitism was common. It came in many forms—racial, economic, and cultural. In 1885, Georg von Schönerer had proposed a bill restricting Jewish emigration to Austria, modeled on the United States Congress's exclusion of Chinese workers: at the time, Jews themselves were frequently depicted as "Oriental." They were prominent in the bourgeoisie; their mercantile skills were seen as fatal to the *Bürgertum*, Senator Mann's class.

Meanwhile, from Kant to Wagner, there came reiterations of a tired complaint: Jews were creatively deficient. They lacked imagination, they could only invent. They were without soul, a cold, legalistic, hyperrational tribe. Not all Germans agreed. Goethe argued that Jews and Germans were ineluctably paired; Germany's role would be to torment the Jews, and act like them—or, better yet, be *perceived* to act like them: conjoined as pariahs. Nietzsche despised anti-Semitism; he considered Jews the only truly European people, transcending borders, nationless, and consequently international.

Mann remembered very few school friends, but the two he mentions were both Jews. One, Carlebach, was a rabbi's son. Thomas was struck by his first name, Ephraim, "so unlike Hans or Jürgen"; similarly, he sought from his Jewish friends "an adventurous and hedonistic note; I saw it as a picturesque fact calculated to increase the colorfulness of the world." The other boy, Feher, was the son of a Hungarian tailor. Thomas enjoyed attending musicales at the Feher home; he describes an atmosphere of theatrical hijinks, "unofficial and quasi-gypsy." It was a happy alternative, perhaps, to the dramas Heinrich invented. A third, unnamed boy, the son of a Jewish butcher, was shown his first verses, and responded with an "understanding" he could have found "nowhere else in the school yard."

Mann also describes Carlebach as slightly unclean, Feher as ugly and cursed by a premature five o'clock shadow. He admits that social prejudice inhibited his inviting Feher home. Elsewhere he alludes to a Jewish house-

* He frequently observed that chameleonic talents had made the Jews "an enduring people." In 1943, after Leslie Howard's plane was shot down by the Nazis, Mann noted that this quintessential Englishman was the son of a Jewish family named Stainer. "His parents were probably the first to immigrate. But nobody could have been more English. . . . It is a peculiar phenomenon that national characteristics frequently find their truest, most convincing artistic manifestation . . . through the medium of a Jewish temperament."

hold's earthy aroma; but with his chronic ambivalence, he usually accompanies a compliment with a deflating adjective. Far more important is that he felt at ease in a Jewish environment, while he despised the conventional nationalism of his Bismarckian instructors.

Jews were both his earliest advocates and his most vicious critics. He displayed great disdain for some "Jew-boy scribblers," but given their attacks, Buddha might have trembled. These running feuds become insignificant when compared to the facts that he began attacking the Nazis in 1921, and that throughout the 1920s he insisted the only exponents of reason left in Germany were the Jews. In 1941 he was among the first to draw attention to the systematic extermination of the Jews, and in 1943 he condemned the administration of his beloved Roosevelt for abandoning European Jewry. (Much of his conflict with German émigrés like Brecht and Paul Tillich stemmed from his insistence that the Jewish question was primary.)

Like the Jews, Mann was called overly rational and without warmth. He frequently observed that artists revise and reinvent tradition, much as Jews do; and that imagination was a child's game, egocentric and socially disastrous. Mann's peculiar role would be that of a Wagnerian philo-Semite.

This is largely because the Jew exemplified a type Friedrich Schiller would consider reflective. He was the master of fabrication, skeptical about settling anywhere, urban, conventionally regarded as mental, not physical, artificial, not natural. In sum, he was a virtual twin of the sexually ambiguous characters in Thomas Mann's early stories. This perception hardly depended on Mann's slant; it was a popular conviction. As much as Christians, Jews themselves bought the idea that they were a rarefied group who could never acquire the virile strength of pure-blooded Germans.

The great exponent of this foolishness was Richard Wagner. Yet despite Wagner's anti-Semitism, many Jews became his champions, among them Thomas Mann's father-in-law, Alfred Pringsheim. Theodor Herzl's *The Jewish State* (1895) was inspired by the author's reaction to *Tannhäuser*. Herzl believed that cultural bliss of a Wagnerian order was forbidden Jews, a response compounded of self-hatred, infatuation, and political shrewdness: Mannian in its complexity. Some years after Herzl's book appeared, another Viennese Jew, Otto Weininger, wrote a work, *Sex and Character*, in which the harshest stereotypes were accepted. Yes, said Weininger, Jewish men are weak, effeminate, incapable alike of aesthetic refinement and brute power. Weininger was a homosexual who hated his sexuality, his Jewishness, his own "feminine" elements. (Isaac Babel's tributes to Cossack warriors, the vicious enemies of his fellow Jews, expresses a similar conflict.)

He hoped to transcend his self-loathing by converting to Catholicism and writing a misogynistic, homophobic, anti-Semitic book. It didn't save him. Instead he committed suicide at twenty-three. Amidst the notoriety, his work became a best-seller, particularly among Jews.

(The Jewish obsession with Nordic glamour proved very durable. Even Walther Rathenau, the immensely wealthy financier and Foreign Minister in the postwar Weimar government, was a fool for it, genuflecting before "this marvelous blond people of the North whose every migration becomes a conquest." This commingling of chauvinism and desire reached its apotheosis in Hollywood, when *shtetl* Jews made deities of pinup queens and all-American boys.)

In a Germany permeated with Wagnerian kitsch, the hero was glorified as Siegfried or Tristan, Greek gods with German accents. Nietzsche's dubious contribution was to posit a magnificent type, liberated from thinking: his blond beast was life personified.

Jews and homosexuals succumbed to a fantasy that excluded them. In Arthur Schnitzler's novel *The Road into the Open*, a young Gentile is praised by an admirer. "Well, yes, a handsome, slender, blond young man: Baron, German, Christian—what Jew could resist this magic? . . ." Mann shared the attraction. As someone "racially mixed myself," he stood with the Jews outside the arena where prowled the blond beasts whom they both feared and adored. He saw the dangers of "ethnic purity," but—again like the Jews—was too much a product of his time not to admire its beauties as well. Sharing so many of Mann's dilemmas, the Jews became his partners in ambivalence and his proxies in cultural outrage.

Mann recognized a verbal dimension to his marginal figures, a sign perhaps of their impotence. As he depicts them, Jews are virtuosos of language, whether they are the glib critics Alfred Kerr and Karl Kraus or the garrulous impresario Sol Fitelberg, who tries to save Mann's Doctor Faustus by "representing him to the world."

Not only Jews talked too much. Women and homosexuals shared the vice. Mann's women, frequently surrogates for himself—and therefore disguised homosexuals—can't keep their loves hidden. In particular, the woman he models on his sister Lula has a verbal "compulsion"; her feelings overwhelm her discretion. She *must* keep talking until she can state her love fully; her quixotic task is both doomed to failure and "soaked in a sensual bliss."

Meanwhile the boys and the "healthy men" are nonverbal. Tonio Kröger and Hans Castorp are chatterboxes, while the objects of their love, Hans Hansen and Joachim Ziemssen, are rugged types who prefer physical action

to pointless "talk." A familiar caricature presents Jews as verbally flamboyant, their effeminacy displayed in tone and gesture. As Thomas Mann depicts them, men obsessed with language exhibit the same traits. But he
often said that literature was both a Jewish act—springing from "the people
of the book"—and profoundly un-German. In his hands it also became
sexually suspect.

3

A SELECTIVE EDUCATION

I

For a world-class author, Thomas Mann liked to say, he was shamefully uneducated. He had been a poor student, twice failing to be promoted. When he graduated from the Gymnasium (high school) in 1894, a year late, it was with barely passing grades in all his subjects: his one "good" grade, in the area of conduct, was modified to "on the whole good" (more accurate than his professors may have realized). He was plainly not cut out for the academy; he told his uncle Friedel that he would be a "journalist, not a scholar."

He spent his life telling tales out of school, in part because he had hated the place. The anger persisted. When he was fifty, he wrote, "For something that happened in my youth I will never forgive myself." In religion class, the students were discussing the golden calf. A seminarian asked for the Egyptian bull's name. Mann, previously considered a dunce, astonished everyone by calling out "Hapi." Speaking aloud gave him a performer's high—"I felt drunk with knowledge." The teacher corrected him: "Wrong. You'd be better off knowing nothing than something wrong. Apis." Mann knew that "Hapi" was the Greco-Roman variant, but "I lacked the courage to defend my superior knowledge. . . . That the happiness of knowledge could be throttled by authority indicates the quiet servitude in which our generation was trapped." Out of such embarrassments a quietly rebellious spirit grew.

"I hated school . . . despised the milieu. . . . I criticized those in power with a literary opposition to their education methods." He loathed equally their emphasis on correct spelling and correct morals: the hollow abstractions of "duty, service, power, career, and Kant's categorical imperative."

Having received barely passing grades, Mann would specialize in defying categories and subverting standards.* At that time in Germany, literary art was entrusted to the lyric poet (*Dichter*) while everyone else, particularly novelists, were demoted to the rank of "writer" (*Schriftsteller*), as in "journalist." It was a distinction between a calling and a vocation, a mission and a job, an artist and a technician. Mann deplored the hierarchy, and he would eloquently defend the incomparable liberties afforded the novelist. He rejected all invidious definition. There was no such thing as Art, "only the artist." Much like Brecht—a writer he otherwise despised—he banished conventional morality from art. The salon-Marxist Brecht rejected "private property" as he blithely plagiarized other men's work. Similarly, Mann believed an artist could "appropriate" whatever he needed: "In art, there is no Sixth Commandment." Who made something up was insignificant. His interest was in aesthetic response, and that was always in flux.

Summing up his life in 1950, Mann declared, "I was never a member of any school or coteries that happened to be riding the crest of the wave—whether of the naturalists, the neo-romantics, the symbolists, the expressionists, the surrealists, or whatever their name. Hence I was never put forward by any school nor often praised by the literati. They saw a 'bourgeois' in me—and not without reason. . . ." He would live out Tonio Kröger's plight, a bourgeois to the left, but to the right a traitor.

At fifty, Mann returned for the seven hundredth jubilee of Lübeck. Meeting a former professor, "I told the white-haired emeritus that while I gave the impression of a good-for-nothing, I managed to profit anyhow." But his education, unlike Heinrich's, was largely self-made, arbitrary, and determined by whim. He was capable of extraordinarily sustained research—the encyclopedic curiosity he later granted Hans Castorp—but quickly as he learned, he forgot what he no longer needed (to the chagrin of scholars who expected a more systematic approach).

In his teens he discovered paperback reprints, and he would read them past curfew. Thus literature became a secret pleasure, discrete from his studies, the particular mode of his "silent refutation." Not surprisingly, when he graduated to his Big Three influences—Nietzsche, Wagner, and Schopenhauer—the stimulus for his appreciation was sexual. His first encounter with Schopenhauer was "essentially a metaphysical intoxication,

---

* When he finally began writing about Freud, he drew special pleasure from the fact that psychoanalysis was an affront to "academic psychology."

closely related to a late and violent outbreak of sexuality (I am speaking of my twentieth year) and its nature less philosophical than passionate and mystical." Other writers celebrate their first loves as if they could recapture in words the unique moment of deflorescence. Instead Mann confuses intellectual discovery with sexual awakening. An introduction to Schopenhauer was his rite of passage: "One only reads that way once in a lifetime." And when he was first exposed to Wagner: "I can safely say that the Stadttheater never gave shelter to a more receptive, entranced listener. . . ."

Already a newcomer, Mann discovered his mentors when they had fallen out of fashion. Cycles in taste turned as rapidly then as now; Heinrich Mann claims that young men of his age read Nietzsche as if he were addressing them personally. But Thomas kept his distance, and he praised Nietzsche as "the victor over self." He loved the language and "took nothing literally." This ambivalence "made my love for him a passion on two planes—gave it, in other words, its depth." He allowed that the blond beast, that sexual incarnation of Nietzsche's life force, "haunts my own youthful work." But his image was less fierce. He tamed the beast and makes the blondness and "lack of mind" adorable.

Nietzsche's Supermen didn't overpower him—or so he claimed—because he reduced them to "objects of that erotic irony . . . in which the mind . . . did not give away too much." (Forget that in the grip of passion, Mann's lovers give away everything.) Ultimately, after the Nazi misuse of Nietzsche, Mann would condemn his "lyricism" in praise of mindless "life" as a pathetic abandonment of reason. He spoke from the heart; only in their transgressions could he identify with professors.

In 1925, attempting to define his relation to the Lübeck tradition, he wrote that his ancestors' qualities could only be "recreated in another form . . . freer, more spiritualized, more symbolic and representative." Nothing would survive unchallenged. He quite literally made the "past" his "passionate present." The imaginative process allowed him to remake his heroes in his own image, thereby constructing an erotic community of saints. So much for scholarly decorum or respect for tradition. Telling tales out of school, he nearly burned down the schoolhouse.

II

The unhappy student found his refuge in art. Nietzsche helped popularize the word *sublimieren*, and seldom have the uses of sublimation been as prominent as in Mann's career. One solution was visual. His ingenuous celebration of male beauty has a poignance unavailable to more experienced

Thomas Mann at age thirteen, with Lula, LEFT; *Carla; and Heinrich,* RIGHT

gay writers. It remains a vision innocent and adolescent. In his forties he wrote that merely looking at young men satisfied him. In later years, he kept Ludwig von Hofmann's *The Spring*, a portrait of naked boys scampering out of a water hole, in his study; they became his Ganymedean muses.

Mann's taste in visual art was never advanced. He liked the great conventional painters of his youth—Arnold Böcklin, Franz von Lenbach, Hofmann. Even the later artists whom he admired, Max Liebermann or Frans Masereel, were figurative painters. (Masereel pioneered a form of pictorial novel later exploited by cartoonists like Art Spiegelman.) His temperament was so thoroughly voyeuristic that he expected art to be a series of snapshots.

New forms of representation attracted him. He liked the cartoons of *Simplicissimus*, the satirical magazine to which he contributed several pieces. Against Jugendstil's diaphanous swirls, Mann's preference for smirking lines and encapsulated anecdotes might seem the mark of a *Schriftsteller*, not a *Dichter*.

Very early he began to amass a collection of photos and illustrations that would provide pictorial inspiration for his fiction. One of the first was a painting of five children, four boys and a girl, in clown costumes. This was one of the earliest reprints to be mass-produced, a forecast of Mann's own adventures in display and distribution. He cut the image out of a magazine and pinned it to the wall, entranced perhaps by the similarity between Pierrette and her "equally pretty brothers." Many years later he met the model, Katia Pringsheim, and wedded her—the marriage of two forms of representation.

The photo file demonstrates his facility in transforming his enduring obsessions over era and pictorial genre. For instance, in the late 1940s, while plotting a life of Pope Gregory, Mann cut out a photo of an adolescent to serve as his model for the medieval pontiff.

Mann began his *Felix Krull* project in 1909, kept it going off and on into the 1920s, and resumed the work in the early 1950s. A glance at his photo collection reveals the level of attention he sustained for decades. In 1911, imagining a great lady of society, he selected a photo of Anna Pavlova, and forty years later his model of feminine temperament becomes Anna Magnani. Similarly, to evoke the pseudo-British tennis players whom Felix will encounter, Mann selected one young man in 1912, properly garbed in white ducks, grasping his racket high before him like a giant microphone. Over forty years later he cut out another image, that of the Australian Lewis Hoad, as he slams the ball from a kneeling position. But uniforms have changed; Hoad wears white shorts, and the position accen-

The four Pierrots and a Pierette: Katia Pringsheim and her four brothers in the portrait
CHILDREN'S CARNIVAL *by Friedrich August von Kaulbach. Mann remembered having seen*
the image when he was fourteen, but it was painted in 1892 when he was seventeen.

tuates his muscular legs. Three summers earlier, during the season of Franzl,
Mann had become visually enraptured with an Argentinian tennis player,
and his diary paid particular attention to the youth's thighs.

Mann's eye for male beauty made him an impassioned moviegoer. In
The Magic Mountain he described a heavily muscled extra in a silent movie.
Almost thirty years later, he was riveted by the sight of Marlon Brando's
naked chest, a rampant display of "sex appeal." (He also appreciated less
voluptuous types; elsewhere he comments on the more "passive" charms of
Gérard Philipe.)*

Mann's mode of aesthetic response was simultaneously sensual and utilitarian. This concentrated focus was extended to other forms. We know of
his great love for music. He played violin for several years in chamber
groups and by himself. His first violin instructor, Alexander von Fielitz,
was rumored to be courting Frau Mann. This may have invested the idea

---

* As late as March 1954, while strolling through a gallery of Renaissance art in Fiesole, he
delighted in the sculpture of Cellini's St. John and Verrochio's David, an aesthetic world devoid
of women, excepting an occasional madonna.

of music with an implicit licentiousness, a theme that resounds throughout his work, most notably when he writes of Wagner.

But Wagner, as Mann experienced him, was the supreme solipsist. While in an early novel of Heinrich Mann, a young couple spoon during the Venusberg scene of *Tannhäuser*, when Thomas's early hero Little Herr Friedemann attends a similar performance, he sits isolated in the audience, nursing his private fantasy.

As quickly as he responded to the movies, Mann became an early champion of the phonograph. In *The Magic Mountain* he describes its technical limitations; music on records is like a theatrical image seen through the wrong end of an opera glass. But he's not complaining: the artificial distortion renders both sound and image more amenable to his fancy. Thus when Hans Castorp selects a series of operatic arias, each one contains an erotic subtext—evident to him alone—and refers to his beloved, now dead cousin, Joachim. Castorp exhibits a vulgar, bourgeois affinity for snippets. Though most aficionados despise the abstracting of themes from their musical or dramatic context, Castorp's approach—and Mann's—is satisfied by Opera's Greatest Hits. Choose an aria or an image, not for the work's sake but for your own.

His great novels are all composed of a series of episodes. His prose becomes symphonic in its never-ending series of climaxes and cadenzas. In lengthy works he may promise closure hundreds of pages before the work peters out. When he does so he resembles an operatic tenor, expiring in lengthy paroxysms, rising from the dead for yet one more ringing high note. He understood as much. When he wrote, "As a composer, Wagner was a great novelist; as a novelist, he was a great composer," he offended patriotic Germans. But his intentions were apolitical; he merely saw in Wagner his twin, a powerfully driven, sensually thwarted personality, bending all aesthetic circumstances to his will.

Mann's powers of selection, arbitrary in the extreme, enabled him to impose the concept of mind over matter on various areas of experience. His adolescent Felix Krull wills himself sick, while Hans Castorp, a delayed adolescent, anticipates the theory of endorphins, the body's self-produced analgesics. The common denominator is a fierce desire that brooks no opposition.

Mann liked to say that certain writers, particularly Goethe and Tolstoy, were "comfortable in their own skin." Evidently he was not. A poor athlete, a timid lover, he appears to some readers the most aphysical of men. One unkind critic says that he "wrote about everything and experienced nothing." Yet what other novelist allows the imagination so many physical satisfactions? He can shock a reader with the numerous ways he makes art and music his playthings. He forces us to see the peremptory, world-consuming nature of literary composition.

III

If *Death in Venice* became notorious for its marriage of Eros and Thanatos, Mann's entire career consisted of yoking Eros and the word. As is usual, writing for him initially constituted a form of erotic expression. He confessed that his first poems were inspired by Armin Martens. Moreover, any excessive use of language signified an outsider's caprice. Healthy men enjoyed their bodies; from the sidelines invalids wrote poems.

At home, often while eating sandwiches, he read the giants of German poetry, thereby satisfying two hungers at one time. He invariably preferred writers who shared his erotic nature. Whether or not their experience was literally homosexual, he read it that way. He was not a proto-Foucaultian, arguing that sexuality is constantly being reformulated. Just as he assigned the face of a 1940s adolescent to a medieval pope, he made his ancestors conform to his understanding of erotic response.

In so doing he disproved the notion that literary influence invariably evokes an Oedipal anxiety.* Mann didn't compete with his ancestors so much as join them in a great unified act of erotic sympathy. This sympathy can be rendered most graphically. Goethe's monologue in *The Beloved Returns* begins with the poet awakening from an erotic dream, congratulating himself on so vigorous a display for a man his age. In his last years, Mann drew pleasure from the discovery that his idols from Hans Christian Andersen to Leo Tolstoy may have—no matter how temporarily—shared his desires. Writing about such men, he turned criticism into, as Oscar Wilde says, the most civilized form of autobiography: indeed, without knowing Wilde's definition, he assumed that good criticism had to be grounded in autobiography. "Criticism that is not confessional in character," he wrote in his thirties, "has no value."

The most audacious expression of this sympathy happened to be the last thing Mann wrote. In a 1955 tribute to *Billy Budd*, he scolded Herman Melville for comparing his villain to Iago. In fact, Mann contended, Melville was superior to Shakespeare, having created in "the beautiful Billy" a more pathetic figure than Desdemona.

---

* Occasionally he displays a competitive spirit, particularly in *Joseph and His Brothers*, when he contends with the Hebrew scribes and God himself: while in *The Tables of the Law*, Moses offers God a chance to *rewrite* the Ten Commandments.

Thomas Mann with Armin Martens, his first love, 1890. The distinction between the "racially mixed" Thomas and the all-German blond Armin is visible. Thomas Mann's affection for such boys would last a lifetime, inspiring the character Tonio Kröger (about whom he once said, having become infatuated with a Martens look-alike, "Tonio Kröger, Tonio Kröger. It's the same every time and the feeling deep"). If none of his beloveds were remarkably handsome, he had a witty explanation: "There were, and are, hosts of {their} like."

During World War I he became the arch-defender of German culture, thereby earning a reputation as fundamentally conservative, notwithstanding his later socialist declarations. Critics overlooked the fact that he viewed German culture as a long history of episodes, many of them homoerotic. Writing became the equivalent of Eros. He described a writer as "someone more sexual and intellectual than his neighbor." Extending the definition to suit his circumstances, he also termed homosexuality "the more intellectual form of love." (*Geistig*, the German word, suggests several meanings: "intellectual," "spiritual," "self-absorbed." All three apply in this context.)

In his late masterpieces, *Joseph and His Brothers* and *Doctor Faustus*, the elaborations grew even bolder. In *Faustus*, the "absolutely questionable" becomes a defining measure of art, as well as a relentless attack on social and sexual norms; its apparent opposite is a "saving irresponsibility." But "irresponsibility" in Mann's lexicon invokes the "useless" ("*nutzlos*") pleasures of homosexual sex and onanism. So the dialectic becomes a tautology. In *Joseph*, Mann characterizes his eponymous hero as "double-themed," the androgynous votary of disparate gods, as if his wisdom depends on being something more than heterosexual.

Politics lay behind these extravagant remarks. The German constitution of 1871 included paragraph 175, which criminalized homosexuality, a situation that Mann deplored on several occasions and that contributed to his view of the artist as morally ambiguous.

The love-struck adolescent sought out poets who addressed his condition. It helped that German poetry, for over a century, had been steeped in Greco-Roman antiquity, in Venice and the Mideast.

His first heroes were eccentric, besieged figures, men who did not have an easy time of it. They included Heinrich Heine, unsure whether to claim his legacy as German or as Jewish, the poet who once despaired that he came from a two-thousand-year line of schlemiels. Heine was both a political radical and an intellectual elitist, thumbing his nose at the German bourgeoisie (in particular his fellow Jews, whom he satirized for their nouveau-riche pretensions). He particularly appealed to adolescents trapped in the provinces; Thomas, in his early story "The Will to Happiness," admits to feeling a " 'pathos of distance' toward most of our fellow students, familiar to anyone who ever read Heine at fifteen. . . ." There was also Adalbert von Chamisso, a French émigré who celebrated a German-Yiddish version of the clumsy, shadowless schlemiel; and, foremost, Schiller, the "restless stepchild of life."

His favorite teacher was a Schiller specialist, Dr. Ludwig Bäthke. A rare liberal among the Bismarckian nationalists, Bäthke emphasized Schiller's artistry—Mann never forgot his words "This is not just anything you are reading, it's the best you could possibly read"—and his politics. He had his students memorize Schiller's verses alongside lyrics of the French Revolution. However, it would take Mann over thirty years before he could apply Bäthke's views of the politically engaged artist to his own career.

But Schiller's essay "On the Natural and the Reflective" (often translated as "On the Naïve and the Sentimental") influenced him at once. In it Schiller divides literature between natural talents like Goethe—untroubled geniuses who speak in effortless tongues—and overly conscious writers like himself, for whom art is a matter of blood and sweat. No German writer would leave a simple distinction alone. Schiller hints at numerous qualifications, and Mann discovered more. Sometimes his Naturals are feminized; but most often his Reflectives appear androgynous. From Nietzsche he derived a similar distinction between "mind" and "life," although "life" was very often a monstrous force requiring the intervention of the "mind."

Mann turned an intellectual debate into a story of unrequited love. As a youth he had more in common with Schiller, the rejected suitor. Tonio Kröger woos Hans Hansen with a plot summary of Schiller's *Don Carlos*, which he condenses to the plight of a lonely man seeking a loving friend. Mann later quoted a line from the play that "singer and prince both live on the heights of humanity," a notion that may have comforted him as he strolled alone, an incognito prince, through the streets of Lübeck.

His last great essay, composed in his eightieth year, was a study of Schiller, not Goethe. He celebrated Schiller's disappointed love for Goethe as "the greatest romance of the early nineteenth century," a love story told yet more circuitously than his own. In the original German version he underlines the sexual element in a passage omitted from Richard Winston's translation: Schiller, "who was so essentially masculine," was drawn to "that other poet, to whom he was inclined to attribute a feminine disposition." (*Echt* German, too, is this dizzying spin of the dialectic, rendering the studious, reflective, and desperately ill Schiller masculine, and Goethe, the archetypal "healthy man," feminine. Perhaps the only "healthy" men Thomas Mann didn't hate were those he desired . . . or those he feminized. In this case, the virile Schiller died at forty-six, while the womanish Goethe lived to be eighty-two . . . and left a corpse that was a physical marvel.)

Homoerotic tropes are inherent in any poetry drawn from the Greco-Roman legacy. But Mann would argue that the choice is not haphazard: he believed that August von Platen, for one, selected precisely the lyrical forms identified with his sexual preference. Nietzsche had similarly argued when he chastised Jakob Burckhardt for ignoring the central role homosexuality played in Greek culture: in "Morgenröte" he says, "No woman could claim a man's deepest love; men lived side by side with men," and proceeds to quote Goethe's praise of *"übergeschlechtiche Liebe,"* translatable as "platonic love."

As a youth Goethe wrote his mentor, Johann Gottfried von Herder, the leading theorist of preromanticism: "Be my Socrates. Let me be your Alcibiades"—flirtatious words given a mere five-year discrepancy between the two men. Friedrich Hölderlin, a hero of the generation succeeding Goethe and Herder, composed a poem about Socrates and Alcibiades. Mann cites it at least twice: first as a spur to political reform, and, much later, during his infatuation with the Bavarian waiter Franzl. Mann's use of Hölderlin has been questioned by two of his most affectionate critics, T. J. Reed and Erich Heller, but since romantic poets unabashedly yoked the national quest to emotional angst, his behavior was not unprecedented—more properly, it was a nineteenth-century gesture made well into the twentieth.

Goethe played no part in that movement: yet another reason why the young Mann did not fall at his feet. In later years similarities between them became conspicuous. Not merely their great range or stamina; as personalities they were similarly depicted. Both were represented as cold, aloof, beyond the reach of normal sexuality. When Goethe advised a friend that poetry is worth sacrificing—"What you lose as a poet, you will gain as a human being"—he sounded like an early Thomas Mann.

Among Goethe's favorite words were *Sehnsucht* (desire) and *Gestalt* (shape): a tension between Eros and form would equally characterize Mann's career. Similarly, Goethe was the proponent of *Haltung*, a rich term suggesting comportment, bearing, self-control. He envisioned the artist as a closed fist, strenuously withdrawn in the pursuit of his calling. While Mann later imagined the artist in precisely those terms, *Haltung* invariably commanded a terrible price.

The two attempted similar projects. Goethe wrote a youthful epic about Joseph, the subject of Mann's immense tetralogy. Both, amidst their many other achievements, kept returning to a single, evidently irresistible subject. Goethe began *Faust* as a youth and completed it in his old age. Mann began *The Confessions of Felix Krull* in his mid-thirties and completed it forty years later. But his Goethean ambition mocked itself. *Felix Krull* is a deliberate parody of Goethe, the world-grasping Faust demoted to the status of a middle-class hustler. Both writers had friends at court, but while Goethe mistrusted democracy, Mann worshiped an American president.

At the time, epic verse and political action were beyond the adolescent Mann, who thought small, and mostly of love. What he would have found in Goethe were stirring paeans to visual beauty, many of them addressed to boys. In his *Roman Elegies* he idealizes synesthesia: "I see with an eye that feels and feel with a hand that sees." In his lyric "April" he makes vision and speech coterminous: "Augen, sagt mir, sagt, was sagt ihr" (Eyes, tell me, tell, what do you tell). At times the visual transcends other communication. Gazing at Schiller's skull, Goethe discerns "a language written plain for me." In his collection *The West-Eastern Divan* he recreates a medieval Middle East where a poet serenades and is serenaded by his youthful cupbearer. At one point the older man says, "No wonder it enchants us, when eyes gaze boldly into eyes; it feels as if we had succumbed in reaching the presence of him who thought us." Perhaps the most astonishing prediction of Mann occurs when Goethe's youth thanks his mentor for showing him the cosmos, but adds, "Your love is dearest of all." Upon which the poet replies, "You have learned so young how an old man thinks."

This colloquy lifts us into the world of *Death in Venice*—although no such pleasing dialogue is heard there—and, indeed, Goethe composed some of his most electrifying poetry after visiting that city. His famous "Erl King" involves a darker encounter between age and youth: the king's fatal power over the sick child is based on sexual menace, symbolized by his *Kron und Schweif* (crown and tail). (I owe this interpretation to Emil Offenbacher.) Given the current understanding of Schubert's homosexuality, his musical adaptation of the poem constitutes another of Mann's freighted choices.

At times Mann read German history as one long queer epic—he alluded to Frederick the Great's homosexuality and depicted Bismarck as "hysterical and high-pitched." When considering literary history, he enjoyed couples, charging the marriage of true minds with a physical Eros. Thus Schiller's courtship of Goethe; or, likewise, his contention that Schopenhauer had found his aesthetic mate in Wagner. Nietzsche, by comparison, was still available.

In 1944 the American novelist Charles Jackson met Mann and his wife at a party. Mann was low-keyed and unassuming, more interested in contracts and advances than in metaphysics. Katia was sterner. To Jackson's avowals, she replied that one could appreciate Thomas Mann only in German—and not even then unless one knew the language, particularly its greatest poems, as intimately as he did.

No poet—not Schiller or Goethe or Hölderlin or Novalis—meant as much to Mann as Count Platen (1796–1835). A Protestant aristocrat, born in the small southern city of Ansbach, Platen began his military career in Munich. Yet another nineteenth-century polymath, he knew twelve languages. His position was isolated. As a consummate formalist, he disdained the romantics' absence of polish. Despite the intense melancholy of his own lyrics, he satirized the provincial melodrama of his romantic peers, whom he viewed as reactionary, and fled a stultifying Munich for Italy. Like Thomas Mann he made few friends: conservatives saw in him a radical; radicals like Heinrich Heine beheld a homosexual. Both writers, at the age of thirty-five, struck outsiders as being very "old young men." In 1907 Mann recalled Goethe's complaint that Platen's polemic compromised his lyricism—a common indictment of Mann as well.

Platen employed a deliberative, mournfully sensuous syntax, filled with languorous echoes and delayed gratification. Not since Keats's "She dwells with beauty, beauty that must die" had a poet made visual pleasure so morbid a condition. In his great poem "Tristan"—a work that Mann loved as much as Wagner's opera—Platen writes: "He who ever gazed upon beauty / Has already succumbed to death." The German doubles the visual impact: "angeschaut mit Augen" literally means "gazed with eyes." The transience of beauty becomes, thanks to such lines, a theme of homosexual art. Projecting such mutability on the landscape, Platen "scents death in every flower blossom."

Mann declared his love for Platen in many forums, echoing the poet's Venetian stanzas in *Death in Venice*'s depiction of the fatal costs of beauty. As a youth he advises his friend Otto Grautoff to read Platen: amazingly Mann finds the poet "cheerful" and links him to the endlessly agreeable novelist Theodor Fontane: a more Janus-faced pair is hard to imagine. Whenever desire for a beautiful youth left him ravaged, he sought consolation in Platen's lyrics.

While the Mann brothers looked abroad in different directions, they were equally committed to Goethe's vision of "world literature." There shortly arose a countervailing tendency among right-wing nationalists, who felt that German letters required no foreign influence. A similar attitude was expressed by Bertolt Brecht. He considered belles-lettrists (among whom he would surely have included Thomas, if not Heinrich) as "Goethe-ingers" and "Schilleringers," fastidiously effete. He preferred the demotic, guttural prose of Martin Luther. As it was, Thomas Mann frequently employed dialect, and his late works *Doctor Faustus* and *The Holy Sinner* include characters steeped in the vernacular, Bible-thumping with a Lutheran gusto. No doubt the naysayers would consider this inauthentic showmanship—in Charles Dickens's great words, "He do the police in different voices." For Brecht, fine writing was a reactionary gesture.

Yet few of his critics remark how often Mann dramatizes the question of verbal competence. Some of his characters, like Hans Castorp, the hero of *The Magic Mountain*, or Zeitblom, the narrator of *Doctor Faustus*, confess that they are overwhelmed by the facile outpourings of their intellectual superiors. *The Beloved Returns* largely revolves around the small-timers in Goethe's entourage, including his pathetically untalented son, August. The result of their sputterings is to make the ceaselessly fluent, perpetually resourceful Goethe something of a monster.

From an unkind perspective, Thomas's dramatization of this matter constitutes a dullard's revenge. Occasionally he could retaliate verbally— once, confounding an enemy, he boasted to Heinrich, "Oh, to be so talented!" More often he was flustered by criticism. For years Heinrich's incisive manner—Thomas often described it as "French"—left him speechless. In 1903, he waged a public and private attack on Heinrich so intense that outside the "fraternal constellation" it might have been libelous. But when Heinrich pursued their disagreement, he fled the arena. "I fall to pieces," he confessed, when it comes to polemic, on the page or, worse, in person. Well into his late seventies, unkind remarks could literally sicken him. At least once a bad review drove him into a sanitarium.

We have leaped decades from the adolescent Mann. But, aged seventy-five, he displays the same longings and self-doubts he had at fifteen. Another literary titan who lived into a triumphant old age, Yeats, writes that, at last, he must make his bed in the foul rag-and-bone shop of the heart. A lifetime of honest work is overshadowed by one wish: to be a lad again, and "hold her in my arms." A very old Thomas Mann was unluckier than Yeats, despite the fact that "Politics" is introduced with a quotation from Mann. He had fewer memories of youthful embraces to sustain him; at seventy-four he remarks, "Why is memory paradise? I must always live freshly in new things." But a year later he sounds a Yeatsian note while musing over a nineteen-year-old waiter: "World renown has no meaning beside the smile on his lips, the look in his eyes, the warmth of his voice."

Mann's career may be read as a tale of profound erotic disappointment, and its diversion into and projection onto the widest range of disparate subjects. The loss informed his lifetime melancholy. But, conversely, it also kept him young, alert to each *promesse de bonheur*, a term he was still using in his seventies. As he wrote of George Bernard Shaw, "Having never been young, he remained eternally youthful."

"Wishes survive decade after decade as if they'd just been made," he wrote in 1929. A sympathetic reading of his diaries suggests that fame rarely compensated for the wishes not granted. Youth would always mean the storehouse of his most painful responses. At twenty-six he complained, "Adolescence hangs on with me." He must have wanted it that way; at seventy he declared that one writes "to keep the wound open." (Mann's Polish disciple Witold Gombrowicz proclaims his gratitude for the "sub-world of sub-feeling . . . for causing the child in me to survive.") There is an almost embarrassing frankness about his revelation that literature is "the sole and painful way we have of getting the particular experience." The experience in question was the refreshening of an open wound. Tampering with the work betrayed the life: "I have a probably inartistic tendency to see in a book . . . a track of my life which it is almost dishonest to touch."

Freud considered Goethe a "careful concealer," teasing his readers with ambiguous disclosures. Mann shares his master's traits. At least twice he burned his diaries, first at twenty, then in his sixties. In 1950, having confided his latest homosexual infatuation, he wonders whether it is time for another fire. The evidence would "destroy me"—yet he reconsiders.

Quoting—whom else?—Platen, he writes, "The world should know me in order to forgive me." By forgiveness he means a compassionate recognition that the young waiter has joined all his male loves in a "gallery of which no 'literary history' will speak." But elsewhere he admits that everything he writes unlocks that gallery. Nothing's hidden "if you have a feeling for it." The incognito prince wore a transparent mask.

II

AN ARTIST WITH A
BAD CONSCIENCE

1

A COLD LOOK

Thomas Mann's favorite word was "longing." In German, the noun *Sehnsucht* connotes an experience both metaphysical and visceral, equally suitable to a mystic or a voyeur. The frustration of his desires stimulated a passionate energy for composition. It also kept him productively engaged—for if nostalgia summons the language of the past, *Sehnsucht* anticipates a language that is yet to be written.

The Wagnerian Mann realized very early that *Sehnsucht* and theater were linked. In a youthful story, "Little Louise," he describes the marriage of a middle-aged, "self-hating" buffoon and a vain little soubrette. The narrator admits that such a union cannot be "conceived." Instead he advises us to regard it as "theater"—then all becomes clear. A decade later, in *Death in Venice*, Mann allows Aschenbach and Tadzio to understand each other without speaking a word. Their knowledge lies in a visual apprehension of roles assigned them in their courtship. With forms and masks, as theatrical bravado and operatic hyperbole, *Sehnsucht* protects—and reveals—itself.

To a striking degree, Mann's characters depend on how others see them. This does not mean that their relations are happy or fruitful, but that they are always on public display, and their image a matter of public dispute. In fictional terms, it means that each of Mann's heroes is under surveillance. From Savonarola in *Fiorenza* to Joseph and God, he surrounds his great men with courtiers, speculating about their motives and commenting on their appearance.

How was the author seen? In his earliest photos, he gazes out sullen and uncomfortable, with sensual lips and the large family nose. At fourteen, the self-possessed "lyric-dramatic" author draws a sketch of himself sporting a monocle and a thick mustache. The nose is emphatic and cartoonlike, sharpened to a point, the chin dips suggestively, the neck is outsized. Mann's combination of adolescent frame and foppish affect is amusing, a charmingly naïve self-caricature.

A photo of him at eighteen shows an incipient mustache and a residue of baby fat. Photos from his mid-twenties indicate he had achieved the image he predicted. As throughout his life, he is elegantly attired. His slightly winged eyebrows surmount eyes that stare with great intensity. Mann never looked so handsome again, though he would retain a trim figure and upright posture. In his autobiographical fiction, he describes his eyes as dreamy; his right eye is slightly off-center, as if naturally suited to the sidelong glances with which his characters observe the world. In a photo at twenty-four, he is shown with pen in one hand, cigarette in the other. He offers well-manicured nails, tapered fingers, and a ring—the pristine professional. But at twenty-five, facing the camera, his look appears both steadfast and vulnerable. It is a face as provocative as any he would describe—its guarded expression would oblige him to constantly interpret himself to the world. Yet with his own words in mind, we can view the face as a supplicant's, still very youthful. The glance can also be read as quietly, hopefully seductive. It murmurs "Love my work, love me."

In another photo, a twenty-five-year-old Mann is seated below his brother Heinrich. Sporting his own stylish coiffure and a goatee, Heinrich stares down, unsmiling, at Thomas. The pose is formal, but it tempts us to read ambivalence and confusion in Heinrich's hooded glance and a willfully oblivious attitude on Thomas's part as he turns defiantly away from him and toward the camera.

How did others see Mann?

Mann's favorite child, Erika, described for him some of his conspicuous features: "strong hands, slender fingers . . . attractive eyes under dark, jagged brows, one of which you like to raise, pensive or astonished, the long upper lip and the head, small and dark, with soft, closely cropped hair." And, of course, "the strong, prominent nose . . . life-saving for your caricaturists . . . the long upper lip with the correctly styled mustache and the long oval chin." (Victor Mann writes that his family often mentioned "the old family nose.") She noted his smell, "a mixture of leather, printer's ink, eau-de-cologne, and cigar smoke."

By today's standards, Mann was short, no more than five foot seven, but he prided himself on his carriage, holding himself very straight. He was generally perceived as firm-backed and imposing, despite his height, although C. P. Snow remembered his "fat legs." An American friend, Frederic Prokosch, remarked that even his back had "a dark, oaken grandeur. The neck, the ears, the shoulders radiated an invincible solemnity." One time Prokosch caught Mann unaware: "his eyes, intently watchful yet turned profoundly inward, were tinged with an inexplicable sorrow and despair."

A less affectionate observer, George Grosz, writes, "Thomas Mann was born a gentleman, as evidenced by his small, longish head, his small, slender feet and hands, his bearing, his clothes, his ties, and even the cut of his collars. There was something English about his clothes. His collar, shirt, suit, hat, and shoes were exactly as he might have worn them forty years ago."

Mann loved food; his diaries contain descriptions of wonderful meals, and occasionally of their vivid after-effects: indigestion, constipation, and dyspepsia were routine. Perhaps this was why he remained slight. Heinrich ballooned with the years: a possible tribute to his well-satisfied appetites. Thomas, despite ample signs of neurasthenia and hypochondria, enjoyed giving an impression of physical fitness. When he was seventy he wrote Hermann Hesse, "Freshly shaved, I look fifty-five."

Thomas Mann's self-caricature,
age fourteen

Mann's obsession with an immaculate appearance was rooted in both precedent and paradox. Elegance was expected of the senator's offspring. It also disguised the artist's fundamentally dissolute nature. In his preparatory notes for *Tonio Kröger*, Mann alludes to his brother's unkempt appearance: "*Typus* Heinrich. As a writer, one is enough of an internal adventurer. Externally, he should dress well, damn it, and act respectably!"

The brothers' vocal styles were also distinctive. His nephews thought that Heinrich's voice always sounded as if he were speaking French. Thomas's voice was slow and plangent. According to Klaus, "The complex music of Thomas Mann's prose hesitates and woos." The voice remained in one register, while Katia's zoomed over two octaves. Within his limited vocal range Mann was capable of microtonal inflections. This is most evident in his German recordings; the voice can be deadpan, courtly, anguished, and severe. The acoustic talent survived exile. Mann was a very popular American lecturer, despite his robust accent. In a 1945 recording for the Library of Congress, he contemplates the nature of German guilt and innocence and finds them inseparable: he cannot "renounce the *wicked*, *guilty* Germany and declare I am the *good*, the *noble*, the *just* Germany. It is all within me . . . I have been *through* it all." The emphases are mine, but each adjective receives an impassioned stress. The theatrical coup is the reading of "through it all," the preposition, replete with rolling *r*, signifying a physical process. There's a split-second pause and the barest shift in register between "it" and "all," but it's enough to convey fatigue, contrition, and the deepest melancholy (an example of an émigré's naïveté about idiom restoring pungency to a stock phrase). As writer or actor, Mann considers tone substantive. But the qualities of a small voice require particularly close attention. Although he tried to cultivate a "larger" style than his initial lyrical manner, the unique charm of his work is its retention of a quiet, personal voice.

Mann could do very little about his body; he considered himself unattractive, ineligible for a handsome youth's attention. But he wielded power with his voice. His syntax, impacted with dense, sensuous impressions, became the equivalent of physical mastery. He admitted as much when trying to win his friend Paul Ehrenberg's attention; he vowed to show him "my power" . . . an exclusively verbal one.

Thomas Buddenbrook is happiest when he manipulates his own image—he loves to address a crowd but hates to answer its questions. Likewise his creator, Mann, could be a most authoritative figure onstage. Some Germans would complain that he was the dullest public speaker they ever heard—a former Berliner remembers faking a coughing fit to release her from the rolling periods and ineluctable voice. Yet others, among them the playwright Carl Zuckmayer, contend that he might have become a great actor. Even his archenemy Brecht was impressed by Mann's melodious voice, the first time he heard him read in his native Augsburg. Like the solo performers of his invention—from the Infant Prodigy to the wizened Magician—Mann required full control of the dramatic representation.

He appeared less formidable offstage. At twenty-two, living in Munich, he initiated a friendship with Kurt Martens, a writer five years his senior. Martens invited Mann to visit.

> He came. Exceedingly modest, almost shy, but bearing himself well, a grave, slender youth crossed my threshold. His sensible, reflective conversation, bathed in mild melancholy, enchanted me as no man's speech had ever done before. . . . From the first word on I loved him, voluntarily subordinated myself to him, the younger man, because he was the greater and at the same time all too modest. . . . I believed in his singularity and his future when he himself was still hesitantly groping his way forward.

Martens evokes a combination of reticence and formality unusual—and not universally appealing—in someone so young. He implies that friendship with Mann required a large degree of sympathy for his peculiar temperament. While expressing the utmost respect, he suggests that an outing with Mann was seldom fun.

Yet Mann loved to be entertained. At parties he much preferred to enjoy other performers—in Hollywood he particularly cultivated Charlie Chaplin—rather than to display himself. As an onlooker, he appeared to many either dry or cold, but his daughter Elisabeth remembers him as frequently laughing himself silly.

Mann would probably say that the important question is not how *he* looked but how he *looked*, his distinctive angle of vision. As a boy, constructing a marionette kingdom, he would squint through a peephole at his imaginary audience—a voyeur and narcissist. In a famous anecdote, Arthur Holitscher claimed that he once left Mann's house and turned back to catch his host observing him with binoculars. Katia dismissed the tale; she claimed that with his superb memory and analytical powers, her husband had no need to spy on anyone. Mann himself believed that he could observe more in a few minutes than most people could ascertain over a period of years. However, at least one other person, the American Edith Jonas, recalled a similar experience from when Mann was living in Princeton.

The stories of Holitscher and Jonas ring true, because the surreptitious glance is so typical of Mann. Whether staring through shop windows or

trailing a handsome youth, the way Mann's characters regard others is itself a mixture of voyeurism and narcissism. The adolescent Hanno Buddenbrook's gaze is described as "cold"—a cold look, "kalter Blick"—
superficially unfeeling. Actually it is the coldness of the uncanny, an X ray
into emotional interiors. It dare not expect a response. Yet when the glance
is returned, the bliss is beyond words—Aschenbach is nearly delirious once
Tadzio acknowledges his gaze. Similarly Mann notes in his diaries an intense pleasure when he locks eyes with some young man during a concert
intermission or while signing autographs.

Mann's earliest recollection of himself as a character in history was
during the centennial of the Johann Siegmund Mann firm in May 1890. It
commemorated "a century of middle-class diligence" from which he felt
himself alienated. "My heart was full of anxiety. . . . I knew then that I
would not follow my father and my father's fathers, at least not as it was
silently requested of me that day." In 1890 Heinrich had moved to Berlin
and begun working for Samuel Fischer, the publisher of *Freie Bühne*, a
journal devoted to the dramatic naturalism then identified with the left-
wing playwright Gerhart Hauptmann.

Senator Mann's death at fifty-one came quickly. He had undergone
an operation for the removal of bladder stones (performed in the family
ballroom) on July 2. He survived long enough for one more vacation in
Travemünde, and died on October 13, reportedly from blood poisoning,
though there was speculation that he committed suicide upon learning
that he had cancer. In a sketch, Heinrich draws himself weeping before
his father's deathbed, embracing the corpse's hand, while Julia Mann looks
on, solemn but less than devastated. Despite his father's opposition to a
literary career, Heinrich remained convinced that he had received a final
"blessing." The benediction may have occurred while their father was still
alive, but Thomas, in an angry hour, remembered Heinrich dashing out
of the house, leaving—as always—Thomas himself to protect the home
front.

His father's "Amen" had been a form of gallows humor. But at the
funeral, Pastor Ranke, the vicar of Marienkirche, cited it as an instance of
piety, a virtue not, he added, shared by "this decadent family." Writing in
1931, Mann found this a comic example of religion bent to rhetorical
purposes.

Three months before his death, the senior Mann made out his will.
There was no question of the senator's anger at his family. He found them
a trifling lot, and punished them all. His wife inherited everything, but
two officious guardians were appointed to make financial decisions. They
were instructed to sell the company and the Mengstrasse and Beckergrube

houses and furniture within a year. Since the law denied Julia any right over her children he assigned one guardian to

> direct the children for a practical education. As far as possible one should oppose my eldest son's literary inclinations. In my opinion, he lacks the requisite education and knowledge. The basis for his inclination is fantasy and lack of discipline and his inattention to other people, possibly resulting from thoughtlessness.
>
> My second son will be easier to talk with. He has a good disposition and will adjust to a practical occupation. I can expect that he will be a support for his mother.

He warned against Lula's "passionate nature," while advising that Carla would be "next to Thomas, a calming element." Actually Carla would pair off with Heinrich. For baby Vico he offered a mild encouragement: "Often children who are born late develop particularly well. The child has good eyes."

He concluded with a command: "Towards all the children, my wife should be firm, and keep them all dependent on her. If she should become dubious, she should [forthwith] read *King Lear*."

He delegated an impossible task. The family's financial decline meant that Julia could not bind her children in material dependence. She also lacked the requisite strength. Only the nonheterosexual Thomas would marry the kind of powerhouse his father envisioned. Katia Mann raised six children with unimpeachable authority.

The will was an unfriendly document. Heinrich tried to avoid his father's prophecy. Filial homage took the form of right-wing politics. During the 1890s he composed indictments of his father's class enemies, the new breed of Jewish capitalists. The elder Mann had apparently paid Thomas no attention, and the son did not obey his wishes. In short order he rejected a "practical occupation," and in his first novel he presented a father very much in Senator Mann's image, closely watched by a son he considers a hopeless case. In Thomas's last years, the will had a Shakespearean echo. Demoralized by a series of personal tragedies, he began to quote Prospero: "In my ending is despair."

Frau Mann spent the next year enmeshed in the family's complicated finances. In 1892, she moved to Munich with her three youngest children, Lula (then fourteen), Carla (ten), and Victor (three). Although their fortune had been reduced by almost sixty percent, she was able to rent an eight-room apartment, complete with a veranda and garden. She also began writing sentimental stories. Unlike her late husband, she believed in her children's talent, at least Heinrich's. In 1894 she subsidized the publication of his first novel, *In a Family*. She was less sure of Thomas. Her "profound disappointment" over his miserable grades led her to "discourage his poetic urge."

Back in Lübeck, Mann completed his final school year boarding at the home of Professor Timpe, the father of his second great love, Willri Timpe. He recalled the time as good. His professors left him to his own devices: "Feeling myself quite hearty and clever, I was not cast down. I sat away the hours. Outside school I lived very much as I liked, and stood well with my fellow boarders, in whose premature drinking bouts I gaily condescended to take part now and then." He was also stocking up a museum of impressions, as evidenced by the "dreamlike" ease with which he would summon up Lübeck years after he had left.

His only serious friend was Otto Grautoff. Grautoff was homely, not very talented, and socially questionable, his father being a failed bookseller. Thomas himself had suffered a change of fortune. Senator Mann was dead and the family's prospects vastly reduced. Still, he recognized a social gap between Grautoff and himself. Three years later, befriended by some young aristocrats, he neglected Grautoff. On March 28, 1895, he wrote an apology: true, he had been slightly disloyal—"Did I forget you personally?—Yes and no, no and yes." He added, less than tactfully, that the counts had despised Grautoff, and that, by their refined standards, they were not wrong! But he could never be ashamed of his friend, for that would be "tasteless." He added, unkindly, that in Lübeck even his professor had objected to Grautoff's appearance.

In 1935, upon learning of Grautoff's death, Mann recalled "my school-boy chum and confidant during my passion for W.T., later elevated into Pribislav Hippe. For a long time I had given no thought to this pompous man who had come to bore me. But now the death of one who shared those youthful years so rich in sorrow and laughter, is chilling and sad."

W.T. was Willri Timpe. In *The Magic Mountain* Hans Castorp develops a crush on his schoolmate Hippe. They have the briefest of encounters when, for exactly one hour, Castorp borrows Hippe's pencil. In 1950, love-besotted, Mann compared the waiter Franzl to Timpe; he admitted enjoying Franzl's letter as much as he once had cherished "W.T.'s pencil shavings. In that respect nothing has changed." Undoubtedly the Timpe years included many more episodes. The nature of the relation, "so rich in sorrow and laughter," cannot be specified. But when Mann announced to Grautoff that he had burned his diary—and that Grautoff ought to do the same—

the allusion may have been implicit. This happened shortly after Oscar Wilde's trial.

When he was seventy-eight, Mann returned to Lübeck, where he visited the old school-yard. Thinking back to Willri, "the second one after Armin," he concluded, "the eternal love of boys." (The adjective may have been an allusion to Goethe's Eternal Feminine.)

Ludwig Ewers, the friend to whom Heinrich had entrusted his message that Thomas's love for another boy was "nonsense," spread rumors that the Mann brothers were estranged. In September 1895, Mann wrote Grautoff that "friendship between my brother and me has recently turned into a fraternal intimacy." But concerning intimacies about Timpe, he had but one confidant: "There is only you."

Mann and Grautoff also shared a private language, "Gippern." Throughout his twenties, Mann exhibited nostalgia for their days of Gippern. Still poised between commerce and literature, he advised Grautoff to acquire some office skills; he mentioned stenography. So Mann in his late teens was attuned to both private codes and shorthand. His letters make clear the proximity of the two, and their origins in those intimacies he now refused Heinrich.

The era of Mann's youth was hospitable to new movements, particularly those forms of expressionist art and drama that drew on Wagner's example: the city was drunk on his music; young fops whistled his arias in the streets. There were new investigations of adolescent love, including homosexuality, in the plays of Canozza and Wedekind. The title of Wedekind's drama of pubescent homoeroticism, *Frühlingserwachen* (*Spring's Awakening*), was echoed in that of the school journal, *Der Frühlingssturm*, that Mann edited along with Grautoff and some other boys in his senior year.

The journal's preface announces its intentions. It begins with a schoolboy's jottings: "It was noon. After school. Between one and two. I had no desire to go home, and strolled, my copy of Caesar under my arm, a cigarette dangling between my lips, through the streets and up to the city gate. Which gate? It doesn't matter." The speaker is bored, contemptuous. He blames school for making him "thoughtless—if one leaves school, it's always like that." His posture is plainly anti-authoritarian.

He evokes an atmosphere of "sleeping drought" and "idiotic fatigue," which he seeks to "arouse . . . from its torpor." Suddenly he detects a "rumbling murmur," approaching ever nearer until the storm arrives, "crashing and blustering through the trees." This downpour supplies the metaphor for his manifesto: "*Spring Storm*. As a spring storm blows through an oppressive landscape, we shall sweep with words and thoughts through the morass of musty brains and ignorance and narrow-mindedness, the pompous philistinism that oppresses us."

Throughout his career, Mann would employ weather imagery to demonstrate extreme changes in consciousness, as revivifying as a spring storm. Or, in an equally tendentious fashion, he would use nature's example, the provocative humidity of Travemünde or Venice, to demonstrate his characters' willful estrangement from physical life. His famous remark that his prescience was due simply to "something in the air," a spring storm of cosmic proportions, united the tactile and the visionary.

The magazine introduced his first published story, "A Vision," a facile sketch about the joys of smoking, a habit Mann kept to his death (limited, however, to no more than twelve cigarettes a day. At the end of his life a very despairing Mann said that he ate primarily to nourish himself and keep smoking. Though, when he was happier, he also prided himself on his capacity for penile erection). More resonant was a short essay, "Heinrich Heine the Good," in which he assumed a combative stance. Identifying with the self-exiled poet, Mann derided the attempts of "Philistines" to turn an apostate Jew into a conventional Lutheran. Ethics don't apply to artists; Heine isn't "good," merely great: art supersedes morality. Echoing the Francophile Heine, Mann switches tongues: "Dieu me pardonnera, c'est son métier." As for the moral arbiters, they sound "so dull and worthy" that they deserve to be made "professors." With that, he thumbed his nose at authority and prepared to begin the world.

2

"THE BEST 'MÜNCHEN' THERE EVER WAS"

Mann arrived in Munich in March 1894. Within a month he began working as an apprentice at the South German Fire Insurance Bank. It was a dull job, spent "surrounded by snuff-taking clerks," and it seems to have left no impression on him, none of the excessive account-taking of Franz Kafka, who spent a lifetime in a similar office. In the fall of 1894 he enrolled as an auditor at the city's Technical High School, planning to major in journalism. In November "I registered at the university and attended lectures which seemed fairly likely to forward me in the rather indefinite calling I proposed: courses in history, political economy, literature, and art. From time to time I attended these, with fair regularity and not quite without profit." He would make use of what he studied, up to and including courses in Middle High German he would recall fifty years later while composing *The Holy Sinner*. "Without being formally a student . . . I lived like one." As could be expected, the auditor's happiest memory was his participation in campus plays.

Also not without profit, he registered the differences between Munich and Lübeck. Twenty years later, in his *Reflections of an Unpolitical Man*, he wrote that his birthplace was a "politically independent, oligarchical city democracy of the northwest" in which the old "burgherly ceremonious community endured, in defiance of the newer tendencies of capitalism, nationalism, and imperialism that had recently swept through Germany."

Munich exhibited, in a theatrically entertaining form, the triumph of all that. "The penetration of a new German spirit, the Americanization

of the German life style, expressed itself there in a certain clumsy corruption, in profiteering and enterprising ventures of a characteristically naïve
tone. . . ."

Munich—to borrow Mann's later antithesis—symbolized modern civilization rather than traditional culture: "Its deep-rooted artistic culture is
less spiritual than material; Munich is the city of applied, indeed, of fes-
tively applied, art, and the typical Munich artist is always a born festival
organizer and carnival-man." This urban alloy of Germany and America,
show business and the Middle Ages, Catholicism and the theater was also
the home of baroque churches and Mad King Ludwig's architectural
follies—the grandiose stage set for a band of performers.

During World War I, Mann apologized for having remained in so
frivolous a climate by saying that it had stimulated his capacity for irony
and resistance. Where better, he implied, to test a Gothic Protestant than
in this Vatican of temptations? (During the next world war he was tougher:
"ridiculous" Munich deserved its bombed destruction.) But his wallowing
in paradox denied the Mann who always loved festivals and was endlessly
intrigued by carneys and con men. He was both an easy mark for
charlatans—briefly sharing his generation's obsessions with graphology and
séances—and a self-professed "Magician." By 1929 he would recall the city
of his youth as "the best 'München' there ever was."

I

Klaus Mann, born in Munich, attempting to imagine it from his father's
perspective, called it "serene, beautiful, and obtuse. . . . It entirely
lacked the feverish verve of Berlin . . . and never quite lost its savor of
enjoyable sloppiness."

Berlin, Klaus declared, was quite another case, imperiously unsenti-
mental. It had outgrown the Munich communal divisions, being without
a Bohemia. "The artists were too commercial to be veritable bohemians;
the bourgeoisie too smart to be outright philistines." Too smart and—too
Jewish. Both Thomas and Heinrich had been disturbed by an urban irreverence they specifically associated with Jews. One critical voice of Berlin
Jewry was Alfred Kerr. Already, at twenty, Thomas mentions in a newspaper review that Kerr is gratuitously unkind, attacking well-meaning,
defenseless authors. When Ludwig Ewers advised Grautoff to become a
journalist, Mann replied that his friend lacked all the qualities: "practical-
ity, cunning, subtle and shameless irreverence, impertinence . . . the art of

making oneself popular, the 'ass kissing'—all the vulgar characteristics which make Jews so suitable to this profession."

This is the most flagrant instance of anti-Semitism in Mann's work. Yet it must be added that the hardest, most ungenerous critical voices in German—Kerr, Karl Kraus, and Maximilian Harden—were all Jews. In 1948 he wrote of Harden, "Just because he was a Jew he leaned strongly toward snobbish conservatism and Prussianism and inclined very much toward the paradoxical." Mann considered himself a softie; he was endlessly obliging to his fellow writers, and always exhibited a respect for the sheer effort that Kerr might dismiss with a ruinous put-down. The late-adolescent Mann, still nursing his father's prejudices, understood something else. He saw that his disposition and Kerr's were irreconcilable. Somehow he guessed that his enemy awaited him; and sure enough, Kerr would become his scourge. A kind of regional—or even class—prejudice would obtain. Uncle Bräsig, a character created by the Plattdeutsch novelist Fritz Reuter, had come to symbolize the provincial oaf. Berlin's meaner critics would represent the Mann brothers as Uncle Bräsigs in the big town.

Germany had many urban centers. But if Berlin was its capital, Munich was its second city. Mann lived there for years, though rarely at ease. If he recoiled from Berlin's hyper-modern veneer, he felt alienated from his Munich neighbors. Obviously he found no pals among the brewers and shopkeepers. But he didn't find any elsewhere, among the "long-necked clowns" who lived in Schwabing, the local bohemia.

For at least twenty years Munich had been an international center catering to unknown artists and writers. It was the great place to be young, with its agreeably laid-back tone, and its famous holiday seasons. Fasching—the period preceding Lent—was carnival time, party time. The connection between worship and license perplexed Thomas Mann, but it made Klaus toy with conversion to a church that offered both a compassionate mother and Fasching.

Munich reveled in a mind-body dualism. Gymnastics and modern dance complemented an interest in graphology and hypnosis, expressionism and psychoanalysis. One wit described the town's ethos as a blend of art nouveau and turnips. At age twenty, Thomas wrote Grautoff: "This Munich, I never confessed this before, but I've had enough of it. It's the most illiterate city par excellence—filled with banal women and healthy men. God knows how much contempt I put into that word, 'healthy.' " It invoked all the horrors of physical education: "And the last straw . . . is the fresh, pious, delirious attitude toward gymnastics."

Yet the cult of the body engaged even him. Munich was enraptured by various forms of physical therapy. The smart moneyed aesthetes frequently took cures, accompanied by Spartan, usually vegetarian diets. Thomas and Heinrich made several trips to the sanitarium at Riva, a small town outside Munich. In his letters Thomas Mann describes the intrusive treatments—for instance, an electric hose forced deep into his rectum. Years later he referred to a Zurich clinic as a "hygienic penitentiary."

Munich was bubbling over with vanguard art, particularly the *Blaue Reiter* expressionists with their riotous colors and frame-leaping composition. Thomas Mann continued to prefer the illustrators, Lenbach and Böcklin. His musical taste was similarly rear-guard. Schwabing liked Arnold Schönberg; Mann remained obsessed with Wagner. (The aftermath, a meeting of Schönberg and Mann in Los Angeles, ended with the composer bitterly objecting that his work had been misrepresented.) In 1901 the first political cabaret, The Eleven Executioners, opened in Munich. Bruno Walter, who later became Mann's neighbor and friend, played piano, while Frank Wedekind and Erich Mühsam appeared as poet-singers.* Thomas Mann would wait twenty-five years before even alluding to such nightlife. But his children Erika and Klaus would both become stars of cabaret. As if to rebuke Mann, popular culture kept invading his home.

The intellectual milieu was dominated by a series of outlandish figures, self-appointed prophets and Utopians, cult leaders and charlatans. The most brilliant was Otto Gross, a living example of *Lebensphilosophie*. He was Schwabing's "king." A proud feminist, he adhered to Johann Jakob Bachofen's theories of *Mutterrecht*, the mother's law traduced by patriarchal excess. (His own father once had him arrested.) Gross had serious intellectual aspirations. He saw himself as Freud's rival, emboldened by his study of Nietzsche. He preached sexual freedom and practiced it with his numerous lovers. (Among them were D. H. Lawrence's future wife, Frieda, and her sister, Elsa. Max Weber, Elsa's brother-in-law, called their affairs "naked piggishness.")

Unlike his colleagues Ludwig Klages and Alfred Schuler, Gross was neither antiscientific nor politically reactionary. Rather, like Freud, he read history and myth as a journey, frequently diverted, to enlightenment. He

---

* Wedekind, best remembered today for the play *Lulu* from which Alban Berg derived his opera, was the master of sexually explicit dramas. In 1899, he was arrested effectively for committing literary crimes, and he would fight a lifetime battle with the censors. Besides pushing the border of theatrical expression in dramas that combined a Wildean gift for epigrams with a revolutionary approach to physical action, Wedekind made fun of his fellow artists. In plays like *The Tenor*, he represents them as the bourgeoisie's paid clowns. He included himself; in the ways he parodied his own accession to respectability, he predicted both Mann and Brecht.

considered Cain the first revolutionary, with his double assault on God's commandments and the nuclear family. His vocabulary became politicized; in 1920 he argued that the first "white revolution" was the patriarchal expropriation of women's rights. By inference that made women the first Bolsheviks. He was less sure about homosexuals. He decried the modern state as inherently homosexual: hierarchy made it so; the comic-opera uniforms of the rococo palace guards might have swayed his opinion. He was more tolerant of "primary"—i.e., undisguised—homosexuality.

Ludwig Klages also expected men to capitulate to women. Three years Thomas Mann's senior (he outlived Mann by a year), he was a full-fledged irrationalist. Klages hated modernism, which he considered a Jewish plot. He didn't care, either, for Wagner's *Parsifal*. The alternative to modernism and capitalism lay in an unspecified elsewhere. For Mann, Klages's anti-intellectualism, combined with his sexual tirades and anti-Semitism, made him a proto-Nazi (Klages flourished under Hitler).

A clear line connected antirationalism and anti-Semitism. Yet such Jewish intellectuals as Hannah Arendt and Theodor Wiesengrund Adorno (all right, half-Jewish) exhibited a similar disdain for the Enlightenment. The idea that rational organization defiles the spirit is wonderfully resilient. It informs attacks on both communism *and* capitalism: Arendt and Adorno saw them as virtually indistinguishable. The historian Henry Pachter remembered such intellectuals as always affixing "so-called" to the word "Enlightenment."

While Gross ruled over Schwabing, a tiny, bizarrely selective, and blatantly homoerotic group named the Seventh Circle congregated around the scholar and poet Stefan George. His lyrical genius was such that it humbled Mann, whose best friend for almost two decades, Ernst Bertram, was a member of George's inner sanctum. The master had fallen in love with a Jewish boy named Maximilian Kronberger, who died at fourteen. In death Maximilian became the subject of George's lyrics; Rilke had to settle for an angel as his muse.

Fifty years later Mann revealed that Bertram had felt uncomfortable in the Seventh Circle. "His Protestantism and Germanism rebelled against the Imperial Roman and Jesuitical tendencies of that sacred clique. Also, there were probably too many Jews in it." The handsomest member, Friedrich Gundolf, became a leading critic, but according to Mann, Bertram would not have let this heterosexual Jew become a full professor. Bertram's lover, Ernst Glöckner, was a member of the Circle, though apparently he was considered at first insufficiently attractive.

George's influence extended to Mann's great friend the Jewish scholar

Erich Kahler, and to Count von Stauffenberg, one of the conspirators against Hitler, who was killed in 1944. Thomas Mann would seem an ideal fellow traveler of the George-Kreis with its hermetic and "spiritualized" homoeroticism. But he found the poet's attempts to render the physical metaphysical grandiose. In 1919, comparing George with Platen, he praised the latter as "wholly lacking in the sacerdotal manner and without pretensions of being anything but an itinerant rhapsodist"; a singer not a priest.

Thomas Mann belonged to no movements, had no allies in the premier circles, and still observed everything. (Likewise he wrote in 1948 that he remembered each block and house.) He had an outsider's revenge in later years when he dramatized the Schwabing bohemians as, at best, dilettantes and lunatics; at worst, incipient Nazis. But he also would exhibit Otto Gross's tendency to read both myth and history in sexual / political terms.

To his astonishment, while he distanced himself from the school of literary decadence, describing it later as an "all-too-modest and somewhat flippant formula to convey a sense of ending, the end of an era, the bourgeois age," he remains more identified with themes of decline (the original title of *Buddenbrooks*) and decadence than with rebirth and transcendence. During World War I, he called himself "a chronicler and interpreter of decadence." The salient distinction is that he was an "interpreter," not a participant.

Forty years later, in *The Beloved Returns*, Mann let Goethe fight his battles: "I was twenty years old then, but I left my hangers-on in the lurch and I laughed at the 'genius' school and its caricature of originality. . . . Originality! That kind is just crazy, distorted, art minus creation, barrenness, vanity, dried-up spinsterishness." Goethe's alternative is "the productive, male-female force, conceiving and procreating, susceptible to the highest degree." The professed decadents were poseurs: Thomas Mann, wrapped in the armor of his bourgeois disguise, was the real "androgyne."

Mann's intellectual hero was Friedrich Nietzsche. True to form, he came to Nietzsche a generation late. While Schwabing chose to emphasize the philosopher's vitalist, Dionysian tendencies, Mann preferred the acerbic social critic. From Nietzsche he acquired the idea that each generation superseded to the point of invalidating its predecessor, but was itself an ephemeral product. This enabled him to regard cultural representations with an anthropologist's distance. But he was a complicit taxonomist, loving whatever he dissected.

Both Mann and Nietzsche couldn't get Wagner out of their systems. After championing the composer, Nietzsche became disgusted by the hero worship he had inspired. He found the operas suffocatingly German. "I need to open the window a little! . . . Air, air!" Like Dürer and Goethe he needed a vacation. He envisioned "light feet, wit, grace, the great logo . . . the southern shivers of light, the *smooth sea*." (The imagery of romantic poetry was hereby represented as anti-Wagnerian.)

Thomas was nineteen when he first read Nietzsche's critique of Wagner. Nothing afterward so piqued his interest or confirmed his disdain for the Munich philistines. Nietzsche's original affection for Wagner was intense and deeply personal—it resembled the homoerotic conflict Mann discerned in Goethe and Schiller.* The philosopher first heard the composer in a Swiss village, when an enthusiasm for Wagner was defiantly vanguard and anti-German. Nietzsche perceived the artist of his dreams as a decadent: *Tristan und Isolde*—Act II of which was composed in Venice—became his example; and he considered it appropriate that Wagner's first ("and perhaps best") defender was the French poet of vice and dissolution, Baudelaire. Alas, Wagner returned to Germany. Nietzsche was horrified to see him become a spokesman for political reaction and anti-Semitism. German bad taste conquered its greatest enemy. As *Parsifal* demonstrated, Wagner even grew "pious."

Nietzsche's critique expanded into an indictment of all German culture. The Germans were boors, tone-deaf, psychologically illiterate. Their heroes were the monsters of Europe. Whenever enlightenment threatened to break out, the Prussians killed its spirit. Not only had they introduced nationalism—the warfare of small states against Napoleon's dream of a united Europe—but they gave the world Martin Luther. Nietzsche despised Luther for removing Christianity from its institutional apparatus and placing it deep within the hearts of men, from which it would become virtually impossible to extract. The neo-pagan idol worship of the Roman popes was less a threat to human progress, Nietzsche remarked, than the peremptory self-regard of German Protestantism.

Not surprisingly, Thomas Mann hung a portrait of Erasmus of Rotterdam, Luther's archenemy, on his wall: Heinrich later called it a "prophetic" gesture. A portrait of Tolstoy, however, could be read as counter-Nietzsche, though equally counter-Munich. Mann's heroes were a varied lot, united only in their opposition to the reigning ideology of their times.

Mann loved Wagner, but he loved Nietzsche as much, precisely for exposing Wagner's folly. "Nietzsche made extravagant fun of the misunderstandings Wagner gave rise to amongst us Germans. Reading [his analysis] was the keenest critical experience of my life." What a mess. You

---

* After their friendship ended, Wagner spread the word, acquired from Nietzsche's doctor, that the philosopher's problems were due to a small penis and excessive onanism and pederasty.

dream of Valhalla and end up in Bayreuth. After reading Nietzsche, Mann would never be sentimental or pious about tradition. While the philosopher inspired a Gross or a Klages to hyperbolic reaches, he made Thomas Mann a skeptic.

Frau Julia Mann had begun to live it up. She possessed a few good pieces of furniture—although in *Doctor Faustus* we learn that they seemed forty years out of date. Word reached Lübeck that she had become a "merry widow," the enterprising mistress of a salon. But (again we rely on *Faustus*) the daughters were embarrassed by her penchant for racy, double-entendre tales of sailors, artists, and models. They had inherited Lübeck's sense of propriety. She had other worries. In 1893 her father died, and Vico became ill with rheumatic fever. Thomas felt the disease damaged Vico's heart; he would be the first brother to die, at age fifty-nine. His elder brothers both lived till eighty.

At home the family continued to be extravagantly theatrical. Carla had determined to become an actress; Heinrich would be her playwright. Lula, the most high-strung, chose to enact a self-cast role as votary of the traditional graces.

Thanks perhaps to Nietzsche, more likely to their childhood games, they all had a profound sense of the ways self-presentation reflects a change in the social order. In 1895 Thomas made the actor, despite himself, an intellectual. "The actor is an artist," he wrote, "a critic in the most exalted sense. His personality disappears and, consciously absorbed, illuminates his role. . . . He is nothing but a critic." (In 1929 he cites Nietzsche's disrespectful words "The actor is the paradigm of the artist . . . one extremely vain and sexual monkey.") But play-acting in his family could be a full-time occupation. His father had died, he believed, of the strain. Now he began to fear for the elder of his sisters. In *Doctor Faustus*, Ines Rodde is modeled on Lula. Unlike her sister, the actress Clarissa (Carla), Ines has no bohemian inclinations.

> She represented—or shall I say: yet she represented?—the conservative element in the little family, being a living protest against its transplantation, against everything South German, the art-metropolis, Bohemia, her mother's evening parties. She turned her face obstinately back to the old, paternal, middle-class strictness and dignity. Still, one got the impression that this conservatism was a defense mechanism against certain tensions and dangers in her own nature. . . .

In 1895 Mann would not have used Freudian jargon. But did he recognize that his female self was being bled dry by her self-inflicted task? "Strictness and dignity" were precisely the virtues he wished to instill in Grautoff. Lula, denied a man's outlet, domesticated the problem. "Shall I say: yet she represented?" is an implicit admission that representation involved hypocrisy and self-denial, and that by 1895 the Manns had nearly forfeited the right.

II

A concern with mode and affect, perhaps derived from his new environment, characterized Mann's first published stories. Their authority resides in sumptuous descriptions and a narrative ease that finesses unpromising material. In "Fallen," an implausible discussion about a woman's virtue, he situates four adolescent roués at a table graced by fine silver, flowers, fruit, and wine: Mann knows the objects better than the putative emotions. (Similarly in "A Vision," the moderately stoned smoker hallucinates a girl's disembodied hand arranging one perfect red flower—shades of Dorothy Parker—in an exquisite vase.)

In October 1894, "Fallen" was published in a Leipzig magazine, *Die Gesellschaft*, and earned its teenage writer some attention, including a generous letter of support from Richard Dehmel, a famous writer.

By February 1895 he had begun work on "Walter Weiler." This story, later expanded and retitled "Der Bajazzo," in its evocation of cultural ambivalence and a declining social status, offered a rather neat reflection of Senator Mann's son, beginning the world abroad. He also dallied with lyric poetry. He wrote Grautoff that "one does not have to possess either industriousness or perseverance to write poetry. I usually write it while going to sleep": this blithe remark indicates that his fourteen-year-old self had been wrong about his calling as "lyric-dramatic poet." Nor were there any dramas, although Mann impressed his friends in plays such as Ibsen's *The Wild Duck*.

A more unpleasant role was ahead. Heinrich Mann had begun publishing short stories revolving around world-weary young men, defeated by circumstances they had yet to live through. His oversophisticated youths were teenage scholars of Heine and Nietzsche. They suffered from a "sickness of the will" and mental "instability." In April 1895 he became the editor of a right-wing periodical, *The Twentieth Century: A Journal of German Art and Welfare (Das Zwanzigste Jahrhundert: Blätter für Deutsche Art und*

Wohlfahrt), and continued for thirteen months when he quit. Thomas contributed occasional pieces, while the twenty-four-year-old Heinrich served as the journal's mouthpiece. *The Twentieth Century* was both advanced and rear-guard. It was anticapitalist, but the class it defended was the *Mittelstand*, the burghers like Senator Mann, overwhelmed by a new breed of entrepreneurs. The attack was frequently anti-Semitic, since Jews exemplified the new, apparently rootless subclass.

The magazine published many anti-Semitic tirades, several written by Heinrich. By 1895, Jew baiting was a well-worn theme. Decades earlier, the German Karl Marx and the Frenchmen Pierre Joseph Proudhon, Auguste Blanqui, and Charles Fourier had attacked Jewish finance from the left. Right-wingers found time to attack Jewish radicals, like Marx himself. A few discerned a Jewish cabal that transcended class divisions. For example, the Russian anarchist Mikhail Bakunin decided that the Communist Marx and the archcapitalist Rothschilds were equally disposed to centralization. Eureka, it must be another Jewish plot!

By comparison, *The Twentieth Century* was a sophomoric effort. Heinrich drew caricatures of wealthy Jews and intellectuals, and he attacked the power of the Jewish press. In his first novels he makes fun of arrivistes fresh out of the ghetto; and even in *Der Untertan*, his most famous novel, he satirizes Jewish self-hatred. A lawyer is so eager for assimilation that he has his ears fixed: "I'm about to change my appearance to fit my national identity." As early as 1896 Heinrich imagined a physician who specialized in nose jobs: "Nasen-Joseph." It's worth repeating that the Manns were highly sensitive in this area.

Why this change in Thomas after his early friendships with Jewish classmates? A certain envy perhaps: the Jews appeared to have inherited the mantle of leadership from the burghers. Satirizing their pretensions was akin to William Faulkner's unmasking of the Snopeses. A few scholars point to the influence of the French novelist Paul Bourget. Bourget was an early master of a now-common device: the trick is to use the tone and idioms of a vanguard to express right-wing prejudices. His vivid novels depict a Paris of artists and aristocrats, a lively community still recognizable in the salons of all major cities. But, despite his cosmopolitan manner, Bourget was primarily a spokesman for Catholic reaction and Bourbon restoration. He was also a raging anti-Semite.

While Heinrich's first novel was dedicated to Bourget, the Frenchman also gave Thomas the terms with which he could attack his greatest rival. In his notebook he copied out a passage from Bourget, condemning the cynical aesthetes "whose religion is pleasure, . . . refined epicureans, aristocratic in both their nervous and intellectual reactions." For almost thirty years, he would use similar words for Heinrich.

Mann's 1896 story *"Der Wille zum Glück"* ("The Will to Happiness") exhibits traces of Bourget and Heinrich. The daughter of an ugly, nouveau-riche (Jewish) mother loves Paolo, a frail artist of mixed ancestral stock: like Mann, he is part German, part South American. Despite her parents' objections, they marry, but Paolo dies after the wedding night, overcome by an excess of joy. (In many tales of adolescent writers, sex is too gross an experience for the palpitating sensibility. It is best kept in the head. Bombarded by such tales, the editors of *Simplicissimus* offered a prize for the novella in which sexuality played no part.)

Overlooking the rude satire—and therefore the marriage itself—we find a familiar pattern. The narrator first befriended Paolo when they were classmates, outcasts amidst the Philistines. Their affection endures, indeed survives through the narrator's composition, while the heterosexual love is literally fatal. Mann strayed into bathos and slapstick because he was avoiding his natural subject.

Mann's letters to Otto Grautoff express his distaste for bohemian Munich. He lived there "in silent refutation," as trapped and defenseless as in his school days. He had found no friends. "I haven't Gippered with anyone else. On the contrary, I'm rather serious and melancholy. . . . Often I long for our meetings in the Cafe Bavaria. Why shouldn't I say it? For you. Here I have many, many acquaintances but real friendship, real intimacy, I had with only one person. That's you. . . . With nobody else can I talk as openly as I talked with you—and just recently I had so much to tell you, but it's impossible in writing. . . ."

Grautoff had literary aspirations. Mann tried to be encouraging—suggesting at one time that his friend become skilled in "plotting" and "invention," though he later would disdain "originality" as another Nietzschean fad. He was blunt about Grautoff's lack of talent. But he preferred to describe his own successes. "Sometimes my stomach turns over with ambition." After the publication of his first sketches he reported that he had become an object of attention. When he entered the university reading room, "all eyes turned." The incognito prince was now being *seen*. He dreamed of having his head crowned with laurels. On January 8, 1895: "You know how childishly vain I am. . . . My ego is rather large but it always remains within the bounds of good taste, and doesn't become ridiculous."

He declared, immodestly, that an artist's subject is always himself. "Understanding . . . is to be had in no other way than by self-devotion, by the route of passion, by loving absorption into his own work." His subject would be an "ego supported by intellectual ideas," discovering "the superior pleasure of self-analysis."

Superior to what? Other routes of passion. In March, the nineteen-year-old advised Grautoff, "Concerning love—about which you talk—you don't need to despise your lower regions entirely—but concerning those chambermaids and whores, I tell you wholeheartedly, Phui to the devil. However, the lower regions contain quite a bit of poetry. . . . One has only to transform it beautifully into feeling and atmosphere." He quotes a French proverb that in true love the soul commands the body. The homely Grautoff hadn't acquired the knack. "But you can do it. I do it too. Lately I've become an ascetic. I adore my beautiful hours. They are purely aesthetic. Sexuality has become a sexuality of the spirit—for the spirit, the soul, the feelings. I say let's separate the lower regions from love and so on. One could write volumes about that. But mine is a very personal attitude. That one cannot generalize into a philosophy."

The sibling rivalry with Heinrich now extended to letters. Heinrich's first novel had been published, and Grautoff was not alone in finding it lurid and tasteless. Thomas leapt to his brother's defense. On May 16 he wrote, "What you write about my brother's novels is very simplistic. Please don't be offended. Probably you still don't understand his style." Good friend Grautoff had preferred Thomas's prose. Thomas admits to having "a certain pleasing sentimentality that he lacks" but insists that he's not in Heinrich's class. "No, my boy, Heinrich Mann is an artist, a poet, and the two of us cannot reach his knee."

Later that month he offers news of the family. "Vico is happy. Thomas alone criticizes him as not very musical." The thought of music inspires a bird's-eye view of history: "My father was a businessman—practical but with an inclination to art, and unskilled in commerce—his oldest son [Heinrich] is already a poet and writer with a strong intellectual gift for criticism, philosophy, and politics—followed by the second son (me), who is only an artist, only a poet, only a man of moods, intellectually weak, a social good-for-nothing."

After such a diminution, "no wonder if finally the third son, the latest born, will be claimed by that art which is most distant from intellect, which consists only of nerves and senses and is without intellect whatsoever. Music? That's what I call degeneration." But Mann likes the prospect; he uses a piece of Bavarian dialect to suggest the decline will be "devilishly good."

This is a great letter. Mann foretells his development by recapitulating his family's history. His first title for *Buddenbrooks* would be *Verfall*— "Decline," i.e., "Degeneration." He, the man of feeling, would outshine all the intellectual resources of his brother, and find in music, particularly Wagner's leitmotifs, a method of organizing experience. Out of the battle between moods and ideas, intellect and music, would issue his first masterpiece.

After Heinrich made his first trip to Italy, in 1894, the Mann brothers had begun to spend long periods away from Germany. In 1895, they visited Palestrina and Rome between July and October. At home he complained of his limited circumstances: "I am not a rich man; if I'm decadent, it's not because of my wealth." Circumstances changed somewhat after he came of age and received a sum of 319 marks. In June 1896, shortly before the publication of "The Will to Happiness," Thomas traveled to Vienna. In October he spent three weeks in Venice and next visited Ancona, Rome, and Naples. In November 1896 he wrote "Disillusionment," a story ostensibly gleaned from the narrator's travels. Mann projected an image of himself as the experienced tourist, a foreign correspondent recording the emotional travails of Germans abroad. He felt comfortable with the pose. When an admiring editor began a letter of acceptance "What a gifted creature you are," Mann laughed at his astonishment, "which curiously enough I found naïve."

In December he joined Heinrich in Rome. They shared a large room with a stone floor, wicker chairs, and a piano. "My brother, who originally meant to be an artist, sketched a great deal, while I, in the reek of endless, three-centissimi cigarettes, devoured Scandinavian and Russian literature and wrote." Gradually he acquired a certain authority—"My attitude toward life was compact of indolence, bad civic conscience, and the sure and certain feeling of latent powers."

Thomas acquired a dog, Titino, who became his "inseparable" companion. Heinrich recalled that its doggy life provided a constant jolt of reality, a "cheerful corrective" to the tedium of Thomas's literary apprenticeship. Mann would kill a very similar dog in a story he published shortly after returning from Rome.

It was a productive period not without its tensions. In 1918 Heinrich recalled a quarrel in Rome when Thomas, his back turned, declared them "in inimicos."

They had many discussions about literature. Extrapolating from Thomas's letters of 1903–04, we learn that they considered literature an exalted pastime. Heinrich was the professor: he insisted on high standards. It was forbidden to pander, to strive for sensational "effect," merely to land one's book in some provincial "store window." An implicit aesthetic can be derived from Mann's letters. Somewhat like Henry James (one-half of an equally famous brother act), the Manns stressed tonal consistency, a verbal texture unmarred by inappropriate diction, a truth to character and situation. The product was designed for the "finer reader." At that time neither confessed to high expectations: fine readers were a rarity in Munich.

There were bitter debates, supposedly over literature, although the subtext was, in Thomas's words, "personal ethos." Heinrich believed an artist must be ruthlessly cold and objective; he demanded the abolition of personality. Thomas already knew that the springs of his art were autobiographical, that he could never arrive at a place beyond subjectivity. He also recoiled from Heinrich's verbal fantasies of Renaissance palaces and obese women. His own tastes ran to the Gothic and young men.

Outsiders found Heinrich a typically aloof Mann, but to Thomas he became the embodiment of brusque virility. "There was a continual dinning in my ears about the 'strong beautiful life' in sentences that ran something like 'Only people with strong brutal instincts can create strong works.' " (Aptly enough, the lover of Italian culture briefly anticipated futurism!) Thomas was more swayed by *Anna Karenina* or the Sistine Chapel, art produced by "people of the highest moral Christianity, scrupulous characters who were willing to suffer." He was too embittered to recognize that Heinrich also suffered. Instead he remembered a barrage of patronizing advice: " 'You are staying too long with the criticism of reality,' I heard very close at hand. 'But in good time you will get to art too' "—even though "criticism of reality" constituted his notion of art, unlike Heinrich's "programmatically ruthless gesture of beauty." A love of beauty that exacted no price could not be trusted. Its amorality was downright unpatriotic! Years later he described the German's preference for "ugliness" as "ethical."

This was a battle over exquisite literary distinctions, and over judgments he would later disown, as when he satirized Tolstoy's morality or added Michelangelo to his list of supermanly homosexuals. He spent a lifetime exhilarated by beauty, as did Heinrich, who would be luckier, but not much. The "critique of reality" became a family specialty, most obviously when the brothers risked their lives in challenging Hitler. Yet over such differences they would argue violently; and some years later, according to Thomas, they came close to blows. The pretext then was literature; the timing, shortly after he broke off relations with a man he loved.

As Thomas began plotting *Buddenbrooks*, he recognized the need for a more capacious and ambitious style than his efforts had previously demonstrated. The risk was great: a few years later he claimed that he understood the difference between "long and long-winded." But by then he was also convinced that literary dignity—and its commensurate laurels—were his possessions, forfeited by Heinrich, whose many novels (that literature came easier to Heinrich was never in doubt) he found overwrought and vulgar.

Though he admitted to Grautoff that sexual desire drove him crazy, Mann spent all his time with Heinrich: "We made no friends." They came to Italy as eccentric German burghers. "We regarded Rome as the refuge of our irregularity, and I, at least, lived there not on account of the south, which at bottom I did not love, but quite simply because there was no room yet for me at home."

Thomas was about to join Heinrich in book form. At the request of a Munich editor, Oskar Bie, he prepared a collection which would include "Little Herr Friedemann," "Der Bajazzo," "Tobias Mindernickel," and "Little Louise," a series of masterly inventions for a writer barely twenty-one. It is not clear how much the brothers influenced each other during this time. They did collaborate in 1897 on a keepsake book of satirical poems, caricatures, and fantasies, composed for Carla's Palm Sunday confirmation and dedicated to their younger sisters and brother. "Seventy-five works of art by the hand of Masters, among which [are] twenty-eight colored pictures and forty-eight engravings, beside which [are] sixteen accompanying works of poetic art, and many captions containing instructive and illuminating morals, collected and published with care and special regard for the moral mind of Germany's growing youth": *The Picture Book for Well-Behaved Children.*

In the tradition of great children's literature, the adult order was satirized: Kaiser, pope, beggar, and worker all make fools of themselves. As in the morbid fables of Wilhelm Busch or the Grimm brothers, there was ample blood and gore. Particularly caricatured were the symbols of authority. A parody of Schiller, entitled "Murderer Bittenfeld Overpowered by Sunset," included a professor's *explication du texte*. There were even a mock allusion to "The well-loved poet Thomas Mann" and a satirical drawing of the tragic hero of his short story "Little Herr Friedemann."

In private the brothers named their irreverent opus *The Life Work*. In 1931 Thomas characterized their joint effort as a product of nineteenth-century ambition. He made a similar point in 1949 when he claimed that writers born in the previous century were capable of "greater, more illuminating documents of the age."

The Life Work exemplified a Rabelaisian audacity; the Manns left out no person or condition. Thomas may have felt himself an outsider at the Munich festivities, yet he often compares narrative to a "festival," a carnival addressing every human appetite.

In a 1927 essay addressed to "the youth," he recalled his early twenties. "We were young, which means brittle and turned inward. Our passion was recognition and fame. In the ascetic relations of morality and art we pursued the heroism all youth desires." Reflecting that ambition, his first stories had been self-involved to the edge of solipsism. But *The Life Work* pointed a way out. The much-quoted critic Mikhail Bakhtin also relishes the idea of "carnival," and—like Thomas Mann—compares it to the multivocal, omnibus nineteeth-century novel. Mann's longer works are frequently propelled by a sense of carnival. In *The Magic Mountain* he makes illness a festive occasion—a time of license and experiment, an invalids' Mardi Gras.

When he was twenty, he wrote about himself in the keepsake album of Ilse Martens, Armin's sister. Like his alter ago, Tonio Kröger, he compared himself to Hamlet, crippled by an excess of ratiocination. He also identified himself with both Faust and Mephistopheles, a rich prediction of his later work. He felt born in the wrong time; he would have preferred the early part of the century—when, he didn't add, Goethe, Schiller, Kleist, or Platen would have been his peers. Already he was divided between attacks on the establishment—"insurmountable disdain" for "Kant, the categorical imperative and the philosophy of state officials"—and acceptance of its standards. His choice of favorite writers (Heine, Goethe, Nietzsche), composers (Wagner, Richard Strauss, Grieg), and painters (Guido Reni and Lenbach) was unexceptional. He did add a couple of obscure local composers, including Fielitz, and two contemporary writers of opposing spirit, Paul Bourget, the reactionary Catholic, and Ernest Renan, the idol-busting author of *The Life of Jesus*. He gave no hints of *Sehnsucht* in this sketch (perhaps because Fräulein Martens reminded him too much of his first unhappy love). His "idea of happiness" was "to live independently in terms of understanding within myself." Independence was frankly an economic matter: he feared a life of dependency, "without means." A quiet, contemplative life on a fixed income was all the clandestine prince would admit to wanting.

At the age of twenty, in the very capital of youth, Thomas Mann had disdained youth. In particular he had rejected the Dionysian element. He wrote a review that year knocking the poet Richard Dehmel for a Dionysian art, "dripping with sentimentality." Nobody could become an artist "who does not transcend his feelings but only tries to vent them. . . . I welcome poets who speak simply." (He added that Alfred Kerr could probably formulate this better—as if they disagreed about everything but the noxious misuse of kitsch.)

That same year he supported the censorship of a play by Oskar Panizza in which God punishes human sexuality with an epidemic of syphilis. Perhaps he did so because Panizza's indictment of Wagner's homoeroticism a year earlier had hit too close to home. Priggishness is a familiar mask. Condemning Panizza, the twenty-year-old presented himself as a disciple of "good taste in art"—rank hypocrisy from the author of "Heinrich Heine the Good."

In Mann's fiction desire always betrays the moralist. The same occurred in his life. In October 1896, a few months after his condemnation of Dehmel and Panizza, he traveled to Italy. His letters to Grautoff from Naples reveal a highly sexed, deeply frustrated youth, losing his "good taste" by the minute. The city is preferable to Rome, he writes, because it is "a select and sensational mixture of Rome and the Orient . . . more plebeian, but with a naïve, lovable, gracious, and amusing vulgarity. It does not have the bold and imperial Caesarian profile of Rome; its physiognomy has a somewhat turned-up nose and puffy lips, but very beautiful dark eyes." Polymorphous perversity saturates the travelogue. (In his shorthand, "Oriental" usually signifies "homosexual.")

Finally the boy cannot contain himself:

> I think of my suffering, of the knowledge of my suffering. What am I suffering from? From knowledge—is it going to destroy me? What am I suffering from? From sexuality—is it going to destroy me? How I hate it, this knowledge which forces even art to join it! How I hate it, this sensuality which claims that everything fine and good is its consequence and effect. Alas, it is the *poison* that lurks in everything fine and good. How am I to free myself of knowledge? By religion?— How am I to free myself of sexuality? By eating rice?

Years later, he characterized this period as haunted by a "psychological susceptibility, a power of vision, a melancholy, which even today I hardly understand, but under which I had to suffer indescribably." Returning to the 1896 letter, we discover a hyperalert tourist: "Here and there, among a thousand other peddlers, are slyly hissing dealers who urge you to come along with them to allegedly 'very beautiful' girls, and not only girls. They keep at it, walk alongside, praising their wares until you answer roughly. They don't know that you have almost resolved to eat nothing but rice just to escape from sexuality." Eat rice or read Schopenhauer; cultivate an ironic mode; condemn sentimentality; never vent your feelings. All that might protect him from the temptations beckoning from each street corner.

Brecht contends that irony is a bourgeois device; Mann proves the case. Irony afforded both self-protection and distance from the "sentimental" Dionysians—and the sidewalk panders. In yet another of Mann's late-blooming episodes, he only began to celebrate youth in his forties—although the new public of democratically inclined students were most unlike the right-wing irrationalists of Schwabing.

Some time in his late teens or early twenties, he read Arthur Schopenhauer. While his neighbors argued over Otto Gross or Sigmund Freud, Mann had skipped back two generations. (He later placed Freud in a pantheon that began with Schopenhauer and Nietzsche.)

Reversing the normal procedure, Mann needed to grow old to distrust Schopenhauer. On December 30, 1946, he wrote Emil Preetorius: "I have had patience—which Schopenhauer called heroism. Good fellow, he thought his one-and-all, clung to through thick and thin, heroic. Poor fellow, much good he did humanity with his particular song of life. Whereupon things went up to the icy heights of Nietzsche, and then they went incredibly fast, incredibly deep down."

Ten years earlier Mann had written that Schopenhauer must have had a tremendous sexual drive: "The essence of the creative artist is nothing else—and in Schopenhauer himself was nothing else—than sensuality spiritualized, than spirit informed and made creative by sex!" Goethe knew this and it made him happy. The deeply pessimistic Schopenhauer chose patience and self-denial, instead exalting the will's triumph over its baser instincts. "Much good it did him," Mann concluded in 1946; as in 1950 he wished to trade "world renown" for the smile on Franzl's lips. On such occasions he may have remembered a youth who had foolishly declined to "vent his feelings" and live his life.

3

NOBODY LIKES THEM,
NOT EVEN THEIR DOGS

Mann's first heroes, as a group, are child-men haunted by threats of public humiliation. Shame and self-hatred, a cynical veneer that breaks at the touch, are their common attributes; none of them get to enjoy Paolo's night of love.

His heroes fail at everything, but Mann's prose is suave and facile. The "magician" had mastered a wonderful trick. He could reveal a dubious, pathetic character without undermining his narrative authority. Formal control protected him, made him seem wiser, more mature than he knew himself to be. Surveying this transition, he informed Grautoff that he had previously "communicated from myself to myself" in a "secret diary." The range of his feelings had included "my love, my hate, my sympathy, my disdain, my pride, my scorn, and my accusations." Yet with the acquisition of literary power, he boasted that "I am suddenly able to find the discreet forms and masks with which I can walk among people with my experience." A few years earlier, he had wandered through Lübeck secretly impersonating Prince Karl. Now he moved "among people" masked and formally, as if craft demanded a vocational charade.

These early stories predict Kafka's vision of the individual overwhelmed by the flux of modern society. But while his antiheroes inhabit a state as dreamlike as Kafka's, the details of their social nightmare are rendered with journalistic precision. If Kafka's oneiric tales point toward fable and allegory, Mann's convey a mixture of social realism and case study. His characters appear static, arrested, but the world around them keeps changing. At twenty-one, Mann specialized in superannuated youths.

His first triumph was to situate his eccentrics in a world so vividly rendered that they became gadflies of a culture in transition. This juxta-position of society and the outsider was to influence his best readers, among them Kafka, Bruno Schulz, and Witold Gombrowicz. All three might ap-pear more overtly political than the young Mann, barely escaped from his unfortunate association with *The Twentieth Century*. But his type is theirs —effete, bemused, deprived of his social function, prone to cold sweats and stomach cramps.

The political victim in their works—and arguably in all of Central European fiction—is conspicuously unlike the creations of Aldous Huxley or George Orwell. He's a maladroit schoolboy dodged by schoolyard bullies. His ambivalence derives from a combination of erotic attraction toward his enemies and internalized acceptance of their criticism. This is starkly por-trayed in Kafka's depictions of the inexorable father with his brutal, in-sanely arbitrary pronouncements.

But it's Mann who introduces the notion of a "vague, irresolute" burgher as the perfect modern victim. No writer before him had captured so well this emotional state or drawn so frankly upon his own erotic confusion.

Adorno located Kafka's genius in his ability to imagine everything as if he were the smallest boy in a classroom. Nobody could be smaller than Little Herr Friedemann, the eponymous hero of a story first published in May 1897 in the *Neue Deutsche Rundschau*. He is physically stunted, hardly more than a midget. Mann begins his story by showing that Friedemann's condition is due to a tipsy housemaid who dropped him in his infancy. The shock of this opening section is its apparent callousness, deformity as an-ecdote. It also exhibits Mann's usual treatment of the working classes as sources of comic relief, folk wisdom, and vulgar prejudice. Although he can memorably depict the impoverished, they tend not to be ordinary laborers; he shares this imaginative limitation with Proust, Kafka, and his brother, although not with Döblin, Joyce, or Lawrence. (Acknowledging Richard Dehmel's letter of encouragement, Mann had distinguished his work from those writers obsessed with the *"miserà plebs."* They would never be his subjects.)

The narrative tone is Mannian: casual asides like "to be sure" and "make no mistake of it" deflate the emotional hyperbole while placing this modest tragedy in ironic relief. Scholars enjoy Mann's quiet satire of naturalistic devices and his allusions to Fontane's *Effi Briest*. ("The Old Fontane" always charmed him.) But he puts a new spin on the familiar. Friedemann's house abuts a garden saturated with "the sweet stench of burnt sugar from a refinery close by." The proximity of garden and factory (as in some paintings of Manet) gives a mercantile edge to the sultry aroma.

Johannes Friedemann is nobody's hero. But it is typical of Mann to allow him some physical appeal. So, despite Friedemann's humpbacked, pigeon-chested physique, he has an "almost pretty face," with large, melting brown eyes, the better to regard the world. As a boy he sees his fellow students at play. He decides that he can't join them, not at these games or any other. Years later, when he spies an attractive couple, he concludes that sexual love is, like gymnastics, "a category of things from which he was excluded." Mannian is the blend of adolescent insecurity and intellectual rigor: the conviction—a theorem derived from an intuition—that one is doomed.

When he is twenty-one, Johannes's mother dies, a sorrow "that he cherished." Mann's narrative intrusion, "a connoisseur, if you please" is unappealingly snide. For just as the boy Thomas Mann strutted through Lübeck, unacknowledged by his townsmen, so the incongruously foppish Friedemann strolls theatrically, cocooned in his "quiet and tranquil happiness." This hero of a closet drama loves opera. His little body atremble in the dark, he applauds the heroic passions he has forbidden himself. He is Mann's first delirious fan.

The temperament remains the same when the fantasy changes. Gerda von Rinnlingen, the wife of a district commander, becomes his new obsession. Resembling no siren of heterosexual fancy, Gerda is remote, unflirtatious, even androgynous. She "scrutinizes" the timid fellow with a masculine confidence; her alto sobriety overwhelms his soprano fervor. With blue shadows around her close-set eyes and a slight tic, she exemplifies the damaged, moribund beauty. Her coldness thrills Friedemann, who would be terrified by a more robust woman.

He artfully positions himself so he can spy on Gerda during a performance of *Lohengrin*. The mock heroics are blatant: this is no Wagnerian tenor. Instead, sneaking a "quiet, furtive, sideways glance," he becomes Mann's first voyeur, window-shopping in a public space. Passion overwhelms Friedemann. He flees the theater, his "prudently cultivated sensibility" shattered, and cries Gerda's name to the lampposts. But if love makes him crazy, it doesn't make him stupid. Like almost every one of Mann's lovers, he feels an "impotent, sensual hatred" for the person who destroys his equanimity. Liberated into a world of sensual response, his profit is to hate. Mann's pairing of emotional antitheses was remarkable from the first.

After this incident, Friedemann acquires a sensitivity to each gradation of his beloved's feelings. In the turn of her head, he spots "a cruel, barely perceptible expression of mockery." Finally an actor in a real drama, he comes to see his life as a story. He develops a romantic "nostalgia" for his lost bliss and, as its complement, takes a polymorphous pleasure in his physical environment. Sexual union appears impossible; Eros resides simply in his capacity to be stirred.

If the story had ended there, Mann would have traced the development of a singular sensibility. But the climax is far gloomier, an authorial punishment of emotional hubris. Friedemann reveals himself to Gerda. He admits the dishonesty of his life, the despair he obscured with "lies and my imagination" (his own forms and masks). But as he confesses, she flings him aside, laughs scornfully, and vanishes. This blue-veined *dame sans merci* doesn't allow him the consolation of jealousy. Her rejection is total.

"What were his sensations at the moment?" asks the narrator as he describes Friedemann's suicide, performed in an "excess of self-disgust." The question is Mann's first admission of the inexpressible, a realm of feeling beyond language. Enigma dignifies the melodrama.

Yet melodrama it remains, a panicked adolescent's view of adult emotion. Why grow up at all? You lack the talent. Better revert to a "glad unhappiness," a benign form of "sensual hatred" measured by the low-grade fever of a passionate latency. However, once initiated, you can't go back. Your will is always threatened by the tremendous force of desire, a drive as propulsive, as "muscular" as Friedemann's suicidal plunge.

In this story, Mann attempts a musical arrangement of themes and images. ("Friedemann" was first accepted by a music critic, Oskar Bie, doubling as magazine editor. Mann recalled decades later that "perhaps more than chance willed that it was a musician and connoisseur of music who performed this decisive function in my life, bringing to light a writer whose work was from the first marked by a deep inward affinity to the art and a tendency to apply its technique to his own field.") The technical authority was to increase at a dizzying pace, although the characters would remain static, arrested figures. In tracing the varieties of their social estrangement, Mann had a topic that attracted both the journalist and the lyric poet. Each story posed and met a specific challenge, yet was dense with implications for his later work.

The sketch "Disillusionment"—composed earlier than "Friedemann," though Mann placed it later in his collected stories—manages to both share and mock its eponymous attitude. A tourist in Italy encounters a fellow German who assumes the narrator's role. This fellow speaks bad French (the multilingual narrator answers him in English) but demonstrates an excellent

German. In fact he lives in language: "Speech, it seems to me, is rich, is extravagantly rich, compared with the poverty and limitations of life." And even that life is generated by language: "pulpit rhetoric," a Kantian congeries of laws and tropes. Hypereducated, emotionally undeveloped, he affects a universal ennui. He anticipates death as terminal boredom: "So this is the great experience?" Hardly worth dying for. Mann makes a drama out of the perpetual anticlimax. The tourist's monologue becomes a form of essay, an early indication that Mann's actual essays would themselves be dramatic monologues.

Likewise, in "Death," another sketch composed that year, a blasé count anticipates his death while vacationing at the seashore. When death finally arrives, he resembles a dentist, "so jejune, so boring, so bourgeois." This is a German parody of French ennui: the words of a Teutonic Huysmans. It's also unconvincing. For someone so disaffected, the count has a passionate interest in numerology. He wants to die on October 12 (Senator Mann had died a day later). Mann shared that interest—he saw his life in five-year cycles. His obsession with dentists also survived the story, most horrifyingly when Thomas Buddenbrook's stroke is triggered by a toothache. Mann had to withdraw this story after he was accused of plagiarizing the plot from Jakob Wassermann. However, he retained the ennui and the disappointment with death, having learned the virtue of recycling a good idea.

The most resonant early story is "Der Bajazzo," a title variously translated as "The Dilettante" and "The Joker." It is the first to analyse—and question—a literary, i.e., Mannian, sensibility. Where the previous narrator fled from pulpit rhetoric, the Joker trusts language to order his reality; he contends that "the more placid, detached and solitary a man's outer life, the more strenuous and violent his inner experiences."

Mann combines the etiolated intellect of his narrator with a vivid sensuality. His rendering of visual movement is cinematic; when the narrator recalls his childhood home, the literary equivalent of an Ophulsian pan shot carries him up the winding stairs to the very spot where his mother plays Chopin, an image in quotes, made all the more stylized by her resemblance to Renaissance madonnas. (Max Ophüls's last proposal was a filmed version of *The Magic Mountain*.)

His greatest childhood pleasure is a puppet theater in which he enacts all the roles and soundlessly plays the imaginary instruments, as well as designing the real, if primitive, sets and lighting. In his solitary fantasy, he gazes through a peephole at an invisible public. He grows so accomplished in his obsessions that he can improvise the details. Mann understands, without any tutoring from psychoanalysis, that the truly insidious aspect of monomania is the variety of expression possible within its self-imposed confines.

The narrator's memories of his youth are Thomas Mann's. "I was an usually brisk and lively lad . . . an adept in the art of imitating my school-masters." He is a novelist in training, a mimic of voices and gestures. He is also a musical dilettante, infatuated with the key of F-sharp because he likes its "color." Basking in "the atmosphere of books," he finds ubiquitous "reflections of myself." So far he's a perfect little acolyte of Huysmans or Oscar Wilde, an arch little fop and poseur.

What distinguishes Mann's treatment of this joker is the social analysis of a psychological condition. Only wealth distinguishes him from his "poorer contemporaries." In an aside he boasts that it's his "birthright" to regard the "poor" and "unlucky" with "benevolent contempt." Yet he craves their admiration and envies their entrepreneurial flair. While Mann tended throughout his life to keep a benign distance from his social infe-riors, his characteristic play with the word "contempt" invariably turns the attitude into a circuitous form of desire.

The Joker describes his parents' deaths with extreme coldness. After they die, he begins to travel, although without the "good bourgeois com-forts." In Palermo, he makes a brief impression by improvising a Wagnerian opus, with lavish semaphore and recitative. Only in a theatrical represen-tation can he express himself; Mann wittily treats Wagner's dilettantish work as a form so popular that our hero can "improvise" around it.

The Joker returns to a modest-sized German city that is still uncon-taminated by modern business. There he rents a large room and becomes obsessed with the acquisition of objects. Continuing his boyhood fantasies, he crams his room with antique mementos. He believes that those who lead complicated lives need an extra supply of beautiful goods, and he treats himself to fine linens and imported tobacco.

Like Tonio Kröger, he admires the beautiful "children of light." But he daren't introduce himself. They have no interest in his sort. Nor should they; they exist to evoke sensations, not to feel them. He dreams of a *Gesamtkunstwerk* that would synthesize his talents and combine sound, word, and image; he confesses a desire for "recognition, praise, fame, envy, love." The division between social ambition and sexual desire is fragile. He be-comes infatuated with a young girl he sees in the streets. But she is not for him; he compares himself to a beggar standing outside a jeweler's shop window.

She has a suitor, and Mann describes his physical ease and blond self-confidence with an envy that barely masks his attraction. Trailing the couple, the Joker is "tortured" by his ridiculous behavior: evidence that his irony lacks conviction; this is the first instance of Mann, the celebrated ironist, revealing the mode as a feeble defensive gesture. One glance and irony shrivels into despair. He next sees the young lovers at a bazaar. Mann depicts a carnivalesque setting in which the Joker finds himself "intruding, a stranger, not one of the elect."

Recalling the theatrical bent of his youth, he realizes that his desire cannot be "dramatized"; he's doomed to monologue. He also sees that the love itself is a product of "vanity, envy, hatred and self-contempt." Far more than "Little Herr Friedemann," this story demonstrates Mann's prodigious knowledge of a certain type.

In the end, his confusions are interpreted in class terms. He meets Schilling, a poor boy who has lucked out financially and yet continues to admire the aristocratic manner our hero displayed in school. As they sit together, the Joker knows that he can't keep up the act. Sure enough, Schilling departs early. The final humiliation underlines Mann's recognition that his hero's "split" nature is a function of his declining status. Since Mann had been recently influenced by Paul Bourget, one might see the Joker as a reactionary playboy without the confidence of his prejudices. While he exists in a state of impotent leisure, he perceives in the new classes, workers and entrepreneurs alike, sexual and emotional vigor. Imagine, Faulkner's Quentin Compson lusting after Flem Snopes.

The Joker's reflection is not to be found among the active members of his society. If he has an alter ego, it might be found in "Tobias Mindernickel," another 1897 story. Tobias is the Joker without money; impoverished but clearly of middle-class origins. His singularity is definitive; he is equally isolated from men and from things. Lacking "the natural superiority with which the normally perceptive individual looks out upon the phenomenal world, he seemed to measure himself against each phenomenon and find himself wanting; his gaze shifted and fell, it groveled before men and things."

Not even his dog, Esau, likes him; it prefers to eat dung in the road and avoid his glance. Allowed a certain power when he nurses Esau, he stabs the dog as soon as it recovers. Once again, Mann insists coyly on the inexpressibility of untoward events: "That which now happened was so shocking, so inconceivable that I simply cannot tell it in any detail." Mann loved dogs, and Esau's demise is at least as touching as Little Nell's. But the tragic figure is Tobias, a man driven crazy by the material world. This brief, almost repulsive sketch indicates Mann's affinity for self-abasement.

A final story from 1897, "Little Louise," is more philosophically ambitious than the others. It impressed Heinrich Mann (as Thomas recalled in a 1908 letter), and its plot anticipates Heinrich's most famous work, *Professor Unrat*. The story begins with a by now familiar caveat: "There are marriages which the imagination, even the most practical literary one, cannot conceive but must just accept." Literature having failed before the irrational, it must now keep still before the grotesque—although, Mann adds disingenuously, if you just give in to the spectacle and treat it as "theater," the problems dissolve.

An obese lawyer named Christian Jacobi is married to Amra, a pretty, voluptuous woman whose "presence suggested the harem"; her sensuality is actually enhanced by a thick nose. Jacobi is burdened with a large rear-end, a ludicrous parody of anal sensuality. He is both vain and obsequious in his attempts to "disarm the scorn" of potential allies. His masochistic pleasure is to be regarded as his wife's " 'good doggy.' "

A young hack composer with pretensions, named Alfred Lautner, becomes Anna's lover. He's simply a provincial musician. But Mann is fascinated by the world of small culture—the area in which the second rank contend as if they were titans, receiving instead of laurels the devotion of bored housewives. At twenty-two, Mann had no guarantee that he would rise above this sphere; for all he knew he might read his sketches forever to an audience of bluestockings and Bovarys while sneaking a glance at the handsome child of light who yawned conspicuously throughout.

This attention to provincial culture allowed Mann to introduce an editorial aside quite unlike anything he had written before. In a tangential exposition, he addresses "the present-day race of small artists." These men aim only to please; they enact "the naïve genius." Where Mann's jokers truly suffer, these "entirely immoral and unscrupulous" hacks are "healthy enough to enjoy even their disorders." As if in preparation for his play *Fiorenza*, Mann assumes the guise of a bourgeois Savonarola confusing a provincial musicale with the bonfire of the vanities.

His anger bespeaks irritation with all those who haven't shared his suffering. "But woe to these wretched little poseurs when serious misfortune befalls them, with which there is no coquetting"—this from Thomas Mann, perpetually prey to a child of light's coquetry. "They will not know how to be wretched decently and in order. They do not know how to attack the problem of suffering. They will all be destroyed. All that is a story in itself." Mann is infuriated by the hacks' glibness when he is sweating heart's blood. Perhaps most remarkable about this undeveloped outburst is its intrusion into Mann's disciplined narrative. By allowing a personal eruption, he crosses the line between story and essay.

It ends with a costume party which, like the bazaar in "Der Bajazzo," serves the oxymoronic purpose of isolating the hero in public. The evening, hosted by amateur performers, is an occasion for wild parodies. Curtains part to reveal a "horrifying tableau of actors in blackface." Mann's racist description expresses a common prejudice, used here—in Bourget style— to further ridicule the impersonators. Another actor does impressions of Goethe, Bismarck, and Napoleon, a burlesque of high culture and the state. The ultimate parody is Jacobi's appearance in drag. Complete with blond wig, he sashays forth and sings the siren lyric "I am the popular pet, Little Louise," unwittingly accompanied by his wife's lover.

Mann underlines every humiliation. Even the boorish crowd is depressed by this "lamentable" display. In a musical extension of Wagner's leitmotifs, Lautner's kitschy accompaniment grows dissonant as the curtain parts again to reveal "something nude." Disrobed of his dignity, the lawyer flashes his plump, defenseless bottom. The cuckolding of Jacobi becomes the rape of Little Louise. In a moment, he associates the music's satirical jabs with his wife's betrayal, collapses and dies. A "serious young Jewish doctor" arrives to declare, "It's all over," while Jacobi's rival, the heartless musician, attends to the dying echo of an F-major chord.

All these figures of the young Mann's imagination are doomed by a gaze. Tobias can't get Esau to return his glance any more than the Joker can oblige the children of light to notice him. Reciprocity is even worse. From Gerda von Rinnlingen's imperious dismissal, Mann has moved to a situation in which "hundreds of pairs of eyes" contemplate the pathetic Jacobi with a "knowing expression" that destroys him. It would be difficult to humiliate characters more completely. For someone proud of his own masks, Mann had no compunction about ripping away his character's disguises.

Among those readers struck by Mann's early stories was the Berlin publisher Samuel Fischer. In the spring of 1897, he proposed that Mann next turn to longer fiction. So far his stories had involved little interaction, resembling essays more than miniature novels. But Fischer recognized Mann's ability to present the implications, social, historical, and economic, of his characters' behavior.

(Glenway Wescott, without knowing Mann's dreams of self-analysis, praises "the artist's temperament feeding on itself. . . . I love his talent at the beginning of the century—all the astonishingly natural, small-scale ability and entrancing technique, so precocious that one may be tempted to call it innate.")

The fakery and overreaching, the incapacity for the workaday of his early characters, remain enduring traits of Mann's fiction. Combined, they make him a veritable connoisseur of latency, the archivist of those suspended, inchoate powers that fill up our lives. Critics have followed a trail of renunciation he laid out for them. But a Mannian slant, more yes/no than no, would also see him as the great author of single people, the unattached, the wallflowers, the not unhappily isolated people who gravitate to cities. A celebrated family man, the father of six children, he was most comfortable dealing with those who live by themselves. Who else could imagine both Tobias Mindernickel, the universal outcast, and Joseph, the power behind Pharoah's throne, as comparably estranged from their surroundings, nowhere comfortably at home?

4

DREAMS OF LAUREL WREATHS

A
lthough Mann's stories were astonishingly fresh, their appearance did
not make his name. Publication in book form occurred while he was
in Rome. The tourist could see his German work displayed in a
Roman store window, complete with a seductive if irrelevant cover illustration of a pretty woman reading some book. His sold a mere four hundred
copies. He was still a contender for the world's approval: he revealed, half-
proudly, half-sheepishly, that it was laurels he was after. (In March 1900,
with *Buddenbrooks* well-launched, he admitted to Heinrich that his "secret
and powerful ambition" had always been "greatness.") Given his poor education, his intense but limited grasp of character, and his weak sales record,
Mann's ambition seemed excessive.

In October 1897, still a tourist in Rome, with Samuel Fischer's suggestion in mind, he began a novella about Lübeck, which would develop
into an epic-size work. He wrote some years later, "When I began to write
Buddenbrooks, I was sitting in Rome at the Via Torre Argentina trenta
quattro, four floors up. My home city had little reality for me and I was
not very convinced of its existence. It seemed to me with its inhabitants
nothing essentially more than an earlier dream, both ludicrous and respectable, and *in the most proper way my own* [italics mine]."

Mann frequently asserted that finishing a book was like awakening from
a dream. *Buddenbrooks* was his first reported instance of a zone into which
he could slip, momentarily paroled from the world.

The copious research provided a trace of his entrepreneurial ancestors;
the immense preparation he always assigned himself for his novels mim-

icked the organizational skills involved in running a small business. Of all
Mann's forays into the precincts of scholarship, *Buddenbrooks* required the
least application. The subject was his own family. He examined the history
of Lübeck economics, cultural patterns, business cycles; he combed wills
and recipes, and drew upon his relatives' memories. (He used some of Lula's
notes on Aunt Elisabeth's unhappy career verbatim.)

Much as a dilettante lives off his income, Mann's dreamlike condition
was materially grounded. The erotic animus of youth inspired his work.
And a monthly check from his mother supported him. Finally it was money
that gave him entry into the zone.

En route to Munich, he stopped briefly in Florence. He was there in
April 1898 when a large commemorative stone was placed on the site of
Savonarola's bonfire of the vanities (the public burning of the toys and
baubles of the wealthy), to mark the four hundredth anniversary of that
fiercely ascetic occasion. While in Florence, he began taking notes on Savonarola's rebellion against the spiritual excesses he now identified with
Heinrich. A year earlier, in "Little Louise," he had begun to attack. Now,
after seeing the stone in the Piazza della Signoria, he had acquired an
objective correlative for his anger as well as a potent dramatic symbol.

He returned to Munich at the end of April and took his first bachelor
apartment in the bohemian section of Schwabing, living first on the ground
floor before moving to the second and finally to the fourth. When you live
alone, nothing counts but the details. He described his digs as a "bohemian
ménage," where he spent days "squatting" before wicker chairs purchased
in the raw and "painting them with red enamel." There was also his parents'
mahogany bed, his father's cigar case, a rented piano, and his violin. Like
the dilettante, he found consolation in possessions. He lived simply and
bought his supper at a local delicatessen. Meanwhile the onset of several
dental problems—a lifetime agony—kept him awake.

Never a good athlete, he derived great pleasure from bicycling through
this "half-rustic, half-cosmopolitan town." Other times he would ride into the
wood "with a book on my handlebar. I was such an impassioned rider . . .
that I scarcely went a step on foot, but even in pouring rain went on all
my errands in loden cape and rubber overshoes on my machine. . . . Mornings, after my work, I used to stand it on its saddle and clean it." Richard
Winston interprets this as an attempt to ward off a breakdown like the one
that had already placed Heinrich in a sanitarium. But it's also of a piece
with Mann's lifetime fascination with novelties. Thomas boasted that he
witnessed the first electric lights, telephone boxes, and bicycles to reach
Germany, and Heinrich remembered traveling with his father in an auto-
mobile in 1890: "Only the nouveaux riches disdain novelties," he quipped.

Thomas shared the dilettante's interest in pretty furniture. In "The Wardrobe" (first published in 1899), a Heinrich-like neurasthenic is visited nightly by a naked wraith escaping from a large, backless armoire. The object is more substantial than the fantasized woman. So are the splendid meals the hero consumes, detailed from herbal soup to Gorgonzola and pears, fortifying Cognac, and Russian cigarettes. He's a sickly fellow with a passionate urge to sleep; indeed the woman seems to him "as sweet as the lips of sleep." She tells him stories but disappears as each one ends. When he finally embraces her, Mann vouchsafes no details: "How long it lasted, who knows?"

The wraith resembled his youngest sister, Carla. That highly theatrical girl was always closer to Heinrich, and had been the dedicatee of the brothers' joint production, *The Picture Book*. The illustrations included Thomas's drawing of a lewd, lip-smacking Mother Nature—an apparition recalled decades later in *Doctor Faustus*, but perhaps evident in "The Wardrobe" in the form of an old woman covered by fungal growths, "repulsive" except for her long, lovely, white hand. Juxtaposing these images, the ghostly muse and the obscene earth mother, suggests that Mann could not yet create a real feminine presence. He was more comfortable with drawers and closets; the story's hero boasts, "No man has ever been so alone." ("The Wardrobe" was Mann's first American publication. It appeared later that year in a New York German-language newspaper.)

Before his marriage to Katia Pringsheim, Mann would go through a series of six apartments, none of them luxurious: one place was described by Kurt Martens as "a paltry little room." Victor remembered a portrait of Tolstoy, Heinrich one of Erasmus. There was also a laurel wreath placed near a manuscipt of *Buddenbrooks*. This bid for attention recalls the practice of Proust's Mademoiselle Vinteuil, who keeps a songbook on the piano turned to her father's composition.

Occasionally he gave literary soirées in which he tried to re-create the ambience of a public reading, although his audience was usually limited to Lula, Carla, and Ilse Martens. Dressed in tux or tails, he would enter his candle-lit chamber, bow to his elegant guests and read long passages from his novel. Afterward the young people would snack on delicacies sent over from Frau Mann's pantry; Ilse recalled particularly a huge ox tongue in aspic. Obviously the author's idea of fun was to dress up and act out; even at leisure, he was rehearsing for stardom.

The Mann brothers had long quit their association with *The Twentieth Century*, a magazine Thomas now described to Grautoff as a "simpleminded little rag." After his return to Munich, in April 1898, he had graduated to *Simplicissimus*, assuming a job as acquisitions editor and copy reader.

(Korfiz Holm, a former schoolmate and co-founder of *Frühlingssturm*, was one of the editors.) He was not a demanding editor: he admitted some years later that he accepted far more than any magazine could publish. He would remain an overly tolerant reader. During his exile, he provided many effusive blurbs for his less successful compatriots. His generosity then might have had a whiff of noblesse oblige: his enemies pursued his endorsement, then dismissed it as insincere. They ignored his expression of a comradely fellow-feeling. For Mann's perpetual subject was the immense difficulty of writing, and its few and transient rewards.

The cheeky tone of *Simplicissimus* epitomized modern irreverence. For Mann to pursue a representative status, despite his association with the magazine, was akin to a youthful satirist aspiring to the role of poet laureate. Even more modern than the tone were the numerous advertisements for unfamiliar products—bicycles, motor cars, American "Brownie Kodaks," laxatives, potency tablets, and condoms. There were even treatments for drug addiction. Nihilism was supported by a newfangled commerce; it was a moot question which was the greater outrage. The slow starter Mann had leapt into the ranks of the avant-garde. Not incidentally, the journalism of *Simplicissimus*—and the advertisements—prepared him for both the new century and America. During the early 1920s, he would support his family by composing German cultural dispatches for an American journal, *The Dial*.

While he would later recall a gregarious period in his teens, the era of Grautoff and Timpe, he was now a loner; his significant friend remained Heinrich. Through his work he acquired important literary acquaintances. They provided a cheering section for his nascent career. Kurt Martens, for one, served as both his mentor and his promoter. But he still impressed people as unrelaxed and tense. Mann hated such responses. He would declare to Martens that he was not seen correctly; in truth he overflowed with passion. The world might view him as a closed fist, but his heart was open, and he was, if anything, too emotionally susceptible.

In September 1899, he returned to Lübeck for the first time in five years. Instead of visiting relatives, he chose to stay at a local hotel. While there, he was briefly detained by the police, who apparently mistook him for a fugitive confidence man. He would milk this incident. When Tonio Kröger is similarly detained, he concludes in an essayistic riff that the artist and the criminal are brothers; Felix Krull, about whom Mann kept writing off and on for almost fifty years, is himself a confidence man.

There is an eminently bourgeois infatuation with the mud in Mann's affinity for outlaws. There may also be a subtext; his furtive strolling may have appeared a sexual amble. This would certainly explain the need to return to his hometown incognito. Whatever the case, he had begun a series of unpleasant encounters with the authorities that would extend from the Lübeck police to Adolf Hitler and the FBI.

He began to move freely among the lions. On September 9, 1900, he reported to Grautoff, "I went to the beer house—with many other literary people—Wedekind, Martens, Holitscher, Count Keyserling, among others." He no longer felt overwhelmed by their reputations. Six months later he informed Grautoff that Holitscher's notebook was all right, "but I do it better"—and proceeded to do so by using Holitscher as a model for "Tristan."

A draft summons could not have been more inopportune: both his career and his personal life were thriving. Days earlier he had written Grautoff, "I have decided to avoid the infantry service with its foul-smelling, repulsive exercises. Martens made them seem terrifying. He told me to avoid it at any price. I don't want to revive the Schramm lessons; they were the worst, most awful times of my life, despite Willri."

Mann had only remained in school to acquire a certificate (one-year-volunteer's certificate) limiting his military service to a year. He had written Grautoff from Rome in 1897 that he didn't intend returning to the " 'esteemed Fatherland' again" for a year; he was an unashamed draft dodger. The quotes suggest he considered German jingoism worthy of satire. He griped that "unless the army surgeon has a heart, there awaits me the gruesome Moloch of 'militarism.' But I don't much like to let my mind dwell on that and it crouches, gray and horrible, a puffy-eyed monster, behind the colorful, attractive games of the immediate future." Necessity would be the monstrous mating of Mother Nature and the puffy-eyed Moloch.

He was twice rejected for his narrow chest and nervous heart. But a brewing conflict with England over Germany's support of the South African Boers made the authorities less rigorous. Mann was amused that they were desperate enough to consider him: "On October 1, to the consternation of the enemies of the Fatherland, I shall shoulder a gun." To some an outlaw, to others a hermetic aesthete, to himself a poseur and homosexual, Mann knew that he was a most unlikely volunteer for the Prince's Regiment of the Royal Bavarian Infantry.

At first he reported, "I am completely acquiescent (believe it or not). . . . Only in this way can these nervous crotchets of mine be exorcised." The army would make a man of him yet. This bravado was expressed to a new friend, Paul Ehrenberg. The self-ridicule was a seductive ploy: Thomas

Mann remained, only knew himself as, a "nervous exception." But for a while, he enjoyed military wardrobe: his snug uniform was a costume to replace the regal outfits of his childhood princes. Be prepared, he wrote Ehrenberg, to find me a "romantically costumed and brutalized mercenary."

In his first letters to Heinrich, Mann described his army service as a calamity. The work was tedious, and there were no kindred spirits. But twelve years later he remembered the months as paradoxically invigorating. "[I felt] an extraordinarily enhanced enjoyment of inner freedom—when, for example, in the barracks, while cleaning my rifle (which I never learned how to do properly), I whistled something from *Tristan*." In 1900 he had been desperate for assistance from a pliant doctor, who would agree that his flat feet made him unfit for service. But the army's junior medical officer was rude and disrespectful. While examining Mann he declared that he needed a cigar or he would succumb to nausea. He found nothing wrong and directed Mann back to duty. A few days later Mann was hospitalized for a case of "inflamed flat-foot," but again no problem was detected. However, Frau Mann's doctor had intervened with the chief medical officer. This gentleman arrived at the infirmary, pulled rank on his junior, and "commanded him to see something that wasn't there." In 1900 Mann viewed his release as a deliverance. Yet by 1907 he could laugh over the episode: "The body is to a certain extent subject to the mind and if there had been the slightest liking for [this military] business within me, the ailment probably could have been overcome." Such objectivity was not granted everyone. Mann was enraged when his mother's financial adviser questioned his early release. As throughout his life, he reserved the right to ridicule himself. In 1912 he summarized the whole episode as "an amusing case of corruption."

Another explanation had appeared in 1904. Mann remembered himself as a "cripple of the state" with absurdly "inflamed legs." He recalled trembling before his commanding officer: "I lose my composure before those I love," and he appended a quotation from Schiller (addressed to Goethe), "If I love you, why should you care?" These words either allowed him a graceful way of saving face or betrayed his longing for the clear-eyed blond beasts, resurrected in his World War I propaganda.

On July 18, 1900, Mann informed Grautoff, "Today I wrote the last line of my novel." He was on the verge of his military service and in the first throes of his involvement with Paul Ehrenberg, the great love of his life. This double tension may contribute to the urgency of his novel's final pages. But the dazzling achievement of *Buddenbrooks*, composed by a man who seems to have lived sparely, far surpasses its biographical sources. It drew upon the history of the Lübeck Manns, a family, he intimated in his work's subtitle, that was now "in decline." Such language infuriated those around him. But he contended that "indiscretion loses all its sting as soon as it is also (and primarily) directed against the author's own person. In my work I expose myself with such passion that by comparison the few indiscretions against others scarcely matter."

5

BUDDENBROOKS

As Proust has his madeleines, the author of *Buddenbrooks* has his marzipan, a confectionary emblem of the bourgeoisie. This delicacy symbolizes Lübeck *Gemütlichkeit*, but its references are not merely local. Mann observed happily—if inaccurately—that the word derives from "Marci panis," the bread of St. Mark's. Etymology linked Lübeck and Venice, grammar and commerce. Just so, his novel, with its acknowledged debts to English (Dickens), French (the Goncourt brothers and Flaubert), Russian (Turgenev, himself a pupil of the French), and Scandinavian (Andersen, J. P. Jacobsen) authors, became more than the record of a local family's decline. In 1904, Mann offered a bluntly German confession: "My literary colleagues will be astonished to learn that my [real] master is Wagner." But, as early as "Der Bajazzo," he had demonstrated that Wagner was a trans-European phenomenon.

The same patterns of marketing and distribution that homogenized the Western world made *Buddenbrooks* a universal document. Often regarded as a belated example of nineteenth-century fiction, it actually predicts most of the issues—of culture, politics, and the self—that would preoccupy modern writers. All of Mann's later work can be traced to this early, most reader-friendly of his novels.

Buddenbrooks is supremely a novel about language. From its opening lines, when Tony Buddenbrook's grandfather coaches her attempts at the Lutheran catechism in a mixture of Plattdeutsch and French, the book details the myriad ways language informs our lives. Yet for a novel that revolves around such a highly intellectual issue, *Buddenbrooks* is doggedly materialistic: indeed the combination of abstract thought and sensuous detail is what makes Mann so appealing—or, to readers like Nabokov, so middlebrow. All the big subjects are treated: religion, philosophy, national politics. But they are grounded in the routine, assimilated to anecdote and gossip. The most imposing activities of adult men are sabotaged by infantile neuroses. Every attempt at overreaching is checked by an intractable nature and a rebellious human body. In few previous novels had decaying teeth and nervous stomachs so viscerally represented a state of spiritual collapse.

The narrative leap from short story to massive novel was eased by the book's format. Thomas told Heinrich that he had enough material for several novellas, and the first sections of *Buddenbrooks* resemble a collection of short stories. These proceed with the inexorable drive of a daytime serial. (Following the success of the family sagas *Upstairs, Downstairs* and *The Forsyte Saga*, *Buddenbrooks* was itself serialized for television.) The abbreviated format mimes the characters' uneventful days while later, lengthier chapters culminate in a series of tragedies as melodramatic as Little Herr Friedemann's suicide or Christian Jacobi's death. True to the narrative rhythm, even the metaphysical is domesticated.

Mann had acquired a knowledge of family minutiae which he conveyed with the attentiveness of a Japanese novelist. Each Buddenbrook activity is investigated; the assorted hobbies and fads comprise a form of cultural anthropology. Their pursuits merge high and low, serious and trivial, for as needy burghers they turn everything to their immediate advantage. Whether swooning to Wagner or misreading Schopenhauer, they are a typical clan of bourgeois consumers. It was another of Mann's lucky breaks that the forces that regulate the Buddenbrook lives were so universal that their history became a world classic: the triumph of bourgeois appetite.*

Within three generations, and four decades (1835–1875), the Buddenbrooks are brought to ruin. At their height, the family of shipbuilders and merchants incarnates the burgher values of thrift, piety, and cunning—but, also, at least initially, a fair degree of independence. Precisely because the senior Johann subscribes to the French Enlightenment, he employs French—and low German—to ridicule the Lutheran catechism. He "makes fun of sacred things" in demotic slang. His irreverence is joined with tolerance (he tells Tony to accept "each one according to his own light")—qualities that elude his son and skip at least two generations. His son Johann, the Consul, derives his piety from his mother. As indicated by his motto, "Work, pray, and save," he combines a social directive with a re-

---

* Buddenbrook was the name of a relative of Armin Martens, as well as of a character in Fontane's *Effi Briest*.

ligious obligation. Mann draws a fascinating connection between religion and introspection, exemplified by Grandmother Buddenbrook in the hour of her dying.

Johann, father of the three siblings, endorses a rigorous combination of capitalist principles and fundamentalist Christianity. (Were he alive today, he might join the Full Gospel Businessmen's Convention.) Mann prided himself that he had unwittingly created a character in the Max Weberian mold, a man for whom commerce and faith are interchangeable.

Johann wrecks his children's romances when they stray across class lines. He upholds reactionary politics and reduces all family matters to a question of financial prospects. Yet this proud man is vanquished by the weather. While he is vacationing with his family, there is a sudden burst of humidity, menacing and tropical. When it ends, Johann Buddenbrook is found dead, apparently of a stroke. As if Mann wished to assert the physical sensations Johann had denied his offspring, he punishes the tyrannical father with a beach idler's revenge.

Besides Buddenbrook's three children, Thomas, Christian, and Antonie (Tony), major characters include Thomas's wife, Gerda, and their son, Hanno. Among them Mann distributed the qualities he recognized in himself. They are variously womanish, nervous, musical, word-intoxicated, and death-obsessed. Tony alone is gifted with resilience, and that trait derives from her apparent insensitivity to the most ghastly personal setbacks.

She has other powers. From her first appearance, worrying over the catechism, she is identified as the guardian of a sacred text. She grows into a pretty, adventurous girl who falls in love with a young revolutionary. Her father forbids the match and forces her to marry a scoundrel. After the divorce, she survives two other bad marriages: the first, her own to an amiably vulgar Munich entrepreneur; the second, her daughter's—stage-managed by Tony as if she herself were the bride—which ends with her son-in-law's criminal conviction. With the years, the girl who danced at the revolution becomes a snobbish, silly woman, a chatterbox and a bore. By the end, we've seen her sprout a mustache and vomit on the lawn.

Yet she remains so defiantly a Buddenbrook that she winds up a near-mythic character. During her time in Munich, she learns that she is a Lübeck product—like marzipan. The *Münchner* don't share her language or her recipes (clearly hers is an oral personality), and if they won't call food by the right name, she doesn't want to eat it. She decides that her native language is Buddenbrook-speech: the family's history of Bible study and Plattdeutsch fables produced a local idiom. Only when she talks that talk can she be herself.

Tony becomes the custodian of language and customs because she can-

not live without them. In merging her identity with that of her family—
"I am they"—she anticipates the mythic figures in Mann's later work who
see themselves recapitulating their tribe's history in a new land. Tony is
nothing like the Hebrew Joseph: "We should never be transplanted, we
northern folk." (Of course it's her parochialism that makes her a particularly
universal character.) But then Joseph is an androgyne and a chameleon;
Tony is nothing more, nothing less than a Buddenbrook.

By modern standards, invisible to her if not to Mann, she enacts a
particular feminist role. For despite her lateral dip from revolutionary politics to family chauvinism, she is colored for life by her youthful rebellion.
She insinuates political lyrics and slogans into the family idiom, thus keeping the language alive. Her undying nostalgia for the old songs is familiar
to survivors of the 1960s. An unfriendly observer might take her residual
liberalism as some more of Tony's *Quatsch*. But her nostalgia for the revolution is indivisible from her personal tragedy. The liberal student was the
only right man for her. In Tony's case, the political is always the personal—
with her it could not be otherwise.

Late in the novel she attempts to sum up her experiences for her
nephew:

> "Travemünde is and always will be a beautiful spot. Till I go down
> to my grave I shall remember the weeks I spent there when I was a
> slip of a girl—and such a silly young girl! I lived with people I was
> fond of, and who seemed to care for me; I was a pretty young thing
> in those days,—though I'm an old woman now—and full of life and
> high spirits. They were splendid people, I can tell you, respectable and
> kind-hearted and straight-thinking, and they were cleverer and better
> educated, too, than any I've known since, and they had more enthu-
> siasm. Yes, my life seemed very full when I lived with them, and I
> learned a great deal which I've never forgotten—information, beliefs,
> opinions, ways of looking at things. If other things hadn't interfered—
> as all sorts of things did, the way life does, you know—I might have
> learned a great deal more from them."

This wonderful passage grants Tony her dignity. She has lived an unfulfilled life; the interjection "the way life does, you know" would break
her heart if she listened to herself. Schiller thought art could provide a
vision of happiness, but poor Tony dreamed that life itself would do the
trick. Whether Mann endorses her youthful politics—he certainly praises
its adherents for their intelligence and spirit—he registers her emotional
defeat in political terms. Johann says no; she has as much chance at an

independent life as a small nation attempting to break free of a superpower's control.

In her father's death might there not be a political vengeance on Mann's part? When rebellious workers capitulate to the town leaders during the 1848 revolution, Mann immediately shows a dignitary, Johann Buddenbrook's father-in-law, Kröger, felled by a stroke. Each stage of his decline is mercilessly depicted, as once again the claims of the body—and heart—assert themselves.

Tony's insistence on Buddenbrook decorum helps ground her brothers, Thomas and Christian. The two are endlessly at each other; there are few literary precedents for such murderous displays of sibling rivalry. The actor Christian considers Thomas a prig; the businessman Thomas sees in his brother the collapse of all standards. They snort and rankle like members of a particularly vicious therapy group. Christian's broad family head and large nose make him too homely for stardom. He specializes in character roles; he is particularly adept at Anglo-American forms of comedy. Thomas considers his mimicry a sign of immaturity. But they remain as much alike as when they were boys rolling on the Travemünde beach. In one passage, Thomas admits that Christian is a walking example of his own suppressed tendencies.

Christian's histrionics are founded on hyperbole. As a child, suffering from stomachaches, he vows never to eat: "I'm sick. I tell you damned sick." He's finicky, whining, hypnotized by his theatrical posture. As an adult he delights in scaring his relatives with tales of a red-headed demon. (Little Hanno inherits the nightmare, and imagines a red-bearded fellow with dirty fingernails "waiting to discipline him in the detested" mathematical equations. In such ways, sexual imagery enters the Buddenbrook collective unconscious.)

Like Tony, Christian can't shut up. Thomas observes, "He lacks equilibrium, mental poise—he can't cover up . . . but . . . tells his most intimate thoughts. There is such a lack of modesty in so much communicativeness." But these words are unconvincing, one of the novel's many ironies at the expense of language. Thomas would love to express himself as easily. His problem is that he's so much more complicated than his siblings that no words prove adequate. As Tony's eyes brighten with the name "Buddenbrook," Christian is excited by the very word "theater." But Thomas, whose role is to impersonate the Buddenbrook ideology, is cheerless.

Christian has one grand moment, when Thomas dies and he kneels before the corpse with unpremeditated emotion. But he survives to be hoodwinked by an actress and end in a madhouse. No wonder Mann's Uncle Friedel was not charmed by the resemblance. (Mann didn't much like his

uncle, judging by references in his letters to Heinrich, but he does endow
Christian with some of the traits he recognized in himself, and recreated
in his favorite Buddenbrook, Hanno.)

Mann's fiction is animated by the conviction that it takes one to know
one; the spotting of a dissolute "brother" is a perennial event. In this, its
earliest instance, the Buddenbrook brothers are wise to the other's tricks.
If Thomas understands too well Christian's faults, Christian knows how to
read him:

> "You are self-righteous. Oh, wait, that is not what I am going to say,
> nor what I accuse you of. I don't know where to begin, and however
> much I can say is only a millionth part of the feeling I have in my
> heart against you. . . . Your equilibrium is the most precious thing in
> the world to you. But it isn't the most precious thing in life,
> Thomas—no, before God, it is not. You are an egotist, and that is
> what you are. I am still fond of you, even when you are angry and
> tread on me, and thunder me down. But when you are silent . . . and
> withdraw yourself, quite elegant and remote, and repulse people like
> a wall and leave the other fellow to his shame, without any chance of
> justifying himself—. Yes, you are without pity, without love, without
> humility.—Oh . . . how sick I am of all this tact and propriety, this
> pose and refinement—sick to death of it."

This outburst serves as a superb dramatic monologue—true to the fre-
netic, stop-start rhythms of Christian's speech—and as a dramatized form
of social critique: a soliloquized editorial. It also resembles the indictments
frequently directed against Thomas Mann.

For the first time he dramatizes the question of *Haltung*. The Buddenbrooks are manipulators and slaves of their image. It would have been
enough to have Thomas and Tony victimized by their concern with "the
déhors," a pathetic echo of their grandfather's Francophiliac discourse! But
he also shows that *Haltung* is a social product, the midpoint between Grandfather Johann's lack and Hanno's excess of self-consciousness, and that it
constitutes a triple vise, social, psychological, and—inasmuch as Thomas
Buddenbrook is the town consul—political.

Shortly after Christian's tirade, we learn that

> in truth, Thomas Buddenbrook's existence was no different from that
> of an actor—an actor whose life has become one long product, which,
> but for a few brief hours for relaxation, consumes him unceasingly . . .
> while he stubbornly clings to the determination to be worthily rep-

resentative, to conceal his inward decline, and to preserve "the *dehors*" whatever it cost him. All this made of his life, his every word, his every motion, a constant irritating pretense.

A definitive statement from the novelist who symbolized—to his critics—the shams of representation.

Thomas is so much the actor that he can perform only when he is in complete charge of the "self-production." In other words, he represents only himself; his appropriate commentator is less Max Weber than Freud. Impersonating Senator Thomas Buddenbrook requires him to design the costumes, angle the lights, collect the props. He is invariably thrown off when his audience, by responding, introduces a new element into the spectacle. As Mann had made clear before, self-production is self-protection. His artifice exhibits an attention to details bordering on "pedantry": a reader might add "monomania" and "pathology."

Thomas knows his act is killing him. Sometimes he tells Tony, "[Life's] passing me by. It's lost all sense. I can't control it." But the practical Tony won't hear him; she insists that one can't *say* such things. In these scenes, Mann makes two breakthroughs: turning the representative into an expert witness against himself, and suggesting that an honest admission is outside the realm of social discourse.

In Proust's novel, Marcel sheds involuntary tears while tying his shoelaces, because the act summons the image of his doting grandmother. Something quite other occurs when Thomas Buddenbrook sheds his involuntary tears—not the recovery of past emotions, but visionary release from the routine of self-denial. This distinction matters; it suggests how much Mann is the writer of *Sehnsucht* and not of nostalgia, how much his impulse is to move away from the past.

In the summer of 1874, while his wife conducts a discreet flirtation with a musically inclined soldier, Thomas has a brief epiphany. He picks up an unnamed book—a volume of Schopenhauer's—and becomes enthralled by its gloomy pronouncements. As he reads "On Death and Its Relation to the Indestructibility of Our Essence in Itself," his life assumes its meaning. In a language of alienation that stretches from Rousseau and Wordsworth to Karl Marx, Thomas sees his life as a prison sentence. The release is death, "a great joy . . . a return from an unspeakably painful wandering, the correction of a grave mistake."

If alive he was trapped in his individual, historically determined fate, once dead he will express every human potentiality—the disappointing Hanno is of no consequence. He doesn't need a son—his seed will bear a spiritual fruit. Somewhere he has a perfected self, his twin, his comrade, his true son. Thus Thomas Buddenbrook anticipates Thomas Mann, who referred to his creation as "my father, my brother, my double," in a conscious echo of his own words.

Granted this confidence, Thomas welcomes death. Previously "I have hated life" because it would not bend to his purposes. Now death will unite him with the Other—and implicitly the self—he had denied. I love you all, he declares with the expansive fervor of adolescence; dying into you, "I shall live." Inspired by literature, his faith goes beyond language: he feels charged with "a sudden rapturous illumination of his innermost being."

Well he might, for, read coldly, his vision is metaphysical gibberish, a Mannian dream of homoerotic union abstracted out of existence. It's probably a misreading of Schopenhauer as well. Whatever its intellectual validity, Thomas forgets the experience. He does not finish the book, and the maid eventually replaces it, no doubt next to Tony's lending-library romances.

With Thomas Mann, the accuracy of somebody's reading is insignificant. His characters' response is what matters. Few authors probe so well the intense, visceral coming to knowledge of an essentially passive, aesthetic experience. The modern artwork loses what Walter Benjamin calls its "aura," but acquires a mundane utility, drawn to the measure of each consumer's needs.

Like his father's death, Thomas's end is triggered by a physical accident. His dentist is Dr. Brecht; much is made of his onomatopoeic name (while the reader winces at this unwitting forecast of the playwright, Mann's despised nemesis: the ironies of language were as breathtaking as Mann believed). The Buddenbrooks suffer from tooth decay and exposed nerves, a transparent symbol of their decline—and perhaps a comment on their bourgeois diet. Under Brecht's scalpel, Thomas experiences a whole new dimension of pain—an epiphany far more shocking and graphically represented than the vision out of Schopenhauer. It is a new sensation, and he literally cannot live with its existence. The preened and perfumed senator collapses in the gutter.

Thomas's wife, Gerda Arnoldson, is an outsider. She is imagined as an Ice Maiden, a Hans Christian Andersen figure. Although sympathetic to her troubled husband, she is clearly inhibited by the provincial setting of Lübeck. Her pleasure is making music, and she responds to Wagner with a passion absent in her marriage. Sometimes she accompanies her young son, Hanno, and Mann intimates a deeper communication between mother and child, that bypasses speech. Gerda is commonly seen as frigid.

The true problem is that Thomas has no words for her. He is so influenced by his father's commercial idiom that when he writes his mother about Gerda, he cannot distinguish between his love and her financial prospects. Likewise, when Gerda performs duets with her friend the cultured military adjunct, he is verbally stymied. Theirs is not a conventional affair, and he can't define it. Gerda can be regarded as an intellectual Madame Bovary or as an oblique tribute to Julia Mann: mother, madonna, and muse. No doubt she would have been better off single.

Hanno is the last of the Buddenbrook line. Until the creation of Adrian Leverkühn, Hanno would remain Mann's favorite character, and he showers him with tremendous attention, while indicating that he is doomed. We see him briefly happy in the period of childish games whose meaning no adult can grasp. But as if to overwhelm the poor fellow, Mann brackets this description of youthful pleasures between an evocation of *two* wars and a preview of unrequited love.

His health proves fragile—the familiar stomach and dental problems —and his will still feebler. Precociously morbid, he draws a line through his name in the family Bible, as if to write himself off. Like his mother, he wishes to emancipate himself from language. In a series of beautiful passages, Mann suggests an unspoken communication between father and son. Both share the gloomy conviction that their character is their fate. But Thomas can't bear to acknowledge the similarity of temperaments. He requires the abnormally shy boy to recite Christmas poems. When Hanno embarrasses himself, Thomas goads him, "Are you a little girl?" After that Hanno pledges his retreat from language, particularly the pulpit rhetoric Thomas employs for his own motives of self-disguise.

Hanno's death is as physically gruesome as his father's, a similarly psychosomatic collapse in which a demoralized self blocks the body's capacities of immunization. Coming after his remark that "I want to die," his typhoid seems willed. Readers have wept over that death, but perhaps not so much as over Echo's in *Doctor Faustus*, because Hanno seems complicit. His death is usually read as a definitive ending to the Buddenbrook saga. This appears most unsubtle, given that Hanno was Mann's favorite and that *Buddenbrooks* is the opening salvo of a long career. Hanno's character and desires overshadow Mann's complete oeuvre. He was anticipated in 1895; he leaves traces in 1955.

Hanno Buddenbrook is something new in literature. He is the first "Little Boy Blue," the aesthete, bad at games, socially maladroit, suffused with a voracious and forbidden sexuality. By comparison, the sorrows of Dickens's orphans are easily alleviated. Like all the sad young men who will succeed him, Hanno sees that his misery is intrinsic. "So it is and so it will be always and everywhere."

Yet Mann allows him some relief. The purest communion in the novel is between Hanno and his only friend, Count Kai Mölln.* The two embody Schiller's split between sentiment and nature. Hanno is the precious aesthete: the mud-loving Kai makes fun of his soft, white, feminine hands. In his avoidance of potential bullies, Hanno disdains gym class because of the physical stench of his fellow students. But he's not bothered when Kai refuses to bathe himself. The same bodily odors can revolt or arouse. Desire provides the context.

Their flirtation does not break the class barrier. Kai is an aspiring writer, living out the nature Hanno refuses to assert. Thomas Buddenbrook supports their friendship. His hope is that while Hanno refines Kai's manners, Kai will toughen up the sissy. (Such exchanges haunted Mann at this time; he boasted that he was cultivating Paul Ehrenberg while Paul was making him more earthbound.)

Yet Mann places him in a setting that he can observe with an acuity worthy of its author: Kai is the writer but Hanno has the writer's eye. He gazes at the world—his family, his fellow students, even Kai—with an obliquely cold look (*kalten Blick*), the austerely sensual glance that always conveys Mannian *Sehnsucht*. Thus gifted, Hanno becomes the most typical Mann figure, a precursor of all those, from Tonio Kröger to Felix Krull, Hans Castorp, and Joseph, whose task in life is to penetrate the world's glittering surfaces.

Since Oscar Wilde (or in German, the lyrics of Mann's favorite poet, August von Platen), gay melancholia has fragilely balanced the grandiose, the campy, and the genuinely afflicted. Tricked and wounded by the philistines' assaults, seeing themselves as little Saint Sebastians (Mann's preferred saint), some youthful fops exhibit a form of aesthetic Catholicism, reveling in their misery. Hanno displays operatic excesses of self-pity unmitigated by humor, along with a precise sense of the life around him. It is a knowledge specifically predicated on his sexual nature.

The novel's longest chapter recounts Hanno's schoolday. Mann evokes a tedium that makes everyone crazy. The school hierarchy resembles a Great Chain of Being that peaks with the "Father God"—the headmaster—a figure so arbitrary that he prefigures the God Mann imagines in his Joseph books, a jealous male-bonded deity who requires the foreskins of his chosen people. The atmosphere is grimly Prussian, consecrated to xenophobia and

* The model for Kai was Mann's schoolmate Count Hans Kaspar von Rantzau.

greed. The Father God threatens to destroy his *"sans-culottist"* students' career. (In 1950 Mann remembered when his principal accused some "pranksters," "You've behaved just like Social Democrats.") The teachers intimidate the weak, suck up to the strong. Employing Hanno's perspective, Mann definitively renders the horrors of Prussian schools.

Slight, soft-spoken, and a Buddenbrook, Hanno becomes a provocative presence. One time, while swimming, he is attacked by the Hagenström brothers, sons of the town's new leaders. (A family of go-getters, their name signifies for Toni the triumph of the barbarians; the echo of Wagner's *"Götterdämmerung"* is deliberate.) Count Kai swims to his rescue, dives underwater, and bites the offending Hagenström on the leg. This action is by far the novel's most shocking physical action. It's not clear whether the battle is over sex or class, or both.

Most of the instructors are hacks and bullies; they share the master's warped ideology. But one, a student teacher, Candidate Modersohn, is more vulnerable. He is timid, clumsy, "insignificant looking," and he teaches English, not German. The students pick on him, mimicking his speech impediments. As he carries on, ignoring their hostility, Hanno finds that he "loved him in that moment, sat quite still, and looked up into his worried, helpless face." With the same insight that revealed his father's nature, Hanno has deduced from Modersohn's appearance "the whole pathetic, inadequate figure he made." He sees more: "he saw into the man's inner self." How is he repaid? Modersohn recognizes the boy's unspoken sympathy, but when his tormentors provoke him beyond endurance, he turns on Hanno.

Throughout Mann's fiction, he dramatizes an unspoken awareness between the leaders of society—from Buddenbrook to Aschenbach—and certain less privileged men, of whom Candidate Modersohn is the first. These men either pander to their tastes or share them. Invariably the understanding involves isolated men, drawn together by something vaguely—but unmistakably—homoerotic. It is a tribute to Mann's realism that the class tensions always intrude. Hanno has no more luck with Modersohn than with his father.

" 'But so it is, and so will be, always and everywhere,' " is the boy's conclusion, "and fear, and that sensation almost amounting to physical nausea, rose again in him. 'And the most dreadful thing is that I can't help seeing through you with such disgusting clearness.' " This combination of an almost clinical attack of anxiety with a double epiphany about two spiritual brothers, divided by their self-hatred, demonstrates Mann's extraordinary psychological reach.

Music is Hanno's sole means of communication, but he won't dare perform in public; as he tells Kai, "I can only improvise a little when I'm alone." That isolated improvisation builds to an orgasmic crisis. His final performance is emphatically sexual, a refined form of masturbation. First he introduces a motif, then allows it to disappear beneath an onslaught of overwrought harmonies, always to return, "now like a raucous laugh, now like an ineffably sweet promise." During a cacophonous passage, a hallucinatory moment occurs—"as though curtains were torn apart, doors sprang open, thorn-hedges parted of themselves, walls of flame sank down." There follows a dizzying succession of images out of German fairy tales or Wagner and blatantly sexual symbols. When the motif recurs, the mood changes to one of religious exaltation and "festival." All the elements combine; the music resounds through every octave, "triumphantly adorned with all the bursting, tinkling, foaming purling resources of orchestral pomp."

We become as embarrassed by the recital as if we'd caught Hanno at penile play. Mann observes "a quality of the perverse in the insatiability . . . a sort of cynical despair . . . a longing for joy, a yielding to desire, till exhaustion, disgust, and satiety supervened." It's a bird's-eye view of someone trapped in a waste of shame.

From *la petite mort* to the big one: Hanno's typhoid becomes the coda of his onanistic virtuosity. As he lies dying, Count Kai visits him and falls to his knees, showering kisses on the white, girlish hands. In its unashamed directness, this homage of nature to sentiment is the novel's most passionate gesture. The prospect of happiness may be frustrated and renounced in Mann's fiction, but it is always a palpable presence. In similar scenes in Edith Wharton's *House of Mirth* and Klaus Mann's Tchaikovsky novel, *Symphonie Pathètique*, men can only acknowledge their emotions after their lover has died. At least Hanno feels Kai's lips on his hands. This embrace is the novel's last dramatic action. As such, it is an astonishing revelation on the author's part, giving pride of place to a homosexual embrace. But most readers have failed to recognize his act of self-exposure. A little like Poe's purloined letter, the evidence of Mann's tendencies was too visible to be spotted.

Mann's works are uniformly subversive of convention. But the distinguished language and the author's reputation tended to mute the books' most outrageous implications. A novel like *Buddenbrooks* came to represent all that progressive German novelists despised: they found it stately, morbid, melancholy, smug, the bible of the loathsome bourgeoisie. Yet what an indictment Mann had produced. Although the progressive politics of 1830 and 1848 came to naught—hardly Mann's fault!—he demonstrates that liberal values have seeped into the culture, together with the changes in taste and patterns of consumption. The decline of the Budden- brooks can be read as a valedictory to families in general. The future that Gerda, Thomas, Christian, and Hanno predict is one of single people work- ing out their salvation alone. They won't marry; they will burn.

Buddenbrooks is saturated with religious imagery. From Toni's opening stabs at the catechism to a final affirmation of faith in the hereafter, mouthed by the pathetic dwarf Sesemi Weichbrodt, it reflects the central position of Lutheranism in this household. Yet from the period of Johann's fanatical piety, there is a precipitous drop to the last pages, when religion has become the stuff of sewing circles, the consolation of embittered women. Ministers prove to be fortune hunters; pious slogans become the last mut- terings of con men. Hanno finds church as stifling as school, its myths equally irrational.

During a bad time, Thomas flirts with Catholicism, but his nature is too inbred to dissolve into the church's universal communion. The nexus that Weber defined lives on in Thomas, even after he loses his faith and his taste for business. Protestantism endures as a skeptical form of intro- spection. For instance, when Thomas's mother dies, this decent, pious woman is shown monitoring her physical decline. This is a subtle echo of the biblical command to "watch as well as pray," suggesting the route from piety to self-reflection. Ultimately her death is so agonizing that it leaves her barely conscious, much less prayerful or lucid. Mann changes the terms of solace and then snatches it away entirely.

If *Buddenbrooks* diminishes personal and institutional authority, it pres- ents a world in which objects vie for the characters' attention. Once more shop windows act as mirrors; it's almost predictable that new owners should open a store in the old family mansion. The lonely make do with inanimate objects. Good furniture, good clothes, good food compensate for what shouldn't be felt, must not be spoken. But the skeptical Mann withdraws this consolation as well. The novel is so crammed with splendid meals that Mann joked he was becoming known as a food writer. But his well-fed burghers suffer unrelenting dyspepsia. Mann suggests a purging in lieu of catharsis.

Long after the novel's publication, another sexually conflicted product of Mann's class, Ludwig Wittgenstein, argued that the human world is not ordered by any codified, institutionalized principle of discourse. Instead he saw a multiplicity of forms of life, each of them characterized by its own "language games." The philosopher's suggestive remarks were not spelled out. But in Mann's novel, the perpetual conflict between what Wittgenstein called "signifying practices" is rendered on virtually every page.

There is no common language available to pious entrepreneurs, political radicals, aspiring writers, and self-appointed "representative men," not to mention musicians, for whom truth is by definition nonverbal. Yet what Wittgenstein considers a social failure is for Mann the novelist's great chance. His views parallel those of Bakhtin, who celebrated novels for their unique incorporation of a multiplicity of languages—the dialects and idioms of the many subgroups that compose a society.

Only the novelist could see it all and tell it all—even the stuff that resisted telling. With his first novel, Mann declared his particular interest in the strains and failures of language. Throughout the book, characters muse on what may be properly said. Toni refuses to hear Thomas's confession of inadequacy because "one" doesn't talk like that. He speaks in public a language so artificial that it shuts off the chance of dialogue, the prospect of which terrifies him. Hanno is so bullied by words that he escapes from language to music. From early childhood he has received musical instruction from the church organist Herr Pfühl. His best times are when he is sequestered with Pfühl, high above the congregation, deaf to the preacher's "twaddle."

Four years after *Buddenbrooks* appeared, Henry James published *The Golden Bowl*, a novel in which the heroine laments the distance between "what she took in and what she could say." James fills that gap with involuted examinations of motive. The much younger Mann anticipated James's theme, and with far greater immediacy. His family ultimately goes to ruin because there is no clear path from what they know to what they're allowed to say.

Rare moments occur when they can plot their liberation. Always something intervenes—"the way life does, you know." Thomas closes his Schopenhauer and forgets his vision. If a way out exists, it is provided by art. The art form par excellence is music, and it provides both a structural ballast for the novel and its only viable image of freedom. Hanno writes himself out of the family history by sketching a double line diagonally across the page, "as he had been taught to embellish the page of his arithmetic book." He's estranged from words and numbers. The kind organist Pfühl hopes that "in later life when Hanno's mouth will probably be shut even tighter, he might have some kind of outlet—a way of speaking—." Pfühl exhibits a musician's gaze, absentminded, soulful, the mark of his devotion to "a purer, profounder, more absolute logic than that which shapes our verbal conceptions and thoughts." Music becomes a Utopian form of speech.

Gerda notices that Hanno has a wide digital grasp—he can strike the ninths and tenths—but runs the risks of a thoughtless virtuosity. What saves the boy is his unerring sense of harmony: "It was only a confirmation of what he had always known." His earliest composition provides "an extraordinary contrast between the simple primitive material . . . and the impressive, impassioned, almost over-refined method with which that material was employed." This is superb musical criticism which doubles as a comment on Hanno's unarmored sense of adult life.

It also refracts on Mann's career: his great fluency, his limited subject matter, his tendency to harmonic elaboration at the expense of rhythmic— i.e., dramatic—excitement. There may be an implicit manifesto in the description of Hanno's technique: "He gave every simple harmonic device a special and mysterious significance by means of retardation and accentuation; his surprising skill . . . was displayed in each chord, each new harmony, by a suddenly introduced pianissimo."

Years later, when Hanno improvises for the last time, his music has grown darker and more compelling—"precisely by means of the meticulous and solemn precision with which it was defined and produced." Looking forward to the diabolical chorales of *Doctor Faustus*, Hanno's music is "torn by shrieks, like a soul in unrest." He introduces "ever different harmonies, questioning, complaining, protesting, demanding, dying away . . . shrieks of fear recurred. They took form and became melody." At last Hanno achieves his eloquence, and, in so doing, distinguishes himself from all the earlier adolescents in Mann whose anguish remains undeclared.

Mann dooms Hanno, although he can imagine an escape for his beloved. Even during the bout of typhoid, "life calls to the patient, may well up in him something like a feeling for a neglected duty; a sense of renewed energy, courage and hope; he may recognize a bond existing still between him and that stirring, colorful, callous existence which he thought he had left so far behind him. . . ." The blinded Milton lamented above all the loss of "human face divine"; and Tonio Kröger, poised on the verge of suicide, is summoned back to life by the prospect of "stirring, colorful, callous existence." One can feel Mann encouraging Hanno to revive himself. At least he fulfills the boy's "longing for joy." He dies after Kai has kissed his hands.

When the Buddenbrook women hear of Count Kai's embrace, they sit absorbed in thought. The last gesture, the image of a dream lover adoring the dying Hanno, heedless of public disapproval, like all the displays of emotions that have gone before, cannot be discussed.

The ultimate irony about an author perpetually saddled with the burden of paradox is that when he wrote most ingenuously, he wasn't taken seriously. So he could write about the unseemly satisfactions of literary composition. His novels showered numerous gifts on their readers, and they left him with the sad, sweet fantasies for his personal amusement. For him, too, art provided the breakthrough, allowed the expression that life denied. Like Hanno's "perverse" musicianship, Mann's literary art sprang from "longing," aspired to a "festival," and ended with the performer exhausted, written out, and alone. Until, reanimated by the Eros of literature, he began to write again, the "intervals" were "gruesome."

Mann specializes in startling juxtapositions of tone and subject matter. Like a canny soap opera scribe, he can juggle plot lines: as Thomas Buddenbrook reads Schopenhauer on one floor, his wife conducts her musicales with the young lieutenant on another, and on a third, Hanno silently composes a new tune. The contiguities are most astonishing in Mann's treatment of death. For him, there are deaths and there are deaths. Those of the Buddenbrook patriarchs don't signify much, outside of nature's caprice. However, by drawing from Wagner and Schopenhauer, Mann makes the deaths of Thomas and Hanno seem subjectively alluring.

Most surprising is the way he rhetorically undercuts the pathos of death. When Grandmother Buddenbrook painfully expires, the reader may feel as physically drained as her mourners. But immediately after, Mann introduces a note of low comedy: the servants abscond with her treasures.

Similarly, the delirium of Hanno's last cadenzas—conveyed in a language of willful excess—is succeeded by deadpan descriptions of typhoid. Like an excerpt from a medical journal, the neutral, colorless prose diminishes the suffering individual and reduces Hanno to a distant, abstract figure: the loved one becomes a footnote. This dissolution may be what Mann intended. He had considered using a Platen poem for the novel's epigraph. It begins "In the end I grow calmer and cold": the prose's icy tone may thus be read as a form of assent to death's destruction of identity.

Mann likes to play with the language of mourning. In *The Magic Mountain*, a harrowing death crisis will be succeeded by vaudevillian routines or by ironically inflected prose that almost rob death of its sting: Mann boasted that he had succeeded in making death "comical."

But there's another, more artistic problem with endings. Mann's treatment of closure is singular; a rare parallel is D. H. Lawrence, who resembled Mann more than either would care to admit. In Lawrence's novels, the life lived afterward is frequently more provocative than what takes place within the work. What kind of life is possible for Birkin and Ursula after he confesses his longing for a second relation with a man? All we're left with is a tremendous, albeit conflicted, psychic energy. The conclusion is at best an assertion of personal autonomy that leaves nothing settled.

The same may apply to *Buddenbrooks*, even if we limit our judgments to a novel that seems to end most conclusively. Yet Hanno's death signifies more than the fall of the house of Buddenbrook. It's the *sehnsüchtige Sprache*—the language of desire—that tells the tale. Just as the pessimistic tone of *Great Expectations* makes Dickens's coda unpersuasive, the barely suppressed energy of Mann's erotic prose contradicts the novel's air of finality. A modern reader finishes the book convinced of Mann's talent and his impatience.

Buddenbrooks is latent with possibilities for Mann himself and for all those writers who shared his particular slant: Proust and Kafka, as much as Wittgenstein and Bakhtin, are anticipated in the novel's pages. One might add that while the musical sections at first combine Wagner's aesthetic with Nietzsche's dissection of the bourgeois public, they undergo a profound change. In the last passages harmonic resolution is almost impeded by a sustained dissonance, and delirious virtuosity is examined as a pathological symptom. Among other things, Mann was composing the transition from Wagner and Nietzsche to Schönberg and Freud.

6

THE RIVALS

Mann had little confidence in the novel's chances. He wrote Paul Ehrenberg in June 1900 that after *Buddenbrooks'* completion, "I shall probably have to throw it into my publisher's maw for a song. Money and mass applause are not to be won with such books."

On the verge of submitting his manuscript, he experienced great misgiving: "I see it coming that whole chapters at the beginning, which now strike me as repulsively stupid, will have to be reworked." Actually not much revision was necessary, and shortly afterward he mailed his only copy to S. Fischer in Berlin. He was too exhausted to recopy the manuscript, so he sent it off, as Richard Winston records, "written on both sides of the page in his curiously sloping and sometimes difficult Gothic script . . . it looked shorter that way." (Mann knew the tricks of his trade.) He insured the work for one thousand marks but "burned myself fearfully with wax while sealing the novel."

Fischer wanted the book cut in half. After they learned of his demands, the Manns considered the publisher a villain for, as it were, wishing to abbreviate their family history. Mann refused to yield on length, but he gave some elsewhere: publish the book as is, he informed Fischer, and you can dictate your terms. Fischer agreed to publish it uncut in two volumes; his contract offered a high royalty rate (20 percent of retail) but no advance whatsoever.

Mann felt impoverished—"a church mouse," he told Heinrich—since his mother had deducted taxes from his quarterly income. (An annual income of 640 to 720 marks, supplemented by earnings from *Simplicissimus* and occasional magazine sales, had marginally sustained him.) He was now a free-lancer with miserable prospects. "I shall see nothing at all until September 1902. . . . If the edition sells out . . . I shall be receiving 2,000 marks, for the bookstore price will probably have to be around ten marks. But who is to say that even as many as one hundred copies will be sold? Incidentally I expected nothing better, and in fact nothing so good." His worse fear was that he would end up as a bank clerk.

Of course *Buddenbrooks* eventually sold millions. But perhaps in memory of Fischer's initial caution, Mann would later strike a hard bargain. All during his exile, he demanded that Fischer's successor, his son-in-law Gottfried Bermann-Fischer, adhere to the terms of his contract. Although Mann was financially responsible for six children and—more often than not—Heinrich, Bermann-Fischer pleaded for mercy: other refugees were financially strapped. Mann held out. He required the tangible forms of worldly success.

In the 1940s he knew his worth, but in 1900 he was another nervous writer, risking all without confidence in his publisher's support. Meanwhile Heinrich's novel *Im Schlaraffenland* had been published and was enjoying a great promotional campaign. By February 1901 it had appeared in a French translation. A disgruntled Thomas wrote his brother: "In a word, you are flourishing while at the moment I am going to pieces." Sibling rivalry had acquired a vocational aspect. The stakes were no longer parental affirmation but that slender laurel wreath.

Thomas Mann faced his greatest generational threat at home. Heinrich became someone to applaud, encourage, and . . . overcome. Yet his rival was also his confidant. He told Heinrich that he was insufficiently prolific: everything with him was slow and studied. Elsewhere he condemned Heinrich's rate of production—nobody could write well at that pace. Like many authors, he could simultaneously envy and condemn his peers.

Heinrich lost the war; Katia Mann says that he ultimately acknowledged Tommy as the superior artist. Yet in some circles this is not the received wisdom. Thomas's rival was a formidable one, particularly threatening because he shared his sensibility. (Though both subscribed to the belief that, as Heinrich put it, "as an artist one is bisexual," the heterosexual Heinrich frequently chose a female persona while Thomas rarely treated women except as surrogates for his own homoerotic tendencies.) Some word is necessary, then, about Thomas Mann's brother.

Their critic friend Hermann Kesten observed of the Manns that Heinrich was wiser and Thomas deeper. Heinrich was initially more facile but in the end less ambitious. A Francophile, he declined to become an essayistic

Thomas Mann in 1899, on the verge of fame

novelist in the German manner; he left intratextual commentary to Thomas.
Nor was he a linguistic athlete; he agreed with Montaigne that language
should be enriched, not expanded, and he deplored the German weakness
for compound words: Thomas had no such qualms. Heinrich's style is distinguished by his smuggling of rhetorical and analytical judgments into
fictions that consist of rapid scene changes and highly charged dialogue.
His work is invariably theatrical and its greatest flaw is melodrama.

Despite his constant attention to intellectual matters, he never becomes
a Shavian Prussian, all dazzling intelligence and no heart. Instead, a penchant for the bizarre, the arcane, and the lewd complicates his most abstruse
arguments. He shares Thomas's knack for unwittingly embarrassing himself. In a career of wild swings from aesthetic distance to political engagement he remained *l'homme moyen sensuel*. In the Aschenbach of *Death in Venice*
and Heinrich's Professor Unrat, the Mann brothers created two archetypal
voyeurs in their own image.

Like Thomas, Heinrich seeks a common denominator between high and
low art. Simply put, this meant that a nightclub singer can be as thrilling
as an operatic soprano. Whatever the musical arena, Heinrich's theater provides a spectacle of beautiful, liberated women whose performances manifest
the promise of happiness that German romantics once sought in high art.
His erotic depictions may not arouse a modern reader, but they cannot be
avoided. Early critics condemned the ubiquitous hijinks as vulgar; the
young Thomas found them repulsive.

Yet sexual curiosity is one of his most appealing traits. He is more like
his brother than the young Thomas realized. In fact, there is an almost
clinical interest in seeing how a similar temperament coincides with dis-
similar sexual preferences. Heinrich's women suffer from the same jitters as
does Madame Bovary; they have urges that find no reflected forms of desire.
He never doubts that the political nature of their loss makes them incipient
revolutionaries. More human and adventurous than their men, his women
are "the bolder and more clear-sighted sex."

As his views of community changed, Heinrich saw erotic response as a
political metaphor: perverted, it led to fascism; liberated, it enabled a progressive and social happiness. But he could never assume a disinterested
pose. His great words on satire sprang from the kind of intellectual who is
an embarrassed patron of burlesque, a voyeur satirizing himself and his
fetishes: "No one has ever written good satire without having some sort of
affinity with the object of his ridicule. He is either an apostate or one who
has been excluded. In satire there is envy or disgust, but always an outraged
sense of community." Thus a furtive man with his raincoat in his lap
becomes a social critic and political philosopher.

Heinrich published his first novel, *Within a Family*, when he was twenty-two. His first important novel, *Im Schlaraffenland: Ein Roman unter feinen Leuten*, appeared in 1900. Compared to the Tolstoyan achievement of *Buddenbrooks*, Heinrich's novel may seem comparatively light, but contemporaries like Rilke felt it had ushered both expressionism and social criticism into the German novel. For his admirers Heinrich's early work, more topical, vivacious, and unfinished than his brother's—as the journalistic rate of production might guarantee—provides a more useful guide to the era as well as prophetic views of Germany's future. (These readers would contend that *Buddenbrooks* points backward.)

Schlaraffenland is a playland; the English translator renames the novel *Berlin: The Lack of Cockaigne*. While parallels can be found with French novels, particularly works by Zola and Maupassant, Heinrich's depiction of a young writer has a special tang. He was himself an outsider, a Lübeck burgher moving in a world of parvenus and hustlers. More than that, he wrote much of the novel in Italy while his political criteria were shifting— and Thomas was reinventing their family's roots (in a novel Heinrich might also have written). Heinrich described the Berlin of 1893, but it is recognizably the same place Döblin and Brecht portrayed in the 1920s. Above all, he captures a variety of speech styles, from aristocratic to working-class, and discovers a common tone in that irreverence sometimes called *Berliner Schnauze*. Like the Munich of Thomas's early stories, Berlin is a city where everyone's an actor.

In this "lazy man's heaven," a society is inventing itself, cut loose from ethics and history. This may be the first novel to fully depict a capitalist metropolis where money is the universal lubricant; the Berlin novels of Theodor Fontane portray a far less materialistic society. The Jewish speculator Türkheimer—a portrayal not without anti-Semitic traces—is compared to Roman generals and Renaissance princes, and while the allusion is sheer parody, his power over investors, employees, and the Kaiser himself makes this crude trader Cockaigne's regent, a pope of capitalism.

His minion, court jester, and rival is Andreas Zumsee. This newcomer despises his provincial roots: he even renames himself Zum See (it sounds more distinguished), although he already feels a racial superiority over the Jewish parvenus whose favor he seeks. The social ranks that Mann had celebrated while editor of *The Twentieth Century* had fallen: in Cockaigne, one is a bum or a millionaire; the *Mittelstand* has vanished.

The stock market bankrupts investors, skyscrapers are built for obsolescence, furniture deconstructs, and the beer smells like poison. Yet Heinrich's recitation of capitalist evils does not make this a radical novel. Communism is one more stale metaphor: it translates into a trickle-down economics for top people. The proletariat hastens to sell out its principles, not to mention its daughters. Even the cultural icons are shot down with wisecracks. A pretty parvenu contemplates statues of Heine, Nietzsche, Poe, Baudelaire, and Verlaine and says, "Don't let those guys spit in our soup."

If Mann composed *Buddenbrooks* in an oneiric state, he awoke quickly from the dream and began to orchestrate his book's reception. First he made sure that Grautoff and Martens would review it. With an instinct for horse trading that would please Grandfather Buddenbrook, Mann instructed Grautoff to praise Martens's latest work. Not a great book, he confided, but the fellow can be useful.

As wily a hustler as Andreas Zumsee, Mann shows Grautoff how to represent the novel. Play to the galleries: "Stress the German character of the book. Mention as two truly German ingredients . . . music and philosophy." Give the writer an exotic pedigree: "Granted the author . . . has not found his mentors in Germany. For certain parts of the book Dickens, for others the great Russians, may be named." But don't confuse the public. Insist that this eclectic work is "truly German in its whole mode (intellectual, social) and in the subject itself: in the relationship between the fathers and the sons in the different generations of the family (Hanno and the senator)."

Hedge your bets. "Censure a little (if you will) the hopelessness and melancholy of the end. Say a certain nihilistic tendency can sometimes be detected in the author. But his affirmativeness and strength is his humor." That is as much as to say that Hanno need not have died. Coldly observing his product, Mann sees the ending as an aesthetic and commercial liability. This letter reveals a very knowing writer. He forestalls criticism by dismissing his defects as minor infelicities.

Grautoff's review faithfully echoed Mann's words. Martens was more independent. He praised the novel and was especially struck by the facility with which Mann treated no less than ten deaths. But he confessed that he found the philosophizing superficial. This caveat signified his integrity, though Mann could live with such a reservation; Tony Buddenbrook would not be diverted from buying a novel simply because it wasn't *profound* enough.

The first major review from an outsider came from Rainer Maria Rilke in the *Bremer Tageblatt*. The young poet was overwhelmed by the work's realistic detail—its "sociology"—and its evocations of family decadence and morbid introversion (the subject matter of his own *Notebooks of Malte Laurids Brigge*). He found it larger than its doomed characters: it was a veritable "act of reverence toward life—life that is good and just in its enactment." (Poet and novelist shared a sensibility nourished at a common source: Rilke's favorite writer, J. P. Jacobsen, was also one of Mann's early influences.)

Mann had initially sought acclaim for his humor and insight, perhaps a slender laurel. Rilke had endowed him with a prophet's mantle. Even the most skeptical writer would be thrilled by such praise. Years later, defending himself from Heinrich's political criticism, Mann exclaimed, "But I have shown people how to live." After Rilke, and the thousands of critics in his wake, an unironic Thomas might regard himself as a healer of the soul's disease. Yet Heinrich could have offered a more informed reply, "Physician, heal thyself."

Buddenbrooks sold slowly in its first nine months. Sales picked up after a review in the *Berliner Tageblatt* from the well-known critic Samuel Lublinski. As if Sesemi Weichbrodt had a twin, Lublinski was a hunchback (and Jewish). He defended the novel against complaints that it lacked structure or was insufficiently dramatized. He praised its encompassing vision and supple dialogue. He also forecast that it would become a classic, "read by many generations." This was Mann's favorite review. It was smart and kind, and it appeared where it could sell books. The novel required no further manipulations on his part.

He further benefited from publishing innovations. Fischer, reckoning he had a potential best-seller, issued a one-volume edition at half-price. By 1904, Mann imagined that "eight or ten thousand people" had "patiently" read *Buddenbrooks*. Some years later, it appeared in a mass-produced edition, one of the first of its kind. Katia Mann remembered seeing a parade of trucks packed with copies of her husband's novel. This valedictory to the nineteenth century enjoyed the newest means of promotion and distribution. Tony Buddenbrook might have been horrified by the trucks and delighted by their cargo. Thanks to a literary representation, the Buddenbrook / Manns had regained their celebrity. It came at a cost—the anger of many townsmen—but the pragmatic Tony had lived through worse. Indeed, Aunt Elisabeth, the original Tony, positively gloated that the Manns were again the talk of Lübeck. Trade, publishing; homage, satire: it was all the same to her as long as the subject remained her family.

Mann recalled in 1939 that "in this book the German novel first laid claim to acceptability by the rest of the world. This was the German novel's breakthrough into world literature. . . ." This may seem inordinately vain, but in fact he was correct. Anyhow, by then he was troubled by the question he had posed for Grautoff: how German was it? Whose Germany was depicted, Hanno's or the Father God's? In his last years, Mann contended

that *Buddenbrooks* was so thoroughly German that it could inspire a rapprochement of his divided homeland. He was unconvinced that West Germany had been de-Nazified and bitterly opposed its remilitarization. Even
so, he imagined that his words could outmanuever armies and nullify trea-
ties. It was a campaign bolder than anything he had dictated fifty-five years
earlier. But by 1954 he had a lifetime's knowledge of politics, culture, and
salesmanship behind him.

7

"THAT CENTRAL EXPERIENCE
OF MY HEART"

The period of his literary baptism by fire coincided with the most disturbing emotional episode of Mann's life—his involvement with Paul Ehrenberg. Both courtships demanded the representing of a complicated self to a skeptical public.

Previously, he had sought men's favor with forms and masks. In the summer of 1899 he wrote "Monologue," a poem that displayed his ambition and immaturity:

> I am a childish and weak person
> And like to attack myself on every front, and seek a strong hand.
> And still I hope that something I thought and felt
> Will one day be received in glory and go from mouth to mouth.
> My name is already a little known in the country.
> Some intelligent and discerning souls approve of it.
> A dream of a slim laurel wreath
> Which will decorate my brow for work done well
> Such a dream makes my nights restless.

(For a wicked parody of this lyric, see Alfred Kerr's 1925 "Thomas Bodenbruch.")

A need for something more than laurel wreaths was expressed in "Gerächt" ("Avenged"), a story he wrote that summer. The narrator has a platonic friendship with a Russian journalist named Dunja Steegemann. He finds her unattractive but is gradually seduced by her literary skill—though no follow-up occurs. This was a rare jest for the young Mann, imagining a free-spirited woman and granting her the verbal power to offset a homely face, a skill he often wished for himself, and, during the affair with Paul Ehrenberg, may briefly have acquired.

Before Paul, there had been at least two schoolboy crushes: the first on Armin Martens, the model for Tonio Kröger's first love; the second on Willri Timpe, the model for Hans Castorp's. The affair with Ehrenberg, the model for Adrian Leverkühn's single *adult* affair with a man, dwarfed these episodes. In 1934 Mann recalled them as adolescent foreshadowings of the "youthful intensity of feeling, the careless rapture and deep shock of that central experience of my heart when I was twenty-five."

He recognized the continuum at once. In February 1901 he wrote Grautoff, his confidant from the days with Timpe, that history was repeating itself: "It's crazy and ridiculous. I'm already writing nothing but 'he' and 'him'; all that's left is to write it in capital letters and draw a golden frame around it, and the 'Timpe' era will be resurrected in all its glory." (It can be inferred that like any teenager, he had scribbled his beloved's name during school hours.) In March he wrote Heinrich that Grautoff dismissed his "infatuation" as "adolescent," and admitted that these days he was feeling "very pubescent." He wasn't complaining; in his notebook he writes, "I have enough dignity to squander quite a lot."

Twenty-eight years later, he depicted the friendship with Paul as a sunnier version of his infatuation with Armin Martens. By then Mann was an old hand at partially disclosing the most intimate things about himself. As his diary notes indicate, he always knew better. How he represented the story to the world was not how he understood it . . . or how he would reveal it in *Doctor Faustus*.

In late 1899 he had met Carl (born in 1878) and Paul (born in 1876) Ehrenberg, the sons of a Dresden painter and college professor. Carl was a musician studying in Cologne; Paul was a student painter and violinist at the Munich Art Academy (in *Doctor Faustus* he reappears as Rudi Schwerdtfeger, a violinist). The three young men made bicycle trips together and attended costume balls in Schwabing. Mann could party and clown with them: their friendship signified how far he had moved from Lübeck's stuffy interiors.

Mann wrote Grautoff that Paul was "decent, untroubled, childlike, slightly vain, but guileless." As his temperament differed from Mann's, so did his language. Paul employed whimsical idioms that Mann would have abominated coming from another's mouth. Spoken by Paul they seemed charming, and he couldn't resist quoting them to Grautoff.

The Mann women were also charmed. Shades of the Armin Martens

LEFT TO RIGHT: *Paul Ehrenberg, unidentified woman, unidentified man, Carla Mann (the family actress), and Carl Ehrenberg (the future Nazi), circa 1902*

days, Paul was attracted to Lula. He became infuriated when she married a banker, Josef Löhr, nineteen years her senior and hopelessly bourgeois. (Katia Mann claims that Löhr had courted both Julias, mother and daughter.) In *Doctor Faustus*, Ines Rodde, the Lula character, falls in love with Rudi Schwerdtfeger. She has a rival: not Thomas—the Roddes don't have a brother—but her mother! Here were enough triangles and quadrangles to keep a soap opera spinning for years: Löhr-Lula-Paul; Julia-Löhr-Lula; Julia-Paul-Lula; Thomas-Paul-Julia; Thomas-Paul-Julia-Lula; Thomas-Paul-Julia-Löhr.

Zeitblom, *Faustus*'s narrator, remarks that Ines's chagrin upon seeing her mother flirt with Rudi may be imagined. If Frau Mann really made a play for Paul, Thomas's despair would be almost unimaginable. His rivals would have been the two women closest to him.

Mann cultivated a friendship with the Ehrenbergs' half-sister, Hilde Distel. When he wrote her after a New Year's Eve party, he observed disingenuously, "Through his personality, Paul is the dearest fellow, but Carl has music on his side, the art which I pursue amorously because of the unrequited love in my heart." The truth is that his love was all for Paul; the homage to music diverted attention from the significant attachment. Moreover, as if to make a chamber opera of his soliloquy, Mann performed in musical groups either with the Ehrenbergs or with the sister of Armin Martens. The volleying impressions were dizzy with associations meant for him alone.

Despite these labyrinthine elaborations, his early letters to Paul reveal, almost for the first time, a young man having fun. On June 29, 1900, he writes Paul that he will shortly commence his military service. Because he knows how well Paul understands him, he feels obliged to demur: "[I] assure you that the spiteful and mocking expression with which you have been reading . . . is out of place. First of all, I recognize that in the long run the German army could not possibly manage without me. Second, arrogant decadent that I am, I imagine that it will be extraordinarily refreshing to be bawled out ruthlessly and vigorously for a year. Which I shall no doubt deserve." Doesn't it amuse you, Mann implies, that I'll be humbled, made fit for ordinary company? Once "those nervous crochets of mine [are] exorcised," I'll "undoubtedly add ten more years to my life." Strong, healthy, normal: Mann makes partially ironic use of the army's slogans to ingratiate himself.

Don't be surprised, he jokes, if I appear as a "romantically costumed and brutalized mercenary" at Lula's wedding. He shares with Paul his pleasure in dressing up, in play-acting. He later describes an exhibition of the Munich Secession, apologizing for going on so: "May I take another sheet of paper? you don't mind"—a most coquettish tone for him. He confesses the limitations of his taste: one painting "made a big impression upon me, from which it probably follows that it is not worth two cents. . . . I should have liked to hear your precocious professional opinion of it." He takes for granted his reader's everlasting irreverence: "I am now willing to turn [another painter] over to your tender mercies. You are right, he is just an idiot after all."

There is more family gossip: he and Carla (who had also been wooed by Paul!) attended *Götterdämmerung* "and moreover, to ingratiate ourselves with the common folk (only for that reason, of course) took seats in the gallery," an allusion either to his limited funds or to possible discussions of class and status—did Paul encourage him to mingle with the crowd? He advises Paul to stop worrying about Lula. "With all due respect for 'love,' one does get further without it. A truism, by the way, that is rather repugnant to me personally. But what can one do on this inferior planet?" Here is a prime instance of Mann saying several things at once, so quickly and disingenuously that he must edit himself. The impulse may be due to his correspondent. For even as he advises Paul to dismiss romance, he reveals that his cynicism is hard-won. And, as in his fiction, while he may doom his lovers, he won't demean their passions . . . or his own. He must signal, no matter how obliquely, his true feelings. (He conveyed his displeasure with Lula's marital choice by dedicating to her Book III of *Buddenbrooks*, wherein Tony also chooses unwisely.)

He makes gloomy predictions about *Buddenbrooks*, but the communion with Paul lifts his spirits. Whatever the outcome, "I'll be proud and grateful. (May I take still another page? If you don't mind. But don't worry. I won't fill this one up immediately.)" He mentions playing violin again, "unquestionably thanks to you." He concludes with "the most important thing." It is not Lula's marriage, not his military career, not the fate of his novel, but a lover's request. "Both of us know a certain person, a writer, single, eligible for conscription for military service, a native of Lübeck"— see, see, I won't risk the chance of your mistaking me—"residing here, who would be very pleased if in the course of the summer he were actually to receive the promised drawing from you." He ends with a casual invitation to spend next winter in Munich. Alternately bold and shy, Mann's letter might have embarrassed him with its ardor. Perhaps only Heinrich could fully appreciate this identification of "the most important thing" as neither literature nor family but another man's gift.

In his notebook Mann declared Paul "my first and only human friend." Earlier acquaintances had been "unkind and imperceptive." They had been "demons, clowns, deep monsters, and ghosts. . . . In other words, literary friends." He had lived among them in "mute unrecognition." But now all that had changed and he was profoundly grateful:

> These are the days of a vital feeling.
> You have enriched my life. It burgeons
> And hark, music—in my ear
> A ghostly Sound breathes blissfully [*wonnevoll*–a Wagnerian
>   word for rapture]
> I thank you, my savior, my joy, my star!

And:

> What took so long?
> Frozen. Desolate. Ice. And spirit! And art!
> Here is my heart, and here is my hand!
> I love you! My God—I love you!
> Is it this beautiful, this sweet, this kind, simply to be human?

Mann's initial desires were modest. He writes about the pleasure of a hand-clasp or a shared lovers' glance, one presumably of "mute recognition."

He describes their affinities: "We talk about sexuality, about the precarious situation of those who don't go for loose women but prefer high-class ladies, although a cozy relation [with them] is simply too expensive. Also that both of us were advised by doctors to have a liaison with a married woman. I want to tell him, to reveal my feelings to him. I want to tell him—even if it isn't quite so—that his friendship—indeed from a psychiatric perspective—is for me . . . a purgative, a cleansing, and a sexual release." To which he adds in quotes, suggesting that he told Paul outright: "If you didn't feel this secretly, possibly without knowing it, then the way I tried to direct our relation would have seemed comical to you which I hope it didn't!?!"

He evokes periods together: "Especially in the morning, after rising, or washing his sleepy face, Paul has a way of looking at somebody that is simultaneously expectant and angry. His blue eyes almost burrow into your face."

Though Mann was released from military duty in December 1900, his mood was bad. On the seventeenth he wrote Heinrich that while *Schlaraffenland* appeared on Best of the Year lists, the prospects for *Buddenbrooks* were poor. His other work came slowly: the play *Fiorenza* was, as yet, "a formless dream." In January he alludes to "fits" of despondency in which he anticipates the worst: his book doesn't sell and he winds up a clerk. From then on, in every letter that details his nervous collapse, he makes some reference to Heinrich's professional good fortune.

The origin of his despair was not literary. It was the evident impossibility of an affair with Paul. On February 13 he writes, to Heinrich, "I go through ups and downs. When spring comes, I shall have behind me a terribly turbulent winter. Really dreadful depressions with quite serious plans for self-elimination have alternated with an indescribable, pure and unexpected inner joy, with experiences that cannot be told and the mere hint of which would naturally sound like boasting." In the course of one sentence, he replicates the manic highs and lows of his obsession. "But these highly unliterary, very simple and vital experiences have proved one thing to me: that there is something sincere, warm, and good in me after all, and not just 'irony,' that after all everything in me is not blasted, overrefined, and corroded by the accursed scribbling."

It is a mark of fraternal trust that he writes these words to Heinrich. Similar declarations occur only in his diaries, or when he recalls the men

Thomas Mann and Paul Ehrenberg on bicycles, circa 1900

he has loved and assures himself, "Yes, I too have 'lived.'" For a few months, he had responded in a full-throated manner, as love-drunk as a schoolboy. Adult life was measured by work. Resuming that life meant the sacrifice of everything spontaneous and heartfelt. In February 1901, Mann found work a prison, a horrible form of the obligations that strangled Thomas Buddenbrook. "Ah, literature is death! I shall never understand how anyone can be dominated by it *without* bitterly hating it. Its ultimate and best lesson is this: to see death as a way of achieving its antithesis, *Life*." But no more than Buddenbrook can he escape the demands of his métier. "I dread the day, and it is not far off, when I shall again be up alone with my work, and I fear that the egotistic inner desiccation and overrefinement will then make rapid progress."

Yet he leaps into his good news. *Buddenbrooks* is scheduled for an October publication, along with a second small volume of stories. "I shall have my picture taken, right hand tucked into the vest of my dinner jacket; the left resting on the three volumes. Then I might really go down happy to my grave." To correct any impression that the suicidal mood persists, he exhibits a vital confidence: "So much of what is characteristically my own is there that it will really define my profile for the first time." He will be doubly represented—in a photographic image and in the assertion of his literary profile. Literature may deny him one man's affection, but it supplies instead the public's approval: a decent exchange. He names the stories he's working on, and adds parenthetically after the title "Tristan," "Isn't that something. A burlesque named 'Tristan' . . . "—a sensational joke for the Wagnerian siblings.

Mann tells Heinrich that Tony Buddenbrook reveals "an almost comic pride in her misfortunes. She remains a child with a child's unbelief in her reality, yet with a child's seriousness, a child's self-importance, and, above all, a child's power to throw them off at will." That was his case, too.

Upon contemplation, he was less sure that Heinrich would understand him. On February 22, he wrote Grautoff: "I really would like to answer my brother immediately in detail and confess the scheme of my novel— but I have no time now—and am afraid of a written confession and capitulation because I know from experience that information in such a case doesn't clarify but exaggerates and deepens [the confusion]. On the other hand, naturally I have the desire to explain the whole thing in detail." But would Heinrich, who had called his love for Armin Martens "nonsense," have sympathized?

S. Fischer had just informed him that his previous collection would go out of print. "First, I thought, this is the last straw. Because right now I can't handle misfortune. But then I demonstrated my ability to bounce back. After five minutes I was up again, and back at work on 'Tristan.'"

He planned to dedicate a section of *Buddenbrooks* to Paul. "This dedication has become an idée fixe—I want it passionately. It is the self-evident desire to do something, to offer him some sacrifice." The impulse was not simply generous. He admits "my desire to let him see my power, to make him a little bit ashamed that I 'can throw' his name around." Since "Paul imagines he can love a woman simply for her opinions," Thomas's intellectual power has become a strategic asset in his pursuit of the young flirt. Following that line, he convinces himself that he need not fear the hostesses of Munich. "After, all, I'm more 'important' than his women."

Just because Grautoff knew him in the Timpe days, he can employ the language of a lovesick adolescent: "Believe me, only with you do these matters assume the style of a sixth-grader. Really things are by far less infantile, far simpler and more manly, and only the damned weakness of nerves revives my painful yearning."

The February 22 letter recapitulates Mann's ambivalence about "venting one's feelings." It is ludicrous and unmanly, this need to explain it all— in *Doctor Faustus* he makes Ines's verbal compulsion a pathology. Meanwhile, he hopes that a cooler, more distant language will make Paul love him, or at least acknowledge his "power." In his notebook, fearing that love has made him lugubrious, he reminds himself, "Don't forget the humor in [his autobiographical story] *Die Geliebten.*"

Alarmed by Thomas's depression, Heinrich replied at once to the letter. Thomas instructed him not to worry. On March 7 he recalled the passage when Thomas Buddenbrook dismisses the suicide of a ruined aristocrat: " 'There's the nobility for you!' This is highly characteristic, not only of Buddenbrook, and should serve to reassure you for the present." Good burghers don't kill themselves. He ridicules his morbid infatuation. "I don't want to hear anything about the typhus. It is all metaphysics and adolescent sexuality—adolescence hangs on with me." Hanno dies of that typhus, but I won't. He trivializes his feeling in order to deny any motive for suicide: "At the moment there is little practical reason to go through with it, that you may rest easy." Fear not, I won't embarrass our family with so banal an outcome of "[late] adolescent sexuality."

But his mercurial nature leads him to add—almost coyly—"I cannot vouch for what may happen someday": the Wagnerian obsession with the "wondrous realm of night" is "a question that disturbs me myself." He revives the idea of literature as a cul-de-sac: "I'll spare myself any more detailed confessions because writing and analysis only deepen and exaggerate these things." Five years earlier, he had conflated "writing" and "analysis" as his literary ideals. Now he recoils from them both.

He dissembles a bit: "What is involved is not a love affair, at least not in the ordinary sense, but a friendship—how amazing!—understood, reciprocated, and rewarded—which I candidly admit at certain times, especially in hours of depression and loneliness, takes on a character of somewhat excessive suffering." Grautoff says that it's a late-adolescent fling; "but that is putting it in his own terms." The Manns know that emotions cannot be labeled. "My nervous constitution and philosophical inclination have incredibly complicated the affair; it has a hundred aspects from the plainest to the spiritually wildest. But on the whole, the dominant feeling is one of profoundly joyful astonishment over a responsiveness no longer to be expected in this life. Let that be enough."

These may be the most intimate words Thomas Mann ever wrote to another person. His evocation of "a hundred aspects from the plainest to the spiritually wildest" constitutes a literary critique of the emotions: the multivocal language that was *Buddenbrooks'* animating force. But the fundamental cry is plain enough, "profoundly joyful astonishment" over another man's concern. At twenty-five Mann had felt himself cut off, apparently for life. Echoing the despair of Hanno Buddenbrook, he had gauged his lot as fixed, "now and forever." If what he felt now wasn't love "in the ordinary sense," it's only because anyone with his "nervous constitution" couldn't love simply.

Three weeks later, on April 1, he writes Heinrich, "I go on being 'negative' and ironical in my writing largely out of habit, but for the rest, I praise, love, and live." In one of his favorite terms of praise, "everything is simply one grand festival. If I leave [to join Heinrich in Florence] it will be over for the present and won't come again this way; *we know how it is* [italics mine]." This is a light allusion to the brothers' chronic melancholy. But for now, "I want to hold on to it to the last moment."

He alludes casually to Paul without naming him. He is sitting for his portrait "by the good fellow to whom (assuming that one should not talk about fate all the time, but may also thank specific persons) I owe such an incalculable debt of gratitude. He's doing it because it's fun for both of us." He proposes to dedicate some work to Paul: "I feel such boundless gratitude. My sentimental need, my need for enthusiasm, devotional trust, a handclasp, loyalty, which has had to fast to the point of wasting away and atrophying, now is feasting." A famished Mann was finally seated at the table. He had entrusted his representation to another—more than any Buddenbrook had allowed—simply because "it's fun for both of us."

Yet the notebooks also contain expressions of anger and despair. In one long passage he describes a lingering quarrel with his friend. He was embarrassed to see that Paul could always pacify him with "empty, nice words." Or, upon meeting a disgruntled Thomas at a party, he could simply put his arm around him and "again I was conquered." Once he wrote, "Why shouldn't I make him suffer too?"

After he had requested Paul's photo, he began to fear that the boy would attach a clumsy and pretentious autograph. Yet when Paul neglected to bring him anything, Thomas complained, "Wasn't I enthusiastic enough?" The intellectual discrepancy appeared insurmountable. When Thomas spoke of Hamlet's discontent with man and woman alike, Paul chimed in, "Ah yes. I'm just like that." In private, Thomas wrote, "He's as much a Hamlet as I'm a Hercules." Coming upon Thomas one day, Paul asked, "What have you been doing?" "Thinking." "Definitively?" "Definitively and not definitively." Baffled by such writerly indecision, Paul called him "unfriendly." Indeed, thinking of his novella *Die Geliebten* (*The Loved Ones*), Mann wrote that the lovers "basically don't like each other." He also imagined another novella in which a "pessimistic poet" marries the embodiment of "life," and, Samson-like, loses his creative strength. In these notes, pity, disdain, and abject need coalesce, foreshadowing the "desire and contempt" with which Mann's lovers would confront the world.

In May he returned to Florence and Venice with Heinrich. Richard Winston feels this proves that the friendship was not sexual enough, or, at least, not powerful enough to keep Mann in Munich. Winston tries to downplay Mann's homosexuality, even suggesting that he exaggerated it. Isn't it a more interesting question why Thomas, in the midst of his passion for Ehrenberg, needed Heinrich's company? It suggests the same dangling between alternatives that may have led him to perform with Paul one week and with Armin's sister the next.

While in a Florence pension he met an English girl, Mary Smith. He wrote Heinrich, "She is so very clever, and I am so stupid always to love those who are clever, although I cannot constantly keep up with them." In his 1929 *Sketch of My Life*, Mann suggests that it was probably too soon then to marry, and that cultural differences kept them apart. A year later he dedicated a story, "*Gladius Dei*," "to M.S." This brief heterosexual episode left obscure traces. Mary Smith attracted him because she resembled a Botticelli painting, but in the story contemporary paintings of the Botticelli school appear blasphemous and obscene. Mary Smith—the name itself seems apocryphal—does not figure in his diaries; in 1929, he's not sure if her name wasn't Molly.

In October *Buddenbrooks* appeared with three dedications: Lula (Part Three), Heinrich (Part Eight), and Paul (Part Nine). The next months were some of the happiest in Mann's life. He was not productive—although by manipulating his book's reception, he was creating an audience for his future work. He didn't need literature. Paul satisfied him. He wrote Hilde Distel, "I have grown and straightened out somewhat, humanly speaking— for example, sociability no longer makes me completely melancholic. . . . Undoubtedly the influence of your brothers can be felt in the change— chiefly that of Paul. I have made him a little more literary and he has made me a little more human. Both changes were necessary!" He introduced Paul to Nietzsche, much as Tonio Kröger courts Hans Hansen with Schiller. Thomas Buddenbrook would have approved the trade, so much like the one he desired between Hanno and Count Kai.

It was hard to remain melancholy when his literary prospects appeared so good. On November 6, 1901, he wrote Grautoff: "Always around this time, when nature dies, autumn brings rivers of deep feeling. I am artist enough—let everything happen. I can use it all." The next sentence appears elliptical: "By the way, Brother Girolamo had a friend who worshiped him and whom he loved, Giovanni Pico della Mirandola, the blond humanist. . . ." It becomes a classy version of Gipper once you know that

Mann was preparing to write about Girolamo Savonarola, or that Paul, his beloved friend, was blond.

He had read in a Munich paper "a note about TM, the 'well-known contributor to *Simplicissimus*,'" whose forthcoming book will be "a novel in the grand style, a real German work of art. That is almost all I want to hear."

Fame was the spur and the curse. On January 28, 1902, he wrote Paul that he wished to be liberated.

> In truth I am tired of my talent being praised because it cannot compensate for what I lack. Where is the somebody who says yes to me, a person not very lovable, bad-humored, self-destructive, incredulous but full of feeling and abnormally voracious for sympathy? Who says yes? A constant question. Without being impeded or alienated by the cold possibility of rejection?
>
> Where is the person? Deep silence? A discussion would do me good, and I almost invited you to come and visit me, assuming that you were not like all the others who respect my talent and find the actual man disgusting.

For the first time the virtuoso of representation presented himself to another person, disguising nothing. In this letter he sacrificed his "power." Damn literature, damn critical praise; nothing mattered but Paul's love.

In June Mann wrote Kurt Martens that "I haven't worked this winter, I have merely lived, simply as a human being, and assuaged my conscience by filling my notebook with observations." These experiences included numerous concerts, three during one week in March. "It is almost too much, but I don't want to let anything slip past me," he wrote Hilde Distel. Among the notes he was taking were the preliminary outlines of *Die Geliebten*. It would have dramatized the affair between Adelaide, a married woman, and Rudolf, a dashing young violinist. Rudolf was obviously modeled on Paul; Adelaide on Mann himself; and her husband, a Nietzschean devoted to "Life, Beauty, Power, and Mindless Instinct," on Heinrich (his name was to be Albrecht, the name of the Heinrich character in *Royal Highness*). In his notebook, he intermingled observations about his fictional triangle with details about himself and Paul and Heinrich, so that fiction and autobiography kept chasing each other's tail.

By March 1902, he had decided that Rudolf must die.

In Dresden, a married woman had shot her lover on the train. When Mann requested from Hilde the background of the Munich shooting, he asked, "What finally precipitated the catastrophe—a love affair or an engagement on his part? . . . Of course, I could work it all out for myself, and when I have the facts I shall probably deal with them in my own way. The facts interest me only for their stimulating effect and their possible usefulness. If I really should do anything with the incident, the chances are it will be hardly recognizable in my version." Any confusion with real life would be coincidental, he claimed. But given the volatile nature of his affair with Paul, the curiosity may not have been disinterested.

Adelaide's obsession belies her stated sexuality. She is the more ardent, more virile lover, jealous of every hour Rudolf spends away from her. "The suffering on days when she doesn't see him. Not to be near, with, or in him. To know that the other lives, smiles, speaks, busies himself—without her participation. . . . One doesn't want to live alone. One doesn't want to move. Every action seems a direct betrayal of life. He too should feel the same way. One should only be still and love."

Rudolf doesn't respond and she grows desperate. Any gesture becomes the final rejection. "The smallest treachery on his part breaks her heart. . . . Suspicion of the most petty infidelity can almost destroy her, and make him seem painfully unworthy of her love." Half-mad, she becomes a genius at overinterpretation. No psychiatrist or literary critic ever read more into a casual glance or shift in tone. She prefigures a century of fanatically observant lovers, headed by Mann's Aschenbach and Proust's Swann.

Before, in Mann's work, desire had been omnipresent but "nameless." Now it appeared in a manic guise, dissolving all notions of propriety and decency. Had he completed Adelaide's novel, he might be acknowledged as, in his words, "an adventurer of the emotions." But he couldn't make a novel of such undiluted passion, and he temporarily abandoned the project.

Yet these pages throw light on his entire work, since he would employ them in two of his greatest novels, *Joseph in Egypt* and *Doctor Faustus*. They offer us a new way of reading Mann, linking the later works with the early stories inspired by his love for Paul. Like Goethe or Proust fixating on the same themes and subject matter over decades, Mann kept returning to *Die Geliebten* for almost fifty years.

Once read in that manner, with each work elaborating and refining the basic theme, the complete saga constitutes an examination of obsessional love as intense as Proust's, with a Mannian (and German) attention to social history and politics.

In 1951 he described the phenomenon, as it occurs in Gide: "The same psychological motive appears again and again, in new contexts and newly illuminated and thus the characters join, after all, into an interconnected unit—just as the life work which they interpret and which, like few others, demonstrates that what counts is not the single book even though it makes a claim to finality, but the opus in its entirety."

He employed the *Geliebten* material in *Doctor Faustus*, where Adelaide becomes Ines Rodde. He endows this woman, a fictional recreation of his "female self," with a Mannian schadenfreude. Like Aschenbach gloating over Tadzio's bad teeth, she revels in her lover's defects—he has had a bodily organ removed. It consoles her that he'll have fewer hours to betray her. Up to a point, her friend Zeitblom is sympathetic: "One does not at bottom 'understand' this. . . . However hard it is actually for a man to enter into the feelings of a woman on fire with love for somebody of his own sex."

Rudi dies, shot on a tram car by a distraught Ines, in an episode engineered by his other denied lover, Leverkühn. As he dies, Rudi makes a final conquest when Zeitblom sees the corpse: "Bubbles of blood welled out between his lips, whose gentle fullness seemed all at once so touching to me." Zeitblom's enduring affection for Leverkühn is chaste, but it is self-acknowledged "love," as intense as Schiller's pursuit of Goethe. Mann dramatizes two forms of homoeroticism, the physical kind and the spiritual. In both the lover lives through his beloved: as Adelaide dreamt, "near, with, and in him." Thus Zeitblom believes that he must undergo Leverkühn's political Gethsemane: "I accept the terrors of time in which I myself continue to live on. It is to me as though I stood here and lived for him, lived instead of him." The crazed Ines and the scholarly Zeitblom are both on fire with an impossible passion.

Judging by its preliminary form, *Die Geliebten* would have focused on its titular subject. But it also would have anticipated *Faustus*'s larger concerns. In one note, Mann described the Munich artist colony as diabolical— "demons, clowns, and ghosts of literature," the same phrase he used for his so-called literary friends. The animus he felt toward "heartless" Nietzscheans like Heinrich would be transferred to the proto-fascists surrounding Adrian Leverkühn. He even predicted *Faustus*'s great discussion of music: the spirit of Mozart's *Magic Flute*—one of "virtue, duty, enlightenment, humanity"—had been "eaten and gnawed away," he wrote, while *Tristan and Isolde* had been reduced to a bourgeois entertainment.

Missing, of course, was the alternative provided by modern music, especially the twelve-tone system the hero receives from the devil, and Mann actually derived from Arnold Schönberg through the mediation of Theodor Wiesengrund Adorno. Surprisingly, Adorno did not greatly admire the Schönbergian section, which struck him as over-deliberated. He found more art in the hissing blue light under the tram in which Rudi Schwerdt-feger is killed. In fact, Mann, who was most concerned with depicting Adelaide's murder of Rudi ("his death must be immensely sad") had composed that description in his notes of 1902!

Mann gave other expression to his love for Paul Ehrenberg. *Tonio Kröger*, published the year after he wrote Paul that literature had denatured him, was first titled *Literature*. In February 1903 he sent a letter to the Ehrenberg brothers, signing it, "Yours, Tonio Kröger"—as if to show Paul his "power." Even rejection had its literary uses.

In the earlier letter he described his yearning as voracious, literally as *heisshungrig*, burningly hungry. Physical hunger was a familiar subject. In September 1900 he describes it more dryly to Grautoff: "My respect for hunger is really great. It would be even greater were there not things one cannot heal with a beefsteak." The quip is what you'd expect from Paul Ehrenberg; in those days, his needs being satisfied by Paul, he might have talked like him.

But in the intervening months had come the recognition that left him *heisshungrig*. While *Tonio Kröger* can be read as a distillation of the Ehrenberg affair, a contemporaneous work presents a more flagrant version. In late 1902, after attending a ball with the Ehrenberg brothers, he composed a sketch, "The Hungry." A Munich artist, Detlef, condescends to a public that pays him no mind. "You are after all mine, and I am above you. Can I not see through your simple souls with a smile? . . . The sight of your artless activities arouses in me the forces of the word, the power of irony. It makes my heart beat with desire and the lustful knowledge that I can reshape you as I will and by my art expose your foolish joys for the world to gape at." Literary license has never seemed so close to erotic sadism. But the rush of excitement is momentary: "Then all his defiance collapsed again quite suddenly, leaving only dull longing in its wake." A painful form of *Sehnsucht* reduces him to size.

Having seen his beloved Lilli (Lily Teufel was Paul's girlfriend and future wife) dancing with a painter, Detlef leaves the ball. Mann-like, he smokes a cigarette, and finds himself observed by a man with a "red-bearded, hollow-cheeked, lawless face, with wretchedly inflamed red-rimmed eyes that stared with savage scorn and a certain greedy curiosity into his own." He regards Detlef knowingly, with the *kalten Blick* of a disdainful sexual cruise: "His gaze traveled over Detlef's whole figure from opera-glass to patent-leather shoes." Detlef apprehends the other's "envy and longing" and finds them a reflection of his own nature. "You thought

Paul Ehrenberg, "that central experience of my heart," in 1902

to show me a horrifying warning out of a strange and frightful world, to arouse my remorse. But we are brothers." Like a Dostoyevsky detective, he demonstrates an expert knowledge of the other's soul. "Why did you not hug your misery in the shadow instead of taking your stand under the lighted windows behind which are music and laughter? I too know the morbid yearning that drove thee [out into the streets], which may just as well be called love or hate."

There is no gap between the bourgeois artist and the renegade: "Nothing is strange to me of all the sorrow that moves you. . . . What is mind but the play of hatred? What art, but yearning in act to create? We are both at home in the land of the betrayed, the hungering, the denying, and common to us both are those hours full of betraying self-contempt, when we lose ourselves in a shameful love of life and of mad happiness." We brothers crave "the simple and the instinctive, dumb life itself, ignorant of the enlightenment which comes through mind and art, the release through the Word." We know that—so to speak—literature is death, and the mindless embody life. "Ah, we are all brothers, we creatures of the restlessly suffering will, yet we do not recognize each other. Another love is needed, another love." The story ends on a note of false pathos: "These gentle words: 'Little children, love one another.'" But until then, it has presented a moment worthy of Gide or Proust, as one starving man recognizes another, and self-hatred clashes with the need "for sustenance."

Apparently the story offended the Ehrenberg brothers; they chose not to see themselves as "dumb life itself." It conveyed both Mann's desire for Paul and his fear that he had been expelled from the feast. But there was also a defiant note: the "restlessly suffering will" cannot be suppressed. Inside the public arena, sexual roles must be inverted, and Paul become Lilli. Outside, in the streets, the will realizes itself, speaks its name. Mann asserts his true profile by taking his place in a brotherhood of the hungry.

Instead of uniting with Lilli—or Paul—Detlef-Thomas finds his companion in a kindred spirit. His previous heroes were either solipsists or cuckolds. Detlef is no more fortunate, but he displays an empathy they lack; the product of love is the ability to imagine another person's need. As when Hanno pities Candidate Mödersohn, Detlef's sympathy extends to someone from a lower class. In his apolitical period, this reaching out was Mann's form of socialism: "Little children, love one another" becomes here a preliminary form of political organization.

Love allowed Mann to expose himself, albeit in his usual convoluted manner. Yet he hadn't exiled himself permanently from the feast. In the summer of 1903 he ended a letter to Paul with these verses:

Here is a man with warts and all,
And full of passions great and small,
Ambitious, love-starved, and conceited,
And touchy, jealous, easily heated,
Excessive, factious, hardly stable,
Now far too proud, now miserable,
Naïve and so sophisticated,
World-fleeing, world-infatuated,
Nostalgic, half-moron, blind indeed,
A child, a fool, a writer too
In fantasy and will entwined.
But with the virtue that to you
With all his heart he is inclined.

For over three years Mann had felt comfortable enough with Paul to satirize himself. Now he could employ light verse to express the antipodes of his personality. These would constitute the subject matter of his fiction. The Mannian persona is represented, "warts and all"—no critic is more exacting—and entrusted to Paul Ehrenberg. He makes the offering without any of the *Weltschmerz* that characterized his pathetic letters to Heinrich—perhaps because he assumed that he need not remain "love-starved." (However, in a letter to Paul he presented himself more grimly, as compact of "ambition" and "indolence," "passion" and "so much heaviness.") His poem was a sweet apology (written, it should be added, some months after he had met Katia Pringsheim).

What kind of quarrels lurk behind it? We have some indication in his literature. For the public he retold the episode as a parable of immaturity. Later, in his *Sketch of My Life*, he assimilated the events of his mid-twenties to "my twentieth year." He claimed it was then he toyed with ideas of suicide, prompted by his first reading of Schopenhauer, "a metaphysical intoxication, closely related to a late and violent outbreak of sexuality."

The recent Nobel Prize winner could blithely regard his suicidal period: "Ah, youth, with its sacred pants, its urgency, its disorders! It was a happy chance that these supra-bourgeois experiences of mine came at a time when I could weave them into the close of my bourgeois novel, where they served to prepare Thomas Buddenbrook for death." At least the dates seem closer, although *Buddenbrooks* may have been completed before the love for Paul inspired any suicidal thoughts. Mann's gloss reads like a caricature of bourgeois smugness. The good burgher lets nothing go to waste; suffering is absorbed into the novel, becomes its "happy chance." A tactful paragraph break suggests that the morbid episode was done when he wrote it out.

In *Doctor Faustus*, he dramatizes the relation he referred to in his diary as "that central experience of my heart." (In a 1951 diary, he admitted that in *Doctor Faustus* he composed, at least partially, "my memoir.") The novel's hero, Adrian Leverkühn, is an immensely gifted composer who seems incapable of warmth or affection. He drifts into an affair with a successful young violinist, Rudi Schwerdtfeger, whose pretty head never harbored a metaphysical thought or a world-conquering ambition. Rudi is affable, glib, casually flirtatious with both sexes: the prudish narrator, Zeitblom, allows that "he was one of those people who always have to touch and feel—the arm, the shoulder, the elbow. He did it even to me, and also to women, most of whom did not dislike it."

In a highly poetic novel, Rudi's verbal style is, at best, antic and banal. When Leverkühn makes an eloquent remark, he can only reply, "Did you hear that? The way the man talks! How he knows how to use words! He's a master, our Master." In a vicious, ultimately fatal caricature, Leverkühn sends Rudi to his doom with the campy admonition "Mach's nett" ("Now be nice").

Rudi is not attracted by the composer's beauty or charm. Genius alone wins his fancy. He begs his friend to compose a piece that he can perform. Our collaboration will be covertly sexual, he says, with you playing the father and I the mother. Unlike Leverkühn's usual work, the concerto Rudi inspires is so blatantly melodic that it verges on parody: "a feast of melody in which the parody of being carried away becomes a passion which is seriously meant." Its effect is "somewhat embarrassing"—though Mann might add that Leverkühn had plenty of dignity in reserve. Function followed form. Even the narrator, no friend of Rudi's, admits that this "apotheosis of salon music" became a prime stimulus to flirtation.

In a moment of ardor Leverkühn confesses that no one "in love with every, I really mean every, organized noise" can feel " 'too good,' for any sort of music." Goethe thought art must be difficult, he explains, but "light" music can be as virtuosically accomplished as "heavy." It's a question of technique: "One must be very well anchored in the good and 'heavy' to take up with the light."

"The blue-eyed mediocrity" blushes. Quicker than Leverkühn himself, he gets the point: light music—and musicians—may break your heart, but you can't take them seriously. While Mann patronizes Rudi, he allows him a degree of sublety: "He was illogical enough to use his native gift of coquetry—and then to feel put off when the melancholy preference he aroused showed the signs of ironic eroticism." (Hidden here is a sly echo of the term "erotic irony" Mann used during World War I to justify his conservatism.)

In 1905, Mann's initial plan for the novel had involved a Dr. Faust who, in a state of diabolical intoxication, creates "brilliant, wonderful works in enraptured enthusiasm." That a "brilliant, wonderful work" could resemble "salon music" indicates how much erotic irony had since invaded that scheme—or, possibly, as Mann admitted to Bruno Walter, "I am committed to romantic kitsch from head to toe."

Zeitblom alludes to a letter Adrian mailed to Rudi: "I refrain from quoting it, merely characterizing it as a human document which affects the reader like the baring of a wound and whose painful lack of reserve the writer probably considered an uttermost hazard. It was not." Casting off his dignity, Adrian begs Rudi to visit him, as Thomas had begged Paul. This is a very rare moment in Mann's fiction; someone actually says what he feels, and is rewarded for his honesty. At once the violinist appears. Adrian's subsequent "revelation of a simple, bold and utterly sincere bearing" marks the temporary withdrawal of irony *for* eroticism, parody for passion. Rudi gets his concerto and Adrian achieves a sexual consummation he italicizes as a *miracle*, echoing Mann's own words to Heinrich about Paul.

Self-exposure is not an "uttermost hazard," and "the way it proved not to be was most beautiful."

But shortly after, a darker confrontation occurs. The two men argue about marriage. (In September 1903, Mann informed Grautoff that he and Paul had quarreled violently over his courtship of Katia Pringsheim.) Adrian tells Rudi that he will marry in order to obtain "a real home, a companion congenial in the fullest sense of the word; in short a warmer and more human atmosphere. . . ." With the animus of a spurned lover, Rudi replies, "Forgive the simplicity of the remark, but I would not want to hear any humanly inspired work from you."

Did Paul Ehrenberg say such words? When Leverkühn hears them, his blood runs cold. "Don't you think it's cruel to let me know that only out of inhumanity I am what I am and that humanity is not becoming to me? That I have nothing to do with humanity, may have nothing to do with it, that is said to me by the very person who had the amazing patience to win me over for the human and persuaded me to say *Du*, the person in whom for the first time in my life I found human warmth." This is the language of Mann's letter to Heinrich, "praise" and "joyful astonishment," exposed as self-indulgent rhetoric. After forty years, he remembers exactly when his hopes were dashed.

Rudi replies knowingly, "It seems to have been a temporary makeshift." And Leverkühn switches his attack in words that recall Mann's gratitude for even a temporary siege of happiness. "A man came into my life, by his heartfelt holding out he overcame death—you might really put it like that. He released the human in me, taught me happiness. It may never be known or be put in any biography. But will that diminish its importance, or dim the glory which in private belongs to it."

Rudi shrugs off Leverkühn's plea. He has no desire to go "public" or enter his lover's "biography," and he switches the topic to a woman whom Leverkühn will employ as the vehicle of his doom. The circuitous action mimics the novel's tricky composition. For although Mann uses a heterosexual episode to destroy Rudi, Leverkühn's affirmation is one of the great homosexual love arias. A man cursed with consciousness is granted the simple passions of ordinary people; a god becomes human. For a moment, he feels liberated; and then he learns—forcefully instructed by his lover— that he can never be "simply" human. (Imagine a young Thomas Mann pleading with Paul, "Yes, I can be like other people," and Paul, wise at last to his talents, disagreeing: "You don't belong with us." Back to literature, death-in-life: "alone again naturally.")

As part of a "cold, secret, automatic revenge" he has Rudi court Marie Goreau, a woman they both admire. Like figures out of D. H. Lawrence, they use a woman to mask their homosexual flirtation: "I had played *you*, and was feeling warm and susceptible," says Rudi, describing his first encounter with Marie Goreau. (Mann frequently gave heterosexual rivalry a homosexual spin: in *The Transposed Heads*, he even let two passionate rivals switch body parts, thereby achieving a union beyond intercourse. The origin of this convoluted activity may have been his chats with Paul during the latter's courtship of Lula.)

In 1950, answering the queries of Professor Henry Hatfield, Mann admitted that Leverkühn precipitates "a *murder* in more than one sense." Knowing that "Rudolf is endangered by the passion of Ines," he provokes Ines into killing the violinist. The "murder" of his lover becomes Adrian's most diabolical act. *Doctor Faustus* has been considered both Mann's masterpiece and a work damaged by theological symbolism, particularly the appearance of the most fluent Satan since *Paradise Lost*. But Mann's Lucifer, whatever else he signifies, is also the devil in the flesh. Adrian's gesture ends up a murder-suicide. He doesn't win the bride: "As in the old story he is not allowed to marry." But, more telling, "Nor is he allowed to love."

In 1943, Mann came across a brief synopsis of the Faust project that he had made in 1901, a memento from "the Tonio Kröger period, the Munich days, the never realized plans for *The Loved Ones* and *Maja*. 'Old Love, old friendship rise along with these.' Shame and strong sentimentality at remembrance of these youthful sorrows. . . ." The discovery was shattering, "accompanied by a degree of emotion, not to say inner tumult, which made one thing very clear to me; that the meager and vague nucleus had been surrounded from the beginning by a belt of personal concern, a density of biographical feeling." This emotional core is frequently overlooked by critics, bemused by *Doctor Faustus*'s "G E R M A N allegory." Yet Mann made the failure of Leverkühn's love for Rudi a cipher for the German's incurable "loneliness" and, even more, the political naïveté that, as he saw in 1943, had ended so disastrously.

Virtually the same feelings had been aroused in 1934, and put to less political use, when his love for Ehrenberg inspired Mut-em-enet's obsession with Joseph. At that time too, reading his notes reopened the wound. "The passion and the melancholy psychologizing of that long-lost time came flooding back familiar and deeply saddening." He was struck by "certain utterances," including the confession he had never again repeated: "I love you. My God, I love you." Such "overpowering intensity . . . has happened only once in my life, which is doubtless as it should be."

At least in his diary, he was not ashamed of this passion. Indeed it confirmed his humanity, despite the subsequent renunciation and denial: "Ah well, I have lived and loved, have in my own fashion 'paid' for being human." He added that one such love was "doubtless the normal course of human affections, and owing to this normality I can feel more strongly that my life conforms to the scheme of things than I do by virtue of marriage and children." If Paul had actually said that Thomas did not belong with the conventionally "human," these words proved him right. The father and husband were less real to Mann than the lover.

Proving that he was indeed artist enough to use everything, Mann wrote in his diary of January 9, 1935, that the *Geliebten* notes were filled with details, "economically" conveyed, that would suit his current novel's style. Having by then read Proust, he decided that the abbreviated jottings, the mercurial twists of logic and emotion, were "modern," even if the setting and characters of *Joseph in Egypt* involved a "mythic-primitive world."

Following the Bible, Joseph is propositioned by Mut-em-enet, the wife of Potiphar, the Pharaoh's steward, and is severely punished for rejecting her. Expanding a scriptural anecdote into a novel allowed Mann to observe a beautiful youth from the perspective of his female lover. Thus Adelaide, the Munich hausfrau, evolved into Mut, the Egyptian aristocrat.

We will consider her story in due time, but it's worth noting that her irrational gratitude to Joseph, "O paradise of feeling! Thou has enriched my life!" recalls Thomas's poetic address to Paul. And yet again when she awakens from a series of "endlessly resumed dreams" she says words that Mann first gave to Adelaide, "My God, my God, how is it possible? How is so much agony possible?" Having fun with himself, he satirizes her impulse to call Joseph a God, even as he quotes from the poem in which Paul became his "savior."

As a coda to the Ehrenberg affair, there is an obscure 1948 letter to the American novelist Charles Jackson. Written in stumbling, heartfelt English, it is one of Mann's most direct letters to an American, covering an area never broached in his correspondence with friends like Agnes Meyer or Alfred A. Knopf. Mann wrote to acknowledge receiving a copy of Jackson's novel *The Fall of Valor*, in which an affair between a Marine and a college professor ends when the soldier kills his lover. He thanks Jackson for "never denying the knowledge we have retained of the so-called perversions and aberrations of this sphere," assuming the hip tone of his daughter Erika's American friends—"namely above all the homosexual component, a phenomenon which, as Goethe says, is in nature, although it seems to be directed against nature."

Mann is especially interested in the relation between Professor Johnson and the young Marine captain. Such a relation plays a part in *Faustus*, he says. "Those involved are a lonely artist, a figure somewhat like Nietzsche, whose clinical fate he also shares—a young man of impish traits to whom every human relationship becomes a flirt, and who courts the loneliness for so long and with such boundless and uninhibitable confidence until he overcomes and seduces it. However he does not grab the poker but is very proud of his conquest. It is the other man who takes deadly revenge for his defeat."

These lines express what may be his last word on the episode. The love affair ended in a "defeat." Paul set him free and then—whether bewildered by Mann or sexually disengaged—he drifted away. Mann's regret was immense; every citation of the Ehrenberg years laments what was denied— not simply because it was homosexual, but because, as Rudi concludes, happiness is not the artist's proper condition.

Later there is another horrific death—far more brutally drawn out than Hanno Buddenbrook's—of a beautiful child, little Echo, Leverkühn's nephew and last great love. Echo's model was Mann's grandson Frido, whom he called his own "last love." (There would be others.) Echo's death agony stunned Mann's family, already shocked by the detailed re-enactment of his sister Carla's suicide.

Perhaps the child's death was prepared—not only narratively but within its author's psyche—by his "deadly revenge" on Paul. When he began the Rudi Schwerdtfeger section, he wrote that "now I will have paid for it all," a remark that follows Leverkühn's insistence that artists do "penance" for the suffering they cause others. Reliving that "love affair" was part of the ongoing purgatory of *Faustus*'s composition. In a novel that rooted Nazi horrors in the glories of German culture, Mann spared none of his greatest loves: music (the Ninth Symphony was revoked), his family (his mother and his sisters were disgraced, his grandson tortured to death), Paul, or himself.

Did Paul and Thomas make love? The temptation for some commentators is to see the relation as yet another botched attempt at intimacy. It is true that while reading Gore Vidal's *The City and the Pillar*, Mann wondered how one could sleep with a man; yet he found Vidal's depiction of teenage gay sex "glorious."

A case for arguing that the affair was physically complete was made by Mann himself. In 1946 while composing the Adrian/Rudi episode, he expressed dissatisfaction with "the homosexual section," clearly intending their relation to be read that way. Further confirmation came in 1946 when he learned from a mutual friend, the writer Walter Opitz, that both Ehrenberg brothers had been Nazis, though, as always, Carl was the more adamant and Paul the less committed. With great sadness, Mann replied on February 28, 1947, "Paul was an ordinary painter, just one like many, many others." Yet, he added, "he was a charming fellow and one of my greatest love affairs—I can say it no other way." In German, as in English, "love affair" (*Liebschaft*) is usually, if not always, sexual. Since Mann had just completed a novel in which he demanded the utmost in truth-telling from himself, since every diary citation suggests the origins of Adrian's love for Rudi in Thomas's love for Paul, and since those diaries describe the literary affair as homosexual, it appears a safe bet that the real affair was of the same nature. If Mann could say it "no other way," we should, paraphrasing Lawrence, trust both the tale and the teller.

8

HYSTERICAL RENAISSANCE
AND INFANT PRODIGIES

In 1903, Frau Mann moved to Polling, a country town where she boarded at the farmhouse of a Herr Schweighardt. She still kept her grand piano and various mementos of the old days. But, at fifty-two, no longer attractive—in *Doctor Faustus* we learn of her toothless gums and thinning hair—she had fled from a delayed youth into a premature old age. Lula was properly married; the boys were literary celebrities. Carla had committed herself to the stage, an avocation her mother understood, if she didn't wholly approve.

In *Doctor Faustus* Mann writes that Clarissa, the Carla figure, was more suited to "the uprooting out of her hereditary middle class" than was Ines/ Lula. Taller and more buxom, "with large features whitened by cosmetics, a full lower lip and underdeveloped chin . . . she wore her golden-yellow hair in bold and striking style, under hats like cart wheels, and she loved eccentric feather boas." Flamboyance notwithstanding, she was too reserved for the stage. The Mann drama was meant for a chamber, not a theater. (Heinrich adored Carla, but he was objective about her limited talents.)

Mann had better luck in print. During the years of his tormented relations with Paul, he composed a series of short masterpieces. Having represented his ancestors in their decline, he proceeded to introduce a new sensibility, post-bourgeois but not quite bohemian. With immense skill, he transformed his peculiar case into a general condition. The artist—more precisely, the Mannian artist, living in comfort, but estranged from his class and his origins—became the modern type. A large audience identified with this ambiguous figure. In *Tonio Kröger*, Mann likened his admirers to early Christian martyrs; he himself preferred the image of Saint Sebastian.

His new subject performed an unfamiliar role. He didn't belong to the commercial class of his ancestors. Nor was he an employee of the newer service industries, although he discerned countless parallels between himself and those who worked in hotels, stores, clinics, and theaters. Collapsing the hierarchy, Mann identified writers, child prodigies, dancing instructors, waiters, and con men as brothers, partners in crime, because there was always an economic underpinning to their plight. The artist was then a newfangled scoundrel, a compound of Hermes, Saint Sebastian, and the Romanian bank robber Manolescu.

He was among the first artists to question his job. By the end of the twentieth century, novelists would strip the writer of all dignity, catch him in his lies and deceptions, at times make his composition a barely sublimated form of masturbation. Thomas Mann anticipated these professional muckrakers. His literary coup was to make drama of his mental work, *precisely* as he revealed its alienation from physical life. With some perversity, he wrote stories that would persuade a reader like Paul Ehrenberg that artists are simply not like other men.

Before he joined the army, he had written "The Way to the Churchyard," his first story about a member of the working class. The absurdly named Lobgott Piepsam is a physical grotesque, boasting a "carnival nose" and "pathetically inflamed eyes." An unemployed laborer and a drunkard, he travels a route "parallel to the highway," to the cemetery where his wife and child lie buried. Everything enrages him; Mann sees that for those deprived of a role in society, any modern phenomenon becomes a personal insult.

On his way to the graveyard, Piepsam encounters a young bicyclist sporting a "perfect joke of a cap," speeding toward him "like Life itself." He sees this harmless chap as insolent, threatening. It might be noted that, at the time, Paul Ehrenberg represented for Mann an immensely alluring and threatening form of "Life itself."

As a countervailing force to Piepsam's hysteria, Mann assumes a light, mocking tone. He appears to compliment the reader—distancing his hero from "happy people like yourselves"—by presuming they don't know such folk: "I do not like even to mention such things, but they are after all very instructive." While Piepsam goes mad, the narrator goads us into another kind of discomfort. Life itself speeds toward the drunk and he snarls, "I will report you." When the placid youth asks why, Piepsam replies, "You must know it"—an outburst worthy of Dickens or Kafka.

He admits his vices: "Sure I drink, I even booze. So what?" Even so, he's quick to call down judgment on his listeners: "There'll come a day."

Like a demented Pentecostal, he dances in rage, "his face swollen with roaring." His anger is murderous, evangelical: " 'I'd like to skin you alive, you with the blue eyes, you . . . you windbag . . . you ignorant, ignorant, ignorant puppy.' " He unleashes a paranoid glossolalia. His words won't stop, he can't breathe, his sounds "long passed from the particular to the general." At last he collapses from verbal exhaustion. By the time an ambulance appears, he has died, killed by language.

Mann juxtaposes three kinds of speech, the smart-alecky words of Life, the pragmatic commands of the ambulance driver, and Piepsam's frenzied syllables. His language is steeped in medieval fanaticism. The final image of his corpse shoved into the ambulance, "like a loaf of bread into an oven," recalls the grisly children's tale "Max und Moritz." The metaphorical reach comprehends motor vehicles and autos-da-fé.

Piepsam's rage, so familiar to Mann, looks forward to the demented zealots of his next stories. They all share the grievances that would characterize Adolf Hitler in the audacious 1939 essay Mann titled "A Brother."

He had resumed public readings. In January 1901 he read "The Way to the Churchyard" in Munich. He informed Heinrich that "Piepsam with almost every sentence caused lively excitement and was constantly applauded," perhaps because his impersonation of the madman allowed him to perform in dialect. Dickens specialized in such histrionics, and Piepsam recalls Dickens's character Krook, the walking time bomb who literally explodes from rage. Mann was particularly happy that the director of the Schauspielhaus attended his reading and "seemed extraordinarily entertained, applauded me loudly, and received from me a special bow. Such a theater director is a very important power." Mann had begun to work on his play, *Fiorenza*, whose leading character, Savonarola, might be called Piepsam's spiritual father.

A very similar story, *"Gladius Dei,"* appeared in July 1902, complete with a dedication to Mary Smith, whom he had met in Florence while researching Savonarola's career. As early as 1899 he had shown interest in the motif of young religious fanatics strolling through an art shop.

The narrative masquerades as a tourist's guide to Munich, "this picturesque, languourous town," where young men croon Wagner arias like cabaret ditties. Mann wends his way through the streets until he reaches the most famous store windows. Through similar windows Tony Buddenbrook saw her family's decline represented. In a materialist society, the store window is both transparent and reflective, enframing the object of desire as it mirrors the desiring subject.

A prosperous tourist beholds in the local art store's windows "reproductions of masterpieces from all the galleries in the world," painting and

sculptures beside facsimiles of modern works in which the classical epoch
is examined with "humorous realism": myth as cartoon. There are manu-
scripts enclosed in "iridescent colors . . . exquisite bindings, triumphs of
modern publishing." Appearance is all; books are judged by their covers.
Among these random offerings are portraits of local artists, musicians, philosophers, actors, and writers. These creative figures are like their art, com-
modities suitable for reproduction. As their works lose a Benjaminian aura,
the artists disappear into the history of publicity.

   The window's pride of place is a reproduction twice over: a photograph
"in an old gold frame," conflating tradition and novelty, like some post-
modernist collage. What's reproduced is a lubricious Christ child, a nude
infant stroking his mother's breasts while he glances knowingly at the
viewer. This stylized reproduction of a modern blasphemy shocks nobody.
Religious worship is reserved for the "cult of line, of decoration, of form,
of the senses, of beauty." So Mann exposes Catholic Munich's symbols as
store goods, classy items for the carriage trade. (He was also mounting
another attack. Katia recalls Munich as a painter's town "where writers
didn't count for much.")

   One person alone finds this scene disturbing. He is Hieronymus, a
young man stepped out of the Middle Ages, with his hooded cloak, his
name, his suppression of sexual impulse, his "full and fleshy lips" coexisting
with another of Mann's "hooked and prominent nose[s]," in a face that
expresses "a constricted spirit and vast suffering." Amidst the giddy flâneurs
he stands out like a parody of *Fiorenza*'s Savonarola; he is himself a reproduction.

   This religious zealot sidles into the store with its Miltonic "dim religious light," a blasphemous use of illumination for purposes of display.
There he hears two young aesthetes exclaiming over the Madonna's beauty,
comparing it to her model's, and quipping that the living person is more
"innocent-looking"; art has introduced the "depraved" quality. They glibly
alternate between sexual innuendo and gallery chitchat: "The treatment of
the flesh and the flow of the lines are really first-rate." Enraged, Hieronymus
leaves.

   But he returns, his eccentric outfit contrasted with the uniform of a
young, underpaid salesman. This time he spots an English tourist stroking
"a graceful nude statuette of a young girl . . . her hands crossed in coquettish innocence upon her breast." Meanwhile another customer chuckles
over some French drawings. Clearly these works of art are, in both intent
and effect, pornographic. I know of no earlier argument that the commod-
ification of beauty is a disguised form of rape.

   Like some demented prophet, he rages at these assorted blasphemies and demands their removal. The salesman shrugs; the store manager insists that what he calls "naked sensuality" has garnered universal laurels and state sponsorship. Hieronymus is a philistine, and his pious demands for censorship predict the drive to burn books and exile writers. As in "The Way to the Churchyard," Mann is imagining the type that would drive him out of Germany (an ironic coda to this attack on the Americanization of Munich!).

Yet Hieronymus is granted some debating points. The true work of art is not a sexual toy. It is deadly serious, devoted to "knowledge . . . the profoundest torture in the world . . . the purgatory without which no salvation is possible." Art is not "naïve impudence," a formulation remarkably similar to Ursula's criticism of the artist Loerke in Lawrence's *Women in Love.* She derides his contention that art is about itself; for her and Lawrence, art's truth is "the truth of the world." Hieronymus claims no less: "I tell you I am not blaspheming art. Art is no amoral deception," but rather the "holy torch" which "mercifully illuminates each sad and shameful abyss." He instructs the store manager to burn every item on sale. Our prophet quotes scripture, Latin ("Gladius Dei super terram"), and German ("Die Ernte ist reif für den Schnitter"). His reactionary position and fustian prose earn a swift boot out of the store from a huge, heavy-breathing "son of the people."

Outside he has a final vision of a "great flaming pyramid" in which his townsfolk expire with all their store-bought vanities. He's absurd, archaic. But his attacks draw on Mann's ambivalence about the new conjunctions of art and commerce (as well as the suspicions of his contemporaries that course through his early letters, his 1909 critical project *Geist und Kunst*, and stories like "Little Louise"). This homoerotic artist—so rarely the creator of convincingly passionate women—briefly becomes an advocate of feminine dignity, condemning their reduction to sexual objects.

Thomas wrote Heinrich that *Fiorenza* would turn *Buddenbrooks* on its head. This time intellect would supersede art, something a "writer" like him could dramatize, while an "artist" like Heinrich would never yield so much to the philistines. (He added that he hadn't turned against culture, and had been busy reading Flaubert's drama about Saint Anthony.) The play (1905) invokes the doom Savonarola prophesied for the Florence of Lorenzo de' Medici. It is very talky; the tendency to essay does not play well. There is a Shavian attempt to make drama of intellectual arguments; Shavian too is the use of a monolithic female to embody the abstractions and to aggravate the tensions between Medici and the priest.

Fiorenza looks forward to Mann's reactionary tirades during World War I, when he tried to reconcile cultural innovation and political conservatism.

He would later describe Savonarola's revolution as "the decline of an aesthetic epoch and rise of a society of suffering, the triumph of the religious over the cultural." He also heard in the monk's jeremiad his own "protest against the material, entertainment culture" of Munich. But Savonarola, the spellbinding showman, anticipates not so much the triumph of religion as the transformation of culture into personality cult. If de' Medici is a scholar pope, his nemesis is a Holy Roller employing new media to convey old errors.

It's up to Lorenzo to see that they complement each other: "You know the hero's garland is not won by him who is merely strong. Are we foes? Well, then, I say that we are warring brothers." In keeping with this leitmotif, the dialogue is heavy with operatic and Shakespearean echoes. Renaissance language survives, as does its humanistic intent. Savonarola wins, but the other's spirit prevails.

The introspective sensualist Lorenzo is modeled on Heinrich Mann. It may be an extravagance to see Thomas in the zealot Savonarola, but the play demonstrates a by now familiar blend of repression and complicity: The monk tells the contessa, "I too have loved you with a hopeless love." Three years later, defending himself against Catholics who thought he had satirized the Counter-Reformation, Mann wrote, "This is not a tendentious play . . . it shows the representatives of heathen beauty as a group of jokers, dreamers, and children against the knowing and ambitious spirit of my hero." Who, then, was the villain?

In 1919, Mann remembered writing the play's last scene while living alone in his mother's house in Polling. He was so pleased that he inscribed it in "violet ink." Savonarola, a "hopeless" lover, outlives Lorenzo de' Medici—so there, Heinrich!

As he had promised Grautoff, he allowed Savonarola a loving male companion, Pico della Mirandola. This dashing and rather campy artist flits from scene to scene, a member of every circle, while echoing Savonarola's attack on free thinking and immorality. Heinrich enjoyed the character—recognizing, Thomas would later recall, the amount of self-parody in its creation. Was something else going on? By making Pico Savonarola's convert, was Thomas in wistful code showing Paul his literary powers of persuasion?

Mann often makes inspired fiction out of the dialogue between flesh and spirit. But he couldn't translate it to the stage, as Alfred Kerr noticed in a 1913 review that ascribed the failure to an overzealous application of *Sitzfleisch*.

There would be several performances in German and Austrian cities, and Mann persisted in championing his only play. Yet by comparison with the exploration of the biblical commandment "Choose ye this day whom ye shall serve" in *"Gladius Dei," Fiorenza* lacks Mann's customary pithiness. It's also exceedingly dull.

A livelier companion to *"Gladius Dei"* is a 1903 story, "The Infant Prodigy." Unlike the doomed cuckold Jacobi or the humiliated politician Buddenbrook, the Infant Prodigy is Mann's first depiction of a public performer who does not disgrace himself. The young pianist is not corrupted, although he is clearly a pedophile's delight. With his "slim little hips," this "charming little creature" is the lewd infant of *"Gladius Dei"* grown prodigious. Or he may resemble an emancipated Hanno; he even bows, as did that Buddenbrook, "like a little girl."

Mann places us in an overheated, unnaturally bright concert hall, a public place in which the pianist's artifice finds a visual correlative. Musical performance becomes the articulation of an "individual differentiated soul" rising above the "heaving, insensitive mass soul." But, happily, the materialist Mann knows all about that mass soul. Bibi's little fingers evoke many forms of *Sehnsucht*. A frustrated piano teacher compensates for her career disappointments with pedantic criticism. A professional critic parodies Mann as he dissects the artist's divided nature: "Yes, you are already quite complete, the artist par excellence, [with] all the artist's exaltation and utter worthlessness, his charlatanry and his sacred fire, his burning contempt and his secret rapture." Mann satirizes the critical sensibility: "I'd have been an artist if I hadn't seen through the whole business so clearly," in a sneaky commercial for himself, the artist who sees through it all, and still performs.

Other kinds of desire are mentioned. A young girl fantasizes about kissing the child: "Is there such a thing as passion all by itself, without any earthly object?" "No," says the crowd. At the concert's end, the impresario gives Bibi a "resounding kiss, square on the mouth." The kiss drives the audience wild; it makes them "shiver." If Hanno's concerto, improvised in private, resembled masturbation, Bibi's performance borders on a striptease. As an encore, he plays a patriotic Greek hymn. The critic groans that these showmen don't miss a trick. Yet he grudgingly admits, "Perhaps that is the most artistic thing of all. What is the artist? A jack-in-the-box. Criticism is on a higher plane. But I can't say that." No writer equals Mann in his attention to the vulgar effects employed by a skilled musician, whether he is the child prodigy Bibi, the shipboard musicians Mann heard on his first trip to America, or the charlatans of nineteenth-century symphonic composition with their demagogic aptitude for a rapturous "ah-h-h effect."

Mann particularly enjoyed this story, and it supplies a witty complement to the apocalyptic frenzies of Hieronymus, Piepsam, and Savonarola. It has its own pendant in a late essay Mann wrote on Pablo Casals. In 1954, the seventy-nine-year-old celebrated an Aged Prodigy who was not a creature of publicity but an ethicist. Casals's refusal to play in fascist nations emblemized for Mann the bond between art and morality. The Child Prodigy grows up and discovers, as Mann would learn over the next fifty years, that art cannot be divorced from politics: as he intuited in 1903, the aggrieved critic was wrong.

Meanwhile Heinrich was dramatizing similar themes on a much larger scale. *The Goddesses* appeared in 1903. It is a trilogy (*Diana, Minerva, Venus*) about an Italian noblewoman, Violante. In each novel she incarnates a form of modern culture, appearing first as a political activist, then as a patron of the arts, and finally as a love goddess. In 1901 Heinrich wrote that he intended to portray "a whirl of paganism, modern swindle affairs, voluptuous artifices, classic mysteries, etc." The result was a mix of graphic scenes and prose poems evoking the conspicuously nonhuman charms of sun, wind, and sea. But for an adventurer of the emotions, Violante is notably hard to move. After her first sexual experience she wonders why people desire "something so unimportant." (Only a Mann would dub such a woman "Violante.")

As Heinrich located himself between races and cultures, Violante sees herself as belonging to no family, country, or community. During her childhood, an old Voltairean counsels her never to believe more than half of what she hears. So "naturally she questions facts, she believes only in dreams." She is anachronistically Ravelian (having been born in 1850), falling into reveries of a nude Daphnis while chatting with some companionable lizards. She feels herself the frail descendant of giants, the spawn of primeval monsters. If such emotions were ever felt, they surely would not prepare one for radical politics.

Indeed, her political commitment dissolves when she realizes that the people do not want education and justice. Revolutionaries make themselves "obnoxious," interfering with the masses' natural conservatism. She no longer sees them as animal half-gods, strutting heroically between "heaps of garlic and olives and gigantic, round jars of clay." She comments, "On so much beauty I wanted to found a realm of liberty."

In the novel's most quoted passage a painter describes his art as Hysterical Renaissance: "Modern paucities and perversions I dress up and put powder on with such superior cleverness that they seem to share in the full humanity of the golden age. Their misery arouses no disgust but rather titillation. This is my art!" Violante's erratic behavior makes her less a Renaissance woman than a hysteric. However, the allusion to cosmetics is *echt* Heinrich Mann.

A superior work of art may be the very short "Three-Minute Novel" of 1904. The narrator is a wealthy aesthete who moves from Germany to Paris. There he receives a masochistic thrill when he is swindled by a prostitute and her pimp. He moves to Florence, where one night he attends a pantomime and falls for the Pierrot, a woman in disguise. He desires her so much that he becomes her beautician—a form of identification that may be unique with Heinrich Mann. As long as she is a star, she ignores him. Eventually she develops syphilis, loses her job, becomes a streetwalker, and is reduced to boarding with him. As she sleeps, he gazes at her moribund form . . . and writes. (The parallels with *Death in Venice* are clear.) He admits, "I had never loved her; I had only wished to love her," but he nevertheless considers the hour spent weeping over her corpse his greatest moment. Like a Thomas Mann character, he regards his private activity as inherently theatrical, something to be seen.

His next lover is generosity itself. But he finds her benevolence stupid, and she quickly tires of him. Precisely then he "compels" her to become his mistress. Although the story predates Marcel Proust's great novel, it reaches a similar conclusion: Proust's Swann weds Odette after the fact, his love a thing of the past. Similarly, it takes the death of love to make the narrator experience desire. For him, as for Swann, union becomes "proof of . . . unbroken solitude." The masochist's dream comes true: nothing is sadder than a happy ending.

Heinrich's best-known novella may be *Pippo Spano* (1905). A summary of its plot reads a bit like a shaggy-dog story. Mario Malvoto, a self-conscious writer, meets an uninhibited girl, a "miracle" in Mann's rather sentimental phrase (he may have been echoing Thomas's praise of Paul Ehrenberg). When the tabloid press exposes their affair, she decides they must commit suicide. He encourages her and even guides the knife as she stabs herself. But as she commands the poor clown to join her, he pauses. She dies, cursing him as a murderer, while he insists that he is almost ready. But he is not; the "curtain" will not set on this "player."

Years later Heinrich referred to *Pippo Spano* as a dress rehearsal for fascism. Although critics have noted the hero's identification of art as warfare, a modern reader may as easily infer Mann's sense of the artist's amorality, a perception he shared with his brother. Malvoto knows that he will exploit Gemma's love to his aesthetic advantage. In a characteristic Heinrich Mann formulation, he finds himself "translated body and soul into the strength of a woman's being." This is Mannian empathy, just as Malvoto's self-criticism of artists—of their vindictiveness, their vanity, and their passion for fame—resembles his creator's strictures.

While Thomas sought to ingratiate himself with the public, Heinrich assumed a hermetic posture. For a 1904 publisher's catalogue, he wrote in an autobiographical statement that "being caught between two races strengthens the weak, makes him single-minded, difficult to influence, obsessed with creating for himself a little world, a homeland which he cannot find elsewhere." He offered no entry to this homeland, no hospitable invitation: "The aim is not to amuse others; where would others come from? No; he creates sensations for a single being. He is out to make his own life richer, to improve the bitter task of his own loneliness."

Thomas had felt like that, imagined dilettantes living no other way. But now his eye was on the prize, and he eschewed public displays of melancholia. Heinrich's sales remained poor, and the reviews of *The Goddesses* were decidedly mixed. Frau Julia Mann wept over every unkind word written about her sons, but she wished Heinrich would lighten up a bit. Thomas simply considered *The Goddesses* a travesty. In March 1903 he wrote a "small review" in which he lambasted the current fad in breathless, Italianesque fiction. He particularly attacked a most un-German devotion to Renaissance ideas of beauty, which he associated with his brother. As he wrote Heinrich that December, "Certain points . . . were quite consciously aimed at you."

Titled "*Das Ewig Weibliche*," Goethe's phrase for "the eternal feminine," the review is of an obscure novel, *The Marriage of Esther Franzenius*, by Toni Schwabe, whose heroine displays a profound ardor and a "tension of innocence" that evoke for Mann "the second act of *Tristan*." She suffers more deeply than her lover, to the point that she wishes to become a man, or at least as unfeeling as the other sex. The review culminates in lines dense with personal meaning for Mann. "We poor plebeians and outcasts who believe in love as suffering are regarded with smirking laughter by the superficial Renaissance-men" (at least he didn't write "Hysterical Renaissance"). Therefore, artists who "believe in pain, experience, profundity, and sorrowful love and who stand somewhat ironically in relation to the beautiful surface of life" must look to the women of the future. He forecasts that "one day they will become the leaders and greatest artists among us. . . ." A feminine culture will have nothing in common with "what cold and stiff hearts call 'Beauty.' "

This was an allusion to a corrupted, post-Renaissance pursuit of beauty, an unfriendly reading of Heinrich's fiction. Did it suggest an incipient feminism on Thomas's part? Not very likely. His daughter Elisabeth claims that he always regarded gifted women as "talented second-raters." The womanly achievement would have to come from Mann himself. For wasn't he using a language of suffering drawn from his recent experiences with Paul Ehrenberg?

Heinrich's latest novel, *The Hunt for Love*, was another roman à clef about the Mann family. Where *Buddenbrooks* stopped in the moment before yesterday, Heinrich depicted the contemporary Manns as a family bordering on the philistine, and in Lula's case, toppling over. The characters of Löhr and his friends were uniformly boorish. The Carla figure was a sexual adventurer, who kept—as did her model—a skull on her night table as her household deity. The family waxed indignant, adding to the racket caused by Uncle Friedel, who had not forgiven his depiction as Christian Buddenbrook.

On December 5, 1903, Thomas wrote Heinrich a most damaging letter. His impressions of the new novel were not pleasant. Reading it was a torment; he found himself tossing the book aside, resuming, becoming infuriated and reduced to tears. There was a time, he remembers, "five, ten years ago," when Heinrich had been his ideal. "A refined connoisseur— next to whom I regarded myself as a plebeian, barbaric, and buffoonish." The new version traffics in vulgar jokes and melodrama: "desperate attacks on the reader's interest."

"I read them and don't know you anymore." There is no verisimilitude, and therefore no pathos: "Everything is distorted, screaming, exaggerated, 'bellows,' 'buffo,' " operatic in the worst sense. Heinrich has been corrupted by his own pursuit of "effect and success." Remember the time you said one of my titles would look well in a shop window, "while I, without wanting to appear sanctimonious, had not until then given the 'shop window' a thought." I know what's happened, you've become obsessed with my critical successes: "your anxiety [is] the result of your neurotic concern that you'll achieve less than I do." Your "hygienic discipline" makes you a prolific wonder; but a good story is worth many bad novels.

Your novels fail because they are inauthentic. You have no place "in this grotesque world of crude effects." Instead you employ vulgar diction: for example, "horseteeth." Your attempts at idiomatic expression are strained and unnatural—a yoking-together of Gallicisms and the street slang of Vienna and Munich.

All of these objections are "trifles" compared to Thomas's more personal complaints. "In Riva, in the rowboat," the battle lines were drawn. You had used my formulation "loved—unloved" [an allusion to *Die Geliebten*] in *The Goddesses*, "word for word as something established and in general use. When I objected that I could no longer use that as a title, you omitted the 'loved,' but retained the 'unloved.' " (A double swipe, perhaps, at Thomas—underlining his sense of rejection by Paul?) Likewise, where in *Tonio Kröger* I long for the "bliss of the commonplace," you indicate in *The Hunt for Love* that all true artists loathe the "commonplace." Since that formulation had swept literary Germany, Heinrich's elitism might well have been perceived as *ad hominem*.

The most telling passage involves Frank Wedekind. Although the playwright's work has been called obscene, it is less so than Heinrich's, simply because it encompasses "the demonic . . . the uncanny, the depths, the permanently questionable nature of sexuality, and feels the suffering that sex may cause; simply, one feels the passion." By comparison Heinrich's flabby bodies and perfumed lust are "disgusting." "Thighs," "breasts," "loins" on virtually every page—enough!

Someone familiar with Mann's oeuvre might turn to *The Magic Mountain* with its abundant physical life compounded of skin, flesh, and the adiposean tissue that allows a body its "charm." At twenty-eight Thomas Mann's love of the body had been sufficiently conveyed. The real point of the letter was in the depiction of "passion" as "demonic," terrible, and incapable of resolution. This was the lesson he had derived from his affair with Ehrenberg. Heinrich's glib promiscuities denied the "central experience of my heart."

Naturally Heinrich was upset. In notes he prepared for his reply, he wrote that all the graphic details were irrelevant "phenomena" compared to the psychological "interiority" at the novel's core. He also admitted he was "so much sicker" than Thomas, with such a large portion of "Gypsy artistry . . . more Roman, stranger and less stable." He was the one with desperate prospects. Yet his reply, now lost, was so tactful that Thomas could write on December 23, "We two do best when we're friends—certainly I do. My very worst hours are when I feel hostile toward you."

On January 8, 1904, in a longer follow-up, Thomas complained that recent whimsical remarks on his part may have been misunderstood by

you, whom I know to be so far superior to myself in human refinement. . . . [Anyway,] you know that I'm no good at disputations; I'm just as bad in writing as speaking. I'm incapable of isolating a train of thought, of carrying through a conversation artistically. I fall apart inside from hundreds into thousands of pieces, everything I know psychologically gets stirred up, surges in my head, the world's complexity overwhelms me, the recognition that ideas may have artistic values without providing value as truth makes my throat choke, I begin to tremble, my stomach starts to beat (not the heart, it's my peculiarity), my brain turns around on me, and if I don't want to go crazy on the spot I have to pull myself together and say the hell with it.

This passage illuminates Mann's distraught condition, and, unwittingly, his literature. The virile mastery of structure would be the equivalent of an artistically deployed "conversation." Mann's familiar habit of introducing new elements at the apparent expense of logic or order is the literary equivalent of his inability to sustain an argument. This can be very winning, a source of constant narrative surprises, but it made him an infuriatingly elusive opponent. How do you dispute someone who admits that the "intellectuality" of his critique is "probably just a corrective to the gloomy and sluggish musicality" that bedevils all his heroes from Hanno Buddenbrook to Dr. Faustus? Or answer someone who claims that since "my organizational skills . . . bear no relation whatever" to the rapidity and depth of my responses, "my best letters to you have not been written."

He tries to mock himself. A young conservative has called him boring and journalistic. Why can't Heinrich dismiss him that casually, so we can return to "the world of Lübeck, the family, the humane," and, Wagner-style, make good Saxon jokes. After all, Heinrich, you weren't heaven-sent "to represent on earth that gloomy and questionable blend of Lucifer and a clown that one terms 'artist.' "

You don't know your own power. Why, these days at the Löhrs, all they do is talk of you, proving, as I tell them, that "he's more than all of us put together." No matter what I say or write, "next to you there's nobody else in the running." Therefore my "arrogant Hanseatic instinct, with which I think I have sometimes made myself ridiculous, is that compared to us everyone else is inferior." If I'm "haughty," it's only toward the outsider. Anyway, you can't demand "dignity and modesty" from me, since "I'm too pathological and too childish, too much the 'artist' to have it." You're so good, such a "holy man of letters," that you could never stoop to my contemptible behavior. Thereby Thomas admits the cruelty of his public attack, adding, "I have worse things to forget."

He closes by observing that "we are both on either side of thirty, an age when one easily takes for ethos what is simply pathos." You know I'm not a witless, tone-deaf Nazarene [Heine's term for the philistines who opposed the enlightened Greeks]. Didn't you admire Pico, the character in *Fiorenza* based on Paul Ehrenberg? "In my best moments, I feel myself capable of the most surprising changes of mind and reactions." This power stems from "my irony, which I deploy more aggressively against myself than against anyone else, and which is gradually becoming a simultaneously vain and superior delight in my own dubious personality." Heine said Nazarenes were capable of "a funny, squirrel-like cheerfulness—even charmingly capricious, even sweet, sparkling too. . . ." With such formidable allusions and quicksilver transformations Thomas sued for peace.

Yet that same month he informed newspaper readers that he shared Nietzsche's respect for "the atmosphere of ethics, the Faustian flavor, the cross, death, and the grave," a preoccupation that derived from traditional Lutheran culture. This was both a swipe at his brother's ethos and an implicit claim that he read Nietzsche better than Heinrich did.

The irony was that he, the apparent prig, was potentially more dissipated than Heinrich, who was indeed his father's first son, while he resembled the hysterically unkempt natures of "poor dear Mama" or Lula. He was also, by now, the greater careerist, despite his vaunted indifference toward the shop window. In 1909 he would write, "I may be a soft-hearted plebeian but I have far more lust for power" than Heinrich. Not for nothing was Savonarola his hero.

9

"HOW CAN YOU SEE IT
AND NOT PLAY IT?"

Thomas couldn't outtalk Heinrich, but he could outwrite him. While both "Tristan" and *Tonio Kröger*, his masterpieces of 1903, resembled Heinrich's fiction, they were richer, more integrated, incomparably more touching. In the house of art, immaturity need not be an impediment. The same adolescent energy that infused the stories persuaded readers that Mann's heroes spoke for them. To mitigate his grief, just when Paul Ehrenberg rejected him, a new generation found in him their prophet.

Although Mann initially described "Tristan" as a "burlesque," such a term barely covers his final product. The first edition boasted a cover designed by Alfred Kubin, a Munich artist who had impressed Mann with his "uncanny and obscene" work; Mann saluted his contribution as "grotesque and somber." Yet these adjectives don't capture "Tristan" either. Perhaps "a grotesque, obscene, uncanny, and somber burlesque" will do.

He chose a melody with very intimate associations. While Paul Ehrenberg had painted his portrait, "Carl in his admirably sustained and harmonious style would play to us both out of *Tristan*." Mann couldn't work the music out of his system. Klaus Mann averred that whenever his father improvised on the piano, it was always to "the same rhythm [of] that swelling, weeping, jubilating song. It was always *Tristan*."

As the Vinteuil theme trails Proust's lovers, so Wagner's *Sehnsucht* motif haunted Mann. To burlesque the sensibility was tantamount to blaspheming his love for Paul. At such moments, he was, as he claimed, toughest by far on himself.

The setting is a sanitarium, Einfried, its name a pun on Wagner's

Bayreuth residence, Wahnfried. Like Mark Twain's Connecticut Yankee or James Thurber's Walter Mitty, Mann's characters dream themselves into a mythic past. But instead of defiant warriors and lovers, they are petit-bourgeois invalids, medicated by prescription drugs. Throughout, dramatic images that evoke Wagnerian stagecraft or Jugendstil paintings devolve into scenes bordering on slapstick. In the end he exposes several forms of myth as both patriarchal and adolescent; and, shades of *"Gladius Dei,"* literally fatal to women.

The hero of "Tristan," Detlev Spinell, has been compared to Heinrich. (He talks a blue streak while his lover declines into an eternal silence; similarly Heinrich's Pippo Spano can't shut up while his lover expires.) Another putative source is Arthur Holitscher, Mann's disgruntled former friend. As before, physical traits notwithstanding, Detlev most strongly resembles Thomas Mann. He is a Jewish Wagnerian, one of several dubious roles he plays—the others include artist, lover, and invalid. Overweight and underdeveloped, he is referred to throughout as a "putrefied infant." His absence of bodily hair suggests that he is lacking in testosterone. (The name of his rival, Klöterjahn, is a local idiom denoting ample testicles.) Mann's most outspoken heterosexual resembles a castrato.

Detlev is vain, pompous, with a dilettante's pleasure in antique furniture and gourmet meals. He works slowly—"Considering the man was a writer by trade, you would have to conclude that a writer is one to whom writing comes harder than to anybody else." He's no fairy-tale prince but an overzealous fan.

The sanitarium is as well equipped as a department store, catering to virtually the same needs and customers. Within this hermetic society, the only dissatisfied patients are Detlev and Gabriele Klöterjahn. In a burst of operatic enthusiasm, he decides to remake her life. First he suggests that she has wasted her youth. Instead of serving the philistines as wife and mother, she should have been a "sublimely useless" vestal of the arts. He seduces her with language that predicts Rilke: You denied your essence when you "renounced beauty"; I must show you how to live. Their communion occurs as she performs a piano arrangement (unnamed) of *Tristan.* Wagner's marriage of Eros and Thanatos is reduced to a sad, wan flirtation between two invalids.

The prospect thrills and exhausts her. Later she becomes critically ill, and Klöterjahn is summoned. Spinell writes him an outrageous letter in which Mann again mounts an argument of feminist proportions. As Hieronymus deplored the sexual treatment of women in art, Detlev contends that sexualizing Gabriele destroyed her. Sex reveals her husband's gluttony; lust is a "peasant's taste." A self-appointed courtly lover, Detlev declares that his writing will redeem her pathetic life. "My words will for the first time make a vivid story of Gabriele Eckhof's [her maiden name] eventless life." He wishes not to offend but proclaims it his "appointed task to call things by their right name." (Rilke argued as much when he condemned the dead Paula Modersohn-Becker for denying her Angel.) His words will prove more potent than Klöterjahn's semen.

For dramatic purposes, Mann makes Klöterjahn a real adversary, solid, not stupid, and physically vital. This philistine devastates the aesthete with literary criticism—confronting Detlev, he misquotes his favorite, most belabored phrases; he condemns his penmanship; he interprets his quiet imagery as a sign of envy and cowardice. Worst of all, he shows Detlev what Gabriele *wrote* about him. Quoting the author, she wrote that he looks at women "sideways"—the askew glance of Hanno Buddenbrook—a gaze that reveals to Klöterjahn Detlev's fear of "reality." Then she stopped mentioning him. The artist plays a minor role in another text.

Alfred Kubin's book jacket alludes to this scene. It shows a bearded man with a gargantuan stomach, using as his footstool a bald, effeminate clown. The former is puffed up with pride, his nose turned to the ceiling. The clown appears weightless, literally deflated.

Detlev flees the building to avoid word of Gabriele's death. But the shrieks of her terrifyingly healthy infant pursue him. In a final vision the poet is defeated by vulgar life, just as his Isolde dies. Between them, husband and lover have destroyed her. In the terms of Detlev's vocation, she has been doubly misread.

As in *Buddenbrooks*, death becomes a tragicomic affair: tragic for Gabriele, comic for her survivors. Also reminiscent is the multifarious use of language together with an eloquent lamentation for all that words cannot express. The prose is rich with musical sounds: chuckles, lip smacks, onomatopoeic names, a lascivious interplay of vowels and consonants, noise and silence. Only music allows a spiritual communion. This becomes clear when Detlev discusses Wagner with Gabriele. Till then his language has been affected, overripe. Now it assumes a quiet dignity. The simplest parts of speech are fabulously mingled—"du" und "ich," the "süsses und" (sweet conjunction "and").

Gabriele is confused by Wagner's cosmic narcissism: "Then I *myself* am the world." How does Detlev help her to understand? All Mann says is that "he explained it to her, in a few soft words." At such moments, the master of lengthy sentences knows the virtues of discretion. But paradoxically he discovers a literary resonance in the unspoken, charging it with negative energy. This is not a cinematic, theatrical, or operatic silence. It is silence that acquires a literary meaning.

Immediately afterward, Gabriele compliments Spinell for his vision while alluding to his impotence. "How can you see it and not be able to play it?" she wonders. In reply, Spinell speaks for Mann, the frustrated musician, the rejected lover: "The two seldom go together." He hears the song, nobody hears it better, but he can't play it. This is a comic pathos but the knowledge had broken Mann's heart.

*T*onio Kröger conveys a deeper sense of the artist's role. It is partially an autobiographical statement, directed at both Heinrich and Paul Ehrenberg. It is also a literary manifesto, ending with a call for a more worldly vision that echoes his recent letters. Tonio/Mann's development also parallels the replacement of a merchant class with new mandarins, commerce and stately mansions yielding to journalism and hotels.

The idea came to him while he was working on *Buddenbrooks*. "The impressions" drawn from a visit to Denmark "was the nucleus around which the elements of the allusive little composition shot together." There were numerous autobiographical details as well, including his brief detention by the police. The most difficult portion to write was "the middle part, lyric and prose essay in one . . . the conversation with the entirely imaginary Russian woman friend cost me months." Some readers feel the strain; they find the exposition tedious. But for Mann, the despairing lover of Paul Ehrenberg, the issues were not abstract.

Denmark also provided a literary model in Jens Peter Jacobsen (1847–85). Jacobsen's novel *Niels Lyhne* impressed Mann ("I am quite Nordically inclined, and perhaps it is J. P. Jacobsen who has had the greatest influence on my style so far"). Its hero is a wealthy aesthete filled with passionate longings but cursed with ambivalence and a bourgeois "level-headedness." Everything about him is divided. He is torn between the bohemian glamor of Copenhagen and the beautiful if forbidding countryside with its awesome fjords. In his love affairs, poetic rapture gives way to cynicism and contempt. His purest love is for another boy, Erik: "Is there anything more delicate, more noble, and more intense than a boy's deep and yet so totally bashful love for another boy? The kind of love that never speaks, never dares give way to a caress, a glance, or a word . . . a love which is longing and admiration and negation of self. . . ." As an adult, he has an affair with Erik's wife, Fennimore, which ends after Erik's untimely death, and the pair's recognition that he was always their true love. Clearly this was a development to compel Mann's interest.

Jacobsen's clinical attention to physical suffering (a product of both his poor health and his translations of Darwin) looks forward to *Buddenbrooks* and *The Magic Mountain*. His Nordic dialectic between passion and ambivalence resembled Mann's condition far more than anything he might find in French literature.

Tonio begins with a student's love for another boy. Adolescent homoeroticism, insinuated in *Buddenbrooks*, becomes unmistakable here. Perhaps his novel's success had emboldened Mann; he does not apologize for Tonio's crush on Hans Hansen. Instead he presents it with the assurance of someone who considers his own problems symptomatic. (There was also a romantic tradition of intense youthful friendships: Mann could reveal himself while making Tonio seem yet another child of Schiller . . . or cousin of Niels Lyhne.)

Tonio Kröger's name bespeaks his mixed origins, as do his swarthy complexion and Mediterranean features. Consul Kröger's son is a dreamy child with "heavy-lidded eyes," given to reveries of "the fountain, the old walnut tree, the violin and the Baltic Sea in the distance." In class he's barely conscious, but outside he exerts a theatrical power; he combines Hanno's vagueness with Count Kai's drive. His appearance is exotic, but he considers the conventionally Aryan features of Hans Hansen "extraordinarily good looking." This is desire crossed with social envy.

Even as a lovestruck adolescent, Tonio has a sense of status. He respects his father's critique: one should be like others, thinking proper thoughts, the kind that can be spoken aloud. After all, "We're not Gypsies in a green wagon." Gypsies, Hungarians, prostitutes, homosexuals, vagrants, and exiles—in many cultures, these appellations are coterminous: any reader of Mann knows that these men are his brothers. (One of his first school chums, the Hungarian Jew Féher, regaled him with tales of Gypsy circuses.)

Tonio woos Hans with dramatic poetry. He tries to sell him Schiller's *Don Carlos*, but Hans prefers to look at horse photos: "Life itself" doesn't read. Tonio's analysis of Schiller's hero is a *cri de coeur*: "He's always so alone, nobody loves him, he thinks he has found one man, and then he betrays him." In this little dialogue, Mann does two remarkable things: First, he dramatizes a conflict between verbal and visual expression. Next, he dramatizes a tendentious reading of literature—the homosexualizing of Don Carlos—to show the private uses of art.

Because Hans considers his name un-German, Tonio wishes that he were called Heinrich or Wilhelm. He is fated to be another creature of language, betrayed by his name. This precocious knowledge is painful—"How it hurt to understand all this so well"—but not, despite the echo of Hanno Buddenbrook, hopeless.

As if love were a seminar, he prepares new topics to discuss with Hans; language will reconfirm their intimacy. His stroll home is an adolescent version of Aschenbach's furtive trips through Venice. In both cases, a lover's perspective endows spatial objects with significance.

A new section introduces a new phase. Tonio's latest crush is a girl, Ingeborg Holm. This development greatly relieved Richard Winston, who saw it as evidence that Mann had outgrown homosexuality. Yet little has changed. Ingeborg Holm, the pretty blond daughter of the town doctor, is a cipher. The real news is Tonio's recognition that since love causes "sadness and humiliation," he must quietly—and privately—transform his memories into literature.

He's an oaf in dancing class. While Ingeborg glides across the floor, Tonio's partner, Magdalena Vermehren, trips over her feet. Mann's joke— and insight—is to pair the homosexual and the wallflower. The dance master is the unforgettable François Knaak, an hilariously officious queen. Knaak favors startling pirouettes; with his "beautiful . . . stupidly charming eyes" and sensuously plump hips, he dazzles every spectator. The only exception is his bored accompanist; again Mann ushers the world of small culture types into literature. Knaak resides between classes, cultures, and languages; he announces pompously, "J'ai l'honneur de me vous présenter." Self-presentation, Mann's obsession, appears farcical once it becomes Knaak's knack. When Tonio mistakenly joins the girls' line, Knaak calls him "Fräulein Kröger," further proof that names will be his undoing. Disengaged, he recalls a poem of Theodor Storm's, "I long to sleep, to sleep, but you must dance. . . ." He would rather dream in private than enjoy physical life.

A new section shows him traveling alone, "whistling to himself, gazing into vacancy with his head tilted to one side. And if it was the wrong way, well . . . for some people there is no such thing as a right way." The peculiar stare of Detlev or Hanno is accepted as a special angle of vision. Tonio travels south and leads a life divided between intellectual pursuits and the mastery of "unconscious, inarticulate, life" in "carnal affairs." But he surprises himself. "How did I get involved in all these eccentric adventures? I don't come from a line of gypsies in green wagons."

While his moral health suffers, his art thrives. His name becomes a synonym for excellence, for craft, for pain allied to a cathartic praxis. But writing depletes him, leaves him an actor without his makeup. Such a figure "counts for nothing as soon as he stops representing someone else."

Toying with the conceit, Tonio tells his friend Lisaweta Ivanova, "I shall behave [and dress] like a representative citizen," in order to disguise a fundamentally bohemian nature. The shrewd Lisaweta calls him a "bourgeois manqué."

She is Russian, a product of the literary culture he regards as "holy."

She's also very smart; as in "Gerächt," their literary conversation, devoid of any sexual flirtation, suggests a new form of Platonic friendship between the sexes.

"Sometimes now I have days," Tonio tells his friend, "when I would rather state things in general terms than go on telling stories." His long dialogue with the clever Lisaveta is a tour de force, albeit one that skirts tedium. The abstractions raised look forward to the convoluted dialectics of *The Magic Mountain*, pages that few readers have wished longer. Yet, as in the novel, Mann does his best to dramatize the abstractions: "general terms" spring so fully out of his particular story that he makes thought appear the equivalent of dramatic action, the stage business of a closet drama.

The symbolic portents are comically grandiose. Here is the nominally half-caste Tonio debating with the all-wise Russian muse until he becomes "sickened" by insight, a cultural and psychological malaise that he hastens to identify with the Danish Hamlet, thereby making his ennui Baltic rather than French—anything but French, Heinrich. (During his trip to Alsgard, Denmark, Mann read Goncharov's classic evocation of sloth and ennui, *Oblomov.*) Literature becomes a maze leading to a trap. Originality requires endless introspection, anguished hours of thankless work. And for what? More of the same—words, words, words. A man of letters is like a papal soprano, neutered in the service.

Therefore personality must be banished, a statement one imagines conveyed with a voice-cracking tremor. "What the artist says is never the point. It is only the raw material, indifferent in itself, out of which the work of art is made and the act of making must be a game, aloof and serene." Otherwise, "you will become solemn, you will become sentimental, you will produce something tedious, plodding, pompous, insipid, dreary and provincial. . . ." (Tonio has a writer's gift for pre-empting his critics.) The problem is that "warm, heartfelt feeling is invariably banal and useless; only the irritations and frigid ecstasies of a corrupted nervous system can produce art." *Und so weiter, und so weiter.*

Literary refinement—the "crystallization" or "distillation" of an emotion: the metaphors suggest a chemical change—exalts the writer but dishonors the feeling. The cul-de-sac grows claustrophobic; no wonder Tonio feels a "nausea of knowledge"—or the unfortunate lover Thomas Mann. His plea that he only wants "a little familiar human happiness, the bliss of the commonplace," has a double purpose, persuading his reading public *and* Paul Ehrenberg that he is like them, *l'homme moyen sensuel.*

So far he has failed. When he gives readings, he encounters "my own flock . . . the same old gathering of early Christians . . . with fine souls in clumsy bodies." The blue-eyed beauties never attend; they don't need literature. While the Tonios and Magdalenas enter the "sickly aristocracy of letters," vulgar life glows with health.

Kröger returns to the road. He doesn't like Italy; there's "no conscience in their eyes," and the culture makes him nervous. (In July 1903 Mann wrote a Munich historian that his temperament was Nordic while Heinrich's affinity was for the southern "romantic.") So he heads north. For the thirteen years since he left Lübeck, he has often thought of his cheerful, unworldly townsfolk, especially when he suffered from indigestion. But when he returns, everything has changed. His home is now a public library, an ironic homage to his questionable vocation. The police mistake his name for a criminal's. They demand his papers but he has none. From Heine to Hitler's émigrés, exile would be the fate of German writers who defy categories and lack documents. The Lübeckers reject Tonio's name: it appears foreign to Hans Hansen, effeminate to Knaak, criminal to the police.

Having informed Lisaweta that Hamlet is the literary artist par excellence, Tonio lives out his Shakespeare by sailing to Elsinore. The severe Danish houses, with their gables and turrets, prompt a nostalgic rush. But, unlike Proust, Mann fixates on what didn't happen, and the reminder of lost chances depresses Tonio.

Abroad, he encounters Thomas Mann's first Americans, a group of doltish football players. (In the 1930s, Mann complained in his diaries that American men were not good-looking; after years in the country, his opinion changed.) Tonio attends a dance and is startled to see Hans Hansen and Ingeborg Holm waltz by. Actually it's their figurative twins. Spying on the couple with his furtive sideways glances, he enacts Mann's vision of the writer: a timorous onlooker at the festival of life.

In the novella's most moving passage, Tonio admits that everything he wrote was for these beauties. His literature was always a foredoomed courtship. "Don't read *Don Carlos*, Hans—the lonely weeping king has nothing to do with you." The subject was always me, the object always you. His dream was to marry Ingeborg and have a son like Hans (a typical Mann diversion; the partner he desired was Hans). But life has not allowed it. Certainly Mann's did not. To wish for a son like Hans Hansen but father Klaus Mann instead is irony enough to confirm the deepest pessimism of Buddenbrook/Kröger/Mann.

He can't summon up the courage to address them; he has no words. So he dances with another shy, awkward girl while they disappear. "Would you still laugh, even though I've become a famous man?" he muses. But he knows better. They would keep laughing, and be right—even if he became another Michelangelo, Beethoven, or Schopenhauer. He retires to his room. In bed he senses the musical cadences "lilting" from below. Popular culture is equated with life; the intellectual is vanquished by a waltz.

The story concludes with a gloss on his trip. He writes Lisaweta that she was correct: "My bourgeois nature and my love of life are one and the same thing." But he immediately amends the formulation. He's a "bohemian homesick for respectability, an artist with a bad conscience." These problems are not equivalent. The first is glib, easily addressed; simply change your wardrobe. The second is intractable: in Mann's work, bad conscience is indivisible from consciousness.

"I stand between two worlds. I am at home in neither, and this makes things a little hard for me. You artists call me a bourgeois, and the bourgeoisie tried to arrest me. . . ." But while the plebs reject Kröger, he won't ally himself with the "proud, cold beings," those dabblers in a meretricious psychology who set out to name what should best go unspoken. The proud, cold ones resemble another Mann, and Thomas would shortly paraphrase these words in his indictment of Heinrich's work.

At the end, after banishing emotion from art, he welcomes its return. Unlike the "littérateur" type Heinrich, Tonio rises above "mere literature." "Life in its seductive banality," "the bliss of the commonplace," enable him to tame the aesthetes and outdo them. "For if there is anything that can turn a littérateur into a true writer, then it is this bourgeois love of mine for the human and the living and the everyday."

And if he follows his bourgeois love of the ordinary, he will surpass the mere littérateurs—so much for Heinrich with his casts of exotics. "What I have done so far is nothing, or not much, as good as nothing." Sometimes an artist must disown his past; the former decadent now gazes "into an unborn, formless world that needs to be ordered and shaped." He envisions many characters, some tragic, some comic, some "both at once—and to those I am most powerfully drawn." The tragicomic has become the mode of a bourgeois artist with a bad conscience.

Malgré tout, his deepest longing remains for the blue-eyed, "brightly alive." Don't laugh at me, he pleads; my love comprises "longing and a gentle envy, and a little touch of contempt." That is his most authentic formulation yet (and possibly an homage to Jens Peter Jacobsen). Before those too dumb to love him, contempt becomes a means of saving face. The artist reclaims his powers of discernment; his dignity is another matter.

Following Mann's lead, it's easy to find in *Tonio Kröger* a Nietzschean confrontation between art and life. But this boon to scholarship diminishes the pathos. Mann makes the artist's dilemma both gruesome and funny—with a Russian woman pinpointing Tonio's complaint as characteristically

German, bourgeois, and adolescent. It is also sexy: "this bourgeois love of mine" could be read as a summation of his affair with Paul, something salvaged after all.

In October 1903 Mann wrote S. Fischer after he had met the playwright Gerhart Hauptmann. He feared that he had made a miserable impression of "confusion, conflict, tension, and extreme torpor." Mann had Tonio's self-consciousness, his knowledge that he appeared dull or cold. "Perhaps I shall continue to compensate . . . by the diligently forged symbols of my life, which is less uninteresting than my mustachioed personality." In other words, I'm to be read, not seen. In May 1903 he instructed Walter Opitz, another author who had solicited his friendship, that "no one can come closer to me than he . . . who reads *Tonio Kröger*." He was not being coy or self-promoting. In a notebook of the period, he says, "When I wrote in Tonio Kröger that quite a number of people go astray because there is absolutely no right way for them, I didn't think that would be the most revealing thing I could say about myself." For Mann to understand something, he had to write it out. The story may have been so convincing because the author shared his public's self-discovery.

With *Tonio Kröger* Mann became the voice of the "sickly aristocracy," the wallflowers and the discreetly homosexual. Tonio became the most representative figure of Mann's early career, as weighted with significance for his generation as Holden Caulfield for a later one. His posture toward the modern world comprehended insecurity, contempt, distaste, and envy. No sensitive bourgeois was unfamiliar with these emotions.

More than any earlier work, the story allowed Mann a discursive freedom that verged on the personal essay, a tendency evident in his original title, *Literature*. This was Mann's happiest form of abstraction, intellectual prose qualified by the tragicomic personality of its speaker. What passes for "general terms" is covertly autobiographical, a tendency he would refine, although forty years later he was still quoting Tonio to justify his move from fiction to political essay.

Another development was the interplay of flat and rounded characters, with a Mannian caveat that the "flat" were enviable, and their ignorance bliss. By the time Mann finished with the Hebrew gypsy Joseph, his gallery of types had expanded into a fully socialized mythology, capacious enough to fit the bright-eyed beauties and the febrile aristocrats. In mythology Mann could have things both ways, "there being no right way."

Mann was delighted whenever life reflected his fiction. At times, however, the parallels went unremarked. In 1950, while he longed for Franzl,

Katia and Erika brought to his attention the youth's rude behavior to his co-workers. Another waiter, a polite, soft-spoken fellow, asked for Mann's autograph. Mann obliged, though he was distracted. Like his hero, he disdained the ones who understood him. Of course the youth held a paperback copy of *Tonio Kröger*.

10

MARRIAGE! HAPPINESS!

The disappointed lover drew solace from an ever-widening laurel wreath. On April 3, 1903, he wrote Carl Ehrenberg that he had already received "400 (four hundred) marks" in royalties for *Tonio Kröger*. He wanted the news spread abroad: "Please tell everyone about it."

Following the publication of the collection *Tristan*, Mann was introduced to the salons of Munich's wealthiest Jews by Elsa Bernstein, a writer also published by S. Fischer and the wife of a prominent attorney, Max Bernstein. In the spring of 1903, he met Professor Alfred Pringsheim, a converted Jew, his wife, Hedwig, and their twenty-year-old daughter, Katia.

There was an ironic parallel between the Mann and Pringsheim households. Alfred Pringsheim, scion of a Silesian railway entrepreneur, had traveled a route from commerce to *Geist*, roughly similar to the Manns. In both families a tenuous social status coincided with theatrical ambitions. Hedwig Pringsheim, the daughter of converted Jews, had been an actress, the career later chosen by Carla Mann, the daughter of a dying class. While the Mann brothers sketched their relatives, the five Pringsheim children had become national pinups. There was even a common penchant for romans à clef. In 1894 Heinrich turned his family history into a novel. Two years later Hedwig Pringsheim's mother wrote *Sibella Dalmar*, a thinly disguised indictment of her daughter's marriage.

But where the Manns represented the decline of a particular class, the Pringsheims glittered as symbols of—in Thomas's words—"pure culture . . . with nothing Jewish about it." Though the parents and grandparents had all converted, their assimilation was solely cultural. They were temperamental Marranos, exemplifying a rapid, nervous irreverence that scandalized the Manns. German Jews have compared themselves to iron. The Pringsheim stock proved stronger than the Manns. Katia's grandmother Hedwig Dohm lived to eighty-eight, Alfred Pringsheim to ninety-one, his wife to eighty-seven. Of their five children, Erik would die at thirty, possibly killed by a jealous husband. But the second son, Peter, lived to eighty-three; Heinz to ninety-two; Klaus to eighty-nine; and the indomitable Katia to a regal ninety-six.

The younger brothers had distinguished careers: Peter became a physicist, Heinz a musicologist, Klaus a conductor. Hedwig Dohm, still upset over her daughter's marriage into the bourgeoisie, was twice disappointed when Katia gave up her studies for wedlock.

The family's palatial mansion at Arcisstrasse 12 astonished Mann. In his autobiographical sketch, he writes that he had known the opulence of great houses from his childhood, but he admitted that it had now been "transformed and intellectualized in this stately society compact of art and literature."

The exterior of their home was a melange of influences, Dutch, Italian, and neo-Gothic, with two contrasting towers, elaborate friezes, and sculpted figures above the entrance. "Pure culture" prevailed within. The music room could have graced a doge's palace. Its double-height ceilings allowed for two levels of horizontal and vertical action, a painted frieze interrupted by sculpted figures. It looked like a pagan cathedral or some monstrous architectural engine.

The truth is that Mann married upward. The Pringsheim mansion, filled with Gobelin tapestries, rare books, and family portraits by Munich's best-known painters, made his Lübeck home appear, at most, haut-bourgeois. Katia lived in a virtual museum. "Each of the five children . . . had his own beautifully bound library."

Alfred Pringsheim was professor of mathematics at the University of Munich. He was also a Jewish Wagnerian, rumored to have fought a duel over the composer's honor. His wife came from an illustrious family of Jewish origin. Her parents were both journalists. Ernst Dohm had founded *Kladderadatsch*, a Berlin-based satirical broadsheet that anticipated *Simplicissimus*. His wife, Hedwig, was Germany's most prominent feminist. Berlin provided a second home for their grandchildren. Katia's twin brother, Klaus, a student of Gustav Mahler's, would eventually become the music director of Max Reinhardt's theaters in Berlin.

Alfred Pringsheim excelled in the area of personality where Mann considered himself most deficient. Upon Pringsheim's eightieth birthday, his granddaughter Erika commented that he still had "the wittiest eyes in the world, a mouth which never gives one peace but streams with jokes and merry puns . . . he plays the piano like a young man . . . still studies mathematics in his little mysterious study with its gallery and astronomical equipment. . . ."

But the family had its troubles. Pringsheim was both a martinet and a philanderer. According to Golo—who specializes in placing his relatives in the worst light—"Opie" Pringsheim had "broken his two eldest sons' spirits in childhood." For many years he kept a mistress, the opera star Milka Ternina; the family knew about it. One time, eight-year-old Katia is supposed to have interrupted dinner to address her father. Speaking words impossible to imagine from Lula or Carla Mann, she said, "You're like a widower on the prowl. . . . Maybe you need to divorce us, marry Milka for a year, and have a child. Then you can come back and boast that it's smarter than we are." Golo admits that at least his mother's spirit was unbent; she inherited and matched her father's "irate temper."

Hedwig Pringsheim suffered in humiliation and became a patron of the arts. Unlike her mother, she was not a feminist, preferring great men from Napoléon to Walther Rathenau. Golo said this spilled over into a brief infatuation with Hitler; but Klaus remembers her giving him a book by the pacifist Bertha von Suttner. (During the 1930s, she distressed Mann with her excessive tolerance of the Nazis.)

As a child, Katia did not know she was of Jewish origin. Although she informed Thomas, at least twice, that his attempts at philo-Semitism bordered on the opposite, she may not have been immune to prejudice. Whenever he teased her that their babies looked Jewish, she became angry. In the 1960s, a scholar reprinted some scurrilous passages from *The Twentieth Century*. She saw no need for apology, explaining that they were typical of that era. Everyone, possibly even the Pringsheims, made fun of the Jews.

Arcisstrasse 12 gave Mann an immediate entry to journalism, theater, music, the whole artistic world of Munich and Berlin. It was also a shade daring since the Pringsheims made few compromises with bourgeois culture. He was startled to see the twins, Katia and Klaus, holding hands at the dinner table, a habit their family took for granted. In addition, Katia's grandmother was considered a subversive figure. German conservatives regarded feminism as a socialist conspiracy; the masterminds were predictably identified as Jews. Five years earlier Mann had been scribbling for an anti-Semitic "rag." Now he would marry into the first rank of progressive, assimilated Jewry.

His address now appeared in Munich guidebooks: he had been embraced by the city's publicity apparatus. With poetic logic, Katia Pringsheim initially entered his life as a publicized image. A reproduction of a painting of the five Pringsheim children had first captivated him when he was a teenager. The artist Friedrich August von Kaulbach had disguised Katia and her four brothers as clowns; she was a little Pierrette, a girl-boy. Mann next spied her at the opera house. A bit like Little Herr Friedemann, he used binoculars to observe her, accompanied by her handsome twin brother, Klaus.

How much these early impressions counted may be gauged by the tribute to Katia he wrote fifty years later. He recalled her as "the twin sister of an almost equally pretty fellow." Mann made precise use of this memory. In the 1950s he imagined Felix Krull falling in love simultaneously with a brother and sister. Krull asserts that the siblings' appeal lies in their doubleness. (In 1903, the siblings appear, smitten with their reflections, in "The Infant Prodigy.")

Katia was handsome, athletic, another bicyclist. She remarked in later years, "I now think I must have been quite pretty as a girl. I wasn't aware at all. No one in my family ever had the kindness to inform me." The smart Jewish beauties of Berlin considered coquetry demeaning. In the Berlin style, Katia had a masculine directness, a disdain for sentimentality, and a riotous sense of humor. She combined a boyish appearance with an intelligence not conventionally female: educated at home, she was the first Munich woman to take the *Abitur* (Mann never did), a test that covered the equivalent of two years of college. Subsequently Katia studied mathematics with her father and physics with Wilhelm Conrad Röntgen, the discoverer of X rays.

Fame spurred Mann to thoughts of marriage. In December 1903, he wrote a friend, "I feel as though I have fallen within range of an immense spotlight which has made me visible to the public eye and that I am now burdened with the responsibility of using my talents." He was a local celebrity on the verge of national and international fame. He began plotting a novel about royalty, since "one leads a symbolic, representative existence, similar to that of a prince." Tonio Kröger had spoken facetiously of actors, princes, and authors as brothers; Mann conceived *Royal Highness* as a counterpart to the novella. Its prince marries a young American heiress with a penchant for bike riding.

Five months earlier, Mann had confided to Grautoff that his introduction to Katia's fabulous home was inspiring "wonders and wild tales . . . fairy tales." *Royal Highness* developed from those initial fantasies, much as his other work expanded on his infatuations with Martens, Timpe, and

Ehrenberg. (In August, he also dedicated Part Eleven of *Buddenbrooks*—the Hanno section—to Grautoff, his confidant during the Timpe and Ehrenberg episodes, acknowledging an emotional history that had been exclusively homosexual.) But while the novel engages many interesting questions, Mannian *Sehnsucht* is notably absent. Regarding the marriage of another difficult writer, Samuel Johnson claimed that Milton's lack of affection could be adduced from the mediocre sonnet in which he mourned his wife's death in childbirth: all prosody and no heart. Johnson was wrong about the poem, one of the great English laments. But if we tentatively apply his method, *Royal Highness*, the driest of epithalamiums, bespeaks much nervous energy and little sensual attraction.

In February 1904, Thomas wrote Heinrich a letter about politics and marriage. Heinrich had moved to the left; reversing the usual development, he became increasingly radical as he aged. Thomas considered this "a kind of youthfulness," as if Senator Mann's children were finally sowing their oats, a decade later than normal. He granted that the change might be the product of mature contemplation. But as the subject of public attention, he required the safety of institutions. He claimed that he didn't understand freedom, having been influenced by Russian literature, traditionally the product of political oppression. Personal freedom with a small *f* made some sense. But as a social policy, it bewildered him. Freedom required an inhibiting context to define itself.

He makes an easy transition to his current success: "*Buddenbrooks* has just reached the eighteen thousand mark, and even *Tristan* is up to three thousand now. I first have to get used to my role of 'famous man.' It is very exhausting. . . ."

He introduces Katia. She is "indescribably rare and precious, a creation whose simple existence outweighs the cultural activities of fifteen writers or thirty painters." He is intoxicated by her family, about whom there is nothing Jewish, only an air of distilled culture. But intoxication doesn't promise any "happiness," a concept as elusive, it would seem, as freedom.

Yet something like happiness can be imagined. It's a fantasy: "Humpty Dumpty marries the princess." He assures Heinrich that he's not attracted by her wealth—nor scared of it ("I'm not afraid of being rich"); he's making enough money these days. Heinrich was not and found Thomas's good news oppressive. He revealed his jealousy to his mother. Frau Mann wrote in November 1904, begging him not to show Thomas or Lula "that you feel less recognized by the literary world." She also suggested he offer the public more pleasing representations, modestly adding, "I feel pretentious telling you what to write." Thomas's courtship of Katia, a turn toward conventional behavior, was a form of distancing himself from his brother. Marriage made him more representative, and robbed him—how well Heinrich knew—of his freedom. "Happiness" was unfreedom, sanctioned by the institutions Heinrich most distrusted.

When Thomas Buddenbrook becomes engaged, he writes his mother that Gerda's wealth increases his joy. An echo of this remark appears in Mann's autobiographical sketch. He attended a ball at "the golden High Renaissance salon of the Pringsheims." There "for the first time I was conscious of basking in the full sunshine of public favor and regard. It ripened in me the feelings upon which I hoped to base the happiness of my life." Not wealth but the requirements of his public role compelled Mann's pursuit. A self-appointed prince required a consort with the status of a secular princess. "Happiness" was equated with the mimicry of normal life, although there was very little normal about Thomas Mann or Katia Pringsheim.

Mann's love letters to Katia range in mood. But they are intensely literary, rehearsing the themes of his fiction, as if they were mediations between *Tonio Kröger* and *Royal Highness*, not between lovers.

Yet whether the love object was male or female, Mann seemed to require a salutary ambivalence to get him writing. A note written just before one dated April 9 reads: "Detail for a love story. As passion wanes, the power to conquer increases. For days he had suffered terribly over her. . . . Then, after seeing her again in a big hat which did not flatter her, he suddenly felt healthier, refreshed, freer, more in charge, less filled with yearning, stronger, more 'egoistic,' able now to challenge, score points . . . make an impression."

The power of literary irony could be exerted over Katia too. This passage, like so many others, recalls Swann's decision to marry Odette *after* he no longer loves her. Of course, as with Paul, Thomas's literary "control" was temporary. More often he pursued Katia despite scant encouragement on her part. Another note speculates about "this strange, kindly and yet egoistic little Jew-girl, so polite yet without a will of her own"—which is not unfair to Katia's mood at the time; the racial slur is less vindictive than his attacks on Jewish critics like Kerr, who exhibited none of Katia's humanity.

In April 1904, he suggests that he's won Professor Pringsheim's approval: "You're always telling me of your father's tigerish temper only because you don't like me." He fears a new rival later that month. "You must not make me wait like that again, Katia. Waiting is horrible." She's no longer busy with her studies: "I wholly approve of your not giving too much attention to your tomes on mathematics and physics. . . . I am a little jealous of the sciences and secretly experience a diabolic joy when you

Interior and exterior of the Pringsheim home on Arcisstrasse in Munich

thoroughly neglect them." He'll play the humanist clown to lure her from scientific pursuits. By the month's end, he begins to feel confident that she likes him: "and *even though* you say so, I think you mean it halfway seriously," a formulation he had already placed on Tonio Kröger's lips. It's a good writer's trick—endowing her words with his meaning. On May 16, he proposed.

During this period, Mann published an atypical story, "A Gleam," composed before he had met Katia. It was inspired by an anecdote Kurt Martens recalled from his army days. At a public dance, a wife gazes longingly at her handsome, faithless officer husband. His eyes rest on a young soubrette, Emmy, the little "Swallow." But in an expression of shared victimization, the two women draw together. Finally Emmy gives the baroness her husband's bracelet. The woman realizes "that her own feeling for the little Swallow was warmer and deeper than Harry's own."

Baron Harry is a soldier, grandly displaying his "glorious scars." But, at the end, feminist sympathy has ennobled the Swallow. She tells Harry, "You are coarse," murmurs "Forgive" to Anna, and kisses her hand. The baroness is stunned. She can only wait "for this unexpected event to assume shape and meaning within her." The narrator also steps aside in astonishment to behold "two worlds, between which longing flies, touch each other for one fleeting, illusory moment."

Mann begins the story with a self-referential aside; he's just arrived from Florence, where he's worked on "high and tragic and ultimate concerns." This subtle tale, arguably more dramatic than *Fiorenza*, is one of his rare excursions into heterosexual narrative. But even when he explores Heinrich's turf he plants his own seeds. The feminist alliance against the insensitive male beauty replicates an enduring form of Mannian sympathy. As in "The Hungry," the members of two different classes are united in their hopeless *Sehnsucht* for an elusive beauty. He grants the women an ambivalence reminiscent of Tonio Kröger's, a mixture of desire and contempt for the seductive male.

In May he confirms to Katia that he is not simple. But that's his attraction:

> I am quite conscious of not being the sort of man to arouse plain and uncomplicated feelings. I add today that I do not exactly regard this an objection to myself. To inspire mixed emotions, "perplexity," is, after all, if you will forgive me, a sign of personality. The man who

never awakens doubts, never causes troubled surprise, never, *sit vernia verbo*, excites a touch of *horror*, the man who is always simply loved, is a fool, a phantom, a ludicrous figure. I have no ambitions in that direction—.

Elsewhere, he quotes the playwright Hebbel's diaries on the independence of an image. Then, characteristically, he rewrites Hebbel: some images acquire "the independent self-sufficiency of hallucination. When I think of you, Katia, as I do always, I see you so vividly alive in magical detail." His most persistent vision is of the opera house where he would spy her "through my opera glasses before we knew each other." He adds a description of her entrance, pale, black-haired, silver-shawled, oblivious, exhibiting no self-consciousness whatsoever about being seen.

In June he writes his most ardent letters. Quoting their previous words, he confesses

> how guilty I am of causing that "kind of awareness of something" (this touching "of something") which you feel toward me, how my lack of "innocuousness," of unconstraint, of un-self consciousness, all the nervousness, artificiality, and difficulty of my nature, hampers everyone, even those who are most well-meaning, from becoming closer to me or in fact from dealing with me in any tolerably comfortable way.

Only Paul had earned such an admission.

All the guilt is his. "It is my fault, and that is the reason for my incessant craving to analyze, to explain, to justify myself to you." Perhaps he tries too hard.

> It may be that this craving is altogether superfluous. You are intelligent, after all; you are perceptive out of kindness—and just a little fondness. You know that I could not develop myself personally, humanly, as other young people do; that a [talent] can act like a vampire: bloodsucking, absorbing. You know what a cold, impoverished existence mine has been, organized purely to display art, to represent life; you know that for many years, *important* years, I regarded myself as nothing, humanly speaking, and wished to be considered only as an artist. . . .

Given the years of personal frustration, Mann's italicizing of "important" is a valedictory to an emotionally wasted youth. Tonio Kröger had condemned this writer's urge to spell everything out, to be waylaid by rhetoric. But Mann has the solution denied Tonio.

> Only one thing can cure me of this *disease of representation and art* [italics mine] that clings to me, of my lack of trust in my personal and human side. Only happiness can cure me! Only you, my clever, sweet, kind, beloved, little queen. . . . What I beg of you . . . in short, is *love*. . . . Be my affirmation, my justification, my fulfillment, my savior, my—wife! And never let yourself be put off by that "awkwardness or something"! Laugh at me and yourself if I awaken such a feeling in you, and stay by me!

This proposal reads as if Mann wished to turn the tragicomedy of his life into a sophisticated farce: a wisecracking heroine would humanize a gloomy neurotic, and as the curtain fell, they would embrace.

But Mann knew that his sequence was a bit too pat. Life continued to resist his literary ordering. He informed Kurt Martens—who had become his emotional mentor, greeted as "Du"—that when he chose "K.P. of all people for love and marriage, I could not expect that everything would run as smoothly as between Hans Müller and Käthchen Schulze."

On June 13, he confided that Katia had not accepted him yet. But he was patient. As for any gossip about him and the Jewish princess: "I've been a reserved eccentric long enough and not very generous about feeding people's craving for sensation. Their talk can scarcely harm us after all, for since when has it become a disgrace for a man to pay court openly to a girl?"

Perhaps for literary purposes, he was forcing events. In her *Unwritten Memoirs*, Katia declares, "I didn't give marriage a thought, not even when I met Thomas Mann and he showed interest in me. I didn't take it very seriously, and it would never have occurred to me to marry him. Marriage was his idea." Idea seems *le mot juste*.

Mann was carefully cultivating each section of his public. In his letter to Martens, he says that he has just shown a new story, "At the Prophet's," to his prospective mother-in-law. The story is both a survey of the new bohemia and a public wink that he's given up childish things. Frau Pringsheim became the first, most important surrogate for the public. Through her he would tell the world that the gloomy Kröger had been retired.

It begins in the mode of a feuilleton sketch. The first paragraph evokes a seedy precinct where policemen walk in pairs. At twilight, pallid visionaries, "criminals of the dream," congregate in smoke-filled studios. Mann focuses on a particular set inspired by the circle of Stefan George, the grimly homosexual poet. Its members are a familiar crew. In the world of haut bohemia, several groups overlap. This is a durable phenomenon, from 1900s Munich to 1960s Cambridge or 1990s New York. A great chain of being links political radicals, artists, gays, and—to pay the bills—socialites. Mann sees the groupings but fits into none; his particular audience, whether "sickly aristocrats" or "cultivated Jews," is unwelcome here. He has a superb ear for the distinctions in tone and politics that separate cliques.

Underlining this distance, he introduces two foreign perspectives. A rich and beautiful woman, "as beautiful as her daughter," attends out of an amateur's curiosity. Her daughter, Sonia, is, of course, Katia. The other intruder is a young novelist, "a man from another sphere . . . on good terms with life, having written a book read in middle-class circles." Mann goads his bohemian critics by exulting in his bourgeois public. The Gypsy in the green wagon has moved to the catbird seat. If his enemies are mortified, all the better. He sells books, they don't; he's marrying Katia, and they're not.

The local guru of the story is Daniel, a twenty-eight-year-old prophet, "short-necked and ill-favored." (His model, Ludwig Derleth, was a Catholic reactionary who traipsed around in a monkish outfit, excoriating the vices of Schwabing bohemia.) In a room crammed with reprints, Daniel is himself a reproduction—of Luther, Nietzsche, Robespierre, and Savonarola. In other words, he's a killer, pouring forth an "endless succession of technical phrases, military and strategic, as much as philosophical and critical." Piepsam and Hieronymus acquire an intellectual brother, another medieval type residing miserably in the wrong century. "A fevered and frightfully irritable ego here expanded itself, a self-isolated megalomaniac flooded the world in a hurricane of violent and threatening words." Although born again into normal life, Mann has some feeling for Daniel's anguish. "The solitary ego sang, raved, commanded." A year ago that solitary ego had been Tonio Kröger.

In the figure of Daniel, Mann perceives all the requisites of genius: an encyclopedic vision, a relentless will, even "the proximity to madness and crime"—a capacity Nietzscheans take for grace. But finally it all seems so humorless, so "lacking—perhaps the human element. A little feeling, a little yearning, a little love." Mann knows that the prophet's circle regards such words as schoolboy gush. He solicits their disapproval. His public resides elsewhere. "Greet Sonia for me," says the novelist in a declaration of fidelity.

This story was composed at a rare time in Mann's life. He could slough off the ironclad certainties of a latter-day Savonarola because he'd found a superior representation. The novelist says of his sweetheart, "She's alto-gether too good to be true, a marvelous creature, a consummate cultural product, an achieved ideal." While he lusted after Hans Hansen's physical vigor, his notion of female glamour was the refinement Detlev wished for Gabriele.

Mann's letters grew more intense. On June 6, his birthday, he recalled a blissful moment when her cheek had rested against his. Leaving her induced a "mortal sadness." But when he reached home, his senses were ravished by "the mild, entrancing perfume that emanates from her letters and her hands." By the month's end, he believed he had offended her with "certain possessive nouns and pronouns." Once he waited all day for a reply. Finally, beside himself, he mounted his bicycle and rode off "at an insane pace." When he returned he found her "dear, dear, blessed letter."

He nudges her by quoting a friend (Martens) who implied that she has misled him. But, having indicted her, he becomes her advocate. He cri-tiques Martens's letter by quoting his own reply. He won't act a Baron Harry: "to play the venal lord and master" would ruin matters. Anyway—"haven't you given me reasons for hope?" Mann's literary instinct is to play two voices against each other—to provoke anger at Martens and gratitude for his defense.

When he needs it most, his verbal fluency does him no service. As Tonio Kröger told Lisaveta, literary skills arouse the world's suspicions. So Mann assures Katia that he's not too good for her . . . just because he's eloquent. He hasn't "overestimated" her; she won't disappoint him. (Ac-tually Katia understood very well that his obsession was largely a matter of auto-suggestion.)

I love you—Good Lord, don't you understand what that means? What more is there to expect and to be? I want you to be my wife and by being so make me madly proud and happy. . . . What can I "make of you," the meaning I attribute to you, which you have and will have for my life, is my affair, after all, and imposes no trouble and obligation on you. Silly little Katia! Babbling on quite seriously as if she—now, really!—were not worthy of me—of me who asks timorously each time after we see each other: "Do I come up to her? Can she possibly want me? Am I not too clumsy for her, too unworldly, too much a 'writer'?"

No author ever proposed more honestly.

Later in June he writes that the "refractoriness of life, of substance, of matter" is maddening. She says " 'it' is happening too quickly," two months after he first spoke his love "in plain words." Obstacles keep rising.

On July 14 he informs Martens that he's "thoroughly miserable." She is visiting her sick father in a Swiss clinic. Worse, she cannot "imagine a union." In her own words, everything is fine and simple until he raises the issue of marriage. Then she retreats. He's consulted a psychologist, who agrees that the indecisiveness betrays "a decidedly morbid element"—as if Thomas Mann needed an expert opinion on ambivalence! He feels like death, prefers it to life without her. He'd even sacrifice a performance of *Parsifal* for a quarter-hour of her company.

Separation allows him to analyze their courtship. "We would like to dash our visions down rapidly with a big brush, as fresh and perfect as we first saw them, but everything resists, blocks, checks, intrudes difficult details, demands compromise and renunciation." In August he determines that they cannot rely on the simple expression of feelings. "Between us, reason must have its say." A literary discourse will have to serve; it is their only mode of communication. He discusses his public image, how other artists see him. A writer has revived that old canard about "cold-heartedness." Of course she will "confirm . . . out of your own experience" how cold-hearted he really is. In case she mistakes this blatant irony, he emphasizes the joke: "In all seriousness there are no more than five or six persons in Germany who know what irony is, and understand that it need not necessarily stem from a desolate inner life. If a writer knows how to make his work pungent and to be economical with his means, he is dismissed as an emotional trickster. . . ."

A happier coolness results from his newfound objectivity. At first, living without her had seemed an eternity. But he's survived three Katia-less months "in a tolerably good state of mind. Man is a remarkably tough vertebrate."

In late August the writer quotes his own fiction. "In you I saw a minor miracle of harmonious education, a realized cultural ideal . . . artistic and demure, free and full of grace." But he's discovered something better: she is *"good . . . kind. . . ."* Before, Tonio-like, his love had always mingled "longing and contempt." He offers an inspired take on that story: Tonio's was "ironic love," nostalgic, mocking, hopeless. Never before had Mann loved anyone bright or kind. The combination of decency and intelligence was "something absolutely and incredibly new."

"This love, the strongest there can be, is from this point of view—*whatever may happen*—my first and only *happy* love." In his diaries, surveying the great affairs of his heart, Mann doesn't even list Katia. The love objects are all male. But "from this point of view," those loves were morganatic episodes, encounters with men who didn't speak his language or return his affection. Such emotions would remain "ironic" and secretive; the love for Katia was happy, a lapidary bliss for public display.

In a sign of his intellectual respect, he confides his literary dilemmas. The mark of an artist is unending melancholy. Only "ladies and dilettantes . . . 'effervesce.' " He quotes a favorite line of Flaubert's, "Mon livre me fait beaucoup des douleurs." "For talent is nothing easy, nothing playful, it is not an ability to perform without more ado. It is necessity . . . an insatiability which creates and intensifies the ability it requires at the cost of some torment."

Katia would become the helpmate of Thomas Mann's life by alleviating those torments. She would manage worldly affairs, freeing him for work, and she would provide a sophisticated acceptance of his complex personality. Seeking a wife, he was training a reader.

So when she calls herself "stupid," he corrects his pupil with a new definition. If "stupid" means the opposite of "smart," "by all means be so. For 'smartness' is something deeply nasty." A smart person limits himself to two rolls a day, and Mann wishes to be well fed. "Everything naïve, noble and devout is 'stupid,' all intrepid devotion on this earth. *Let us be* 'stupid,' my Katia!" But by placing the word in quotes, Mann implies, "Let us be ironically stupid; it'll be our joke."

In one more August letter, he remembers a time at the theater when, from a distance, she observed his response. He suddenly felt "liberated, objective," because she had chosen to notice him. For a rare moment, Mann caught someone regarding *him* with a furtive, sideways glance. He had told her when they first met that "I almost never am consciously aware of my own worth." But he did not lack confidence. He might not know his merit, but others did, "and arrogant as it may seem I regard a person's conduct toward me as a criterion of his own inner cultivation." This would be insufferable vanity if Mann didn't add that he feels "distracted, derailed, alienated from myself."

As her letters grow warmer, "I wept like a child." He gives vent to "a primitive and vital instinct . . . [speaking] in a kind of colloquial and unsophisticated language." Shortly after, he writes, "I feel young and strong in feeling as never before in my life. . . . I love you beyond all creatures and all virtues!" In a final resolution he writes, "You belong to neither the bourgeois nor the Junker class." Her cultural refinement makes her a "princess," as he—"you may laugh now but you must understand me"—has always seen himself as a prince. At the end of September, he speaks his "favorite word," *Sehnsucht*. It is "my holy word, my magic formula, my key to the mystery of the world. . . ." Katia recalled these letters as "very passionate by his standards." On the third of October, they were engaged.

As in a Mann novel, the world reasserted its mundane presence. Thomas told Heinrich that since he was "Christian" and from a good family, not to mention a literary celebrity, there was nothing to disturb the Pringsheims. He failed to anticipate the parents' jealous affection, the grandmother's irritation that Katia was throwing away her career, and the brothers' conviction that he was a mixture of pompous ass and fraidy-cat.* In November, Thomas, Frau Pringsheim, and Katia traveled to Berlin to visit Hedwig Dohm. Forty years later Mann would remember the feminist as the most striking personality of his life. She was less charmed; she had not wanted her daughters wed, and was infuriated that marriage would terminate Katia's studies. (Some time later Mann's joy over the birth of a son deeply offended her—although Katia admitted, shamelessly before her own daughters, that she was happiest bearing sons.)

Berlin was also the home of Alfred Kerr, the Jewish theater critic, who had recently courted Katia. After Mann read passages from *Fiorenza*, Kerr made fun of someone with a North German accent attempting a Renaissance dialect. Later Kerr expressed scorn for Mann's bourgeois creations and his unnatural women.

There was also an evening at a Berlin Jewish salon presided over by the husband of the writer Else Lasker-Schüler. The gentleman was something of a dilettante. He had composed a piece named after Thomas Mann; Katia found it "a very strange buzzing on the cello." Having a low tolerance threshold for the pompous, she began to laugh, which the sibyllic Else tried to silence by lobbing candies at her.

It was fitting that her sense of comedy manifested itself in Berlin, whose Jewry had cultivated a particularly biting version of the town's patented *Berliner Schnauze*. It would prove a salutary gift throughout their history, extending into exile. (Once in New York, at the funeral of a refugee professor, a mourner whispered to her husband, "Now it's time again for *Death and Transfiguration*." As the well-scratched recording began, the husband burst into uncontrollable giggles. Katia Mann would have joined him.)

At the end of October Mann wrote Professor Philipp Witkop that he now feared the idea of " 'happiness.' " He wasn't cut out to be simple. No doubt Witkop endorsed his "surrender to life"—after all he was interested

* In later years he grew closer to his brothers-in-law. Peter Pringsheim would become a scientist at the Argonne National Laboratory in Chicago, and acted as a scientific consultant for *Doctor Faustus*. During World War I, Klaus Pringsheim considered Mann a right-wing militarist, but by 1930 he applauded the latter's fervent anti-Nazism and proudly relayed demands that Mann run for presidency of Germany. After Mann's death, Klaus's son wrote an essay praising his uncle's political development.

in the welfare of laborers. But Mann suspected the posture was a "kind of dissoluteness." Madness and crime had infiltrated the realm of the stupidly happy.

Heinrich began to voice fears that a surplus of good fortune would distort his work. Mann replied that his happiness contained too little peace to endanger his artistry. Happiness was a burden: "strict, difficult as life itself. I didn't win it; it befell me. I accepted it as a kind of duty, an innate imperative." He could imagine Heinrich as not quite jealous but suspicious, "shrugging your shoulders over my new role. Don't do it. I didn't make it easier for myself." Since marriage was a "service," akin to military duty or some vague literary advancement, one could imagine this self-confessed "neurasthenic" glad to be unhappy.

In December he returned to Lübeck for a reading of "The Infant Prodigy" and portions of *Fiorenza*. The first went well; the second failed to stir. (After his reading, he was given a laurel wreath, at last realizing the dream of his poem "Monologue.") If, as he later wrote, *Fiorenza* captures his mood at the time, he didn't approach marriage with a placid spirit. Who can imagine Savonarola as somebody's husband? The public occasion allowed him to announce his wedding in a stylized manner: "A wholly new chapter in the novel of my life is about to begin, a chapter that was conceived in a lovely delirium and that now must be shaped with love, art, and faithfulness." He had spent months preparing it, but, as so often, he anticipated the reception with profound misgivings.

On February 11, 1905, twenty-one-year-old Katia Pringsheim married twenty-nine-year-old Thomas Mann. The wedding took place at the city registrar's office, attended by the Löhrs, Otto Grautoff, Frau Mann, and the fourteen-year-old Viktor. Julia Mann attended the ceremony, but she wrote Heinrich that she wept silently throughout: "I was *never* in favor of this choice." The Pringsheim family jokes and nicknames made her feel an intruder. She feared that Katia was cold. She was certainly not typical: Tony Buddenbrook would have disapproved. Katia had demanded an informal, nonreligious ceremony and declined a veil because "it would make her feel like a sacrificial lamb." Professor Pringsheim had wept for days; his wife lamented that she had lost her only friend. Even so, Katia would be living near her parents. Frau Mann suspected she would "resent" Thomas's attachment to *his* clan.

Julia Mann recognized that her family was not emotionally demonstrative. But Heinrich knew that, "exteriors" notwithstanding, they were never "separate" in their feelings. Still, neither Carla, then performing in a provincial theater, nor Heinrich attended the wedding. He was occupied in Rome, where he would shortly meet a girl of mixed German–South American origins, born in Brazil, like his mother. This Ines Schmied was an opera singer and a bohemian—i.e., an embodied riposte to Katia. The brothers' preferences in women signified the philosophical distance between them. Frau Mann felt abandoned. Carla and Heinrich believed Thomas had sold out.

From Zurich the bridegroom recalled his wedding as a "strange and confused affair. All day I was amazed, typically like a man, at the fix I'd gotten myself in." A week later, "neither my stomach nor my conscience {was} entirely in order." He was baffled, bemused—"happy" at last.

III

RENUNCIATION AND EROS

1

MAKING SENTENCES
OUT OF THINGS

Were they well matched? Klaus Mann thought so: "They belonged together since they were somehow different . . . ironic, problematic, vulnerable . . . [not prone to] convenient sentimentalities." Katia says she married because Thomas Mann proposed and she happened to want children. She enjoyed his love letters but reports no great passion. Their romance was cool and steady.

As they had immediately recognized, they shared a dry and pitiless humor. Both were skilled mimics, particularly of their in-laws. Katia specialized in doing Uncle Heinrich for her children, capturing him at his most inane: "Ah, the rich! They have so much money." The family also made sport of their pretentious friends, like Hugo von Hofmannsthal. For years, they would repeat lines like "Papa was so very sick, you know," to mock the Hofmannstahls' conviction that the world revolved around them.

Perhaps because he wasn't tempted, Mann informed Katia whenever importunate women (Grete Litzmann in Germany, Agnes Meyer in America) flirted with him too intensely. But his homosexual yearnings were also conveyed. Just as Heinrich had known about Armin Martens and Paul Ehrenberg, she learned about the boys who attracted him. In almost all matters she became his dearest confidante, except for their daughter Erika and that only in later years.

While the marriage suffered numerous strains, there was always one worse nearby to confirm their comparative bliss. Professor Pringsheim's affair with the opera star Milka Ternina was public knowledge and embarrassed his wife; several years later, when the battling Löhrs moved next

door, Thomas and Katia became captive witnesses. In America they were
forced to observe hysterical quarrels between Heinrich and his second wife,
Nelly, as well as "grotesque" squabbles between Mann's patron, Agnes
Meyer, and her husband, Eugene. These outbursts had Wagnerian out-
comes; Lula and Nelly committed suicide, as did Eugene Meyer, though
he may have killed himself because of physical illness. Thomas and Katia
stayed together for over fifty years. In no recorded forum did she ever call
it a bad marriage.

At first, Thomas may not have realized her strength. In his notebooks
shortly after their marriage he writes, "I can't tell her everything. She isn't
strong enough to share my pain. But without such an abyss, I probably
would love her less. I don't love someone like me, someone who understands
me."

After a short honeymoon, the young couple moved in February 1905
to an elegant Munich apartment at Franz-Joseph-Strasse 2, equipped, as
Julia Mann boasted, with two water closets. Because Mann liked heights,
the apartment was situated on the third floor—a miserable distance for
Katia during pregnancies. All the furnishings were provided by Alfred
Pringsheim, and Mann was no longer pleased with his father-in-law's taste.

Or much else about Katia's family. Initial impressions were unfavorable
on both sides. Upon learning of Thomas's neurasthenic complaints, Hedwig
Pringsheim wrote a friend, "My son-in-law is a sissy."

Within a month of his marriage, he was back telling the truth about
himself in literature. Almost at once, he wrote "A Weary Hour," a story
about Schiller for *Simplicissimus*. As the first product of a marriage, it would
have alarmed most wives. Characteristically, he incorporates material from
his love letters to Katia in which he expresses the longueurs of his vocation.
But he goes much further. As Schiller stands over the sleeping body of his
young wife, he silently warns her that a part of him cannot be hers. It
belongs to literature, and if it contains room for two, the other is a man,
that nameless figure in Weimar whom every German reader would understand as Goethe.

Such admissions might not have disturbed Katia, who knew that his
career was studded with rivalries, beginning with Heinrich. But what ambivalence about marital bliss is evident in Schiller's gloomy perception:
"Here was the despairing truth: the years of need and nothingness, which
he had thought of as the painful testing time, turned out to have been the
rich and fruitful ones, and now that a little happiness had fallen to his lot,
now that he had ceased to be an intellectual freeloader and occupied a
position of civic depth, with office and honors, wife and children—he was

exhausted, worn out." At this moment, Mann predicts his large family and his hallowed reputation with something approaching terror.

Six years before *Death in Venice* probed the morality of dissipation, Mann has Schiller speculate that "precisely sin, surrender to the harmful and the consuming . . . seemed . . . more moral than any amount of wisdom and frigid self-discipline." Discovering in Schiller his own conflict, Mann makes it seem a uniquely German attempt at self-awareness, one that anticipates Nietzsche and Freud, not to mention Gustav Aschenbach. (In retroactive terms, Tonio Kröger's years of vice had been a fount of inspiration.)

Schiller would prefer to be single, unhappy, lost in unrequited love. Instead, he assumes the authority of his discontents. As he had in earlier stories, Mann chastises "my friends down in the audience" while he interpolates the sentences from his letters to Katia. Art is not mere facility —a possible knock at the voluble Heinrich? "At bottom it is a compulsion, a critical knowledge of the ideal," and, in a striking new formulation, "a permanent dissatisfaction."

Much as Trotsky proposed a permanent revolution to stave off a bureaucratic caste, Mann expects "permanent dissatisfaction" to prevent his growing smug and banal. "Happiness" for Mann is like institutionalized socialism for Trotsky, a dangerous fantasy. "Permanent dissatisfaction" is a curious way to contemplate a marriage. Such thoughts carry Schiller away from the bedroom and toward the study.

As a worker, the dutiful husband is both narcissistic and homosexual. Schiller regards his own hand with "the liveliest tenderness." He loves himself for the art that self produces. As self-love turns outward, he recalls the Weimar man, and in "the inevitable sequences of his thoughts" he realizes he can only "assert and define his own nature, his own art against that other." This is the true literary consummation: not marriage to a sleeping bride but contention with a rival who never sleeps.

Mann makes a hero of the solitary author sweating over his prose: "Did anyone realize what discipline and self-control it cost him to shape a sentence or hollow out a hard train of thought? For after all he was ignorant, undisciplined, a slow, dreamy enthusiast": we've heard that *lied* before. Goethe's language matches the visible world's splendor; he can simultaneously see and name "the bright, unshadowed things." But Schiller / Mann's struggle into form engages a more subjective experience. He can draw lyric "out of nothing, out of his own breast." A poem originates in "a pure, primitive essence long before it puts on a garment of metaphor. . . . History, philosophy, passion [are] no more than pretexts and vehicles."

He is so unconcerned with the world that he disdains its liberation. The word "freedom" means little to him, once reduced to the emancipation of his class. A better freedom is the freedom from all conventional rewards, "even from happiness, from human happiness." Some consolations are available: namely honor and admiration, "to be known, [chastely] loved by the peoples of this earth." Schiller / Mann considers the pursuit of fame a sign of inner merit. "Everyone who is out of the ordinary is egotistical. . . ."

In a letter to his wife, George Bernard Shaw explains the dryness of his literary production with the remark "You drain my desires." In "A Weary Hour," Mann says quite the opposite. Just because heterosexual marriage cannot fulfill him, he inhabits a state of productive melancholy. Forecasting his next fifty years, he finds the Eros life denies him only in his work. Subsequent events did not shake this conviction.

As a companion to "The Loved Ones," Mann had begun to plot a longer novel, *Maja*, which would incorporate everything he knew about urban life. It would have applied Schopenhauer's Buddhistic notion that life is an illusion (maya) to a frankly erotic situation. As he would often do, he used a philosopher's authority to support conclusions that he, better than anyone, knew were overdetermined by emotion, and virtually immune to logical analysis.

Maja would have deposited a modern Tristan or Parsifal in the big city. (It might also have included autobiographical passages. In his notebook he describes a "demoralized" writer, whose young wife can't quite understand that "happiness is 'forbidden' to him"; only after considerable stalling does he make "the half-true admission, 'I am happy.' ") Given Mann's superlative grasp of quotidian detail, not to mention his passionate involvement, it remains one of the great unwritten novels. But in 1906 he told Heinrich that he couldn't write "just any modern novel." He was meant for nobler efforts—for instance, a study of Frederick the Great.

Invariably Thomas Mann corrected himself. A few years later Aschenbach, the hero of *Death in Venice*, is credited with a treatise on maya—and on Frederick! As we shall see, the novella demolishes Schopenhauer's argument. Rather than depicting the vanity of sensual desire, it represents its triumph.

Nor does it cast a happy light on the first year of marriage that Thomas could contemplate a grand novel of renunciation, prompted by his having "experienced and suffered so much," or, for that matter, next turn his attention to the deeply misogynistic and homosexual Frederick. He later confessed to Heinrich that *Royal Highness*'s happy ending was something of a commercial fraud, meant perhaps for shop-window browsers, but unbelievable coming from Frederick's biographer.

In May 1905 Mann spoke of working on a "longer short story." Scholars have not determined whether the work was *Royal Highness* or a novelized biography of Frederick.

That summer he visited Berlin with Katia, staying with her grandmother Hedwig Dohm, still overwhelmed by "the most astonishing person" he would ever meet. She was the first of Katia's relatives to whom he responded positively. In his notebook he praises "this petite, progressive Utopian of an old woman, trusting in her future, who wants to glimpse a Zeppelin. Touching, graceful, and lovable symbol of the life force. Her pleasant toothless speech." He lists her political allegiances: "Women's rights. Social Democrat." He also spots a tension between ethics and aesthetics: "Weak writer—emphasizing the human at the cost of art." He later applied the same criticism to Heinrich.

He also spent time with Katia's wealthy relatives the Rosenbergs, who lived in the Tiergarten section of Berlin. He had planned to return to work, but Katia was six months pregnant and was "shy of exposing herself to the curiosity of her husband's fellow townsmen." So instead of to his beloved Travemünde, they traveled first to the Baltic coast, and then back to Berlin and the Villa Rosenberg. Here, he wrote a friend, "we lead a sheltered, superior life. Ah, say what you will, wealth is a good thing after all. I am enough of an artist, corruptible enough, to be enchanted by it. And besides, the contradictory tendency to asceticism on the one hand and luxury on the other is probably part and parcel of the modern psyche. One can see it on the grand scale in Richard Wagner." As had long been clear, the ascetic Mann had pronounced sybaritic tendencies. This half-sheepish admission sets the tone of "The Blood of the Walsungs," which he composed during Katia's pregnancy.

The story was published in the magazine *Die Neue Rundschau* in January 1906, but Mann had the issue withdrawn when he learned that his in-laws were profoundly offended. (Only a very big name could stop the presses, and Fischer's new contract of March 1906 paying an unprecedented 25 percent royalty established that he was that.) His surprise appears disingenuous at best. Yet, amusingly enough, the reception of *"Wälsungenblut"* links him to Jewish writers from Heine to Philip Roth who were similarly accused of exposing family secrets to the gentiles.

Mann's treatment of this Jewish family has been cited as the anti-Semitic display of a writer insufficiently weaned from the xenophobic *Twen-*

tieth Century. But it's arguable that the story bespeaks his close, occasionally loving attention to the Jews around him. Mann encountered several instances of Jewish self-hatred. An early champion of *Buddenbrooks* was Samuel Lublinski; some years later Lublinski would be attacked viciously by another Jew, Theodor Lessing, for, among other things, praising Mann. (Lessing later wrote a book called *Jewish Self-Hatred!*) In 1921, Mann observed that critics like Alfred Kerr saved their most savage indictments for their fellow Jews—and him. As in Berlin, so in Vienna, where Karl Kraus ridiculed the social follies and bad taste of the Jewish bourgeoisie.

The ethical dilemma, if one existed, was whether to reveal the Jews' private scorn for the benighted goyim. The story's tone and milieu are exemplary: the eye that surveyed the Lübeck bourgeoisie misses nothing of the Berlin Jewish haute bourgeoisie. The sizable number of Jews among the Schwabing bohemians provide other antecedents of the family Aarenhold, as may the Jewish parvenus of Heinrich's *Im Schlaraffenland*.

The Aarenholds inhabit a decadent, hermetic world available only to

Hedwig Dohm in her old age: Mann's Jewish grandmother-in-law and Germany's foremost feminist

the very rich. It's the domain of Huysmans's *A Rebours*, with all its financial underpinnings made explicit. From the first sentences, Mann's language is atypically crisp and matter-of-fact: a mimetic reflection of the no-nonsense language of Berlin. The parents are barely removed from eastern shtetls, and their children view them with ill-concealed disdain. The first child, Kunz, appears "in a braided uniform, a stunning tanned creature with curling lips and a killing stare." Elsewhere he might be the object of Mann's desires, his stares passionately returned. The second child is the resident feminist, Marit, "an ashen, austere blonde of twenty-eight, with a hooked nose, grey eyes like a falcon's, and a bitter, contemptuous mouth. She was studying law and went entirely her own way in life." She suggests the kind of woman—independent, sexually disinterested—Mann was best equipped to portray. A hussar dandy and a feminist lawyer: even before the Wagnerian siblings appear, Mann signifies that this is a completely assimilated household.

Siegmund and Sieglinde are nineteen-year-old twins, "graceful as young fawns," with immature, androgynous bodies: "his long slim hands [are] no more masculine than hers." She is engaged to a sallow-complexioned government official, a stereotypical German clerk. (Is this a private joke? The Pringsheim brothers had called Mann "liverish.") The family is ambivalent about her marrying a gentile: Marit opposes the church ceremony because she is "enlightened"; her father's opposition stems from his low aesthetic estimate of Protestant ceremony. Either view suggests a clan of Marranos—Christian in name only.

They are thoroughly modern, the young Aarenholds, employing a patois that excludes Beckrath, the hopelessly square fiancé. But having read "A Weary Hour," we realize that their aesthetic—"for the vision, the intention, the laboring will they had no use at all; they ruthlessly insisted upon power, achievement"—is not Mann's. Nor is their language, pivoting on the fine points of grammar and logic, one he finds sympathetic. In *echt* Berliner fashion, their speech exhibits a "pitiless clarity," a relentless irreverence that dismisses enthusiasm out of hand. Unlike Thomas Buddenbrook, they will never lose themselves in literature: enthusiasm is for them a joke; passion, bad form: "it made them laugh."

Mann must find some character to love. Not surprisingly it is Siegmund. He follows him to his boudoir and depicts his absurd, almost fetishistic need for purification. The youth stands before his mirror, the Tiergarten evident outside his windows. A circle of milky light bulbs softens each detail: the paneled tables, the polished bottles, the "chaos of ties"—objects so exquisite that they leave "almost no place at all for life itself."

Like his father, Siegmund has mastered "the art of never getting used to anything." He has no friends but Sieglinde, and his only pleasure is to be with her, glorying in "their own rare uselessness" and their shimmering repartee: "All they uttered was pointed, neat, and brilliant; it hit off the people they met, the things they said, everything done by somebody else to the end that it might be exposed to the unerring eye, the sharp tongue, the witty condemnation." F. Scott Fitzgerald was no harder on his golden youths.

Mann dresses the twins with lavish care, while noting that the boy's immature body is already "shaggy with black hair." They greet each other with family nicknames, a Pringsheim trait, and share a first embrace which smacks more of narcissism than incest: "They loved one another sweetly, sensually, for sheer mutual delight in their own well-groomed, pampered, expensive smell." After this interlude, they depart for the opera. As they enter their coupe, she bids him draw the curtains. This enclosed space, much like their box at the opera, seals them off from "the machinery of urban life" and the hostile glances of their "lost" fellow citizens.

Perhaps only Thomas Mann would imagine such an intersection of nineteenth-century decadence and modern technology. The cab is as much a claustral box as the coffin where French dandies sleep or the carriage wherein Emma Bovary commits adultery.

The opera that night is a Wagnerian epic of blond, rough-hewn Germans: as if Tonio Kröger were watching Hans Hansen belt out an aria! More precisely, the Jewish Siegmund and Sieglinde are watching their Aryan models.

During the intermission Siegmund has an epiphany. He draws a Rilkean lesson of his own life's hollowness from the impassioned work of art. His existence is "so full of words, so void of acts, so full of cleverness, so empty of emotion." He may scorn the orchestral bombast as "sentimental"—not the roughest indictment of Wagner—but he realizes that "Creation, Experience, Passion" are beyond him. This satirical passage is gratuitous, a relapse on Mann's part into the editorializing attacks of his earlier stories. Fortunately he rescues himself. The twins wander languidly into their box as eight buxom Valkyries, "not exactly stars in appearance," frolic clumsily on the rocks. Brünnhilde intrudes, but their brief appearance evokes a world of ordinary show business—of operatic extras and chorus members—that stands in comic relief to the Wagnerian grandiloquence.

The twins return home to snack on caviar. Siegmund exults in an atmosphere redolent of soap, cigarettes, and toilet water. Back in his boudoir, he stands before an open-winged mirror and studies his two profiles. This is the cold glance of Hanno Buddenbrook beamed directly at himself. He reclines on a bear rug. His sister enters and bends over him, a gesture that defines his fundamental passivity. When she regrets her engagement, he assures her that "you are just like me . . . what you have . . . to experience is for me, too": through her he will acquire a wife's feelings. (Is it farfetched to suspect here a circuitous encounter between Beckrath / Mann and Siegmund / Klaus, the fellow Mann described as Katia's "equally pretty brother"?) As he caresses her, he murmurs that their lovemaking is a "revenge." "Trying to clothe with reason" a seduction she has already willed, "his words envelop her senses like a mist."

What ensues, Mann's most graphic description of intercourse, may seem to modern readers a diversion from the carnal. The lovers' favored sexual organ is the nose. Once again they adore "their own spoilt and costly well-being and delicious fragrance. They breathed it in, this fragrance, with languid and voluptuous abandon, like self-centered invalids, consoling themselves for the loss of hope." Riotous passion gives way to sobs. The reader doesn't know whether to gasp or sneeze.

Afterward, Sieglinde wonders about Beckrath. Her brother replies— "and for a second the marks of his race stood out strong upon his face: 'We have begoniffed him—the goy!' " Mann excised this rather tasteless lapse into dialect almost at once, despite Heinrich's feeling that "to sacrifice typicality to propriety is kitsch." On December 5, 1905, Thomas explained that the Yiddishism was out of keeping with the "ironic discretion" of upper-class Berlin Jews. In January he raised the subject of self-censorship. With "a couple of imperious telegrams to Berlin," he had seen to it that the story would not be published. Heinrich would probably call him a "cowardly bourgeois," but he was still answering criticisms that *Fiorenza* was anticlerical, and he couldn't manage two cultural provocations at once.

The story was finally published in 1921, but Siegmund's remark was suppressed until 1958, as if it were an obscenity. (At the Mann family's insistence, the filmed version of this story changed the Aarenholds' name, expunging any trace of Judaism.) Actually these words displayed Mann's prophetic talent. He wrote them three years before Schnitzler, in *The Road into the Open*, dramatized the Jewish nouveaux riches' alienation. Nothing in Schnitzler expresses so vividly the outsider's need to "get over" on his enemies. It takes one to know one. Mann had been fooling the goyim for years.

But, perhaps scared off by the story's repercussions, he withdrew for almost twenty years from the contemporary world. (Although he wrote Heinrich that his depiction of the Berlin haut-bourgeoisie, the "only valuable and really new thing in the story, can probably be used elsewhere.") Not until "Disorder and Early Sorrow" would he return to a similar milieu.

This reader, fascinated by his observations, wishes he had figuratively stayed in Berlin.

Mann had tainted his new family with scandal. It would trail him for years: literary gossip recounted how Katia strolled hand-in-hand with her brother Klaus; while the Manns' oldest children, Erika and Klaus, with their penchant for shared wardrobes, appeared to some observers the 1920s' answer to Siegmund and Sieglinde. (Considering their shameless play with images, the allusion was probably intended.)

Mann's candid representations of the lives he depicted brought him more trouble. He found himself cited in a Lübeck court case involving a provincial novelist who had supposedly libeled his townsmen. An undistinguished writer, Fritz Oswald Bilse, had served six months in jail following his fictionalized exposé of military corruption. The prosecution cited the Lübeckers' resentment over *Buddenbrooks* as if Mann were simply another hack in the Bilse mode.

Still nursing his "Wälsungenblut" wounds, Mann composed a powerful self-defense, "Bilse and I," for a Munich newspaper. He doesn't argue in support of free expression—freedom was still not a valuable concept. Instead, he defends his method of transforming the quotidian. He draws a distinction between *finden* (factual discovery) and *erfinden* (the imaginative use of facts). Previously he contrasted his kind of novels with Heinrich's overplotted melodramas. Now he distinguishes his fiction from conventional romans à clef. Bad novelists like Bilse are glorified reporters. But an inspired artist infuses his material "with his essence"; his discovery is drawn, like Schiller's, from his own breast. *Erfinden* is all. "If I make a sentence out of a thing, what does the thing have to do with the sentence? Philistinism. . . ." He is a formalist, a visionary, not a journalist.

He goes on to argue that the models for great literature do not regret the roles they play; Goethe's Lotte did not gripe about her literary apotheosis. (Thirty years later, in his Goethe novel, she would.)

Mann turned from generalizations inspired by Bilse to memories of his first novel's composition. This autobiographical interjection helped turn his essay into a statement of the artist's "privileges," which included "a sublime revenge on his experience." In a postscript, he cited a sculptor who felt his words applied to all serious artistic production. It's a kind of greatness, Mann acknowledged, to represent others simply by remaining true to one's own principles. "It [was] the austere happiness of princes and poets," the very subjects of the novel he was at this moment composing: his manifesto contained a sneak preview. Bolder still was his explicit comparison with Goethe.

"Perfect," my fellow townsmen will say, "he's comparing himself with Goethe." Heaven forbid, no. But Goethe was not always the genius immune to libel suits. He too was once present, modern, just a young man from Frankfurt who "wrote," who put his life into poetry and fiction, who formed the impressions he garnered from the world and people, just like me. And if I am asked to which of them I feel more closely akin, to Goethe or to Bilse, I shall answer wholly without megalomania; to Goethe.

In his previous works he had conceived men like himself. As his ambition expanded, he began to entertain the idea of "personality," by which he meant something robust and assured, quite unlike the sickly, doubt-obsessed nature he shared with his characters. While the origin of this obsession may have been literary—Schiller's depiction of Goethe as nature triumphant, or even Nietzsche's invocation of the *Übermensch*—the precipitating factor was his meeting with the playwright Gerhart Hauptmann, at his publisher's home in Berlin, during the fall of 1903.

As he wrote to Heinrich on December 5 of that year, he had become entranced with the older man's "personality, the spell it casts." Hauptmann's "luminous" intelligence, his manner, alternately "dignified," "gentle," and "soft," his total self-confidence and showmanly ease made him "exactly my ideal. That's what someone could have been if he hadn't been 'damaged.' . . ." (Twenty years later that ideal becomes Peeperkorn, the grotesque, Olympian—and "damaged"—character who commandeers the last section of *The Magic Mountain*.)

Precisely two years later (thus exhibiting the slow pace by which he approached enlightenment), on December 5, 1905, Mann delivered a manifesto about such personalities. He imagined a new kind of literature of "great men." In a letter to Heinrich he contemplates a book about Frederick, although, till now, historical fiction has been the former's specialty. Carlyle's *Frederick the Great* is splendid, but it lacks my post-Nietzschean view of heroism. *Fiorenza* has prepared me to write something unprecedented, a work that "represent[s] a hero as human-*all-too*-human, with skepticism, even with *malice*," with psychological detail and yet evident respect, "written out of deep experience. I don't think this has been attempted." He adds that Frederick's opponent will be his brother ("the brother-problem always provokes me").

Decades later, after exploring the nature of outsized figures, both real (the biblical Joseph or Goethe) and imagined (Peeperkorn or Dr. Faustus), Mann reviewed the force that drove them. "Personality. Goethe called it 'the supreme bliss of mortal man'—but what it really is, in what its inner nature consists, wherein its mystery lies—for there is a mystery about it —not even he ever explained. . . . Certainly this phenomenon . . . takes us beyond the sphere of purely intellectual, rational, analyzable matters into the realm of nature, where dwell those elemental and daemonic things which 'astound the world' without being amenable to further elucidation."

In fact his novels defied this essayistic commentary. He had dramatized the inexplicable, applied spirit to nature. How else could he, Schiller-style, court the titans, or, through the figurative device of language, reduce them to size?

In January 1906 he indicated where his strengths lay. In an amazing sequence he describes the pleasures of public reading—with practice even he, mobilized by "my nervous elasticity," can become a master of the podium—an activity that is sheer theater; and then declares that his greatest aspiration is "dignity." *Maja* would have been insufficiently ambitious or dignified; *Frederick* will be. Does it matter that "my 'historical instinct' is not very well developed"? Well, neither was Wagner's. If you have my exquisite sense of "tone," then you can make triumphant intuitive leaps. (Art historians cannot believe that he captured the Florentine tone so casually, "with a minimum of research." Later, physical scientists and anthropologists would be equally baffled.)

Nowadays he reads biographies, memoirs, and collections of letters, not fiction. He has also read a letter of December 29, 1797, in which Schiller connected artistic symbolism with the prospects of modern opera. He advises Heinrich to read the document. "You won't believe your eyes": a nice instance of finding one's echo in the past. As Wagner imbricated history in opera, the self-proclaimed "lyricist" Thomas Mann feels called to "represent *greatness*." Tone will provide the music and "animate" the story— once more he summons the acoustic advantange.

He had acquired another identity on November 9, 1905, having become the father of Erika Julia Hedwig Mann. (The date of her birth was historically significant. November 9 would also commemorate the start of the Munich revolution in 1918, the date of Hitler's Beer Hall Putsch in 1923, Kristallnacht fifteen years later—and, we might add, the tearing down of the Berlin Wall in 1989! A resonant birth date for the daughter of a man endlessly fascinated by cycles and coincidence.) As he wrote Heinrich, the birth proved "frightfully difficult and my poor Katia had to suffer so cruelly that the whole thing became an almost unendurable horror. I shall not forget this day for the rest of my days. I had a notion of life and one of death, but I did not yet know what birth is." When in *The Tales of Jacob* he later evoked the agonies of Rachel's death in childbirth, he drew upon memories of his "lovely child" Katia in her forty hours of labor. The baby was very pretty, Mann noted, with a glancing trace of Jewishness that delighted him (Katia's response is not recorded). The Jewish looks reminded Mann of his dilemmas involving the word "gonif," and he addressed Heinrich as a fellow guild man, not as his child's uncle. For all his immersion in the biological reality of a woman's experience, Mann was no wiser about the sex. "Perhaps this daughter will bring me nearer to the other gender, of whom—despite my marriage—I still know very little."

As if he were the mirror of Thomas Buddenbrook, Mann became exhausted from the task of self-production. To Heinrich alone he confessed the strain. He recognized that personal neuroses had blocked a wide range of aptitudes, from the visual to the political, and a comparable range of subjects. Citing Schiller, he declared that a formalist must be skeptical of political commitment; after all, what does a "thing" have to do with the "sentence" he makes of it? (Heinrich wrote in the letter's margin, "There goes an enthusiastic skeptic.")

"I admit that I cannot shake off a feeling of unfreedom that in hypochondriacal periods becomes very oppressive, and you'll call me a cowardly bourgeois. Easy for you to talk. You are absolute. I, on the other hand, have deigned to give myself a constitution." As a close reader of his brother's work, Heinrich could link such remarks with the idealization of unhappiness, the heroicizing of unfreedom.

Heinrich had fallen in love with Ines Schmied, the blond opera singer from Brazil. Culturally and temperamentally the polar opposite of Katia Pringsheim, she elicited from Heinrich a response similar to the one Katia had inspired in Thomas. In December 1905, shortly after composing an essay about George Sand's humanizing friendship with the imperious Flaubert—the very model of "austere" devotion to art—Heinrich wrote Ines that his cynical novels had been the products of despair: "No love was available for me, nor was anything that seemed worth loving." Until now the absence of "tenderness" had made his sexual depictions shrill. To her he acknowledged the validity of Thomas's criticism.

That same year he published *Professor Unrat*, one of his most famous works, most happily read today as an expression of the same doubts, self-contempt, and unsatisfied longing that plagued Thomas Mann. Its putative hero became a symbol of all the ghastly teachers who ruined the youths of sensitive Germans from Albert Einstein to Fritz Lang. His real name is

Wolfgang Raat, which his pupils vulgarize into Unrath ("garbage"; an English translator calls him Mut to allow the wordplay on "mud"). Language undermines this grammarian. Lohmann, his archenemy, is a student who idolizes Heine and Zola. They contend over a woman, but their conflict is primarily cultural. A dialectic worthy of Thomas Mann becomes almost vulgarly graphic.

Raat is a monstrous victim. His tyrannical aspect is evident; we learn immediately that he is called a "tyrant with a bad conscience": Heinrich's parodic homage to *Tonio Kröger*. His isolation is so great, his pleasure so fleeting, that the reader is shocked into a kind of horrid sympathy. Many people were unhappy in their childhood. Friendless, ridiculed by their classmates, they considered school days torture. But for Raat the extremes of infantile panic multiply in adult life. With every corner he turns, he anticipates the awful syllables "Unrat." School is hell, and school is everywhere. When he looks down from the town prospect, he imagines fifty thousand students rising up with jokes at his expense.

Tracking Lohmann and his friends to a cabaret, the Blue Angel, he meets their idol, Rosa Fröhlich. She becomes the wrinkle in his pattern, the siren of his downfall. However, she is not the naughty Lola who destroys Emil Jannings in the movie. She has a working girl's fast, sharp tongue and is not unkind to her "old fellow." In a prediction of *Sunset Boulevard* appropriate to an author who ended up in Hollywood, Raat discovers the source of her allure: cosmetics. The pots, puffs, and paints transform her. Seeing this, he grows "disillusioned and initiated." Sounding more like a Mann brother than a provincial bully, he concludes that artifice is wonderful—the most complex response allowed him—and becomes a makeup artist.

For a while, Garbage pollutes the neighborhood. Attended by his muse, he becomes a master of revels, king of the underworld. But she betrays him. In a scene anticipating Proust, Unrath spends a night waiting for his unfaithful consort, whom he has tricked into an assignation with yet another foe. When he hears her footsteps, he hops into bed and fakes sleep. Manipulating appearances but terrified of consequences, this is the same masochist who turned corners half hoping to hear his name blasphemed. He considers going straight, but it's too late; "the tyrant had turned anarchist." His nickname becomes an underworld moniker: "Remember," he tells his victim, "you're dealing with Old Garbage."

It can't last. He discovers Rosa with Lohmann, goes mad, and tries to strangle her. As the novel ends, a former student shouts his name, stripped of its cachet, a renewed obscenity. Read as a political parable, this is a qualified happy ending. But Lohmann's own plans to rise above the fleshly, "like Parsifal," and join the cavalry, a Wagnerian knight, make him a dubious savior.

Thomas was appalled by the work. In his journals, he wrote a section, "Anti-Heinrich," attacking *Unrat*'s stylistic flaws and lapses in tone. "I consider it immoral to write one bad book after the other from fear of the anguish of idleness." Both brothers were intrigued by charismatic divas— the more shopworn, the better. However, it's Heinrich one imagines sneaking into a burlesque house, perhaps because no emporium of male strippers then existed for Thomas's pleasure.

Mann was frightened by analyses of his character that might challenge his public image, as when, in October 1905, his quondam friend Richard Schaukal wrote an unsympathetic review of *Fiorenza* that ended by dismissing the author as "not prolific, not versatile," and comparing him to an "adolescent snob."

In 1903 Thomas had been only mildly disturbed when Schaukal turned a piece on him into an attack on Heinrich's novel *The Goddesses*. After all, Schaukal had been his self-declared "friend," even paying homage to "my 'fine, nervous nose!'" But two years later Schaukal's criticism of *Fiorenza* prompted a virtual breakdown. Schaukal concluded his pan with the prediction that "Mann will not surprise us again and again; he is not protean, not versatile."

The Manns were not the only writers who knew how to hurt each other. Schaukal's observation that Mann lacked sufficient versatility or boldness spoke to all his self-doubts, his fears that he had not achieved the "larger" style that would carry him from satire to epic. On March 13, 1906, he wrote Heinrich, wishing that somebody would punish "this self-righteous fop." Heinrich couldn't do it; that would smell of nepotism. But just to provoke his brother he mentioned that Schaukal considered the latter's fiction "insolent hackwork." Always the more generous sibling, Heinrich forgave Thomas's previous disloyalty and wrote a devastating rejoinder. In terms common to both brothers, he depicted the Medicis as the victims of restless thought, their "self-confidence" diminished by a surfeit of "subtle insights." Wasn't that big and surprising enough? Schaukal's notion of literary range was not an artist's concern; the latter's work would always be self-referential, drawn from within; written to "make known . . . his own, always nothing but his own destiny." Heinrich understood that the arguments in *Fiorenza* were between Mann and himself.

Within a week he had Heinrich's vigorous reply in the form of a letter to the editor. He was overjoyed that, as in a Lübeck schoolyard, his brother had rescued him. Overstimulated by Thomas's words, Heinrich even defended him against a criticism of "hackwork." That, of course, had been Schaukal's word for Heinrich, and Thomas excised it from his brother's letter before it was published.

Thomas became, as he might say, "hypochondriacally" sensitive to any criticism. In early 1906 Kurt Martens published an article, "The Mann Brothers," in a Leipzig journal. When Martens mailed him a copy, Mann was beside himself. He ignored the copious flattery, so enraged was he by the "many distortions, exaggerations, misunderstandings, premature judgments."

Martens remembered him as a literary cenobite, a monk uncontaminated by "crude life," concerned exclusively with the material he derived from within. He described a world-view of "icy misanthropy" and "lovelessness toward everything of flesh and blood," in which normal responses were "replaced" by a frantic worship of art. On March 28 Mann wrote Martens, defending himself. Didn't *Tonio Kröger* or *Fiorenza* display sufficient irony toward the self-obsessed artist? Wasn't Tonio's confession of love almost embarrassingly honest? Martens was wrong, he says, in his appraisal of *Buddenbrooks*. "Critical" and "sardonic" might fit, but "it is too affirmatively artistic, too lovingly graphic, at its core too cheerful" to be labeled "destructive." Any good book that criticized life was actually "tempting its readers on behalf of life"—its Utopian promise was as thrilling, one might say, as Count Kai's final embrace of Hanno Buddenbrook. Martens had further distorted matters by saying that the novel was essentially un-German. What other national atmosphere, he wondered, could have produced such a work?

"You will admit that I have some gift for detail, some liveliness and contemporaneity, some keenness of vision, and *energy of conception*. And what does that amount to if not imagination? (I say nothing of linguistic, stylistic imagination.) *Creative* imagination? But I have created, you know! Terribly little as yet—four medium-good books [he was including three collections of stories] but they do *exist*. What are you asking for?"

Martens had accused him of glorifying "mere resistance to physical complaints." But in truth he has always valued the heroism of ordinary people, the achievement "in spite of real obstacles." His idea of heroes encompass Caesar and Thomas Buddenbrook, precisely because of their superhuman endurance. Even the sybaritic Lorenzo de' Medici acknowledges in *Fiorenza* that "no greatness comes effortlessly."

Addressing Martens's remark "T.M. by his whole nature condemned to be an ascetic," Mann admits it is "not wrong, but it is extreme." He allows that he distrusts happiness and pleasure as unproductive. "One cannot serve both masters, pleasure and art; man is not strong and perfect enough to do so." Tonio Kröger's dilemma is resolved in an epigram. He chooses the path of achievement. Martens caricatured this attitude as Quakerish, but he must know that Mann is too skeptical or, putting it more proudly, "too free *to preach anything in my books.*" His presentation of the debate in *Fiorenza* was absolutely neutral; didn't he pour much of himself into Lorenzo?

Martens predicts that Mann's reception will involve "more cool respect than heartfelt affection." It's not so, Mann asserts; I'm not the creature of reviews, some critics' darling whose books are bought but never read. *Buddenbrooks* and *Tonio Kröger* are "*loved,*" so much so that it almost scares me: "Am I so soft, so insipid, so mediocre" that I should be so popular? But "since I am neither frivolous nor crotchety nor tart nor stiff, I do not see, if I should somehow prove lasting, why Germans should refuse me love in the future."

After all, I've given them no cause to condemn me. "I was a quiet, well-behaved person, who won a measure of prosperity by the work of his hands, took a wife, begot children, attended first nights, and was so good a German that I could not stand being abroad for more than four weeks." What more do you want, that I "go bowling and drinking on top of that?" He chastises the portrayal of Heinrich as "egotistically solitary." Doesn't Martens know about his recent political activism?

Mann closed by hailing Martens as still his best critic. But the knowledge that a reasonably intelligent man could know him for years and still misapprehend everything about him was discouraging. A few days later he received bad news from Katia about a dearer friend. Following a scandalous affair with Lula, Armin Martens had been dispatched to the German colonies in Africa, where he barely supported himself as a salesman. On April 1, he died there, at twenty-nine, his possessions limited to the ragged clothes (worth less than three marks) on his back. Six days later, Mann wrote Ilse Martens, employing the familiar *Du* of their youth. "Armin and death don't go together. I can't make any sense of this. You know that my earliest, purest, most tender feelings were for him": a striking admission from a newlywed husband.

After the bleak predictions of Schaukal and Kurt Martens had come the news of his first love's death. Mann was sickened by fear. In May 1906 he entered a Dresden sanitarium to recover.

On June 7, he wrote Heinrich that life had been easier without a wife or child. Now he felt "exhausted and drained and dead and finished. . . ." He was "tormented by the thought that it was wrong to become attached and tied down." He had always suspected that winning "happiness" had taken "the *last* of my energies." Indeed, he, "the happier one," had it incomparably harder than the bachelor Heinrich. "I am bound and have a gold weight on each leg."

Bad spirits still prevailed between Mann and his in-laws. Four days later he mentioned "terrible" times he had recently undergone with the Pringsheims. He was sensitive to the fact that Katia was underemployed. In July 1907 he requested that Heinrich send over some volumes of Flaubert for her to translate.

E very two months or so periods of depression and insomnia would vanquish him. He suffered gastrointestinal upsets, from which he recovered over a period of days. Once regarded as neurasthenia, Mann's complaint has received more arcane diagnoses from contemporary physicians; perhaps these are best disregarded—one of them explains Mann's lack of interest in heterosexuality as evidence of an undeveloped pituitary gland! Mann's nervous stomach is a familiar complaint of the unloved and overworked.

Though it was not a good time, Mann derived some pleasure from the occasional public performance. In May he gave a reading in Dresden: he later described the trip in a story. "It was a literary and artistic pilgrimage, in short, such as, from time to time, I undertake not unwillingly. You make appearances, you attend functions, you show yourself to admiring crowds—not for nothing is one a subject of Wilhelm II." In one of several occasions when the external world reflected his emotional state, the train broke down: naturally he made a story of that. After the lecture tour, he entered the sanitarium.

He knew that more than a bad review had prompted his breakdown. He wrote Heinrich that he should never have married; he wasn't ready for a normal family life. In another letter he praised Heinrich's new story, "Abdication," which spoke immediately to his depression. As mentioned earlier, its subject was adolescent homosexuality. The story ends with the hero's suicide. Heinrich's sympathy was laced with satire, but Thomas missed the humor. Enthralled by the self-abasement over a worthless object, he declared that it was Heinrich's best story, one so vivid he felt he had written it himself—though he intimated that he'd have done it better.

Heinrich exhibited great tact when he responded to Thomas's sarcastic jibes at his "rushing tempo, your famous verve, the delightful pungency of your language"—i.e., your hot air—without equally sneering remarks. Thomas proved grateful. Now that his old friend Otto Grautoff was leaving Munich for Paris, he hoped that Heinrich would marry his sweetheart, Ines Schmied, and move near him. Recalling his marriage's first days, he ob-

served, "You are united, you are sure of yourselves . . ." as he and Katia
hadn't been. He didn't add that he might never grow sure; praising "Abdication" was confession enough.

On November 18, 1906, his first son, Klaus Heinrich, was born, named
after his latest hero. By now, the spillover from his work took many forms.
A letter reporting Klaus's birth contained an exegesis of his new novel:
"The artist is akin to the prince in that, like the latter, he leads a *representative* existence. What etiquette is to the prince, the lofty obligation to
create form is to the artist. The artist, as I know him, is never the man
who can 'let himself be seen' freely and without much ado. He needs pru-
dence in passion, idealization in self-depiction, or in short—art. That is his
human weakness."

Was art then merely a subterfuge, a refusal to be seen? Shades of Tonio
Kröger, Mann alternately disdained and wallowed in self-revelation.

He began writing critical essays, a natural expansion of the literary commentary that ran through his fiction. Mann's irreverent wit led some
readers to dismiss him as *Schriftsteller* rather than *Dichter*, a proficient critic
rather than an impassioned artist. He ridiculed such criteria; Winston nicely
observes, "he also anticipated this criticism, assimilated it into his legend,"
as, in fact, he had been doing since *Tonio* and "Weary Hour."

Between February and May 1907 he wrote an "Essay on the Theater"
which would be published eight months later. In it he drew a distinction
between the theater, a form of public, popular art that was both lovable
and frivolous, and the drama, a serious literary form. It was highbrow
propaganda for his play *Fiorenza*; but he faltered when he tried to separate
high and low art. The author of the wildly successful *Buddenbrooks* made
an unlikely knight of the ivory tower.

The essay conveys his misgiving about the proximity of art and entertainment. He writes, admittedly, as a perplexed fan. In his youth he had
been the most ardent of theatergoers, thrilled by the spectacle at the Tivoli
Theater, and often reduced to tears afterward. He describes a night at the
theater—the dizzying succession of perfumes and movement, sound and
sight. As fastidious as Siegmund Aarenhold, he manages to enjoy the spectacle while distancing himself from his neighbors, those beer-drinking
boors. "Can it be good, can it be sublime if it appeals to those other people
as well? The ideal is not without its comic side."

The drama of Schiller, Goethe, Ibsen, or even Mann's contemporaries
Hauptmann, Wedekind, and Hofmannsthal, is actually better read than

seen. But Wagner, ah, Wagner—he is nothing without the stage. The *Gesamtkunstwerk* can not be broken down or contemplated in isolated detail, while drama on the page allows introspection.

A stage can't be dignified; it is too geared to the sudden thrill: "it exists in the here and now; it has no yesterday." Sounding the very model of an elitist snob, Mann observes the theater's scandalous toadying to the lowest common denominator. Yet snob or not, he exposes himself as susceptible to those same appeals. The adolescent who found in the Tivoli a world of "novelty, adventure, and license" is the most vivid figure in his essay. Mann recaptures his pleasure and makes literature of his guilt.

With its numerous contradictions, the essay exhausted him. It's one of his rare forays into theory, and though it fails, it also honors a complicated nature. Ambivalence may not be a theoretician's strong suit, but it's almost the essayist's lifeblood.

On another matter that year, his position was unambiguous. A right-winger had guessed that he was Jewish; something about his irreverence gave a Jewish impression. Mann used a magazine forum, "On the Jewish Question," to correct the error. His racial mixture was Latin, not Jewish, he pointed out, but he disdained racial chauvinism of any sort. He identified himself, "though not otherwise richly blessed with wholly unequivocal convictions, a convinced and unequivocal 'philo-Semite.' " He regarded a mass exodus of Jews, such as the one called for by Theodor Herzl's Zionists, as a potential disaster for European culture.

Mann sees the "Jewish question" as "a personal, human conflict, a purely psychological problem." A stranger and outcast everywhere, "the Jew distinguishes himself in a sublime or an offensive way, despite all humanistic-democratic leveling." The Jew's strength is his indomitable personality. He can never be typical, normal, like his neighbors. In a Mannian sense, he represents "revolutionary tendencies and warped snobbism," both "a rugged, communal feeling" and "heretical individualism," "insolence and insecurity, cynicism and sentimentality, sharpness and melancholy."

By now Mann knew that he did not cut a charming figure, that something about his presence irritated almost everyone. He recognized a similarly forbidding personality in the arrogant Jew with his "frequently annoying superiority." The Jew does not hide his talents. Mann had argued on Schiller's behalf that the truly great possessed a right to their ambitions. Therefore, when he expressed an "artist's affinity for the Jews," he was praising a mirror image of his own personality, audacious and forlorn.

In 1907 he saw "progress" as the only solution to the social prejudices of Western Europe and the far bloodier pogroms occurring in "barbarous" Russia (only its literature was "holy"). Once the Jew was fully assimilated, he would lose his disagreeable habits, the whiny, davening voice, the nervous eyes and hands, those unhappy products of "two thousand years of terrible exclusion." The stereotype could be retired now that the Jew was permitted to become a full-fledged German, if not a European. Of course the Jews Mann admired were members of an elite, whether financial or Nietzschean. He was a philo-Semite only by their standards.

Mann can point to young Jews with an English talent for "physical culture" (Katia was far more athletic than he). Alluding to his own situation, he praises the concept of mixed marriage. The Jew should be assimilated—and "baptized" to make things economical—in order to break any ties with the unsavory Chasidim, those medieval invaders of modern cities. He predicts that assimilation need take no more than three generations. Today, he says, it's possible for Germans to balance aristocratic and "modern" tendencies; tomorrow Jews will move as casually between the eras.

For its time, this was a progressive statement. Modern readers will detect his class and cultural prejudice, not to mention his personal animus: he allows the Jews only those offenses that resemble his own. But this was not his last word on the subject. Among many surprising developments would be his espousal of Zionism: in the late 1940s, he wrote several pieces urging the creation of a Jewish homeland.

In early May he visited Venice and found the Lido "a pretentious dive." He returned in time for the Frankfurt production of *Fiorenza*, and regarded it a success. Having proved himself in two new media, criticism and drama, he sought to refurbish his public image. During the summer of 1907 he wrote a lengthy discussion of his work habits for the Bonn Society for Literary Criticism. Each morning without exception was devoted to writing. Although this lifetime routine made him appear a literary automaton, he always limited activities to these hours, when he was freshest, in part because he placed such tremendous pressure on whatever he wrote then: "Every passage becomes a 'passage,' every adjective a decision." It was demonstrably a case of holding fast and overcoming. "As for myself, the watchword is: clench the teeth and take one slow step at a time. The watchword is: practice patience, idle through half the day, go to sleep. And wait to see whether things may not flow better next day with the mind rested."

In an echo of *Tonio Kröger*, Mann admits that he needs to write slowly—and in undisturbed comfort—because "given the way I work, to stick to it requires a patience, or rather an obstinacy, a stubbornness, a discipline, and a repression of one's will that is almost unimaginable and that, believe me, stretches the nerves to the screaming point." The moment of composition is so draining that it's almost beyond rational discussion. He can't assess his work properly: "Faith in it becomes artificial . . . a galvanic twitching. The greatest part of one's nervous energy is consumed in *simulating* that faith" (italics mine). Throughout his life Mann would distance himself from the work he'd just completed. Perspective might take years; his usual tendency was to doubt his achievement and proceed swiftly to the next piece. In such a way, the sustained efforts of a miniaturist produced a lifetime oeuvre of many volumes.

A less exceptional self was presented in the short sketch *"Im Spiegel"* ("In the Mirror"), in which he confessed himself a poor student, an uncertain public speaker who had felt an "elusive superiority." He made fun of his natural indolence, his apprenticeship in the insurance office—"I left before I was thrown out"—the "mixed bag" of courses he audited at the university; the late adolescence when "like a real vagabond, I walked around for a year." By day he would write; by night, play dominos and drink punch, content with the bare essentials as long as he could purchase sweet Italian cigarettes. He satirized the "flat feet" which got him kicked out of the army. "My feet couldn't get used to the ideal manly walk called parade stepping." Once more a civilian, he became an editor of *Simplicissimus*: "You see how I deteriorated."

But now "nobody is as lucky as I am" with my "princess" of a wife, my beautiful children, and my large apartment "in the best neighborhood," and with "electric lights, most beautiful furniture and pictures." He commands three maids and a Scottish sheepdog. For breakfast he eats sweet rolls, and he wears patent-leather shoes almost daily. What else? He admits that he's a nervous public speaker, but audiences applaud when he arrives: he sold out the Cabaret Casino—they gave him a laurel wreath (a nice joke for those tracking Mann's pursuit of laurels is that he receives them in a casino).

But he confesses that success puzzles him. "I haven't changed, I have not improved. I have only kept doing what I did in school—dream and write poetry." His poor teachers would consider his good fortune a scandal.

This self-portrait was the product of someone in a very good mood, self-mocking and self-promoting. The construction of a personal myth required an agenda. On February 6, 1908, he wrote Heinrich one of his most revealing letters. Admiring his brother's love of beauty, he suggested that it was due to a trouble-free youth (Heinrich didn't see things that way). Thomas had never acquired the gift because he'd been plagued by "inner problems." Yet now, coming out of himself, he was learning to appreciate beauty—an understatement for this world-class voyeur. If his luck held out, "if my body keeps up," he would achieve even more ten years from now. "Sometimes I believe . . . I will do my best work between fifty and sixty." Aged thirty-two, he began rehearsing for old age.

2

THE LEFT-HANDED PRINCE

Anticipating a calmer future, Mann began to see that he was threatened by something more than bad reviews. In his typically slow way, he acquired a social perspective (the more advanced Heinrich was by now an outspoken radical). In his letter of February 6, 1908, he describes the libel trial of Maximilian Harden, a journalist who had attended the soirées of Katia's Berlin relatives. Harden had exposed a homosexual clique at the Kaiser's court. Dominated by Prince Philipp zu Eulenburg und Hertefeld, the German ambassador to Vienna, the so-called Eulenburg case hastened the ruin of many wealthy and powerful men, most of them married. In Berlin, several suicides followed the revelation of Eulenburg's pranks.

A muckraking nationalist, he considered Eulenburg insufficiently vigilant and bellicose toward France. In other words, gay men were selling out their country (an argument revived in America during the 1980s by Norman Podhoretz). Harden discerned a Masonic order composed of Bismarck's queer followers. His exposés had an unintended effect. Patriots now railed against both Jews and homosexuals, messenger and message. From observing these events, Mann learned that homosexuality could destroy a career, and that neither right nor left would defend his kind of love.

The aggrieved wife of Count Kuno von Moltke sued Harden for defamation. His defense attorney was Max Bernstein, whose wife had acted as a matchmaker for Katia and Thomas. Mann deplored the court's "shameless tendency" to side with Countess Moltke by rejecting every second question of Bernstein's. A hostile atmosphere engulfed the witnesses, including Magnus Hirschfeld, the pioneer gay activist.* As the establishment rallied against its critic, Harden's journal, *Die Zukunft*, lost most of its subscribers. (Eventually he was acquitted.)

What a story for Thomas Mann! Like the gays who broadcast tales of right-wing homosexuals in order to destroy their political power, he was applauding an act of "outing" that he refused himself. (Forty years later, in a letter he intended to be "completely private and personal," the seventy-three-year-old Mann wrote that Harden's "methods of fighting the court circles, or more personally speaking of the Count Eulenburg, were not exactly in good taste.")

Meanwhile, he learned that the scandal had provoked a reactionary group of Berlin socialites—"of whom our uncle Friedel would say 'the worst.'" He regretted that the group's leader was Richard Wagner's son-in-law, Privy Councillor Thode. In a forecast of later Wagnerians, Mann deplored the man's beer-hall cadences, his "unbelievably poor German." As would the Nazis a few years later, the group proposed a hygienic culture: the German soul's health would be measured by its art. "It's the most disgusting stuff one can imagine. That Wagner's name is linked to this affair saddens one but is finally right. I always feel kind of ridiculous about the bourgeois world's misunderstanding of Wagner."

Mann spent the rest of 1908 finishing *Royal Highness* while living in high style. In September, he commissioned Gabriel von Seidl, a well-known Jugendstil architect to design a summer house in the fashionable resort town of Bad Tölz, thirty miles south of Munich. In late November he visited Vienna, where he joined his colleague Jakob Wassermann and encountered for the first time Arthur Schnitzler and Hugo von Hofmanns-thal. All three were Jewish writers, and Mann asked them to privately comment on "The Blood of the Walsungs." Their response is not known, but since friendly relations were established, one guesses that they were not overly harsh. It's a sign of philo-Semitism that Mann sought their approval. It was also a shrewd move, since the three Jews were, along with Heinrich, his major rivals in the German language.

The friendship between Hofmannsthal and Mann was decorous and studied. Mann was impressed by the Austrian's splendid residence; he also

---

* Magnus Hirschfeld adduced effeminate characteristics as proof of a "third sex." Mann demurred, although he had already created a majestic queen in Herr Knaak. By contrast, Hirschfeld underlined the gay subtext of Goethe and Schiller's friendship long before Mann called it the nineteenth century's great romance.

confided to Heinrich that Hofmannsthal handled his reading glasses just like him. The two corresponded for years and met on several occasions. When Hofmannsthal died, after returning from the funeral of a son who had committed suicide, Mann described the youthful beauty of the poet's corpse.

There was little warmth between the two men. Their private comments aren't recorded. But Elisabeth Mann Borgese recalls her parents' laughter over the Hofmannsthals' lugubrious outbursts: northern Germans have often found Viennese hyperbolic. Hofmannsthal's daughter, Christiane Zimmer, one of the great hostesses—and gossips—of the literary emigration, provided her own take. She could inform you about the sexual escapades of Klaus and Erika. Until she read the diaries, she hadn't known of their father's homosexuality. But she once said, "He observed them . . . *very carefully*," as if his attention bordered on the prurient.

While in Vienna Mann gave a reading of passages from *Royal Highness*; by February he had finished the novel. A month later he became a father for the third time. Angelus Gottfried ("Golo") Thomas Mann was born March 27, 1909. A new novel and a new son: the public couldn't expect more substantial achievements.

He composed a sketch for the Easter supplement of a Viennese newspaper. "Railway Accident" exhibits his capacity to turn almost any event into literature. More essay than story, it draws on the accident he had experienced some years earlier en route to Dresden. During the tumult, the narrator fears he has lost his manuscript, "my honeycomb, my spiderweb, my nest, my earth, my pride and pain, my all, the best of me." He doesn't have a copy, but he's not disturbed. If the piece is lost, "I should set to work again and perhaps this time it would come easier."

In May intestinal difficulties returned with such severity that he repaired to a Zurich sanitarium, and a regimen of raw fruits, nuts, and vegetables, along with considerable outdoor exercise. Initially Mann derided the cultish ambiance: he described himself as "a grass-eating Nebuchadnezzar going on all fours in the air-bath." But the treatment seemed to work. More useful yet may have been his discovery of a new universe where therapeutic procedure became a mix of vacation, hobby, and ideology, and where money and technology converted sickness into a highly stylized way of life.

Mann the good patient was a reflection of Mann the fan. In August he met Max Reinhardt, whose Munich theater he had previously attended: "My acquaintance with Reinhardt himself quite excited me, in the same childish way I am always excited whenever I come into contact with an inspired man." Withal his irreverence and skepticism, Mann's preferred mode was enthusiasm. Virtually at the same time that he celebrated the

Jew Reinhardt's thoroughly modern—and socially progressive—approach to theater, he attended a Bayreuth performance of *Parsifal* and recognized that "though I never really believed in Wagner, my passion for him has greatly diminished in the last years. . . . But . . . isn't the mood, the tendency and taste expressed in [*Parsifal*] regarded already today as merely of historical interest?" Perhaps the solution to feeling outdated was to throw oneself completely into the present. Hello Reinhardt, goodbye Wagner.

Between January and September 1909, *Royal Highness* was published in serial form in the leading literary journal *Die Neue Rundschau*. Negative responses came at once. The book was seen as a flawed entertainment. Mann aimed for a whimsical fairy tale of modern life, but he introduced as morbid and eccentric a crew as ever inhabited a comedy. The problem wasn't humor; Mann is often witty. But the melancholy of his concerns permeates the work. He later claimed that its tone reflected his feelings during his courtship of Katia; and it rehearses notions he had offered in various forums for the last few years. Granted that for a work of light fiction, its characters are notably heavy of heart and thick of brow, its singular charm may be a demonstration of light fiction's potential for the grand gesture. A narrative manner more suitable to feuilleton sketches or Billy Wilder films is employed as "a transparency for ideas to shine through."

Mann's characters inhabit a world so inbred that even an overly refined collie winds up "unbalanced" and "insane" (unlike the sweet-tempered family dog he would memorialize a decade later). By 1939, Mann recognized that his sympathy inclined to satire and caricature. "The book has a light-hearted attitude towards mental aberration: that, it seems to say, might happen to anyone! For a 'high-life novel with a happy ending,' it has a disconcerting way of referring to the border-line in whose seductive proximity all individualism dwells, being saved only by the steadfastness of the constant tin soldier from overstepping the boundary." This passage alludes to the "crisis of individualism" which Mann understood by 1939 as the *necessary* surrender of the individual perspective to the "communal, the social, the democratic, yes, the political at the will of the times." By then he was a confirmed if unlikely democrat; in 1908 he had a way to go. His novel thus depicts "a perfect orgy of individualism," both satirizing and glorifying its "aristocratic monstrosities" as the last of their breed.

In Prince Klaus Heinrich the Tin Soldier combines with the bridegroom on a wedding cake. He is physically impaired, with a shriveled left arm that a Gypsy had prophesied. Although Kaiser Wilhelm II had such an arm, Mann must have known that "left-handed" and "shriveled" were al-

most clichéd signs of homosexuality and impotence. (He later insisted that
the arm was a moral, not a psychological, motif, evoking Andersen's fairy
tale, not a Freudian case study.) The first important thing we learn about
our prince is that he moves through society with studied indifference. "He
looks straight ahead through the crowd with the air of a woman who knows
she is being looked at."

Klaus Heinrich feels overshadowed by his brother, Prince Albrecht, a
figure so depressed that he makes Klaus Heinrich seem like a cut-up. Albrecht lives in a Kafkaesque hovel: "an exceptionally unhomely and repellent room, small, with cracked ceiling-paintings, red silk and gold-bordered
carpet, and three windows reaching to the ground, through which the
wind blew keenly." He eschews all the comforts dear to his brother (or
Mann himself) because he despises his own position. He won't cater to the
masses—"I don't care for their 'Hi!' . . . my reason rises superior to all
considerations of popularity or unpopularity." There are princes—and best-
selling novelists—who may endear themselves to the public: "they see
themselves in you." But out of tact and humanity he prefers to stand aloof.
Albrecht is an obvious salute to Heinrich—he even shares his lisp. As in
life, his presence reminds his brother of the demeaning compromises he is
obliged to make. But while he is admirable and pathetic, he's also a dubious
model, isolated from life and friendless.

The courtiers of this diffident prince are all outsiders. Klaus Heinrich's
mentor is Dr. Sammet, a Jewish Nietzschean. When they first meet, the
prince insists on tolerance and equality: "equal chances for all." He's another
philo-Semite. Sammet goes a step further. Equality or not, some folks are
"exceptional . . . abnormal." But he's a benevolent elitist: "distinction
imposes an exceptional obligation toward society."

Balancing such moralistic discourse is Klaus Heinrich's airily ingenuous
chitchat, a speech pattern indebted to Hans Christian Andersen and, perhaps, Paul Ehrenberg. Echoing his prince, Mann graces the novel with
casual asides. A typical passage reads: "And now you know what the town
was like, what the country was like, and how matters stood."

Klaus Heinrich's youth is performed on a stage "remote from the public," populated by phantoms in flux. His parents leave a vague impression,
so with his brother and sister he exists "continually on the level of . . .
stories": even royalty needs a myth. While Klaus Heinrich is "tender-
hearted and prone to tears," Albrecht can't weep: without emotional affect,
he is unimpressed by his surroundings, the fabulous objects or the "gorgeous" courtiers. But Klaus Heinrich—like his creator—takes delight in
these splendid men.

The palace becomes a cross between a mental asylum and "the halls of the snow-king." When the queen laughs at her husband's jokes, she glances at the mirror to catch her performance. Klaus Heinrich learns early that "our nature is not to have simple feelings"; his role is to represent emotion, "make our tenderness visible"—to display and not feel it. When he grows older and begins attending balls, he concludes that his role is "to show himself and be stared at." Since he's constantly ducking his arm out of sight, his public appearance resembles a vaudeville routine, as he simultaneously tries to show his person and hide his hand.

Of course he suffers in school. Like Tonio Kröger, he's bothered by his name. In his case, it's too plebeian: unlike "Bogumil" or "Dagobert," "Klaus Heinrich" could belong to "the shoemaker's sons who blow snot into their hands." Neither his body nor his name suit him for the task of representation.

At school he meets the novel's most complex figure. Dr. Raoul Überbein sports a red beard, ugly protruding ears, a greenish-white complexion, and watery blue eyes; his hands are delicate and small. He performs the familiar role of both Jews and homosexuals, adviser to the court. More than Sammet, he gives the prince an identity: "I am a categorical unit—but you are a conception, a kind of ideal, a frame." (Mann wooed his Princess Katia by calling her a "cultural ideal.") He warns the boy that "formality and intimacy are mutually exclusive"; and proceeds to celebrate "the marked men, those one can see are not as other men, all those whom the people stare at open-mouthed." Überbein wills himself to be the guardian of "reserve, etiquette, obligations, duty, demeanor, formality." Yet he understands, as well as Thomas Mann, that he's basically a "born gypsy," not a likely candidate for the "squire of princes."

Anyway, the all-too-human Klaus Heinrich proves a poor student. He acquires a capacity for simple pleasures: he attends a ball and gets drunk, for the first time "whirled around by a feeling of contentment." He also sees that there is "misery in the world," though he confides to Albrecht that he doesn't understand "hunger and want, the war and the hospital horrors."

He attends a fair held at a model village, where he becomes unduly impressed by the ducks and pigeons, beets and cloves, "an entire overpowering world of ingenious utility." Anyone flabbergasted by plants has led a very sheltered life.

A second alternative to court life is provided by the writer Axel Martini, who extends Überbein's analysis of representation into the literary realm. He declares a writer's requisite to be his sense of "unsuitability." Like

Mann, he didn't get on at school. His father disowned him, his mother helped him, believing he couldn't survive "hunger and harsh winds."

Martini's confession allows Mann to make fun of Tonio Kröger. Writers like Martini dare not experience desire. They get "peeks," and these ephemeral glances whet their "hunger for the actual," for hunger itself. Or for sorrow—any simple emotion will do. They expend their energies on the dubious task of representation. "Renunciation is our compact with the muse," he argues, Mann's pithiest statement of his eternal dilemma. "Life is our forbidden garden, our great temptation, to which we yield sometimes, but never to our profit."

Once we authors choose to live, we make "greedy excursions into the festival halls of life," but we leave in a hurry, as morally compromised as Tommy Mann fleeing the Tivoli Theater. Martini is Tonio Kröger's artist-as-eunuch: he admits that he has experienced very little sensual pleasure. But lack of experience doesn't inhibit him; hunger—or at least the idea of hunger—keeps him prolific.

In a burlesque of the prevailing tendency in sanitariums, Martini insists that "hygiene is our whole ethic. Nothing is more unhygienic than life." His routine recalls an unending round of physical therapy, wholesome to the point of vice. (In a sketch "On Alcohol," Mann had recently asserted that he didn't need alcohol for inspiration: he didn't believe much in the good moods liquor induces but then he didn't believe much in good moods.) Martini shuns the bottle and retires early. His skittishness reads like a caricature of Mann's excessively regular habits. Like his creator, he admits to sieges of "idleness, boredom, peevish laziness." In Mann's Bonn speech he described the long dreary pursuit of eloquence. But when Martini confides that "a sentence may be a whole day's work," and that writers sleep a lot, when they're not "idling about with heads that feel like lead," the complaint comes across as "a little repulsive."

Mann provides a counterirritant to Martini in the person of a popular soubrette, Mizzi Meyer. Like his subjects, Klaus Heinrich is a fan of "our Mizzi." She is described as barely attractive, but gifted with an "uproarious manner." Albrecht believes that the people see themselves in Klaus Heinrich, but it's really Mitzi who is "flesh of [their] flesh." They aren't jealous of this homely woman's triumph: "She was the glorification of the people itself . . . indeed the people applauded itself when it applauded her."

While in his essay on the theater Mann questioned any art that panders to popular taste, Mizzi serves as a charming alternative to the bourgeois artists with their hermetic principles. Like them, her task is representation, but she performs it with good spirits: she doesn't mope around all day polishing a sentence; public appearances don't humiliate her. Heinrich

Mann also has his soubrette, the Rosa who destroys Professor Unrat. But "our Mizzi" harms nobody.

In one of Mann's favorite stories, Theodor Storm's *Immensee*, there is a discussion about the power of folk tunes. They speak to the heart because they seem to have been composed by everyone: "They are not made, they grow . . . it is as if we all had helped to write them." This is very far from Noël Coward's quips about bad music. It addresses a natural, communal power that is the envy of any self-conscious artist.

P hilosophy, education, literature fail to socialize the prince. It's time for the heroine's appearance. She is Imma Spoelmann, a fabulously wealthy American heiress of mixed lineage, part German, part Creole. (True to form, Mann makes her a cultural freak: "she's a creature of many colors" to the Germans, while some Americans regard her as black.) She evokes Katia's premarital independence, a product of great intelligence and wealth. Incapable of casual flirtation, boyishly athletic, she is as serenely assured as the prince is feckless.

Her father is an interesting figure, in view of Mann's exile in America. Spoelmann is an immigrant profiteer. He's made a killing in the States, built a palace on Fifth Avenue, and acquired both renown and the hatred of his "out-distanced competitors." He was once Dr. Sammet's great man-as-entrepreneur, but now he condemns capitalism and returns to his homeland to shower his American treasure on the natives.

The Spoelmanns are attended by a high-strung dog, Percival, and the demented Countess Löwenjoul. The latter draws attention to herself by walking through the streets, muttering softly with semaphoric accompaniment. It turns out that she is a textbook case of homosexual paranoia. Convinced that lewd women conspire against her, she hires a man to box the ears of an old lady who has supposedly propositioned her. In America, she attempted a legal action against the female camp followers of an army barracks. Spoelmann rescued her from making a further ass of herself. Now she acts as Imma's companion, and reckons her life as "blessing," except for "the women sitting at nights on my chest and forcing me to look at their disgusting faces." Mann enjoys her aberration because he understands its source, a morbid fear of sexuality. Dr. Überbein and Countess Löwenjoul may be the most perverse chaperons in literature!

One day Klaus Heinrich sees Imma make a shortcut to her algebra class right past his castle. When a soldier tries to block her path, she cries, "I'm in a hurry!" The prince is enraptured by her gumption, "the honest, passionate, irresistible anger" suffusing her words. More courageous than any man, she still impresses him as "slight and lonely." He's smitten, but she is less than enthralled. When they meet, she returns his glance, "without any respect . . . absolutely unembarrassed and free," this American version of a Berlin feminist.

She accompanies him on Dr. Sammet's guided tour of a children's hospital. Here Klaus Heinrich has his first lesson in worldly horrors. One boy was found in a river; another was shot by his impoverished father. Not since the unemployed alcoholic Piepsam railed at the world in "The Way to the Churchyard" has Mann so forcefully evoked the economic determinants of social tragedy. Sammet guides them into a laboratory to view the dissection of a strangled child's larynx; they are also shown the pernicious enlargement of a child's kidney. Under a microscope they see bacilli, a visual spectacle as mind-boggling to the prince as it will be to Hans Castorp. Next they visit a nursery, where they find hilarious the sight of "bald-headed little creatures" with "their naked gums." Biology is one construct Klaus Heinrich has not anticipated—although this excursion seems a grim introduction to physical life.

Imma treats the prince with a sly amusement. When he suggests that mathematics must be "terribly brain-racking," she demurs, "It's just splendid; it's like playing in the breezes, so to speak, or rather out of the breezes in a dust-free atmosphere. It's as cool there as in the Adirondacks." When he looks confused, she informs him, rather condescendingly, "The Adirondacks. That's geography, Prince." Their flirtation borders on hostility. In one of the novel's best passages, he flips through Imma's notebook, recognizes her "childish round hand," and finds his head swimming in the atmosphere of "cabalistic signs and ciphers," interspersed with sentences in ordinary German, "whose sense was equally beyond the normal intelligence, and conveyed no more to the reader than an incantation." Seldom has a writer described so sensuously material about which he understands nothing. The image is a striking tribute to an emancipated woman's intelligence; where else would a sign of emotional distance be literally algebraic?

The flirtation proceeds obliquely; they seem more siblings than lovers. Embrace occurs after she notices his crippled hand. "Were you born with that?" she wonders, and, touched by her sympathy, he descends to his knees, "Little sister—." She proceeds to stroke the deformity he has spent a lifetime hiding—and kisses it. The scene resonates with Mann's faith he would outgrow the vestiges of shame once Katia saw him whole.

Imma is Dr. Sammet's ideal realized, a princess whose sense of noblesse oblige compels her to sponsor public kitchens and orphanages. On a level easily as high as the prince's, she does not take his proposals seriously. "You went to school for show . . . you came into the world for show": how can

I take you at your word? He admits there's been "a lot of fiction to my life." Then comes the accusation Mann had heard too often. "You prevent me from letting myself go . . . it makes me shiver. You hold yourself erect, and ask questions, but you don't do so out of sympathy, you don't care what the questions are about—no, you don't care about anything, and you take nothing to heart . . . in reality you have no opinion and no belief, and the only thing you care about is your princely self-possession." Was Mann making fun of his acknowledged deficiencies? Like the prince, he couldn't prop himself up with an ideology, but resistance was less a question of principle—he had termed it "formalism"—than one of excessive self-regard.

Most men would fear Imma's pitiless gaze, but it's just what the prince needs. Her tirade works its spell; overnight he learns his figures. He settles comfortably into "the simple and rude texture of interests, the system of down-right logical needs." Meanwhile academics and journalists invoke the Gypsy's prophecy that a shriveled arm will bring glory to the nation. They construct a modern myth out of necromancy and robber-baron capitalism.

There is a happy ending, a marriage, but clustered around that event are two disquieting episodes. Albrecht advises his brother, "You're a Sunday child," easy to love. For him, though, love of any sort is a deception. Be happy, my brother, but "not too much." Anyhow, with this "very strange, very original" woman, there's no chance of an "easy time."

This homage to a singular woman is followed by news of Dr. Überbein. After his colleagues force him out of the Teachers' Union, the loss of his students—his version of the author's public—drives him to suicide. His only mourners are Dr. Sammet and Klaus Heinrich. Überbein and Albrecht recede in the background, these isolate celibates, but they will haunt the prince. (As if he can't imagine a gregarious figure, he makes Imma's father a reluctant entrepreneur who prefers to collect glass and play organ arrangements of Wagner.)

The night of their wedding, the young couple admit their immaturity. She says, "We are so stupid and so lonely, Prince—on the peaks of humanity, as Doctor Überbein used to say—and we know absolutely nothing of life." He's less gloomy—haven't they come through, didn't she inspire him to "study so practically the public welfare?" Now he will apply the lessons in love and management: "That shall be our business in future: Highness and Love—an austere happiness."

Having invaded the public realm, Thomas was very pleased with himself. His 1910 remark "I believe I have only to talk of myself to release the spirit of the time, the tongue of my community," bespeaks a prince come into his kingdom.

In 1939, a time when none of his "very German productions" were
available in their homeland, Mann greeted an American reprinting of this
particularly Old World document. He regrets that it has been comparatively ignored, unlike the novellas he tossed off so quickly. He believes it
was misread, that it is as "blithe" as youth, written in a spirit of affectionate
parody. He might have done better turning out more sagas like *Buddenbrooks*, "but that was just what I could not do; it did not satisfy my own
demands on myself."

Readers don't understand that a work is not absolute in an author's
career. Instead it's a way station, "a means to an end." This novel made
Magic Mountain and *Joseph and His Brothers* possible (always Mann sneaks in
a commercial for his more salable products). He explains his strategy: "I
think all criticism should have this biographical flavour, as a necessary
human element." He sees the novel's resemblance to *Tonio Kröger* with "that
favorite theme of my youth, the theme of the artist as isolated and 'different,' " and finds a solution in the "harmonizing of happiness and discipline." The novel's method is allusive: the royal world parallels, "in a word,
the existence of the artist."*

Although he used his knowledge of the Wilhelmine court in Berlin,
he didn't dare name the city in fear that any specific reference would
break the spell. Yes, he had forecast tremendous social changes, but
unknowingly.

> Is literature a swan-song? No, rather it is a prophecy, though not in
> direct and explicit form. The artist's nature prevents him from being
> in the very least the servant and harbinger of new things, even when
> his words betray his unconscious intuition of the future. What happens
> is rather that the old and the new . . . play upon him and with him,
> and this play is his work, a dialectical product, almost always, of old
> and new, wherein his sympathy, yes, his love, is conservative and faces
> the old, and only the artist's sensitive responsiveness hints at the new.

By 1939, Mann's formulation for the reconciliation of high art and politics
was no longer "austere happiness" but the "harmonizing of the individual
and the social in the human." Rereading "this odd little book" showed
him that at thirty, he had dramatized social transitions he would need three

---

* In 1910, Mann tried to underline the connections between the universally acclaimed *Tonio*
and his new novel. He recalled that after *Tonio*'s appearance, a reader sent him a painting of a
lonely Spanish king [Philip II] in tears, anticipating this novel before it was conceived.

decades to appreciate. Typically he congratulated himself for standing between eras and getting things half-right.

The serenity of this introduction confirms Mann's prophecy to Heinrich: If his body held out, and his spirit remained firm, even an apparent failure would assume its organic place in his development. As he said in "Railway Accident," each time out provided a new occasion to perfect the work. And each rereading would surprise him with the prophetic thrust of his "sensitive responsiveness"; his books invariably seemed to know more than he did.

Royal Highness didn't resolve his confusions. He had enough second thoughts to propose a new aesthetic. But when Mann attempted theoretical speculation, it was always self-referential, an explicit defense of his own method. By now he understood his work as an act of resistance against both present forces (reactionary politics, rival authors, the redoubtable Heinrich) and past ones (the tradition he had affectionately challenged since high school).

He began making notes for the critical essay "Mind and Art" (never completed and only lately foraged by scholars) while vacationing in Livorno with Heinrich. In a series of terse, abbreviated jottings, Mann considers literary history. German romanticism is heavily ironic and analytical: its "naïveté is a calculated one." Belabored, it lacks " 'plastic' effects"; stylized, it avoids psychological truth. German literature honors arbitrary distinctions between critical (*Schriftsteller*) and creative (*Dichter*) writers—comparisons rendered particularly invidious by the so-called *Dichter*'s failure to serve his times. Long before it became an intellectual commonplace, Mann decided that aesthetic procedure was implicitly political. By pretending that his work wasn't grounded in mundane reality and determined by larger interests than mere literature, the so-called "pure artist" revealed himself as a charlatan and demagogue, a purveyor of *Volkstümlichkeit* (popular clichés).

If Mann still didn't understand freedom, he no longer drew an absolute distinction between the things of life and the sentences he made of them. Political freedom might not exist for him, but he knew that aesthetic purity was factitious, a folly with political consequences.

Another kind of sobriety was demanded by right-wing nationalists. Friedrich Lienhard, founder of *The Twentieth Century*, was agitating for a new category: *Heimatkunst*, the expression of healthy, patriotic men rooted in German culture, and not of effete, hyperconscious and overly critical (i.e., Jewish) aesthetes—something like the hygienic art endorsed by Wagner's son-in-law. This proto-fascist demand reminded Mann that only the Jews of Berlin took literature seriously. The nationalists might see him as decadent, a traitor to his class. But the Jews shared his ambivalence and praised his work. He concluded that among the philistines and Junkers, they alone knew how to read.

He suspected younger people. In a 1910 extension of these notes, he declared, "We who were born around 1870 are too close to Nietzsche, from whom we acquired our psychological sensitivity, our lyrical criticism, the experience of Wagner, the experience of Christianity, the experience of 'modernity'—experiences from which we shall never completely break free." But while they still suffered the aftershocks, the next generation took Nietzsche's revolution for granted, selectively retaining only his "affirmation of the earth, the affirmation of the body, the anti-Christian and anti-intellectual conception of nobility, which comprises health and serenity and beauty." In other words, they made him a yea-sayer. Their readings were hardly less tendentious than those of Friedrich Lienhard.*

Both left and right seemed to agree that art delivers the artist from self-conscious critique. Mann was not convinced. In a note for *Fiorenza*, he identifies the born Protestant as a figure temperamentally in opposition. Viewed in the context of German history, Mann imagined an enduring conflict between the protesting individual and his conforming neighbors. A Lübeck Protestant in Catholic Munich, a disciple of Nietzsche in the age of Whitman, he found himself alienated in space and time.

But therein lay his opportunity. As the essay proceeds, he insists on the "necessity of 'literature,' especially in this country: development of an understanding of human nature, moral education, refinement, improvement, weakening of stupid convictions and value-judgments, a growth of skepticism and humor. As far as morality is concerned, *at the same time* development of a subtler sensitivity and an education in doubt, justice, tolerance, *psychologization*"—the latter most sorely needed, because "there is no psychology in Germany, no deeper knowledge, no sensitivity, no bite to analysis, there is no critical passion." In other words, nobody writes like him. His prescriptions constitute a hidden manifesto.

Dichter and *Schriftsteller* meet in the composition of an intellectual fiction—what I would call the essayistic novel—in which ideas spring to dramatic life. Since Mann's ideas are so often elaborations of his psychological conflicts, separation of "critical passion" and self-examination in his

---

* Mann shared some of their concerns. From his intensely erotic descriptions of Hanno swimming with Count Kai to the painting of naked adolescents that graced his study, he was preoccupied with male nudity. (It was a common interest; in 1903, the world's first nudist park was opened in Travemünde. By 1910, sunbathing in sexually segregated groups was a national fad.)

work becomes an exercise in circular logic. But this doesn't damage his enterprise. His failure to break through becomes representative of the inhibited bourgeoisie: Mann's most devoted critic, the Marxist György Lukács, loves him precisely because he doesn't make the next step into a truly social fiction. Mann's Big Idea may be the irrelevance of Big Ideas to *l'homme moyen sensuel*, as one of his great themes is the political fate of a nonpolitical man.

Mann summons his beloved enemy Richard Wagner. With pompous claims for his unprecedented artworks, Wagner introduced "an important craving for the great, the poetic, the *more-than-literary*, the sublime, which is not to be found in any other country." (He immediately appends the Italian d'Annunzio's name.) From him stems the foolhardy attempt to rewrite "literary history." Self-consciously obsessed with the new, novelists today call themselves " 'narrative writers' . . . it sounds less literary"—as today writers produce "texts" (according to critics who have assumed Wagner's promethean attitude).

Mann notes the deficiencies of Wagner's music and dramaturgy. Compared to Mozart or Beethoven, he's a vulgarian. Yet how representative a figure in his blend of Teutonic culture and Christianity with a Jewish admixture (Wagner was rumored to have a Jewish father: in the philo-Semitic glow of 1940, Mann would credit Wagner's "sensuousness and intellectualism" to his Jewish legacy). The composer is particularly German "in his unfailingly brilliant grasp of the role of authority." It's true that the post-1870 generation, trained by Nietzsche, finds him "dubious, suspect." But, in a rhetorical somersault, Mann admits his love for Wagner precisely *because* his successors mount such outlandish claims for his innovations: "these gentlemen have strangely engineer-like notions of progress."

Then again, Wagner revealed his ignorance when he proclaimed "his *Ring* the greatest thing that had ever been written." Mann ridicules the composer's boast with a devastating list of great works, from the *Odyssey* to *Faust*: "all purely literary, of course, pretty dry old stuff." The best alternative to Wagner is provided by Schiller, whose "Discourse on Naive and Reflective Poetry" is "an artistic achievement compared with which Wagner's writings are nothing but vainglorious self-advertisement." Schiller becomes Mann's literary ideal as Wagner's success is credited to the Germans' "lack of literature."

There's a more contemporary alternative. Max Reinhardt is as modest as Wagner was vain. He's the Schiller of impresarios; his "modern approach, minuteness, accumulation of details, lack of genius, intellectuality, allied with tenacity, work, endurance of will" have produced an exemplary art, one that stirs the people without degrading them. His success proves you can have "the dummies" and not give up your principles. After the demagogic Wagner, it was a case of innocence by association. Mann also relished the irony that a Jew had superseded an anti-Semite. (A more horrible irony would have Wagner's admirers exiling both Mann and Reinhardt.)

The attempt in "Mind and Art" is finally more confessional than theoretical. Mann concludes that matters are improving for his kind. The poet Stefan George has been condemned as "more than literary, discursive, critical, not poetic," but George's critics will simply have to catch up. In a parenthetical outburst he delights in confusion: "I adore this age of ours. Nothing could be more interesting!" Elsewhere he quips that Germans take matters too seriously. You see, Thomas Mann addresses himself, we must begin to play.

Royal Highness was finished; he had a work to vindicate his theories, a theory to justify his work. The left and right would have to make room for his austere entertainments. The time would then be his: "I adore this age of ours."

3

THE EDUCATION OF A
CONFIDENCE MAN

As the children tell it, the first decade of marriage was good for Katia. They invoke an "unalloyed happiness" with her husband and an easy proximity to her still youthful parents. Gabriel von Seidl had designed a summer house at Bad Tölz with picturesque views of Munich, the Isar River, and the mountains. Here Katia and the children spent their happiest days. The architect had achieved a Jugendstil balance of geometric lines and ornamentation; the grillwork over the transom arched above a stylized monogram and the date 1909. Attached to a residence with ten rooms, servants' quarters, a balcony, and a veranda was a private park containing its own tennis court.

Yet in those years Katia suffered two miscarriages, learned that her favorite brother, Erik, had been killed, and saw her husband dramatize their experiences in three works of fiction, none of them completely flattering. (In the 1960s she told her children that Imma was "a very distorted portrait," "overdone.") She also accompanied him to Venice, where he became, in her words, "infatuated" with a young boy. Not everyone would call such events "unalloyed happiness."

During the summer of 1909, while struggling through his critical treatise, Mann began preparations for *Felix Krull*. In a September interview, he referred to "a smaller short story, 'The Confidence Man,' which will be a kind of psychological supplement to my novel about court life." It was a quietly subversive act to propose similarities between a ruler and a char-

Katia in 1908 with Erika and Klaus

latan. Both Klaus Heinrich and Krull were preoccupied with self-creation: youthful chameleons maneuvering their way into the spotlight.

In October *Royal Highness* was published simultaneously with Heinrich's *The Little Town*. Thomas congratulated Heinrich on his most successful work, perhaps because its Verdian elements were so unlike his own comic opera of a novel.

The milieu agreed with Heinrich. His 1908 novella *Die Branzilla* is the story of a diva. In the course of her life she murders a rival, declines lovers, and, with an idiot savant's concentration, masters her art. Age does not disturb her: "Who says that we are old! You, sure, you are old! . . . I am still Branzilla." Forty years later Heinrich Mann was an exile living in Hollywood when Billy Wilder, another émigré, helped conceive *Sunset Boulevard*, whose heroine, Norma Desmond, is a latter-day Branzilla ("I am big; it's the pictures that got small").

A year later, *The Little Town* examines the fusion of life and opera. It is Heinrich's most technically complex novel. Polyrhythms and counterpoint prevail: he realizes a simultaneity unusual in literature, limited in cinema to crosscutting but uniquely possible on the stage. A large cast pops in and out, regrouping in operatic formations. Even their monologues resemble arias, conveying a heightened passion at the price of realism.

Mann's narrative method reflects his characters' vocation. A touring opera company arrives in a small Italian town; it includes a melange of giddy chorines, romantic tenors, wizened managers, and cynical sopranos. In short order they provoke a minor civil war between the devotees of art and progress and the supporters of a reactionary priest. The troupe's sponsor is the town lawyer, a liberal committed to the service of "humanity" and, like Heinrich Mann, terrified of anarchy or class warfare. But his legalistic rhetoric verges on song. *The Little Town* may be read as a contra-Wagner (and contra-Thomas) novel, with the public-spirited melodies of Giuseppe Verdi complementing the text.

Once again this is a performers' world. Even the lawyer is dismissed by his enemies as a disguised actor. Nello, the lyric tenor, is an appealing juvenile lead. He is not very bright or talented, simply a poor boy from Verona whose spectacular high Ds provide a passport out of the ghetto. The novel contains three impassioned women, two of them in love with Nello. But he leaves the soprano and the mezzo to fight it out. His true lover is too "great" for him; she would sing out a real-life tragedy, but he is only "fit for stage blood." She lures him anyway to what resembles a Verdian *Todeslied*.

The novel's most interesting duet is performed by Don Tadeo, the village priest, and Flora Garlinda, the prima donna. Their conflict is not sexual. He pines for a soubrette while she flirts with the conductor. But as high priestess of art she becomes his Whore of Babylon. While her lover yearns to compose for the masses, her attitude toward the public is ambivalent: she love-hates them because they are "wicked and dangerous." Conductor and soprano recapitulate the lifelong dilemma of the Mann brothers: they crave a public whom they fundamentally distrust. As in Thomas's *Fiorenza*, dialogue between a religious fanatic and a passionate beauty quickens the text.

Tadeo disappears after a fire. The local demagogue—a journalist—turns the town against the lawyer and the singers. A vigilante mood arises. But the priest returns and summons the faithful to church, where he preaches a sermon of such vehement self-abasement that women scream and roll in the aisles. He admits that he has loved God in the spirit but not man in the flesh. He rips off his cassock to reveal—not a scarlet letter but similar evidence that sin has consumed him: holes burnt in his cassock. This display is meant to inspire a new social vision in the parishioners.

It doesn't work. An old writer observes that nothing really changes: "Again and again, humanity will have to overthrow its masters, and spirit be matched against might." The novel concludes with a rapid sequence of virtuoso arias. The conductor pounds the piano like some delirious genius in a 1940s movie; Tadeo dedicates himself to society at large, having cut himself off from more intimate satisfactions; Nello and his lover lie dead in the town square while a senile old man bows to his invisible public.

Though both Mann brothers would say that *The Little Town* is Heinrich's best work, it remains a very dated tour de force. This peculiar marriage of *Weltschmerz* and *verismo* feels more ponderously German than *Royal Highness*. Thomas's lightest work holds up better than Heinrich's "masterpiece."

The sibling conflicts of 1903–04 had a literary correlative; personal animus kept developing into a debate about creative principles. A few years later the confrontations descended to a soap-operatic mode, unashamed, and in the case of Lula downright hysterical. The Löhrs disapproved of Heinrich's mistress, Ines Schmied. There were a series of perceived insults—gifts exchanged and insufficiently appreciated, invitations not acknowledged, criticisms made behind people's backs.

Thomas and Katia encountered Heinrich and Ines in Munich as well as on vacation in Bad Tölz and Venice. She chastised Heinrich's in-laws, but Thomas declared that he and Katia had not taken offense. On April 1, 1909, he wrote Heinrich that despite Lula's wayward behavior, she was "five times more controlled than Ines. . . ." The latter had criticized Thomas to Frau Mann. "Poor silly Mama," as Thomas now called her, had grown "weaker and more anxious with each year." Why upset a pathetic old lady?

As for Lula, Mann declared elsewhere it was unthinkable that any Mann could simply be a bourgeois. True, she was noticeably eccentric—her favorite topics of conversation were cancer, war, and poverty. But she had assisted in the preparation of *Buddenbrooks*, and was sufficiently literary to anticipate that *Fiorenza* would be the means of reconciling her brothers. Moreover, her impossible husband would drive anyone batty. Heinrich, he commands, ease up, remember our good times at Beckergrube 52. On August 7, 1910, he accused his brother of being "too literary," the very crime Schaukal had attributed to him.

What about Ines's side? On January 6, 1909, she had written Heinrich: "I can still see your brother's face, how cold, indifferent, and yet somehow discontented his *gaze* is" (italics mine). The vacation home at Bad Tölz struck her as "utterly unpoetic," an assortment of desiccated snippets, a glimpse of mountain, meadow, and woods. Nothing grand or visionary, everything "sober, bourgeois, cold." They hated her, all right, "but that I can't stand them is no wonder either."

Royal Highness was condemned by right-wing patriots as irreverent toward the ruling Hohenzollerns. When his Lübeck friend the novelist Ida Boy-Ed rallied to his defense, Mann was most grateful. "It's incredible how concerned I am about Lübeck. Would you like a bold comparison? Napoleon once said that before every act, every battle, his first thought was: What will the Faubourg Saint-Germain say about it? Lübeck is my Faubourg Saint-Germain. I always think: What will Lübeck say about it?" In her review, the older writer had congratulated Mann for discovering a new literary subject: "the improbability of a prince's existence in the framework of modern life . . . {royalty's} deepest alienation from the simplest realities." She intuited that Mann spoke from experience when he evoked "the latent tragedy of such loneliness." She gave him a reading that reflected his own standards: "for the second time [he has] created a form of his own for a subject uniquely his own."

Mann's reply was both humble and self-serving: her favorable review was "among the very best, most brilliant, warmest and finest things you have written. . . . How sensitive is your remark that the vitality of a work of art consists less in superficial liveliness than in that organic coherence which is a function of memory, of circumspection, and of consciousness." Meanwhile a younger contemporary, Hermann Hesse (whom he had met

six years earlier), gave the novel a negative review. Hesse saw a falling off
from *Buddenbrooks*; he found the work coy and mannered. Boy-Ed's reading
was the more compassionate. Where Hesse saw an overly intellectual bel-
lettrist, she discovered a master of wit and pathos.

Hesse followed his harsh review with a more cordial personal note, and
Mann replied, "I sometimes think that what you call my 'playing up to
the public' springs from my long, passionately critical enthusiasm for the
art of Richard Wagner—that art, as exclusive as it is demagogic, which
may have permanently influenced, not to say corrupted, my ideals and
artistic strivings." He cited Nietzsche's observation that Wagner's "shifting
perspective" allowed him to appeal alternately to the crudest and the most
refined tastes. Mann wondered whether he had the "willpower" to resist
the temptation of a devoted public. Ultimately Hesse faced the same
problem.

There was other negative criticism. Hermann Bahr, an early idol, wrote
that Mann's characters were class representatives, lacking in individuality;
he even implied that the barely liberal Mann was a Marxist. Mann had
backed into political commentary without realizing it, simply by means of
psychological analysis and parody. In January 1910, Mann wrote Kurt Martens that his "passionate democrat" of a brother was delighted with Bahr's
criticism. Young German writers tended to be progressive; most had signed
an appeal for electoral reform in Prussia. And so Mann, his politics still
tentative, was willing to be labeled a radical: the "intellectual or ethical
merit" of his work was a dividend.

Yet "an artist can give certain trends of their times their due . . . and
then show himself entirely independent of them afterwards." He wasn't
quite ready to join Heinrich behind the barricades. Condemned as a Marxist, Mann was described by another right-wing, *völkische* writer as "a champion of Jewish racial policy." Otto Schmidt-Gibichenfels emphasized the
sympathetic treatment of the Jewish physician; he also identified the Spoelmanns as Jewish (perhaps because of Katia Pringsheim's origins). Mann was
preaching racial miscegenation, but the pure-blooded German peasants and
nobility would, "sword in hand," defeat his schemes.

Writing irreverently of royalty—how could Mann not have expected a
political response? He continued to juggle various literary subjects, all of
them implicitly radical, whether he realized it or not. On January 10, a
day before his letter to Martens, he wrote Heinrich that *The Confidence Man*
"will probably be my strangest work. Sometimes I am surprised at what I
pull out of myself."

Later that month he began corresponding with Ernst Bertram, a *privat-
dozent* (nonsalaried lecturer) at Bonn, who would become an important

friend. Bertram, an intellectual aesthete and a homosexual, was for years both Mann's mentor and his disciple. Since Bertram had lectured affirmatively about *Royal Highness*, Mann confided that he had a "shameless plan for a novel about Frederick the Great." If not shameless, it still promised an audacious pendant to his recent work. Mann knew that Frederick was another homosexual as well as an untouchable hero of German tradition. Any Frederick of his devising would infuriate right-wing nationalists.

Mann had a considerable talent for overreading. Schaukal's critique of *Fiorenza* might have been sincere, but there was no explanation outside of sheer hatred for Alfred Kerr's relentless attacks. On January 16, 1910, Thomas wrote Heinrich, quoting an essay in which Kerr had alluded to a kind of mediocre novelist, "an eccentrically neurasthenic clerk or old sanitarium patient" who writes in order to advance his social position and disguise his "Achilles tendon." The references to Mann's army days—and to his penchant for rest cures—could not be coincidental. This was verbal torture, inflicted by a "refined" sadist, who figured that nobody would crack his code but its subject. Mann admitted that it had left him "ill for days. I have no psychological use for enemies. . . . I'm not prepared for it." Alas, Kerr was not finished with him, and his later outbursts would be brusquely—*ad hominem*.

Mann next suffered at the hands of Theodor Lessing, a well-known Munich writer alternately viewed as a "polymath" or a "dilettante." (They had met previously, and Lessing, like Kerr, had frequented the Pringsheim salon.) In January 1910 Lessing, himself a Jew, mounted a vicious attack on Samuel Lublinski, complete with mean-spirited references to his physical deformities and Yiddish accent. Out of loyalty to the critic who had initially championed *Buddenbrooks*, Thomas Mann composed "Der Doktor Lessing," in which he, in Richard Winston's words, "revealed a capacity for polemics that foreshadowed the literary activisms of the war years and the Nazi era." It also invoked his own alienation from swinging Munich. Among other digs, it reported that Lessing and "a few other Schwabing ecstatics danced stark naked around a fire."

Arguing that his humorous intentions had been misunderstood by a tin-eared prig, Lessing wrote a series of anti-Mann essays he published as a pamphlet, "Samuel Draws Up the Balance and Milks the Morality Cow." Mann was enraged and composed further provocations; Lessing kept replying, and, in one febrile moment, reportedly challenged him to a duel, an invitation Mann declined.

It was all a bad reminder of past arguments. In 1903, Heinrich's use of "psychology" to explain the Manns' history had struck Thomas as vulgar sensationalism. Deployed by Kerr or Lessing, it seemed as threatening as a physical assault. (On January 30, 1913, three years after the initial blast, Mann wrote Bertram that he was still contemplating "A Study in Abjection," his final rejoinder to Kerr and Lessing.)

Perhaps this preoccupation with unkind critics was a means of forgetting artistic problems: *Felix Krull* was temporarily stalled. But surely more was at stake. Mann was always most selective about self-revelation: he had to determine the extent and the nature. From now on, he would exert such control over literary interpretation that even as frank a rendition as *Death in Venice* would appear ambiguous—indeed, its very triumph and redemption supposedly was its ambiguity. Balancing autobiography and symbol, the insidiously fleet Mann would outpace his lumbering critics.

In this acrimonious period, he produced his first significant study of another writer, "The Old Fontane." As would become a lifelong pattern, he went abroad to find himself. For just as Schiller resembled the insecure newlywed, Fontane prefigured the tentative liberal's political development. An outsider by virtue of his French Huguenot ancestry, Theodor Fontane (1819–98) was the foremost German exponent of realism in the novel. He arrived at his metier very late, having been a drama critic and a foreign correspondent (as well as a prisoner) during the Franco-Prussian War, before turning to the novel when he was approaching sixty. Like Mann, he was comparatively uneducated and a slow worker.

From this late-blooming career, Mann concludes that some men need to find themselves in old age: "There are . . . temperaments whose only appropriate age is old; who are, so to speak, classic old men, ordained to show humanity the ideal qualities of that last stage of life: benignity, kindness, justice, humor, and shrewd wisdom—in short a recrudescence on a higher plane of childhood's artless unrestraint." Mann's analysis is blatantly autobiographical. He presents Fontane as "tortured by nerves . . . not suited to youth," melancholy, constipated, insomniac. Age made him solid, productive, contentious: he developed into a "cranky" old man. His self-doubt was enabling: he is "one of those who attain perfection because they always feel they are unsuccessful." (Unlike his heroic peers Wagner, Bismarck, and Tolstoy, he lacks megalomania—he's one of the permanently dissatisfied.)

Already in his letters to Heinrich, Mann had seen himself overcoming a barren youth in a prolific old age. Fontane's example offers a frigid consolation: social life may not get easier, but you will acquire fame and the company of powerful men. Much as Heine admired the Rothschilds, Fontane confessed that he enjoyed being with "people who employ five thousand miners, build factory cities, and dispatch expeditions to colonize Africa."

As his style evolves into a "deft play of wit and atmosphere," Fontane acquires a perspective which allows him to see "at least two sides of everything." He disdains chauvinism, preferring the indolent pleasures of Munich or Bayreuth to the oppressive energy of Prussian cities. But he has a special affinity for the "Berlin public," particularly those urban Jews who are his best readers. Mann links the relaxation of tone to Fontane's evolving liberalism. When he is "seventy, and growing younger all the time," he begins to identify with the left.

In 1868 Fontane wrote his wife deploring attempts at compulsory education; the masses required a strong church and monarchy. But by 1896, when he was seventy-seven, he had concluded that "the fourth estate heralded a new and better world," and that "what the workers think, write, speak, has far outstripped the thinking, writing, and speaking of the traditionally ruling classes. Everything is more genuine, truer, more living." Mann loves this "amazing growth into youth and the future." Just as his own political evolution was a thing of stops and starts, the old Fontane was "the kind of man in whom both opinions, the conservative and the revolutionary, could exist side by side. His political awareness was complicated by the temperament of an artist; it was, in a very elevated sense, not reliable." So it was that he celebrated his seventy-fifth birthday not with working-class radicals but with admiring members of the nobility. And that while privately calling Bismarck "a bulldog and a cry-baby," he continued to support him.

Even so, he was not presented at court like his contemporary the painter Adolf von Menzel. Katia recalled that the Munich of her youth valued painters over writers. Inverting the hierarchy, Mann asserts, "A great painter may become official, a great writer never. For everything that constitutes the rank, the charm, and the value of his personality, the subtle intellectual distinctions, the problem-posing, the willful undiscipline, must make him seem in the eyes of the ruling classes both disloyal and suspect."*

The protean Fontane both glorified war-loving aristocrats and railed against militarism. In his pacifist guise, he asserted "that part of him which was rationalistic-humanitarian eighteenth-century (and twentieth-century?)." This preview of the new century is deliberate: Mann sees that

---

* Maximilian Harden, who had commissioned the piece, was enraged by Fontane's "duplicity." Any admirer of Bismarck, no matter how halfhearted, was no liberal in his view. He published the essay but, like many readers, he was suspicious of the politically ambidextrous duo Fontane and Mann.

"men of his sort must always be complicated and unreliable in their political behavior; for the contradictions in which they are pushed by contemporary events can be resolved and reconciled only in the future." Even as
Fontane jumps from the eighteenth to the twentieth century—his ration-
alist humanism finding no place in his own—so Mann, aged thirty-five,
believed the literary and political apotheosis of old age would allow the
recovery of a youth he had never enjoyed. Old age would settle the fabric
and reveal his life's design.

Fontane reappears in 1944, when Mann compares him to another Berliner, the Jewish painter Max Liebermann. He finds in both "the moral-
symbolic, the human example, the soulful guidance of art and poetry. . . .
Gallic Fontane and Jewish Liebermann refine and humanize." The words
are partially self-referential; his *Joseph* tetralogy honors the same qualities.
It's also a tribute to Berlin, a city he once disdained precisely for its impious
Jewish tone. Max Liebermann trumps Harden and Kerr, with Fontane's
blessing.

Close to his death, Mann wrote again about the old Fontane, no longer
a model but a peer. That was an affectionate coda exemplifying a charm he
had foreseen as one of the gifts of old age. The 1910 essay served another
function. It clarified Mann's existence by subjecting it to historical, psychological, and political development. Without referring to himself, he
turned a critique of Fontane into an elaboration of "Mind and Art" and a
circuitous defense of *Royal Highness*. To paraphrase Martin Luther's Bible,
all things worked together for the artist's good. It was a brilliant essay, and
its composition—promising so bright a future if he didn't weaken—
pleased him greatly.

On June 7, 1910, Mann's fourth child, Monika, was born. He wished
to be done with fatherhood: "God willing no more will come along;
it already verges on the ridiculous." The summer was spent in Bad Tölz,
amidst firs, ponds, and "the bittersweet fragrance of conifer, tonic herbs,
and raspberries." Mann was working on both the Fontane essay and *Felix
Krull*, a sweet-natured critique together with a burlesque Bildungsroman.

On July 30, the younger of his sisters, Carla, committed suicide. She
had fulfilled her brother's youthful fantasies by going on the stage. Heinrich
remembered her saying that "those who read you see people. I want to be
seen myself, really present myself to them. What you are with your mind
alone, I am with my whole body." As if to say, I'll show you what exhi-
bitionism really is. For all her professed need to expose herself, she lacked
a theatrical flair: in their stylized way, her brothers did it better.

Carla left the stage to marry a young manufacturer. But a previous suitor arrived and threatened to reveal her sordid past if she didn't comply with his wishes. Although she surrendered, he proceeded to inform her fiancé. She chose to turn this melodrama into a tragedy by taking cyanide. "Coming from an interview with her lover, the unhappy creature hurried past her mother with a smile, and locked herself into her room, and the last thing that was heard from her was the sound of her gargling with water as she tried to cool the caustic burning in her throat." Frau Mann and Heinrich were devastated. In her grief she wrote, "What suffering she kept from me—oh my Carla-baby!" Despite Heinrich's Marxism, he retained a mystical conviction that he had heard Carla's dying cries.

Initially Thomas was less sad than angry. In the family wars, Heinrich and Carla had served as bohemian critics of his bourgeois marriage. He was infuriated that she should hurt their mother so badly. Not too long before, he had experienced a suicidal depression himself, prompted by his feelings for Paul Ehrenberg. Now married, Ehrenberg re-entered his life to offer condolences. On August 12, Mann wrote Ehrenberg thanking him for his "sympathetic lines." He surmised that Carla had been play-acting at first: "She must originally have bought [the potassium cyanide] as a sort of aesthetic caprice and idiosyncracy—you know, the way she kept a skull on the dresser as a young girl." He presumed that Ehrenberg remembered the Manns' eccentricities. He closed by wishing to continue the story "face to face." It would be wonderful to see Paul again. Of course, both men were now married, and Carla's suicide would dissuade anyone from risking all for love.

Yet we know he had not outgrown his infatuation. Decades after the fact, he writes in his diary that Paul had been the great love of his life. Six years would have provided insufficient balm for his wound. Real life offered him numerous correlative subjects in that season of teenage outlaws and old Fontanes, of Carla's suicide and Paul's reappearance. Mann could represent the joys of fatherhood, and in Katia he had chosen an extraordinarily sympathetic companion. But he knew that marriage had not revoked his desires. The "unreliable artist" and confidence man were familiar figures that summer.

On September 3, he wrote Paul again, thanking him for a new letter which proved "what a loyal good friend you are." By then Frau Mann had joined her son's family at Bad Tölz. They were all recovering, having just celebrated Alfred Pringsheim's sixtieth birthday. He spoke of plans to attend a Mahler symphony. (On the twelfth, Mann joined Mahler and Max Reinhardt after the premiere of the former's Eighth Symphony: on this occasion, he viewed the face that inspired Aschenbach's.)

The Manns with baby Golo, Erika, and Klaus at Bad Tölz,
the children's favorite home, 1909

Too busy to visit Paul, he still hoped to see him "more often." Meanwhile he had resumed "the toilsome and passionate playing that is called artistic work." The language, a belated echo of his love letters to Katia, would remind Paul of his mercurial self-presentation. One moment he appeared pathetic: "My feelings have been in sad order." The next, he exhibited a morbid Realpolitik: "Yes, life goes on, and as long as one is not also lying in a black, rectangular pit in the ground, interlaced by tree roots, one must go along with it a little." Writing such sentences to Paul must have been "toilsome play" indeed.

Carla's suicide began to haunt him. On January 26, 1911, he wrote Heinrich, "It is the worst that could happen to me. Through her suicide, our existence has been questioned, our anchor loosened." He implied that her death had shattered any hope that Senator Mann's children could lead normal lives. Heinrich had written that "warmth is not for Carla, she is not made for happiness, for sociability, for *life*," words that applied, as much to Lula, Thomas, and himself. By her act, Carla had validated Kurt Martens's assertion, not to mention Thomas's belief, that conventional happiness would never be their lot.

Heinrich chose to see her death in literary terms. In a final letter, she had written her lover, "Je t'aime. Une fois je t'ai trompé, mais je t'aime." As a francophile, Heinrich was impressed that she had spoken "her first true words of love in a new language." He might have added that the language and gesture were both redolent of boulevard drama, theatrical romance before Wedekind. In fact he shortly composed a play, *The Actress*, based on her life; and, three years later, would marry the leading lady. In 1930, Thomas incorporated a description of her death in his autobiographical sketch. More remarkably, the description appeared verbatim in *Doctor Faustus*, an admittedly "shameless" work in which he also dramatized his relations with Ehrenberg. Ostensibly a reckoning with German history, the novel had more private significance. It was an attempt, almost forty years later, to exert literary control over the worst events of his youth: Carla's suicide and the loss of Paul.

Following this tumultuous summer, the Manns moved into a new apartment (actually two adjacent four-room flats) in Herzogpark, a newly built suburban development across the river Isar from Munich's English Gardens. The warily up-to-date Mann became a pioneer of this modern phenomenon, a luxury establishment in a previously uninhabited wilderness. Along unspoiled areas beside the Isar, Mann pursued his daily *Spaziergang*, a bracing, contemplative walk, often accompanied by the animal he would memorialize in "A Man and His Dog." For a voyeur like Mann, the intermittent sight of another man was not unpleasing. (In his Californian exile, the

Spaziergang led him across Muscle Beach, where he noted the bottle caps and condoms strewn beside the extraordinarily pumped-up bodies.)

Whether in retreat from the exhausting triumph of marriage—Klaus Heinrich's and his own—or as an expression of the feelings evoked by Paul Ehrenberg, Mann spent the next year composing homoerotic fiction. At least in literature, wives were abandoned.

Throughout his life, there were periods when Mann seemed on the verge of a great confession. His abiding decorum prevented an overt disclosure, but he left his clues. The year of his most homoerotic fiction, 1911, was also the year when, speaking of another writer, Chamisso, he observed, "Writers who give of themselves at bottom want others to understand them, for they are concerned not so much with the fame of their works as with the fame of their lives and sufferings."

About this time, he contributed to a forum on pornography and offered "Pornography and Eroticism," a bold defense of the very art he was composing. The quondam censor of Wedekind had matured. He now argued that those who invoke community values mimic the police. Perhaps the authorities were right to inhibit "pornography" in public, but with its grace and daring, art transcends their laws.

The censors knew nothing: at the moment they wished to exclude the *Decameron* from book catalogues. He ridiculed the zealots and Philistines, "foaming at the mouth," in paroxysms worthy of the fanatical Hieronymus. The salient autobiographical detail was this: even as Mann admits he writes to be understood, he declares that sexual passion—impossible, disorderly, a public offense—is art's primeval source. This sounds like a man eager to be found out.

In February 1911, "The Fight Between Jappe and Do Escobar" appeared. Not widely known, it is one of his most provocative stories. The setting is the Kurhaus at Travemünde, Mann's favorite resort; the time, "not long after the war, when strength, courage, and every hardy virtue stood very high among us youth and all sorts of conduct were banned as effeminate." In this atmosphere, upper-class boys of various nationalities work out their sexual and political tensions. The occasion allows Mann to examine the narcissistic display and erotic signals of adolescent games. What critics must extract from *Huckleberry Finn* swims on the surface of his tale.

The narrator is a passive observer. The first thing he beholds is an English boy lying naked. He is too old to expose his genitals, but Johnny Bishop reclines unconcerned. His friendly blue eyes and lazy smile make the narrator regret his inhibitions. The aristocratic Johnny is both a flirt, making eyes at the other boys, and a fop, wearing what resembles "girl's clothes."

Johnny informs the narrator that some fifteen-year-old "loafers," Jappe and Do Escobar, are going to fight each other. A practiced little voyeur, Johnny has observed the German's broad chest and muscular calves while swimming. As he describes them, the narrator focuses on Johnny's defenseless, child's arms. Reveries of power and sexuality begin to merge: that night he dreams of fighting another boy, "an adversary just as inhuman, I drove my fist into his hated jaw with all the strength of my being, so that all his teeth were broken, I received in exchange a brutal kick in the stomach and went under in a sea of blood."

The fight takes place on the dunes. Johnny appears, always the provocateur, elegantly clothed, his throat and legs bared, singing obscene ditties. The narrator focuses his attention on the two pugilists. Do Escobar is a Spanish dandy; in fact, his outfit impedes his performance. Jappe is less pretentious, a "natural" boy, although nature is itself a cultural pose: real German boys wear a studiedly casual uniform. Whatever political significance lies in the battle is dwarfed by the arrival of a most surprising referee. It's none other than Herr Knaak, the ballet master who enjoyed humiliating Tonio Kröger.

Knaak is one of Mann's most astonishing studies, a figure unlike any character before Proust. He is effeminate, rather pretty, with a heavy, undulating behind. Much like Prince Klaus Heinrich, he enters a room "as if it were a stage."

The boys distrust him. But since he leads an irreproachable life—he's even rumored to have a wife and children—they accept his authority. (Such are the benefits of living "officially.") Mann's description of the fight is overshadowed by this extraordinary figure. However, the fight allows Mann one of his favorite literary devices, piling up aggressive images that resemble physical blows. Not until *The Holy Sinner* forty years later does he provide so many instances of bodily combat. Yet, for much of the fight, the two boys seem rather sweet and frail: their pants keep slipping off.

Jappe leaves Do Escobar bloodied. Neither is knocked out, to Johnny Bishop's disappointment. When the diplomatic Knaak offers the "delicate fiction" of a draw, the audience demands another round. The narrator admits that he has awaited the challenge "with shivers of delicious anticipation." Aroused by Johnny, he'll fight his way to a physical release. To paraphrase Clausewitz, violence becomes another means of lust.

The boys decide Herr Knaak must fight. But in a beautifully anticlimactic development, the dancing teacher declines: "No, thanks, very

much—I had enough beatings when I was young." (Of course, an effeminate, working-class Knaak would have been abused by other boys.)

Mann does allow him a patriotic outburst: when Do Escobar derides
wrestling as a cowardly sport, fit for Germans, Knaak offers the "capital
retort" that Germans can "give pretty good beatings sometimes too." It's
an immense leap for Mann to identify with someone like Knaak. "Virile"
homosexuals have typically resented the Knaaks as flamboyant embarrassments. Mann's homosexual friends tended to be retiring scholars—although
Klaus and Erika introduced him to more theatrical gays. But Mann reveals
more about himself than about Knaak—wonderful and unprecedented as
that character is. The political implications of his recognition that the
guardians of society's mores are frequently its pariahs—previously Jews,
now homosexuals—are very rich, as is the recognition that militarism is a
diversion of sexual energies: if you can't sunbathe with Johnny, you need
to knock someone out.

In the history of the gay sensibility, an important milestone occurs in
Proust's *Cities of the Plain*. When the Baron Charlus meets the little tailor
Jupien, the two men engage in a dance of courtship, literally rubbing
behinds, to indicate their membership in the same tribe. Herr Knaak's
plump bottom struts into literature before Jupien's, and the complicated
attention he receives is another breakthrough. More than *Tonio Kröger*, "The
Fight Between Jappe and Do Escobar" was Mann's tribal signal.

I n June 1909 Mann informed Katia that his reading of the confessions of
a Romanian criminal, George Manolescu, had inspired a new tale, *Felix
Krull*. A first section appeared in 1911, and additional episodes appeared
in the 1920s. He resumed the work in his late seventies, and it became his
last novel. Readers have often marveled at the seamless composition, as if
Mann had immediately recaptured a sensibility and subject matter he had
apparently abandoned thirty years before. But this should not be surprising.
Mann regarded *Felix Krull* as his most personal work, and his obsessions
never changed.

Moreover, Hans Wysling has shown that already in 1909 Mann had
planned to have Felix change places with a nobleman, the "prince and the
pauper" switch that constitutes the most dramatic development in Book
III. A more startling exchange occurs in Mann's 1940 novella *The Transposed
Heads*, when Mann makes a fusion of separate selves both metaphysical and
homoerotic: how better to love someone than to turn into him? Of course,
impersonating a Felix would come close.

Mann intended the Bildungsroman of a criminal to be a parody of Goethe's *Wilhelm Meister* and *Poetry and Truth*. The narrator is an austere sybarite—a familiar Mannian figure, even if he's a crook. He receives a sentimental education in the diverse forms of social hypocrisy, while exhibiting the sensibility of an ingenue; his tone is languid, even passive, and rarely cynical.

Above all, he's sexy. Krull is the only Mann narrator who refers to himself as physically desirable. At first he's a coquette, posing in the nude for an uncle who places him in classic positions, reviving the clichés of homosexual imagery (a possible allusion to the preposterous poses the Baron von Gloeden demanded of his impoverished Sicilian models). Krull allows Mann to become the object of his desire.

Unlike Herr Knaak, he's not a poor boy. Instead he's a bourgeois con man, a traitor to his class's already bankrupt principles. Raised in the provinces, he aspires very early to the conspicuous leisure of the titled aristocrats. His father is a vintner, given to adulterating his wine with fuel oil (still a habit among some Austrian exporters). Felix will ultimately stake his claims in the precincts of taste and breeding. This will require a move to the city, to the court, to other lands. By circuitous routes, Mann creates a modern picaro.

In temperament, he could be Mann's more sanguine twin. Like his author, "I have always been very sensitive, susceptible, and in need of cherishing; and everything I have accomplished in life has been the result of self-conquest." He considers self-obsession—in his case, a strategic form of narcissism—"a moral achievement." This absurd boast is a parody of Mann's Schiller, of Mann himself, for the story is universally disrespectful. Anticipating Freud, Mann denies the sentimental myth of childhood innocence. "Even at my nurse's breast, I displayed the clearest evidence of certain feelings," an early sign of "the eagerness of my nature."

This is matched by a precocious talent for satisfying himself. He orchestrates his solitary pleasure with the same attention to details that marked his predecessors' manipulation of puppet theaters and stage lighting. He's a boudoir apprentice, with an artist's patience, calculation, and —even here—discipline.

Those desires and sensations he dubs "the Great Joy" and "the best of all" are balanced by a "healthful austerity." His love of food, music, and creature comfort borders on the polymorphous perverse. Everything is sexualized, but sex itself affords a limited pleasure: "My desires were always upon a broader, larger, and more general scale; they found the sweetest feeling where others might not seek; they were never precisely defined or specialized—and for this reason among others it was that . . . I remained so long innocent and unconscious, yes, actually my whole life long a child and dreamer."

The fantasy world of this masturbatory adolescent is populated by figures real and imagined. In this realm, Goethe, whose short legs resemble Krull's, merges with cherry tarts, rectal thermometers, and greased violin bows—not to mention a flirtatious chambermaid and a lascivious uncle. His "great joy" is Joycean in amplitude.

As a vision of youth, Felix Krull offers a bracing antidote to the miserable Hanno Buddenbrook. He also stands with Herr Knaak as one of Mann's boldest inventions. Hanno was a classic "sissy," the ideal prey of schoolyard bullies. Like Hanno, Felix Krull has no friends—he finds his schoolmates coarse. But he's quite able to entertain himself, secure in his own independence. The cultural gap between Krull and the representative boys of American literature is huge. Felix is the polar opposite of Huck Finn, isolated, bad at games, easily humiliated. What they share is a cultivated ambivalence; like Huck, Felix is willing to "go to hell."

The story refers to his eventual imprisonment. Jail doesn't signify a well-earned punishment; it's the site of one more bed where Felix rests splendidly; for, like his author, he derives an orgiastic pleasure from sleep. In another of the story's implicit self-parodies, Mann connects indolence and crime. While yielding uncritically to the flow of impressions, Felix keeps his eye on the main chance. He's one Mannian voyeur who understands the follow-up.

The parody alludes to Mann's recent experiences. In the year of Carla's attempted marriage into the bourgeoisie and her suicide, Mann dramatizes the engagement of Krull's sister, Olympia, a failed actress like Carla (Felix envies her capacity to change her identity by changing her name: a transmogrification legally forbidden to men), and the suicide of their father. The story is filled with self-referential echoes—when Felix performs in public, he is hailed as "the Infant Prodigy"—and a kind of proleptic parody—Felix masquerades as a Grecian shepherd much as Aschenbach casts Tadzio in a neoclassical myth. With his soft hands, girlishly blond / brunet hair, and golden brown skin, he is a combination of Johnny Bishop, the Florentine dandies, Goethe, and Hermes. Above all, he is Mann's wittiest commentator on the dangers of representation.

As a child, he learns how to misrepresent himself. He shams illness so well that his appearance changes: "I had improved upon nature . . . out of a combination of nothing but fantasy and . . . personality." He's so preoccupied with making an impression that when he sees his father's corpse, and "[pays] him the abundant tribute of my tears," the grief seems theatrical, a miming of the obligatory emotion. Likewise his seduction by a servant girl is sketched with minimal enthusiasm: he provides no "lightness of tone or lewdness of expression." Anyway, with his capacious libido, he's more stimulated in a theater or a boutique.

An episode in a delicatessen is one of the high points. Upon entering, Felix announces his arrival. When nobody attends him, he becomes a thief by default. The abundance of goods conspires to tempt him; the absence of a salesperson gives him his chance. He's the proverbial child in an unguarded candy store. And not just candy: a kingdom, an empire is displayed on platters and behind glass showcases:

> dishes of Italian salad, lobsters spreading their claws on blocks of ice, sprats pressed flat and gleaming goldenly from opened boxes; choice fruits—garden strawberries and grapes that could have come from the Promised Land; tiers of sardine cans and those fascinating little white earthenware jars of caviar and foie gras. Plump chickens dangled their necks from the top shelf, and there were trays of cooked meats, ham, tongue, beef, and veal, smoked salmon and breast of goose, with the slender slicing-knife lying ready to hand. There were all sorts of cheeses under glass bells, brick-red, milk-white, and marbled, also the creamy ones that ooze in a golden wave out of their silver foil.

This is as lubricious a passage as Mann ever wrote.

Krull recalls the various poses he assumed as a model: Greek god; Roman flute player; Spanish bullfighter; German mountaineer; French abbé; Florentine dandy. These dabs at representation comprise a con man's *Bildung*. (They also demonstrate crass commercialism lurking behind idealized imagery, including homoerotic icons: the Greek god becomes a pinup boy.)

In the period before androgynous youth matures into Adonis, he attends the theater with his father. Wilhelm Meister also learned from theatrical artists. But Krull's lessons are distinctively modern, uniquely Mannian.

One actor, named Müller-Rosé, is the crowd's favorite. He makes a series of appearances, involving changes in wardrobe, from full dress to silk underdrawers; along the way, he touches all the emotional spots. The audience is enthralled. "Müller-Rosé heightened our joy of life—if the phrase is adequate to express that feeling, mingled of pain and pleasure, envy, yearning, hope and irresistible love which the sight of the consummately charming can kindle in the human soul." Very little ambivalence here; Krull is simply a fan.

He goes backstage with his father and is quickly disillusioned. The actor is not handsome. He removes his wig and "I saw that he was red-haired," by now a familiar sign of disreputable morals. His mascaraed eyes wink lewdly, a forecast of the old fop Aschenbach encounters while traveling to Venice. Worst of all, his back and torso are covered with suppurating carbuncles.

A Mannian artist, the actor dreams of winning his public's love. Despite his triumphs, he remains insecure, and barrages the Krulls for their opinion of his performance: like Schiller or Fontane, he's perpetually dissatisfied with his work. An erotic union occurs between him and a public of "little shop girls . . . simple fathers . . . and young soldiers." Müller-Rosé succeeds as did Mizzi Meyer, and as no serious artist can: he simultaneously wins the Krulls "and the dummies too." The exchange is neat: "He gave us joy of life, we in turn sated his craving for applause; and was this not a mutual satisfaction, a true marriage of desires?"

Müller-Rosé is a proper companion to that other public servant Herr Knaak. Both men traffic in idealized representations; low-born experts in the rituals and routines that move a culture.

There's more at stake. The Eros transmitted between the performer and his public exemplifies Krull's "broader" sexuality at its widest limit. Müller-Rosé seduces a crowd that would individually reject his courtship with scorn. Theatrical sensuality is immense, unparalleled, and completely unreal. Analogies to the mesmerizing powers of authors like Tonio Kröger or Mann himself are self-evident. On a smaller scale, Herr Knaak plays a highly stylized role with his public. He flatters like a courtier, insults like a peasant. He's a new social phenomenon, an avatar of the service economy, although his ancestors include both Figaro and Hermes. (To use the modern jargon, his service is the conveying of information: cultural codes.)

There's an abrupt, shaggy-dog feel to the story's ending, as the narrator weeps self-consciously over his dead father. Mann complained in his letters that he had a hard time dreaming up escapades for his crook, and the collocation of events may seem random, with no narrative development. But the subject is the acquisition of a tone and slant. Felix Krull weeping uncertain tears is merely exchanging the roles of artist's model, truant, shoplifter, and fan for that of mourner.

In 1911, in preparation for Krull's later adventures, Mann began clipping images of the new urban culture out of newspapers and magazines, with folders devoted to Resorts, Elegant Festivities, Hotel, Travel, and Sports. This dependence on visual aids—both as inspiration and as compensation for the perceptual deficiencies of his youth—continued throughout his life.

Early or late, Felix Krull remained a love object impersonated by the one who loves him. Thus it was aesthetically right that Mann should next turn from Krull to Aschenbach, from the one who practices seduction to the unhappy victim.

They represent the two aspects of Mann's disposition, blithe and morbid, yielding and obdurate. Their culture inhibits them, but it also transforms their most intimate responses into acts of erotic resistance. It's an astonishing example of self-knowledge—not necessarily conscious—that Mann could imagine both men in the same year, as if Krull, not Tadzio, were summoning Aschenbach.

4

DEATH IN VENICE

In January 1911 Mann gave a lecture tour of Westphalia, reading from *Felix Krull* and his other stories. By March there was a recrudescence of his stomach upsets. (Katia wasn't well, either.) He thought of returning to the sanitarium but decided instead that he and Katia would join Heinrich on a tour of Italy. The first stop was Brioni, an island off the coast of Istria. But the atmosphere at their hotel was not pleasant. Whenever one guest, an archduchess, entered the dining room, her retinue remained standing a moment after she had been seated. The no-nonsense Katia found this behavior absurd.

The three travelers left the resort quickly, and by May 26 were settled on the Lido near Venice at the Hôtel des Bains. There "a series of curious circumstances and impressions combined with my subconscious search for something new to give birth to a productive idea, which then developed into the story *Death in Venice*. The tale as at first conceived was as modest as all the rest of my undertakings; I thought of it as a quick improvisation which should serve as an interlude to my work on the Krull novel."

Mann claims elsewhere that he had imagined a more conventional tale: not the story of a man's love for a boy but a novella drawn from the aged Goethe's infatuation with a seventeen-year-old girl, Ulrike von Levetzow. (Vladimir Nabokov regarded Mann as strictly middlebrow. Something of a homophobe, Nabokov famously quipped that if *Lolita* had involved a man and a boy, he would have had no problems. It's amusing that a *Goethe in Marienbad* would have anticipated his travelogue-cum-pedophilia.)

Virtually every detail in *Death in Venice* was based on fact, from the shipboard encounters to the rumors of cholera. In the 1960s, Count Wladyslaw Moes, the original of Tadzio, the beautiful Polish boy, confirmed the accuracy of Mann's depiction of his mother, sisters, and older friend. He also recalled that the two boys had been conscious of an "old man" watching them attentively. Validation comes from another source. In her memoirs, Katia Mann declares quite coolly that her husband was intrigued by the ten-year-old Pole. He may well have drawn her attention to the lad. (Monika Mann remembers how he dispatched his entire family to help observe another striking youth, who would serve as the model for young Joseph.)

Katia Mann's acceptance of her husband's infatuation is one detail missing from the story—as is she. In other stories drawn from their lives together, "Mario and the Magician" and "Disorder and Early Sorrow," the wife may not play an active role, but her presence is acknowledged. But the hero of *Death in Venice* has no wife and is alienated from his daughter. Since everything else reflects Mann's experience and temperament, one might contend that on a profound level he remained unmarried. But concerning this implication, the shrewd Katia tells us nothing.

Aschenbach was physically modeled on Mahler, whose death Mann had learned about in Brioni. (Mann had sent a copy of *Royal Highness* to Mahler, inscribed: "To Gustav Mahler: In whom, as I believe, I recognize the most serious and holy artistic will of our era.") He also resembles Mann, from his mixed racial heritage to the specifics of his oeuvre. Though his motto, "All great achievements are acts of defiance," sounds like Schopenhauer, it comes from Mann's essay "About Alcohol." (Therein, surprisingly, Mann counseled moderation.)

Within the novella's lyrical passages he deposited allusions, paraphrases, and even quotations from earlier poets, in particular Goethe (*The West-Eastern Divan*) and Platen. From one perspective, the homosexual element in German poetry reaches its culmination in Venice, the site of Goethe and Platen's most impassioned lyrics. Schopenhauer and Nietzsche also leave their traces in the story.

Of the last, Schopenhauer's ascesis is thoroughly interrogated, and—it can be argued—rejected. In composing the novella Mann may have seen the impossibility of reconciling Platen and the grim philosopher. (His contemporaneous rejection of Wagner, Schopenhauer's "artist," was more than coincidental.) Aschenbach's world is not Will and Idea; it is, simply, the boy Tadzio. In his poetic configuration Mann allows desire to banish Wagnerian cobwebs and Schopenhauerian toads.

While Mann conceded that all the story's details were drawn from life, "I had to arrange them . . . as elements of composition." There were other, more literary sources. As David Luke points out, Mann's notebooks show that he "immersed himself in the study of the Platonic theory of love. He read especially the *Symposium* and the *Phaedrus* and Plutarch's *Erotikos*— all of which he interestingly and perhaps knowingly misquotes in the text of the story." Of course, Mann, a smart shopper in the literary marketplace, had previously claimed the right to creatively misread for his story's purposes.

To support his claim that *Death in Venice* did not originate as a homosexual tale, Mann also declared he reread Goethe's *Elective Affinities* at least five times. By October 1911, he was steeped in György Lukács's *Soul and Form*, a book that addressed and reflected his concerns—so much so that he would later suggest that its analyses of the relationship of "burgherly nature and l'art pour l'art" in the career of Theodor Storm was derived from his own example: "Doubtless we have special claim to the knowledge to which we ourselves have contributed by our existence, and when we accept it as our own, we are somewhat in the position of a father who smilingly lets himself be taught by his learned son." (In such ways, Mann would always turn the table on the professors.) One of Lukács's chapters, "Desire and Form," cited Socrates and Plato to illuminate the condition of the modern bourgeois artist.

In a work note, "Connections Between Chapters Two and Three," Mann offers a summary that shows the influence of Lukács's formulations. The bourgeois artist achieves "dignity," i.e., fame, only at the cost of "insight and second innocence." This lack of self-reflection leaves him open to a demoralizing passion. "Form is the sin. The surface is the abyss. How deeply art again becomes problematic for the artist who had attained dignity! Eros is the guide for the artist toward things intellectual, spiritual beauty; for him the path to the pinnacle goes by way of the senses. But this is a dangerously delightful path, a wrong way and a sinful way, although there is no other."

Sehnsucht leaves the artist exhausted and disgraced. He can never enjoy his passions, he "*can never* attain dignity . . . he necessarily goes astray, remains a bohemian, gypsy, libertine, an eternal adventurer of the emotions." Therefore, Aschenbach must die: "Dignity is rescued only by death (this is the 'tragedy,' the 'sea')—as a solution, a way out and refuge of all elevated love. The fame of the artist is a farce; the trust of the masses is sheer idiocy . . . the irony that the boys are reading him, the irony of his official standing, of his being granted nobility. . . . *At the very end*: state of decadence, enervation, demoralization."

Another intellectual source was the short-lived "neoclassicism" fad championed by, among others, Samuel Lublinski, Mann's Berlin admirer. Mann's need for a drier, "classical" alternative to the hyperventilations of naturalism led to an essay he composed while in Venice, in which he admits his affinities with Wagner—"the recurrent motif, the self-quotation, the symbolic phrase, the verbal and thematic reminiscence across long stretches of text"—and compares Wagner's *Ring* and his *Buddenbrooks* as "epic pageants of the generations." Yet he no longer believes in him, "if indeed I ever did believe." The modern generation rejects Wagner's writings on art because they are "propaganda rather than honest revelation." What this generation requires is a new "representative" spirit, as Wagner represented the nineteenth century. "Something conspicuously logical; well formed and clear, something at once austere and cheerful"— isn't this "propaganda" for *Royal Highness?*—"[and] no less imbued with strength of purpose, but more restrained, refined, more healthy, even in its spirituality—something that does not seek its greatness in the monumentally baroque, nor its beauty in the sweep of emotion. A new classicism, I believe, is on the way." This is the essay Aschenbach / Mann composes while on the beach, gathering his inspiration from the presence of a beautiful boy. The result seems contradictory: a decadent occasion prompting a neoclassical manifesto. But, Mann explains, Wagner had always provoked an ambivalent response: "As a thinker and personality he seemed to me suspect, as an artist irresistible. . . . My love for him was a love devoid of belief, for *it has always seemed to be pedantic to insist that one cannot love without also believing* [italics mine]. It was a liaison, an affair—skeptical, pessimistic, clear-sighted, spiteful almost, yet full of passion and indescribable charm."

This kind of affair—"spiteful" yet passionate—closely resembles the forms of desire felt by Tonio Kröger, Hanno Buddenbrook, or Aschenbach. The Wagner sketch, neoclassicism and all, is itself a powerful disclosure of Mannian *Sehnsucht*.

Despite all the material Mann processed while composing *Death in Venice*, he really didn't have to look abroad for inspiration. He had been blessed again by the muses. An actual event—along with a selective scholarship—had triggered barely dormant responses. No matter how often he declared the writing of *Death in Venice* fortuitous, all the circumstances of his life—and career—pointed to its composition.

When Aschenbach wordlessly contemplates Tadzio, his action is the apotheosis of the gaze, of Mann's obsession with seeing and being seen. A lifetime of hard, cold glances, aslant at opera houses, directly through store windows, by a series of voyeurs from Johannes Friedemann to Hanno Buddenbrook, Klaus Heinrich, and Felix Krull—is evoked as the old man pursues his idol through the byways of Venice. Ever since "Der Bajazzo," Mann had articulated a poetics of consumerism. Where better than Venice to exercise a taste for history inflected by the knowledge that commerce had overrun tradition? Mann's choice of setting has an inevitable logic. The city where all views are compromised, shadowed by mortality, becomes the site of Aschenbach's sea change.

Venice is also "where composers have been inspired to lulling tones of somniferous eroticism," the place where Wagner composed Act II of the fatally seductive *Tristan*. Like the other fine arts burlesqued—the poetic stanzas transformed into a pederast's come-on, the Renaissance images erased by advertisements—music loses its dignity. Late in the novella, Aschenbach dreams of a Dionysian orgy accompanied by guttural shrieks and the song of goats. Mann continues to burlesque *Tristan*—or to discover the obscene grunts drowned out by Wagner's orchestrations.

The Venetian setting emancipated him. Recent accounts of his creative dilemmas had grown involuted with self-regard. (For that matter, not every reader enjoys the essayistic complaints dating back to *Tonio Kröger*.) But the same theme enacted here, with its delirious erotic undercurrent, inspires his richest prose. It is a multifarious language, including an elegant discourse that acts as a counterfoil to the hero's passionate disorientation—as Mann observed, correct for once in his smugness, filled with "such inexhaustible allusiveness as to dazzle the creator himself."

The prose is often mimetic, as nauseatingly overripe as the cholera-infested fruit that poisons Aschenbach. It ranges from the prolix to the inarticulate, the barely understood vowel sounds "-iu" which precede Aschenbach's recognition of the name "Tadzio."

Criticism of the novella's more fulsome passages eventually obliged Mann to declare the work a partial parody. He was a playful satirist, not to be confused with the love-drunk Aschenbach. Mann had reason to fear that younger writers considered his style old-fashioned. Actually, it's amazingly daring prose. He achieves effects that are virtually cinematic, including some that would tax any film director. Amidst the normal bustle and gait, Aschenbach's movement toward Tadzio proceeds at a slow clip, as if underwater. In a crowded room, he only has eyes for Tadzio. The lover balances two discreet forms of looking: what might be called normal vision, which takes in the crowd, and ecstatic vision, which beams, with preternatural attention, on the beloved object. ("The boy [returned] his gaze . . . with a seriousness that seemed a copy of his own; it seemed oblivious to the general mood.")

The story's composition allowed Mann to reveal a "sympathy" with two particular publics, neither of them the homely losers who comprised Tonio Kröger's readership. Aschenbach is "the writer who spoke for all those who work on the edge of exhaustion, who labor and are heavy laden, who are depleted but still hold themselves upright, all those moralists of accomplishment with stunted growth and scanty resources." These people are "the heroes of our age. And in his pages, they saw themselves; he justified, he exalted them; he sang their praise." The classic and pagan allusions come later; Aschenbach's German achievement is ratified by a secularized church. But Mann addressed another crowd. In an elegantly elliptical form—which would be transparent to any "sympathizer"—he declared a set of feelings that has evoked immediate recognition from generations of gay readers. The role of spokesman for an inarticulate mass was scarcely new to German literature. But excepting Platen, no previous artist had spoken so boldly for homosexuals.

In recent times, this sympathy has acquired a political nature. For some proponents of gay liberation, *Death in Venice* is marred by Aschenbach's attempts at subterfuge, as if the city constituted a shimmering closet. (It's not unfair to call Mann the poet of a half-open closet.) Even without the pioneering critique of Magnus Hirschfeld—whom he initially disliked— Mann understood homosexuality in political terms. To begin with, Paragraph 175 made it illegal in Germany, as the Eulenburg trial and the consequent ruin of many famous men had lately demonstrated. This knowledge contributed to the story's authenticity; Aschenbach couldn't pursue Tadzio with such equanimity outside Venice.

Already in "The Fight Between Jappe and Do Escobar," Mann had drawn a connection between Eros and warfare. This grows clearer in the novella; whenever Tadziu is assaulted by his older friend, the attack borders on rape. In the Venetian potpourri of cultural style, an English travel agent's sobriety is juxtaposed to the naïveté of Austrian tourists, the aggressive camaraderie of Russians, the aristocratic hauteur of Poles, and the devious hustling of Mediterranean panders. Nationalist rivalries flow through the story.

The opening conveys a sense of imperial decline. We learn that Gustav Aschenbach has been recently knighted; after fifty he became Gustav von Aschenbach, a title he has earned—thereby making him an artificial aristocrat. As he celebrates Germany's most famous ruler, Frederick the Great, he has come to embody Frederick's discipline (*Zucht*) and composure (*Haltung*), virtues identified with the warrior who conquered Aschenbach's native Silesia.

Mann conflates a political, indeed militaristic, stance with a moral one. He presses the connection so hard that *Haltung* becomes a figure of both heroic self-discipline and pathetic repression. It conveys a sense of physical dignity worthy of that universally acknowledged representative of German culture, Aschenbach—and increasingly Mann—himself.

Mann also ascribes *Haltung* to Saint Sebastian—"the most perfect symbol . . . of composure under the blows of fate, grace constant under torture." Sebastian, Mann's favorite saint, is the first of his paradoxical warriors, "seemingly passive" yet heroic. (That Sebastian was also a homosexual icon would not have escaped his attention.) Long before Hemingway, he valorized the grace of quiet endurance.

Even in Munich, Aschenbach inhabits a world that is exclusively male. While at a tram stop, outside the city cemetery, he exchanges glances with a red-bearded stranger. Somehow this wordless communication evokes thoughts of the river Ganges and the jungle, the geographical sources of the cholera that kills him. The powerful male figure prompts a desire for travel: Aschenbach's visions are blatantly sexual. Hairy palm trunks and thick, fleshy plants become phallic extensions of the stranger with his throbbing neck muscles.

Aschenbach's "European psyche" fears "the colorful, external world." His story resembles Mann's. The product of a respectable bourgeoisie, a "union of dry, conscientious officialdom and ardent, more obscure impulses," he has transferred his ancestors' perfectionist urges to literature. But, much like Schiller, in the process of "settling down for work" he has lost the "sparkling and joyful improvisation" that made work play.

"He had been young and raw with the times." As such he exhibited all the traits Mann condemns in "Mind and Art": overly intellectual and analytic, he "called genius into question, held art up to scorn." But he matured into the Nietzschean consciousness that "knowledge lames the will." His estrangement from "an age indecently obsessed with psychology" was marked in his story "A Study in Abjection," in which a repulsive hero drove his wife into the arms of a younger man (a foreshadowing of *Doctor Faustus*, this Dostoevskian fable also limns a diverted sexual encounter between the hero and his younger rival—in Thomas Mann's work, no association between men seems above suspicion). This story signified that he had renounced a sympathy with the abyss—as Mann had done in "At the Prophet's"—for engagement in the world of normal men. Yet, older and wiser, Mann questions such conversion. "Is form not two-faced?" the narrator wonders. Wasn't Aschenbach's rejection of "all shattering and corrosive insight [a] dangerous simplification, a morally simplistic view of the world and of human psychology, that strengthened the hold of the evil, the forbidden, and the ethically impossible?"

As Mann instructed us previously, art is an "intensified life." Its weight is apparent in Aschenbach's brow: his brushed-back hair, large scarred forehead, and aristocratic nose all resemble Mahler's appearance. In an ecumenical act of imagination, Saint Sebastian's experience, as inscribed in Christian metaphor, is physically registered on a Jewish face. (Mahler was fifty-one when he died; Aschenbach is fifty-three.)

Having shown Aschenbach as he is perceived, Mann now shows him rehearsing the act of voyeurism. En route to Venice, he observes a crowd of young men. Among their number is a man as old as he, ludicrously made up to resemble his companions. The boat trip culminates in a cinematic closeup of the queen's "senile underlip."

Upon his arrival, he recalls Platen's original vision of the city. But this "passionately shaped language" has an obscene echo: the fop winkingly salutes Aschenbach and "your sweetheart, your sweety-sweety-sweetheart." This parody provides a spectacular transition to Aschenbach's trip on a gondola. Mann evokes the "dread," the "sense of terror" that accompanies one's descent into coffinlike blackness. He appends a friendly question, as if he were the ultimate travel guide: "Has anyone remarked that the seat of such a boat . . . is the softest, the most voluptuous, most relaxing seat in the world?" The lassitude of his trip leaves Aschenbach powerless. Surrendering to inertia, he becomes easy prey for the gondolier: "evidently not of Italian origin," with a "brutal appearance" and reddish eyebrows, a new incarnation of the stranger who first tempted him to travel.

Once ensconced at the hotel on the Lido, Aschenbach begins to survey the other guests. He is immediately transfixed by the sight of Tadzio. But though it's easy to reduce *Death in Venice* to the love of an old man for a young boy, Tadzio has several other attributes. He's not just a beauty, he's also a Pole (in vigorous distinction to the other Eastern Europeans); rich; charismatic, easily outshining his sisters; an object of attention; and apparently frail. Forgetting his symbolic role as Hermes, the messenger between two worlds, he is almost as specific a cultural type as Imma Spoelmann.

Aschenbach's first appraisal of him is aesthetic. He compares the boy to Greek statues and applauds his observation, "assuming the patronizing air of the connoiseur to hide . . . his ravishment over a masterpiece." (Within that sentence, scholarly rectitude is exposed as hypocrisy and dissolves into rapture.) He is an erotic figure, though not a pornographic one;

his sense of decorum resembles Aschenbach's. With the "angry contempt" of a Polish aristocrat, he stares at the fleshily "overripe" and "indolent" Russian tourists.

Aschenbach loves him before he knows his name. (First he makes out the "iu" sound; this develops into "Adziu.") Many of the bathers are naked, "contentedly enjoying the liberal local customs." But when Tadzio appears, his legs are naked only to above the knees. Aschenbach sees the boy build sand castles with a friend. Afterward they walk arm in arm, "and once the lad 'Jashu' gave his beautiful companion a kiss."

This scene may be unprecedented in literature: a mature homosexual observing what Freudians consider a preliminary stage of sexual development. No writer before Mann had played so artfully with the contrasting desires of adults and adolescents. The poignance lies in Aschenbach's sympathy for "Jashu," a feeling the boy cannot share; the sympathy is all in one direction. Mann's equally tremendous insight is that society allows Tadzio only one passionate friend; the enjoyment of youth is legally forbidden to age. If previous Mann characters felt themselves banished from the festival of life, none was as excluded as Aschenbach.

Later, after Tadzio has finished swimming, he runs out of the water, and Aschenbach swoons before this image of a "living figure, lovely and austere in its first signs of manhood." Still, he must impose a scholarly design: the vision suggests "the birth of form" and "the origins of the gods."

Aschenbach returns to his hotel room. Gazing at his image, he remembers that a famous man stares back at him. This irruption of narcissism may explain the positive glee he takes over Tadzio's jagged teeth, a physical sign the boy won't live long: the older man need fear no posthumous rivals. The story's mood darkens. From a vision of Olympus, we plunge to the Venetian canal where signboards carrying the names of "commercial enterprises [are] mirrored in water where refuse [bobs] up and down." Vice and capitalism are real, Tadzio a dream. The scholar decides he had better leave.

But, of course, he doesn't. Through willful procrastination, he misses his connection. When he returns to the Lido, he can barely suppress his joy. He manages a sober countenance, still alert to the impression he makes. But his performing mask conceals the "panic and thrills of a truant schoolboy" (Mann understands that the schoolboy's outlawed pleasure is anxiously enjoyed).

He was earlier described as closed-fisted; now, "quite unseen," he opens his arms to the boy he spies "coming up from the sea." The gesture is one of invisible acceptance.

He spends the next days in quiet contemplation, coming to know his beloved in every aspect of play and repose. He beholds Jaschiu "caressing him"; he sees him at the water's edge, "rocking . . . on the balls of his feet," his translucent, hairless arms within Aschenbach's grasp. While a very conscious flirtation takes place, Aschenbach feels compelled to generalize. His "store of culture . . . in a state of flux," he recalls that "ancient tradition" in which "the love god" uses "the shapes and colors of young men" to inflame their admirers' hearts with beauty.

That image leads to a vision of its cultural sources, Athens, and the replay of a Socratic dialogue in which ugly wise men court handsome youths. Because it is the one divine element fully visible, Beauty supersedes the abstract essences, Reason, Virtue, and Truth. But its experience is reserved for the beholder. Mann puts on Socrates' lips "the subtlest thing of all, that sly wooer: the lover is nearer the divine than the beloved, for the god is in the one, but not in the other—this perhaps the most scandalous thing ever thought, and the source of all the guile and secret bliss a lover can know." It's quite beside the point if this Mannian construct, formulated in phrases that echo so much of his previous work, is incorrect. Like Thomas Buddenbrook's misreading of Schopenhauer, it's a creative misappropriation for the lover's benefit, an error that serves as a confession.

There follows a paragraph in which Aschenbach composes a magisterial essay while within embracing distance of Tadzio's almost-nude body. It aptly includes a paraphrase of Platen, the poet whose feelings most closely resemble Aschenbach's. It begins with a joyful defense of the *Schriftsteller*: "Thought that can become emotion, emotion that can wholly become a thought, are the writer's highest joys." Confident in his own powers, Mann is also showing how—with "critical passion"—the *Schriftsteller* can surpass the *Dichter*.

While other men might seek a physical fulfillment, "felt a sudden desire to write . . . his excitement was driving him to produce. The occasion was almost a matter of indifference." This is how a Mannian voyeur seeks consummation: "He craved . . . to work . . . in Tadzio's presence, to take the youth's body as a model." He wishes to carry the boy's mortal beauty into spiritual realms, much as Jupiter abducted his Ganymede. The act of composition resembles love-making: "Never had the joy of the word been so sweet to him, never had he known so clearly that Eros resides in the word." The brief essay he composes, "his idol still in view and the music of his voice in his ears," would be widely admired for its "chaste and lofty prose." But, like Felix Krull exhausted by his private indulgence in the "Great Joy," Aschenbach finishes his work "drained, broken, debauched."

By now, Tadzio and Aschenbach are fully aware of each other. They flirt in silence; Aschenbach fears that speech would produce "disenchantment." Desire springs from a "defective knowledge." It is a voyeur's truth that "the relationship between people who know each other only by sight" is the most provocative of all; its members are forever desiring, forever invigorated by fantasy. Mann understands that in this silent, visual world, they are equally green connivers. Aschenbach is no older or wiser; his cunning is acquired on the spot. (Elsewhere he calls Tadzio "a model and mirror.")

In Max Ophüls' great movie *Letter from an Unknown Woman*, the heroine finally encounters the man of her dreams. When Louis Jourdan walks toward Joan Fontaine, his stride is so invested with her years of longing that the camera almost swoons with her. Something similar happens in *Death in Venice*. When, quite unprepared, Aschenbach and Tadzio nearly collide with each other, each one involuntarily smiles. Only with the careful preparation of Mann's narrative could so harmless a gesture appear so shattering. Aschenbach is defeated by the smile. He whispers after the departing boy, "You dare not smile like that!"—the planets will rocket out of space, the universe will explode.

Only after language has been dethroned as a register of feeling, can poor Aschenbach utter "the hackneyed phrase of the heart's desire— impossible here, absurd, depraved, ludicrous and sacred nevertheless, still worthy of honor even here, 'I love you!' "

Love makes him an outlaw. He follows Tadzio to a church, where, of course, the boy had expected him. He pursues him in a panderer's gondola, oblivious to the smirking attention of his diabolical ferryman. (The gondolier's maneuvers through the side canals of Venice look forward to movie chase sequences; Aschenbach's commands "Follow that gondola" are both alarming and ridiculous.) He realizes that his ancestors would be appalled by his behavior. But he invokes an older tradition represented by those cities where strong, valiant men shared his desires. What is anathema to Munich was Sparta's joy.

Demonstrating the timeless nature of homosexual desire, Mann turns from myths of Grecian cities to modern urban vices. Aschenbach attends an evening recital. He catches Tadzio seeking him out and is struck with a "vertiginous sense of triumph and horror." Not knowing what to do next, he almost resents Tadzio for obliging him to act. His attention is diverted by the leading performer, a grotesque comedian. Another redhead, another foreigner—a Neapolitan in Venice—this obscene figure is "half pimp, half comedian, brutal, blunt, a bad character, and wildly entertaining." We quickly learn what he represents.

The next day, an English travel agent explains to Aschenbach the cholera epidemic's trajectory. From the Ganges delta he had fantasized in Munich, the disease traveled throughout Asia, up to Moscow, was rerouted to Naples, where it was easily transmitted through "a breakdown of moral standards." Venice has been invaded by forms of "professional vice" normally found only in southern Italy, home of the red-headed comedian, and eastern countries. The vice is most likely homosexual prostitution: this description may allude to the temptations Mann perceived in Naples when he was twenty. (Thirteen years after *Death in Venice*, he uses the same formulation to describe an influx of homosexual activity in Paris.) In a terrible yoking of symbols, the exalted love he feels for Tadzio is inextricably bound up with venereal infections, as Aschenbach becomes a highbrow john teased by his little Polish tramp.

Only now does he become criminally culpable. Aware that the disease is fatal, he declines to warn Tadzio's mother. He's too far gone to protect himself, either: "someone beside himself disdains the idea of regaining his senses." At this time, having betrayed conventional morality, he has a dream of a sensual apocalypse. In a nighttime setting, accompanied by the plangent reiteration of "ooo"-ended shrieks, a wild congregation pays obeisance to "the stranger-god."

There is an obscene synesthesia, utilizing all of the story's sensuous details. Phallic symbols are everywhere; "the acid stench of goats" prepares the way for a huge, "obscene symbol." Hairy men, smooth-skinned boys, and shrieking women fondling snakes prostrate themselves. Celebrants of a black mass, they roll before the altar, foam at the mouth, lick blood from their limbs, and indulge in "an orgy of promiscuous embraces." Previously *Death in Venice* has consecrated a chaste, impossible love. This nightmare liberates the sexuality that can no longer be idealized in myth.

Mann allows Aschenbach to analyze his nightmare while he dreams it. Like some patient of Freud or Jung, he realizes that all the delirious worshipers are "himself." The Great Joy of Felix Krull turned masturbation into a kind of seminar involving high and low culture. Aschenbach's nightmare congregates a universe populated solely by manifestations of his desire. (Even at his most solipsistic, the Mannian persona is compelled to represent.)

For the last time, Mann modulates his tone. First, Aschenbach's vice is rendered harmless; word of the cholera epidemic is out, though Tadzio's mother chooses to remain in Venice. No longer monstrous, Aschenbach becomes frivolous, banal. "Like any lover," he seeks to please, and so he winds up at the barber. After a series of commercial blandishments that have not dated—let cosmetics "restore your natural color"—the barber applies two kinds of toilet water and rouges his lips. The man who regarded himself in a mirror and saw dignity incarnate now beholds "a younger man looking back at him." The obsequious barber assures him, "Now the signor can fall in love." He's become the repulsive, shipboard queen: the irony is glaring, and by now gratuitous.

One day he follows Tadzio, drunk with excitement, because the boy won't give him away. After eating some rotten strawberries, he stops to nap on the steps of a dilapidated square. Mann regards this latest image: the literary model of schoolboys, a man "who had outgrown the ironic pose" to become the establishment's ideal, is a physical wreck, nodding with his eyelids closed, droning a romantic gibberish compounded of dream logic and classical verse.

In this dream Phaedrus is warned, "The magisterial poise [*Meisterhaltung*] of our style is a foolish joke." We can't be trusted, "we are like women . . . debauched adventurers of the emotions." Artists possess an "inborn tendency toward the abyss," and their knowledge "sympathizes with the abyss, is the abyss." What's more, there is no superior, neoclassical alternative. Form and a reborn naïvete still lead to "intoxication and lust." Eros, our companion in the pursuit of beauty, rapidly becomes our *"Führer,"* inspiring our art and snatching our soul. "We writers cannot overcome the self, we can only waste it in shame."

A few days later, Aschenbach, sickly and filled with a nameless dread, makes his last trip from the Hôtel des Bains to the beach. Tadzio's family is finally preparing to leave, but he is allowed one more glimpse of his beloved. While it occurs, an "apparently abandoned camera" rests on the beach, unmanned, so no human photographer will capture the hallucinatory gleam of his last moments. He sees a final erotic combat between Tadzio and Jaschiu, their bodies twitching convulsively. Tadzio wanders off, ignoring his friend's pleas, and strolls gracefully into the water. Then, "as if he were compelled by a sudden memory"—a wonderful reminder of the routine he and Aschenbach have invented—he turns to view his lover. Even as Aschenbach had invisibly embraced him, Tadzio removes his hand from his hip and points outward to another invisible communion, "an immensity of richest expectation." No assignation ever promised such a mythic and metaphysical release. "And as so often, he set out to follow him." This final stroke is Mann's cruelest, for the sexual prowl is revealed as a death trek. (In her translation, Lowe-Porter simply removes these words, a curious deletion, as if the idea of a pederastic excursion into death upset her. Likewise when Jaschiu kisses his "beautiful companion" Tadzio, she drops the adjective, thereby muting the adolescent Eros.)

Aschenbach collapses. Minutes pass before anyone comes to assist him; he is, as always, solitary. But death restores him to his fame. The shocked world that learns "the news of his death" recalls us to the sphere of politics and publicity, and to the multiple ironies of representation.

Mann spent the year between July 1911 and July 1912 writing *Death in Venice*. By December, he confided to Heinrich that he was having trouble with the ending—one might wish that he'd found another—and Erika claims that the work was submitted only at Katia's insistence. But Mann realized quickly that, as the Bible says, he'd dug down deep and found pure gold. He'd written something "extremely successful," even if he'd later have to dissociate himself from the work's plummy style and its transparently homosexual sympathies. On March 24, 1913, for instance, he wrote Boy-Ed that the story shocked him, too, particularly its elegance. If such craft was possible, Germany must really be a decadent country—and "perhaps a war is needed." The teller was treating himself as a specimen in order to distance his public persona from his tale.

Death in Venice was published in the October and November 1912 numbers of *Die Neue Rundschau*, and in book form in February 1913. The response was immediate and overwhelming. It was clearly Mann's greatest success since *Buddenbrooks*. During Mann's lifetime it would appear in twenty countries, in thirty-seven editions. The history of its reception comprises an astonishing chapter of sexual politics. Although a certain public has never had trouble with the text, it rapidly acquired an intellectual patina that overwhelmed the affair that comprises its very heart. *Death in Venice* has been treated as purest symbol—to paraphrase Mann, a treatise whose subject is a matter of indifference.

Thus the fact that Mann had sympathetically depicted a homosexual was dismissed as irrelevant. Stefan Kanfer in *Time* condemned Visconti's film version because it emphasized the story's homosexuality, when it was no more about something that disreputable than *Metamorphosis* was about entomology. In the late 1940s, Leslie Fiedler wrote unsympathetically of the work, begrudging some meager praise for Mann's exposure of the crippling neuroses of homosexuality. (With the years, Fiedler has apparently mellowed; in 1977, he hailed Mann as the prophet of a myth he found attractive, the Dirty Old Man. Apparently, one such guy will tolerate another.) As recently as 1989, a veteran scholar declared any emphasis on homosexuality "superficial." Better to contemplate the metaphysical implications than the sordid reality.

More sophisticated critics have been troubled by the lines Mann included in an epic poem, "Song of the Little Child," he wrote to commemorate the birth in 1918 of his youngest daughter, Elisabeth.

Do you remember? A higher intoxication, amazing
Passionate feelings once visited you as well, and they cast you
Down, your brow in your hands. To hymnic impulse your spirit
Rose, amid tears your struggling mind pressed upward
Into song. But unhappily things stayed just as they had been;
For there began a process of sobering, cooling, and mastering—
See, what came of your *drunken song*? An *ethical fable*!

Now, if one can bypass the remarkable expression of homosexual memories in a poem addressed to one's infant daughter—perhaps a routine event
in a family where Katia encouraged the story's publication—the lines of
this poem remain problematic. For while Mann asserts his professional role,
"sobering, cooling, and mastering" the elements of composition, he also
seems to regret that "things stayed just as they had been." If the cold hand
of convention forced him to tame his drunken song, then *Death in Venice*
can be read as a muffled plea for emancipation. At the very least, a drunken
song offers an alternative to the extremes of chaste sublimation and insane
orgy.

About such possibilities, three of Mann's best readers disagree. The
senior figure, Erich Heller, is uncomfortable with anything resembling liberalism on Mann's part: he particularly deplores the unabashed politics of
Mann's late years. Though Heller is extremely sensitive to the homoerotic
currents in Mann's work, he seems to prefer that they remain a trade secret.
He's disturbed by the diary's revelations; the work's implications are clear
enough. Apparently he fears that Mann's admissions of homosexual desire
will place him in some army of gay liberationists, further politicizing a
writer whom he prefers to honor for his "conservative imagination."

In his diary of January 26, 1951, Mann was outraged by Heller's attempts to give him such an imagination and to demean his more radical
statements as "trivial." (Had Heller lived to read the later diaries, he would
have been mortified not so much by their revelations as by their liberated
tone: "Erika finds [*Felix Krull*] homosexual. So be it.")

T. J. Reed, a brilliant observer of Mann's literary method, admires
Mann's liberal development. He views Aschenbach's sublimation as unfortunate, and, drawing on Mann's work notes, makes a case for the drunken
song. David Luke is one of Mann's finest translators. Based on his exceptional attention to the complexities of Mann's prose, he argues that *Death
in Venice* merges "drunken song and ethical fable." Mann would probably
concur.

In a Mannian—or Jamesian—comedy, the author's representation by others became the subject of controversy. Benjamin Britten's opera *Death in Venice* is more about pederasty than philosophy: one production made Tadzio a symbol of AIDS.

Whatever the quality of Britten's music, his understanding of Mann was textually informed. Yet objections arose from conservative homosexuals like Allan Bloom or Heller, who preferred their author closeted. (Bloom's reported death from AIDS, coming after his attacks on the gay movement's "misuse" of Mann, wreaks of Mannian irony.)

Other scholars applied therapeutic dicta to Aschenbach's condition. In the 1930s Harry Slochower, a Marxist turned Freudian, discovered in the novella a case of "esthetic onanism," in which Aschenbach the artist fell in love with his own creation. (Was it ever otherwise? Would Slochower have been so judgmental if Tadzio were a girl?) Fifty years later a sociologist, Harvey Goldman, argued that *Death in Venice* revealed less about homosexuality than about vocational failure. These critics ignored what many readers saw at once. Tadzio, the summoner, sets the tone; after the mating dance begins, Aschenbach's vocation is irrelevant.

Yet other critics find implausible Aschenbach's love for the Polish boy; if they countenance the pederasty, they remain uncharmed by this Apollo with decaying teeth. Mann later joked while praising a comely youth that the planet was filled with equally agreeable fellows. And so what? One is all it takes. The drama lies in the emotion, what in *Doctor Faustus* he called the baring of a wound. That Aschenbach could be destroyed by passion still terrifies the bourgeois public.

Harvey Goldman also contends that Aschenbach "lives only in symbols" and that his misplaced devotion to abstract principles "prevents the called person from facing others and self truly." This might be valid in group therapy, but Aschenbach can hardly face his love "truly" if he doesn't want to be arrested. Mann's art conveys all the obstacles to consummation, of which Aschenbach's pompous credo is among the least inhibiting.

A modern reader may well be disheartened by the imposition of moral criteria, and downright bored by the misbegotten classicism, neo- or otherwise. Yet, whether Apollonian fable or Dionysian song, *Death in Venice* comprised a revolutionary breakthrough in the expression of gay desire. Mann was seldom convincing in his depiction of heterosexual love. But his own passions were not etiolated. Indeed, *Death in Venice* does more than evoke a pederastic episode; it constitutes a virtual Baedeker's guide to homosexual love.

Consider what Mann introduced as literary subjects. He captured the

complex social compact inherent in "cruising." The activity allows Aschenbach entree into a world that merges ages and nationalities, a gay underground where all cultural hierarchies topple. Aschenbach's magisterial past
has no bearing on his new role; he's complicit with clowns, barbers, and
pimps.

Since *Tonio Kröger*, Mann had dramatized the intellectual, cultural, and
social gaps between lover and beloved. Swann might be mystified that he
wasted his affections on Odette, a woman who was not his style. But Mann
suggests that homosexual passion is inherently asymmetrical, linking the
wise and ugly with the beautiful dummies. Had anyone before him captured
the homosexual's need to *justify* himself? Mann observes the signals and
translates the codes that reveal gay men to each other. (He also indulges
in his own codes—e.g., "beauty" in his story always means male beauty.)
But he also conveys a self-hatred which obliges Aschenbach to despise himself. It is not only social convention that turns the song to fable, or makes
a brief fascination morbid.

At first Mann seemed to endorse a symbolic reading. In September 1915
he thanks Paul Amann for an intelligent critique of the novella: "I am
scarcely a competent interpreter by now; I have almost forgotten the work."
He believes himself universally misunderstood. What he offered as "caricature" was taken as confession. The cultural Hellenism was a literary trope;
the work's tendency was Protestant. "When I deal with an artist or even a
master, I do not mean 'me.' I am not asserting that I am a master. . . . I
am merely saying that I know something about the nature of the artist and
master." Nietzsche taught him to understand art by making it. "When I
examine myself closely I realize that this and this only has been the purpose
of my 'creativity,' to acquire the sensibility of the masters. It has been a
game, just as I played 'prince' as a boy in order to acquire the princely
sensibility." In order to dissociate himself from Aschenbach, he must become the imposter Krull.

This meant exploiting the one Mannian trait absent from *Death in
Venice*: humor. A hilarious coda surreptitiously appeared twenty-five years
later in *The Beloved Returns*. Mann believed that novel contained "more of
love and erotic union" than his earlier works, albeit in a spirit of light-
hearted parody, tonally disjunct from either *Death in Venice* or his literary
essays.

In a flagrant act of identification, he rewrites Goethe's lines and attributes his own projects to the poet. The parody reaches its zenith when

Goethe fantasizes a procession of mythological figures, explicitly not "wild and repulsive": Aschenbach's nightmare become a gorgeous dream. Leading the ensemble is a chariot driven by "a perfect cupid of a boy," a "lovely lad" in thrall to King Pluto, god of riches and the underworld. This youth plays the symbolic role of Poetry: he is a pint-sized emblem of aesthetic inspiration, complete with rings on his fingers and beads in his hair. Lest one miss this spoof of Mann's novella, Goethe adds that "the relation between poesy and riches, giving and spending—calls up a picture of Venice."

Mann then surpasses himself by assigning to Pluto an exhilarating blasphemy: "This is my beloved son, in whom I am well pleased," God's words after John baptizes Jesus. (God himself behaves like a petulant lover in *Joseph and His Brothers*.) While his scandalized son, August, fidgets, Goethe imagines "tongues of fire" springing up at the charioteer's behest, an orgy of glossalalia ignited by Phaedrus. Improvising on the blasphemy, he envisions a Father, Son, and Holy Ghost trailed by the great god Pan, "prick-eared fauns and shrunk-legged satyrs." The ecumenical orgy concludes with his words "If you don't have a sense of humor, I'm not the man for you."

This antinomian riff simultaneously undercuts biblical piety and Mannian pathos. Aschenbach's tragedy was the product of a thirty-six-year-old; but Goethe's spirit of parody *and* his adoration of youth embody the "wisdom" of old age. Thus Mann gives his saddest story a devastating critique, ending with a slap at the prissy August and his "modish scruples."

Mann's last word on the issues he raised in *Death in Venice* was composed when he was seventy-five. His critical essay "Michelangelo's Erotic Poetry" expresses the same emotional tensions and employs cultural analogies—including references to Plato's *Phaedrus*—for similar purposes. But with the passage of forty years, his views had grown far more benign.

Mann still argued that the artist's knowledge of love was limited to *Sehnsucht*. Michelangelo is old and ashamed of his body. Those he loves, men and women, are young and beautiful. Mann contemplates a Michelangelo still sexually aflame at seventy; "die Lende gespannt," Michelangelo moans—"the groin leaped up." Like Mann, the friend of presidents (or Aschenbach, the nation's cultural arbiter), he is a political figure, indebted to the Medicis. But his utterances are similar to the outcast Platen's. Even in Italy, his is the "exile's complaint"; he's a tourist in his homeland.

His quest for perfection leaves him constantly depressed; the only source of his productivity is a "godlike eroticism" manifested in his "adoration of pictorial beauty." He has the "hopeless addiction of genius," the joy, long after age has rendered it ridiculous, in a "beautiful youth or gorgeous woman." But the god he serves is cruel; it keeps sending new temptations. "How could I lose myself again?" Michelangelo complains. His worship is focused on the face, most particularly the eyes. In a "classic example of Platonic eroticism," he worships the "immortal soul irradiating the body."

But the leaping groin always threatens the established order. Ecstasy robs Michelangelo of his good sense; like all morganatic lovers, he can waste his affections on a worthless object: "ounce for ounce, she's not worth much." He spends a decade adoring the youth Cavalieri ("naturally he has beautiful eyes"). Observing Michelangelo as he gazes upon his beloved, Mann offers the optimistic alternative implicit in *Death in Venice*. "Hopefully the boy was amiable and had an idea of the honor." Like Aschenbach on the beach, Michelangelo has a fleeting sense that Cavalieri's spirit "reciprocates." But it's no matter if he doesn't. "For him, in the Platonic way, the god is in the loving and not in being loved. Being loved is only the vehicle of divine enthusiasm." The grammar is deliberate: the beloved is passive; all virile activity is initiated by the lover.

Michelangelo's idea of eroticism seems to have been Mann's as early as 1911 (and may have been prefigured in *Die Geliebten*). The love of youth for age is a meager compound of "pity and generosity." But age's triumph resides in visual worship. So when his mistress enters a convent, Michelangelo asks her to pray that God will make "his ugly body all eyes." He promises a fulfillment in time. Work will "conquer death"; in a thousand years, his art will serve as a witness to "your beauty and my ugliness and that I was not a fool to love you."

The ancient Michelangelo is, like Aschenbach / Mann, drawn to the androgynous, the union of *"männlich und weiblich."* Boldly alluding to his own career, Mann says of the artist that "none of his works fully expresses his eroticism." He scolds Michelangelo for his "melancholy rhetoric." The language, if you will, of ethical fable leads the painter to accuse love of "tormenting his soul." But he is "never wiser" than when he admits his vulnerability: "You expect to seduce me when I can defend myself so poorly." His late genius "glows with sensuality" and, thrillingly potent, produces "super-manly, super-human work." St. Peter's Basilica was built only because Cavalieri's "beautiful lips" requested it. Obeying his lover's command is Michelangelo's consummation: "In your breath I form my work." Michelangelo's religious art is metaphorically inseminated by a visual act of homosexual desire. The drunken song becomes an ethical fable.

So this coda to *Death in Venice* provides a solution to the problem Mann posed in the *"Gesang vom Kindchen."* Aschenbach died for love. Michelangelo lives for it. Admittedly his bliss is remote and austere, perhaps the only kind Mann could imagine. His love is barely spoken, unreciprocated, but it ennobles him.

Physical beauty alone inspires Michelangelo; politics, history, religion, merely provide the occasion. T. J. Reed quotes this work note for *Death in Venice*: "A man can only share in art if Eros instructs him. His art too was a sober service in the temple of Thespiae [a temple to Eros mentioned in Plutarch's *Erotikos*]. Eros was always in him. Tadzio was always his king. His love of fame was Eros too." Although the final composition of *Death in Venice* provides a darker view of art and Eros, these work notes exactly prefigure the conclusion of the Michelangelo essay. Mann always insisted he moved slowly. He may have needed four decades to finally declare himself.

If the 1950 essay connects so gracefully with the 1911 story, there may be a biographical explanation. Both visions of the artist were inspired by Mann's unspoken love for a handsome youth. In 1911 it was an aristocratic Pole. But in 1950, the night before he composed his essay, Mann dined in the restaurant of a Zurich hotel and became smitten with the waiter, Franz Westermeier. In 1911, Mann wrote for himself that the "love of fame was Eros too." In 1950, in his diaries, recalling his newest love, Mann wrote, "World renown is wonderful but it cannot compare with the smile in his eyes."

During the season of Franzl, Mann began to speak more confidently about homosexual passion. In the fall of 1950 he read "The Hitchhiker," Donald Windham's story about a gay pickup. The tale charmed him. He congratulated Windham on the ways his "surprising little story poeticizes with serene composure the naïveté of the flesh and its warmth." That the lifetime advocate of *Haltung* would discover "composure" in soft porn was a "reborn ingenuousness" vouchsafed in extreme old age. Aschenbach should have been so lucky.

In an irony that would have amused Mann, an echo of his most famous story would resound in the last piece he wrote. His tribute to *Billy Budd* ends with ecstatic praise of the sailor's ascension to the gallows, above him a rising sun, below the crew members "who all love their Billy." Tadzio resembles Ganymede; Billy, according to Melville, "God's lamb." No matter, the American sailor, like the Polish aristocrat, beckons his lovers to a

"World renown cannot compare
to the smile in his eyes."
Franz Westermeier, 1950

radiant and "atoning" death. "Oh could I have written that," declared the eighty-year-old Mann.

T hey comprised a peculiar trio of vacationers, the three Manns: Katia, often sickly; Thomas, preoccupied with a Polish youth; and Heinrich, whose relations with Katia remained formal, and with Thomas, strained. This family drama never became a Mann subject, though it's as vivid as Aschenbach's interlude. Mann had depicted a scholarly, reticent, but finally ecstatic lover. Had he also given us the scholar's brother, and—even more—his wife, he would have gone where no writer has, before or after *Death in Venice*. Like everything he wrote, the story's interest extended to all that was known and remained unsaid.

Neither Henrich nor Katia could fail to see certain resemblances between Mann and Aschenbach. Mann credits his hero with works he had previously contemplated and rejected composing. These include *Maja*, the novel that grew out of his affair with Paul Ehrenberg, and "A Study in

Abjection," an attack on the "indecent games" he had previously associated with Kerr, Lessing, and—at least in 1908—Heinrich. In the latter Aschenbach had shown "a whole younger generation" the possibility of "moral resolution." But "will and tenacity" rather than "strength and stamina" had enabled him to "hold out for years under the pressure of one and the same work."

In 1913 Heinrich reviewed the novella for a Munich journal. Typically, he begins by citing Emile Zola's vision of literature as social history. He stresses that Aschenbach had become identified with the institution he represents, the state. Aschenbach was knighted only after he had outgrown his "gypsy ways and the amoral pursuit of experience." This description may be a sly allusion to a younger man who refused to be a gypsy and condemned his brother's fiction.

There are other telling remarks. Thomas's great dream of a dignified and productive period in his fifties is laid to rest: "A fruitful old age . . . upon which his work and life were aimed" will be "shortened." The reward is purely formal, "the worship of beauty." Aschenbach's "high solitude"— precisely the trait ascribed to the Heinrich figure in *Royal Highness*—will prevent embrace: his will be "a wordless, unfulfilled love."

In this depiction Aschenbach descends to the amoral realm of all the Heinrich novels Thomas deplored, without even the relief of sensual gratification. Heinrich ends his review with a summation of "sweet heat, glorious colors of decay, a fate spun out of lust and fear, a suppressed breath filled with the voices of wild birds and sweet human form, resounding in death, this death in Venice," that could have sprung from *The Goddesses*: the voluptuously febrile style that had driven Thomas to despair now applied to his own condition.

Heinrich comes close to celebrating Aschenbach's infatuation with "the boy he desires." Despite everything, "should he regret? The question is never asked." With these words Thomas Mann's closest reader concludes that *Death in Venice* is neither allegorical nor moralistic, that it fully accepts the sudden rush of desire, ignoring the cost.* It is a superbly generous, nonjudgmental assessment, but it conceals a stinger. With his good Mannian eye, Heinrich saw the profoundly unhappy implication of Thomas's work: by the time we know what—or whom—we want, he has escaped our grasp. Locked grip or open arms, Aschenbach will never embrace. It was as if Heinrich too were beckoning an old age of despair, not of premature death but of a lingering death-in-life.

---

* Hedwig Dohm also praised the story in a Berlin newspaper. Is it too much to see the eighty-year-old feminist actually approving Thomas's homosexuality?

5

MAKE WAR, NOT LOVE

Not until he was back home in Bad Tölz could Mann transform his fascination with the Polish youth into literature. Paradoxically, a familiar setting allowed him to express his wildest fantasies. Some portion of the confusion he felt in his return to normal life is evident in an essay he composed that summer on the French-born Adalbert von Chamisso, the author of a favorite schoolboy text, *Peter Schlemihls wundersame Geschichte*. Like Fontane, the descendant of Huguenots, Chamisso symbolizes a pan-European spirit; he provides an antidote to the post-Wagnerian obsessions with "blood and race." As Mann tells it, his story provides a rational inoculation against Aschenbach's disease.

Mann selects the biographical details that suit his mood. "A tall, mild man with . . . noble, almost beautiful features," Chamisso became a world traveler, "capable of friendship with children and savages," and cultivated a special relation with a South Seas Indian, Kadu, whom he considered one of the great loves of his life. (Over a decade before Lawrence's *Studies in Classic American Literature* drew attention to Melville's infatuation with exotic males, Mann noted the phenomenon.)

Chamisso's greatest creation, Peter Schlemihl, not the blunderbuss his name suggests, is a man robbed of his shadow. This leaves him defenseless before "the pity of women, the mockery of the young, the scorn of grown men, especially the portly ones, 'who themselves cast a good broad shadow.'" Since Mann believed that none of these groups truly saw him, he found an endearing pathos in the diminished Schlemihl.

But Chamisso gave up his childish fancy. He got happily married and became a model citizen. Mann ends the essay: "It is the old story. Werther shot himself, but Goethe remained alive" (the proper nouns could be changed to "Aschenbach" and "Mann"). "Chamisso, after producing a book from his sufferings, hastened to outgrow his problem-child phase. He settles down, becomes the father of a family and an academic master of his craft. Only the eternal bohemians find that boring."

In "At the Prophet's," Mann addressed similar remarks to his mother-in-law. Now he addressed the world—and himself: "One cannot be interesting forever. Either you die of your interestingness, or you become a master." In Venice, you can be interesting; at home, stick to your work, masterful but dull. He implies that the only way to escape Aschenbach's fate is via a dreary middle age.

Mann increasingly measured his development by the newest bohemian generation. In 1912, he wrote a young man that his work evoked experiences he had once "struggled through, or to put it less heroically, *got* through. . . . Just think: I'm nearly thirty-seven! These days people at that age begin to feel academic inclinations. . . . Well, don't think I'm quite fossilized yet."

This invidious need to distinguish himself from younger people while asserting his continued significance and his enduring youthfulness flashes through Mann's writing in the next few years. It was heightened by his conflicts with Heinrich. The latter had become a greater success with the bohemian young than with their bourgeois parents. Mann knew that a writer must cultivate the next generation if he intends to last.

There were occasional periods of cooperation. In November 1911, they attended the Munich premiere of Heinrich's play *The Actress*, based on the life of their ill-fated sister. Others found the composition of the play, much less Heinrich's close participation in its staging, an act of callous exploitation. But the brothers thought it an act of family solidarity; Thomas wrote Heinrich that Carla would have approved. She who had envied the ability to transform life into art had provided a model, albeit at a frightful cost. (During this period, the brothers exchanged professional tips on the treatment of military routine; Heinrich was working on *Der Untertan*, Thomas on Felix Krull's attempts to dodge the draft. He exhibited a sadomasochistic nostalgia: the physical circumstances were lousy, but he had enjoyed an "inner freedom" impossible for a civilian to understand. He would expand on this idea during the next years.)

Meanwhile Katia remained sickly. In September 1911 she took a cure accompanied by her parents. From March to September 1912, she was hospitalized at the forest sanitarium of Dr. Jessen in Davos, following an attack of tuberculosis (catarrh of the tip of the lung). In May and June

1912 Mann spent three weeks with her there. The altitude made him temporarily feverish, and the director, "smiling with an eye to profit," suggested he prolong his stay. In *The Magic Mountain*, Hans Castorp accepts
the invitation. Mann escaped, but he had received the inspiration for his
next major novel. Typically it was conceived as a short story, "another brief
interlude" to *Felix Krull*, and "as a satyr play to the tragic novella of decay
just finished."

For the next six months, his mother managed the country house at Bad
Tölz while he finished that novella. So it was as a grass widower that Mann
first read his homoerotic tale to a gathering of friends. Despite his risqué
subject, Mann had acquired such prominence that he was appointed a member of the Munich censorship council. He became quickly embroiled in
attempts to censor *Franziska*, a play by Frank Wedekind—whose *Spring's
Awakening* had been a favorite of his youth. Three years earlier, Wedekind
had applauded *Fiorenza*'s "sublime, brilliant drama," a minority opinion for
which Mann had been grateful. In December 1912, he wrote Wedekind a
rather stuffy letter to the effect that his role was "to warn the superinten-
dents of public order against infringing on works of literary status." In
other words, dear Herr Wedekind, I'm on your side. Unfortunately the
police commissioner "did not feel that he could accept my recommenda-
tion." But, Mann added, the dialogue in question might well be sacrificed.
Hadn't he observed Wedekind unnerved by the audience's inappropriate
laughter? (Wedekind must have felt spied upon.)

The idea of *Venice*'s author serving as a guardian of public morals was
risible. Perhaps Mann was directing toward the elder Wedekind his anger
at impertinent younger writers. But in April 1913, he reasserted the liberal
positions of "Pornography and Eroticism." When Wedekind's "Lulu" plays
were subjected to editorial censorship, Mann again wrote the police commissioner. This time he argued that the drama was no "worthless piece of
hackwork aimed at sensationalism, sensual titillation, and glorification of
vice, but a modern work of art," widely hailed for its "profundity, seriousness, and value." Mann traced an encouraging development. A 1904 production had created a near riot; a 1910 performance was a triumph.
Wedekind's public had also expanded; it now included both the "superior"
haut-bourgeoisie and the middle-class tourists who keep theaters open. Very
shrewdly, Mann combined an aesthetic defense with a commercial appeal.

Apparently Wedekind had not forgiven him. Mann confided that his
defense was genuinely disinterested: "I have not the slightest personal reason for advocating Herr Wedekind's cause. Ever since I joined the board,
he has behaved with extreme hostility and has irresponsibly and indeed

insanely picked quarrels with me." But even disagreeable men can make "significant cultural contributions."

A comedy of errors ensued. According to a letter from Mann to Kurt Martens, "radical loudmouths"—mostly Jewish left-wingers—took his membership on the board as " 'the most important question facing writers today!' . . . That is the limit." He decided to resign from the board—and from the League of German Writers; to hell with the lefties, to hell with the Establishment. "So let there be an end of my social activity and the pretty fiction of solidarity among writers."

As it was, by resigning, Mann solidified his reputation, at least with Wedekind. He wrote the playwright on May 29 that a "bourgeois element"—of which he was not ashamed—had persuaded the authorities to place a "crude confidence" in him. He had chosen to "mediate politically between genius and authority," as if he, and not only Felix Krull, were a little Hermes, the artist's envoy. Well, he hadn't succeeded, but since their friendship had resumed, he felt content to remain "without any official position whatsoever." The Mann and Wedekind families grew very close, and the playwright's daughter, Pamela, would become an intimate of Klaus and Erika.

His best friendships were with younger men. In February 1913 Ernst Bertram visited him at Bad Tölz, their first private meeting. Shortly before, while in Berlin, he had met Hans Reisiger, a Silesian law student who had switched to journalism. While Bertram stood at the fringes of the George circle, Reisiger was a friend of Gerhart Hauptmann's: Mann met him first at the home of Samuel Fischer, his and Hauptmann's publisher. Where Bertram personified high seriousness, Reisiger was all laughs. With the scholar, Mann could discuss Nietzsche, Wagner, and Schopenhauer, "the cross, death, and the grave." With the journalist, he could play cards, tell jokes, and—especially after the war—discuss liberal politics.

Through Fischer he made another friend. In the summer of 1913 the publisher decided that Mann deserved a biographer. Mann recommended Julius Bab, a Berlin Jewish critic, with whom he shared many interesting letters and who would eventually join him in exile. "You," he told Bab on August 31, could write about "my restless hero-type," a sign that he was itching for some kind of change.

He needed these friends since his enemies had expanded to include a generation of Young Turks who saw him as aligned with the police. His old foes remained. In January the indefatigable Kerr had demolished a Berlin production of *Fiorenza*, directed by Reinhardt, calling it a "poisonous howling," filled with a "vindictive bloodthirstiness" that revealed to a perceptive viewer Mann's true nature. Whatever small talent this ominous figure possessed Kerr ascribed to his "thick-skinned *Sitzfleisch*." He particularly derided Fiore, the play's heroine, as the creation of a "philologist" not a lover.

Meanwhile, reactionaries linked him to his radical brother; by 1913, they had identified him once more as a Jew. Mann felt rudderless. That September he wrote with great sympathy about a young novelist who had recently died.

The occasion was a foreword to *Night and Day*, Erich von Mendelssohn's novel of school days and first love. Mann most admires the recollections of schoolboy cruelty. Another critic had argued that such behavior is a necessary preparation for manhood. He continued in the manner of good old boys the world round, "Anyone who doesn't laugh to tears over this 'cruelty' is a hopeless misanthrope." Mann replies, "Then I'm a hopeless misanthrope." He explains that while he loves Kipling's *Jungle Book*, he can't stomach the sadistic games of Stalky and company. (In 1917, he would discern "an artistry of cruelty, a cold, nervous and intellectual cult of the hideous" in the literature of England, France, and America.)

How then did Mann wind up mimicking the strident cadences of Junkers and Philistines? A clue lies in the sense of helplessness he felt during the prewar days. On November 8, 1913, he wrote Heinrich one of his most anguished letters. Everything political confused him: "The whole misery of our time and our fatherland is on one's shoulders," as Heinrich had predicted in his novels. "I am happier about your work than mine. Morally, you are better off than I am." While the older brother had acquired an ideology, Thomas confessed "an inability to orient myself politically or spiritually as you have done. . . . My whole concern is with decadence and that, of course, hinders me from being interested in progress."

Thomas feared himself not yet forty and already "burned out. Probably I should never have become a writer. *Buddenbrooks* is a bourgeois book and has no more meaning for the twentieth century. *Tonio Kröger* is simply lachrymose, *Royal Highness* a work of vanity, *Death in Venice* half-educated and wrongheaded." (His critics could not put matters more succinctly.) He realized that he had placed Heinrich in a hopeless position. "That I write like this to you is tactless, because you can't really answer. But since it had to be written, please forgive me."

Heinrich responded so quickly to Thomas's distraught letter that his brother was overwhelmed. Once again the oldest had set things right. Gratitude inspired him to contemplate a book about their lives. It would be a sequel to *Buddenbrooks*: "We're worth it. All five of us." (In the midst of all his other worries, Mann still had the familiar satisfactions of male beauty.

On June 27, 1914, he wrote Ludwig von Hofmann that during the previous winter he "fell madly in love" with his painting of naked youths. His remark a year later that, among other things, militarism comprehended pederasty may allude to his purchase of *The Spring*.)

Both brothers had financial problems. On February 17, 1912, Thomas asked Heinrich to begin repaying loans he had made some years before. Katia's annuity had been reduced; he had made unwise loans; paying the rent seemed impossible. Heinrich repaid a sum at once. In his depressed letter of November 11, 1913, Thomas mentions a seventy thousand–mark mortgage looming over an income of ten thousand marks—and a not incidental "sympathy with death."

At thirty-nine, Mann was demoralized by Katia's illnesses, his alienation from the "interesting" young writers, his fear that his career was a string of artistic failures. The Tin Soldier had specialized in holding fast; now he needed to break out and through. War provided the chance. Like many members of his generation, Mann rallied to the German effort. His initial public utterances were uninflected, almost shrill: he called them "journalism," not "essays."

The Mann family witnessed two marriages. On August 1, 1914, shortly after he was called up for military service, the twenty-four-year-old Victor married a nineteen-year-old Magdalena Kilian. Eleven days later, the forty-three-year-old Heinrich married Maria Kanová, a twenty-eight-year-old Czech Jewish actress, who resembled Carla, and had played the leading role in *The Actress*. She would bear his only child, Leonie ("Goschi"), two years later. Their marriage ended legally in 1930; he had left "Mimi" some years earlier. But she remained loyal to him; during the first years of exile she returned to Prague, transporting his library with her. She was later interned at Theresienstadt and died shortly after her release. Victor's marriage lasted until his death, and *his* wife became a Nazi. The fates of these two sisters-in-law comprised a metaphor for the collapse of German society.

By August 7, 1914, Mann anticipated that the war would ruin him. On September 13 he announced that Katia's allowance had been cut in half. Land values had plummeted, and his country house at Bad Tölz was "unsalable." Yet he was exhilarated by the vision of chaos, a national trial by fire. If ruin lay ahead, "we'll live through the wildest things," he wrote on September 18. Still, couldn't Heinrich help just a little bit? Heinrich replied that his circumstances were even bleaker. Without "Mama's allowance" he couldn't make it at all; and he reckoned that the war would destroy whatever small public he now had.

Thomas assured him that the war was "great, fundamentally decent, and in fact stirring." He looked forward to defeating "the vilest police state in the world, Czarist Russia." To his friend Philipp Witkop he admitted that never having experienced a war, he couldn't anticipate its epic thrills. He was grateful for the lesson. Why, if people lost their belief in war, they'd stop believing in all the institutions that make them "decent."

By the winter of 1914 Heinrich was outnumbered. Without Carla, he stood alone against his mother, Thomas, and Lula. Thomas was now the undisputed head of the family. His need to defend German honor intersected with his victory in the sibling battle.

Very few writers were immune to patriotic slogans. As Mann wrote Richard Dehmel, a volunteer at the age of fifty-one, he felt no shame for his fellow hawks. They shared a "joyful curiosity" about the future. The war would produce "a stronger, freer, happier German soul."

Overflowing with military spirit, Mann wished Dehmel "a strangely lovely Christmas under such harsh circumstances." This was exactly the "vindictive bloodthirstiness" Alfred Kerr had denounced—except that, for the moment, it was shared by Kerr and almost everyone who mattered but Heinrich.

Sometime during the first months, a bitter quarrel occurred. According to Golo, Mimi Mann said that her husband had spoken "gently in full control of himself, 'Don't you know that Germany will lose the war, that the German ruling classes have the chief responsibility, and that the inevitable result will be the fall of the monarchy' and TM indignantly stormed out." The brothers wouldn't speak again for almost ten years. Katia's brother, Klaus Pringsheim, also turned against the war, and suggested the return of Alsace-Lorraine to France. Katia came to share her brother's antimilitarism. But no other opponent irked Thomas like Heinrich.

In January 1914, Mann had moved into a new house at Poschingerstrasse 1, facing the Isar River. This house, where they lived from 1914 to 1933, was closer to the lines of Lübeck than to the baroque display of the Pringsheim palace. It incorporated English elements with a Dutch double-hipped roof and a bayed section on the first two floors; a small decorative terrace was topped by a grander one for sunbathing. In Mann's study, light poured in from three directions; next door was a drawing room with a grand piano. This signified haut-bourgeois living, though not too "haut"; the Pringsheims had *two* grands.

He had overextended himself. That month he wrote Ludwig von Hofmann, whose painting he coveted, "Like a real new German, I live above my income." (The merchant's son could still cut a deal; Hofmann lowered his price.) The housewarming was attended by Heinrich, Professor Pringsheim, Bertram, Heinrich's lawyer, Dr. Maximilian Brantl, and Bruno Frank, a Jewish novelist and playwright, who had been Mann's friend since 1910, would become his next-door neighbor in 1925, and wind up, like Mann, in California. For the moment, his next-door neighbors were the Löhrs and their three daughters, Eva Maria (1901–1968), and the twins Rose-Marie (1907–) and Ilse-Marie (1907–).

He had a new project: the first third of *The Magic Mountain*'s first volume had been written by August. By the time he stopped his initial work on the novel in December 1915, Mann had reached the Hippe section, where the hero, Hans Castorp, recalls his first love for another boy. Many changes occurred after 1919, when he thoroughly revised the opening pages. But the poignant appeal of the stricken warrior, Joachim, and Castorp's divided sexuality were already in place. This special and "secret" pathos would inform Mann's work during the Great War. From the start

LEFT TO RIGHT:
Samuel Fischer, Mann's publisher; Mann; Hans Reisiger, the counter-Bertram; Annette Kolb; and Fischer's daughter, Brigitte Fischer—circa 1920

Munich, Poschinger Strasse 1

he endowed Joachim with the homoerotic lure to which an entire nation, emphatically including Thomas Mann, would succumb.

Mann also had an ally in Bertram who by 1914 had joined the family circle. They played together in a chamber group until work obliged Mann to give up the violin. Sacrificed too was the novel and his other literary projects. Wartime propaganda took precedence over art: as a militant nationalist, Bertram approved.

In September 1914, Mann delivered a harsh attack on the Entente Cordiale, "Thoughts in Wartime" (*"Gedanken im Kriege"*), in which he defended Germany's bellicose actions by comparing them to Frederick the Great's battle for Prussian national identity. War signified Germany's "right to be."

Germany deserves to win because she's more spirited and less intellectual than her enemies; the overloaded German word *Geist* has seldom been so fractured by contradictions. Even more personal is Mann's general take on culture. Who else but he would defend it as potentially anything, "magic, oracle, pederasty"? While joining the nationalist bandwagon, Mann prepared a special place for the hermetic, oracular pederast.

Elaborating on the distinction between Germany and her neighbors,

Mann explained that the Germans preferred "culture" with its more "human content" to "civilization," a frankly political concept. The German soul was "deep"; the enemies were "shallow nations." He added that Germany's peculiar values, "demonic and heroic," would make her seem "repulsive and wild." Just to be different, Mann exulted in the violent impulse; just to be the same, he concerned himself with representation, how Germany appeared on the international stage.

Other Germans would employ culture as a battering ram, evidence of their inherent superiority. Rilke's prose poem *The Cornet: The Manner of Loving and Dying of the Cornet Christopher Rilke* sold a million copies. German soldiers went off to battle with Rilke in their knapsacks. The poet's hero dies a noble, sensual death. Not since Goethe's Werther had a premature demise been rendered so alluring. Clearly Mann was not alone in the morbid fixation on a death-serving culture.

Although Mann's wartime writings exhibit little sympathy for Germany's victims, since Germany demands none for her own, he is never bloodthirsty. As he later observed, it is easy to contemplate battle from an armchair in one's library. He wrote movingly of the death of Katia's twenty-year-old cousin, Andreas Rosenberg, imagined the boy's despair ("for what inner resources could have helped him?") and terror ("as a common soldier in hand-to-hand combat with [Russian] muzhiks"). He also regarded the military system's survival as something "fantastic" in "our civilized world"; his rejection of civilized values was always qualified.

He revealed no enthusiasm for imperialism or colonialism. The Lübeck of his ancestors had not "derived much material advantage from the creation of empire." Capitalism and imperialism, the handmaids of democracy in his view, had ruined the burghers' legacy and turned it bourgeois. In his *Reflections of an Unpolitical Man*, he denies ever indulging in the banal "demand for annexations," usually phrased as " 'we' must not have bled in vain." The paradox he overlooked is that so modest and apolitical a nation should have the right by force of will and fate to dominate the Continent.

He followed this attempt at journalism with a more serious essay, "Frederick and the Great Coalition of 1756," which occupied him until December. It appeared the next month. At his most chauvinistic, Mann still wrote like nobody else. Those same right-wingers who attacked *Royal Highness*'s irreverence toward court life considered "Frederick" a libelous satire. They were not completely wrong.

Who else but Mann would pay attention to Frederick's youthful effeminacy? Or note so carefully the means with which this aggressively non-heterosexual monarch confronted the formidable dowagers Maria Theresa, Elisabeth, and Madame Pompadour, whom he dubbed "the three whores of Europe"? We first see him as "boyish of feature, elegantly built, if rather plump, the nicest little creature in the kingdom": as if Herr Knaak had ascended to the throne. Throughout the essay, he's a figure wracked by ambivalence—as well as gout and diarrhea. He's insufficiently socialized and dies, "burnt out," unmourned, without a clean shirt to his name. Yet the people love *"den alten Fritz"* and his quixotic ways. Like another old fellow, Fontane, his disagreeable personality and inconsistent politics have grown lovable. This is a Frederick who may owe more to the examples of Tonio Kröger, Gustav Aschenbach, and Thomas Mann than to history.

Mann's attempt at patriotic apology is initially playful. "Well, where shall I begin?" he wonders dryly. How best to treat the Seven Years' War now that it has been repeated with virtually the same cast? He slides into his defense of Frederick by acknowledging, at once, the "well-founded mistrust" evoked by this problem child of royalty. Later Mann wonders, "Is it possible to trust him? Probably not." But for Mann—or his enemy Brecht—that's no deficiency. Artists and rulers—Mann's representative men—are usually suspect.

Mann also lists Frederick's real achievements: "He created the common law of the land, a great and bold reform, a model of reason and fair-mindedness." A friend of Voltaire's, he was an advocate of tolerance, an opponent of religious superstition. Admittedly he lacked sympathy for the exhausted laborers who plowed marshes and built canals at his command. But he worked himself hardest, rising at three a.m. (He was not, Mann notes, burdened by conjugal duties—a possible allusion to the months he'd spent without Katia.)

Mann imagines a perverse affair between the misogynistic Prussian and his powerful women rivals. Mann doesn't specifically allude to Frederick's homosexuality. But, in a gossipy aside, he quotes Voltaire's remark that Frederick liked a certain dancer because she had a man's legs. This effeminate youth grew into a man so virile he despised the company of women. From these observations Mann leaps to a remarkable inference. Sexuality determines politics. Was Frederick bad because he didn't love women, or did he dislike them because he was bad? Whatever, Mann is convinced of the connection. The eighteenth century was "the Frenchest of centuries, a woman's century, par excellence, saturated in the perfume of the Eternal Feminine." But Frederick, a precursor of the next century, despised the "atmosphere of French femininity."

If one follows Mann's logic, a distaste for the eighteenth century is tantamount to a rejection of womanly feelings, of heterosexuality itself. Mann's later identification of himself as a child of the nineteenth century, dismayed by the amorphous humanism of the eighteenth and twentieth, is usually read as an assertion of his—temporary—conservatism. But, given his view of politics as sex-linked, it's also an identification with misogynists and homosexuals (not that these two are a natural pair).*

Mann uses his analytic powers to capture the vital contradictions of the king's personality. He employs lesser gifts—rhetoric in the service of propaganda—to bury the opposition. He dismisses all of Prussia's enemies as soft-headed hypocrites. Frederick alone stands above the simplistic distinctions between offensive and defensive. He couldn't disentangle the two ("If I thought my shirt or my skin knew anything of my intentions . . ."), and Mann prefers "to say nothing." Frederick's invasion of Saxony is not lamented. Much later, historians combing the Dresden archives would find evidence of Saxon maneuvering between the contending nations. "She" was no more neutral than the Belgium whose ravaging by German soldiers horrified the world at the very "hour" Mann wrote. Frederick acted correctly, as—in an implication no contemporary reader missed—had Germany in 1914. Saxony and Belgium were duplicitous women: attacking them was a pre-emptive strike. Then and now, "Europe shrieked, as with one voice. It was terrific to hear." Mann is rarely this sarcastic, almost never such a bully.

Later he employs a more interesting device, redolent of both Hegel and Marx, when he acknowledges that Frederick "was not in the right as far as right is a convention, the voice of the majority, the judgment of humanity. His right was the right of a rising power, a problematical, still illegitimate, untested right, which had to be fought for and won." Mann argues with the historian Leopold von Ranke, who asserted that Frederick's "defense" made him the great man of his century. No, says Mann, the defense was really an offensive, "superficially defensive," because Prussia was encircled, "then again offensive," because he was the first to attack, "yet, once more, defensive." The revolving definitions confer a literary ambiguity on political crimes. It's a fine old German trick, predating Nietzsche, surviving Heidegger, to substitute vitality for ethics.

Frederick reconciled "passive and active qualities, endurance and patience, invective and resourceful energy, as never before or since, to my knowledge." He was the iconoclastic leader of a national vanguard, endowed with "a distinctly thrilling" awareness that enabled him to turn "memory in a contrary direction, namely forward." He was morally superior to his

* Mann imagines a similar combination of sex and politics in women: e.g., his creation of Tamar in *Joseph the Provider*.

enemies, because "it was always with him a question of life and death."
Mann's last, "most German thought" is that Frederick's " 'secret instinct'
was the urge of destiny, the spirit of history."

Although Mann hedges a bit, this "Abstract for the Hour" can be read
as an elegant call to arms. During the war he would get entangled in
sophistical attempts to distinguish might and right. But this essay clearly
grants all the advantages to the newest, youngest, least hypocritical
nation—once Prussia, now Germany. Nationalism having restored his confidence, Frederick's biographer, Mann, defines himself as young, while those
who subscribe to the womanish liberalism of the eighteenth and twentieth
centuries are old.*

His positions were rarely consistent. In March 1915 he wrote that *despite*
his "sly and skeptical" glorification of Prussianism, he knew that it was
finished: "after this war Prussianism, politically speaking, will belong to
the past." In May he wrote a letter to a Swedish newspaper expressing the
hope that after the war, Germany would "no longer need to build as she
has done previously upon Prussianism, the principle of power, but will be
able to afford the cheerful lunacy, the joy of the liberal spirit."

But in the same letter he defended his attempts at propaganda while
attacking his country's enemies. He was particularly offended that the Bel-
gians had let one of their colonial subjects, a Senegalese "animal with lips
as thick as cushions," stand guard over German prisoners and call members
of this noble race, "barbarians." (A similar racism was expressed twenty
years later when he caricatured Franco's Moorish troops. Only in America,
where he became a nominal ally of Paul Robeson and W. E. B. Du Bois,
did he speak out for the rights of black people.) A few months later, the
Swedish letter together with "Thoughts in Wartime" and the Frederick
essay were published in a small book. It became a minor sensation and
German soldiers began carrying it into battle. Frau Mann, Lula, and Victor
were overjoyed, but Heinrich was mortified to see the Mann name used for
militaristic purposes.

In September 1915 Thomas admits that he makes a questionable pa-
triot, "thoroughly antisocial, nihilistically unpolitical artist that I am." He
sees all of world liberalism arraigned against Germany, while the "conser-

---

* In 1916 he reviewed a biography of Frederick by the nineteenth-century Scotsman Thomas
Carlyle, who by introducing essayistic technique into the writing of history anticipated both
Schopenhauer and Nietzsche. (Therefore German culture acquires a foreign ancestor.) Alluding
to his own essay, Mann declared he had made his Frederick "naturalistically bad" to the displeasure of conservatives, while "our radical literary people" had taken his choice of subject as
a gesture of "social-climbing conformity." He felt misunderstood by both sides, although he
was being disingenuous after the fact.

vative and retrograde powers . . . for example the papacy," support her. But he assures himself that Western liberalism is yesterday's news; his proof: "Even . . . savages . . . are already raving about 'freedom.' " He's obviously straining, as is apparent in the willful grammar of his remarks: "I feel sure that world liberalism will be defeated—no, is already defeated," as if a change of tenses could do the trick.

He grants that he's not really sure of himself. After all, the Western cause is "so thoroughly intertwined with literature" that he "ought more or less to feel it as my own cause, or at least as the cause of the Latin literary man within myself . . . for such there is." But that's the Europe of the shallow, merely "amusing." The truth is that "I am antirevolutionary." No doubt recalling Heinrich's melodramas, he finds in revolution "operatic gesture, inhuman sensibility, lack of honest reservations, lack of love for truth and therefore lack of freedom. . . ."

Yet barely three weeks later, he again reverses himself. An Austrian Jew and devotee of Romain Rolland, Paul Amann had composed a review in French of his career, giving special emphasis to *Royal Highness*. Mann was delighted. "It often seems to me that French is the only language in which to talk about literature. . . . A musician ought to be a German, and a writer a Frenchman, or they are only half-baked specimens. What power there is in language!" Indeed, *Royal Highness* "can best be discussed in French, and perhaps only in French." The German critics hated the book; the French found it *charmant*. Which revives his old conviction that "at bottom the 'Reich' is inhospitable to writers, most inhospitable." He could accept an "amusing" literary Europe—in fact, he'd make out like a prince. "If I were conceited, I would perhaps wish for an Allied victory. But there has always been too much irony in my temperament for me to be properly conceited. . . ." Something more serious: for Germany to win may require so much bloodshed that "I should take little pleasure in belonging to a nation that has its foot upon the neck of Europe."

Actually, it would be two decades before that prospect materialized. Despite their political disagreements after World War I, Mann and Amann shared the fate of Hitler's exiles, both settling in America. (By then an art historian and college professor, Amann would die in 1958, three years after Mann.)

As the war progressed, the Mann family became prone to physical and mental disturbances. In June 1915, Klaus was stricken with appendicitis. At the height of his illness, his intestines were removed, examined, and replaced. Not surprisingly, he nearly died. From that moment, or so he would claim in his autobiography, death ceased to be a stranger to him. This was Mann's closest bout with tragedy since Carla's suicide. Two other children, and finally Katia, were stricken with peritonitis. In March 1916, Mann became ill with influenza ("Never have I had such a high fever"). The following August, he suffered "a quite serious attack of nerves, which forced me to stop my work for a week." In November 1916, the army declared him unfit for military service, citing his nervous and stomach troubles, although many Germans older than he had become soldiers. In October 1917, he suffered a bout of dysentery and was hospitalized.

He grew querulous as Germany's fortunes waned. Golo got the worst of it. He recalls fierce tantrums, "outbursts of terror and brutality." At the dining table his normally composed father would pluck at flowers and tell the child he was ugly. The only happy moments came when he invited the children into his study and read to them, told them ghost stories, and whistled themes from Wagner.

Mann became impatient, complaining about the children's "incredible lies." He would march around in a gray smock they dubbed his "service jacket." To Klaus the period was one of "silence, sternness, nervousness or anger." More indulgent than Golo, Klaus admits that his father temporarily lost his usual "kindness and irony," but that all of them, Mann included, had been war victims. "Even the inadequate food and chilly temperature in his studio" seeped into Thomas's wartime prose.

However, Mann's neighbor Bruno Walter remembered spending "many an unforgettable hour on that wide terrace during the warm season and in the comfortable sitting room adjoining the author's fine library and study during the winter." The Manns and the Walters were frequently on the phone, consulting about their children's sundry "misdeeds."

The children turned to Katia. Golo decided she was the smarter parent. Rereading her diary notes, he was struck by "such telling formulations, such perceptive observations and gentle amusement." He also concluded that Mann was "no match for [her] alert, legalistical, logical intelligence." He was Spirit; she was the Law, "too strong and naïve . . . to honor him."

Like most people, Mann reserved his worst behavior for his loved ones. As a patriotic gesture, he opened Herzogpark to young artists and intellectuals, among them the playwright Ernst Toller. For the first time he had a clique of handsome young men dependent on his graces. It vindicated the loneliness of his school days, and strengthened his patriotic resolve.

But re-entering the public world also brought out his reflective side. Already in February 1916, he anticipated Germany's defeat and his need for literary purgation. He wrote Paul Amann, "I am as little an intellectual [meaning an ideologue] as Romain Rolland. I will never be the slave of my thoughts, for I know that nothing which is only thought and said is true; the only unimpeachable truth is the image. [Tadzio thereby defeats Hindenburg.] Whenever I am engaged on essayistic work my motto is: 'You must not seek to confuse me with my contradictions. The moment one speaks one starts to err.' " He followed this quotation from Goethe with another from Schopenhauer: "As soon as our thoughts have found their way into words, they are no longer heartfelt, nor are they, at heart, serious anymore." The philosopher begins to sound like Tonio Kröger!

Sure enough, he had begun to miss literature. "The essayistic expression of my thoughts is . . . the only safe way of getting rid of them, of getting beyond them to other, new, better and where possible completely oppositional ones—sans remords!" To paraphrase Goethe on Platen, composing ideological essays would enable him to write novels free of rhetoric.

Heinrich was now completely identified with such French pacifists as Rolland. Mann wrote Ernst Bertram, "I do not know how to treat my brother, who would welcome the Rhine as a border ('In those days we had a great literature'). . . ." Yet even in his period of greatest reaction, Mann was not illiberal. In January 1916, he wrote an article for the *Frankfurter Allgemeine* protesting the suppression of Maximilian Harden's by now left-wing journal, *Die Zukunft*. Moreover, he wrote this after reading Heinrich's essay on Zola, with its implicitly *ad hominem* attacks on Mann himself, in the dissident journal *Die Weissen Blätter*, edited by an Alsatian-German, René Schickele.

Where Thomas's exemplary figure had been a lonely autocrat, Heinrich chose a muckraker. And where Thomas had derived an apology for German militarism, Heinrich used Zola to mount an assault on his bellicose countrymen. He began his essay by indicting most of his generation. Those literary intellectuals who defended the German war effort were "entertaining parasites" who posed "in elegant array against truth and justice." Among this number he singled out those who had achieved a precocious success. Having burned out, they deployed nationalism to maintain a public that would otherwise dismiss them as yesterday's news.

Although Heinrich might insist with a vast and rather suspect dignity that he meant nobody in particular, Thomas read these words as addressed directly to him. He was beside himself with the public humiliation. Heinrich had punished his politics by disclosing his deepest fears. He reckoned the Zola essay an act of fraternal disloyalty bordering, quite literally, on the murderous: having been devastated by the attacks of critics like Alfred Kerr, Mann now believed that words could kill. He must have had support from Katia; years after the deaths of both brothers, she told her children that Heinrich's words were deplorable.

In September 1915, Mann had begun work on an extended essay, *Die Betrachtungen eines Unpolitischen (Reflections of an Unpolitical Man)*. The Zola essay was published in *Die Weissen Blätter* in November, but it was two months before Thomas read it: wisely Heinrich had not mailed him a copy. In January Maximilian Brantl, Heinrich's lawyer, loaned him the magazine. Six months later Thomas returned it, covered by scribbled notations. He had begun to erase them but found the results sloppy; anyhow, the essay practically begged for such a response in order to complete the implicit dialogue—Mann wrote Brantl that most readers would miss "the choicest double entendres." But after years of close reading of Schaukal, Kerr, *and* Heinrich, he didn't miss a thing.

As he wrote out his anger a modest enterprise became gargantuan; the final work runs to almost five hundred pages.

Yet Mann's nature still remained divided. Patriotism didn't coarsen his sensibility. His tutor in conservative principles became Ernst Bertram. Their conversations were sufficiently intense that Mann imagined a literary symbiosis. Having temporarily lost a brother, Mann acquired an intellectual sibling in Bertram. No typical jingoist, the young soldier (having been called up late in 1916) was as cultivated and refined as Heinrich. This devotion to German culture spoke to Mann's needs during the composition of his *Reflections*. So did Bertram's homosexuality, for, even in this ostensibly public work, Mann later recognized his own "inversion."

Evidence of Mann's trust in Bertram can be found in a letter dated August 28, 1916. He apologizes for not responding earlier. Letter writing comes harder now, precisely because he is no longer spending his mornings on "something three-dimensional," namely fiction. As an artist, Mann can address—and please—himself. As a public man, he grows sick of his own voice. "Time is swift and I am slow. I must think everything out minutely and pedantically, and I fear I am growing old and tired in the process."

He sympathizes with the intellectual Bertram's exposure to the rigors of military service: to adapt to this "fantastic" system, so contrary to "our civilized world," "demands either the most vulgar apathy toward experience or unusual strength of mind." But while he alludes to mundane matters, like his daily tramp in the park (where they say an "open-air theater" will open shortly), the small talk is limited; in the end "it always comes back to the work." He cherishes Bertram's support for the *Reflections*. Alas, the sympathetic audience Mann had won for Aschenbach has been reduced to a small circle: "I am writing a big fat book for a few *friends* like you." Not to fear, though: once the war is ended, "the value of friendship will have risen very high." Seven years later a vision of friendship would make Thomas Mann a democrat.

6

THE POLITICS OF A
NERVOUS EXCEPTION

Very late in his huge volume of reflections, Mann recalls a joint review of *Buddenbrooks* and one of d'Annunzio's novels that "juxtaposed the pessimistic moralism of my story to the voluptuous estheticism of the Latin one." Mann carried the clipping in his breast pocket. "This was it. This was the way I was and wanted to be. I also wanted to be *seen* in this way. . . ." But he also describes his "monologue" as "a glance back at what I was . . . and what I, without feeling *old*, can obviously no longer be." Or seem to be: the present tense is already outdated.

Reflections of an Unpolitical Man is a most perverse work, interrogating its procedure, advertising its faults, leaving the reader as confused as its author. If the monolithic *Zauberberg* sometimes feels as oppressive as Hans Castorp's seven years on the mountain, the *Reflections* are crushed by a wartime's worth of mental turmoil. No question is raised lightly; Mann says it would be un-German to make things simple.

At half-point he observes, "I know that future events are somehow foreshadowed in me and through me." He adds defensively, "as they are through every somewhat sensitive instrument," but the self-promotion is unmistakable. He always insisted that the work should be read as an episode in cultural history, that it distilled an experience he was fated to undergo along with his fellow Germans.

The work haunted him throughout his lifetime, and has been rejected out of hand—if it has even been read—by generations of progressive Germans. They have missed utterances that anticipate such diverse thinkers as Leon Trotsky and Theodor Adorno. In this intellectual hodgepodge, he

comes up with something for any side from the far right to the far left.
The prose itself betrays its author's ambivalence. In any paragraph, it moves
from brilliant observation to embarrassing disclosure, from ad hoc argument
to *ad hominem* abuse.

Every tonal coloration in Mann's palette is here, not always under his
control: magisterial, coquettish, plaintive, maudlin, vain, melancholy, bullying, and practical. The verbal juggernaut propels him through logical
fallacies, historical errors, and massive contradictions.

In the prologue, written in February and March 1918, Mann offered
his political manifesto as an admittedly weird literary hybrid. He confesses
that its "light and sovereign manner of speaking" conceals his failure to
master the subject. The result lies between "composition and hackwork."
If it succeeds artistically, it will achieve an "essayistic resolution." More
likely, it will be weakened by traces of "the actor, the lawyer, of play,
artistry, detachment, of lack of conviction and of that poetic sophistry that
allowed the one speaking at the moment to be correct, and who in this
case was I, myself." For, as he tells us, "someone used to creating *art, never
takes* spiritual and intellectual things *completely seriously.* . . ."

Has there ever been a political broadside so crammed with self-
abnegation? Critics like T. J. Reed have analyzed in detail Mann's misreading of Kant, Schopenhauer, and Nietzsche; his disingenuous
appropriation of their ideas for his political purposes. But three pages into
the prologue, Mann himself admits that he uses quotations as "affidavits of
support." He has a "childish urge" for "consolation," and if he finds it by
misreading, well, he already told you he's not an intellectual. Two hundred
pages later, in a confessional digression, we learn that he will accept "everything offered him and . . . not worry much about the readability of his
composition."

Mann had often made a dramatic motif of the limits of language. Here,
the critique is directed expressly against himself. On page 38, he admon-
ishes, "But let us get to the point." One hundred pages later, he throws
up his hands: "But no more!" Ten pages later, "Everything has been said."
Perhaps, but he's three hundred pages from shutting up. He remarks, after
nearly two hundred pages of dense speculation, "To reach the goal too easily
is not to reach the goal properly. We must begin again." And so it goes
throughout: "one more point," "we have digressed," "I have been very
exhaustive"—the statements recur like taglines. Mann intends his reader
to suffer the consequences of a maddening obsession.

In these wartime reflections, the enemy is personified for Mann by another figure, "civilization's literary man." He is a glib exponent of liberal

clichés, a jaunty Francophile, "amusing," smug, trivial. Of course, he is Heinrich Mann, who was none of these. The rage at Heinrich devalues Mann's politics: it turns a world war into an extension of sibling rivalry. (As Mann wrote Bertram, his "need to regard things in intimate terms" led him to see the fate of Germany "symbolized and personified in my brother and myself.") In the narrator's jousts with an inimical "you," the work grows most impassioned, absurd politics but thrilling polemic.

The "you" is never specifically identified, though we learn that he is "a little more than kin and less than kind." But Heinrich's presence is an endless incitement. Mann attacks him in heartfelt outbursts. These exhibit a *post hoc* fluency; they resemble the superb rejoinders you wake up making after your opponent has fled. This "you," this "brother"—the metaphorical disguise is that transparent—is guilty of statements that "from a human point of view" demonstrate "simply outright meanness," and "destroy all his chatter about love." The *soi-disant* pacifist kills the spirit; the prophet of universal brotherhood demonstrates a murderous hatred *en famille*.

To assuage his suffering, Mann quotes the Zola essay, as if doing that would remove the sting: "It belongs in this book which is to be a document and will remain so when the waters recede." Out—in italics—come the worst indictments: *"deep babbler who provides intellectual support for irrationality." "Vainglorious advocate of ruthless force." "Those who are destined to dry up early step out . . . when they have scarcely entered their twenties." "{They} profit . . . from their pretended patriotism even more loudly than they would have perhaps done if it were not intended to drive us into oblivion." "Your ambition is preaching . . . or, what is even worse, your vanity . . . by pushing to become national poet laureate for half a lifetime, if your breath holds out."* Each remark was a dagger aimed at his breast. From Mann's quest for laurels to his dream of a great career if his body didn't weaken, Heinrich had published their most intimate correspondence.

He writes a book to prove his superior ethics and *discipline*. Almost at once, he equates conscientiousness with "loneliness" and links them to the burden of representation, of "how I wish to be seen." The artist's "life element is a public loneliness." He exists, as it were, on stage: "The literary public life . . . is both intellectual and social at the same time, as in the theater." Because it's a role, the actor can indulge in "the prostitution and revelation of his personal life, [with] the most complete Jean-Jacques shamelessness," and still keep his dignity. Having "sacrificed, surrendered, yes, even abandoned himself personally," he can still walk among men without compromising his "civic existence." It's a matter of tact and decorum, both of them breached by Heinrich's scandalous indiscretion. Campaigning for support, the author who told us not to trust him now offers his "public loneliness" as a certification of good faith! (In January 1918 he attended a performance of *Fiorenza* in German-occupied Brussels, where he was greeted as a "comrade-in-arms." He considered himself twice blessed.)

As in *Tonio Kröger*, he regards his work as criticism infused with sympathy, unlike the vicious satire of nameless aesthetes.

> If I have understood anything at all of my times, sympathetically, it is the type of heroism, the modern-heroic life form and attitude of the overburdened, overdisciplined *moralist of accomplishment* "working at the edge of exhaustion," and here is my psychological contact with the character of the new burgher, my only contact, but one that is important and moving to me.

Beginning with Thomas Buddenbrook, his business has been "creating symbols" of an heroic bourgeoisie.

An Englishman said poets were the "unacknowledged legislators of mankind." Similarly, Mann presents himself as the match of any sociologist.

> I place some value on the fact that I sensed and discovered this idea that the modern capitalistic businessman, the bourgeois, with his *ascetic* idea of duty to his career was a creation of the Protestant ethic, of Puritanism and Calvinism, that I came to this idea completely on my own, without reading, by direct insight, and that I only discovered afterward, recently, that it had been thought and expressed at the same time by learned thinkers. Max Weber in Heidelberg, and after him, Ernst Troeltsch, have treated [in Weber's terms] *The Protestant Ethic and the Spirit of Capitalism*, and the thought is also found in greatly exaggerated form in Werner Sombart's book of 1913, The *Bourgeois*— which interprets the capitalistic entrepreneur as a synthesis of hero, merchant, and burgher.

But until now Germany has not recognized its prophet. Almost from the start, he laments that it is an "unliterary country." From his youthful reading of Schopenhauer ("One only reads this way once") to his infatuation with Wagner, Mann had learned that "passion is clairvoyant"; blind love is unworthy of its name. But the large view demands a literary posture, "synthetic-plastic and analytical-critical," that is anything but German; for example, the supremely Teutonic Hauptmann lacks both qualities. While attacking literary intellectuals like Heinrich, he confesses, "And yet, I too have a part [of them] in me."

He surveys his own oeuvre and finds a persistent tension between the entertaining "clarity of form" that wins the burghers' approval and the "problematical," which lures "passionately uncompromised youth." *Buddenbrooks*, exhibiting the influence of Schopenhauer and Wagner, captured the fathers; *Tonio Kröger*, with the admixture of Nietzschean principles, seduced the sons. Put another way, *Buddenbrooks* was an organic work, quintessentially German, therefore "Gothic, not Renaissance" and "untranslatable," while *Royal Highness*, fatally smitten with Francophiliac "literary formulas," and inhabiting Heinrich's emotional sphere, was "Renaissance, not Gothic." He's willing to declare it a failure because he has found his true, his first self; *Tonio Kröger* becomes the crucial text. It is "my real work," the source from which all others radiate. There he first limned a mind-saving "irony" and pleased the "youth" by giving life a prettier face but intellect a better image—for demonstrating that "the god is in the lover." This highly literary perspective endows his reader with irony toward both sides, a sense of "this-as-well-as-that." To borrow a much later catch phrase, Mann salutes a pluralism of voices and positions, a posture generally defined as liberal.

Nonetheless, reviewing his work, he invariably chooses the interpretation most conducive to wartime propaganda. Thus his critique of *Royal Highness* includes most of the words he would employ in his 1939 preface. But while then he saw the novel's homage to eccentric individualism as a last-ditch effort, and its austerely happy ending as a halting gesture toward democracy, in wartime he rejects so progressive an interpretation. "One cannot think that I am so common, so *political*, that I seek an argument in 'happiness.' . . ." That would be downright "virtuous," a position he considers kitsch. If nothing else, these remarks cast a peculiar light on the "happiness" that accompanied his marriage to Katia. In the heat of literary battle, Mann can at last admit that he finds the "happiness of [marital] love" a banal joke.

Next he draws from *Death in Venice* an attack on beauty, the worship of which he attributes to "Italians and tricksters of the intellect." The profound German writer honors the "ugly." He claims to have been misunderstood when he declared in his youth that the artist must retire from life. "In truth, 'art' is only a means of fulfilling my life ethically." Even his attempt at autobiography—of which this work is a prime example—"has ethical origins, but that, to be sure, does not exclude the most lively aesthetic will to impartiality, distance, and objectification, a will, then, that is again only the will to faithful workmanship." During this period he even characterizes Felix Krull as a militarist. In his words, do these statements constitute "ethical fable" or "pulpit rhetoric"?

He so dislikes the smug pieties of his opponents that he defines Germany as fundamentally pagan. The twilight of the gods obscures a risen savior; "the only real Christians in Germany are Jewish." The twentieth century cannot intrude on this last act of the nineteenth. Therefore, if in the third year of war, "a mechanical-democratic plebiscite" showed most Germans in favor of surrender, they must be overruled by the historical imperative.

Echoing Tonio Kröger, he writes "an artist is perhaps only artist and poet as far as he is *not* alienated from the primitive, and even if he is a 'burgher,' he is still perhaps only an artist and poet as far as he . . . has not completely forgotten how to observe and feel in a nationally primitive way." He confuses militarism with the violent bloodletting of childbirth, evoking Katia's near-fatal labor. Conversely, he thrills to war's display of the "masculine component."

Disowning the hard-won anti-Wagnerian theories, he rejects the "civilizing" powers of analysis in favor of the "mythic-primitive" and hails "art's tendency to beauty-creating 'barbarism.' " Along with religion, art becomes the supreme "anti-intellectual power" . . . yet another blow against the hyperrational "you." Reason is willfully annulled. Thus, when he first reads Schopenhauer, "not a logical but a sympathetic anticipation" enables him to predict each turn of the philosopher's argument.

Straining to prove his loyalty, he imposes a new pattern on German history, a line that runs from Luther to Goethe, Nietzsche, and Bismarck. Forget that Nietzsche detested Luther and Bismarck—or that Bismarck's acolytes destroyed Hanno Buddenbrook's childhood! They are all "powerful expressions of the German character" in its various guises, metaphysical, artistic, critical, and political.

The gestalt is happily misogynistic. He turns Nietzsche into a latter-day Frederick the Great; the philosopher's numerous attacks on democracy, the eighteenth century, and particularly feminism reveal "the colossal manliness of his soul." (Schopenhauer is also quoted ridiculing American politics with its "simple-minded veneration of women.") The goddess-loving Heinrich stands corrected.

Having shown that his art is more vital, he next contends that it's more profound. To do this, he assumes an attitude derived from eighteenth-century England. Writers like Edmund Burke and Samuel Johnson—both militant opponents of revolution—had argued that conservative politics is wiser, more rooted, truer to human nature. The world of their descendants is melancholy; it accepts imperfection, and generally opposes political intervention as a lost cause, more lately as "social engineering."*

The idea that humanity is fatally constrained—whether by original sin, biological urge, or cultural habit—has often thwarted attempts at liberation. Their defeat is greeted by conservatives with a triumphant schadenfreude, a tsk-tsking over the optimistic hubris. As if it had never known disillusionment and its history weren't populated by millions of martyrs, the left's advancement of social progress is seen as banal, shallow, and, Mann would add, bullying.

During conservative eras, the pessimistic view may appear more profound and informed than the Utopian. Mann implies that, while he's no intellectual, he's a deeper thinker. To such arguments, Brecht once quipped that "depth" is merely another level, unfairly privileged.

Edmund Burke saw the superiority of his cause in its organic nature; he chose the image of a stately tree. Similarly, Mann writes that *Buddenbrooks*'s "organic growth" made it German, as he recalls informing critics who mistook him for Jewish. As for that upstart democracy, its roots lie "nowhere except in 'reason,' " while something substantial like the "feudal principle" arose out of landed property.

With Heinrich in mind, he declares that the German is not merely more rooted and profound but also more skeptical, ironic, even childish than his opponents. He does this by citing *From the Life of a Good-for-Nothing*, a story by the nineteenth-century author Joseph von Eichendorff. The willfully amoral hero is a poor boy who leaves home to seek his fortune. "He also has such a pretty face that in Italy, where as a result of the plot he spends a time without being aware of it, as a disguised girl, an enraptured student falls in love with him, and absolutely all hearts are friendly to him." Fundamentally serious, unswayed by Italian bohemians, he becomes a violinist (a brief chance for Thomas to commemorate Paul Ehrenberg?) and cultivates a romanticism that is "neither hysterical nor phthisic nor lascivious nor Catholic nor fantastic nor intellectual." He won't fall at his beloved's feet, as young students did before him. Instead he woos his sweetheart, a doorman's niece, with unshelled almonds. He recalls figures out of Wagner or Kipling, but without their abnormal traits; no mythopoeia, no saintliness, no undue animal strength. He is simply human, unaffectedly prosaic—"truly the German character."

Following in the steps of Luther, Nietzsche, and the Good-for-Nothing,

---

* In 1951, Mann admitted that during his conservative phase, Burke's words, in translation, were often on his lips. He was also charmed by the "reactionary glamour" of Joseph de Maistre.

Mann joins forces with the German *Volk*: he considers the word a beautiful, German oxymoron, for this is a very lonely, self-doubting *Volk*, not a typically Western mob. Even the German admission that they have committed war crimes is reckoned more honorable than the Allies' attempts at self-exoneration.

Throughout the work, he voices his dislike for democracy. He speaks ill of the people it serves; en masse, they resemble a "menagerie," whose "happiness" is "gorging and boozing."

He can live comfortably with economic justice. In fact, he's proud that Germany's innovations in education and social protection far surpass the West's. He likes the German penchant for "social tidiness," a vast body of laws protecting the sick and poor which logically compliments a "deep disgust for the over-valuation of social life." Meanwhile he exposes "democracy" as so comfortably affiliated with power that its name is almost a code for capitalism and imperialism. He summons as a witness Goethe, who showed that the British opposed the slave trade only because it interfered with their "large Negro colonies."

Anticapitalism does not make him a socialist. The working class, he argues, is itself conservative. It cannot function without an intellectual vanguard. Left to its own devices, it is too ensnared in domestic politics to free itself. It recognizes the privileges of rank; "the people perceive—aristocratically," much as his father's employees worshiped Senator Mann. His son speaks correctly to a point. From the peasants who chased Russian liberals out of their villages to the German workers who supported the war down to the blue-collar Tories who enthroned Reagan and Thatcher, the working class has continuously betrayed the left's expectations. Even its class identity is derivative. Mann considers the love of work a burgherly concept, linked historically to the Nuremberg craftsmen. (Hannah Arendt draws a similar distinction between "work" and "labor.")

His most cunning argument is that Aristophanes and Dostoyevsky ("I pride myself a little on this combination," he remarks parenthetically) are more authentic spokesmen than any left-wing propagandists. They reveal the stubborn conservatism of the lower classes, and in Dostoyevsky's case, their abiding faith. Without a religion, Mann predicts, the masses will fall prey to any "spiritualistic swindle." They are simply not "intellectually and morally prepared for the enlightenment, for progress." This is dreadfully condescending, but the persistence of religious orthodoxy and superstition among the poor remains a universal phenomenon.

All the while, Mann has paid occasional homage to his intellectual antithesis. Halfway through the book, he welcomes a "self-chastisement of all nations." By then he sees democracy as the obvious culmination of this war. Could he do otherwise? He identifies himself as a city man, and even if Lübeck had been uncontaminated by imperialism or capitalism, its political evolution was foretold: city life is by its nature democratic. He veers between endorsing Germany's attraction to the overly potent leader, whether Siegfried or Bismarck, and defending "civilization" 's urge to "get rid of the great man." He even quotes, as would Brecht, the Chinese poem lamenting any nation which needs such monsters.

Overturning high culture, postwar life will be a gallimaufry of "lascivious estheticism and exoticism . . . taboo crazes in clothes styles and foolish infantilisms in . . . art . . . anthropophagic sculpture and South American harbor-saloon dances." Reverting to type, the postwar radical artist will want, as all artists want, "fame, money, love, applause, applause" (the latter so nice, Mann cites it twice). Before the "lens of a movie cameraman," the radical will proclaim his politics, but he'll leave the dirty work to "desperate Jew boys."

The literary hustle will be technically altered: "megaphone advertisements are coming, the yellow brochures of mass distribution, theater festivals," the democratizing of mass culture. "Here's to you! Here's to me!" We'll both need help.

As a last conservative gesture, he reveals a new sympathy with religion, contradicting his earlier analysis of Germany as pagan. The church is a "religious asylum," "two steps away from the amusing highway of progress." Here one sees "the kneeling human being—what a blessing—what satisfaction." Mann had not converted. He admitted that he was not religious: "Doubt has not made me fat." Religious submission is equated with military service: and that, he argues, is inherently homosexual.

In the midst of "war's terrifying masculinity," he finds "the widest room for love." Service, submission to a ruling officer, becomes an erotic "intoxication." Mannian *Sehnsucht* proves irrepressible, as he turns his country's defenders into lovers staring in rapt attention. The most infatuated is, predictably, the one who salutes. "Knightly-masculine obedience" becomes the war's answer to Aschenbach's Greek passions. "Aristocratic order" and "the cult of distance" complement this "romantic play."

Mann imagines the postwar difficulties of a warrior's "pitiful wife." "Will she be enough for his nerves? The war has made him accustomed to freedom and absence of material concerns. . . ." The soldier has "developed voluptuous emotions, high-minded comradeship, heartfelt piousness and *other* things we do not know about." This male bonding, purified of workaday greed, signifies for Mann "an elevation, intensification and ennoblement of human life by the war." Forcing soldiers to love each other will transform the national character.

By the book's end, Mann's tone has modulated considerably from the more strident passages. He welcomes a form of democracy and insists that like Klaus Heinrich in *Royal Highness* he himself has always disdained rank. But if democracy comes, as it must, let it descend from above. "It should not be pretension, arrogance, insulting demand, but resignation, modesty, renunciation, humanity . . . once again . . . what it was before the invasion of politics into God's world: brotherhood *above* all differences and with the formal preservation of all differences."

Realizing that postwar culture will be noisy, he praises the "quiet culture" of Erasmus, which was silenced by Luther's evangelical brigades. Nietzsche contended that the Reformation was actually a relapse into the Middle Ages, worse than what it replaced. After all this tumult, the ceaseless battering on the poor eighteenth century, Nietzsche—and Mann—wind up hoisting "the flag of Enlightenment" against its enemies throughout the ages.

Politics devolves into one last sibling quarrel. Mann remembers the time in Italy when he was composing *Buddenbrooks*. Heinrich kept drilling into him a respect for the "strong and beautiful life," but he knew even then that his approach was moral. What the other dismissed as an apprenticeship—"the criticism of reality"—he saw as his goal: *"criticism of reality, plastic moralism."* He rebelled against "the aesthetic, renaissance Nietzscheanism."

The Nietzsche Mann loved was "morally possessed" by Dürer's woodcut engraving *Knight, Death, and Devil*. He envisioned an art saturated with "ethical air, Faustian smell, cross, death, and grave." Mann seized on this phrase "as a symbol for a whole world, *my* world, a northern-moral-Protestant *id est*, German one that is strictly in opposition to that world of ruthless estheticism."

As if to prop up the lonely, "my world" is crowded with mirror images and ubiquitous echoes, Nietzsche being only the most famous. He mentions a recent critical analysis of the novelist Conrad Ferdinand Meyer as "a burgher gone astray and an artist with a bad conscience." So deliberate a quotation acknowledges that he's figured out his culture. He will not be superseded. Should the northern Protestant confidence evaporate, ambivalence as he *defines* it—as he virtually invented it—will remain.

Further consolation is provided by the composer Hans Pfitzner. When analyzing his opera *Palestrina*, Pfitzner arrived independently at Mann's phrase "sympathy with death," to describe the hero's longing for his dead wife. The opera itself was a last romantic gesture; its "beautiful, nostalgic-fateful . . . motif," the *"final word* of romanticism."

He dismisses Heinrich's Zola as a sanitized fiction that, for purposes of propaganda, domesticated "the most impetuous man of power and violence in the history of art, an epic giant of animal sensuality, stinking extravagance, and filthy strength." A bad novelist and critic, Heinrich also fails as a biographer. For a superior chronicle of the Promethean personality, Mann offers his own essay on Frederick the Great. Because he knows himself to be incorrigibly ambivalent and sees that "art is truly the most problematic area of human nature," he can represent "as never before" Frederick's confounding personality. *His* empathy bespeaks a passion that rises out of suffering. "*Passion*, involuntary, not literary-like, striven-for, hawked-out passion, but heartfelt passion, masked perhaps with irony and humor, is the only thing that . . . produces something new, something that has never before existed—suffering then, pain, sacrificial devotion to something purifyingly suprapersonal."

It is 1903 all over again when, with casual obscenities and facile analysis, Heinrich denied passion's "uncanny" edge, or when Thomas foresaw that his "damaged" self would vault into the company of great men like Frederick. It all happened simply because he had "entered the world a little noble and old, with a natural calling to skepticism, to irony, and to melancholy."

In the end, he's the artist as truant child fleeing from his schoolmasters. Contradicting his moralistic affirmations, and echoing his most famous work (he wins either way), Mann writes, "An artist, I think, remains to his last breath an adventurer of feeling and of intellect, tending toward deviousness and the abyss, open to the dangerous, harmful element." He remains more Gypsy than burgher, a dialectician bound to no fixed principle. Such a figure will always be threatened by powerful men, no matter what their politics. Their triumph will mean "the end of all bohemian life, of all irony and melancholy, all that is loosely bound together, that does not belong, all gallows humor, all innocence and childlikeness, in short, all that one had previously considered 'decent,' artistic; it means 'masculine maturity,' solid and transfigured masculinity, which no longer has much to do with artistic nature. . . ."

Democracy is the "amusing" state for novelists. It is also the territory for "masculinely mature" husbands and fathers, as in 1909 he had called Heinrich "mature" after the latter's political conversion. But it is inherently barred to "nervous exceptions," single men all. Mann never mentions his own wife and children, but he is "intoxicated" by warriors freed from the bonds of matrimony. Whatever his conservatism protects, it's not the nuclear family.

Mann's patriotism drew on two opposing aspects of his sexual disposition. On one hand, it let him imagine a world of loving, virile warriors;

on the other, it afforded protection to the childlike bohemian. The German *Volk* alone could defend him, perhaps because he had defined them in his image.

The "nervous exceptions" had always been intimidated by healthy men. But if they were themselves half in love with death, they became fellow invalids. Moreover, the bully and the sissy, the hypermasculine cadre and the effeminate draft dodger, united in opposition. Two years later Mann wrote that, defying stereotypes, the great homosexual figures embodied "a masculinity so pronounced that even in erotic matters only the masculine has importance and interest." A superman was not typical, not healthy, not happy, not heterosexual.

As he later noted in his diary, the *Reflections* displayed with particular boldness "my inversion." Erich Heller, normally most sensitive to Mann's emotional state, found this incomprehensible. But already in the prologue, the intellect's loving submission to life becomes a retreat from oppressive thought, "enthusiastic, erotic intoxication, a submission that was no longer quite masculine but—how shall I say—of a sentimental-aesthetic nature."

Mann had often conjoined aestheticism and erotic intoxication, and declared the union "not quite masculine." In his attack on Heinrich, "*Das Ewig Weibliche,*" he identified sentiment as "feminine." But seldom before had he employed so many terms—"aesthetic," "intoxicated," "ironic," "conservative"—as elaborate sexual codes. If he loved in a closet, the war expanded that space to national proportions.

The work concludes with two chapters, "The Politics of Estheticism" and "Irony and Radicalism," in which a literary manifesto is sexually charged. Both active and passive, the artist inhabits a state of autoparthogenesis: "every artist's life work, whether small or large, has been a cosmos, resting in itself, stamped with the mark of its creator. Impression and expression have always been necessary elements of art, one without the other has been helpless." Therefore, life and intellect must be lovers, not rivals, their relationship "erotic without a clear sexual polarity, without the one representing the masculine, and the other the feminine principle. . . . There is no union between them, but only the short intoxicating illusion of union and misunderstanding, eternal tension without resolution." Mann sees the dialectic as a case of endless foreplay.

He grows peaceful once he accepts his irresolution as permanent. "Intellect that loves is not fanatic, it is ingenious, it is political, it woos, and its wooing is erotic irony. One has a political term for this: it is 'conservatism.' What is conservatism? The erotic irony of the intellect." Others comprehend irony and skepticism within the normal array of conservative responses. But only Mann imagines them in sexual terms.

Since his days in Rome he had focused on a "double effect" that resulted from the synthesis of an "international intellectual emphasis" and a "national emotional emphasis." Starting with the *Reflections*, this double effect became yet another metaphor for same-sex love. In the final chapter's third paragraph he cites a recently published study, Hans Blüher's ingenuously titled *The Role of Eroticism in Male Society*. Quoting but not identifying Blüher, he writes, "Someone has defined Eros as 'the affirmation of a man apart from his [objective] *worth*.' Now this is not a very intellectual, nor a very moral affirmation, and neither is the affirmation of life by intellect. It is ironical. Eros was always an ironist. And irony is eroticism." Barely implicit is the fact that Blüher and Mann are talking about homosexual Eros—since heterosexuality, as the social norm, requires no defense, "ironic" or not.

Shades of Tonio Kröger, the erotic ironist woos beauties he will never possess. Whether these be disembodied ideals or rosy-cheeked youths, German nationalism or Hans Hansen, the pursuit remains the same. For a few years, the war effort joined Mann and his countrymen in a common goal. As the war ends, that identity dissolves, leaving him as lonely as before.

Mann's immense argument winds down in a series of resolved antitheses. Though art previously stood in opposition to modern politics—i.e., democracy—in the end, a similarity between the two appears; they both mediate between life and intellect. Neither dares remain purely conservative or radical. He fears that the narrative mode best suited to democracy will not be friendly to mandarin intricacies. An exclusively political-critical view denies "the childlike, naïve and believing attitude toward things in the world" and buries the "less than masculine" artist. Heinrich will have won.

How can a nature like his apprehend life with sufficient force? Mann looks to his own work and observes "the little prince of decline and of too much music, Hanno Buddenbrook." In his most chauvinistic passages, Mann had sided with the Bismarckian schoolmasters. While he doesn't quite deny the earlier position, he simply remarks that Hanno's retreat from the militaristic Gymnasium was the sign of a "nervous exception." Yet "pride and honesty," arising from his nature, immunized Hanno from the political rant. Mann almost sees this. The judgments of the "impossible," "lonely," "problematical," "artistic," "nervous exception" were correct from the start.

Irony becomes the intellect of conservatism only when it incorporates "a bit of democracy, of literature." Finally bidding farewell to the "robust . . . simple . . . and strong" conservative militarism, along with its spiritual / ethical Dostoyevskian variant, Mann realizes that every playful change of mood signifies his disloyalty to the cause. He's a man of letters;

and literature is "analysis, intellect, skepticism, psychology; it is democracy, the 'West.' " So when it finally comes down to it, "Conservative? Naturally I am not."

The *Reflections* appeared in October 1918, at "the most unfavorable, indeed the most impossible of moments; the time of the collapse and the revolution. But in reality it was the right moment." So Mann argued in 1929: he had anticipated the move to democracy that the members of his bourgeois class would make, following his example. Because these readers found it "helpful," he confessed a pride in his work, in its depiction of "steadfastness" and its panoramic display of a "last great retreat action." "Last" was accurate; within weeks the war was over.

Defeat involved mundane difficulties. Like many Germans, Mann lost his entire investment in war bonds. He became dependent on the women around him. Twice a week Katia bicycled in search of food. From Polling, Frau Julia Mann began mailing parcels. He was assured of a certain income from his works, *Buddenbrooks* having been reprinted fifteen times during the war. But Heinrich was outselling him. *Im Schlaraffenland* had found its public; in 1916 it sold more copies than the accumulated sales to date of *Buddenbrooks*. Meanwhile, *Der Untertan*, a savage attack on German militarism, had made Heinrich the literary hero of advanced German youth.

In the Christmas 1917 issue of the *Berliner Tageblatt*, Heinrich contributed a piece, "Life, Not Destruction." Two days later, Thomas replied with an article, "World Peace?" seeking to justify his behavior, still scorning the idea of democratic politics in Germany, and implicitly attacking his brother's hollow words: "In its rhetorical and political form, love for humanity stands at the edge of real feeling, and is most lyrically advanced when it is weak at the core." He paraphrased the biblical passage that if a man loves God yet not his brother, his words are but tinkling cymbals. Nevertheless, encouraged by the fact that Thomas had also welcomed the prospect of world peace, Heinrich decided to resume their relations.

In 1916, Mann had predicted a postwar era of "friendship" succeeding "this intellectual caldron." Apparently that era had not yet begun for the Mann brothers. On January 3, 1918, Thomas replied in a letter filled with patient explanation and extravagant self-pity, similar to the tone of *Reflections* but without that work's rigor. He claims that it's "physically impossible" to reply promptly, but that any time would be inadequate to distill the "mental torment of two years into a letter which would have to be much longer than yours."

Like two people resuming an argument after years, recognizing that neither has forgotten a thing, Thomas leaps into the specific. All right, he believes Heinrich "implicitly" when he confesses no hatred toward him. But his use of the term "fraternal hate" refers to "more general discrepancies in the psychology of the Rousseauiste." If Heinrich calls him a difficult brother, "I naturally have found you even more so; that was in the nature of things; and I too did my honest best." As a sign, he praises "at least two of your books [Heinrich had composed a dozen] in the teeth of everyone else [so much for your critical reception] as masterpieces." There may be an implicit distinction between the fluent Heinrich and the tongue-tied Thomas: "You forget or are silent about the way you so often mishandled my simplest and strongest feelings with your justification of passion, before I could react with as much as a sentence."

At last, Mann can address the "you" of his *Reflections* directly. You may claim your animus was not "personally directed." But this public display, with "its truly French spitefulness, the defamations and slanders of the glittering piece of sham whose second sentence was already an inhuman excess," far surpassed any previous attack: "No, I have never allowed myself such liberties or expected any man to put up with such." Others may have disagreed with Heinrich. But none related the Zola essay to their work; everyone saw it as an attack on "me." If you seriously believe this political battle can be forgotten, your essential "frivolity" stands revealed, you who have "lifted [your] heart far into the distance."

Mann defends his wartime actions. They weren't "extreme," but yours were "utterly detestable." I haven't spent two years neglecting my art while I "probed, compared and asserted myself" to let my enemy disarm me now. Sounding very much the sore loser, he dismisses Heinrich's appeal as "moral smugness and self-righteousness."

Now he arrives at Heinrich's deepest insult. "You and your sort can call me a parasite, if you like." But he has served far more honorably than his critics. Lately he had read the bourgeois writer Adalbert Stifter, who described his own works as "not simply poetic creations, but as moral revelations." Mann applies Stifter's criteria to himself. "I have a right to repeat those words, and thousands whom I have helped to live . . . *see* it, this right."

For us, there remains only "the tragedy of our brotherhood." He finds the sorrow "bearable." After Carla's suicide and Heinrich's break "with Lula for life," abrupt divorces are no longer novelties in "our family circle." He closes with an ambiguous reference, "I have not enjoyed this life," not indicating whether he means the Manns' discord or his own miserable state.

"But one must live one's life to the end as best one can": and, for the duration, his will be brotherless.

Heinrich's reply was never mailed. The letter begins, "Dear Tommy":
one imagines that even this intimate greeting would rattle the hypersensitive Thomas. The first sentences are conciliatory. Heinrich wishes to "try
every channel," so that later Thomas will see the injustice of his actions.
"I never deliberately part forever," and, turning the other's rhetoric to his
own advantage, "That is the nature of my zealot's frivolity."

He complains that for all his many attempts to defend Thomas against
his critics, "I got almost nothing in return," forgetting the many signs of
affirmation. He also says that he had never "retaliated" for the 1903 review
in *Freistatt*—an admission that perhaps this time he had finally gotten his
revenge.

And this unmailed letter contains its share of cutting remarks. Heinrich
still knew where Thomas was most vulnerable. "With great regret I learn
that one single statement of opinion on my part has caused you to spend
two years formulating a reply"; lurking beneath the sorrow, one detects
pride in the power to dominate his brother's consciousness.

Their animosity is traced to a day in Rome when, his back turned,
Thomas declared them "in inimicos." Enemies for life in a war Thomas
started. "But you are still young, I can still dissuade you from it before it
is too late, for it wasn't good for you then, nor is it now. Stop relating my
life and actions always to yourself, it has nothing to do with you, would
be precisely the same if you did not exist."

Heinrich describes the sibling rivalry as one-sided. He'd be only too
glad if Thomas wrote something new about the French, "other than ab-
surdities." But he knows that if he tried his hand on Frederick of Prussia,
Thomas would "throw all [his] notes . . . in the fire." He implies that every
literary gesture of Thomas's expresses an act of resistance to his larger
presence.

Instead of "self-righteousness," he acknowledges the universal guilt of
his intellectual generation. A "triumph" purchased at the cost of ten million
corpses may satisfy an "ideologue," but it fills him with despair. "I do not
believe the success or victory of any matter is worth discussing where we
human beings perish." He wouldn't dare claim his work had helped readers
"to live," but surely literature must not lead them to die!

When it comes to first-person attacks, Heinrich's arsenal is much the
better stocked. He argues that less refined minds than Thomas's have
thought their way through to a democratic commitment and a "renewed
energy." But Thomas is mired in fruitless actions of "self-assertion" and
"suffering," all "for the sake of yourself, this furious passion for your own

'I.' " (Mann had sought to avert this attack, perhaps because he had heard it before. Early in the *Reflections*, he discriminated between his mere self and a great nation, and requested an antithetical Other to "show me" where he wrapped himself in an imperial "we." A sense of propriety obliged him to beg, "Save me from pigheadedness.")

If Thomas can allude patronizingly to Heinrich's two good books, Heinrich's retort is as damaging: "You owe several narrow but private works to this passion." The social novelist accuses his brother of an imaginative failure. After Thomas's confessions of self-doubt, such an utterance would have been the *coup de grâce*, a private coda to the ruinous Zola essay.

At the end of Kafka's story "The Judgment," after the son confronts his monstrous father, the old man turns the table with a half-sad, half-contemptuous remark: "I was expecting you to say that." An ironic culmination to Mann's *Reflections* occurs when the "you" mercilessly exposes the "I" as an immature solipsist, all the time awaiting his master's critique.

Heinrich depicts his brother as incapable of imagining another person's existence. He guesses that his absence has forced Mann to seek out new companions. But they have proved to be mindless yes-men, "irrelevant extras who signify the 'people' to you." They don't see what I do.

For example: "Your own ethos, who says I did not acknowledge it? I have always known it, I respected it as your subjective experience, and where portrayed in your works I did not long trouble you with my reservations about its value for other people." But while Heinrich allowed Thomas his experience, whenever he asserted his own, Thomas scorned him as "a play-acting braggart and glittering hack. You poor fool!" In a devastating fusion of literary and psychological analysis, Heinrich shows that "the inability to take another person's life seriously in the end leads to monstrous things."

After their reconciliation, both brothers would acknowledge—characteristically in an oblique fashion—that they had been dirty fighters. New editions of the *Reflections* toned down the *ad hominem* insults; a 1931 reprint of the Zola essay dropped the references to youthful burnouts. Thomas's right-wing enemies accused him of bowdlerizing history and denying his better, conservative self. He replied that the politics were still visible; he took nothing back. History didn't require the spectacle of intellectual fratricide; some sentences didn't deserve reading.

In a letter to Erika, tacitly admitting that the "belated offshoot" and "nervous exception" was a delayed adolescent, Thomas Mann would observe, "How young we were at forty-three."

IV

PARODYING NATURE

1

BEGINNING THE WORLD AGAIN

With literary precision, the defeat of Germany bifurcated Mann's life. As he guessed in 1917, from now on everything would change. His attitudes toward politics and culture would undergo extensive revision, along with his view of the artist's role. Mannian representation meant something very different when all the old stabilities had vanished.

At first, like most Germans, he was both ashamed and embittered. Years that he could have spent on *The Magic Mountain* had been diverted to an exhaustive statement that was already outdated. His reputation, literary and political, had grown problematic. Meanwhile Heinrich's fortunes were zooming. November 1918 marked not only the publication of *Der Untertan*, his satire on Wilhelmine life, but, as well, the formation in Munich of a new government, for which he contributed an inaugurating document filled with the woozy rhetoric Mann despised. The novel brought him great fame, a prophetic image, large earnings—not until 1922 would Thomas approach Heinrich's new wealth—and a dazzling social success. Regarding these triumphs, Thomas Mann grumbled, "Habeat. Habeat." Let him have it.

In March 1918 Thomas had returned to more conventional literary pursuits with a self-professed "idyll," *A Man and His Dog*. It would score a large international success, furthering his image of bourgeois propriety; meanwhile *Buddenbrooks* reached its hundredth edition. Even so, the diaries, at this time, are filled with despair over his prospects, the "uselessness" of his work, the evaporation of his public.

He continued to loathe his Berlin enemies, the Jewish critics Kerr and

Harden. But Munich proved no friendlier. On March 16, 1918, he attended
funeral services for Frank Wedekind. While Heinrich gave the eulogy, Thomas was conspicuously ignored, snubbed by Wedekind's friends. A year
later, he learned that another writer was broadcasting "his pleasure at my
being unnoticed at Wedekind's funeral. Utterly wretched."

Although he attended several political meetings at the posh Herrenklub, he kept still during the debates, recognizing that any position he
assumed would earn him new enemies. By 1920 some forgiving Berliners
spoke of inviting him back to that city's Academy of Arts. He found the
idea "interesting," but it aroused "thoughts of death. Moreover, Kerr will
manage to block it."

He moved in the highest circles. His diaries are filled with references
to professors, lawyers, doctors, artists, directors, and writers he would encounter at the Herrenklub. For example, December 20, 1918, found him
in the company of, among others, Rilke, his old friend Kurt Martens, and
the political economist—and later émigré—Moritz Julius Bonn. Munich's
haute bourgeoisie comprehended artists and scholars. But this distinguished
confederation remained a men's club, fundamentally inhospitable to "nervous exceptions." After one political seminar, Mann determined to "retreat
from the world of action."

If he didn't trust his peers, his fans horrified him. He confided in his
diaries that they were invariably sentimental, mindless bigots. With xenophobic ardor, they condemned Heinrich and glorified him, but their compliments merely increased his "self-deprecation." If these were his best
readers, his career was finished.

His gloom was momentarily alleviated with the publication of Ernst
Bertram's long-awaited study *Friedrich Nietzsche: Versuch einer Mythologie.*
Bertram's Nietzsche is locked in an "incurable tragic dualism," poised between Dionysian and Apollonian impulses, irrational and superbly critical,
ecstatic and willfully sublimated: a character as much out of Thomas Mann's
fiction as out of the philosopher's own words. Mann's critical essays may
also have made an impression. Bertram's introduction extends Mann's intuition about literary reception: "We know only what we look at, and we
look only at what we are . . . What appears to our consciousness is only
for today, and only for us, only for this moment." Applying Nietzsche to
Nietzsche was a very Mannian thing to do.

Mann found it a dazzling academic reflection of his own ideas: one such
acolyte justified years of political contemplation. At a time when he felt
underachieved, he turned Bertram's work into his own triumph. (This book
finally earned its author a salaried position at Bonn.) The study provided

"something dignified, prudent, magisterial, unassailable, irreproachable, yet *brotherly* along my imprudent, untutored, stammering and compromising artist's book" (italics mine).

In a similar tone, he speculated about the *Reflections* chances with a playfulness—"much laughing up my sleeve about almost everything"— reeking of gallows humor. His most insightful comment on the work— that it expressed his "inversion"—came only after his reading of Hans Blüher's study of homoeroticism and the military. It could be read as an attempt to prove that even in defeat he was still representative.

Sure enough, the work's reception would surprise him. He found an unusual warmth in the left-wing press; on September 29, 1918, he noted that "the two democratic newspapers are the first to show interest in the book. Ironic. But it is literature, even though anti-democratic." One of the strongest attacks came from a friendly source; in February 1919 Paul Amann, his wartime correspondent, savaged the book. He particularly in- dicted the way Mann had avoided responsibility for his words by contend- ing that he no longer believed them. His friend's response upset Mann. "This business with Amann is affecting me strongly, especially his glib, tactless, and nasty way of treating the fraternal conflict, this leading motif of what is an intellectual work."

So Mann wrote on April 7, but eleven days later he exhibited a fraternal solidarity that would surely have moved Amann or Heinrich. A Berlin critic, Karl Strecker, had praised the *Reflections* as evidence of Thomas's artistic superiority, and then slammed *Der Untertan*; Mann would have none of this Heinrich bashing. In his diary he admitted that "kindnesses of this sort have a soothing effect, but only on the nerves, and are quite dubious even at that." He proceeded to write Strecker that the "antithesis" between his brother and himself

strikes me as too important and symbolic for me really to welcome the intrusion of the question of rank and worth. I frankly do not believe in my superior rank and worth. I believe only in differences of tem- perament, character, morality, experience, which have led to . . . an opposition of principles—but one based upon a deeply felt brotherli- ness. In me the Nordic-Protestant element is uppermost, in my brother the Roman Catholic element. With me, accordingly, the emphasis is more on conscience, with him more on the activist will. I am an ethical individualist, he is a socialist. However this antithesis might be further defined and formulated, it reveals itself in the realms of intellect, art, politics—in short, in every relationship.

And so, honoring a spirit of pluralism scarcely vibrant at that hour, "any assignment of rank must be purely subjective, depending on personal affinity and sympathy." Political and military defeats will never settle our conflict.

He came to loathe social events; afterwards, "cursed my amiability" and wished to retreat altogether from public life. Yet the holiday seasons of 1918 and 1919 reminded him that he was no longer a sought-after guest. His neighbor Bruno Walter was "overbooked," but for the once-famous Thomas Mann "invitations not accumulating."

On December 19, 1918, Thomas "recalled that I live a solitary, withdrawn, brooding, peculiar and sad existence. Heinrich's life, by contrast, is very sunny just now." On the following November 25, he came across a letter to their mother in which Heinrich blamed the hissing at his latest play's premiere on Munich right-wingers, and exulted in his fifteen curtain calls. "Horrible," groaned Thomas, and added, "Friendship with critic nets him a crawlingly deferential notice. . . . Horrible." Another time in Frau Mann's house, his eye chanced to fall on one of Heinrich's letters, and the mere sight of the familiar penmanship made him physically ill.

Katia and her mother, Hedwig Pringsheim, had turned against the German war effort. There were frequent arguments, long remembered by their children, in which he appeared high strung, easily aggravated, miserable in defeat. Most of the Mann savings were now lost. Food was scarce; Mann wrote Paul Amann as the war ended, "I nourish myself on honey, which is my favorite food anyhow, although I am not a bear in other respects." As to the latter, his offspring might have disagreed.

While the Pringsheims had suffered financially, they continued to set a splendid table, which he enjoyed. But they still held against him the indiscreet confidences of *"Wälsungenblut."* Golo remembers a 1925 argument over Wagner—a red-hot issue for both Mann and Alfred Pringsheim. Afterwards the boy heard his father exclaim, "They have never liked me nor I them!" This was not the whole story. Mann frequently noted the pleasant hours spent with "Katia's mother."

Whatever else, the Pringsheims offered a glamorous alternative to his own family. Heinrich was out of the picture; the youngest brother, Victor, had never been an intimate, and he found "Vico's wife . . . horrible." Saddest of all, he realized that his mother, having become "muted, fragile, and old," was now the family eccentric.

The children remembered a silly old lady who showed up bearing candies, overdressed, her lost beauty hidden beneath dotted veils. She would sometimes mention Carla's death, proclaiming it not a suicide but the result of a "broken heart." (They knew better. Years later Klaus described it as an exquisitely botched attempt at theater.) Julia Mann's fears had been realized. The worldly Pringsheims now set the tone in her son's household. Thomas may have distrusted them, but he found "poor foolish Mama" pathetic and Lula almost grotesque.

The banker Löhr appears often in Mann's diaries as a generous host, but Mann knew that Lula found marriage to him physically intolerable; she had a penchant for unhappy affairs. Unlike Carla, she assumed a pose of social rectitude. When she visited his summer home, she arrived with her pompous, overdressed children. Their elegance seemed to underline the Manns' general scruffiness, a semibohemian relaxation prompted as much by Katia's style as by Thomas's poverty. But Golo adds that Lula's daughters were little viragos, fighting and screaming within moments, ignoring their mother's outlandish self-pity, her declarations that they were all out to kill her.

Mann recognized the foolish impression Lula made, but in September 1918, when she continued to support the German cause, Katia became frankly indignant. He found the contrast between "Lula's lachrymose credulity" and "Katia's often harshly expressed skepticism" simply "embarrassing"; he admitted his own impatience with Lula's "hysterical dejection." Yet he also defended her. In July 1919, writing as "Pielein," his children's latest nickname for him, he assured Erika that Aunt Julia was a splendid person.

While his mother and sister evoked, at best, "disgusted sympathy," Katia still knew how to amuse him; in April 1920, after their fortunes improved, she advised him to marry again, this time a truly rich woman, "so we can have even more kopecks."

Katia Mann's life was not easy. Mann describes her many illnesses and sieges of melancholy. Her sons caused her particular grief. One time, Mann writes, reading Klaus's diaries, she discovered a fundamental coldness that caused her to weep as despairingly as when the boy had come close to death. Mann, too, was upset. "Myself sick at heart. I attempted to reassure and comfort her. I will never play the infuriated father. There is nothing the boy can do about his nature, which is not of his own making." His hijinks were "simply tasteless showing off." Later on, Katia had a talk with Eissi (Klaus's nickname). "He also wept bitterly. I think it did him good to realize we were aware of some of the difficulties faced by young people." Klaus would remain Katia's favorite son.

In her diary, she wrote with exasperation about Golo's tantrums and sloppy appearance; Golo admits he was a very dirty child. Mann recorded

Katia with her six children, 1919. LEFT TO RIGHT: *Monika, age nine; Golo, age ten; baby Micahel; Klaus, age twelve; Elisabeth, "the image of my wife," age one; and Erika, age thirteen. About this time, Mann became infatuated with Klaus—a "highly natural situation," in his view.*

her disapproval of his urge to confide family intimacies in print. The greatest intimacy he reserved for the diaries: his failure to satisfy her sexually.

Despite her regal youth, she proved to be wonderfully practical. Mann liked to joke that hers was not a spiritual temperament: she might have been a lawyer or a mathematician, but not a philosopher. Philosophy was not required when her children went hungry. Instead she began long daily trips on her bicycle, tracking down possible sources of food. For this veritable princess, raised in her Munich palace, household affairs had never been of concern. Even during the early war years, she was accustomed to at least three servants. Now, like a working-class mother, she was obliged to barter and finagle. Poverty domesticated her intelligence.

On April 24, 1918, a third daughter, Elisabeth Veronika Mann, was born. She would become, together with Erika, Mann's favorite child. Indeed, for her first years she seemed to him "my first child"—i.e., the first to arouse the conventional fears and joys of parenthood. In his diaries he worries that he may lose her infantile trust; he quotes her first words with guileless pleasure.

Virtually a year later, on April 21, 1919, Michael Thomas Mann was born. About this arrival he was less enthusiastic. He writes that he detects a resemblance to Katia's brother (probably Klaus Pringsheim), while others would find a resemblance to Heinrich; neither association would lift Mann's spirits. Michael's birth was one more gratuitous event bestowed by the fates. Moreover, since radical politicians promised an end to inherited wealth, he could leave his youngest son nothing.

Most often he was in despair, unable to sleep, doubting whether he had twenty more years to redeem himself. (On September 20, 1918, he describes "Deathly melancholy . . . how good it would be to die now"—albeit, with manic speed, he finds "reaffirmation" in thoughts of his future work and memories of his beloved child.) His self-image was momentarily bolstered in August 1919 when he received an honorary doctorate from the philosophy faculty of Bonn University. Now here was a cause for amusement, so exalted a degree bestowed on a dropout. Ernst Bertram and his lover, Ernst Glöckner, were ecstatic; in their circles a doctorate was something monumental.

He also received a private solace from nature. During the summer of 1918 in their villa on the Tegernsee, he enjoyed rowing the children about, and even climbed the imposing Hirschberg (5,511 feet high). Golo waspishly commented in his own diary that this might have been the only mountain Mann ever climbed; he also suggests that Mann's famous love for the sea was exclusively voyeuristic, to be enjoyed from the shore. Mann writes occasionally of the simple pleasures of wandering outdoors, without a jacket, the breezes caressing his skin. "For the overly civilized, there is something downright voluptuous about nature." (On July 20, 1934, he wrote in his diary that he practiced "calisthenics in the nude"—a physical life about which Golo must not have known.)

His greatest personal satisfaction may have been the composition of his diary. We possess those of 1918 to 1921 only because he spared them from the flames to which he consigned his early diaries in the summer of 1945. As when he instructed his schoolmate Otto Grautoff to burn his own journals, Mann realized that they would compromise his reputation. (In 1933 he feared worse; if the Nazis uncovered his homosexuality, his very life, not to mention his public image, would be endangered.) Mann used the 1918–1921 diaries as source notes for *Doctor Faustus*.

Richard Exner, one of his most perceptive readers, describes their composition as "auto-cathartic." Virtually nothing is left out. In early 1919 he vows to exclude trivia: "must be more selective." He didn't take this advice. In totally random—or, at best, chronological—order, he presents everything, equally deadpan, equally weighted. His physical problems, the perpetual insomnia, constipation, and toothaches, received as much attention as the arguments with Katia, the doubts about his work, the fleeting crushes on handsome youths, the rivalry with Heinrich, the infatuation with Klaus.

These diaries have been read as documents of a supreme egotist, obsessively self-regarding. But there's a literary justification. In a diary note, Mann concludes that in a large novel—something as ambitious as the book he's composing—"all strands must be present." The diaries may be artless, but they are undeniably comprehensive. Even the hypochondria is characteristic; indeed, Mann is seldom so representative as when he worries about his recalcitrant body. The physical is never a trivial matter for him; he contends that "human failures always have physical causes."

The supreme physical event is sex; the diaries reveal more fantasy than action, but their author is neither squeamish nor a prude. Sexuality colors his response to the most disparate experiences. As an example, on September 20, 1918, he reports finding Klaus "in bed with the light on and in a fantastic state of undress." He presumes a bout of masturbation ("puberty games") and wonders, "What form will the boy's life take?" Obviously he relates Klaus's solitary pleasure to his own existence, since he adds, "Admittedly, someone like me 'ought' not to bring children into the world." But he concludes that the supremacy of human will places that normative "ought" in quotes, thus using Schopenhauer to refute Freud.

The next paragraph moves from the pubescent Klaus to depictions of "adolescent" soldiers parade-stepping outside his home; he finds them "charming" and "delicate." That evening he attends a performance of *Parsifal*, which he thinks an uncomfortable alloy of "Christian simplicity" and "pompous ritual." He characterizes "the whole" as "the dream of an exceedingly high-flown, tired, and sensual old man." The journal ends with the forlorn adjective "tired." Spying on Klaus, admiring the soldiers, and identifying with Wagner seem virtually equivalent.

In March 1919, he becomes aroused by a young man who attends one of his readings. He is a "Hermes-like dandy" with "a slight, youthful figure . . . a prettiness and foolishness that amounts to a real classical 'godlike' look. I don't know his name and it doesn't matter." For Mann's readers, however, it does matter. Hermes will become not merely his favorite mythical type but the image of his subsequent heroes—Hans Castorp, Joseph, and the adult Felix Krull. In them, the god of trade and theft acquires a Mannian persona.

The relation between desire and theory was self-evident. On September 13, 1919, Mann received congratulations on his doctorate from Paul Ehrenberg. He was moved: "I loved him and [it] was something akin to requited love." That afternoon he began the second volume of Hans Blüher's *The Role of Eroticism in Male Society*, one of the books—along with Bertram's Nietzsche study and Spengler's *Decline of the West*—that most impressed him in the years between 1918 and 1921. Blüher divided society into the private realm of family and domestic emotion and the public world of male society, wherein, at that time, women played no part. (Hannah Arendt makes a similar distinction in *The Human Condition*.) He excluded Jews from this hallowed society of German men, although, as in Otto Weininger's case, many Jews were intrigued by his ideas. While he was a prophet of the German Youth Movement, and, by rights, a father of the Hitler Youth, the Nazis disowned him because of his sexuality. In turn he condemned the genocide because he did not consider stateless Jews worthy of such attention.

Seven months earlier, on February 11, Mann had attended a lecture by Blüher where he was pleased by the applause when his name was announced, and even more when Blüher used the phrase, "civilization's literary man," as if it were part of the language. Blüher's message touched him greatly: "spoken almost word for word from my soul," as did his "school-teacher" presentation. The new book impressed him so much that four days later, on September 17, he decided that all his work, including the *Reflections*, expressed "my sexual inversion." He added, "No doubt in my mind."

Mann reserved other secrets for the diary. (Even Erika was scolded years later when she intruded while he was writing it.) The most striking element may not be the revelations of melancholy and ambivalence, even those of incestuous longing: his published work may express all of that. Rather, one is astonished by the brusque, no-nonsense prose, the almost telegraphic jottings about emotions of surpassing complexity. None of the diaries read like Mann's literary efforts. Entirely missing is the elegant clutter of his interminable periods; there are none of the "stylistic beauties" that unfriendly readers considered middle-brow *Schmus*.

It is the language of the household, Katia's language.* But Mann could work out the desires he had renounced only by composing a densely elaborated prose. His literary circumlocutions reflected his situation far more accurately than did the affectless staccato of his diaries, factually illumi-

---

* In *Ascent of Woman*, Elisabeth Mann Borgese argues that a womanly prose is direct, pointed, unrhetorical.

nating as they remain. Reading Tolstoy's diaries prompted him to say, "Art
[expresses] all the secrets that cannot be said in simple words."

Measured by the standards he set himself as a youth, Mann's return to
literature was tentative and modest. He granted that he was biding
his time. The Mann of the hour was Heinrich. *Der Untertan* he regarded as
already "dated satire," good for the occasion but not made to last. Still, he
wasn't sure that his own work had any staying powers.

In fact, Heinrich's success was a temporary phenomenon, the product
of a fleeting moment when all things conspired to favor him. As soon as
his friends assumed the leadership in Munich, the publisher Kurt Wolff
rushed out 100,000 copies of *Der Untertan*: within a month, 75,000 had
been sold. Thomas had never enjoyed such a rapid and stunning success.
After many years, he resumed his original role, that of Heinrich's younger
brother.

For Heinrich's defenders—who are usually detractors of Thomas—*Der
Untertan* demonstrates his superior knowledge of the German character. A
product of his early liberalism, composed between 1906 and 1914, it rehearses the familiar themes of his prewar fiction. At one moment, the novel's mouthpiece, Wolfgang Buck, declares that the actor has become his
era's representative man. This is *echt* Heinrich but perhaps a mite irrelevant
to the chaos of postwar Germany.

The novel's first sentence introduces Diederich Hessling, "a dreamy,
delicate child, terrified of everything." For a moment he seems like another Hanno Buddenbrook, a self-absorbed aesthete doomed in his cradle.
By the paragraph's end, he's become a whiner and a sneak. As an adolescent, he bullies the defenseless and cringes before authority. The
Buddenbrook / Mann clan was in decline; the Hesslings are parvenus, one
generation removed from the working class. Something of a German Snopes,
Diederich plots the destruction of his town's most distinguished family,
the Bucks.

As he grows up, his various needs for order and authority merge in a
fanatical devotion to the emperor. When a band of unemployed laborers
petition Wilhelm for "Bread! Work!" the monarch is too preoccupied with
his "personal performance" to notice. Diederich rushes after the Kaiser to
apologize for the benighted masses; he stumbles and plops in a rain puddle.
The ruler takes him for mad; then, recognizing a true subject, bursts out
laughing. Diederich is impervious; he lives to be patronized.

Wolfgang Buck sums up the subject's nature; what makes Diederich
"a new type is simply the gesture, the swaggering manner, the aggressive

nature of an alleged personality, the craving for effect at any price." He refuses to see him in terms of class or politics; the preferred metaphor is always theatrical. Wolfgang speaks in all friendship, "Admit it, Hessling, nobody ever got your number like I did. In fact I am much more taken with your role than my own. Why, I've even imitated you in front of the mirror. The next step is clear. You will take over the town, and I must go on the stage." It's a dramatic confrontation, Heinrich's particular spin on Ibsen, but it conveys a limited understanding of politics.

Heinrich deepens his analysis by endowing Hessling with an inchoate respect for the Bucks and a longing for their approval. The old father, a hero of 1848, recognizes in him the wave of an awful future, but he is too humane, too simply paternal, to condemn any of his figurative offspring. Diederich thus anticipates the lost sons imagined by Kafka, Hermann Broch, and Robert Musil—men who want nothing so badly as a wise father . . . as if this were not itself a form of submission to authority.

There are prophetic passages. Diederich posits eugenic ("hygienic") so-lutions to racial conflicts; he's a perfect twentieth-century rabble-rouser, paying homage to family and church and praising young people as patriotic capitalists. Yet this is not a revolutionary novel; it lacks party and program. Wolfgang Buck and his father regard genuinely great men as more benef-icent than "social legislation." At best the Bucks are republican aristocrats, decreeing social justice from *en haut.*

The novel's ending is a predictable travesty. The dying Buck halluci-nates a "nation" worthy of a last outburst of "spiritual joy"; Beethoven sings him into heaven until he catches a glimpse of Diederich, all puffed up "on general principles," and collapses from the shock. His son quits show business when police chiefs begin applauding his act (a nicely modern touch). But his impotence verges on complicity. In a horrible way, Died-erich is more authentic, and the novel only lives when he performs his clownish routines.

If this were the best Heinrich could do, Mann was right not to fear his competition. Indeed, Heinrich would never achieve a comparable suc-cess. His political fortunes also declined rapidly. In November 1918 he stood behind the Council of Intellectual Workers. But with his "moderate anti-Bolshevist stance" he was no radical. Thomas pegged him correctly as "nothing but an old-line democrat of the Celtic-romantic, Wilsonian stamp—bourgeois parliamentary republic." Heinrich continued to special-ize in the windy pronouncements Thomas had satirized throughout the *Reflections.* In February 1919, Kurt Eisner, the council's leader, was assassinated. Thomas learned that Heinrich spoke at the funeral, "amid the tolling of bells and heavy firing . . . reminiscent of New Year's Eve," and imagined both his discomfort and his political kitsch: "He probably used all the language that is in the air these days, as is only appropriate when paying last respects to a political humanitarian."

Three weeks later, Heinrich spoke at an Eisner memorial and predictably invoked his notions of intellectual responsibility. Thomas paraphrased them: "Eisner had been the first intellectual at the head of a German state . . . in a hundred days he had had more creative ideas than others in fifty years, and . . . had fallen as a martyr to truth. Nauseating!"

The same day Thomas also noted a favorable review of the *Reflections* by Egon Friedell, a Viennese Jewish critic, adding with displeasure that Friedell "at the same time hails Heinrich. We should consider ourselves fortunate to have two such fellows, he says." What he may not have realized was that Heinrich was now as politically alienated as he. When the Munich government turned sharply to the left, Heinrich jumped ship; he did not want a red Germany. After national troops overthrew the revolution, working-class Tories exulted in its defeat. Heinrich fled with his wife and daughter, terrified of the workers he had previously defended; the salon Communist's flight became a popular cartoon in journals like *Simplicissimus*. (Mann compared Heinrich's flight to his inability to face their dying father. In his final days, Senator Mann had extolled Thomas's loyalty; once again he had outlasted his brother.)

By 1920 *Der Untertan* had stopped selling; by 1922 Heinrich's commitment to the Weimar Republic had become equivocal: he wrote Félix Bertaux, a French critic, "For the moment one cannot give people a fully developed democracy—not even economically."

He continued to be regarded as a magisterial figure; Ludwig Marcuse called him "the Hindenburg of the left," perhaps in recognition of his heroically pacifist stance during the Great War. It was not enough to sustain his reputation: in the 1940s Heinrich complained that he didn't wish to survive only as the author of "a lead editorial."

For two years, the Mann Germany read was Heinrich. During this period, Thomas Mann published two domestic "idylls," the starkest possible contrast to his brother's recent work. As a result one Berlin writer dismissed both pieces as beneath consideration. Mann understood that he couldn't deliver Heinrich's brand of goods: when Kurt Martens requested a political essay, he replied, "What could I possibly say? 'Fellows, cheer up, it's not that bad'? I can't, for I find it as bad and repulsive as possible." At the start of the year, he had written Heinrich that he had enabled people to "live." But now "I am simply in no state to comfort and encourage people; I don't feel very much like the man of the hour who is called upon to speak."

A Man and His Dog was written between March and October 1918, while he was coming down from the extended delirium of his *Reflections*. If that work betrayed a lack of narrative distance, this story was placidly disengaged, the musings of a contented homebody. It defied his editor's expectation and became one of his most popular works, conveying an emotional warmth readers often found lacking in his fiction. (In his diary he refers to the story's ironical but sympathetic treatment of the human spirit.) The narrative voice is modest: after depicting a river zone, he declares, "I have covered the whole region and done all I can to bring it before my reader's eye. I like my description pretty well, but I like the reality of nature even better."

In a love letter Rilke wrote, "Can you imagine . . . how glorious it is, for example, to see into a dog . . . to ease oneself into the dog exactly at his center, the place out of which he exists as a dog?" Auden praises the master painters who could depict, in the midst of apocalyptic ruin, dogs still going about their doggy lives. Mann evokes the German pointer Bashan's reality by identifying the specific elements of his canine world.

He struggled to get the details right. He wrote Bertram on June 29, 1918, "The chapter on the landscape in the Bashan idyll is giving me trouble with botany. I have to know how to call the ash and birch trees by name." Despite his daily strolls with the dog, Mann's eye was not attuned to nature, though he noted in his diary the sexual embraces he occasionally spied. The narrator anticipates an urban encroachment on the natural setting: the wilderness abuts a settlement of bourgeois villas, "signs of a hopeful real-estate enterprise"—an indication that this story is meant to be more than a timeless fable.

As in his diary, nature seems voluptuous:

The soil is not what one expects in a wood. It is loamy, gravelly, even sandy. It seems anything but fertile, and yet, within its nature, it is almost luxuriantly so, for it is overgrown with tall rank grass, often the dry, sharp-cornered kind that grows on dunes. In winter it covers the ground like trampled hay; not seldom it cannot be distinguished from reeds, but in other places it is soft and fat and juicy, and among it grow hemlock, colesfoot, nettles, all sorts of low-growing things, mixed with tall thistles and tender young tree shoots. . . . Now, all this is not a wood, it is not a park, it is simply an enchanted

garden, no more and no less. I will stand for the word—though of
course nature here is stingy and sparse and tends to the deformed;
a few botanical names exhausting the catalogue of her performance.
The ground is rolling, it constantly rises and falls away, so that the
view is enclosed on every hand, with a lovely effect of remoteness and
privacy . . . one could not feel more secluded.

Mann folds the traditional German affection for rural solitude into a self-
conscious commentary. (He was pleased when a critic praised this paragraph's
"humorous tone.")

Everywhere in Mann's universe someone is performing. He describes
the time when he and the dog come upon a hunter, "a fine figure of a
man," majestically pacing "like an operatic star." He creates a novel pre-
dicament for himself, the obligation to capture Bashan's confusion upon
encountering a figure totally unlike his master. "I can think of large words
with which to describe it, phrases we use for great occasions; I could say
that he was thunderstruck. But I do not like them; I do not want to use
them. The large words are worn out, when the great occasion comes they
do not describe it." (As if the high-flown verbiage of the *Reflections* served
something less than a great occasion.)

So in an advertisement for his innovative powers, he replaced "large
words"—a German poet's legacy—with a Mannian description, both simple and prosaic:

> *What was that?* He looked and listened with that sort of rage in which
> extreme astonishment expresses itself, listened within himself and
> heard things that had always been there, however novel and unheard
> of in the present form they took. Yes, from this start, which flung him
> to right and left and halfway round on his axis, I got the impression
> that he was trying to look at himself, trying to ask: What am I? What
> am I? Is this me?

If a dog has an interior life, Mann gives it a physical form. His trust in
literature's power to evoke the inexpressible is seldom so winningly confirmed.

The narrator is piqued by Bashan's infatuation with the glamorous
hunter. He advises the dog to flirt with the stranger but to do so forewarned: "There are certain distinctions—that kind of man with a gun is
very keen on them: native advantages or disadvantages, to make my meaning clear, troublesome questions of pedigree and breeding, if I must be

plain." In other words, a hunting man is a snob and a bully. Since you're a thinking man's dog, you must acquire an informed skepticism. Otherwise, you'll fall too easily for a handsome face or a virile posture.

Six months pass, Bashan forgets his infidelity, and the narrator promises him a new hike tomorrow if the "outer world" allows it. "Then I hasten inside, to take off my hobnailed boots, for the soup stands waiting on the table." What Mann doesn't say is that the soup is meager, that in the last months of wartime, most German families go hungry. The idyll touches lightly on his philosophical obsessions, but its transparent aim is pleasure. Rumors of war do not invade the enchanted ground, though they will sweep over the magic mountain.

"Gesang vom Kindchen" ("Song of the Little Child"), the other idyll, is Mann's most atypical work. He frequently admitted that poetry was not his strength—and insisted therefore that the modern *Dichter* required other skills. Yet between November 1918 and March 1919, he composed this epic. It was a reckless gesture; few poets praised his attempt. Indeed, on June 7, 1919, he admits in his diaries, "I have difficulty relating to lyric poetry, at least by my contemporaries."

Toward the best-known of these contemporaries, Stefan George, his feelings were more respectful than affectionate, despite their shared sexual temperament. In 1924, upon meeting George, Mann described the experience, in a letter to George's disciple Bertram, as "weird." Meanwhile Glöckner, Bertram's companion and a member of George's circle, regarded Mann as intellectually unsound and politically suspect. Some years later, Mann admitted that the work of Germany's other great modern poet Rilke struck him as "precious."

Instead he looked to earlier poets: Goethe, whose *Hermann and Dorothea* provided a model for the "Song," and Platen, whose lyrical homoeroticism he continued to draw upon. (He chose an old-fashioned meter as well—dactylic hexameter.)

Mann saw poetry as the recollection of experience; his song was frankly autobiographical. When he read the work to Katia, he reports, she was "very moved and only objected to my describing our most intimate experiences. But it is these intimate things that are really the most universal and human. I don't know any such scruples." Less disingenuous than usual, he didn't declare himself misunderstood, or claim, as he had in 1903, that a sentence's author owed nothing to those who inspired its composition.

The poem's speaker is a man who has surmounted private temptations to achieve an officially sanctioned form of bliss. His claim that *Death in Venice* had evolved from a drunken song into a moral epic satisfied the

Puritans in his audience; Mann cited it himself as evidence that the novella
should not be read as a study in sexual pathology. But he protests too
much. Consider his paean to the wisdom of maturity:

> Longing suits the boy who romantically desires what is not his,
> Love belongs to the man who protects and blesses his own.

The lines descends from pathos to kitsch. The desiring adolescent sounds
throughout Mann's life. *Sehnsucht* remained his favorite word. The upright
husband, protecting and blessing his own, is an artificial construct, a representative figure in the German sense of social display.

In July 1919, shortly after completing the "Song," he was on vacation
when Katia had her birthday. He opened the day's notes by saluting "my
poor little Katia whom I love just as I love my six children": this enu-
meration reads like a plug for his parenthood. But the vast portion of the
entry was devoted to his infatuation with a youth who resembled his first
love, Armin Martens. Demonstrating his ability to distinguish his own
story from that of other men, just after he expressed his attraction, he
mentioned a "rather suspect, somewhat stupid Baron Schenk who wears an
air of melancholic boredom." (Impetus perhaps to return to his family.)

In the spring of 1919 he resumed *The Magic Mountain*. Four years earlier
he had described the project to Paul Amann: "Before the war I had begun
a longish story whose scene was a sanitarium for tuberculosis in the high
mountains—a story with pedagogic and political overtones, in which a
young man comes up against the most seductive of powers, death. . . . The
spirit of the whole is humoristically nihilistic, and the bias leans rather
toward the side of sympathy with death." During the interval, his plans
had changed. A lightweight novella, intended as an amusing complement
to *Death in Venice*, began to assume epic proportions. He was not yet compelled by the subject. It wasn't inherently pleasing, and he questioned his
abilities.

Up to now he had lacked the "goodness, health, humanity" found so
abundantly in the work of Knut Hamsun. At that moment, Mann found
the Norwegian a vital example of "natural communism." During the
Second World War, Hamsun became a notorious supporter of the Nazis;
by then Mann recognized that any flight from civilization was inherently
reactionary.

The competition Mann feared most still came from Heinrich. He was
sure that his novel would surpass *Der Untertan* in ambition and satirical
range. But he also knew that "the subject matter is extremely ticklish and
requires tact," most particularly the "themes of 'time' and 'forbidden love.' "

What threatened to date his work as much as Heinrich's was a "similarly old-fashioned effect, if only because of the pathological undercurrent." In other words, the Manns were ordinary bourgeois neurotics, unlike the new breed of life affirmers, Hamsun being the prime example. (To which one can only reply, Two cheers for bourgeois neuroses.)

2

THE MUNICH REVOLUTION

Despite their charms, Mann's career would survive intact without either of his idylls. Far more important in terms of his development was his experience of the Munich revolution. His diaries provide a history of political turbulence contemplated by someone whose feelings keep changing, almost by the hour.

In the fall of 1918, as the military news grew bleak, Mann hoped that Germany's defeat would not be total. On September 12, Kaiser Wilhelm informed workers at the Krupp factory that the Allies had rejected his peace offer. Mann read the speech with "emotion and sympathy, though also with amusement." It revealed a spirit he might have associated with the world of his father, or of *Buddenbrooks*. "Social humanitarianism, patriarchal": it resonated with a "Schiller-like pathos"—"the whole thing very German in tone and spirit, old-fashioned in that it struck a popular note, not democratically demagogic." But this form of political theater was drawing to a close. By October 4, a new democratic government had been established in Berlin; by November 11, a Socialist was the chancellor.

Mann gladly sacrificed the old Junker establishment. On November 8, three days before the Armistice, he learned that Berlin revolutionaries were taunting Wilhelm II with cries of "shitheel bumpkin" and "bloodthirsty tyrant." He registered a parenthetical "very good"; two days later he admitted no sorrow over "the fall of dynasties" or the dissolution of the "imperial idea and name," seeing them as essentially propaganda tools in Bismarck's invention of the Second Reich. (On September 28, he had advised his brother-in-law, the banker Löhr, that Germany must modernize, democratize herself, sweeping away the old romantic imperial nation.)

He expected a German spirit to survive whatever political or economic turns. It would remain chastened and humbled, a modest national ethos not unlike the melancholy resignation with which he currently faced the future.

But Germany's enemies, he discovered, would not let her off so lightly. He grieved over what newspapers called "the greatest collapse in world history." The defeat was as much cultural as political. On September 16, he writes that "[our enemies would] drive out of us the experience of Goethe, Luther, Frederick the Great, and Bismarck, so that we can 'adjust ourselves to democracy.' " Their arrogance was so great that he immediately added "I do not regret a word of the *Reflections*."

France and America particularly enraged him. After writing a book decrying Heinrich's Francophiliac sophistries, he now beheld the loss of Alsace-Lorraine to France. He feared that the loss of ore shipments (from Alsace-Lorraine and Upper Silesia) would lead to the unemployment of millions of German workers. Initially he hoped that victory would induce the English and Americans to check "a French passion for vengeance." But the nation of Frederick the Great was forced to "grovel." The culture of Luther and Nietzsche depended on the banal graces of an American Quaker, Woodrow Wilson. Mann felt no gratitude for American charity: any kindnesses bestowed on the impoverished and starving Germans betrayed a political subtext. On November 12, he writes, "The assurance of food supplies will presumably have the effect of averting Bolshevist terror. . . . Our Bolshevist-fearing enemies are not helping us out of 'mercy,' but know very well what they are doing." No gesture was pure; they were protecting their economic system against a potentially more appealing one.

As far as his own financial prospects were concerned, on September 28, he appeared nonchalant about the possible curtailing of the rights of inheritance—exhibiting a little concern for Katia's health and Elisabeth's reduced expectations—but by October 21, after expressing his disgust with the widespread "humbuggery," he added that "I don't wish to be impoverished, to that much I can testify."

In a time of general confusion, a so-called revolution came to Germany. It arrived in a haphazard fashion, the product of neither political agitation nor a mass change of heart. (As Mann said, "Out of fear we declare ourselves reformed.") The Social Democrats who inherited a defeated administration had not been an oppositional force for years. In 1914 they had thrown almost unanimous support behind the Kaiser. Their spokesman Friedrich

Ebert (1871–1925) refused to admit any national guilt; he became famous for his remark that German boys had been "undefeated on the battlefield." Unfortunately Kurt Eisner also offered an unsatisfactory perspective. Mann objected to Eisner's attempts to blame things exclusively on the national leaders. All Germans were implicated—Mann knew his own complicity—and acknowledging their universal guilt would hasten their political evolution. (Similarly in 1944 he parted company with émigré leftists by insisting that German guilt could not be restricted to Hitler and his cronies.)

However, a radical movement did exist in Berlin—the Spartacists, the original German Communists, led by Rosa Luxemburg and Karl Liebknecht. Their opposition to parliamentary democracy was principled and vehement, tonally similar to Mann's reservations about Heinrich's politics. On November 10 Mann reports that "the Bolshevist-communist Spartacus group is becoming dangerously active . . . proclaiming its program calling for all power to the Workers' and Soldiers' Councils without elections or a national assembly."

The Moderate Socialists in Berlin and Munich promised a much less radical government. Surprisingly Mann was not opposed to their plans, or their leaders: Ebert, a former saddler and trade unionist who would be the first chancellor of the German Reich; and Gustav Noske (1868–1946), who would briefly serve as its first minister of defense. (Ebert himself would have preferred a parliamentary monarchy to a democracy; and Noske was far more comfortable with counterrevolutionaries than with radicals; under his direction, the army brutally suppressed the Berlin Spartacists.) On November 10, upon learning that a red flag waved over the Royal Palace in Berlin, he admitted that while "I was never a republican," he could tolerate a new Germany, despoiled of its imperialist identity, and transformed into a "free state" that included German-speaking Austria: the familiar dream of *grossdeutsch* patriots. For the moment cultural nationalism eased his fears about the socialist republic. A German revolution was "after all German, though nonetheless a revolution. No French wildness, no Russian drunkenness." The legislative makeup would be eclectic: "bourgeois and objective [sic] elements are taking place" (precisely what the Spartacists feared). The subsequent "evolution" (November 12) will greatly confound the West's "bourgeois imperialists [and] windbags."

As the Bolshevik revolution was virtually bloodless, the Munich one was a combination of pacifism and serendipity. On November 8, Hedwig Pringsheim called with the news that a group led by Kurt Eisner and Gustav Landauer had assumed leadership of the newly dubbed "Democratic and Social Republic of Bavaria." Under the leadership of a "provisional

Workers', Soldiers', and Peasants' Council," they pledged to maintain order and guarantee private property, a socialism that threatened nobody. Landauer (grandfather of the American director Mike Nichols) composed pointed attacks on Marxism, which he regarded as inflexible, antithetical to *Geist*, and devoid of the lyrical power that inspires lasting change. In early 1919, Mann read Landauer's critique with satisfaction.

Throughout the country revolutionary councils took power. One such group was known as the Council of Intellectual Workers. Although Heinrich was a staunch early member, Mann could see no parallel between himself and common laborers. But he was not alarmed. He guessed that the revolution would become "conservative the moment it is accomplished. Extremism then becomes the preventive and shield against what goes beyond the extreme, namely chaos." This witty perception was predicated on Germany's affinity for the middle way. It also anticipated the Kronstadt rebellion of 1921, when Trotsky destroyed the sailors' movement, arguing that it posed a threat of anarchy and chaos during wartime. Conservatives long before Mann had expected the revolution to devour its children.

Bolshevism involved, in Mann's words, an unholy marriage between the largely Jewish intelligentsia and the mob. For once Mann found himself on speaking terms with power. The Munich revolution was led by men from his circle. Their one common element was a Jewish identity; he observed often, sometimes in amazement and respect, other times with active contempt, that virtually every significant figure among the Munich radicals was a Jewish intellectual. (The Berlin Spartacists, led by the Polish Jew Rosa Luxemburg, had a fair contingent of gentiles.)

His ambivalence concerning the Jews had not abated. They remained his constant companions, whether these were his assimilated in-laws, the Pringsheims; his publisher, Samuel Fischer; his neighbor and friend Bruno Walter; or his other neighbors the wealthy Hallgartens. But the diaries express his irritation with Fischer's wife and his disbelief that the "stupid" Frau Hallgarten could be a major peace activist.

He raged privately against his Jewish colleagues. The journalist Maximilian Harden, who had broken the Eulenburg scandal, had been silenced during the war. Now he reappeared: "Filthy buffoon. How is anyone supposed to believe *you* now, no matter whether what you say is believable or not?" (November 7). The Munich scribblers included the novelist Wilhelm Herzog, who wrote unkindly about Mann's apolitical idylls; the playwright Ernst Toller, whose student work he had encouraged during the war; and his close friend Bruno Frank. He condemned them all. Herzog was "a slimy literary racketeer . . . kept by a movie star. Big city piss-elegance of the Jew boy (who doesn't pay his bills). . . ." Frank was "a little confidence man with a dimple in his cheek." Toller was also said to have an actress for his lover. To a man, they were hustlers, gigolos, and salon Communists. (Meanwhile he mourned the loss of his Jewish doctor Loeb, the original of Dr. Sammet in *Royal Highness*.)

While Jews had never been so powerful, anti-Semitism was rampant, thanks to the wartime leaders. At the end of 1916, after the German defeat at Verdun, the generals Paul von Hindenburg (1847–1934) and Erich Ludendorff (1865–1937) had taken over the army, turning the Kaiser into a figurehead and transforming the monarchy into something close to a military dictatorship. The two generals had then mobilized the economy for total war, summoning their countrymen to be civilian soldiers. Appealing to xenophobia and militarism, they had evoked all the tendencies that had made Germany the terror of Europe since the Franco-Prussian War, in which both had played major roles. (This had given Mann an immediate connection with his father's hero, Bismarck.) Now, after the defeat, still prompted by the two generals, the Germans were ready to blame anyone but themselves—Jews, Freemasons, Socialists; Ludendorff ecumenically added Jesuits and the Pope to the list.

The myth of the Jewish back-stabber was already widespread. Mann grew so terrified of the mobs that by November 19 he had prepared these placatory words: "Listen here, I'm neither a Jew nor a war profiteer nor anything else that's bad. I'm a writer who has built this house from money I earned with my intellectual labor. In my drawer I have two hundred marks. Take the money and divide it between you, but don't destroy my books and things." In the same entry, he noted that Heinrich had just been offered the presidency of the Intellectual Workers' Council, and had publicly declined. His only satisfaction was that Pfitzner was coming for tea, full of love for the *Reflections*.

In *Doctor Faustus* Mann contends that the 1918 blockade, which lasted until March 1919, kept Germany "bourgeois-democratic" and prevented a Bolshevik victory. Zeitblom describes the Munich radicals as a gang of "lunatics, dreamers, clowns, plotters, and small-time philistines." At one point he attends a lecture on "Revolution and the Love of Humanity," delivered with "a sybaritic and dimpling relish." This satire indicates that despite his reconciliation with Heinrich, Mann still needed to avenge the insults of 1915. The kitschy title and fatuous bonhomie dispatch Heinrich into the ranks of the small-timers.

Mann's anger was short-lived. Toller, for one, protected him from house arrest during the revolution's last bloody days. Mann reciprocated. In July 1919, after Toller's arrest, Mann testified on his behalf. Two years later, he composed an essay in which he acknowledged the crucial role Jews had played in German culture—and his own life. (During their emigration, Toller, Herzog, and Frank would once more be reckoned his friends.)

He carefully distinguished between Germany's revolution, led by Jewish intellectuals, and those led by French Corybants and Russian drunks. Up to 1917 Marxists regarded imperial nations with their large, well-organized laboring classes as the best prospects for revolution; the impoverished and backward eastern countries made up the train. Had a social revolution triumphed in Germany—and had the scribblers' humanism moderated the darker tendencies of Bolshevism—history would have been vastly different.

For the few months before the revolution sputtered and died, Mann observed up close the century's single approximation of socialism with a human face. True to form he flipped sides a dozen times. On November 28, he became so furious over the Socialists' "idiocy" that he welcomed an invasion by French and American forces to restore order. A mere day later he writes, "No doubt the future belongs to the concept of socialism, even of communism, as an idea—in contrast to the old democracy represented by the West, which incontestably has no part in the future." (As he later elaborated, that conclusion placed old-line democrats, namely Heinrich, in Trotsky's dustbin of history.) In one angry moment, on March 24, 1919, he imagined himself running down the street and shouting, "Down with lying Western democracy! Hurray for Germany and Russia! Hurray for Communism!"—a physical spectacle remarkable to contemplate.

His ambivalence was characteristic. So were the familiar means of escaping the public world. On December 20, 1918, a meeting at his club proved stimulating, but he abstained from the discussion, "since what needed to be said seemed to me too ticklish." Moreover the discussion was "all too political, not moral and psychological," and he found himself "absorbed in admiring an elegant young man [the Hermes mentioned earlier]. . . . Seeing him unquestionably affected me in a way I have not noted in myself for a long time. . . . I readily admit to myself that this could turn into an experience." (The boy resembled a sixteen-year-old student he had recently met and found pleasing.) On March 30, 1919, he declares, apologetically, "In my exhaustion, forgot to note that yesterday the Hermes-like young dandy who made an impression on me several weeks ago attended my reading."

Beginning in the summer of 1919, he frequently repaired to a summer house in Feldafing, usually by himself. The small chalet had been built by Michael's godfather, the art historian Georg Richter (1875–1941), who would later join Mann in exile. The house came equipped to his delight with a brand-new gramophone.

Literature offered another form of solace. On September 18, 1918, he writes, "Purely intellectual thoughts have a soothing effect after embittered brooding on the cheap humbuggery of politics." On November 12, the obsequious praise of a critic, Max Krell, "made me feel good and distracted me from political matters so that I felt a secret sense of relief." On February 26, 1919, amidst fears of censorship and political violence, he expressed his joy upon returning to Goethe. "How at home I always feel in the Goethean sphere, how it gladdens and stimulates me. If I manage to get to *The Confidence Man* I will be able to live and work entirely in that realm." The Goethean sphere, like the realm of sexual fantasy, eased his retreat from political action. Sequestered in either arena, he remained impervious to what was going on in the streets.

The Munich revolutionaries never bothered Mann. Instead, when an insurrection occurred, its origins came from within the household.

Shades of the servants absconding with Grandmother Buddenbrook's treasures, Mann crossed swords with his housemaid Jennie over some missing articles. In the *Reflections*, Mann, lamenting the collapse of standards, had observed that decent help was no longer to be found, and here his words were confirmed in all their arrogance. Klaus Mann recounts how at first Jennie denied any involvement. But when her room was inspected, the Manns discovered a cornucopia of household goods, clothes, rare books, and "two bottles of imported champagne." She had even filched Mann's treasured walking stick. Worst of all, "Jennie tried to hit The Magician. . . . This truly was revolution." Klaus's pleasure at his father's discomfort is palpable.

Jennie sued her employers for libel. In court she appeared a martyr of her class, testifying with demagogic aplomb. The precocious drama critic Klaus Mann dismissed his parents' courtroom appearance as "pitiful"; it was Jennie who stage-managed her own performance, "triumphantly swollen bosom and glaring green satin." The crowd's vocal encouragements for Jennie may have contributed to Mann's excoriations during 1919 against the "canaille." Jennie won the case, but it was a victory as short-lived as the city's revolutionary fervor. Without her old job, she began haunting the Mann family. On wintry evenings, the children sensed Jennie hovering outdoors, whimpering in her cups, occasionally aiming her spit at doors she had once polished.

Klaus was undisturbed by Jennie's kleptomania, and enchanted to learn of her promiscuity: "Why should she not change her lover every other night?" For the future homosexual, sympathy with a female outlaw acquired a political resonance; it extended the revolutionary gesture against his father. This fantasia of adolescent desire and political rebellion evokes the kind of story a younger Thomas Mann might have written in 1919.

The revolution ended first in Berlin. On January 10, 1919, Mann notes the assassinations of Liebknecht and Rosa Luxemburg; a week later, he declares himself "revolted" by her murder. The Munich Spartacists now rallied behind Kurt Eisner despite positions they considered otiose and jejune. On February 21, this native of northern Germany was assassinated by a twenty-two-year-old Bavarian count. An eleven-man government was then formed, comprising various left-wing factions, Moderate Socialists, Independents, and Spartacists. Mann noted, without approval, "Whatever happened, we now have Bolshevism."

He detested both sides. He felt "shock, horror and disgust" over the "idiocy" of the assassin Count Arco's gesture, and an equivalent distaste for the Spartacist posters "branding him a tool of the bourgeoisie": after all, a few weeks ago they had considered Eisner a buffoon. ("The Spartacists have occupied the newspapers; we have a Soviet government *à la russe*.") A civil war threatened. "Planes circling above"; rumors of white counterrevolutionary armies in other cities; and a frightening satisfaction over Eisner's murder that betrayed Munich's traditional anti-Semitism. Klaus reported that his schoolmates, sons of the haute bourgeoisie, "applauded and danced when the news came." Mann and Katia remained on their balcony long after echoes of grenade explosions and wild screams had died out.

On April 17 Mann hoped the White armies under General Franz Xaver von Epp, commander of the Bavarian rifle corps, would march in and restore bourgeois order. It disturbed him that the propertied classes might experience rationing as had their Budapest neighbors. "Student [Ernst] Toller" now commanded the red front; Mann found that "delicious," a clown prince overseeing the barricades.

Flip-flopping by the day, on April 20 he yet again acknowledged the ideological validity of Bolshevism. That afternoon, after reading Friedrich Eicken's 1887 study *The Medieval Weltanschauung*, he determined that its world-view was "socialist-communist." This prompted a rush of sympathy for the international proletariat, as if they joined him in a romantic denial of everything he condemned in modern society, specifically the League of Nations with its "alliance of robbery, exploitation and imperialist counterrevolution."

That day, while anticipating the socialism of his maturity, he also discerned a major reason for the ultimate collapse of Soviet communism. Reading Bolshevik propaganda, he found references to "Dr. Shylock." With

Eicken's study in mind, he recognized that attacks on "usury" were inherently anti-Semitic. "Russia has *medieval* feelings about capitalism, and knows how to communicate its views toward the world."

Toward the end of April Bolshevik forces began to dominate the Munich alliance. On April 27, Mann reports without commentary that the Communists Tovia Axelrod and Eugen Leviné planned to confiscate safe deposits; on April 30, billeting by red armies seemed likely, an invasion of the bourgeois household. Yet even then his attitude remained "ambivalent," as he informed Katia, still recuperating from the birth of her sixth child, Michael. The French now ruled the Saar valley, and the Poles were set to claim Danzig. "Hatred and disgust. How can one help but go over to communism lock, stock, and barrel when it has the tremendous virtue of being hostile to the Allies?"

Chancellor Ebert may have shared Mann's rage. But this did not bring him closer to the Communists, who planned to leap borders and dissolve the class system. He would not allow Munich's secession, much less wholesale financial expropriation, and determined to finish the radicals for good.

On May 1, of all days, the revolution died. Several aristocrats were taken hostage and murdered, among them the Prince and Princess von Thurn und Taxis. The Factory and Soldiers' Councils disowned this "bestial deed" and rallied behind the moderates led by two twenty-six-year-old intellectual workers, Emil Maenner and Toller. Violence had destroyed the image of a republic founded on pacifism. Seeing the Munich reds demoralized and disgraced, Franz Xaver von Epp took his chance. By six p.m. his forces controlled the city.

A familiar thrill stirred Mann. "They are Prussian and South German units in steel helmets, good-looking, and disciplined." (The Munich reds dubbed the white armies "Prussians.") He liked them because they were North Germans teaching the southerners a lesson—and perhaps as much because they were cute. He was still impressed by young men in uniforms.

He misjudged their discipline. The Prussians massacred left-wingers of all persuasions; Leviné was executed, Landauer beaten to death. The soviets could not defend themselves: "The touted heroism of the reds eventually amounted to nil." On May 12, Mann added that "the solidarity of the proletariat seems to be standing the test no better than in 1914." For a few days, a volunteer corps of reactionary students began "acting up," terrorizing the citizens—forerunners of the Hitler youth groups.

Mann drew various conclusions. "The Munich Communist episode is over, scarcely much chance to try it again. Feeling of liberation and cheerfulness, the pressure was abominable—these scoundrelly heroes of the 'masses' murdered hostages." (He didn't know that Toller's intercession had prevented his being taken hostage.) On May 5, he conferred with Ernst Bertram on the need for a "cultural front against all kinds of fanatical extremism." They were "peering into an abyss." The Entente remained "hateful," but the West must be "saved from the horrors of a mass migration from below." Two weeks earlier he had sounded like Rosa Luxemburg, but that was then.

In the same day's journal, he compliments the "discipline" of Epp's marching troops. "Katia's mother feels it is again too 'militaristic' but I am quite in sympathy and find it considerably easier to breathe under the military dictatorship than under the rule of the *crapule*." He was now glorying in reaction, reading with pleasure the French mystic Joséphin Péladan's "antidemocratic" pronouncements, "except where his . . . antimilitaristic ideas come to the fore." These days he was all for a strong army.

As in the last days of the war, Katia's family disagreed with him. Alfred Pringsheim shared his wife's contempt for General Epp. (They were right; he later served as Nazi governor of Bavaria from 1933 to 1945; his less fortunate aide-de-camp, Ernst Roehm, the SA leader, was killed on the notorious Night of the Long Knives in 1934.) On June 1, Katia's grandmother, Hedwig Dohm, died in Berlin, still hoping for a German republic that dwelled "peaceful, progressive" among her "sister nations." Years later, his own politics having greatly evolved, Mann saluted this "touching little mother of mankind."

For now he required a more conservative mentor. By July 1919 he thought he'd found one after reading Oswald Spengler's *Decline of the West*. He was excited by a common interest; the "problem of time" had first impressed him as a literary motif in 1912, the very year Spengler began his study. Mann had found another soul mate: "my unusual sensitivity, linking my solitude to all the more profound thoughts and insights of the times." (By March 3, 1920, he was comparing himself to Einstein: "I anticipated [the problem of time—Einstein's subject as much as Spengler's] in my conception of *The Magic Mountain* just as I had anticipated the political antitheses leading up to the war." But considering the years he had wasted since then, "satisfaction at my seismographic sensitivity . . . is diminished.")

He even found a justification in nature for his intellectual solitude. In February 1920, after visiting his mother in Polling, he recalled a moonlit stroll when "the quarries and the mountain range locked in snow, seemed like a lunar landscape." It was something approaching an epiphany for this agnostic, and he defined it to his taste: "Sense of the pure country life; piety something sensual and physical. 'The religious man thinks only of himself.'" On a similar note, that month he had his first X ray, which allowed him to observe a skeleton of his hand, much as Schiller had regarded the same member with love. The egotistical sublime banished thoughts of politics.

After the whites' triumph, Mann's references to politics decreased sharply. He still grew livid over the Entente's excruciating demands. For a while he contemplated a more humane and intellectual form of conservatism. On January 18, 1920, he wrote Count Hermann Keyserling that "nothing is more important than the infusion of intelligence into German conservatism." Three days later, in his diary, he laments that right-wing students booed Max Weber when he condemned Count Arco, Eisner's assassin: "The antirevolutionary nationalistic mood of the students is basically gratifying to me, although Arco is a fool and the individual proponents of that mood are boors."

Soon enough the right disappointed him. In March 1920, a government official, Wolfgang Kapp, organized a counterrevolutionary coup in Berlin. (Though General Noske, who had brutally suppressed the Spartacist uprising in 1919, offered no resistance to Kapp's troops, they were overthrown within a few days, and Noske was forced to resign.) It did not win Mann's endorsement, despite his belief that "the previous government had already made too much of a mess of things." He detected American financial support behind the putsch. Recalling the preceding year's about-faces, he longed for a political disintegration: "The centralized Republic . . . is a lie." Amazingly, he now hailed Lenin as "the only true man in the world, a Genghis Khan, the incomparably more powerful antithesis of poor Woodrow Wilson."

On March 26, Mann determined that any opposition to Wall Street and the City of London was doomed. "We must preserve the bourgeois republic inasmuch as we cannot survive economically without the support of Western capitalism." So we had best get about our business; cultural resistance has become a farce. On April 11 he marveled that the "educated classes . . . still cling to their fashionable revolutionary, pacifist attitudes." He took Klaus to a performance by the monologuist Ludwig Hardt, filled with stirring revolutionary passages drawn from writers like Heine and Wedekind, and Mann exhibited less sympathy for the audience of true believers than he had extended Toni Buddenbrook in her moments of revolutionary nostalgia.

As if his bourgeois past contained an antidote, he contemplated dropping *The Magic Mountain* for a great "Book of Life" about his own family including the Pringsheims and a *"sehr menschlich"* Mama: this despite his reservations about the whole lot, including Frau Mann.

He decided to withdraw from politics entirely. On May 25, when Katia tried to win his support for the middle-class Democratic Party—the preference of most German Jews despite the radicals among them—he was unreceptive. He opposed alike the Socialist and Catholic parties in Munich. "I'll remain on the sidelines"—even as he had been scared to participate in the Herrenklub debates and fled the manly world of action.

Yet his literary and political fortunes had improved. In January 1920 he reported a great interest in *Death in Venice* among German students—proof of "a turning away from nihilistic demoralization, from Bolshevism of every kind." Thomas Mann was once more a star; on March 23 he announced that "the film people came at 11:30 and took pictures of me [in my study] with the children [Klaus, Golo, and Elisabeth] in the garden."

3

MANN ONSTAGE

During the season of revolution, Mann kept his feelings to himself. Only his diaries reveal his swings from right to left and his dissatisfaction with all forms of power. Once the republic collapsed, he vowed to abandon politics. Yet, with his unerring instinct for paradox, it was precisely then that he went public. After the curtain set on the Munich revolution, Thomas Mann took to the stage.

His children almost beat him there. In 1919 they set up a family troupe, The Amateur League of German Players, joined by their neighbors Ricki Hallgarten and Grete Walter. Bruno Walter mentions a performance featuring his daughters, Klaus, Erika, Ricki, and a ten-year-old Golo playing a lady in mourning: "His earnest endeavor to portray a ladylike sadness contrasted most strikingly with the rakish hint at the clef of a woman's bosom by means of a self-devised charcoal line on his extremely décolleté childish breast." Taking fame for granted, the children requested a critique from their illustrious fathers.

(Yet even these fortunate children would become victims of the war, or so Klaus contended. In 1932 Ricki was the first member of his circle to commit suicide: an act of "immense naughtiness," according to Thomas Mann, that haunted Ricki's lover, Klaus. In 1939 Grete Walter was killed by her husband, the film producer Robert Neppach, who then shot himself. In 1949 Klaus took his own life.)

About this time Mann began to cultivate, more actively than before, a network of literary colleagues. He maintained relations with Martens and Bruno Frank—despite his nasty comments about their politics—and enjoyed a correspondence with the short-story writer Josef Ponten that began in January 1919. Like Jakob Wassermann, all three were masters of middle-brow literature, German equivalents of the Austrian Stefan Zweig—in other words, no threat. In June 1919, he wrote Ponten that he was deeply moved by Hermann Hesse's *Demian*—its homoerotic metaphysics were guaranteed to impress Mann—and soon after he renewed an acquaintance begun when Hesse had panned *Royal Highness*.

In December 1919 he traveled to Vienna for a new production of *Fiorenza*. The rehearsal inspired doubts about his playwriting talent and unpleasant memories of the conflict with Heinrich. But the play was well received by critics and public alike. After the dissension in Munich, Vienna seemed an oasis of hospitality.

While there, he met Robert Musil, then best known for his study of boarding-school homosexuality and sadism, *Young Törless*. As if to underline a congruence of interests, Musil gave Mann a copy of his most recent collection of novellas, inscribed with a quotation from *Death in Venice*. (A few months later, Mann would complain that Musil's stories involved "too much of the female element." He was at that time smitten with Hans Blüher's warriors.)

Musil's great novel, *The Man Without Qualities*, easily challenges *The Magic Mountain* in boldness of conception and visionary reach. Like Mann, he is a master of the essayistic voice. At his best, he is such a rigorous stylist that after him Kafka may appear immature, Mann chatty, Brecht arch, Rilke precious, and Walter Benjamin hermetic. We know that he considered Mann an overrated hack, little better than Musil's countryman Stefan Zweig. They seemed to share at most an interest in adolescent sexuality—Musil's claim that *Törless*'s storyline merely provided the occasion for abstract inquiry can be discounted.

A year later, another Viennese acquaintance, Ludwig Hardt, introduced Mann to the work of a new writer from Prague named Franz Kafka. Mann was not impressed at first but within a few weeks had become a devotee. It's worth arguing that Mann's political development, which began that year, reflected his turn from Spengler to Kafka (and, even more, to Walt Whitman). However, at the moment, he remained a cultural—and, not incidentally, political—conservative. On April 29, 1920, for instance, while thinking of *Der Ring des Nibelungen*, he experienced "a wave of rage at Heinrich and his wanton political blabber against Wagner. Feelings of hatred."

Other professional introductions occurred during this period. In the summer of 1920 he met Annette Kolb. A devout Catholic lesbian, forever living on the kindness of her peers, Kolb remained one of his literary friends

until 1948, when, in *Doctor Faustus*, he described her as resembling a benevolent sheep. Upon their first meeting she alerted Mann to the work of
another new writer, the Frenchman Marcel Proust.

Mann also commenced a highly personal reading of Freud. On May 24,
1921, he notes that Freud's new work "confirms certain historical tendencies" he had observed for himself. Psychoanalysis dealt a fatal blow to any
form of romanticism not saturated with critical insight. "The end of Romanticism, of which I am still a part, expresses itself in all kinds of ways,
including for example a weakening and dying of the sexual symbolism that
is virtually identical with it (*Parsifal*)."

As he recognized in November 1914, his novel's "intellectual humor
[would be] based on the contrast between the mystique of the flesh and
political virtue." Despite Freud, Mann would not give up his moribund
dream, whether it was identified as "mystique of the flesh" or "inversion."
A week later he reports enthralled discussions about Whitman's homosexuality with Hans Reisiger.

And with his particular sense of audience, on that same May 31 when
he contemplated Whitman's homosexuality, he determined to substitute at
his next literary reading the "Hippe" chapter from *The Magic Mountain* for
the section called "Analysis." The introduction of Hippe with his Slavic
cheekbones, the physiognomy that returns in the form of Hans Castorp's
female lover, Chauchat, is unabashed "sexual symbolism." Between Whitman and Freud, Mann's preferences were clear.

Sehnsucht remained paramount. Take the events of October 31, 1920.
Mann attended an open rehearsal of Beethoven's *Missa Solemnis*. His diary
notes the presence of Elsa Walter and a remarkable Princess Gisela, "an
Imperial Highness inasmuch as she is descended from Karl V." He also
recounts that Bruno Walter's lecture was disappointing. Rhetoric never
convinces him of a musical piece's worth, not even Beethoven's; he must
listen "often" and "thoroughly." A range of subject and character worthy
of his novel. Yet in the midst of this plenty, "My chief impression was of
a remarkably handsome young man, Slavic in appearance and wearing a
sort of Russian costume, with whom I established a kind of contact at a
distance, since he noticed my interest in him immediately and was obviously pleased by it."

Mann's public readings served him well. They provided a living during
the worst days of inflation; they allowed him to try out new material
and gauge the response. Above all they let him manipulate the terms of
his own representation. Thus, an off night was like a failed courtship. On

October 19, 1920, after an overly "refined" audience had sat on its hands, he felt humiliated before his family and friends, and, later that evening, suffered "heart palpitations."

The Mannian theater was, predictably, one of monologue; whatever dialogue occurs involves alternate versions of himself. With a narrative voice Mann courted his listeners; he became their instructor, comrade, rabbi, and suitor. In the years between 1919 and 1923, his co-conspirators were often students. He noted with pleasure when the halls filled up with handsome young faces. His prejudices were apparent; he disliked the bluestockings who surrounded him at literary gatherings, though his irritation passed when he locked eyes with some attractive male. The works he chose to read were geared specifically to such a crowd; they usually included the sexiest early passages of *The Magic Mountain*, "Hippe" or the thermometer sequence.

On April 22, 1920, he read some passages from this novel in Augsburg. A precocious twenty-two-year-old critic, Bert Brecht, applauded the work as

> a kind of refined or naïve guerrilla war against death. The careful description is never lacking in metaphysical implications. . . . The story of the dying woman who does not want to die, who kicks her legs in opposition when the priest comes to her, is incomparable in its mixture of profound horror and charming grandeur.

Mann and Brecht wound up bitter enemies, but this early affirmation indicates their affinities. Both men were masters of sensual thought (about Brecht's Galileo, someone notes, "Even his thinking is sensual"), surpassingly alert to the convergences of horror and charm.

These readings shaped Mann's sense of his own power. On February 8, 1919, he comments after an enthusiastic response to the hunting section from *A Man and His Dog* and to the "School-Sickness" section from *Felix Krull* that the latter was "perhaps the most remarkable thing I have written, but the book as a whole can hardly be kept at such a level."

Why should he be so excited over something written so long ago? Perhaps because it captures an intersection of art and the uncanny, whose implications he only now grasped. In this episode Krull fakes illness to avoid the tedium of school attendance, and spend his time more profitably, reclining in the "whispering shade . . . dreaming the dreams peculiar to my youth and state." First he forges his father's signature "so well . . . that the inventor of it could not himself have distinguished between my products and his own." Next he cons the town doctor by mimicking the physical symptoms of disease.

The physician is famously corrupt, but he has met his match. The protean Krull has a unique gift. Others can only imagine the fits and seizures of illness; his moral control allows him to "improve upon nature . . . out of sheer inward knowledge and contemplation—in short out of a combination of nothing but fantasy and . . . personality."

Dr. Düsing becomes a fellow conspirator: "It is even possible that the wretched man enjoyed corruption for corruption's sake and found that a sufficient reason for conniving at my fraud." Krull interjects that Düsing was "actually stupid," a dumb crook. He won his point because "any un-trained person, if he loves and has knowledge of the flesh," can dupe a medical hack. The fever's etiology was purely mental, a highly refined work of art: "I was drunk with the intensity of my own performance in the role of parodying nature."

Siding with truants didn't steal Mann's show every night; at a later reading, on March 2, 1919, he determined that the hunting sequence better suited "the temper of these times." *A Man and His Dog* was then enjoying worldwide success; it was certainly his commercial hit of the hour.

But Felix Krull's trickery continued to absorb him. Sometime before May 31, 1921, he composed a "military examination scene" in which the mature Krull becomes a postdoctoral candidate in Parodying Nature. (Al-though it is commonly assumed to have been written in the 1950s, he mentions it as early as 1912. It was first published privately in 1925, then in 1937 in a somewhat larger edition by the émigré press Querido Verlag, and finally in a 1954 version.) Knowing Mann enables us to appreciate Krull's stroll toward his military inspectors, the graybeards, doctors, and professors who will determine his future: "I . . . inwardly repelled by so many importunate glances turned on me, bemused by the dreamlike sen-sation of being in a highly vulnerable and defenseless position, seemed to myself to be alone, cut off from every relationship, nameless, ageless, float-ing free and pure in empty space, a sensation I have preserved in memory as not only not disagreeable but actually precious." The product of intense application and self-regard is the dreamlike state of art, "at the critical moment something somnambulistic occurs, halfway between action and accident, doing and being dealt with, which scarcely requires our atten-tion. . . ." Is it also possible that Krull, the object of importunate glances, is the successor to Aschenbach, the bestower of such glances? We now learn how the beloved views himself: "pure in empty space."

On May 31, 1921, Mann read the section and was "genuinely surprised at the comedy and wit." He was now receiving affirmation from many quarters. The applauding youths assured him once more that in addressing his delayed adolescence, he made Mannian play of their polymorphous desires. In the *Reflections*, he assimilates even Felix Krull to German militarism. But the Krull that survives is the one who teases and outwits the authorities—in other words, the grown-ups.

I n late 1920 Mann learned that Ludwig Hardt was performing monologues drawn from the work of Franz Kafka. The notion of Kafka as a dramatic, indeed comic, entertainment reminds one that Charles Dickens was the consummate literary performer, driving audiences to shrieks and fainting fits or reducing them to exhausted laughter. A relation between Dickensian and Kafkaesque terror has been frequently observed. In adding Mann to this formidable duo, it's noteworthy that he thrilled his public with matters less terrifying than sexually ambiguous. If Kafka combines horrible implications with comic understatement, Mann's magic lies in the merger of perverse fantasy and bourgeois prose rhythms: cadences to win the professor's approval, actions to grab his students.

Think of him on a podium, reading the dramatic scenes, interjecting the narrative asides as if he were his own chorus, luring the beautiful youths with common fantasies, making love to a roomful of faces while maintaining the physical and professional distance that made his work seem immune to autobiographical interpretation. His "unseemly literary pleasure" became a public disrobing, exquisitely masked by shadows and decoys: parodying nature, theirs and his own.

4

A FAMILY MAN

In his poem "Song of the Little Child" Thomas Mann vowed to protect and bless his family. The first task he accomplished; he went on the road to pay their bills. One can see him as enduring the worst of both worlds, suffering the burdens of his sexual renunciation while assuming the support of a wife and children. None of the century's other great novelists incurred such obligations; it's difficult to imagine Proust, Lawrence, Kafka, or Musil enacting the paternal role. Lacking the talent, Mann depended as usual on willpower . . . and Katia.

The only vehicle he had for recording his true desires was his journal, and it comes without self-censure or explanation. If he only alludes to passionate embraces—as in his 1942 declaration that twice he had clasped a man he loved in his arms—he reveals something far more resonant. Mann lived out his desires in his fiction to an almost unparalleled extent.

In 1918 he spies the Hermes-like youth and wonders if a new experience awaits him. A few months later he's content merely to gaze fondly at the boy's (imagined?) adoration. Yet, by presenting a Hermes figure in various literary guises, he kept his "experience" fresh and the objects of his desire forever young. In July 1919 he spends Katia's birthday away from home on a seashore vacation. Here he notices Oswald Kirsten, the son of a Hamburg shipbuilder, a strapping fellow reminiscent of Armin Martens. This sight evokes a pained response: "Tonio Kröger, Tonio Kröger. It is the same every time, and the emotion deep."

However, this episode is not just a replay of his adolescent *Sehnsucht*. A few abbreviated jottings later, he interpolates the equation "Kirsten equals Hans Castorp." We know that Castorp's first love, Hippe, was drawn from the model of Willri Timpe, the classmate who succeeded Martens in Mann's affections. Now we learn that Castorp's model resembled Mann's first love. Even as the adult Castorp pursues his Hippe through the form of Clavdia Chauchat, Mann possesses both his loves in a literary embrace.

Did anyone know this? Bertram and his lover, Glöckner, played to Mann's conservative disposition, his love of Nietzsche and Wagner, of moribund beauty and hopeless causes. He had many talks with them about his work in progress. Shortly after his encounter with the Hamburg youth, Mann attended a performance of *Parsifal* with Bertram and Glöckner. A few months earlier he had seen the opera as the exhausted folly of an old sensualist. This time:

> Extremely powerful impression: emotion, admiration, and the usual intrigued mistrust. Never was a work of art so naively contrived a product, a compound of religious impulse, sheer lasciviousness, and sure-handed competence that comes across as wisdom. The aura of sickness: I feel "hopelessly at home" in it, I told Bertram. Whereupon both of us, as if speaking with one voice, exclaimed, "Why of course, it's *The Magic Mountain*."

It's a fortunate author who possesses so empathetic a reader.

But *The Magic Mountain* was not yet finished. A countervailing influence came from his other friend. Where Bertram summoned the Wagnerian in Mann, Reisiger introduced him to the democratic Eros of Walt Whitman. Could there be alternatives less reconcilable?

Initially Katia welcomed both of her husband's soul mates, though she later confessed to finding Bertram vague and stilted. (Mann might have said the mathematician in her was rejecting a philosopher.) He served as Elisabeth's godfather, a title she threatened—at first with a smile—to withdraw once he began praising National Socialism.

The marriage was not robustly physical. Mann reports a few encounters with Katia, "sexual excess" that he justifies as inspiration for what promises to be his most "sensual book." On March 12, 1920, she asks for a backrub and he is overpowered by passion. But such incidents are rare. On July 5, 1920, he first notes that he's "in love with Klaus these days." Nine days later he reports an unhappy marital embrace.

> It can scarcely be a question of sexual impotence, more likely the customary confusion and unreliability of my "sex life." Doubtless the stimulation failure can be accounted for by the presence of desires that are directed the other way. How would it be if a young man were "at

LEFT TO RIGHT:
*Ernst Glöckner and
Ernst Bertram,
Mann's closest friend*

my disposal"? Be that as it may, it would be foolish to let myself get depressed by a failure whose basis is hardly new to me. Far better to treat the matter lightly, with humor, detachment, and self-confidence, since these are the best "medicines."

The next day his attraction toward Klaus spills over into conversation on the train "with the attractive young man in white trousers sitting next to me in third class. Very pleasurable. It seems I am once and for all done with women." How Katia took any of this is not clear, though the phrases "customary confusion . . . a failure whose basis is hardly new" suggest that she was prepared.

Mann does acknowledge her feelings, though primarily by discounting them. On October 17, he writes, "Grateful to Katia for her unwavering love for me even though she no longer awakens my desire, and I am not able to give her pleasure, that is the ultimate sexual pleasure, when I lie with her. The serenity, love, and equanimity with which she takes this are remarkable, and thus I need not be that deeply affected myself." With sangfroid, he decides that since she doesn't seem greatly bothered, neither should he.

These words strike a modern reader as callous. Yet the range of marital adjustments confounds generalization. Perhaps Katia was as undisturbed as Mann believes. She continued to remain his devoted companion, the manager of his affairs, the fiercely protective mother of six difficult children. Other women have thrived in marriages to men far more aggressively homosexual than Mann. Likewise marriages endure long past the period of most intense desire. Physical dissatisfaction was probably the lot of many women of Katia's class. Her mother complained that Professor Pringsheim had diverted his passion to Milka Ternina. There were also numerous women married to far older men—the gap might be two or three decades—who served more as nursemaids than as lovers.

On June 15, 1919, the Manns attended a concert; the conductor, Bruno Walter, threw conspiratorial glances at him from the podium. This sign of affection from an international celebrity reminded him of the distance traveled by the young man who arrived in Munich twenty years earlier. Katia, responding to "a certain complacency on my part [speaks] of our splendid situation in general. There is something touching about two such melancholy people spurring each other on to enjoy their bourgeois comforts." In the letters with which he courted her, as in the summons to austere love that concludes *Royal Highness*, Mann acknowledged that Katia and he were deeply complicated, indisposed to simple pleasure (this despite her enjoyment of all things physical). The "bourgeois comforts" allowed Mann to work untroubled by financial need or ugly surroundings, but they couldn't assuage his melancholy. One might add that Katia hadn't needed to have her own melancholia compounded; as she said, marriage was his idea.*

As a father, Mann did better than some. Bourgeois patriarchs usually left child rearing to their wives. Up into the 1950s, émigré fathers were astonished when their American children proposed trips to the ballpark or discussed popular culture. The nineteenth-century British ideal that children should be seen and not heard has only lately been retired.

All the Mann children recall that Father was not to be disturbed during

---

* While on tour in February 1921, Mann discovered that a family friend, Grete Litzmann, the second wife of Berthold Litzmann, a professor of literature in Bonn, had become "frightfully, hysterically" in love with him. Upon his return to Munich, he found a "frightful letter" from her, "which I read to Katia. Embarrassed at how I am to treat her and her husband." (Apparently she settled down—later diary references treat the Litzmanns as before.)

the morning work period or the afternoon hours spent on letters and his diary. Yet Mann reports summer days when he rowed them across the mountain lakes or sprinkled the "delighted" kids with a garden hose. He entertained them with stories, frequently in Plattdeutsch and Yiddish dialect, and terrified them with tales of "the evil consequences of immoderate greed": even his parables counseled renunciation.

Meanwhile they had a large extended family. On one side were the wealthy, brilliant Pringsheims with their magnificent home, "the castle of childhood," the salon with two grand pianos, the social circle of artists and intellectuals. On the other were Aunt Lula and the widowed grandmother. They reported visiting Frau Mann three or four times a year, when she fed them funny-tasting sweets and told them eerie tales in a strong Lübeck accent. Golo remembers her as scatterbrained, failing to "grow old gracefully"; how after the inflation swallowed up her 400,000 marks, "never real gold in the first place, she still insisted on paying for her own meals, but with banknotes that Katia and Erika made fun of." (Her first granddaughter was obviously more Pringsheim than Mann.)

Under the direction of Klaus and Erika, the children continued as a theatrical troupe. They were an imposing quartet; Thomas was greatly amused when he came upon a group of schoolchildren in terrified flight: "Look out! The Manns are coming." In his memoir, *The Turning Point*, Klaus depicts four anomalous but singularly gifted children. He emphasizes their hunger during the years between 1917 and 1922. They were "children of deprivation" who never fully trusted their later good fortune.

Although both his brothers, Klaus and Michael, died at their own hands, Golo's memoir reveals him to be the gloomiest of the lot. As a conservative, he lacked their Utopian optimism. In 1930 he confided in his diary, "What a wretched childhood we had! Sledding, being afraid of other children, of our parents, of school, melancholy evenings. . . ." His youth may have been the saddest. Both parents found him unattractive—he plaintively remarks that when he observes his childhood photos, he doesn't find an ugly boy—although he admits he was for a time a dirty, lying, play-acting child. (In his diaries, Mann is sometimes amused by Golo's theatrics.)

Klaus and Golo shared their father's inclination. He had bequeathed them a unique patrimony: a literary model for their adolescent sexuality. Both use *Tonio Kröger* to describe their schoolboy crushes. When they were older, Klaus advised Golo to follow Kröger's example and stick to harmless types, "arrogant on account of their good looks." Golo didn't know how: "I had no idea what to do with such children."

The daughters fared better—at least Elisabeth, as a child, and Erika, who became his closest literary confidant, the only child to influence his work. For example, she suggested that he include the episode between Felix Krull and a Scottish lord in the 1954 novel. With her considerable tact she may have realized that it dramatized her father's infatuation with the Bavarian waiter.

Monika was the least favored daughter. Her memoirs recount only two instances of his regard for her. When Katia complained about her girlish pranks, he wrote, "Moni's a rogue, that's all," and he inscribed her copy of *Doctor Faustus*, "You'll understand it well enough." Neither warms the heart.

All the Mann offspring except for Elisabeth would compose literary representations of their father. In them the arch-voyeur is himself observed, closely read by his own children. Monika's is the most guarded. In a 1947 Festschrift, *The Stature of Thomas Mann*, she writes that as a child, he seemed to her more grandfather than father, "because his relation to us children seemed to skip one rung of kinsmanship." A devastating remark, made in filial devotion. But she presents him as a natural democrat, respectful and never patronizing toward workmen.

One time she caught him in an intimate moment. He was walking along the seashore and halted, "suddenly seized by panic in face of the silent, monotonous, immense, inconceivable whatever of the dunes. A nameless terror seemed to take hold of him so that his composure resembled the sand, and with agonized, haunted eyes and as if under a protest he toilsomely hastened toward solid ground and human traces." In her memoir she recalls quietly following him as he strolled down Fifth Avenue, stopping in similar surprise before the spectacular storefronts.

In the same collection Erika and Klaus Mann provide a jointly written assessment of their father's nature and development. To them he's a magician, a chameleon, like Felix Krull, "that genius at making faces." They suggest he would have made a fine conductor, a better artist. Despite Mann's admission of his visual deficiencies, they loved the cartoons he contributed to "The Picture Book for Well-Behaved Children," "full of weird dwarfs, of apparitions and comic monsters," and the sketches he drew for them of Brazilian ambassadors and dance-hall Lotharios. They write, "He did not *seem* to trouble his head about us"; the italics indicate that he did.

Their literary insights are of a high quality. They recognize the Hermes-like movement his Eros makes between the spheres of "mind" and "life," thereby uniting princes and swindlers . . . "for he is, after all, an actor too and likes to wear all kinds of strange costumes." They appreciate his irony, the habit of placing everything "within inverted commas." They also discern the erotic source of his morbidity, and produce his favorite lines from Platen: "Whoever has looked upon beauty is dedicated to death." They compare his discovery of Schopenhauer to a "drug fiend's vision."

Klaus contributed a separate piece, "Solemnly Moved," to the 1947 anthology. By then he had spent twenty years in his father's shadow, hobbled by invidious comparisons and his not uninformed belief that Mann disliked his work. Curt Riess, a gossipy friend, writes that he spent many stoned hours speculating on his father's "abnormality," as if that might supply a common bond.

Of course he was right. Much as Thomas Buddenbrook ignored the son who understood him so well, Mann seems to have avoided intimate communication with Klaus, whose sensibility was almost genetically derived from his own. Klaus echoes his father's vocabulary in his *Turning Point*: bourgeois and artist are hopelessly entangled, "constantly irritating, enchanting, missing, and desiring each other. . . . Eros floats between them disguised as envy or scorn or admiration." In rather melodramatic cadences, Klaus bemoans the "curse of consciousness." Taking his place in the Mannian hall of mirrors, he claims that his first memory was "a portrait of my former self," himself as a baby—a representation, not the real thing—and concludes that "our nostalgia begins with our consciousness." Klaus's characteristic blend of voyeurism, narcissism, melancholy, and nostalgia is a self-consciously decadent, if not campy, variation on his father's themes.

Like his father, he was a poor athlete. The other boys thought him a "sissy . . . but not a fool." His childhood politics were tinged with sexual conflicts. He was an early advocate of the Munich revolution, which he saw as a re-enactment of Dickens's *Tale of Two Cities*, to which Hedwig Pringsheim had lately introduced her grandchildren. Yet he also wrote a play about a dashing aristocrat fleeing the Jacobins. He observed the proto-fascistic militarism and nationalist hysteria of his school years: paradoxically the Munich students called him a "Prussian," perhaps because his father was a citizen of Lübeck, not Bavaria. He's terrifically sure in his analysis of the "dramatic conventionalism" of students who screamingly submitted to their masters' "flogging." Both sides participated in a ritual as artificial as a Japanese tea ceremony. But he also wishes he had undergone the experience: "It would have been better for me, perhaps. . . ."

Klaus grew up to become an openly gay man, hiding little from his readers or his family. From the casual references in letters and diaries—in 1946 Mann credits Erika with the information that the "handsome" American writer James Agee is homosexual—we can surmise that Mann felt comfortable discussing homosexuality with his children.

Father and son, the Manns divided between them a pantheon of homosexual icons. Thomas celebrated Michelangelo and Frederick the Great; Klaus, the more operatic and epicene figures of Tchaikovsky and Mad King Ludwig. Mann's discourse was circumspect, wittily indirect, while Klaus's language was at times impassioned, more often strident and humorless. Both viewed romantic happiness as a chimera. Count Kai only embraces Hanno Buddenbrook as he lies near death; Klaus's Tchaikovsky is even less fortunate—he must die before his nephew pledges his love. Neither character hears the words that could have saved his life.

And what might have happened if Klaus had read his father's diaries? He would have learned that Mann's feelings for his son were, for a few months, deeply erotic. Klaus and Erika saw in their father "the face of Jacob, the thoughtful face of the father watching his son, young Joseph, with anxious yearning." They considered the Joseph books Mann's least autobiographical. But they didn't know that Jacob's vision of Joseph re-enacted Mann's infatuation with his son.

In July 1920 he received a letter from Carl Maria Weber, a gay writer disturbed by *Death in Venice*'s unflattering portrait of homosexuality. Mann's reply was lengthy, a masterpiece of dissemblance, admitting much, apparently settling everything, as if he were fixing himself for the schoolbooks. Even as he wrote his letter, he knew it to be incomplete, if not a lie.

Mann praises Weber's poems, "where your emotion attains the highest degree of freedom and unselfconsciousness, as in the 'Swimmers,' which contains much of the humaneness of the younger generation." (Ludwig von Hofmann's painting of nude male swimmers still graced Mann's study.) Recently, he says, he had argued *Death in Venice*'s merits with his friend Kurt Martens. He does not wish to be mistaken: "I should not want you and others to have the impression that a mode of feeling which I respect because it is almost necessarily infused with *mind* (far more necessarily so, at any rate, than the 'normal' mode) should be something that I would want to deny or, insofar as it is accessible to me (and I may say that it scarcely is) wish to disavow." One moment, he defines homosexual love in Mannian terms, desire "infused with mind"; the next, he denies any knowledge of the emotion.

He offers an aesthetic distinction between "irresponsible . . . individualistic" Dionysian lyric and "Apollonian, objectively controlled, morally and socially responsible epic," as if any reader of Mann didn't know he wanted both. "An equilibrium of sensuality and morality" had been his aim, modeled on Goethe's *Elective Affinities*. But quoting his own words from "*Gesang vom Kindchen*," he recalls the "sobering effort" that converted a "drunken song" into "an ethical fable." He claims this was a generational trait, "foreign to you young people." His "naturalistic" tendencies obliged him to alternate the "pathological" details with a symbolic motif, "Tadzio as Hermes Psychopompos." That's Mann the con man talking; remember how he cruised the Hermes look-alike. But then comes an honest admission: Aschenbach, like Mann, was inhibited by his Protestant, "fundamentally mistrustful, fundamentally pessimistic relationship to passion in general."

Hans Blüher, whose analysis of eroticism seems to him "profoundly Germanic," has defined Eros as the "affirmation of a human being, irrespective of his worth." But to so amoral an affirmation of beauty, Mann says, "No thanks!"—thereby contradicting the closing argument in the *Reflections*.

He insists that the story had originally depicted Goethe and "that little girl in Marienbad," and what shifted his presentation was "a personal, lyrical travel experience that determined me to carry things to an extreme by introducing the motif of 'forbidden' love. . . ." He teases poor Weber with the nature of that experience. But after frustrating his reader he offers a catalogue of vigorous homosexuals that reads like a bold—if misogynistic—version of gay pride. Homosexuals are falsely judged to be "effeminate"; medical, pathological explanations distort the "intellectual and cultural side." There are men in whom "masculinity is so pronounced that even in erotic matters only the masculine has importance and interest." These men, he tells Weber, include Michelangelo, Frederick the Great, and Platen: a brotherhood of his heroes. He is touched by a vision of "mature masculinity" protecting "lovelier and frailer masculinity"—represented, he could have said, by Aschenbach and Tadzio, or Mann and Klaus. He disdains certain types—King Ludwig II, for instance (Klaus's favorite)—and he praises the "noble austerity and dignity" of Bertram's mentor Stefan George.

He locates himself in a sphere imagined by Blüher, divided between the family and "associations of men," namely society. "I am a family founder and a father by instinct and conviction. I love my children, deepest of all a little girl who very much resembles my wife—to a point that a Frenchman would call idolatry. There you have the 'bourgeois.' " Perhaps only the words about Elisabeth are unimpeachable. He then switches from epic to lyric as he admits that "if we were to speak of eroticism, of unbourgeois intellectually sensual adventures, things would have to be viewed a little differently." Tonio Kröger, Tonio Kröger, it is the same every time, and the emotion deep.

He quotes his favorite authority, himself, in a long passage from the *Reflections*. It evokes the unconsummated passion of mind for life, ending with the admonitory comment: "The mind that loves is not fanatical; it is ingenious, political; it woos, and its wooing is erotic irony. . . ." This may not constitute a typical confession, but Mann asserts, "Tell me whether one can 'betray' oneself any better than that. My idea of eroticism, my *experience* of it, is completely expressed in these lines." In order to read these words as an admission that Mann shared his nature, Weber would have to see the abstract conflict between mind and life in sexual terms. At that moment, how many readers, possibly excepting Bertram and Heinrich Mann, could do that?

Mann concludes by positioning himself in the camp of George and Blüher, the reactionaries, as opposed to the pacifist, "overintellectual" left-wing journalist Kurt Hiller and the homosexual activist Magnus Hirschfeld. The latter he finds "ghastly"; the former's opposition he explains as "the Enlightenment's [hostility] toward romanticism," while granting that "erotic irony of the mind . . . is a somewhat audacious romantic formulation" ("romantic" in his preferred sense of "imbued with the spirit of criticism"). He would need a treatise to develop his ideas . . . or, he doesn't add, a novel. Meanwhile, he offers Weber provocative intimations of his sexual nature. Now you catch him, now you don't: this conservative, romantic mind-drunk lover of beauty, part hedonist, part Puritan, engages Weber in a flirtatious tease.

Six weeks later, on August 18, he writes the publisher Paul Steegemann another kind of letter entirely. The occasion is a new edition of Verlaine's poems. Mann confesses "the indecency . . . has shaken me. For this is the effect which indecency and voluptuousness usually have upon me when their real abysses become visible." The experience is so profound that any moral objections to the work are simply "stupid." All his life he has contemplated the nature of morality; history instructs him that "great moralists have mostly been great sinners also." Dostoyevsky was a pedophile, a man who loved children, physically compromised by his epilepsy: Mann argues that "nowadays medicine is inclined to explain this mystic disease as a form of indecency." Such medical nonsense can be linked to the notion, propagated in his Weber letter, that homosexuality is a disease, although not one to worry about.

As he offers Weber a parade of manly pederasts, he shows Steegemann that artists as diverse as Nietzsche, Wagner, and Platen—the latter "an austere spirit who, however, precisely because he loved only young men, understood the mysteries of the flesh in a more than 'moral' manner"—were all devout exponents of debauchery. With their imprimatur, he "justifies" the publication of Verlaine's poems because they are wonderfully and "shockingly indecent." He contends that the only reliable moralist is a great sinner, preferably one who shares the tastes of Platen, Verlaine, and Dostoyevsky, all of them lovers of youth.

This is much blunter than his letter to Weber, a frank espousal of "forbidden love" without apology or self-exoneration. In barely six weeks Mann has begun talking like an unashamed lover, broadcasting his desires to the world. In a 1921 review of a potboiler, *Boys and Murderers*, he draws attention to an orgiastic climax wherein a woman pours wine over a boy's penis. He finds such scenes "brave and inspired." The flesh is greater than the spirit; "Man at his highest and purest is a child of nature." The sign of a postwar artist will be his sexual freedom.

Wherefore this change of heart? Exactly one day after his letter to Weber, Mann notes that he has fallen in love with Klaus. (On several earlier occasions, he had commented on the boy's "handsome" appearance, particularly in "tight pants.") Later that day he comes upon Klaus wrestling with Golo in the nude and his "radiant adolescent body" astonishes him. Another time he reads a story of Klaus's, "steeped in *Weltanschauung*," and offers his criticisms accompanied by "tendernesses" that the boy seems to appreciate—much as Milton's Eve prefers literary instruction from Adam, not the angels, because he punctuates doxology with sighs and kisses. "I have fallen in love with Klaus nor do I find this strange." Having written these words for himself, he makes a public affirmation of Verlaine's immorality that seems anticlimactic.

Later that month he received a surprising explanation for his unconventional desire. Upon their first meeting on July 28, Annette Kolb observed that Klaus resembled a younger version of his father. The next day Mann told Katia that he was contemplating a novel about a father's "physical love" for his daughter because she resembled his wife as a young girl. It may have seemed a slightly more risqué version of his words about fatherhood in the "Gesang vom Kindchen": "Surely I loved them for their mother, the fairy bride's sake." Incest could be seen as a highly refined version of marital love.

From sensation to thought was never a big journey for Thomas Mann. But, as he frequently remarked, matters needed to seep long and hard before he could transform them into fiction. Only after several years could he compose the story of Jacob's love for Joseph, the son who resembles his wife, Rachel, as a young girl.

Mann's infatuation with Klaus didn't last long. In September 1921, once more on a vacation by the seashore, he transferred his attention to an "exquisitely formed young athlete from Hamburg still more boy than man." The daily sight of this runner made it "difficult" to think about leaving. Stimulated by *Sehnsucht*, Mann climbed the "fantastic, shifting dunes," mimicking the youth's kinetic bliss. The diaries may not tell us whether he embraced his beloved adolescents, Martens and Timpe, Klaus and the Hermes from Hamburg. But in his fiction they performed at his command. For him, this was—like the momentary love for Klaus—"quite natural," "a highly natural situation."

V

IMPERIAL PASTIMES AND DEMOCRATIC VISTAS

1

THE BLACK SHEEP'S TRIUMPH

By 1921 Mann realized that he was no lapsed wunderkind, his appeal limited to a dying generation. On a local level, his fame was clinched when he acquired the status of a tourist attraction in his hometown. When in September 1921 he returned to lecture on Goethe and Tolstoy, he found that "the house on Mengstrasse had been purchased by the city and restored. On the first floor there is to be a 'Buddenbrook Book Shop.' " (It opened on March 4, 1922.) Though Munich guidebooks had listed his home since 1903, Lübeck had waited eighteen more years to acknowledge his existence. ("I was considered a black sheep of that worthy community" until the curiosity of tourists transformed him into a " 'son of the city.' This is comic," he wrote a French critic in 1923.) Even as Mann discussed the lords of nineteenth-century literature, he became their heir. The boy who barely escaped Gymnasium was now the apparent successor to great Goethe himself.

A plebeian Goethe, that is, spokesman for a defeated nation and disguised as an itinerant lecturer. In January 1922, accompanied by Katia, he visited Prague, Vienna, and Budapest, interpreting Goethe, and by extension German culture, to the former members of the Austro-Hungarian Empire. (There was "a criminal episode": they were robbed in Vienna's Hotel Imperial. But the resulting commotion "contributed to the greater glory of the whole thing, especially since our losses were trifling." The thief, exhibiting the tastes of Felix Krull—or Mann himself—"lingered too long over my small treasures," toiletries, wristwatch, pearl cuff links, neckties, and "did not find the main things, my wife's diamonds and the cash.

Incidentally, the reception in Vienna was overwhelming. We are living like princes, nary a bill sent.")

As the cultural voice of the new Germany, Mann became more of an international figure than Heinrich. In 1921 he had still not forgiven his brother. Though the two lived barely a mile apart, they never met; the increasingly frail Frau Mann had long given up hopes for their reconciliation. Yet a softening could be detected. On March 27, 1921, Heinrich turned fifty, an occasion widely hailed in the press. Mann wrote his old friend Ludwig Ewers, "Your fine article on Heinrich's fiftieth birthday moved me deeply, as I am sure it did him. Heinrich is now being compensated by innumerable honours, for all that was denied him in earlier years, denials which hurt him more than I could ever have imagined." (Had Frau Mann betrayed Heinrich's jealousy over Thomas's superior fortunes?)

Still smarting from Heinrich's perceived insults, Mann turned his brother's political opposition into "the poison which once threatened to destroy his creative artistry." But he hoped that success had mellowed him. "Reconciled with both the world and his fatherland, [he] will perhaps prefer [Ewer's] friendship at the bottom of his heart to that of those Jewish radicals and town criers of his": Mann's last attack on these tragicomic figures, the Munich scribblers.

Thomas reviewed their unhappy history, emphasizing the "highly literary manner" in which Heinrich had publicly humiliated him. He "cannot have had much respect for me if he expected me frivolously and joyfully to accept the recent self-conscious attempts at rapprochement which he made, at a time when all his boldest wishes about Germany had been realized." But he concluded, "A quarrel like ours should be held in honour, no one should try to remove its accent of deadly earnestness. Separate, we are perhaps more each other's brothers than we should be together at the family table."

Loyalty and respect were implicit throughout the letter. In the next few months he received more evidence of his popularity; he also composed an essay on the Jews that more than compensated for his attacks on "those Jewish radicals." In January 1922 he learned that Heinrich had been hospitalized, suffering from appendicitis and peritonitis, ailments that had assailed the Mann children throughout the war years. Doctors feared lung and heart complications. "You can imagine how wrought up we were," Mann wrote Bertram. Katia visited Mimi Mann; Heinrich learned of Thomas's concern and was "delighted." On January 31, Mann sent flowers and a brief note: "Those were difficult days that lie behind us, but now we are over the hill and will go on better—together, if you feel as I do."

In a letter to Bertram three days later, he paraphrased his words to

Heinrich, and the latter's touching reply, "Let us never lose each other again." Mann declared himself "joyful, in fact wildly shaken with emotion," yet unconvinced: Heinrich, he says, refused to take him seriously.

> People tell me that he has never read the *Reflections*. That is good, and then again it is not; for it means that he has no idea what I have gone through. It wrenches my heart when I hear that after reading a few sentences in the *Berliner Tageblatt* in which I refer to those who proclaim the love of God and hate their brother, he sat down and wept. But my long struggle for everything I value, waged moreover for years in a state of physical undernourishment, left me no time for tears. He knows nothing of that, nothing of how time has forged me into a man, how I have grown in the process and even become the support and leader of others.

Knowing that Heinrich would hold against him his immaturity and solipsism, he declares himself miraculously delivered from these conditions. He came through by way of the *Reflections*; the least Heinrich can do is read it.

Still, Heinrich "is said to have become softer, kindlier in these past years." Mann notices an "evolution" on his own part. "The thought which truly dominates my mind these days is of a new, personal fulfillment of the idea of humanity"—language that resembles Heinrich's diction. But he stresses that this "personal fulfillment" has nothing in common with "the humanitarian world of Rousseau," the glib and hypocritical precepts he identified with "civilization's literary man."

Within a few months the evolution was complete, and Heinrich returned to Mann's inner circle. Thomas's political conversion is usually credited to Heinrich's influence, but the movement, as befit his cadence, was more gradual. The "Goethe and Tolstoy" essay, composed while they were still estranged, points to a socializing of Mann's perspective. Another view might be that he reverted to the left-wing principles he had begun to articulate a decade earlier.

The family that welcomed Heinrich back remained as fractious as ever, theatrical in the extreme. Morbidity seemed endemic to the clan. In 1920, Mann's cousin, the son of the aunt who inspired Tony Buddenbrook, committed suicide. Meanwhile Lula continued to bemoan with extravagant self-pity her loutish husband and her insensitive lovers.

To their father's embarrassment, Klaus and Erika proved feckless students, unwilling to obey rules; and they left a state boarding school in April 1922, at the end of their first term. (Erika continued her education at home, as had Katia; Klaus switched schools.) Golo would have a more standard education at a school, Schloss Salem, directed by the celebrated pedagogue Kurt Hahn, an old friend of Katia's, who had previously rejected Klaus as unmalleable.

Herein lies another story of the Mann family that Thomas could have imagined. According to Golo, Hahn was a suppressed homosexual who demanded a masochistic obedience from his charges. He inculcated a sense of honor worthy of the military; according to his former pupils, even brushing teeth became a ceremony. Golo continued to admire his teacher—much as he mourned his father—but he also suggested that Mann was a tyrannical ogre and, with apologies, compared Hahn to Hitler; filial devotion had its limits. (During the 1930s, Kurt Hahn emigrated to Great Britain, where he founded the public school Gordonston.)

Golo and Klaus, Mann's gay sons, both found a surrogate father in other homosexuals. While Golo fastened on the closeted Hahn, Klaus's mentors included André Gide and Jean Cocteau: the two Frenchmen were outspoken about their sexuality. Klaus's choice reflected his bohemian disposition; Golo's, his "inherent" conservatism. Meanwhile Erika became an actress; by 1924, she had a walk-on part in Max Reinhardt's production of *Saint Joan*.

The old Widow Mann observed it all in her vague and forlorn way. On March 11, 1923, she died in Wesseling at the age of seventy-one. Mann wrote Bertram, "I do not believe that I have ever been so sad in all my life." His children were not invited, but Erika snuck into the funeral and boasted that she had seen all three brothers in tears: "Z" and the peculiar uncles Heinrich and Vico. According to Golo, the younger Manns found this hilarious, though they would have been greatly disturbed if Katia's parents had died. Mann's "poor dear Mama" had become little more than a joke to his children.

He kept touring. Financial pressure, as much as literary inclination, turned him into an international figure. Almost precisely as the German inflation hit, he became an interpreter of German culture for the outside world—particularly Americans who read the "Letters from Germany" he contributed to *The Dial*. Tourism was cognate with the forms of distribution and mass marketing that helped him become a celebrity abroad.

In September 1922 he wrote his publisher, S. Fischer, "Without foreign money I should not be able to manage these days with a family like mine. Like everyone else, I am considering how to earn something extra. . . . Thus I am becoming in middle age a bustling businessman. . . ." Sharing his new expertise, he advised Heinrich on the appropriate fees to charge for lectures. In February 1923, he lamented that touring had become a losing enterprise—if he hadn't boarded with friends, his recent trip to Dresden would have left him in the red: "German lecture tours scarcely pay nowadays."

His largest source of income, however, derived not from tours of neighboring countries but from the stipend he received from *The Dial*. Two years earlier Mann had commented on the favorable rate of exchange. It was better in 1922; a decent fee by American standards constituted a Kaiser's ransom.

He made judicious use of his travels. In November 1921, he read a chapter from *The Magic Mountain* and "Goethe and Tolstoy" in Zurich. During his free time he visited the outpatient department of the hospital, doing research for his novel. In May 1923 he lectured in Madrid. His Spanish trip lasted five weeks and left impressions that would resonate a decade later in his essay on *Don Quixote*, and almost thirty years later in the Spanish sections of *Felix Krull*.

Long before *The Magic Mountain*, Thomas Mann was an international celebrity. On September 19, 1924, he wrote Erika that while reading the latest issue of *The Dial*, he came upon an interview with "old Yeats," the last winner of the Nobel Prize for literature. Yeats had learned the previous November that "the Nobel Prize would probably be conferred upon Herr Mann, the distinguished novelist, or upon myself." Mann professed bemusement: "The good fellow thought it highly improbable that he would receive the prize. 'For Herr Mann is in every way fitted for such an honor,' etc."

He had become the model of a professional writer, married to an unswerving routine. Anything compelling his attention would be put to literary use, and usually more than once. Particularly when he dealt with political or critical issues, he would repeat whole passages from earlier works. A Mann reader can often predict the very syntax, not to mention the association of ideas. In "The Railway Accident," confronted with the need to replace a lost manuscript, a writer says, "Next time I'll get it right." Mann clearly believed that something well said can usually be said better. His work became a seamless, Goethean confession, bringing ever new revelations to author and reader alike.

2

"DO WE LIVE IF OTHERS LIVE?"

T he Mann brothers were no longer rivals. Thomas's fortunes soared as Heinrich's plunged; he acquired a huge foreign audience while Heinrich's German readership dwindled to a pre–1914 low.

Mann now saw himself performing in a new drama, supported by a cast of fellow writers. Outside of D. H. Lawrence, there are few great modernists as observant of their peers. But while Lawrence's criticism tends to work overtime as philosophical manifesto, Mann's is autobiographical in the extreme, a simultaneous pursuit and rejection of context. He frequently cited Goethe's egomaniacal remark, "Do we live if others live?" For Mann this meant that he was obliged to justify a highly idiosyncratic—in his own words, "unseemly"—oeuvre. Lawrence seeks to make his readers better. Conversely, Mann wishes to better himself: "the religious man thinks only of himself."

The further removed his subjects, the greater the challenge. His closest literary friends Bertram and Reisiger had influenced him through their respective studies of Nietzsche and Whitman, but neither was a novelist. He maintained relations with more celebrated writers, particularly Jakob Wassermann, and used *The Dial* to promote their books abroad.

His old friend Kurt Martens had offended him years before when he depicted the young writer as hopelessly estranged from ordinary life. After the *Reflections*, he had predicted that Mann would be "still more isolated in his proud solitude." Adding injury to insult, he had also heaped "effete" praise on *Der Untertan*. A chance to retaliate arose in 1921 when Mann reviewed Martens's memoir. With Martens's own words, he reveals his friend to be yet another literary eunuch. Indeed, he sounds so much like Tonio Kröger or Martini, the novelist of *Royal Highness*, that Mann could have invented him. The book opens with a confession of fatigue over "all that I had to kill in myself." Mann calls this writer's life "Brahmin-like." Retreating from the world, Martens achieves the "cool passion" of literary "analysis": a dubious consolation. The spiritual reward is a fake; literature is treacherous, a "fraud of the mind," and its victim is usually the writer himself.

Poor Martens is no literary aristocrat. His memoir lacks the "demonic sense of self" that animates those god-children Augustine, Rousseau, Goethe, and Tolstoy. He provides so few erotic revelations that he seems denatured. He knows that his role is marginal; he declares himself a "precursor" and a "fellow traveler" and offers his memoir as a literary document of the last century. Mann is the kind of attentive reader another writer fears, underlining every confession of self-doubt and impotence. It doesn't matter that he's committed similar treacheries; he assumes a sociological objectivity about his colleagues.

Another friendship of sorts was initiated between Mann and Gerhart Hauptmann. The playwright was first identified with dramas and novels depicting the tragic lives of impoverished laborers. But his work ranged from naturalism to mysticism. As Mann had recognized when they first met in 1903, his personality was as outsized as his oeuvre. By comparison the retiring Mann appeared colorless, a golf course beside a volcano. Hauptmann, thirteen years Mann's senior, had received the Nobel Prize in 1912. Golo says that Mann regarded him as his only peer within German borders.

Hauptmann was also something of a buffoon. He was famous for speaking in a garbled tongue, his enthusiasm invariably getting the better of his syntax. He would become so overwhelmed by the rush of impressions that he stammered and babbled, to the point that only his reputation—or the tremendous force of his physical presence—convinced his auditors that he was not a fool. We know all this because Mann captured Hauptmann's personality in the character of Mynheer Peeperkorn, the Dutch explorer who wins Clavdia Chauchat from Hans Castorp, with the latter's assent. (Mann probably didn't know that Hauptmann once made a pass at Katia as the two entered a box at the opera. She resisted, and only confided the incident to Erika and Golo when she was in her nineties.)

In April 1925, when, despite Mann's efforts, Hauptmann learned that he was the inspiration for Peeperkorn, Mann felt obliged to write the older man. He admits immediately that Hauptmann is right to take offense: "I have sinned against you, I was in sore need, was led into temptation, and yielded to it. My need was artistic. I was seeking a character crucial to my novel as I had conceived it, but whom I did not see, did not hear, did not hold." On vacation, while drinking wine with Hauptmann, Mann recognized that which "I should never, never have allowed myself to accept, speaking in human and personal terms, but which in a state of lowered human responsibility, I did accept, even imagined I had the right to accept. . . ." Mann once said that whenever he needed something badly, it came by post. Writers know the almost uncanny way events accede to their requirements, the occasions when everything seems to apply directly to the work at hand. But the great Hauptmann himself needed an interpretation of his ironic pose. "Dear, revered man," isn't my devotion evident precisely in my language? (Mann does sneak in a parenthetical contention that his portrait was a question of "transmutation and stylization," and that "even the externals were barely akin to reality." But he doesn't risk further offense by reducing Hauptmann to the status of a literary "element.")

Mann was not wrong. His irony enriches the portrait; after Hauptmann's death, his widow, Margarethe, praised Mann's depiction as fundamentally true and sympathetic.

But, as we shall see, Hans Castorp's infatuation with Peeperkorn is fraught with homosexual tensions, released in the suspect form of a shared mistress. "The ironic and grotesque artistic means" are those Mann invariably uses in such ticklish cases. Only with Paul Ehrenberg and Katia did he claim that the style was not the man, entrusting them to find the passion and spurn the irony. Something else occurred here. In this letter, now boasting (Mann is convinced that his novel is as extraordinary as Peeperkorn himself), now obsequious, a great writer offers his "only peer" an apology in which the extenuating circumstance is his literary style—as it were, his talent.

Hauptmann and Mann remained friends. Other writers never forgave Mann his pre-eminence. On the right, former allies considered him an apostate, exchanging German *Innerlichkeit* for the puerile democracy of his American sponsors. The nationalist Josef Ponten had once been a friend. Mann shared his politics and enjoyed his colorful tales; the Mann children report that Katia in her old age continued to read him with pleasure. But by 1924 he was condemning Mann as a false prophet, the symptom of German decadence.

On September 12, Mann wrote to Ponten, in all friendliness, that his politics expressed "good will and feelings of amity toward life." He quoted their friend Kurt Martens's opinion that Ponten ought not to personalize their quarrel: "Perhaps . . . you should not relate yourself to me so much, in general. There are more things in the world than you and I." Almost like Heinrich chastising him for turning a world war into a fraternal conflict, Mann realized that Ponten's opposition derived from intense jealousy. The great narrator of men's obsessions with each other had become the stuff of other men's fantasies.

Either they bore him no respect or they craved his attention. Karl Bohm, a doctor with literary ambitions, begged to send Mann his poems. His request conveyed the fear that Mann would not appreciate the work. On January 4, 1924, Mann reminded him of Theodor Fontane's stricture: "The most important thing is to be able to stand up to one's own criticism," forget anyone else's. But seeing the dominant role he played in Bohm's consciousness, he agreed to read the other's lyrics, adding, perhaps out of pique, "although that seems to be not without its risk."

Mann didn't realize what he had invited. By September 1925 the disconsolate poet solicited more than his approval. Now he expected Mann to tell him whether he should keep living. This was a power Mann declined: "I consider it impermissible to impose upon a stranger the task of deciding whether you are to be or not to be. But as things now stand, I must of course do my best to restrain you from acts of violence against yourself. I cannot understand why you regard your artistic and literary ambitions as so opposed to your profession as a doctor that they must cancel out your life." Thus spoke Thomas Mann, who could never imagine himself as anything but a writer.

If you are no artist, "resign yourself like a man and turn to other forms of ethical action and self-realization. Everything transitory is only a parable, and it does not matter in the least whether a person makes pots or bowls, writes novels, or cures the sick." He suggested as a model Alfred Döblin, "one of our foremost novelists," then employed as "a welfare doctor on Berlin's North Side." If you can't stand Munich, try Berlin; if Europe won't do, there's America. Nothing is hopeless. Evidently Bohm was unconvinced; he killed himself in 1933.

More ironies attend the letter. America would be the destiny, not of Bohm, but of Mann and Döblin. The latter, here a figure of praise, would become one of Mann's bitterest enemies. After the Second World War, Mann became convinced that Döblin's relentless attacks bordered on the murderous. The hypersensitivity that led Mann to create a national enemy in his brother's image, or to comprehend Bohm's and Ponten's fixations, seemed to be an occupational hazard. "Do we live if others live?"

Mann had less turbulent relations with younger writers. He continued to plead the case of Ernst Toller, the former student who remained imprisoned for his activities during the Munich revolution. However, he made it clear that Toller's courage outweighed his talent. He also introduced Toller's friends Brecht and Arnolt Bronnen to American audiences, again with reservations. Meanwhile he served as an early publicist for Franz Kafka, offering unqualified praise for the writer who would become his greatest rival for the crown of twentieth-century German literature.

As unemployment and inflation reached apocalyptic levels, most German writers concluded that literature needed to become a vehicle of social protest. Mann no longer rejected this tendency.

He was thus of a sufficiently pliable mood to encounter György Lukács. No more the literary aesthete whose works Mann had studied when composing *Death in Venice*—and whom he characterized in the *Reflections of an Unpolitical Man* as his figurative offspring, Lukács had become a Marxist. In 1919, following the Hungarian counterrevolution, Lukács suffered house arrest and exile. At the time Mann had written on his behalf.

Now he greeted an intellectual tried by the fire. In January 1922 they met in Vienna, where Mann was scheduled to lecture. He described the meeting in a letter:

> Dr. Georg Lukács is a man whose intellectual nature and attitude toward the world and society are in no way mine but whose strong, pure and proud spirit I honor and admire from an ethical point of view. . . . Once in Vienna he explained his theories to me for an hour. For as long as he spoke he was right. And even if after his talk there remained with me an impression of almost uncanny abstractness, I also felt his clarity and intellectual generosity.

The compelling phrase "as long as he spoke he was right" applies to the mesmerizing rhetoric of Naphta, the Jewish-Jesuit-Communist-reactionary in *The Magic Mountain*. Mann conceived the character shortly after meeting Lukács, and first mentions him in a letter that June to Bertram.

What amazed Mann was that Lukács was a type he had anticipated. On May 3, 1919, even as the Munich revolution collapsed, he speculated about "the type of the Russian Jew as leader of a world movement, this explosive mixture of intellectual-radical and eastern Christian visionary elements. Immediately I thought of incorporating these Russian (Eastern)-chiliastic-Communistic things into *The Magic Mountain*." Already then he had concluded that Jesuits and Communists were brothers under the skin, revolutionaries burning with a cold, ascetic flame. Apocalyptic communism was no contradiction. As Judith Marcus points out, Lukács had ended his pre-Marxist treatise "On the Poverty of Spirit" (1912) with a quotation dear to the Jesuits: whoever "hates not his father and mother . . . and his own life . . . cannot be my disciple"—a holy nihilism, although Lukács also venerated the mild-mannered Saint Francis of Assisi. The Hungarian gave a face and a unique style of verbal aggression to a figure that Mann had observed for years: "Like many clever Jews, Naphta was by instinct both a revolutionary and an aristocrat." The ugly Jesuit is drawn from such disparate individuals as Harden and Toller, although the mediatizing Lukács predominates.

Unlike Hauptmann, Lukács did not object to his portrait. He became Mann's most celebrated critic. In a display of mixed enthusiasms worthy of Naphta, he preferred Mann to more stridently Marxist writers—particularly the hacks of socialist realism—as the most honest witness of a dying class.

Lukács's overview stressed Mann's humor, range of character type, evocation of social milieu—everything that smacked of the great nineteenth-century novels. He glossed over the erotic confusions, and neglected totally the homosexual core. (Lukács was no prude, having had several affairs with extraordinary women—see Judith Marcus's biography.)

In 1949, when, following the appearance of *Doctor Faustus*, his American reputation plummeted, Mann was ready enough to proclaim Lukács "the greatest living critic on the account alone that he means so well toward me." Beyond that, he either caricatured Lukács in the form of Naphta or ignored him. Lukács accepted both slights. He wrote Mann a letter quoting the lyric "If I love you, why should you care?" Nevertheless, the rejection was devastating. After a lifetime of betrayals, having seen Marxism mutilated perhaps fatally, and with his work savaged by Western critics who could not match his acuity or political courage, he confessed only one disappointment: Thomas Mann had declined his friendship.

The great Mannian irony is that he knew that rejection can be a wound that never heals, that some forms of *Sehnsucht* are permanent. How could he understand Lukács so well yet still withhold his affection? A very simple answer is that the critic was not attractive. An ugly soul mate, even one so wise and sympathetic, might have confirmed Mann's insecurity and self-contempt, his fears that no handsome man would ever love him. Or perhaps

Lukács was too much the driven Jewish intellectual, humorless to boot, for someone who craved warmth and relaxation, and who loved to laugh.

Whatever the case, Mann rejected his most devoted interpreter. With its background of political conflict, and its display of apparently kindred spirits divided by the excessive ardor of an intensely Semitic lover, this episode reads like a lost Mann novella, *The Magic Mountain* in a postwar— and, clearly postromantic—key.

If Mann's relations with his contemporaries were both formal and tentative, he was unequivocally bold when encountering those dead men he considered his masters. "Goethe and Tolstoy" (originally titled "The Idea of Education in Goethe and Tolstoy"), composed in the summer of 1921, indicates that his favorite subject remained men who shared his incapacity for normal life.

This essay was his springboard into radical politics. Composed several months before his reconciliation with Heinrich, it marks the breakthrough, and suggests that Mann had to arrive at his most social vision strictly on his own. It is a wonderful piece, exhibiting the capacious range and outsized characters found in *The Magic Mountain*. (The character Peeperkorn assimilates Mann's idea of Tolstoy to the living model, Hauptmann.)

Were it more theoretical, it would earn Mann a place in the critical pantheon with Adorno, Walter Benjamin, Barthes, and Foucault. But it is unabashedly nonacademic, in flight from theory, proceeding by means of anecdote and intuition, anachronism and manifesto, to effectively dethrone the kings of nineteenth-century literature.

Alfred Kerr might accuse Mann of thinking with his *Sitzfleisch*, but the essayist displays the spirit of a showmanly trickster; this is no professor but, in his children's words, a magician at the podium. He speaks as among friends, observing in one aside that "today . . . nobody can live on his income." Another time, recognizing that he's generalizing too freely, he acknowledges his public's objections: "You will deny that. You will not agree to have it so." It's a gesture both modest and cocky, replayed in his next great essay, "The German Republic," when he pretends to hear the rumbling of angry feet.

Of course Mann's sensibility informs his essay from the start. After a neat discussion of the German reluctance to employ "and"—the great equalizer, and, as we know from "Tristan," the conjunction of Eros—he teams the German and the Russian, fully aware that they have nothing in common but a "superhuman" rate of achievement. He plays around with dates, emphasizing how much Tolstoy is rooted in the eighteenth century of Rousseau's *Confessions* while Goethe in his old age becomes a prophet of "class conflict, democracy, socialism, Americanism itself."

He also turns the duo into a quartet; each man has his counterfigure: Goethe and Schiller, Tolstoy and Dostoyevsky. Parallels are found in temperament; his eponymous subjects are classic, their shadows romantic. Both classical figures are resolutely nonsentimental, nonreflective, creative through and through.

He stresses their physical vitality. About no other writers could one remark, "He's comfortable in his own skin" (Mann has to say it in French). They exude health and privilege. But Nietzsche's comment "Man is a sick deer" applies more to Schiller and Dostoyevsky, those thought-obsessed, aphysical doctors' sons. Details as mundane as hygiene and diet reveal the gap in sensibility. Dostoyevsky does not cosset himself; but, Mann notes impishly, Tolstoy, an ascetic gourmet, wants his vegetables prepared in bouillon, his hair shirts tailored.

The children of nature are perpetual adolescents. Mann quotes remarks of their old age: Tolstoy's "As I was then, so am I now," and Goethe's "So here I am with all my thousand thoughts, sent back to be a child again." Of course Mann would love these passages, believing as he did that nobody stayed the same once he knew himself, and yet reminded that, *malgré tout*, "Tonio Kröger, Tonio Kröger, it's the same every time and the feeling deep."

Despite his well-known identification with Goethe, he combines an erotic sympathy with an unfailing sense of his master's limitations. Suggesting that Goethe felt that nature would never kill him off, Mann adds, "Yet die he did," and appends Eckermann's famous description of the corpse, "a perfect human being lying in beauty." And straightaway Mann comments that Goethe and Tolstoy were certainly not " 'normal' in the customary sense of the word."

He establishes the overpowering sexuality of his two subjects while questioning their intelligence. Tolstoy, the would-be prophet, offers "woozy theory imbued with the most penetrating sensuousness." In his time he was condemned as overly "physical." For examples, Mann cites the descriptions of a nude Vronsky in *Anna Karenina* and Napoleon's fat behind in *War and Peace*; his selection is more telling than he realizes. Goethe and Tolstoy are sexual animals—Goethe exhibiting the randy nature of a "beast-god" and Tolstoy delighting in bawdy jokes with "a pagan frankness bordering on the cynical."

But Mann endows them with a sexuality in his own image. He describes Tolstoy pursuing Turgenev's favor "like a love-sick girl" and recalls the "Ganymede-pathos" of Goethe's early poems. The latter's heterosexual ardor is suspect; he "never actually possessed" the women he immortalized in his art—"mostly he bolted." When the old Goethe takes up science, his research has an erotic basis. Despite their medical backgrounds, Schiller and Dostoyevsky give no thought to a "beautiful youth's torso," as will Goethe or *The Magic Mountain*'s author. He detects elements of perversity: Tolstoy finds death such a "sensual, physical process" that it's not clear whether his obsession derives from his "sensual interest in the body" or vice versa.

Both men feel cursed by their hyperbolic appetites; Mann finds in them a "pathos of renunciation" similar to the one constricting the earthbound Martens. Renunciation exacts its price. Schiller is constant while Goethe is mightily fragmented, "conditioned by a hundred circumstances." As a result his "lifework, though almost superhuman, remained entirely a fragment—it is putting it mildly to say that 'not all the dreams of blossoms ripened.' "

"You will not have it so," Mann forewarned his reader. He conveys astonishing judgments about history and culture in a breezy, anecdotal manner; he personalizes everything. The debate between Goethe and Schiller is customarily seen as occurring between classic and romantic, nature and sensibility, royalist and democrat. Mann turns it into another version of *Tonio Kröger*. Although Goethe feels threatened by Schiller's concept of "freedom," Schiller doesn't wish to convert him. He shouldn't read their contemporary Kant, the philosopher who proclaimed, "The sky above me and my conscience—that's religion." The moralist prefers his idol to be unbothered by thought.

He traces two historical movements. Confessional novels like Goethe's *Werther* are the final products of Christian subjectivity: "In the impulse to autobiography, Christian and democratic elements are mingled with that naïve, spoilt-darling claim on the world's affections. . . ." (This is top-rank literary criticism which thumbs its nose at piety—confession becomes a rehearsal for sexual frankness—and reputation—the culturally evolved Goethe is a spoiled brat.) Politically, Goethe's development marks a decline from the humanism of Erasmus to Bismarckian chauvinism. With one stroke Mann devastates the nineteenth century's greatest writer and its greatest politician.

> There is violence and there is sentimentality: crude words both to describe what I mean, crude and naturalistically derogatory; yet it is my humor to use them; for even if I wanted to I could not ignore the hidden irony—quite objective, quite unsuspected irony, of course—involved in their gigantic loyalties, their aristocratic servitude. They were both "faithful German servants of their Lord" (oh my God!). . . .

It was a different story in 1914. During the war years Mann had been all for Russian spirituality and Wagnerian rapture. But now he argues that mysticism corrupted, whether by Tolstoy or by Wagner, leads to barbarism. This is a political judgment, but "I have made no secret of my tendency to interpret the paganism of the children of nature in a primary ethical sense."

While his subjects are "beast-gods" and "beast-men," he belongs to the other party. He identifies romanticism with critique rather than creation, sickness and trouble rather than health and privilege. We may honor the gods, but we reserve our love for human beings . . . "because they have such a hard time."

Mann counterposes mysticism and ethics. The latter he identifies with liberalism, socialism, and democracy, all of which devolve from the romantic spirit of criticism. Thus be begins a process he later ascribed to Sigmund Freud of "demystifying romanticism." Having Marx read Hölderlin allowed him to keep reading Goethe. (His debunking differs from Lytton Strachey's *Eminent Victorians* [1918] since he continues to love his monsters.)

Goethe remained his model because he never seemed to age. In his late work *Wilhelm Meister Wanderjahre*, he found himself rejuvenated by the prospect of American democracy: "they do it better there." Mann couldn't know that he would test Goethe's words himself. The novel also dramatizes Goethe's infatuation with science, revealing an "almost erotic interest in anatomy." No other writer but Mann, the author who confuses an X ray with a striptease, would so enjoy Goethe's physical dissections of the human body, in order to imagine resting on the skeletal frame, "the adipose tissue, the upholstery that lends the form its charm." Out of their mutual renunciation, both men found pleasure in the body's secrets.

On March 1, 1921, Mann confides in his diary that "an interest in biological questions . . . disposes one to be conservative and rigid in political matters. Something similar can be seen in Goethe." At this time, still enthralled by writers like Spengler and Blüher, he found consolation in the unassailable laws of history. Within a few months an erotic knowledge of the body would form his argument for socialism, a change as drastic as his refiguring of irony.

The change coincided with his reading of Whitman's erotic poetry, largely under Hans Reisiger's tutelage. Mann analyzes other writers to know himself better. This may seem a narcissistic gesture. But he never reads at their expense; his essays are usually filled with a great author's professional insights.

Elsewhere he says that critics rely on personality; writers draw strength from their negative capability: "A writer gets progressively duller as he makes other men wiser. He may even often thank other people for telling him something which he had said himself first."

So Mann reimagined criticism as another kind of Mannian fiction. The dividing line was porous, dependent on mood, "and even that is fluid." In the 1920s he wrote an essay on new literature: "When there is nothing to love . . . I feel old, whereas enthusiasm . . . tells me I am not old." As he read, so he wrote. His best criticism was stimulated by pleasure. As he told Hauptmann, "After all, what do we get out of analysis? Let old friends tell each other anecdotes, that is what I shall do now, that is where I come off best."

Anecdotes, unsupported by theory, are truly "tales told out of school." Yet Mann impinges on theory all the time. He anticipates Bakhtin's endorsement of the novel's "prosaic wisdom"; its multiple voices allow for even the author's dissent to register. His fixation on the homoerotic texture of German—and American—literature finds echoes from D. H. Lawrence to young gay scholars.

He vaults over the boundaries of genre with Hermes' frisky aplomb, turning an essay on education into a biographical study.

That Eros and pedagogy had been equally inspirational was evident in his July 26, 1921, diary. While reworking "Goethe and Tolstoy," he heard some "gardeners busy in the garden, one of whom, young, beardless, with brown arms and open shirt, gave me quite a turn. Spent the remainder of the day thinking out further plans, feeling listless, and somewhat ill from lack of exercise. A wealth of thoughts on education—the importance of enthusiasm, love, dedication." The advantages of sublimation could not be clearer.

3

EROS AND THE REPUBLIC:
DEMOCRATIC VISTAS

During the inflation capital became a fable. Billions of marks, carted in wheelbarrows, might secure a family's meal. Five dollars bought six months of private-school tuition. The Mann children turned defeat into a nonstop party. Klaus and Erika entertained their friends with champagne breakfasts and diamond bracelets. One day Mann came upon little Elisabeth perched on a hobby horse. As she rode, she sang to herself, "The dollar goes up, the dollar goes up."

In those years every area of German culture became damaged goods, marked down for a quick sale. Inflation constituted the worst possible revolution, "a new distribution of wealth without system or fairness." Speculation supplanted the old values of craft, patience, and vision. Why prepare for tomorrow? "The outcome was no longer determined by work but by unknown evil forces."

Writing in 1942, safe in America, Mann demystified the market. The unknown forces had names; "the hyenas of economic life" grew rich off speculation: "In those years, powerful industrialists like the Krupps, the Stinnesses, the Thyssens, and so on, liquidated their debts with inflated currency, at the same time buying up objects really worth millions." In 1942 those same families were stoking the engines of Hitler's war machine, abetted by millions of slave laborers. Mann credited Hitler's rise to the inflation. It had weaned the Germans from self-reliance to dependence on the state. This point might appeal to conservatives; nothing else about Mann's anticapitalism would. His socialism had roots in material experience and romantic poetry, empty stomachs and Whitman's verse.

He was no Marxist, certainly not one as driven as Lukács. But by January 1922, when they first met, his wartime conservatism had been largely abandoned. The spectacle of Germany's ruin had turned his thoughts to practical politics. The "ironic conservative" would shortly become a publicist for a government presided over by a Socialist.

History was not kind to Weimar's reputation. But the republic Mann defended had more advanced policies on sexual reform, health care, youth, education, and national insurance than any American administration, including the four-term reign of his beloved Roosevelt.

To go from the heroic isolation of Frederick the Great to the vapid compromises of "Old Father" Ebert in a mere seven years was an astonishing leap for the cautious, slow-paced Mann. His public evolution was far more daring than any gesture he performed in private—its equivalent would have involved, at the very least, a divorce. Its personal ramifications were exclusively aesthetic; he later contended that his vision of literature and myth arose from his new politics.

In the spring of 1919 Mann shared the Nietzsche Award for his *Reflections* with Bertram's study of the philosopher. The prize had been endowed ostensibly to celebrate the philosopher's spirit, but actually to advance the politics of Nietzsche's sister, Elisabeth Förster-Nietzsche, a notorious racist. She "congratulated Mann on his timely warning against the vulgar trends of the times," wrote H. F. Peters. "Mann accepted the prize with an expression of gratitude and pride, assuring Elisabeth that her kind words of praise 'had moved him more than he could say.' " Such thanks were, for Mann, the equivalent of a bread-and-butter note. Even so, the prize kept his name before the conservatives.

A year later, still under the sway of right-wing politics, Mann wrote to Hanns Johst, a fascist novelist, praising his efforts to counter the Gallic and Jewish influences on German culture. Mann's 1944 tribute to Fontane and Max Liebermann, the Gallic and Jewish heroes of Berlin, stands with his postwar essay on Nietzsche—and its indictment of Elisabeth Förster— as evidence of his development since the reactionary days of 1920.

Signs of change were apparent in the summer of 1921 when he wrote the "Goethe and Tolstoy" essay. In September he turned to something more immediate. At a local journal's request, he prepared an essay on the Jews. Katia objected strongly, and it was published only in 1966. It is a typical congeries of autobiographical detail and social diagnosis. But its occasion was frighteningly specific: the rise of Nazism and the attacks on Albert Einstein by students invading his classroom. Mann's declaration of philo-Semitism occurs in defiance of a national abandonment of "liberalism."

The essay begins on a personal note. When friends ask, "How did you make it?" Mann replies, "My hard times through the world have been eased thanks to Judaism." He remembers the Jewish friends of his youth, adding gratuitous—"ironic, grotesque"—details that might easily offend Katia: e.g., Rabbi Carlebach's son was "not terribly clean"; the Hungarian Feher was stereotypically ugly, with a flat nose and a premature five o'clock shadow. Despite his physical misgivings, Mann admired the warmth and vitality of Jewish households. ("A pleasing disposition is more common among the Jews than among Ur-Europeans.")

He quotes Goethe's secretary Riemer that Goethe's best readers were Jews. "I beg your pardon a thousand times," Mann teases, "but this is exactly my experience." He adds that every important artist depends on the Jews. Admittedly he has undergone "bad conflicts between my nature and the Jewish." No doubt alluding to critics like Kerr and Lessing, he complains that Jewish writers have produced "the most hateful caricatures, the most poisonous and witty negations of my existence." (He would never get over Kerr's remark about his *Sitzfleisch*.)

But also "Jews discovered me, published and publicized my work, staged my impossible play." The "poor S. Lublinski" had rescued his first novel, "which had been received with a sour expression." Now that he's a touring author, his most generous out-of-town hosts are Jews. He welcomes their solicitude. "Doesn't this pleasing attention and flattering interest . . . provide a certain guarantee of my value?" He constructs a paradox: only the most refined German pleases the Jews, but middle-brow Jews—like the composers Meyerbeer and Offenbach—delight the Aryan bourgeoisie.

The nationalist professor Adolf Bartels once hypothesized that the Mann brothers were Jewish. Even Mann's World War I conversion to *Deutschtum* has not dissuaded Bartels. It's true that Jews are radical democrats and that—as of this month—Mann is not, but he loves them still; and if the *völkische* professor can't reconcile philo-Semitism with conservative politics, Mann "knows why."

During the war Mann realized that he is an "adventurer, that's my fate," and that, like the Jews, he is an "adventurous world-child," poised between Germanism and European intellectual life. He quotes the Jewish doctor of *Royal Highness* and concludes that the "Jewish attitude is aristocratic-romantic," not unlike the German's. However, a few are hypersensitive; he alludes to "repressive" artists who discern anti-Semitism if "you don't overlook the Jewish phenomenon," by which he means their habits and idioms, a circuitous defense of "The Blood of the Walsungs" (as if the incestuous couple—or their Pringsheim models—were typical Jews!).

From the Walsung novella, he turns to *Death in Venice*, and contends that his "bad" poetic narrative includes a "beautiful" tribute to racial miscegenation, the common fate of Jews and Venetians. "What do you want? The son of a mixed nation, I myself am mixed," a descendant of medieval Germans and Latins. Venice symbolizes the marriage of East and West. Mann's children "share the dream. . . . Hopefully they will be trial examples of the Eurasian-Negroid future race as they follow the way of progress": a remark that alone would devastate the *völkische* professors.*

Mann admits that this is "not quite my road, as I tried to explain in six hundred pages." But he refuses to yield to "cultural reaction and the swastika-nonsense." The swastika may be a popular expression right now, but it fails to "answer my needs." He alludes to the Nazis' attacks on backstabbing war profiteers. True, Jews were among the crooks, but the greatest chiselers of all were "trustworthy peasants." Jews were merely "fellow travelers," no more or less guilty than their compatriots.

Mann remembers his opposition to the Munich reds. "Nobody suffered more under the moral debacle of 1918, the awful radical craziness, than I." He declines all absolutes: "My heart belongs totally to those youths who follow neither Moscow nor Rome as the source of wisdom." But if Munich students have actually drowned out the lectures of "the new Newton" (an unnamed Einstein, probably an allusion to George Bernard Shaw's 1920 characterization of the scientist), attacking him first as a Jew, then as someone who "thinks in spheres of pure abstraction, and finally as a convinced pacifist, it is such a scandal that I desire, as old Claudius said, 'not to be guilty of it.' "

Mann already saw the Nazis' message as a noxious combination of anti-Semitism, militarism, and anti-intellectualism, a "scandal" that would destroy Germany. He concluded with comments guaranteed to please nobody: the Jews' "typical character contains some unpleasantness and some danger. But what folk character does not? Each European people becomes a disaster in its own way. The Jews have something special—which makes them appear stranger than their noses: an inborn love of intellect. This love has often made them leaders in the sins of humanity, but more often humanity's friends and sponsors."

One final paradox. Dostoyevsky's love of literature prevented his be-

---

* Mann's advocacy of miscegenation was more than rhetorical. In 1926, he described Count Richard Coudenhove-Kalergi, a Euro-Japanese nobleman, as "one of the handsomest men I have ever seen."

coming a Slavophile. "Must conservatism always be the cause of intellectual cave dwellers?" Surely the Germans, that most scapegoated of nations, will not imitate their enemies: anti-Semitism was foreign to the cultural masters Goethe and Nietzsche. "Much in me keeps me German," but those very qualities, "the love of spirit, the friendliness toward everything tender and daring," freedom itself, "will always connect me with the Jews."

Dialectical twists and anecdotal details may vitiate Mann's argument. But the acuity of his attack on the Nazis overshadows these flaws. In later years he would defend the Jewish people to such an extent that his death prompted a memorial issue of the émigré publication *Aufbau.* Similarly, the "new Newton" would become his political ally, remaining so until their last years, when they led an intellectual opposition to Senators McCarthy and McCarran.

Together with "Goethe and Tolstoy," the essay reveals that Mann's political development did not require Heinrich's intercession. But it went unpublished. In July 1922 he wrote Bertram, "I am thinking of writing a birthday article about Gerhart Hauptmann [a supporter of the Weimar Republic] in the form of a manifesto in which I shall speak to the consciences of the youth who will listen to me." He saw the challenge: those German students who hated Einstein also despised liberalism.

"On the German Republic" has perplexed commentators. Without a doubt, it's a fantastical manifesto, steeped in poetic imagery and confessional allusion. But, paradoxically, Mann uses these devices to promote a political vision, to argue that politics matters. In 1922, the German republic was barely four years old, inventing itself under the worst imaginable conditions, military defeat and economic chaos. Mann, who was born when the last Reich was only four years old, understood that his countrymen were political infants.

Germans were used to great men absolving them of civic responsibility. Mann quotes Bismarck's disgusted remark "I am tired of driving pigs," but he adds that Bismarck himself bewitched them. As chancellor, he insulated the Kaiser from any system of checks and balances. The prewar parliament had been a smug and docile servant; the socialist capitulation of 1914 could be seen as Bismarck's final rout.

In 1922 young Germans regarded Ebert's government as either too radical or not radical enough. Right-wingers considered it a break with the past. At that time Spengler's *Decline of the West* fed a national appetite for schadenfreude. Spengler offered the dubious consolation of inexorable laws: in his view, the decline could not be reversed, and that was that. Other conservatives simply abandoned rational argument. In Mann's appeal to the

Berlin students, he spars with the *völkische* professors, who attack the republic as fit only for "sharp-witted Jews," prefer "feeling to mind," and condemn Marxists and democrats for their abstractions.

Left-wingers also disliked Ebert, seeing him as ultimately responsible for the deaths of Rosa Luxemburg and Karl Liebknecht. But Mann doesn't contend with them. He argues with the culturally conservative for a simple reason: he knows them. He imagines his auditors as nationalist intellectuals, deeply under the sway of Spengler or Blüher. Therefore he invokes the former's sense of cultural development and the latter's nostalgia for homoerotic camaraderie. Of course he turns their visions inside out, comes up with an optimistic solution, and, in so doing, identifies politics with both romantic poetry and erotic freedom.

Now a literary defense of the republic might not bemuse modern listeners; it could almost be seen as a poet laureate's obligation. It's the erotic nature of Mann's speech that remains startling. Yet each step of Mann's political development had an erotic basis. During his nationalistic period, he shared the common infatuation with glamorous male warriors. In his 1907 memoir of army life, he recalled his presiding officers, and chose— as Lukács would later—to invite their contempt: "If I love you, why should you care?" He wrote these words soon after the Eulenburg trial with its revelations of homosexual circles around the Kaiser, and the heavy hints, propagated by Maximilian Harden, that Wilhelm himself was gay. It had become a journalistic commonplace that an enthusiasm for military life betrayed homosexual inclinations; Mann's rapture, hedged as usual with irony, was therefore quite daring.

During the war, as we have seen, he allowed himself a further expression. In his 1915 "Thoughts in Wartime," he proposed that war meant, among other things, "pederasty." In his *Reflections*, he affected pity for soldiers' wives, displaced in their husbands' affections by fellow warriors. By 1920 Mann's social vision had grown specifically homoerotic and right-wing; witness his admiration for Hans Blüher's "blood and soil" doctrine.

As Mann wrote Carl Maria Weber, he preferred this stance to the left-wing propaganda of Magnus Hirschfeld. The sexual freedom identified with the latter meant little to Mann, who confided in a 1920 journal note his fascination with medieval priests, comely acolytes, cloistered in their monasteries—not precisely the fantasy of a Jewish socialist.

Mann's turn to the left was catalyzed by his reading of Walt Whitman. In April 1922 he reviewed Reisiger's translation of Whitman and called it "noble." Mann saw Whitman as a kindred spirit before he accepted his politics. In his view, the American's tribute to democracy is unmistakably erotic. The city square is a place where he catches "the frequent and swift flash of eyes offering me love." Democracy ratifies a voyeur's cruise: the sole erotic pleasure Mann never denied himself.

Whitman's claim that America introduced a new order of visual pleasure, the promise of love relayed on every street corner, spoke as immediately to Mann as did the lyrics of Platen or Novalis. But while German poets pledged themselves to death, Whitman made of democracy an erotic renaissance. Seeing this, Mann experienced a political conversion with a force reminiscent of Grandfather Buddenbrook's zealotry. In the evangelical tradition, someone reborn has to spread the news. Mann proceeded to do so. His first auditors were friends. On October 6, 1922, he read "On the German Republic" to a Munich gathering that included Kurt Martens, Emil Preetorius, and Heinrich—the latter was deeply impressed.

A week later he delivered the speech in the Beethoven Hall in Berlin. "On the German Republic" displays, in his words, an "almost American freshness." Mann's attempt to convert German students requires an extraordinary range of rhetorical appeals. He speaks as a friend and parent: "Children, fellow citizens, it is better now. Hand on my heart, I say to you we are better off fundamentally." He anticipates their shock, their conclusion that he has sold out his wartime principles, and even their feet shuffling in nervous irritation: he composes passages that will appear improvised. By making their displeasure a necessary part of the ritual, he turns the performance into a ceremony of purgation as well as rebirth.

Yes, he knows they remember his *Reflections*, he can hear their mutters: "Renegade, turncoat! You are eating your own words, you are riding for a fall!" He disowns nothing. "I am a conservative—my natural occupation in this world is to preserve." His book was "conservative, not in the service of the past and reaction, but in the service of the future. Its concern was the preservation of that stock, that kernel, round which the new might crystallize in beautiful forms."

Mann recounts his gradual acceptance of a socialist ideology: "The thing itself was mine sooner than the name," a development that parallels Aschenbach's recognition that what he felt was love. All your opposition is misguided: "your resistance to the Republic and the democracy is simply a fear of words." Mann implies that a master of the language can guide his readers. Their experiences, their aspirations, their ideals are all best conveyed in a foreign language—whose prophet is a New York poet.

Echoing Goethe and Tolstoy, he asserts that "the great and moving experience of education grew unconsciously out of the autobiographical urge to confession and self-portrayal . . . the social may be arrived at through the pedagogic . . . the human being in contact with the social gets sight of what is unquestionably the highest stage of the human—the State." Even

Mann is astonished by his words. "I should never have dreamed that one day I'd be talking like that! But whoever does is a republican."

In defiance of pedants and academics everywhere, he concludes that events, not language, determine consciousness. He's simply found the proper idiom for behavior and attitudes that already exist. Typically, he makes the struggle for verbal consciousness an autobiographical drama.

His political argument doubles as literary explication. He invokes Whitman, as translated by Reisiger, and makes bold to compare the "Manhattan thunderer" and "the godlike Weimarean." This allows him to exalt Whitman at Goethe's expense; "godlike" becomes an archaic word in a republican vocabulary. Whitman understood that "democracy must have some warm hold on men's feelings and beliefs, as did feudalism or religion." He preached a "social eroticism"; likewise, the German romantic poet Novalis commanded us "to live in the State as a lover in his beloved."

For Mann, Eros is ideally a mediating factor. Hence Whitman becomes a prophet of "the German federation . . . or the future European one . . . a human idea . . . as far removed from the political mysticism of a slave state as from the radical and anarchistic individualism of a certain West." The social vision lies between Russian fanaticism and American reaction—notwithstanding its articulation by the most American of poets.

He justifies these poetic flights with an appeal to cultural history. "Romanticism means modernity in Schiller's sense." The romantic poets exhibit the critical animus of modern novelists. It honors no gods—whether these be Odin, Wotan, or Goethe. Mistaken conservatives may have used Nature to refute the ambitions of spirit. But what if "the unchanging laws of Nature were an illusion?" This last question contradicts his remark, a few months earlier, that political conservatism accompanied a "biological interest." But his model then was Goethe, who, this essay affirms, has been overtaken by Schiller and Whitman.

Having deflated the godlike Weimarean, Mann has no problem vanquishing Spengler, the most recent of the lawgivers. Barely two years earlier, he had thrilled to Spengler's "highbrow romance," boasting in private that he responded to the historian's "aperçus" as if they were his own. But now he finds Spengler guilty of "snobbishness" and "extreme inhumanity." Similarly, in a later passage, he refutes Blüher's—and Schopenhauer's—attempt to make homosexual warfare coterminous with reaction. In a witty use of Greek history, he finds two lovers who murdered a tyrant's son.

Spengler denies any process but decline. Whitman knew better; like all romantics, he abhorred stasis. Mann quotes Whitman's "The law is the law of succession," what Trotsky might call "permanent revolution"—a remark so optimistic that it verges on propaganda. His sales pitch for democracy is almost lurid. "The root is love . . . not in any diluted, anemic, ascetic, condescending sense; in the sense rather of the obscene root-symbol which Whitman gave as title to that raging and reverent song-sequence ['Calamus']"—a bizarre attempt to seduce the students with phallic imagery.

His poets share a vision of democracy as intensely physical. He compares Whitman's pleasure in "staying close to men and women and looking at them and in the contact and odor of them" with Novalis's conviction that "Amor it is which presses us together." Nature is no Burkean confirmation of aristocratic principles. It is "biology as a state of being in love," the universal conglomeration of sweat, semen, and excrement.

Politics renders innocent Mann's lascivious prose. He celebrates "unorganic nature, plants, animals, and human beings, the 'excreta' of the consuming force . . . the phenomenon of sexual lust, the yearning of bodily contact. . . ." Whitman's "I Sing the Body Electric" addressed the body's parts "in the exuberant, copious, naïve style of the untrained artist." But his litany was a charmingly rude echo of the learned Goethe, who loved the theater for exposing "the beauty of uncovered limbs," and whose novel *Wilhelm Meister* "regards the free, sensuous, erotic sphere of the theater as a preliminary to the study of medicine. . . ." Theatrical performance or physical disease are simple "variations of the consumingly interesting theme . . . man." Would anyone but Thomas Mann find such parallels?

"Parts of the body are parts of the soul," said the Manhattan thunderer. The Mann who, in hypochondriacal moments, believed that the source of all feelings, much less ideas, was physical, agrees. Whitman's body worship becomes "Hellenism born anew as the spirit of American democracy." Mann can barely restrain himself. He knows that Eros cannot preside over a modern republic. "Yet it would please Walt Whitman if one made the young god president of the new Reich." Could it be otherwise? For all his paeans to the "kind if unsubtle" Father Ebert, the ideal president of Mann's republic is Tadzio!

At this point, Mann's speech becomes the most revealing public statement of his career. Both the political and confessional aspects are bowdlerized in the English translation of H. T. Lowe-Porter. When Mann calls the union of body and soul "das dritte Reich" of "religious humanity," she turns "Reich" into "kingdom," thus losing Mann's specific allusion to Nazi propaganda. When he declares that Eros should preside, he interpolates "as king? no, for that would smack of medieval chivalry"; she drops the words "as king," rendering Mann's negation meaningless, much less ignoring his confrontation with authoritarian homosexuals ranging from Ernst Bertram to Stefan George and Hans Blüher.

She also excises the following three pages, perhaps out of sheer perplexity. Coming at the speech's climax, these paragraphs express the most radical vision of Mann's lifetime. Their absence denatures the speech, much as her subsequent translations downplay the erotic comedy essential to his vision. Lowe-Porter helped establish the official Mann, but such examples indicate how poorly she understood him.

After his quip about the godlike president, a line space indicates that Mann has left whim for theory:

> I will dare, in this connection, which still remains a political connection, to discuss—with all respect for your sensitivity—a topic that has been implicit in my last words. I mean the zone of Eros in which the generally accepted law of sexual polarity proves to be invalid, and in which like with like, whether mature masculinity and adoring youth, joined in a dream of themselves as gods, or young males drawn to their own mirror image, are bound in a passionate community.

Mann carefully distinguishes this "community" from a "society" where sexual polarity prevails. That society has willfully "denied the knowledge," reveals its "prudish detestation." But matters are changing: "the ban of denial and scandal" has loosened—i.e., democracy has emancipated the homosexual. Though he doesn't say so, he is his own best example, for the preceding passage is a close paraphrase of his words about homosexual love in the Weber letter of July 4, 1920.

Back then he accepted Blüher's division of social organization between the family and associations of men. His family role, as husband and father, was seen as vibrant, even idolatrous, but "bourgeois." Homoeroticism belonged to the area of "unbourgeois, intellectually sensual adventures." Doesn't "The German Republic" reverse the order? Now the erotic life can be *officially* celebrated by Germany's foremost bourgeois artist. Even the rapturous synesthesia of his language, the sweaty embraces and stinking root-plants, is unlike such forbiddingly abstract terms as "intellectually sensual adventures." That phrase typified what Lawrence calls "sex in the head." Paradoxically Mann's public statement is earthier, more sexually frank than his personal letters.

Liberation is both visual and discursive. German society can now discuss the "frequency" of homosexual love "in a humane way," as it literally "grabs [it] with the eye"; to be public is to be seen. He allows that such love may connote "a loss of nerve, decadence, illness," and proceeds to reject such terms. How can one call "decadent . . . the sphere of complex feelings that contains the holiest and most fertile elements of culture"?

Mann's need for authority usually requires some high-powered quotations. Out they come: With his dictates about nature and law, Novalis confirms that the "reproach of unnatural" is "trivial." And holy Goethe himself appears for the defense; the sage's remark that homosexuality is "absolutely in—not outside of—nature and humanity, because at all times it has appeared among all people," would seem to clinch Mann's case. But he includes, wafted by self-confidence, Goethe's misogynistic addendum that homosexuality can be explained "aesthetically by the fact that the male presents the purer and more beautiful [image]."

As if that weren't enough, he quotes Schopenhauer's assertion that "what may be casually discussed about this strange phenomenon is inherently political." Is this an addendum to Thomas Buddenbrook's discovery of Schopenhauer, in whose pages he found an image of a beloved friend? Mann's quarrying for affirmation endows all his previous reading with a specific agenda; the erotic sympathy between generations becomes a political strategy.

But Schopenhauer has become linked with the militaristic temperament. "Doesn't one say that war, with its expression of blood and death-camaraderie, powerfully strengthens the heart and unique virility of this form of life, and the atmosphere of this erotic realm?" One who said so was Mann in his *Reflections*. In 1922 he no longer desires the conjunction of Eros and Thanatos. So, after refuting Goethe, the overworked Walt Whitman challenges Schopenhauer. Mann quotes the American's pledge not to "sing any other songs than those of manly friendship . . . to create an example of athletic love." He saw pacifism as the fruit of that love; he dreamt "cities that will never quarrel through the love of comrades."

Imagining that some German youths shared his tendencies—as if Blüher's followers constituted more than a cult—Mann thought his pedagogical role was to transform Spartan warriors into Athenian democrats. For rhetorical purposes, he concedes that pacifism may appear unmanly—"vegetarian," but gives it a Whitmanesque shimmer, grounding it "not in buildings, laws, bureaucrats, or intellectual debate, but in the intimate love of comrades." Not even in the 1960s would a "representative" writer advise soldiers to make love, not war, to each other.

As he always does, Mann escapes from the enemy with a portion of his weapons. Reactionaries like Blüher may long for "Eros as statesman"; their mistake is to cast him in the guise of "monarchic restoration," a new Kaiser instead of Whitman's president. Since they lack "spirit and ingenuity," Mann supplies his own. Can't they be like him? He had been a democrat, a republican, before knowing the words; a radical all those years he called himself a conservative, redefined as an erotic ironist. (In these breathless pages, irony disappears.) That is why he insisted later to friends like Bertram that he had not fundamentally changed. The stable element remained his personality, one that he now displayed to the nation as homosexual to the core.

He winds up the argument by reasserting, "I don't want to leave this subject unnoticed." Is homosexuality "health? Illness?" The master of ambivalence rejects ambiguity. "Be careful of such concepts. They are the most difficult in all philosophy and human knowledge." In republican Germany, normative categories have become anachronisms. Whitman's love of young boys should not be censured; it is "only a beautiful province of his all-embracing kingdom [the 'Reich' returning, unembarrassed] of phallic holiness, abounding phallic ardor."

Thus speaks the author who loves Tadzio and Michelangelo, Jacob and Joseph, who imagines Moses as a musclebound hunk. Whitman's "phallic holiness . . . phallic ardor was surely something more healthy than poor Novalis's love for Sophie, the poet who thought it wise to love a dead person in order to prepare 'for the night' a cozy sleeping arrangement and in whose erotic reveries the lascivious appeals of disease break through."

Better homosexuality, better even the love of boys, than romantic necrophilia. By such verbal trickery, his wit acting as a guarantee of his ideas, Mann attempts to move German students into the republican present. His tactics were politically appropriate, not some crazy lapse of a middle-aged intellectual rendered foolish by the sight of eager young men. Hitler's flack Goebbels would summon "steely romanticism" to gird the loins of Nazi warriors. In this essay, Mann anticipates the virus and provides the vaccine, male friendship.

At this point, in mid-paragraph, Lowe-Porter resumes her translation, making his eccentric argument appear even more disjointed, a tissue of literary allusions rather than a sustained plea for sexual freedom.

He likes Whitman so much that he makes him German. The romantic poets share a "sympathy with death" foreign to "the singer of Manhattan, the herald of athletic democracy, and of free states holding each other embraced." But his love of the ocean betrays a love of death; Mann arrived independently at this Freudian notion of oceanic immensity. Ultimately Platen's "Tristan" tells us, "All poetry is disease since it is profoundly, inseparably, incurably bound up with ideas of beauty and death." (A perfect vision of democracy is simultaneously morbid and buoyant; if there's a logical fallacy, Eros is to blame.)

Just to be consistent, Mann reverses himself. An interest in death and disease, in the pathological, in decay, is "only one form of expression for an interest in life, in the human being, in medicine." Democracy abolishes the distinctions between nature and sentiment, death and life: "a good subject," Mann teases, "for a novel would be that the expression of death is in the last analysis an expression of life, that it leads to the human."

Having shown the young Germans how to read the past in light of Whitmanesque ideals, Mann envisions a uniquely German polity. It will combine "old-fashioned concerns" with a "youthful allure"; the German mean lies "between mysticism and ethics; inwardness and the state; a death-based rejection of ethics and civil values and a purely ethical Philistine rationalism." To modern readers, this dream may appear mired in abstractions, in late-romantic imagery. But as a non-Marxist—moreover, as a representative of German culture—Mann couldn't imagine a better way to have the best of both worlds, romantic introspection and a social conscience. He ends the speech by invoking the unfamiliar, slightly undignified pleasure of partisan politics. Acknowledging their mutual embarrassment, he calls for a rousing salute, "Long live the Republic!"

Every role Mann assumed was colored by his sexuality. It shone through his guises as son and lover. Now it turned him into the queerest of fathers. That was his point. Radicals like Arnolt Bronnen and Brecht were anti-patriarchal, a stance Mann knew well from his Munich days, from Otto Gross and Ludwig Klages. Where the youhg playwright despised parliamentary democracy, the middle-aged novelist wanted to make such a bourgeois form revolutionary. Thereby would sons and fathers join in political matrimony, universal suffrage become erotic license. No generational wall divided his comrades, brothers in arms and in the flesh.

From Berlin Mann traveled to Frankfurt, where he read to great acclaim the "Hippe" chapter from *The Magic Mountain* and the medical examination scene from *Felix Krull*: the first evoked adolescent homosexuality; the second mocked the forces of law and order. Together they dramatized the tendencies he had just declared. As never before he found himself in Heinrich's role, a spokesman for progressive youth. In November he returned to Munich: "The whole trip was quite successful. Saturated with the world, cheerful, and tired, I return to my harbor."

But he felt obliged to explain his amazing transformation to other writers. Before the speech, in September, he had written the Viennese Jew Arthur Schnitzler that "as the author of the *Reflections of an Unpolitical Man*, I believe I owed my country such a manifesto at this moment," and confided that the politics were a byproduct of his latest novel. His old Lübeck champion Ida Boy-Ed was one of the shocked Germans who begged for a fuller explanation. On December 5, he wrote her that the press had misrepresented his ideas. He had supported the revolution, but traced its origins to 1914, not 1918. "It came into being in the hearts of the youth of that time, as they faced death on the field of honor. In saying this [in Berlin] I contributed something toward a definition of the Republic. I mean—I certainly did not hail the Republic *until* I said what I meant by it" (italics mine).

In a kind of shoptalk, Mann still claimed that it was a question of literary definition. "How do I define [the republic]? Approximately as the *opposite* of what exists today. But for that very reason, the attempt to infuse something like an idea, a soul, a vital spirit into this grievous state without citizens . . . appeared to me something approaching a good deed." Though Boy-Ed shared his values, and believed democracy "the ideal of all mature, creative people," she saw his new work as an act of self-betrayal. "I disavow nothing. This essay is the direct continuation of the essential line of the *Reflections*, I assure you." He was right, but who could tell?

He justifies himself with a paradox. "In the name of German humanitarianism I took arms against the revolution when it was starting. Today, out of the same impulse, I take arms against the reactionary wave which is sweeping over Europe," and which finds German expression in fascism. He offers as evidence of his steadfastness "my twice being in the opposition."

He resumed touring in January 1923. His readings were strictly literary, but he could not retire from politics: he joked, "They consider me some kind of campaign speaker for Ebert." That month, after France occupied the Ruhr valley as punishment for German refusal—or inability—to pay wartime reparations, Mann became infuriated. He wrote Heinrich that it was as if the French had deliberately provoked the Germans to do their worst, "giving the lie to everyone . . . who urges moderation." It was an impossible situation. "A French retreat, desirable though that would be, would signify the triumph of [German] nationalism in domestic politics."

On June 24, 1922, Walther Rathenau, the German foreign minister, had been assassinated by reactionary soldiers, after he established relations with Lenin's government, dropping all claims for war reparation.* Rathenau was a wealthy Jew, a modified socialist, and a homosexual. In his writings, he expressed an ambivalence that seemed very literary; in fact Musil would use him as a model for Count Arnheim in *The Man Without Qualities*. In June 1923, eight months after his Berlin defense of the republic, Mann

---

* A secret codicil of the Rapallo Treaty allowed the German army to perform military experiments in the USSR forbidden by the Treaty of Versailles. Rathenau had unwittingly engineered a boon to the future Nazis.

gave a speech at a Rathenau memorial service in Munich: "The Spirit and Essence of the German Republic."

Although the Munich students supported republican politics, the town was deeply polarized; within five months Hitler would attempt his Beer-Hall putsch. Gerhart Hauptmann presides over Mann's Berlin speech, contributing in absentia his good-humored, friendly tone. But this one is delivered in the shadow of Rathenau's murder. Mann offers "somber reflections" in lieu of October's almost giddy exuberance.

He stresses that the Germans' most beautiful trait is *Innerlichkeit*, a mastery of the inner life that makes them more idealistic and profound than other nationalities. But that idea needs to be developed, perfected. Goethe's *Wilhelm Meister* dramatized the route from *Innerlichkeit* to a political sensibility. In modern terms, "republic is [now] the political name for humanitarianism."

A few months earlier Mann presented republican ideas as the newest thing, newer than the language with which he proclaimed them. But now he recognizes that they seem "outdated and relativistic," tentative gestures when the masses demand absolutes. "Community" and "loyalty" *sound* so much stronger than "individualism" and "liberty." He fears that "ideas of revolutionary origin will drive young people into the arms of political obscurantism, i.e., reaction." Nevertheless, in the country of Goethe, Hölderlin, and Nietzsche, "reactionary antiliberalism cannot prevail."

Later that year Mann contributed a long essay, "Five Years of Democracy in Germany," to *Current History*, a magazine published in New York. The previously nonpolitical man had become his country's political gadfly. He used new forums to warn both the Germans *and* their former enemies not to abandon Ebert's republic.

Naturally he repeats himself, interpolating whole paragraphs from his two political speeches. But he also fills in the background for uninformed foreigners, tracing the steps that led Germany to this hour. He accuses Bismarck of exploiting the Germans' infantile need for authority. "Bismarck, the great man who did everything himself, in no way influenced the German middle class to become republican." Now the Buddenbrooks must be wrenched into the twentieth century.

The conditions are not propitious: "Ninety percent of all Germans are not in a position to eat meat more than once a week. . . . German mothers are obliged to wrap their children in newspapers." Yet, as in his Rathenau memorial, he refuses to be overly alarmed. "The union of intellect and sentimental brutality, the association which for a moment appeared to give rise to a German Fascism . . . is not tenable; on both sides it has been recognized as a misunderstanding." Foreign scholars had begun to link

Nietzsche with conventional German reactionaries. For Mann this was "madness! Nietzsche's place is where the spirit of Greece is fused with the lyrical spirit of American democracy, the universal spirit of Walt Whitman." For American eyes, he now placed Whitman and Nietzsche in a "*third reich* of *religious* humanity" (italics mine). In his own version of Goethe's "world literature," he Americanized—and thereby sexualized—his native culture, a gesture of literary statesmanship that persuaded only its author.

Composing *The Magic Mountain*, Mann discerned hidden parallels between the most disparate activities: politics, medicine, "forbidden love." Thus, when he saw the republic as expressing the same impulses that quickened Novalis's erotic verses or Goethe's biological experiments, he envisioned an audience—a public—capable of reading his novel. As he observed later, it could not have been written before then. Neither author nor audience was ready.

Mann's political manifestos have been challenged and ridiculed. His joining of Whitman's eroticism and the mundane reality of party politics appears a stretch; demystifying romanticism seems a grotesquely impractical way to win elections or fight Nazis.

T. J. Reed prefers to emphasize the influence of Ernst Troeltsch, whose attempt to link democracy and natural law was briefly noted by Mann in 1923. But throughout the 1920s, even as he increasingly campaigned for the Social Democrats, an erotic animus remained crucial to Mann's politics. He understood that for all the talk of party platforms, the real battle involved myth and ideology. The Nazis and their fellow travelers professed faith in unreason. Many were drawn to the matriarchal cults, supposedly discovered by Bachofen. Mann deplored equally the irrationalism and the matriarchy, offering as an alternative his democratic ethos.

He was wrong to think that his myth would triumph. But, then, given his public, he might have been right, and given his nature, he had no choice.

His attempt to yoke Marx and Novalis signifies a leavening and humanizing of socialism, an attention to what makes people happy. (As a contrast, see Walter Benjamin's cryptic remark, "Bolshevism has abolished private life.") The obscene and smelly calamus is a metaphor for the satisfaction of physical needs. He dreams of a republic that commands its citizens' loyalty because they are viscerally engaged. Mann understood that a politics that does not accommodate pleasure is doomed. Thirty-five years after his death, the collapse of communism demonstrated the fundamental miscalculation of its materialism. His democracy of uncovered limbs makes the Marxism of, say, Brecht abstract, literally disembodied.

Traces of this argument lingered in a 1925 expansion of "Goethe and Tolstoy." His subject now was German education, not a very sexy topic until Mann got his hands on it. At the moment liberalism was challenged abroad by France, smugly convinced of "the absolute supremacy of Latin civilization and its mission of world domination," and at home by the Nazis, with their disdain for the Judeo-Christian legacy from which, according to Mann, democracy had sprung.

Education might save the day, but not as it was prescribed by Goethe and Tolstoy. Both were elitists who denied the plebs access to high culture. German enough to allow music in his curriculum, Goethe banished studies in dead languages: a rebuke to the classicist Winckelmann. He felt boys should be servants and girls should be mothers: anything but "irritable, advanced and sickly liberals." Tolstoy exiled music and Shakespeare from his ideal school. Learning a trade was fine, Mann thought, particularly when everyone was broke. Still, giving up cultural humanism meant training a generation of cavemen. Tolstoy advocated a form of illiberalism with a religious patina, but *völkische* professors would replace humanism altogether with a "pagan folk religion."

Against such forces, Mann's vaunted irony became a "pathos of the middle," the appropriate political and educational stance for a reborn nation, "a people of the middle, of the world bourgeoisie." To make this irony more German—and Mannian—he compared it to the musical pleasure of "the prolonged note, the teasing melancholy of the not yet." Denial, renunciation, but, for once, without hopelessness.

He refused to distinguish between *Sehnsucht* and *Politik*. In his words, "love of the ego and love of the world are psychologically not to be divorced." Therefore "nobody has ever loved his own ego, nobody was ever egocentric, in the sense of conceiving his own ego as a cultural task, and toiling early and late in pursuance of it, without reaping, almost as though by accident, educational influence in the outer world, and the joy and dignity of a leader of youth." One morning a writer awakens, "incredulous . . . astonished" to see that "he has been teaching while he learned—shaping, guiding, leading, training, setting his own stamp on youth, by the power of words, by that lofty instrument of culture, which is Eros-filled and binds the heart of man." With that assurance Mann rehabilitated Aschenbach. The erotic ironist was no longer a pederast but "a leader of youth."

(Mann employed other rhetorical means of indoctrination. In 1924 he addressed a gathering of businessmen in Amsterdam. After celebrating their "aristocratic" reliability—a hidden salute to the prebourgeois capitalism of his father's generation—he notices their business uniforms, black as the outfits of Venetian merchants. Black is the color of death; "our religious instinct wants it so." But "reason and morality" must unshackle the aristocratic principle, and "the pathos of freedom" counter "the pathos of religion." In other words, Protestants must become socialists. This hope may not have lasted. In a 1932 revision of "Goethe and Tolstoy," he decided that he had been wrong during the Great War to hail Luther. The Catholic church had become "the last bulwark of German freedom and education" —though in America, he would spy a new threat in "Catholic-fascism." The enemy remained the same but Mann's allies changed.)

The extraordinary nature of Mann's political development contrasts with the lack of such development among his peers—for example, Ludwig Wittgenstein. Both were privileged sons; indeed, Wittgenstein was the product of far greater wealth. Both indulged in casual anti-Semitism, despite Wittgenstein's Jewish ancestry and Mann's self-confessed philo-Semitism. Both came from families of suicides; both tended to love men who were their intellectual inferiors. Mann shared Wittgenstein's conviction of language's inadequacy; both men drew careers out of this void. (From Mann and Wittgenstein to Barthes or Foucault, prolix documentation of the limits of language has been a homosexual specialty, as if the love that dare not speak its name must dethrone the authority that silences it.)

Despite a lifetime of generous deeds, Wittgenstein remained politically quietist, uninvolved in the larger world. Nothing about Mann made him more suitable. If anything, he lacked the confidence of Wittgenstein's intellectual power or physical beauty. He knew himself a mediocre scholar, never having advanced as far as the university students he addressed. He was socially awkward, and by his own lights unattractive. Yet from October 1922 to the last months of his life, he remained a public man.

4

IMPERIAL PASTIMES

The postwar era was awash in theoretical speculation. A triumphalist spirit swept through the Allies. The losers, finely attuned to the victors' hypocrisy, offered alternative explanations of their defeat. From all sides came grand historical designs. Marxists and Spenglerians alike banished surprise; any event could fit into their intellectual scheme, as concrete evidence of the proletariat's ascent or the West's decline.

The bourgeoisie never tired of hearing why they were irrelevant, a masochistic pleasure reflected in best-sellers lists to this day. In the early 1920s, right-wing Germans were particularly savage. Spengler, Blüher, George all deplored an irrecoverable loss of standards.

It is not surprising that Thomas Mann should be attracted to such gloom-and-doom theorists. Like Goethe, he was a fragmented self, "conditioned by a hundred circumstances." Such nervous exceptions are often drawn to all-embracing systems. The surprise is that he never adhered for long to any ideology—even his socialism failed the exacting standards of a Marxist pedant like Brecht. Ironic skepticism always rescued Mann; he couldn't be an absolutist if he tried.

The immediate advantage of his political conversion was a loosening and lightening of focus. He now saw that everything was subject to reinterpretation, beginning with all of German culture. It was a sign of his new confidence that he applied the same criteria to extraliterary concerns. Like Goethe, he acted as if he could write about anything, novelties preferred.

This versatility was also a brilliant device for refuting his enemies, those wisecracking Berliners who regarded him as a ponderous square. Mann's involvement with popular culture may be traced back to the soubrette Mizzi Meyer in *Royal Highness*. Its expansion coincided, appropriately, with the birth of his new politics, specifically the erotic Utopia he derived from Whitman.

On December 26, 1919, Mann's journals record his interest in "the wave of the future. Astrology, physiognomy, graphology." A few months later he reports discussing the occult at a party with "a charming young man." In the 1920s, intellectuals caught between Moscow and Rome pursued various forms of highbrow unreason. (The Marxist Walter Benjamin, for example, dabbled in Jewish metaphysics and graphology.) With his usual circumspect gait, Mann took three years to experience the future. On December 20, 1922, he attended a séance. It provided double inspiration, for a famous scene in *The Magic Mountain* and for a lecture he gave on February 27, 1923, called "An Experience in the Occult."

He presents the séance as a dubious event, by no means refined, geared to servants and shopkeepers. A Salvation Army fervor obtains, punctuated by tambourine banging, shouts and ululations: as he will later, Mann evokes a milieu very similar to American Pentecostalism. The subject is a "not unattractive" man of the working class, possessed by a female spirit. As the androgynous medium reclines his head against Mann's shoulder, the writer murmurs, "Nice lad, good lad!"

He's almost persuaded. But unlike the scientists who visit and stand amazed, "[his] skepticism, which in comparison to theirs is belief, a faith in nothing and everything—what name shall I give it?—will have proved essentially unproductive, nihilistic." (Which also explains why Mann could resist appeals that seduced Hauptmann, Bertram, and Ponten.) He feels "nausea" when "a dream-picture objectivates itself." But he reclaims this vision for empirical science: it was "objectivated by psychophysical energy." What began as "backdoor metaphysics" ends as confirmation of Einstein's theories! "Relativity means that the borderline between mathematical physics and metaphysics has become fluid."

This experience allowed Mann to rehearse his novel's structure. It also engaged him sensually. The figure of Willy S., passive and double-sexed, reminds us that the occult was long popular in homosexual circles: the Eulenburg crowd, for one. Describing Hans Castorp's attendance at a séance, Mann writes in 1925 of his great "affinity for vice" and inability to achieve, "even momentarily, a pure concept of human potentiality." The impure always satisfies Mann by acting as a symbol of his "forbidden love."

He didn't tarry long among the occultists. He had discovered a better source of visual pleasure and "objectivated" energy—the movies. He first wrote about them less than two weeks after his Rathenau memorial. A short essay, "Democratic Power," argues that film is an unprecedented resource, with tremendous artistic and spiritual potential. Perhaps because he was then writing a novel about sickness and health, he emphasizes the cinema's documentary functions. He has just seen a filmed operation, photographed as it were from the ceiling. To behold the removal of an appendix was "spectacular!"

Many intellectuals, particularly members of the Frankfurt school, were less impressed by technological wonders. Walter Benjamin said all conceptual terms demanded revision in "the age of mechanical reproduction." He emphasized the loss of an artwork's "aura," its singularity.

But as early as his descriptions of Old Master reproductions artificially lit in their Munich store windows, Mann had made a specialty of placing the artwork in a social—and invariably commercial—context. In other words, there could never be an uncontaminated nimbus circling a pristine aura. Nietzsche had taught him this, with their favorite artist, Wagner, as his example.

In 1923 Mann collaborated with his brother Victor on a screenplay, *Tristan and Isolde*, based on a thirteenth-century poem and not Wagner's opera. It was never produced. In May 1924 Mann defended his foray into the new medium: "I see film as a truly popular medium, an institution with enormous educational potential—a technically and thematically more sophisticated version of the old fairground ballads with picture-and-music accompaniment." The scenario is of little interest, except for its emphasis on the bond between Tristan and King Marke, and the observation that Tristan "deceives himself more than the two ladies whom he deceives one with the other." (This is his only recorded collaboration with his younger brother. Vico had a small literary talent, similar to his mother's, as evident in his gabby and unreliable autobiography, *We Were Five*: the title a reminder that he was the forgotten Mann.)

He knew a lot more about movies, including an unsatisfactory version of *Buddenbrooks* that was released in 1925, when he next wrote about them in 1928. This time, he spoke of film in distinction to literature and the theater. Its "living shadows" effectively cancel its past; since no traces are left, it resembles the flux of both consciousness and narrative—which always takes us from here to there, then to now—while theater traps us in an artificially sustained present setting. (He plays with time in all his postwar novels, incorporating essays on the relativity of its passage, thereby proving the superiority of music and the novel as aesthetic forms. What is striking is that he likes film for the same reason and that he identifies the cinematic-literary-musical sensibility as a "democratic power." He implies that by tampering with our consciousness all three make us better persons: a vision of art's potential that marries Hölderlin to Charlie Chaplin.)

He makes a yet more provocative distinction between genres. "The atmosphere of art is cool; it is a sphere of spiritual valuations, of transmuted values; a world of style . . . preoccupied with form. It summons an equivalent response: You are at court, you control yourself." But in the democratic heat of a film palace, you get "life at first hand . . . it has not been transmuted." Like many Weimar intellectuals, Mann saw movies as a means of uniting the classes; this, more than documentary, was their political function.

Popular culture served a double purpose. It provided a counterirritant to fascism, matching the enemy trick by trick. It was also a means of visualizing the Eros of romantic poetry, as Goethe's cupbearer became a Cecil B. De Mille extra.

In 1931, honoring Heinrich's seventieth birthday, he alluded to the recent "democratic" triumph of the film *The Blue Angel*. Radio was another useful medium. During the 1920s Heinrich and Thomas were both heard on it. In 1929 Heinrich was the first to broadcast the news of Thomas's Nobel Prize. Fifteen years later Thomas's anti-Nazi broadcasts, recorded in Washington and New York, were smuggled into Germany. Mann found the medium friendly: an invisible public obviated the danger of stage fright. Expressing his hatred of the Nazis in this form became his contribution to the war: he joked that such broadcasts were better than a cure.

Was any other of the century's master writers so alert to the overlap and conflict between literature and the products of modern technology? Mann saw it clearly because he was both a Nietzschean gadfly and an unabashed fan. In 1924, writing about Nietzsche's love of music, he remarks the dangers of romantic art, inspired by a love of death that demands "self-conquest." He imagines an escape from this delusion into a world resembling his ideal republic. "Some soul-enchanting artist might give to this nostalgic song a giant volume, and with it subdue the world. Kingdoms might be founded on it, earthly, all too earthly kingdoms, solid, progressive, not at all nostalgic, in which the song would degenerate, if I may say so, into a piece of gramophone music."

The verb "degenerate" conveys his residual loyalties. But who else would envision something like rock-and-roll, "a nostalgic song," its immense volume a means of subduing the world? By now he couldn't raise an aesthetic question without implying a political corollary.

Mann was a literary star in all German-speaking countries. But his "cosmopolitanism," not to mention his Goethean ambitions, required a wider audience. He began to cultivate allies in other countries. Despite his resentment of France's policies, he welcomed the support of its writers. In January 1922, he thanked André Gide for a collection of essays, including "above all the astonishing letter on Nietzsche, this little masterpiece whose insights remind one of the shameful fact that by far the cleverest criticism of Wagner, too, has been done in France."

A year later he wrote Félix Bertaux, a French critic of German literature who had translated *Death in Venice*. "It will be a special satisfaction to me to see it . . . in the language of Flaubert." He described his condition with a frankness that bespoke an international spirit. "There is a Latin admixture in our blood . . . reason enough for our literary Teutons to reject me." That Mann felt a Frenchman could know him better than his fellow Germans indicated a change more startling, perhaps, than his republican convictions.

America remained to conquer. Only *Royal Highness* had appeared so far, in 1916, to modest acclaim. The vehicle that introduced him to a larger public was *The Dial*, a monthly edited and published by Scofield Thayer, "a young man of taste and means." Thayer published Mann in two guises, as a narrative artist—Kenneth Burke's translations of *Death in Venice* and "Tristan"—and as a social commentator, author of the series of "Letters from Germany." America learned about Mann's new politics almost as quickly as Germany. Significantly, *The Dial* represented Mann as both *Dichter*—*Death in Venice* being his most artistically perfect work—and *Schriftsteller*, the voice of German art and Germany's social conscience as well. Within months of his conversion Mann's liberal image became the only one foreigners could remember. (His publisher had advised him not to publish his Frederick essay abroad.)

His first letter is dated November 1922, a month after his "German Republic" lecture, and reiterates that essay's attack on Spengler. Within the first paragraph, Mann stakes his claim by quoting "our own" Goethe's remark about America, "They have it better" (Goethe adds, "No castles"). Saluting his former enemy, he compliments American democracy. War's "historical function" has always been to produce a "closer connection between peoples."

He cites Goethe's dream of a "world literature," and finds its realization in German bookstores. Translations are popular: he mentions, among others, Proust. He now has an extraordinary chance to bring Germany to America. "See me sitting in my room in Munich and speaking of German things to the citizens of another hemisphere. I write this letter, it will travel over the ocean's rolling wilderness, and reappear in the language of Poe, Emerson, and Whitman."

Belles-lettres have lost their function. Modern readers want a "fusion of criticism and creation, which was inaugurated by our romantic school and powerfully furthered by the appearance of that mixture of learning and lyricism . . . Nietzsche." The product of this fusion is "a novel of the intellect." This is a subliminal advertisement for Mann's forthcoming work, but his examples are Ernst Bertram's book on Nietzsche, a study of Goethe by Gundolf, and Spengler's insidiously readable *Decline of the West*.

Mann skewers Spengler in order to preempt any comparisons; he acknowledges that his own hopes remain tentative, but will not "relish the more, by a single grain, the school-masterish insensibility of the Spenglerian brand of pessimism. Pessimism is not lovelessness"—with which phrase Mann informs American readers that his political discourse will be ingenuous, jargon-free, and defiantly literary. Fighting Spengler obliges him to rescue his masters from an historical misreading. "It is ill done . . . to speak of Goethe, Nietzsche, and Schopenhauer as the forerunners of his own hyenalike gift of prophecy. For they were human beings, while he is a defeatist of humanity." He uses a modern artist to refute Spengler: Mahler's adaptation of Chinese lyric poetry, *Das Lied von der Erde*, "knocks into a cocked hat [Spengler's] whole conception of the essential unrelatedness between civilizations." That a Jew gives the lie to an Aryan would enrage Spengler's supporters.

A Spenglerian view in which everything is "appallingly fixed" makes for bad science, dumb history, rotten politics. It must be laughed out of court, since "laughter is the portion of those who believe in good-will and flatter themselves that goodness, spirit and will . . . might have some influence over the course of our world." Spengler's tragic gloom is a sham. He is "secretly conservative," but, in the deadeningly paradoxical way of German intellectuals, he masks this by seeming to accept a loathsome, modern civilization. He may think he's the latest word; he's actually "pure nineteenth century, utterly *vieux jeu*," the lyricist of a "materialistic civilization whose kingdom is of yesterday and not tomorrow." Only the aristocrats of nature—and Mann names but one, Goethe—have the right to side with "nature against spirit and man": the counteraristocracy of the spirit (a proto-democracy?), symbolized by Schiller. He concludes with an idiomatic dismissal—in a word, Spengler is a "snob."

The next letter, dated May 1923, is less contentious. Mann introduces himself as a bourgeois *Hausvater*, longing for a post-Christmas nap on the chaise longue, but obliged to represent German books for his American friends. Relaxed or not, he still quotes Goethe: "Take my word, it's a mess." He continues to applaud the expansion of German taste, and credits this to modern patterns of distribution. He's pleased with the "good business for high-priced editions," but regrets that "prices are colossal," prompting a consumer's strike: reading is "not a luxury. A people in such an extensive educated class cannot dispense with it. Perhaps we'll say good-bye to fine books . . . *Legere necesse est, vivere non est necesse.* [One must read; one doesn't have to live.]"

The September 1923 letter is the most remarkable document. From the first, its tone provokes: "Our theater . . . Oh, do not let me spend many words on our theater! It is in decay, like our highways, and like the whole martyred nation, whose economic and social collapse the world awaits with such indifference." The "Christian" world continues to traffic in "pious lying propaganda" about "Huns and Barbarians": as a result, Germany, "a noble member of the family of white peoples," is dying.

Mann presumes shock at his own language, this ugly echo of his wartime prose—"I beg forgiveness. I am already quiet"—and then resumes on an explanatory note.

Since the inflation, the material conditions necessary for *Geist* to flourish have disappeared. German opera is going "downhill." Its best practitioners, like Bruno Walter, must tour America. "Theater of the spoken word" is threatened by that nonverbal parvenu the cinema. Because money talks, even to aesthetes, the "mimetic talent" quits stage for screen. And now, Berlin has lost its Reinhardt. Mann praises him for subjecting Wagnerian spectacle to a Nietzschean skepticism. The director's work produced "the *most interesting* theater which had ever existed . . . a theater which benefited by appealing to the sense of criticism, since one could not help considering as an asset the intellectual pleasure derived from the exercise of the critical faculties."

You don't have to stay in Berlin to know something's wrong. Any of the provinces in "our culturally uncentralized country" tell the story. Now he condemns Munich. This frivolous burg, "a city of the higher applied arts," could be tolerated once, but its "feasts and carnivals" have turned into rallies of the damned. At best it lives for decoration: "what really interests Munich in the theater is neither the word nor the play, nothing intellectual that is, but the incidental of the plastic arts." He claims to "love Munich too much to risk being the least misunderstood in my judgment of this city which was once so jolly, but which is now . . . torn by political hatreds." It is totally inhospitable to "the critico-literary spirit of European democracy which is represented in Germany chiefly by Judaism"—a bold statement emanating from the Nazis' Vatican and Mecca.

For a large American public Mann now introduces the name of Hitler, "leader of the German *fascisti*," the Italian diction indicating the foreignness of this phenomenon. Munich democracy had predicted the national movement, but "it was and is democratic in the national, racial sense of the word." (Historians might prefer the word "populist.") The Bavarian democracy is conservative, "and herein lies its opposition to the socialistic North, its anti-Semitism, its dynastic loyalty, its obstinacy in matters to do with the republic." Already in 1923 Mann discerned the traits that made Germans susceptible to Nazi propaganda.

Without pausing he describes recent changes in public taste, as if politics and theater were coterminous. "Wedekind is losing in popular interest; Shaw is still a favorite." The latest school, "dramatic expression," arouses more speculation than pleasure. Foreigners already know Georg Kaiser's and Carl Sternheim's satires, "absolutely without warmth." More affecting is his former protégé Ernst Toller, still languishing in jail; but "his artistry falls short of his humanity."

Mann introduces to Americans the most radical Young Turks, Arnold Bronnen and Bert Brecht. These two were allies, perhaps more: when Bronnen changed the spelling of his first name to "Arnolt," Berthold followed suit and became "Bertolt"—a comradely gesture, to say the least. Bronnen's play *Patricide* is "a crass and gloomy work . . . in which all offenses from incest through homosexuality to the dereliction mentioned in the title keep a solemn tryst. Similarly there is much storming and stressing in the drama of young Bert Brecht. . . ." Mann alludes to *Drums in the Night*, one of Brecht's early, homoerotic efforts, and, surprisingly, praises its first two acts.

Munich doesn't like Brecht. "It will not stand for any Bolshevist art." The performance of his latest play, *In the Jungle of Cities*, "inferior to the first from the standpoint of artistic discipline and intellectual 'fineness,'" was disturbed by gas bombs. The theater was cleared, and the public waited half an hour before returning, "still crying from purely physical reasons. . . . That also is Munich."

He was tougher on Brecht in his letter dated April 1924. After attending Brecht's production of *Edward the Second of England*, he made fun of the playwright's method, "literary history with the rouge of the latest modernity in its cheeks . . . scurrilously unreal and over-done until it becomes a style." Brecht's severe diet makes for self-indulgent agitprop: employing a cosmetic image for the great opponent of "culinary theater" is wonderful fun. Mann objects that the part of the king's lover, Gaveston, "whom one must certainly imagine as a winsome, if somewhat loose and immoral chap, was—obviously here again out of sheer malice—taken by an actor whose personal tediousness placed the king's unhealthy passion beyond all human comprehension. . . ." To caricature male desire is to get Mann where he lives. Yet even now he extends the magisterial hand: Brecht's is "a kind of dramatic *Proletkult* very instructive for foreigners who are interested in German experiments in the direction of an anti-bourgeois theater."

Patricide was an apter title than Mann realized. Among the fathers most despised by Brecht and Bronnen, Mann's name topped the list. Brecht never contradicted Bronnen's published memoir of their affair, and his early plays were bluntly homoerotic. But by the mid-1920s, he had added homophobic putdowns to his storehouse of insults; Rilke, for instance, he considered a "faggot" (*schwul*). It's not clear if he knew that Mann had introduced him abroad as a half-gay rebel. But within a year he was promoting Klaus at his father's expense. Many years later he circulated a gay sonnet he had composed under Thomas Mann's name (see Postscript). The homoerotic father figure of "The German Republic" had not predicted this filial response.

What an episode in both men's lives! In later years their kindest estimates would be grudging ones. Brecht on Mann: "He wrote some good stories"; Mann on Brecht: "The bum has talent." Brecht's American journals convey a sense of class warfare between Mann and himself. On June 8, 1942, he writes that Mann's "circle" has segregated his kind of art into "a special concentration camp, the literature of the lowly cannot be high literature." Still, it was Mann who introduced Brecht to America as a Bolshevist, a trafficker in sexual vice, and a despised object of Nazi hatred. With a kind of dramatic inevitability, the two men were to grow further apart during their exile in Hollywood, yet another southern metropolis consecrated to the decorative arts.

Mann's fifth letter, dated September 1925, embodies for Americans his newly minted ethos. The modern Goethe admits "we need more than Goethe." He teams the Weimar sage and the Manhattan thunderer: "These two fathers have much in common, above all the sympathy with the organic, the sensual, the 'calamus.' " ("Fathers" in such a context might strike anyone but Mann as inapt.) The infusion of Whitmanesque democracy has transformed the German writer: "It is not art, not culture in the sense of taste and even inner-worldliness and asceticism which is the important thing today, but problems of co-existence, problems of political morality and human organization." The statement distances Mann from writers like Proust or Joyce—taken at face value, from most modernists—but it may be an attempt to unite Hölderlin and Marx.

It also contains a hint of personal emancipation. "We in our better knowledge shall not let ourselves be misled as to the demands of existence by a pained sentimentality which confuses self-discipline with self-denial." There goes the gloomy moral of *Death in Venice*, one might say, cast into a sea of democratic—and Whitmanesque—forgetfulness. Happiness becomes a requisite of progressive politics; despair, almost fascistic. He now finds a "core of regulative truth" in the principles he had previously seen as "merely utilitarian." Calamus and the enlightenment produce a democracy big enough for Goethe, Whitman, and himself.

We can see Mann as a poet of imperial pastimes and democratic vistas. The first includes both the residual pleasures he associated with the enchanted mountain of German imperialism and, even more, the new technological phenomena, from records to movies, that allowed an unparalleled isolation of focus, by comparison with which German *Innerlichkeit* seems gregarious. (Mann could have predicted Cyberspace's mixture of solipsism and advanced design. Hans Castorp, his sporadically inquisitive hero, was made for the Internet.) "Democratic vistas" connotes the political freedoms, uniquely embodied by the voyeur Whitman, that let Mann fight "mysticism" with "ethics," discovering as he worked out his soul's salvation that "the thing itself was mine sooner than the name." In the act of composition, the unpolitical man came to his senses.

VI

THE MAGICIAN

1

THE MAGIC MOUNTAIN: I

Goethe advised writers to seek first their own pleasure. Politics, ethics, ideology were secondary concerns. Thomas Mann agreed. *The Magic Mountain* was his most formidable accomplishment to date, confirming his reputation as immensely learned, if not dauntingly profound. Yet it was a compendium of his private obsessions, an extravaganza of self-delight.

As so often, he revealed himself obliquely. In the novel's last lines, he grants Hans Castorp "intimations of a dream of love arising out of death and carnal lust." *The Magic Mountain* is a novel about forbidden love, proudly "unclassified," variously represented as homosexuality, fetishism, and necrophilia. Castorp achieves his vision through the intermediary forms of popular culture, stunts, fads, and hobbies entertained with a hedonistic abandon.

Such pleasures are defiantly anti-intellectual. In a 1939 address to American undergraduates, Mann cites one of their classmates, Howard Nemerov, who had given Castorp a new image: "a searcher after the Holy Grail. You would never have thought it when you read his story—if I did myself, it was both more and less than thinking." As if he were daring all the critics who found him middlebrow, the foremost novelist of ideas confessed to something "less than thinking." None knew so well that *The Magic Mountain* was fundamentally a narrative of desire.

For three decades Mann would dream of a film adaptation. He conceded the challenge: transforming the product of an old medium into one barely adolescent. He envisioned a cinematic tour de force: "a fantastic encyclopedia with a hundred diversions in the great world clustered around an epic center, a vision of all areas of existence—nature, sport, medicine and the life sciences, political history, and so on." He could entertain such a quixotic notion because he understood his novel to be thoroughly, if not shamelessly, erotic.

Critics would complain that Hans Castorp, like Goethe's Wilhelm Meister, was less a living character than a vehicle for exploring the wide world. Mann knew what they didn't. Hans's models did not stop with Goethe; he reincarnates every boy Mann himself had loved. Mann's desires, as embodied in Castorp, himself an object of those desires, provide the through-line for the novel. Eros is the ground bass, the ostinato that grants each passage its harmony. Eros inflames the monomaniac's career and converts academic debates into sexualized propositions.

Mann was the first to imagine someone regarding his beloved's X ray with a voyeur's thrill. No forum was sacrosanct; forbidden love forbade itself nothing. So indeed, why not make a movie—that grand documentary tool—of it all? *L'homme moyen sensuel* remained at the novel's heart, Hans Castorp swaddled in his blankets, enjoying visions that surpassed any movie yet produced.

Of course, not only Eros animated the work. Years of research and contemplation, a revolution in Mann's thinking about politics, were necessary. We know how the novel developed. In 1912 Katia spent a few months in the Davos sanitarium. While visiting her, Mann was invited to become a patient himself. He escaped, bemused and a little frightened. (Hans Castorp is more obliging; he accepts the invitation.) But the visit inspired him to begin a novella—something he intended as a comic pediment to *Death in Venice*! He would later boast that his novel made death "a comic figure."

He abandoned the project during the war. After 1918 it ballooned from anecdotal comedy to epic treatise. He resumed work fortified by a perdurable "obstinacy" and "a highly dubious private enjoyment." Virtually every intellectual or emotional preoccupation of those years found its reflection, most particularly the sexual politics expressed in his defense of the German Republic. His narrative conception actually predicted his political conversion. As early as July 1920 he discussed its "multiple concept": it would be a "journey through a world composed of thought, humanism, and the body's voluptuous mysticism." This was a system that hadn't yet found its prophet, Walt Whitman, and its political apotheosis, social democracy. That July was also the month of his letter to Carl Maria Weber and of his recognition that he desired Klaus sexually.

A decade later Mann contended that his novel's success was a function of its era. But, as usual, his generalization covered a multitude of "dubious private enjoyments." Intense self-examination, an honesty that did not flinch at admissions of incest, an awareness that his desires were not heterosexual were necessary before he could relax his notions of literary decorum. As a young man he had informed Otto Grautoff that the "nether regions" were best left out of literature. A bit like Wittgenstein, whose focus shifted from what could only be told in words to what lay beyond verbal expression, Mann now wrote with the conviction that sexual desire informed every interesting action—was, in fact, the only guarantee that he was writing at top form.

That *The Magic Mountain* aspired to its own movie, even including a filmed parody of itself, was a sign that Mann had quit the pantheon for the broad way. His collage of high and low culture transfers Hoffmann's pederastic idylls to Wagner's Venusberg; puts Schubert's lieder on the gramophone; makes the Grecian gods of Winckelmann and Platen movie stars; and calls on Goethe's biology, Einstein's relativity, and Freud's psychology to explain Hans Castorp's broken heart.

Mann transforms Hans Castorp's social and sexual marginality into a worldview expansive enough to comprehend the universe, a veritable "encyclopedia" revolving around a lovelorn, never-to-be-satisfied, perpetual adolescent. Here was immense learning at the service of personal obsession: a Nabokovian theme, Nabokov's contempt for Mann notwithstanding. An exposure to popular media, the forms I previously described as "imperial pastimes," enabled him to subvert the traditions from which he arose. For instance, in a novel filled with musical performances, he seeks to find "the world behind the music." This is not a license to psychoanalyze composers, but rather an attempt to examine intensively the response of music lovers. Hans Castorp, as he whistles Schubert's "Lindenbaum," becomes a stand-in for scholar and fan alike. In cinematic closeups of Castorp's expression while listening to music—drowsy, stupefied, entranced—Mann finds the visual representation of the world behind the music.

Goethe, observing the anguished efforts of his fellow poets, famously identified romanticism with sickness. Mann echoes his master's formula as he inverts it. His novel domesticates romanticism *and* disease by grounding them in physical and social reality. Such an attempt was impossible for Goethe, Mann writes, and Nietzsche could merely predict it when he wrote: "Now the Olympian Magic Mountain opens, as it were, to our view, and shows us its roots." Implicit throughout the novel is the claim that Nietzsche has found his artist-seer, a Goethean polymath with a moviegoer's sensibility.

His comic sense was also liberated. The operatic hyperbole of *Death in*

Venice returns as parody, though parody so emotionally charged that it accommodates a cosmic melancholy. In 1939 Mann informed a group of Americans that he had moved from the novella's *echt Deutsch* "austerity" to an Anglo-American "humor and intimacy." From English-speaking authors he had learned to apply the "coolness of form" to the "heat of universal passion." The representative German had acquired a new stance, one he projects onto Hans Castorp, "unfettered as a Jew, irreverent as an American."

The Magic Mountain has been dismissed as a clumsy leviathan, its novelist as a failed man of ideas. But from the start Mann intends something light and sparkling. His famous irony benefits from the imported "humor and intimacy": almost to a fault, his narrative is suffused with an amiable spirit. Mann becomes the reader's guide, his subaltern and surrogate: at one point he declares, "We have as much a right to our story's meaning as anyone else." The narrator admits to moments of boredom and confusion, a burden he expects us to share.

It's a novel filled with horrors, sickening descriptions of disease, terrifying depictions of the violent prelude to a world war, morbid and supernatural episodes. Yet it begins so easily. Mann's preface is casual and informal: "Let us get introductions over quickly," says the author, who subsequently informs his reader that "not all in a minute" will this story be told. His apology is almost flippant: since "a man lives the life of his epoch," the "simple-minded though pleasing" Castorp has "a story worth telling." We first spot him aboard a train "from his native city of Hamburg to Davos-Platz in the Canton of the Grisons, on a three weeks' visit." The journey from Hamburg to Davos will be "too long, indeed, for so brief a stay." In German Mann writes, "Das ist aber eine weite Reise"—"But that is such a long journey"—the tone of a storyteller who has something up his sleeve.

Upon arriving, Castorp is greeted by the familiar Hamburg dialect of his cousin Joachim. The latter, previously as undistinguished as Castorp, has become a scholar of disease: "How learned you've become!" exclaims Castorp. "Fine kind of learning," is the reply, acquired at the cost of health and sanity. Joachim's colloquial manner familiarizes the horror of his disease. Within a few pages Mann provides descriptions both fey and hallucinatory. The clinic is so honeycombed with balconies that it appears "porous like a sponge." Everything is precisely detailed, but nothing is quite what it seems: even the plants are "androgynous." Once settled, Hans overhears a violent fit of coughing: "It wasn't dry and it wasn't loose," but its sound enables a visitor to "look right into" the patient's lungs; on the magic mountain, synesthesia is the norm. Joachim is unimpressed by the noise; we all cough like that up here, he says, and begins in the same "horribly pulpy manner," reducing Hans to a state between "laughter and tears." At the day's end, Castorp falls asleep on a "common death-bed," a setting he accepts with the chameleonic aplomb of all Mann's Hermes figures, from Felix Krull to Joseph, the young men who can rest anywhere.

Hans is an orphan in time. His parents are dead, and his sympathy has skipped generations, focusing on his grandfather. This gentleman, a superannuated exponent of the Protestant ethic, has "little use for the new" and despises the Hamburg working class; bespeaking his era, Hans, too, is antidemocratic. Recalling Thomas Mann, his politics seem as much a product of sloth and lassitude as of reasoned convictions. As a boy, Hans thrives in this grim, overly masculine atmosphere. An unspoken, sensual intimacy develops. In a passage worthy of Proust, the grandfather with his "wonderful" hands and snowy beard opens a glass case filled with "disused and fascinating objects," silver-branched candlesticks, a broken barometer, an album of old photos. Granted a view of the living past, no longer hidden behind glass—a rare experience for any of Mann's window shoppers!—Hans falls half in love with death and slow time. The ancestral tales induce "a familiar feeling . . . a dreamy, troubling sense: of change in the midst of duration, of time as both flowing and constant, of recurrence in continuity."

When his grandfather dies, Hans is "scarcely sad at all—as things [do not evoke sadness] which have to do with the body and only with it." He can enjoy the embalmed corpse, "a life-size wax doll," a virtuoso display of artifice that defies reality. This estrangement might portend an early form of schizophrenia, but in this novel it signifies Hans's capacity to fetishize his troubles out of existence, a partial dwelling in the supernatural granted only to the compulsively materialistic. A fly buzzes over the corpse. Another writer—say, Poe or Kafka—would evoke something sinister. But Hans inhales the dead man's scent and free-associates it with the strong animal stench of an ostracized schoolmate, the aroma of adolescent sex. For the first of many times, Hans experiences a feeling that eludes "classification."

Two pages later, as the narrator returns to the present, he analyzes Castorp's sensual nature: "He liked good living, and notwithstanding his thin-bloodedness and look of over-refinement clung to the grosser pleasures of life." No Mann character is comfortable with his sexuality; while Castorp lusts aplenty in his heart, in the real world he proves exasperatingly shy. But toward corporal pleasures like food, wine, or cigars ("I live to smoke"), he exhibits no ambivalence whatsoever.

The first two chapters resemble Mann's early novellas—particularly the treatments of death in "Der Bajazzo" and of sanitarium life in "Tristan." But the differences are crucial. He discovers a new subject—"mountain-time"—while treating the physical details of illness as if they too were newly minted. It promises to be his most universal story—more so even than the decline of a bourgeois family—yet it also promises to be *told* as never before. For the more scholarly, there await verbal echoes of Platen, of Heine, inevitably of Goethe; but for the general readers, abundant slapstick and gross humor. Mann lures the cerebral and the sensualist and finds their meeting ground at the altar of "forbidden love."

Hans Castorp's three weeks will become seven years, his excursion into the mountains a trial by fire and sentimental education. For in this modern Bildungsroman the knowledge acquired will be more psychological than intellectual; the problem solved, more a question of feeling than of thought. Up to the final juxtapositions of his last sentences, Mann's novel dramatizes the conflict between unbridled desire and "love."

2

THE MAGIC MOUNTAIN: II

In keeping with his narrative scheme, Mann's characters may appear hyper-realistic or like figures out of opera and fairy tale; they may be endlessly mercurial or Johnny-one-notes out of Dickens or Balzac. Some are emotionally cloistered, gurus of renunciation; others, ambulatory id. At his loneliest Hans Castorp always finds himself part of a larger design; his consciousness provides a tabula rasa on which an encyclopedia could be inscribed, but at the end he remains, in Settembrini's terms, "life's problem child."

The fact that Mann cares so much about this nonentity can be explained by the models he summoned. We know that one figure was Kirsten, the boy "in wide trousers" whom he glimpsed on the beach, who in turn reminded him of Armin Martens. Richard Winston finds in Castorp's name an allusion to Count Hans Kaspar, the original of Hanno Buddenbrook's friend Count Kai. Perhaps somebody else is recalled—Paul Ehrenberg, the great love of Mann's twenties, as Martens was the love of his youth. In a letter to Grautoff Mann described Ehrenberg as "decent, untroubled, child-like, slightly vain"—qualities that fit Hans Castorp, and probably most other literary naifs. But he also notes Ehrenberg's peculiar idiom; phrases like "in netter Weise" (in a nice way) are his "property." Hans Castorp shares this penchant for whimsy. He applies diminutives to abstractions: e.g., time's passage falls upon a *"Jährchen"* (literally "a little year"). Scientific wonders that strike Joachim as "tall tales" he finds "intimate." Someone who embraces a deathbed can make himself cozy anywhere; we last see him whistling on a battlefield.

Hans's first love, Hippe, was based on Willri Timpe, Mann's second love. Martens, Kaspar, Timpe, Ehrenberg, the boy on the beach—to paraphrase his thoughts about Ehrenberg, such literary transformations displayed Mann's "power" (although none of his contemporary readers might detect it) to know the men he loved better than life had allowed him.

Some of this knowledge involves recasting the love object in his own image. Castorp is a mediocre engineer by profession, a habitual dreamer with the quizzical stare of a just-awakened child. Not much of Thomas Mann there. Yet he's also the archetypal German, nowhere more so than in his love of music. Whether attempting in falsetto to reach Wagnerian high notes, or whistling his favorite tune, Schubert's "Lindenbaum," he reveals the German soul to be *dangerously* musical: as Settembrini remarks, with its affinity for the irrational, music can be "politically suspect."

Hans also displays the kind of intelligence Mann last dramatized in Felix Krull. Although he's capable of great bouts of research, his purpose is never scholarly. His discoveries shrivel into little nuggets of detail, retained only if they are emotionally useful; Clavdia Chauchat is not wrong to see him as bourgeois to the core. Yet, like Krull, his intelligence is completely sensuous. He can make astonishing leaps, connecting disparate eras, ideas, and feelings. If the heart has its reasons, Castorp will find them.

The great characters in fiction move in unpredictable ways. The surprises may be late-coming and subtle, catching the reader off guard. The best surprises are saved for the characters themselves. Midway through *Emma*, Jane Austen writes, "It darted through her with the speed of an arrow that no one was to marry Mr. Knightly but herself." The reader knew this from the first paragraph, but Emma didn't, and the process by which she learns makes this sentence one of the greatest lines of self-revelation in nineteenth-century literature. By the time Mann writes, such a discovery would seem anticlimactic in the extreme. More common would be the absence of affect, evident in the characters of Franz Kafka—men who exist, like the jail guard in *The Penal Colony*, to be literally written upon.

Yet Hans Castorp achieves an epiphany at least as remarkable as Emma Woodhouse's. With a publicist's cunning, Mann uses him to argue the preeminence of adolescent homosexual desire. As a boy Castorp developed a crush on Pribislav Hippe, a dignified Slavic youth. For a long time he adored in silence, until one day in school when he asked to borrow Hippe's pencil. Hippe obliged, requesting only that Hans return it. For an hour Castorp was blissful, at ease with the universe, simply writing with the other's pencil. Then he returned the object, and promptly forgot it all, the action, the words, the thrill. Years later, in Davos, he falls in love with Clavdia Chauchat, a Russian woman whose sharp Slavic cheekbones instantly recall Hippe. He makes a remarkable comparison: "Is that why I felt interested in her? Or was that why I felt so interested in him?"

A few pages later Hans continues these speculations: "For a man to take an interest in a woman inwardly diseased—unfit for motherhood . . . had no more sense than—well, than the interest he had once taken in Pribislav Hippe. The comparison was a stupid one; it roused memories better forgotten; he had not meant to make it, it came into his head unbidden." This is a moment of insight as luminous as Marcel's recognition that to justify his wastrel existence he must compose his life. There have been other epiphanies in Mann—e.g., Thomas Buddenbrook's inspired reading of Schopenhauer—but invariably they flickered and died, unmourned, unremembered. Castorp's dismissal, "stupid," is of no consequence; the connection he intuits will make his love of an infertile woman tantamount to the equally "unproductive" love for a boy. All "forbidden loves" are the same.

Emma Woodhouse's self-revelation comes midway through her novel; Marcel's at the end of his. Hans Castorp acquires the "unbidden" insight with seven hundred pages left to go. Mann telescopes the process, employing visual details—pencils and cheekbones—that double as symbols. The process is glaringly psychoanalytic—the pleasure of stroking another's pencil or its fetishistic aftermath, Castorp's fixation on the lead shavings! But after the novel's publication, Mann denied receiving inspiration from Vienna. The analytic impulse was simply "in the air." Whitman, not Freud, had been his mentor. And his own heart had shown him the enduring nature of desire. "Tonio Kröger, Tonio Kröger, it's the same every time and the feeling deep."

C astorp draws on a network of literary allusions, half-remembered song lines, misunderstood theories, and emotional memories, a mélange positively Joycean, though Mann spells out each development with a Teutonic thoroughness. He confronts his hero with a variety of relations, each summoning an aspect of his protean temperament.

The first, and in emotional terms perhaps the deepest, is with his cousin Joachim, the invalid he visits as the story begins. They are physical opposites. Hans, we learn, is an ectomorph gone to seed, with a slightly protruding belly (another Paul Ehrenberg trait?). He is not virile and, for a burgher, lacks ambition or drive: Hanno Buddenbrook without the angst. Joachim, however, is a warrior, the idealized product of the German *Turnhalle*. He has an impassive purity about him, and a terror of expressing emotion, whether for a buxom female patient or for his adoring cousin;

even when he's dying, he thinks it unmanly to lean on Hans's shoulder.

Mann pays great attention to Joachim's physical beauty: during a medical examination, he's likened to a hairy-chested Apollo Belvedere. He loves discipline; *treu* (faithful) is his chosen epithet. A complete soldier, he also reveals xenophobic and anti-Semitic traits. Against him one might hold his inflexible disposition, his bigotry, his obsession with the body.

Yet he is the novel's most poignant character. His fundamental sweetness is displayed when he allows Hans to literally regard his heart: view a cardiogram as it unfurls. Everything is pure and true, if one discounts the violence his presence threatens. Joachim evokes an era of teary-eyed Oliver Norths, killing machines awash in sentiment. That Mann and Castorp adore him is clear.

Hans is less emotionally involved with his mentors, the political essayist Settembrini and the Jewish Jesuit, Naphta. If we remember Mann's notion that Schiller's pursuit of Goethe constituted a great love story, or his belief in the erotic nature of education, then the intellectual contest for Hans's soul may resemble a love triangle. Both men are infuriated by his display of heterosexual desire; women aren't admitted in their club.

On their own they stir up enough heat. As Mann knew from his quarrels with Heinrich and the deadly assaults of his enemies the Jewish critics, words could hurt more than physical wounds. Both characters are masters of murderous rhetoric. In keeping with Mann's history, Naphta represents the pithily brilliant Jew while Settembrini mouths a deadening series of liberal homilies, resembling, as many readers have noted, the glib editorials of Heinrich Mann. For Mann, who never considered himself a fast talker, their creation was an inspired revenge.

The issues raised by these warrior-heroes of the Word retain their urgency. They embrace the classic political dilemma—the incompatibility of freedom and justice, reason and empathy, the imperiled nature of democratic humanism in a society disposed to gigantism, if not totalitarian control. These questions had absorbed Mann since the war: the Naphta-Settembrini confrontation was the fictional product of his internal debate.

He enjoys the philosophers' contradictions. Settembrini comes across both as a Verdian hero—stepping out of Heinrich's *Little Town*—and as an "organ grinder," playing the saccharine melodies of agitprop anthems. Like Heinrich, he makes a fool of himself before women. Yet he is no sybarite. He lives in Spartan digs, resolutely denying the appeals of the flesh. Sick himself, he hates disease; Mann entrusts to him the message that all the attempts to ennoble illness are wrongheaded: illness is no metaphor, "sickness is just sickness."

Settembrini cannot tolerate an absurd universe, like Voltaire, who refused to acknowledge the Lisbon earthquake. Since he believes that "the literary spirit is the noblest manifestation of the spirit of man," he plans an encyclopedic—but "belles-lettristic"—treatise on human suffering. Freud might say that he represents the "masculine . . . abstract principles of justice." He may proclaim, "I affirm, honor, and love the body"—a rhetorical gesture that is stunningly aphysical—but he despises flesh itself as a messy inconvenience. A lapsed Manichean, he believes that in the war of "mind and body . . . body is evil." He condemns the invalids' pastimes, from mindless games to the promiscuous use of irony and parody. Mann dislikes Settembrini's loose categories, thrives on irony, loves the body, and founds his politics on sex. Yet in the end Settembrini survives, and Castorp assumes a comfortable alliance with him.

His opponent, Leo Naphta, is the more provocative figure. Mann lets him paraphrase an argument previously used in his defense of Nietzsche and Dostoyevsky—that sickness, not health, is man's nature, and the source of all "progress." This repellent provocateur is a character worthy of Dostoyevsky or Joseph Conrad, while Settembrini, the mellifluous democrat, is, alas, a character out of a Heinrich Mann novel. Naphta contains all the cultural antinomies Mann had recently pondered; he is the dialectic incarnate. Raised a Jew, he becomes an unfrocked Jesuit; he combines Catholic reaction with communist zealotry. As such he is a product both of Mann's research (expressing the medieval / Russian / anti-Semitic distaste for usury, and thus for capitalism) and of his experience (in his extreme ugliness and relentless argument he is modeled on György Lukács, whose persuasive powers were such that "as long as he spoke he was right").

Mann grants this devil the better tunes. Each retort crucifies Settembrini's humanism: with Jesuitical rigor he challenges definition; with Jewish animus he exposes contradictions—e.g., a self-proclaimed democrat's fear of the masses. (Mann does allow Settembrini the Naphta-like line that malice is the basis of all criticism. Was this an allusion to the wartime essays Mann still found personally vindictive?)

To the reader's surprise, this scourge of humanism is a sybarite. Settembrini, warning Castorp against him, declares, "His thoughts are voluptuous, and stand under the aegis of death." Naphta's study, unlike Settembrini's monastic cell, is richly furnished. There is a medieval Pietà—carefully studied by Mann scholars as a symbol of religious sadism. Everything but the cracked ceiling has been refurbished, and it is glaringly adorned by a Venetian chandelier; the wallpaper is color-coordinated. His home reveals Naphta to be half terrorist, half decadent aesthete. In a rare display of wit Settembrini calls this ugly man "a *joli jesuite* with a *petite tâche humide.*"

The enemies perform a dance of death, each daring the other to make the final, unforgivable remark. When overheated rhetoric leads to a duel, and Naphta's death, Settembrini alone is left to mourn him. Yet Naphta is a monstrous figure. There are few moments as stunning as that when he discloses the one force that can redeem society: "terror." The shock of his words causes his listeners, Settembrini, Hans, and Joachim, to jump up in alarm. Naphta contends that poverty, pain, and torture keep the masses on a Christian track. He prefers the Inquisition to the French Revolution because it killed righteously. The church fathers with their exhortations to universal subservience are more fundamentally democratic than the mob-fearing anti-Communists like Settembrini. Mann gives him the best lines; but closely examined, they invoke the charnel-house.

(Mann would keep noticing a strategic deployment of terror in modern politics. Whenever the voices of reaction grew strident, he despaired that *l'homme moyen politique* had a liking for rough trade. Men preferred to be terrorized into submission rather than assuming control over their own lives. Never using Freudian terms like "masochism," he made political terror uncomfortably sexual, as did his close reader Franz Kafka.)

So many arguments! At one point an exasperated narrator summarizes the Big Ideas at stake; "The Object" here; "The Ego" there; Art versus critique; nature battling with soul. Some readers consider this explication Mann at his most lumbering, the equivalent of Thomas Hardy titling a collection *Life's Little Ironies*. But they ignore Mann's words: "There was no order nor clarity, not even of a dualistic and militant kind. Things went not only by contraries, but also all higgledy-piggledy. The disputants not only contradicted each other, they contradicted themselves." As it is, this marks their final debate; Mann's attention turns elsewhere.

Numerous supporting characters pass through the story. Most display a performer's shtick: the aggrieved mother lamenting the fatal illness of both her sons, "Tous les deux," her Spanish-accented French becoming her signature; the Commercial Traveler who reckons in accounting terms, until death begins to unman him and he responds to the flowers of Joachim and Castorp with the gratitude of a schoolgirl; Frau Stöhr, the everlastingly banal invalid who brings a welcome touch of the ordinary to this febrile crew. Her opposite number, the "Female Job," has a body covered with suppurating eczema. In her brief appearance, she displays a courtesan's wiles. By force of personality, she transforms her dreadful condition into something glamorous, and bewitches Hans and Joachim. (She may be a forerunner of Cipolla, the equally hideous magician, who also hypnotizes youth into worshiping his beauty. Her plight draws on a disequilibrium of power and self-contempt familiar to Mann.)

A miniature League of Nations convenes each night in the dining room. Mann analyzes the shifting configurations with the political acuity last displayed in *Death in Venice*. He assigns them resonant names: among them a Professor Kafka and a lesbian Egyptian princess's companion named after the ill-fated leader of the Munich revolution, Frau Landauer.

The only important female character is Clavdia Chauchat, the Russian with short hair, boyish hips, and a French cat sneaking within her name. Like Frau von Rinnlingen or Imma Spoelmann, she is not a conventional seductress. Her resemblance to Hippe allows Hans Castorp to love another man in the image of a woman. Proust is often accused of disguising Albert as Albertine. Mann is both more honest and more complex; he lets Hans love Albert, Albertine, and Albert-as-Albertine. The same illness that renders men feminine, passive, and impotent denatures her; she cannot become a mother. Some critics argue that she's a maternal symbol, despite her infertility. But Oedipal intimations remove her even more from the realm of conventional romance.

She also represents a new kind of woman, defining her existence with authority and independence. By comparison Hans Castorp is a weakling; of the two she is the virile partner. More than the story's sexual nucleus, she comes to deflate all the posturing males, from the lascivious Polish doctor who displays X rays of her lungs, to the sparring Naphta and Settembrini, both of whom distrust her as a rival for Castorp's affections.

She and Castorp finally spend the night together—in an embrace that occurs off-screen—after a diplomatic series of verbal maneuvers, transacted appropriately in French. Less than persuaded of his ardor, she leaves the next morning. Some years later she returns with a new lover, the Dutch planter Mynheer Peeperkorn. Castorp's affection for his rival produces a new and surprising closeness between him and his former mistress.

This leads to an extraordinary series of dialogues. In one she virtually taunts him for his reticence, his failure to act upon his desires. But she sees this emotional failure as more than personal. Hans is the representative German. And though she has tried to meet Germany halfway—with her "mähnschen" (little mane of hair) rhyming with "Hänschen"—she fears the worst. Someday, she warns, "your coldness will threaten the world." You can read her words as a prediction of Germany's misbehavior during the Great War—although Mann had not yet actually indicted the Kaiser's army for its atrocities—or as one of his several astonishing prophecies of the Nazi era. What's new is the explicit connection between individual psychology and national politics, something also found in D. H. Lawrence's

1920s work. Another Russian woman laughed over Tonio Kröger's bourgeois *Weltschmerz*. But in the interim neuroses had become, literally, world-threatening. In this most German of novels, Clavdia introduces the foreign perspective; in a world divided between the intimate "Du" and the formal "Sie," she is "tu," the "toi" of Hans Castorp's life.

Mynheer Peeperkorn, the other major character, arrives with great fanfare. Mann presumes that readers have sensed so much of his effort, both the horror and the tedium, that they will enjoy the pleasure of his latest breakthrough. Like Naphta, Peeperkorn might be a Conrad character; he's a former cotton planter in Indonesia, an imperialist and buccaneer. His charismatic presence makes Naphta and Settembrini appear spoilsports. He returns the colonialist's temperament to Europe. Mann means for him to appear larger than life: when he invites his fellow patients to delirious orgies of food and drink, he becomes a Dionysus figure. At other times he resembles Tolstoy in his (self-consciously) Lear-like decline: the scenes in which he poses himself against a waterfall, or tries to capture an eagle, have electrified many readers. Others find them grandiloquent and a bit ridiculous.

Peeperkorn excited Mann both as a nonverbal antidote to the hyper-articulate duo and as a challenge to his own gifts of description. His power is a matter of personality and presence, easily captured on film or stage, but usually beyond literary rendition. To the extent that Mann succeeds, it is by making painfully heroic the contrast between the Dutchman's great spirit and his stammering tongue. As a character, he provided Mann the same opportunity he saw in such apparently intractable subjects as music, silence, and death.

We know that Peeperkorn resembles Gerhart Hauptmann, sharing the playwright's verbal and philosophical muddle. Godlike he may be, but his combination of religiosity and overweening sexuality recalls Hauptmann at his silliest. When he complains to Castorp about the tragedies of impotence, and the perfidy of an unsatisfied woman with her legs sprawled out, the tone rings false. A Norman Mailer or a Henry Miller might talk such trash; but Thomas Mann is not given to good-ol'-boy ribaldry. So either Peeperkorn's complaints are Mann's unsuccessful attempts to capture a lusty heterosexuality, or they bespeak a vulgarity distasteful in both Peeperkorn and Settembrini—as in Heinrich Mann and Hauptmann. Within a year of the novel's publication, he wrote that Peeperkorn demonstrates a "majestic inadequacy." Twenty years later he echoed the phrase and extended it to Hauptmann, the discredited supporter of Adolf Hitler.

In 1925 Mann wrote Herbert Eulenburg that Peeperkorn and Joachim were the "most successful and lovable" characters in the novel. But the Dutchman hasn't aged well. Perhaps he enters too late; Mann may have needed to let his material seep far longer—become, as he later wrote Freud, "extremely ripe"—than the few months between encountering Hauptmann and composing the Peeperkorn episode. (His grandiose personality leaves modern readers unmoved the same reason that émigré actors often flopped in Hollywood: a theatrical approach rendered obsolete by popular culture.) Or perhaps a novel charged with German *Weltschmerz* and Anglo-American "intimacy" cannot accommodate an outsized Russian hero. But if his character seems incredible, the old charlatan prompts a surprising development. Castorp and Clavdia become allies, conspiring on his behalf. In other words, an emancipated woman and a homosexual undertake to protect a doomed patriarchy.

Perhaps seeing this, a furious Hauptmann wrote the publisher Fischer, "I'm almost inclined to see [my representation] in Freudian terms." And following this line of circuitous discourse, Mann has Castorp woo Chauchat—in French—with a paraphrase of Whitman's "I Sing the Body Electric": deploying as a heterosexual proposition a lyric whose homosexual essence he was convinced of.

3

THE MAGIC MOUNTAIN: III

Buddenbrooks, almost as long, hews to a simpler line. The action is elegantly circumscribed: more solos than duets or trios; piano accompaniment. But *The Magic Mountain* proceeds via counterpoint and polyrhythm. Mann achieves a dazzling structure—one based on a series of contradictions, narrative and dramatic—that "outwits" and "astonishes" him no less than his reader; the narrator's conspiratorial glee becomes one of the novel's signature devices.

At least as much as Proust's masterpiece, *The Magic Mountain* is about the movement of time. But Mann's focus is more varied. He gives us land time and mountain time, the time of healthy, working people and the time of invalids whose career is their malady. There is a realistic time, punctuated by "flirtations and temperature taking," and an enchanted time, replete with images drawn from Greek mythology and German *Märchen*. Time comes defined by national culture (the "carpe diem" of bourgeois Europe versus dilatory, feudal Russia). It becomes a function of space, geography, and climate—"up here a month equals a day." The novel reflects a temporal confusion: long sections devoted to intellectual speculation culminate in epiphanies so fleeting the reader can easily miss them. The task of reading has its longueurs. Mann admitted that the denser passages bored him as well. He also quipped that "only the exhaustive is truly interesting," and later advised his admirers to read it twice.*

---

* In *Doctor Faustus*, Mann re-examines the artificial regulation of time. Politically the Germans endow it with a specific meaning: their mission ("*Sendung*") is to shape history to reflect the

The narrative texture is enlivened less by incident—"up here nothing happens"—than by an astounding range of verbal expression. Outside of Joyce, few novels are so packed with chatter—from Castorp's Hamburg brogue to Chauchat's Russian-German, from the medieval Latin of medical jargon to the French in which lovers conduct their romance. There are echoes of famous poems, and the malapropisms of Frau Stöhr: an unwitting verbal power that stamps her an idiot savant of the emotions—when, after Joachim's death, she requests the "Erotica," she distills the nature of his appeal in a pun.

Mann's irony almost obliges him to utilize banal speech to express transcendent emotion. The clinic's resident analyst, Dr. Krokowski, gives a lecture on "the power of love." Castorp is enthralled and perplexed— "the speaker employed the word love in a somewhat ambiguous sense, so that you were never sure whether he had reference to the sacred or its passionate and fleshly aspect."

Krokowski employs "a mingled terminology, partly poetic and partly erudite." His manner is "ruthlessly scientific," yet with a showmanly panache that makes the women blush and the men grow still. Castorp is first rendered giddy, "sea-sick," by the varieties of love that Krokowski describes. Then he is mortified by the analyst's "demolition of illusions." No innocence remains for "suckling babes," no dignity for "silver hairs"; everywhere id rides triumphant. Only Mann would make such a drama— and comedy—out of Krokowski's bumbling discourse. For now that everything can be told, "one could go pretty far without shocking anybody."

Just as the tug of war between Naphta and Settembrini goes unresolved for hundreds (!) of pages, the narrative focus may undergo a kaleidoscopic transformation. We learn that nothing is stable; the "exhaustive" may be interesting, but it's never definitive. For example, in one chapter, Hans Castorp makes an intensive study of biological textbooks. The novel seems to have become a blend of nineteenth-century romanticism and twentieth-century science. The atmosphere grows brisk and severe. But in the next chapter, nature and spirit yield to fabrication, when Hans receives his Christmas gifts, a booty of "cravats, leather goods, cakes, candies and marzipan." Life is obviously both raw matter and manufactured goods. His favorite melody, Schubert's lied, is an "artificial folk song," nature improved upon.

There are many such about-faces. Castorp attends a Walpurgisnacht,

national interest. Aesthetically composers find new means of ordering it. Mann describes Beethoven's *Fidelio* as "time articulated, filled-up, organized." His jest is to analogize music, politics, and the systematic timekeeping of sanitarium life.

consecrated to "perversions" (transvestism, sadomasochism) and pagan myths: he quits the sanctuary for the bordello. Once there, he flirts with Chauchat in French. But after his lengthy defenses of the novelist's verbal freedom, Mann refuses to tell us what happens next: "We have elected to intermit the flow of our story along the stream of time, and let time flow on pure and free of any content whatever."

In no section does he toy with our expectations so cunningly as in the chapter called "Snow." It advertises itself as the long-awaited resolution, "dreamed-out to the end," although the reader's hand informs him that one-third of the novel remains. "It's over" seldom means it's finished.

The patients have been warned about snowstorms, the "blinding chaos" and "white dark." Castorp is not impressed; he sees the snow as a transplanted version of "the sand down below." He decides to go skiing, without informing the authorities. Settembrini encourages him, grateful for any sign of rebellion. Once in the snow Hans perceives his folly. "The menace of the elements was not even hostile, but impersonally deadly." He is swept by a "terror which forms the basis of courage." Aha, thinks the reader, Mann's preparing us for something big.

But valor gives way to sexual fantasy. The aquamarine clouds remind him of "certain eyes," despised by Settembrini as "Tartar slits," and belonging to Hippe and Chauchat. He collects snowflakes in his palm and admires their exquisite singularity, each perfect unto itself. But there lies the horror; in the "icy regularity" he finds "the very marrow of death." This uniqueness is "anti-organic," "life-denying"; it makes him appreciate the builders of antiquity who incorporated asymmetry as evidence of their human limitations.

A nature "impersonally deadly" and "life-denying" figures in other novels of this period. When Rupert Birkin, in *Women in Love*, contemplates his estrangement from nature, his instinct is to theorize. When Mrs. Moore, in *A Passage to India*, detects a cosmic nihilism in the cavernous "Boum," she loses her reason. But when Hans finds himself abandoned, he fortifies himself with a schnapps.

Slightly tipsy, he surprises himself once again with thoughts of his two lovers. During their hours together, he remembers returning Hippe's pencil to Chauchat. He switches to French, "son crayon," and the very grammar proves androgynous: " '*Son crayon*'!" That means her pencil, not his pencil, in this case; you only say *son* because *crayon* is masculine. The rest is just a pretty feeble play on words." He adds a characteristically mundane remark: "Imagine stopping to talk about that" while his left leg has just fallen asleep. The reader can fixate on Hans's physical danger or on Mann's contention that sexual norms are simply word games.

Ludwig von Hofmann's oil painting DIE QUELLE *graced Mann's various studies from* 1914 *until his death. It inspired the Arcadian scene in the chapter "Snow," and may have stimulated Mann as he wrote about a series of Hermeses, from Joseph to Felix Krull.*

The erotic tease, the promise of exponentially greater thrills generated by the moment, is embodied in Hans's memory of an operatic tenor whose high notes acquired new harmonic quality while he held them, overtones of bliss that left his ravished audiences in tears, an exhausting, orgasmic ecstasy of sound. At this moment, our hero begins to hallucinate. First there is an arcadian, pastoral scene.* Youth and beauty everywhere inspire an erotic "reverence": the boy who smiles shyly at him is a Hermes.

But the scene darkens into a tableau of cannibalism and death: the "lovely boy" in the field disappears while, deep in a shrouded temple, two gray witches dismember a child. In his description of their misshapen bodies, Mann moves glibly from homoeroticism to misogyny: the crones even curse in the dialect of Hamburg. Hans awakens, and mutters some vaguely Jungian words: "We dream anonymously and communally, if each after his

---

* The inspiration for this scene may have been Ludwig von Hofmann's naked boys. On March 3, 1919, Mann purchased a volume of Hofmann's drawings, which included preliminary sketches of *Die Quelle*, the oil painting that had graced his study since 1914; he was "charmed" by the youthful physicality, and by Hofmann's "arcadian fantasy of beauty."

fashion. The great soul of which we are a part may dream through us, in our manner of dreaming, its own secret dreams, of its youth, its hope, its joy and peace—and its blood sacrifice." All of which we've seen, distilled in his vision, but obviously demonstrated for almost five hundred pages. But Mann rescues the abstraction by juxtaposing to the "great soul" the individual dreams. Hans concludes: "I know all of man, I have known mankind's flesh and blood, I gave back to the ailing Clavdia Chauchat Pribislav Hippe's lead-pencil. But he who knows the body, life, knows death. And that is not all; it is, pedagogically speaking, only the beginning. One must have the other half of the story, the other side."

Now comes what is usually taken as the novel's summation: "I have made a dream poem of humanity. I will cling to it, I will be good. I will let death have no mastery over my thoughts. For therein lies goodness and love of humankind, and in nothing else. Death is a great power. One takes off one's hat before him, and goes weavingly on tiptoe." (Even at his most sententious, Castorp retains his Paul Ehrenberg whimsy.)

Death becomes no longer the completion but the denial of life:

> Reason stands simple before him, for reason is only virtue, while death is release, immensity, abandon, desire. Desire, says my dream. Lust, not love. Death and love—no, I cannot make a poem of them, they don't go together. Love stands opposed to death. It is love, not reason, that is stronger than death . . . from love and sweetness alone can form come; form and civilization always in silent recognition of the blood-sacrifice. Ah, yes, it is well and truly dreamed. I have exercised my power. I will remember. I will keep faith with death in my heart, yet well remember that faith with death and the dead is evil . . . *For the sake of goodness and love, man shall let death have no sovereignty over his thoughts.*

This declaration seems to vindicate Settembrini—and Heinrich Mann; it could be read as a valedictory to decadence, expressionism, to sensual indulgence, "lust, not love." Yet the moral is overwhelmed by witches spitting out Hamburg curses, or by Castorp recognizing that he embraced Hippe in Clavdia's form. Death and love cannot make a poem? Then what of Platen or Dostoyevsky or the mind behind Aschenbach? Only love and sweetness produce a civilization? Tell that to Wagner or Nietzsche. Hans forgets his visionary idyll, just as Thomas Buddenbrook forgets his Schopenhauer.

Sure enough, the next chapter involves a literal yoking of death and love, Joachim's agonizing last days. This is a poem based on silence and denial. When it becomes clear that he's dying, the chattiest patients are at a loss for words. Mann makes another brilliant observation about the failure of language to grasp the outer reaches of experience. Death, we learn, is a mere abstraction for the dying; for everyone else it's the source of "tears . . . those clear drops flowing in such bitter abundance every hour of our day all over the world, till in sheer poetic justice we have named the earth we live in after them." The Vale of Tears supersedes the Magic Mountain; but in these lines' poise, that vale becomes a comic stage. One ironic stroke succeeds another. As Hans weeps, he remembers his biology, the mucus and albumin—and the knowledge that slapstick and holiness share the same material base, excitation of erectile tissue. (Immense shifts in tone, like the grieving over Joachim's "stunk-over" corpse or the visual transition from pretty boy to hideous crone, are recalled in *Doctor Faustus*, when the symphonic "Apocalypse" juxtaposes cries from the pit and a chorus of boy sopranos.)

Much later, as Hans catalogues his favorite records, Mann shows how deeply his roots remain in the familiar soil of German romanticism. Schubert's lied has not served him well: "We add—perhaps rather darkly—that he might have had a different fate" had he loved it less; song cannot be disentangled from the world behind it. Mann summarizes Castorp's life on the mountain:

> The truth was that his very destiny had been marked by stages, adventures, insights, and these flung up in his mind suitable themes for his "self-governing" activities, and these, in their turn, ripened him into an intuitional critic of this sphere, of this its absolutely exquisite image, and his love of it.

Hans's intellectual development has been vexed by (in John E. Woods's translation) "the problems that come with 'playing king.' " The German word *Regierungsprobleme* literally denotes the problems associated with governing, reigning, taking charge. Imperial pastimes, indeed! He becomes lord of the imagination through adventures in the occult and scholarly research. But he has other means to insight, the latest technology from X rays to movie cameras and phonographs. Our exemplary modern Hans Castorp exhibits a nature that changes with the seasons, whether he's watching the movies, listening to music, or taking his temperature. His sensibility is over-determined, so saturated by media-induced impressions that a psychoanalytic explanation seems almost quaint.

After Castorp and Clavdia pledge their devotion to Peeperkorn, Mann observes the varieties of feeling that share the word "love": "It is organic sympathy, the touching sense-embrace of that which is doomed to decay. . . . The meaning of the word varies? In God's name, then, let it vary."

Every narrative strategy Mann employs, every allusive spin of the dialectic, stems from that command. The plainest, most biologically compelling response is overwhelmed by a magic mountain of circumstances. Hänschen doesn't get to keep Hippe's pen; he loses his night with Clavdia to a "time without contour"; he embraces Joachim only after death. No love is realized; no straight line shortens the distance. The story imprisoned within *The Magic Mountain* could not yet be written. Every internal contradiction and narrative diversion tells us that.

Bruno Schulz, who idolized Mann, said that art and philosophy cohabit only while "the blood of the mystery . . . circulates," a comment that Mann would have endorsed. What other novel of this stature is so preoccupied with the body? In 1917 Mann wrote Paul Amann that disease was the poor man's vacation. The wealthy patients of Davos enjoy all the pleasures of a fancy resort together with a physical transformation. The mountain air "revolutionizes the body," an invalid is "all body," "nothing but body." There's a Rabelaisian cornucopia of bodily discharges. We're shocked—and then to our horror entertained—by the description of phlegm and mucus, the itching, sneezing, and coughing, the disfiguring eczema, the lingering dehydration, the stench of death: the very trick of dying, we learn, is to get "all stunk out." As surely as Yeats, Mann configures sex and physical corruption: Clavdia's disease makes her more desirable, "her body rendered twice over body." Hans strokes her X ray with prurient excitement.

Illness destroys inhibitions. Embarrassment is no longer possible in the "anonymous, communal" realm of physical discomfort. As one patient says, "The business of body and soul, the last and highest and most ghastly private matter in the world is also the most universal—everybody can understand it." No scholar's key is necessary; the body topples intellectual hierarchies. In Mann's scheme it is the agent of democracy.

On the Magic Mountain, "disease is love transformed." But it's also inherently aphrodisiacal. Castorp distills the equivalence in a pun, "le corps, l'amour, la mort"—body, love, and death (Platen's vision in Paul Bourget's formulation). When his uncle visits him, he boasts of the "physical gratification" he derives from his suffering. The uncle listens attentively and flees overnight—just in time, it seems, for, as the director Hofrat Behrens observes, the invalid temperament is contagious.

After their mountain enchantments, life below appears insufferable. Former patients cannot resume the habits of land time, somewhat like the warriors in Mann's *Reflections*, grown so devoted to their comrades that they were lost to their wives. Mann fancies sickness and warfare to be twin experiences that "revolutionize the body." The military situation was clearly homoerotic, but in his novel sickness renders heterosexuals passive, "less than men." The invalid's world is a patriarch's nightmare: all play, no work; all process, no product; all tease, no embrace. What makes Castorp a new type is his positive enjoyment of impotence.

Mann is tremendously attentive to the physical world. In 1933 Hermann Weigand noted the range of objects, from chairs to baptismal bowl, each "saturated with the flavor of the life it has served." (Weigand found the same impulse in Rilke.) For a man who once complained of his visual deficiencies, Mann finds subtle distinctions everywhere. In clothes and colors: there's a world of difference between the black vestments worn by Castorp's grandfather, signifying a rejection of the modern era, the uniform of a superannuated *Bürgertum*, and those worn by Settembrini's father, the mourning suit of a frustrated revolutionary.

The voyeur's interest in objects extends to body parts: arms, elbows, breasts, when abstracted, become virtual equivalents of pens, cigars, and thermometers. (A painting of Chauchat so lifelike that each pore stands out almost renders her body a cubist abstraction.) Without assistance from the object relations school of psychoanalysis, Mann examines the implications of his characters' fetishism. The voyeur's perspective is always intentional, whether he spies unwitting lovers through a glass partition or disrobes movie actors who cannot return his glance.

His doctor tells Castorp that tissue rises in the same way to any occasion: "The holy ghost or ice-cold fish, it's all the same." Had any novel before so welcomed physical life at the expense of all the shibboleths of Western civilization? The old man willing to renounce "world fame" for a smile from the waiter Franzl's lips is prefigured in the author who reduces piety to goose bumps.

Mann turns Marx, Freud, and Einstein to his own purposes without citing any of them. He socializes Freud, sexualizes Marx, makes poetry of Einstein's theory of relativity. The central role of the physical sciences distinguishes his novel.

Goethe spent years studying botany and mineralogy. His experiments in color theory look forward to the recent subscience popularly called chaos, which focuses on the contingent nature of human perception. His discovery in 1784 of "Goethe's bone," a tiny structure in the upper jaw, previously thought restricted to nonhumans, anticipates the great scientific idea of the next century, evolution. By contrast, Mann is less interested in biological history than in the ways human response, activity, simply *presence*, affect biology. In a letter to this author, Konrad Bloch suggests that Mann foresaw the discovery of endorphins. (Ever since Felix Krull willed himself an invalid, Mann had made the body subject to his characters' whims.)

The Magic Mountain invents a poetry of science, "lyrical-medical-technical" but primarily Mannian. Among many examples: the way laboratory specimens divide the individual from his type, the lover Castorp from his "anonymous, communal" species; the transformation of science into a middlebrow entertainment co-extensive with movies and records; the individual use of scientific language—mechanical for the engineer Castorp, mystical for Peeperkorn, lascivious for Krokowski, nihilistic for Behrens.

We saw that Mann's views of biology changed with his politics. The "conservative" of 1921 argued a year later that biological laws were subject to revision; this bespoke a Social Democrat's version of Lysenkoism—a folly also entertained by Freud. (Trofim Lysenko was the Soviet biologist who argued that the laws of genetics could be governed by dialectical materialism.) In Mann—or Freud—the Schopenhauerian will encounters few obstacles. Like Felix Krull, miming the symptoms of physical illness, we are all Hermes' double agents between the realms of body and spirit.

Mann's conceits have acquired a scientific basis. Psychiatrists now argue that patients with multiple-personality disorders exhibit a distinctive biological pattern for each persona: a separate body for each soul. In 1934 German scientists introduced the *Umwelt*, a surrounding universe determined largely by each person's biological condition. On a less pathological level, the medical concept of the "self" and the "not-self" illuminates the way we tolerate our most egregious flaws: e.g., the Icelandic proverb "Each man likes the smell of his own farts." Disgust is reserved for the not-self —suggesting why a sexually liberated Thomas Mann would still feel a mixture of attraction and contempt toward his lover.

Naphta says, "Pure science is a myth," a remark Settembrini interprets as antihumanist. He's a late Protestant, still hoping for the Kingdom of God in the laboratory. But almost since 1925, science has confirmed Naphta's remark. When Heisenberg observed that we could not abstract the dancer from the dance, the position of an object from its rate of movement, he revealed that indeterminacy was simply the condition of science. Gödel's theorem indicates that no system is self-contained; it always includes some principle that cannot be internally proved.

Is it possible that Mann arrived independently at the same conclusions? Hans Castorp may be a domesticated version of Heisenberg's uncertainty principle. In his hands science becomes all too subjective; his desire is the catalytic agent that changes the chemistry. Or take Thomas Kuhn's argument that paradigms of thought are subject to historical context and revision—i.e., "pure science" is as malleable as popular taste. Hasn't Mann shown this, most simply in Castorp's ability to transfer the sensibility of romantic poetry to movies and records?

What of Mannian science itself? The interplay of macro- and microcosm results in pathological, "unnatural" excess, "nature red in tooth and claw," an orgy of sexual affinities. It's safe to characterize Hans Castorp, with his love of marzipan and cigars, as contentedly oral. The novel reflects his personality. Biology figures as the tale of bodily fluids, of a universal "sucking and secretion." Mann shamelessly courts psychoanalytic interpretation. Mother's milk, tears, albumin, semen flow together, as he traces the collection of lymph, "most intimate of the body juices," from breast, loins, and belly.

Castorp has druglike reveries in which each part of the body pulses with sexual energy. For the polymorphously perverse pleasure is ubiquitous: "This body [was] a monstrous multiplicity of breathing and self-nourishing individuals." From such knowledge beckons an onanistic joy beyond Felix Krull's dreams. Or a humility of political dimensions: Hans's awareness that from the perspective of atomic physics "smaller than small" means virtually the same as "enormously large."

At the end of a chapter with the eponymous title "Research," he closes a textbook and finds all the data reduced to "just Hans Castorp with burning face and stiffening fingers, lying muffled on a balcony, with a view across the moonlit, frost-shrouded valley. . . ." The body he imagines exists only in his fancy. Under the cold glare of moonlight, life becomes an unnatural interference—"perhaps only an infection, a sickening of matter."

But, a true Mannian, he finds this morbid conclusion "stimulating." After all, sickness is a kind of "intoxication," a winding path to "heightened and unlicensed" consciousness. As Naphta—and Mann before him—says, disease is paradoxically the nemesis of inertia, the force behind all activity, creative, spiritual, or sexual: the latter itself a sickness of the flesh. Perceiving that, our erstwhile scholar falls into a dream. And in this novel, in which the exhaustive is never complete, clinical data inevitably become the stuff of sexual fantasy. He dreams of Clavdia's "organic fragrance," fondles the diseased heft of her "upper arms," and welcomes her bacteria-"moistened kiss."

A parallel exists between Krokowski's lectures and Freud's *Three Essays on Sexuality*. This suggests that Mann's respect for psychoanalysis was not great. As he had told Heinrich in 1903 when comparing the latter's novels to Wedekind's plays, psychological analysis of erotic desire ignored the uncanny elements and the intense suffering. Within the novel, Krokowski's lectures become a kindergarten text in Castorp's sentimental education.

Mann treats psychoanalysis with skepticism. He captures the moment when it was still regarded as half quackery, and he makes it a part of commercial history, a tourist's entertainment along with mountain hikes and afternoon tea. The Freud he invokes, but doesn't name, is a burgher's guide rather than the mythic navigator of Mann's later work. After a patient has an epileptic seizure, Dr. Krokowski analyzes the episode "half-poetically, half in ruthlessly scientific terms." The poet sees the "equivalent of love," the scientist "an orgasm of the brain." This constitutes a "soul's dissection" (*Begliederung*).

Dr. Krokowski conducts a seance, a reminder that psychoanalysis shares its origins with such spurious pursuits as phrenology and clairvoyance. There's a literary joke; the medium Ellen Brand comes from Odense-on-Fuen, Hans Christian Andersen's home. Like the androgynous youth Mann described in "An Occult Experience," she switches genders: assuming the guise of "Holger," a demure lad with "beautiful brown, brown curls." (Is he the "holy" one Mann admired in Ghirlandaio's painting?) The patients are both hyped up and ambivalent. Krokowski explains that mourning is always hypocritical: "not so much grief at not being able to call the dead back as . . . grief at not being able to want to do so." But soon the music and shouting resemble a Pentecostal revival.

What follows is most unscientific: the "non-vital" behaving like a living creature. Joachim's specter appears in the uniform and helmet, yet to be designed, of a Great War soldier. With vocational finesse, Krokowski tries to explain the ghost in analytical terms. The subconscious ought to be called the superconscious, because it leaps over "the conscious intelligence" to link "the individual soul and a wholly knowing All-soul"; as kitschy solecism this resembles Jung more than Freud.

The apparition lacks a material base, yet it derives from a human capacity: thought "drawing substances to itself and clothing itself in temporary reality." Is it a ghost or a waking dream, a wish come true? Hans Castorp selects the musical accompaniment; no more rollicking hymns but Valentine's Prayer from *Faust*. The doctor asks why, and, in a beautiful line, he replies, "A question of mood. Matter of feeling."

During this time Mann, still impressed by his experience of the occult, told a friend that he didn't "*disbelieve*" in séances and that his experiences had not ended in 1923. Without quite ridiculing the supernatural, Mann exploited it for deeply human and—as in Castorp's loving gaze at Joachim—erotic purposes. In 1929 when Hugo von Hofmannsthal died, he wrote that the poet's face appeared rejuvenated in death. Twenty-one years later, following the suicide of his son Klaus, he quoted a friend who had found the corpse blissfully at peace. Ever the materialist, he admitted that this might be due to the "gas." Yet more than a materialist, he added that "lies can speak the truth," the material image expressed a spiritual condition.

(Then again in 1945, he wrote Upton Sinclair that he was "completely lacking in any occult gift." He remembered that his presence had actually "impeded" the proceedings at that famous séance. On the other hand, Heinrich still insisted that he had heard Carla's dying voice calling him by his name.)

As mentioned before, the supernatural had long fascinated homosexuals. Their historical involvement with ecstatic faiths—from aesthetic Catholicism and High Church Anglicanism to the working-class forms of Pentecostal worship—may stem from their quest for an accommodating ritual, one where love is viscerally expressed. Only during the séance can Hans lock glances with Joachim and declare his feelings aloud. (Compare Mann's 1950 diary note linking the "amusing" Holger and "erotic pedagogy.")*

The séance provokes other responses. As Ellen writhes and screams, Mann compares her labor to something "we men [know] if we do not shirk our humanity," alluding to Katia's difficult pregnancy, an episode painfully captured in *The Tales of Jacob* when Rachel dies in childbirth. Mann claims that his novel "passed beyond realism by means of the symbolic." But mountain magic ultimately succumbs to "the sober intelligence of the flatlands." So which counts more, the ghost or the "mood and feeling" that summon him? Or is the salient detail the "goose flesh" that rises as Ellen breathes in Hans's ear? The old erectile tissue, indiscriminate as ever, leaps to the occasion.

---

* Ironically, the occult figures in Mann's biography. Erika had a great friend, the Berlin artist Eva Herrmann. In her middle age, Herrmann came to believe in a kind of Yeatsian automatic writing, a spooky form of graphology. After Mann's death, she was convinced that he was writing through her from the grave. Katia, of as secular a temperament as her husband, humored Herrmann. "Ach, the poor Eva," she told Richard Exner.

4

THE MAGIC MOUNTAIN: IV

From a biographical perspective, it's appropriate that the American edition closes with Mann's 1939 address to the students of Princeton. His novel dramatizes a vision of erotic Utopia, inspired by an American poet and first announced in his appeal to young men. Like that speech, it overflows with propaganda, some of it Settembrini-blatant, but much of it deeply coded, the ultimate version of Gipper, the private language of his adolescence.

The political ideas were duly noted. In 1925 Mann admitted to Julius Bab that he intended "some criticism of prewar capitalism." He added that " 'other things' such as music and the meaningful interweaving of life and death, were much, much more important to me."

At one point Settembrini declares, "There is nothing that is not political. Everything is political." (Castorp demurs, "That's flat.") Mann demonstrates that political ideology embraces questions of culture and language. Naphta enrages Settembrini when he asserts that "grammar and form" are bourgeois tools, instruments of class supremacy. Now this supports his arguments for a new method of education—"a free and public instruction through lectures, exhibitions, cinematographs . . . vastly to be preferred to any school course," an anarchistic curriculum resembling Mann's casual education in Munich. But he also knew that, as Settembrini says, the mere survival of torture demonstrates "how little ground the instinct-worshippers had for their fear that things could ever be too much directed by reason on this earth" (a conviction that directly posed Mann against some of Munich's most famous residents, from Otto Gross to D. H. Lawrence). He could well echo the Baron Charlus's statement "I have always honored those who defend logic and grammar. Fifty years later we recognize they warded off great perils." And during his exile he composed essays that surpass George Orwell's dissection of political lying.

Politics becomes a tale of two cities. Naphta informs his foe that "absolutely everything beloved and cherished of the bourgeoisie, the conservative, the cowardly, and the impotent—the state, family life, secular art and science—was consciously or unconsciously hostile to the religious idea, to the Church with its model of the ideal, the communistic City of God." The humanist and the sensualist are banished from Naphta's city—which may explain why Thomas Mann, for all his vaunted fellow-traveling, could never become a Communist.

The other city is Walt Whitman's metropolis, a place where "ego and personality" walk freely. Hans learns this incrementally. First he discovers that "love suppressed . . . returns in an unrecognized form." Next he sees that his transactions with Hippe remained incomplete until Clavdia: "I have dreamed it out to the end." The working out of his knowledge requires an "orgiastic kind of freedom." At this point, Mann addresses the reader, "Is there any other kind?"

This is a political insight. On Walpurgis Night, Hans admitted to Clavdia that "liberty and freedom" remained foreign concepts. It takes hundreds of pages and seven years; reality must give way to "the picturesque and mythical" to comprehend the orgiastic nature of freedom. The route carries Hans far from Germany; he even exchanges his brand of Maria Mancini cigars for "Light of Asia." Grammar becomes a vehicle of relaxing inhibitions; the formal "Sie" yields to Peeperkorn's "Du"; and Hans pledges to Clavdia, "Tu es le toi de ma vie."

As ever in Mann, both sides of the equation come to light; if politics is colored by the passions, the passions are politicized. Remarkably, Mann advances an understanding of Clavdia that verges on feminist. After Hans yields her to Peeperkorn, he becomes her ally and confidant. Her other admirers, Peeperkorn included, seem vulgar, lecherous, their vitality akin to the big-balled Klöterjahns who always threaten Mann's heroes.

Another patriarch is challenged, for, unwittingly, Mann counterposes Hans Castorp to Sigmund Freud. As late as 1937, the psychoanalyst insisted on the existence of penis envy in women, and argued that the corresponding theme was "man's struggle against his passive or feminine attitude to another man." Avoiding that fight, Castorp becomes the nervous exception to Freud's rule. As he retreats from competition with Peeperkorn, the two acquire an understanding—they become "Du" to each other. Peeperkorn announces that "the period of probation has ended. . . . I offer . . .

a brotherly alliance, such as one forms against a third party, against the world. . . ."

Pace Freud, Hans's forbearance is expressly unmasculine. In the social sense he is not virile and positively exults in his passivity. Confessing his brief infatuation with Clavdia, he admits to Peeperkorn the questionable nature of his "normal" responses: "I must say that when I refer to myself as a man, it seems to me a sort of self-advertising and bad taste. . . ." Without much pain, Hans retires from the battle of the sexes; he won't find "orgiastic freedom" there.

Far sadder is the denial of his love for a man. At the end of the séance, Joachim's ghost singles Hans out with a "quiet, friendly gaze." In life that glance had been "dazed"; Hans had loved to stare at his unseeing eyes. (He resembled a movie icon, impassively displaying himself.) Now his vision is focused and true, directed solely at his cousin. But like that other youth who welcomed Hans in the snow, Joachim will be sacrificed, consumed in a glance. Castorp's eyes overflow with tears; "Forgive me," he whispers, for disturbing your rest. There is no more hopeless exchange in all Mann's work.

Just before the séance we have learned about Castorp's favorite records. At the top is Schubert's "Der Lindenbaum," a heightening of folksong into an enchanted realm of "forbidden love." Celebrating the gramophone, Mann paraphrases his essay "Nietzsche and Music": "Ah, what power had this soul-enchantment! We were all its sons, and could achieve mighty things on earth, in so far as we served it. One need have no more genius, only much more talent"—could one add "obstinacy"?—"to be such an artist of soul-enchantment as should give to the song a giant volume by which it would subjugate the world." The process remains incomplete; the faithful son dies, "on his lips the new word of love which as yet he knew not how to speak."

Not spoken to Joachim in life or death; or at the end, when a bomb rips through two soldiers, "friends who in their need flung themselves down together," leaving them "scattered, commingled and gone." Mann no longer praises their snug uniforms or the perverse camaraderie of the bat-tlefield. Instead he laments all those lost, "commingled" only in death, their "love" still undeclared.

With Ophülsian affection, the camera retreats from life's problem child. In a final tracking shot, we see Hans on the ground, spread-eagled in a sexually provocative position, thirty feet from the exploding "product of a perverted science." His chances? The narrator shrugs, "Without great con-cern we leave the question open." Hear this, Hans Castorp, "Your story was told for its own sake, not yours." But we are not persuaded; too much emotion has been invested in that story. Hans's tune carries over the roaring cannons like a Heldentenor taming an orchestra. To that accompanist, *The Magic Mountain* ends on a Mannian note of apocalypse and intimacy. By his lights the humanistic element constitutes "good will," friendliness to man.

Mann puts these words in Settembrini's mouth: "A man cannot make general observations to any extent, on any subject, without betraying himself, without introducing his entire individuality, as in an allegory, the fundamental theme and problem of his own existence."

Yet Mann shrouds "the fundamental theme and problem of his existence" with literary games. In their immense novels Joyce and Proust frequently employ a first-person narrative. In *The Magic Mountain* our eternal companion is the disengaged narrator. Perhaps this was modesty on Mann's part. But the absence of a warmer personal voice hurts the novel—an irony indeed, but one familiar to all his misunderstood lovers, from Castorp to Leverkühn.

All the same, the novel became Mann's greatest critical success abroad. One of its shrewdest early readers was an American, Hermann Weigand. In a 1933 study he called Mann "the most conscious artist of our time." In seven years his novel had gone from "a work of genius" (Lowe-Porter) to a universal classic; Weigand adds, "No other book of world literature is so perfectly integrated." In 1923, Mann had used the Goethean concept of "world literature" to ingratiate himself with Americans, and a decade later they returned the favor.

Answering his years of self-promotion, Weigand saluted him as the "genius of symbolic biography. His exemplary sense of self-discipline and responsibility qualifies him to render a surpassingly objective appraisal of his own significance to German . . . letters"; like Goethe, he had no need of "false modesty."

Mann's initial assessment of the novel was guarded. In the months after its appearance he felt called upon, once more, to defend his work from misinterpretation. He informed the suspicious conservative Josef Ponten that it never stooped to the level of a tract. Hans Castorp might prefer a "democratic amity toward life" to an "aristocratic alliance with death (history, romanticism)," but such phrases are poetic hyperbole, and, moreover, Hans "promptly forgets it again, in general he is not personally equipped to cope with his higher thoughts." That may be his most endearing quality, and Mann's too. He preferred to emphasize a spirit of play—"Where in all the history of art and literature have you ever before encountered the attempt *to make death a comic figure?"* Mann could remark with pleasure, "Is not my book, despite its own inner fatality, a book of *good will?"*

Mann described the novel as a condition that he and his readers had to get beyond. But this was a message for the editorial page. After eight hundred pages, he had not exhausted the topic or relieved his ambivalence. The ending bespeaks incompletion; if life and health await, it's in the moment yet to come.

Twenty years later Mann returned to the theme of disease and enlightenment. This time he scattered his findings in an essay on Dostoyevsky, a figure he admired precisely because he risked his sanity to make art—a devotion foreign, he writes, to insulated, self-protective egotists like Tolstoy or Goethe.

Or Proust: the French novelist cannot match Dostoyevsky's insights into illness and evil. This invidious comparison occurred just as Mann finished his literary Gethsemane, *Doctor Faustus*, during the composition of which he nearly lost his life. Mann equated this literary burden with the cancer that almost killed him. His remarks about Proust show whom he now saw as rival for the crown of laurels.

In the late novella *The Black Swan* Mann revives the conflict of body and spirit, worked through at such length in *The Magic Mountain*. In this story a middle-aged widow, Rosalie Tümmler, convinces herself that her love for a young American, Ken Keaton, has restored her youth. She has a cynical daughter, Anna, who finds her outbursts of lyrical joy—variants on the Wordsworthian line that nature ne'er betrayed the heart that loves her—kitsch. Eventually Anna condones a rendezvous between her mother and the American. But by then Rosalie's miracles have become pathological symptoms. What seemed like menstrual blood is a sign of cancer. Rosalie dies without bitterness: "I am loath to go away—from you all, from life with its spring. But how should there be spring without death? Indeed, death is a great instrument of life, and if for me it borrowed the guise of resurrection, of the joy of love, that was not a lie, but goodness and mercy."

We have long known that Mann got Rosalie from a story told Katia by a friend. The young American was modeled on an intern who treated Mann during his own bout with cancer. Mann was impressed by the youth's good looks: later, recalling this episode, he declared that beauty should be appreciated in any form. (Ken also exhibits an ingenuous appreciation for the Old World that Mann observed in Edward Klotz, his son Golo's companion.)

His diary reveals other parallels. In the summer of 1950, when he fell in love with Franz Westermeier, the Bavarian waiter who inspired his Michelangelo essay, both Erika and Katia observed his infatuation. The fears he expressed in his diary and essay, if not to them, were later enunciated by Rosalie: "Youth is feminine, and age's relationship to it is masculine, but age is not happy and confident in its desire, it is full of shame and fear before youth and before all Nature, because of its unfitness. Oh there is much sorrow in prospect for me, for how can I hope that he will be pleased by my desire . . . ?" Half-desperate, half-ecstatic, Mann felt nature toying with his flesh. Once more, "after twenty-five years," he awakened each morning in an aroused state. (Erectile tissue would confound him too.)

Like Anna, Erika considered her parent's obsession "undisciplined." But his pain was clear to both women—he even told Katia that he couldn't sleep from longing for the boy—so they conspired to let him see Franzl once more before he left Switzerland. It makes for a rich Mannian episode: the two women observing Mann as he extends his glance to a beloved youth. Moreover, someone else watched: the novelist Carlos Fuentes, dining in Zurich, who merely saw an extremely quiet and dignified old man attended by two convivial women. (Later that summer, the highly "arousable" Mann became smitten with a young Argentinean whom he noticed on the hotel's tennis courts. The angle of vision prevented Mann from seeing his face, but he gloried in the fellow's "Hermes-legs": "who wouldn't wish to stroke them?" Ken Keaton's "long legs and narrow hips" may be modeled on those of this South American athlete.)

Death in Venice receives its final coda in the Michelangelo essay, when Mann discovers a melancholy redemption in age's love of youth. Is then *The Black Swan*, animated by the same muse, the charming Franzl, Mann's attempt to resolve *The Magic Mountain*'s central dilemma? His novella advances the possibility that in the presence of death, we find love. Thanks to Franzl, Mann can imagine a happy ending to his great novel; on Rosalie Tömmler's lips the word is finally spoken.

Whether or not literature allowed the *promesse de bonheur*, Mann continued to associate *The Magic Mountain* with the desires that had frustrated and sustained him throughout his life. Two months after his last encounter with Franzl, he wrote movingly of Platen's sexual timidity: stationed in Naples, where "the love between men was so common" that rejection posed no threat, the poet became trapped in a "philological" maze. He persisted in connecting "love" with women, "friendship" with men, and employed the familiar device of initials to disguise those who fell between. (Mann had not quite put paid to such word games when he decreed that love remain "unclassified.")

With his favorite poet in mind, Mann turned the next day to *The Magic Mountain*. "Amused about Holger's spirit. With this episode the eroticism of pedagogy finally becomes evident. Settembrini's happy and painful smile.* Hans Castorp charming throughout—if you have a feeling for it."

But such a feeling was reserved for those whom Mann elsewhere called "connoisseurs." The less enlightened had other ideas about his novel. In 1949 Sir Alexander Korda expressed interest in a film treatment, but insisted that Mann be "reasonable" and abandon his loyalty to Hans Castorp's adolescent fling. Mann did not wish to sacrifice "Hippe and his pencil." Nothing came of Korda's project, but the image lingered. On September 15, 1950, having returned to the Pacific Palisades, Mann received a letter postmarked Zurich from Franzl. He declared that it gave him as much joy as "W.T.'s pencil shavings" (W.T. was Willri Timpe, the model for Hippe). Life was, for once, kinder than the movies.

---

* This author recently learned that "Settembrini" is Venetian dialect for the "September men," the pederasts who arrive once the season is over and buy the local boys at half-price. If Mann knew this, Settembrini lives up to his name to the extent that his "pedagogy" is happily / painfully erotic. Obviously this draws the organ-grinder out of Heinrich's sphere and into Mann's.

5

DISORDER IN THE FAMILY

From the Alps to Mount Olympus: If *Buddenbrooks* was the first German novel to invade "World Literature," *The Magic Mountain* bade fair to colonize the territory. Success was immediate and, for so demanding a novel, extraordinary. (An American naysayer, decades later, would insist that nobody really enjoyed this elephantine mess, readers' testimonies be damned.) Within two months of its publication in November 1924, Mann could allude casually to fifty thousand readers. A month later he wrote Ernst Bertram: "I must tell you entre nous that I have earned some seventy thousand marks by selling tickets to my mystical-comical aquarium."

The mountain was a display, and the season festive. With his first royalties he purchased a car, "a pretty six-passenger Fiat. . . . I shall travel into the city now with 33 horses, and wave affably in all directions." The chatty but handsome Ludwig served as his chauffeur. In March Mann sailed alone to Egypt, disembarking at Venice, Cattaro, Port Said, Cairo, Luxor, Karnak, and Constantinople. Typically he mixed pleasure with business, steeping in the Egyptian atmosphere as preparation for "ulterior plans which I have laid in secret." He advertised his sobriety. In a travel essay he wrote, "I am living in no luxury suite, and am quite satisfied." His cabin had belonged to the ship's doctor —"It is nice but not too nice, which means it is as it should be for me."

Increasingly Mann's life began to resemble a pastiche, a collage of events so contradictory that they seemed to parody themselves. Starting in 1925, an interweaving of fact and fiction, doctrine and parody, became a permanent condition of his life. Years later, in *Doctor Faustus*, the devil informs Leverkühn that modern life *is* pastiche, cultural parody, a commercialized nihilism.

Nineteen twenty-five was a year of kaleidoscopic impressions, of public images begging for Mann's satirical touch. His fiftieth birthday was one such occasion. There was an official celebration at the Old Council Hall in Munich. The mayor spoke, as did a local writer lecturing on the character Settembrini, followed by Heinrich, the wheezy organ-grinder in the flesh. Mann described Heinrich's speech as "a short, moving remembrance of childhood birthdays [that] brought not only me to tears." But it was also a public reconciliation, a deliberate confusion of life and text.

His own speech was an artful instance of purloined papers, as if he were challenging himself to tip his hand in a public arena. He opened by saying there were certain obligations—"one must marry, have children, and celebrate festivals." Amazingly, he was now the festivals' honoree. And yet, "I was not a social person, not a good colleague. Reticent, much alone, unskilled at social intercourse," suffering from a "timidity and shyness" that were often mistaken for "coldness."

Other artists were born for the spotlight; Wagner could never be honored enough. But Mann took his cue from Shakespeare. "Thou com'st in such a questionable shape." He declared that he didn't think much of his own work. Then, just to imply the opposite, he invoked Goethe, who had also needed to "learn his own greatness." "I always said I was a dreamer and a doubter who never imagined he could instruct or change people." Yet, thanks to a particular combination of "the musical and the moral," he found himself doing just that.

The next day there was a program at the Munich Residenztheater, complete with a performance of Mozart, an academic lecture, and a reading from *Felix Krull* by Mann. For this public ceremony Mann chose his most blasphemous creation, the duplicitous Hermes. Finally a group of young women serenaded the subject of honor and crowned him with a laurel wreath. Even in his twenties, Mann had been faintly embarrassed by the image; in the era of the photogravure, it was enough to drive his enemies —like Brecht and Alfred Kerr—to hoots of contempt.

The aura of pastiche and parody was most evident in Mann's family. While the press announced his official honors, it was more intrigued by a generational conflict. Within a few months he was depicted as both the sovereign of German letters and a befuddled patriarch superseded by his eldest son. A cartoon appeared of Klaus, heavily rouged in the currently popular fashion, informing Thomas, "You know, of course, that geniuses never have highly gifted sons. Therefore, Papa, you are no genius." Klaus became the symbol of bohemian opposition to *bürgerlich* decorum, virtually a literary parricide: Brecht quipped, "All the world knows Klaus Mann, the son of Thomas Mann. By the way, who is Thomas Mann?"

Klaus and Erika both loved Pamela Wedekind, daughter of the celebrated playwright; where their father preached renunciation, hers counseled sexual anarchy. In 1925 the three performed together in Klaus's drama *Anya and Esther*, and were subsequently featured on the cover of *Berliner Illustrierte Zeitung*, Germany's most popular weekly. The photo showed them clownishly made up: Klaus's lipstick gave him the look of a transvestite Harlequin, an image not in keeping with laurel wreaths and greetings from the mayor. What's more, the photo was doctored; the original featured a fourth actor, Gustaf Gründgens, Klaus's lover (he would become Erika's first husband) and the only professional talent in the group. Gründgens disappeared. Where his shoulder lay, the magazine inserted a snapshot of the "poets' children" in street clothes, a nicely—if not deliberately— Mannian juxtaposition of life and theater.*

The Mann household became a veritable laboratory of domestic turmoil. Thanks to Katia, the surfaces still gleamed. As Mann wrote in "Disorder and Early Sorrow," his thinly veiled memoir, "the house is comfortable, even elegant, though sadly in need of repairs that cannot be made for lack of materials. . . . Even so, it is still the proper setting of the upper middle class, though they themselves look odd enough in it, with their worn and turned clothing and altered way of life." Neither Thomas nor Katia would regain the splendid solidity of their childhood homes.

In June 1925 Ida Herz began a lifelong friendship with Mann; she would later organize and systematize his library. She found him gloomy about family matters, still grieving his mother's death, still shaken by Carla's suicide. Laurel wreath or not, the fifty-year-old author remembered that his father had died at fifty-one. She observed that he was the gentlest of patriarchs—"rebellion in the French style" would be impossible against a parent who allowed everything, who subsidized Erika and Klaus in their most antinomian acts. She also saw that his obvious preference for Erika and the baby Elisabeth offended the other four children—to which he replied, "If a man has six children, he can't love them all equally."

(Jealousy wasn't their only problem. Golo writes that by his late teens

---

* Klaus later described Gründgens as a "neurotic Hermes, light-footed with his worn but elegantly shaped sandals . . . haunted by his vanity and his persecution mania, and a frantic desire to please." This exhibits a fair degree of objectivity about the man who was his former lover as well as the ex-husband of his favorite sister. It also resembles his father's descriptions of neurotic tyrants; as Klaus wrote about those prose rhythms: "I have them in my blood."

LEFT TO RIGHT: *Klaus, Elisabeth (holding the dog Lux), Michael, Katia, Thomas, and Erika in Munich, circa 1930*

he was so unnerved by his father that he would stammer in his presence and sometimes, particularly when Katia was absent, prepare notes for their lonely dinners together. Michael was the recipient of physical blows. One time, in an uncharacteristic gesture for the agnostic Mann, he insisted that his youngest son sleep beneath a Bavarian crucifix. This icon terrified the child, but when Katia tried to dissuade her husband, he replied that Michael was getting a lesson in "injustice." In 1925, the six-year-old Michael tore the wheel off the family's new car, and it rolled back into a brick wall. Mann was so angry that he beat his son with the boy's own walking-stick. On several occasions a recalcitrant Michael was banished "under the table with the dog." According to Elisabeth, her father "simply didn't care for the boy."

Like most fathers, he would figure in his sons' dreams. On May 5, 1934, Klaus recorded a dream of "the Magician's secret homosexual life," involving Werner Kruse, Erika's musical accompanist. Where Klaus imagined him in flagrante delicto, Michael, according to Golo, dreamed about wrestling with his inimical parent.

But while Mann rarely supplied *Gemütlichkeit*, he offered his sons a steady intellectual counsel. His letters to Klaus contain rich observations extended by one literary professional to another. Michael may have been the brunt of unreasonable anger, but when he began his musical studies, he received Mann's cherished violin, and when he showed literary inclinations, Mann critiqued his first stories. And in 1939, he let Golo succeed him as editor of *Mass und Wert*, an émigré magazine he had founded two years earlier. This job helped make Golo's name.)

Lula was increasingly unsettled, either confessing her unhappy affairs or acting the soul of propriety. One evening, having just completed *Anya and Esther*, Klaus treated his family to a reading. His elders seemed perturbed by the lesbian relation:

> "Rather on the morbid side, I suppose," my mother added, with cheerfulness that sounded a trifle forced.
>
> Aunt Lula, however, inquired in a brittle little voice, her dainty face rigid with disapproval, "I must confess that I am somewhat puzzled as to the relation between these two young ladies, Anya and Esther. Why are they so conspicuously fond of each other?"
>
> Whereupon my father suggested, apologetically, "Well, you see . . . a sentimental friendship, between schoolmates. . . ."

Forgetting the fact that Mann was a world authority on such friendships, Lula's obtuseness is quite amazing. Yet this was the sister Thomas Mann considered his "female self." Klaus shared the affection. In 1948, after Klaus's latest suicide attempt, Mann wrote Adorno that Klaus greatly resembled his aunt. Father and son echoed her conviction that the world was a vastly threatening place, where image and self-representation provided only a transient safety. Mann found his sister—and his son—embarrassments whose hearts he understood.

To Katia, Lula remained an absurd person. One night they all dined with Gerhart Hauptmann, and he departed from Lula with a "Good night, my good woman." She was aghast; his words struck her as meant for a servant. Impoverished by her husband's death, she feared becoming déclassé. The children laughed at her ludicrous image, hooked nose in the air, the breathless admission "I know I am rococo." She kept inquiring whether they had seen her gastroenterologist, whom they knew to be her lover, and was he alone? The affair ended badly, and her morphine addiction became more pronounced. On May 10, 1927, she hanged herself.

In his autobiographical sketch of 1929 Mann says it is too soon to discuss her tragedy. In *Doctor Faustus* the Lula character doesn't kill herself but murders Rudi / Paul instead, pulling the trigger of a gun loaded, at least figuratively, by Leverkühn—and ultimately by Mann himself: she does the men's dirty work. The narrator, Zeitblom, finds this killing almost admirable; the poor girl went down fighting. In the intervening period Klaus began to resemble Lula—including his morphine addiction and his urge to speak his love aloud. Was it a coincidence that a few months after Lula's death, Thomas found himself once more in love, once more telling the world, or at least Klaus and Erika?

Klaus was less reticent. By 1925 he had made a public drama of events at home. Thomas inscribed a copy of *The Magic Mountain*: "To my respected colleague from his promising father." Klaus "accidentally" told a friend who, not quite coincidentally, tipped off the press, and the story spread from Bremen to Budapest. Like his father when he outlined Otto Grautoff's review of *Buddenbrooks*, Klaus was stage-managing his career. If the gesture seems heartless, remember that at the time he was nineteen.

Klaus's life resembles a novel composed by his father. It too involves a series of representations, a deployment of selves wielded by a terminally melancholy temperament. The self-presentation occurs in a modern key. Unlike his father or uncle, he appears in photos well prepared, ready for his closeup. Perhaps because he was then an actor, perhaps because he consciously assumed a symbolic role as his generation's spokesman (something Thomas did only in the most guarded way), a photo of Klaus tells the story that a photo of Thomas or Heinrich withholds. In one youthful shot, he waves his cigarette in mock ennui, his lips parted flirtatiously, his eyes slightly glazed. He seems "at once" (his favorite formulation) scholar and rake, addict and pilgrim. In a photo ten years later, he has assigned himself a new role, as arbiter of the literary emigration: the pretty boy is now an engaged intellectual, cigarette professionally clenched between his teeth. It is only in the last photos that he no longer appears the author of his fate. He remains elegant, but his long head seems distended and the gaze is blasted.

At the time of the earliest photo, Klaus seemed exceptionally fortunate. With his writing, he challenged the European elders—his cadences were as fleet and spare as his father's were orotund—and got away with it, winning the acclaim of sharp Berliners from Brecht to Vicki Baum. For writers like Alfred Döblin, who despised Thomas, Klaus was an ally, his grammar a means of filial defiance. Through Pamela Wedekind, he linked himself with her father, an "inspired quack and clownish performer," the German D. H. Lawrence, knowing full well his own father's suspicions about the English one; he also chose as mentor his father's Gallic rival André Gide. In these literary allusions, he was either trying to get the whole picture or erasing his father's image.

During the 1920s, Klaus's critics dismissed him as an intellectual sybarite, a perfect little salon pink. (In a 1939 letter of praise, Thomas Mann wrote, "For a long time, people did not take you seriously, regarding you as a spoiled brat and a humbug; there was nothing I could do about that." Now, however, Klaus had shown himself capable of "more than most.") He would shortly astonish them by becoming an early and courageous antifascist. But in both decades, an implicit compact between Klaus and his readers allowed him to treat the matter of his life as both exemplary data and the stuff of myth. It was typical that his most famous novel, *Mephisto*, should conflate a villainous ex-lover, Gründgens, with the Goethean devil.

Klaus was gifted with charm, almost overburdened with status—a canny performer who had learned from cabaret stage and sexual prowl to gauge his public. He made himself at home everywhere, disregarding geographic borders, collapsing one time period into another, history into autobiography. He was almost too easy to psychoanalyze. In 1925, after his first collection of stories appeared, Thomas Mann wrote Erika that he was impressed and troubled: "Our Klaus has a sizable Z. complex," alluding to "Zauberer," the children's nickname for their father. That year Klaus also began work on *Kindernovelle* (*Children's Stories*). In this work Christiane Till, a professor's widow, the mother of four children, begins an affair with a younger man. They make love in the shadow of her husband's death mask. In her study of the Mann family, Marianne Krüll seizes on the Oedipal implications, noting that the widow employs "friction" to arouse her lover much as Katia had rubbed Klaus with eau de Cologne during his childhood illness.

But Klaus provides the more telling detail. He had difficulty imagining this lover until he assigned him the face of René Crevel. Crevel, a strikingly handsome Parisian, was the token homosexual in André Breton's circle of left-wing surrealists. Breton's homophobic behavior has been adduced as a cause of Crevel's suicide in 1935, though as Klaus remembered him the tendency was full-blown in the mid-1920s. Like his father, Klaus always had an erotic muse. At first it was a "metallic youth" who almost played Anya's lover, to whom he dedicated the work. Crevel was one of many successors. Therefore, if Christiane Till is his mother, as Krüll contends, she also becomes his surrogate when she sleeps with his lover.

Klaus's youth coincided with the world's discovery of Youth. Although he appeared to many the very symbol of his era, Klaus saw quickly its potential for exploitation. Bad at games, he never participated in the era's "cult of sports." Bliss it may have been then to be alive, to prowl the world's capitals in pursuit of drugs and pretty boys, to party with Garbo and commune with Gide. He knew the addresses of each city's best-populated baths and enjoyed identifying the male prostitutes of Berlin as sons of Russian princes and Prussian generals.

Despite his notoriety, he distrusted anti-intellectual sybarites; there too he was more like his father than either man recognized. Visiting Budapest, "the most corrupt city in Europe," he dallied at the cafés, investigated the baths, but focused on the Jewish intellectuals, dubbing them an "inner emigration," a term later claimed by those who remained in Germany during the Hitler era. Stefan Zweig, in misguided sympathy with the young people then flocking to Hitler, came close to defending political change for its own sake. Klaus told him, "Not everything youth does and thinks is a priori good and pregnant with future" (lines that could be addressed to any celebrants of puerile rebellion, Viennese novelists or Manhattan rock critics). By his early twenties, Klaus no longer wished to be his generation's spokesman. In their presence he found himself middle-aged, a condition Thomas Mann had also undergone at twenty-three, when, alienated by his sexual preferences and personal shyness, he felt himself an onlooker at the carnival of Munich youth.

In his autobiography, *The Turning Point*, Klaus describes his father as patient, long-suffering, tolerant. "We sometimes suspected him of having more insight into our affairs than he usually showed. On other occasions his aloofness bewildered us. But just when we began to wonder if he cared at all, he surprised and touched us with a casual gesture." One of the journals Mann read aloud contained an attack on Klaus's work. Horrified, Klaus awaited some explanation. Instead, "he discussed the weather, while inside I was raving with tempests." But after dinner, he tactfully commented that "malignant stupidity" ruled the world, adding—in an endearingly pompous allusion—that Flaubert had noted the same phenomenon and counseled forbearance on the artist's part. In effect, he was telling Klaus to ignore his critics.

In 1925, both Klaus and Mann were interviewed by the magazine *Uhu*. Klaus denied any distance between himself and his father, who had been nothing but supportive. In turn, Mann said he was trying to understand the new generation ("I go to the movies"), but that, essentially, all those who had been adults before the war were still living in the past.

Klaus observed Thomas observing him with "an attitude of observant irony, half-amused, half-skeptical, indulgent, understanding, and moder-

Mann and his son Klaus, 1925. A magazine cartoon imagined the young writer telling his father, "Geniuses never have highly gifted sons. Therefore, Papa, you are no genius."

ately curious as to what was going to happen next. I am sure his confidence in the fundamental soundness of my character has always been firm enough to prevent him from being seriously perturbed with regard to my future." If anything, Thomas had been the more lenient parent. Katia was heartsick when Klaus toyed with becoming a cabaret dancer—she had wanted her firstborn son to be an architect, and would have settled for an artist or even an opera singer. But a cabaret dancer was, it went without saying, scarcely better than a gigolo. Thomas was less judgmental but more deflating. He wondered whether Klaus wasn't too gawky; in "Disorder and Early Sorrow" the father laments that his son is singularly "without talent," particularly on the dance floor.

That year Klaus composed *The Pious Dance: The Adventure Story of a Young Man*, a barely disguised roman à clef, dedicated to Pamela Wedekind, with two epitaphs, a couplet from *Anya and Esther*, and a quotation from Ernst Bertram, "You can but live, and living is enough." Its hero, Andreas Magnus, flees his upper-class home and Ursula, the woman he chastely adores, for Berlin. There he moves into a boardinghouse filled with cabaret dancers and prostitutes. One of these, Niels, becomes his god. The casually bisexual Niels fools around with numerous men and women, sparing Andreas a few hours. When the goodhearted Fredericka becomes pregnant with Niels's baby, she declares that the child belongs to her and Andreas, Niels's truest lovers: he will be "our son."

The novel veers between journalistic detachment and metaphysical kitsch. At the end Andreas follows Niels to Paris. The two are briefly reconciled, strolling through Les Halles arm in arm as the day breaks. They walk past the gaping bellies of butchered cows: "This is the way flesh smells," observes Andreas, maudlin even in his sensuality. An old woman tries to sell flowers to the young "flâneur avec son bel ami." It's actually a bold conception, the kind of dewy lovers' stroll you expect in a movie like Ophüls's *Liebelei*, except that here the lovers are male and Klaus instinctively places them in an economic context: "two charming loiterers . . . laden with flowers among the working classes."

After Niels leaves him, Andreas has a vision of the Virgin Mary, her face "kindly as a mother's, gentle as a lover's after the first night, mysterious as the face of a sister." (In his autobiography Jesus lands onto Klaus's Olympus, witty, vivacious, and "incredibly handsome.") He writes Ursula that his sexual experimentation resembles a religious vocation. "Commotion is on the verge of becoming peace. Life is on the verge of becoming death. . . . Besides a festival is not something frivolous or chic, or thoughtless." With no humor at all, he writes, "The human body is beautiful in all places. I love the human body." The novel ends with Andreas running through the streets. He passes a boy in blue shorts, "in all his brief boy's life had he ever been so urgently loved as in this drunken moment. . . ." Farther on, he admires laborers and construction workers. His adoration becomes a pious dance: "He was a runner, praying."

Klaus's later novels are better, though not much. But their quality may be irrelevant. Klaus portrays the operatic extremes that attend a life, situated between the underworld and show business, yet suffused with every passionate utterance from Platen's lyrics to the rosary. As ingenuous as his father, though far less artful, he captures the special forms of gay sentimentality.

He had the family curse of appearing too serious to be good company. Anglo-American homosexuals found him stuffy. On July 21, 1940, in New York he phoned Glenway Wescott, hoping to spirit "poor, dear old Gide" out of France. Wescott found him a "tragic twerp." Likewise during World War II Klaus would argue on the radio with his brother-in-law W. H. Auden. (Auden had married Erika to provide her with a passport: "What else are buggers good for?" he remarked.)* Auden, having grown disillusioned with socialism, felt that artists should avoid politics altogether. Klaus vehemently disagreed. Auden's contempt for his wife's family is evident in the anecdote, perhaps apocryphal, that he would take pickups to the Mann home in Pacific Palisades and make love to them in Thomas Mann's bed.

The animosity was not unidirectional. Thomas and Klaus would refer to Auden's friend Christopher Isherwood as "the starry-eyed one." They considered the Englishmen muddle-headed. Klaus ended his 1943 autobiography with his induction into the United States Army. It was for him a happy ending, despite the war. At last all the contradictions were locked in place; solidarity was no longer a slogan, the imperialists and the socialists were allies, the lion had lain down with the lamb. His English friends Isherwood, Auden, and Aldous Huxley might be paralyzed with skepticism, but Klaus knew what to do. He enlisted even before his naturalization papers were stamped. To his dismay the army rejected him. As revealed in his FBI dossier, he had been identified as a left-wing radical and a homosexual.

So, like Thomas in his 1920 letter to Carl Maria Weber, Klaus was forced to prevaricate. He insisted to the army investigators that he was in no way "abnormal." He was a red-blooded heterosexual. All the misconceptions could be traced to his father's story "The Blood of the Walsungs," he explained, and that was composed before he was born. Years later, after reading Klaus's files, Golo chuckled over his brother's duplicity.

At the one moment when Klaus saw things most clearly, he was obliged to play the hypocrite. Using his father's work to exculpate himself was the ironic fulfillment of a story that had begun perhaps as early as those weeks when Thomas Mann had recognized the nature of his love for Klaus. Klaus used his father's fiction to make things easier for himself—after his induction, he became a correspondent for *Stars and Stripes*, as well as seeing action during the 1944 invasion of Italy. Meanwhile Thomas had already dramatized the plight of a genius's son. In *The Beloved Returns*, proximity to his father nearly destroys August von Goethe. The sage exhibits an Olympian sympathy—geniuses indeed do not have gifted children—and remembers most fondly when August was a beautiful thirteen-year-old, Klaus's age when Thomas had similarly loved his oldest son.

Fame undid Klaus Mann. In 1948, after he attempted suicide, his father wrote Adorno, "It is a good sign that he curses the publicity that followed

---

* A year after Auden married Erika, his friend John Simpson married Thérèse Giehse, Erika's theatrical partner and lesbian companion.

the incident." He expressed some anger for what Klaus's behavior had done to Katia; they both had spoiled him with "understanding." He feared that the boy had too much of his aunt Julia in him. Yet there was a saving grace—a domestic citadel. Whenever Klaus gives up, unlike his aunt "he has a parental home he can always rely on."

The only fictional glimpse of that parental home occurs in Mann's great story "Disorder and Early Sorrow." It was published in June 1925, the month of his fiftieth birthday. His style is as light and easy as a feuilleton sketch—Klaus's world demands Klaus's tone. Yet it is packed with historical resonance, and involves a psychic drama far more perverse than anything poor Klaus could imagine.

As usual he plays up the social ramifications of his domestic sketch. The story is simple enough: Professor Cornelius, an historian, presides over a household brought low by inflation. His wife remains offstage, overworked and exhausted. The professor keeps to his study, trying not to interfere with his four children. The two eldest, Ingrid and Bert—the "big folk"—inhabit a world of actors and bohemians: the haute bourgeoisie intersecting with the denizens of cabaret. The two youngest are Abel and Lorchen: the latter, like her model, Elisabeth, at the moment her father's favorite. The "big folk" give a party, during which a charming friend, Max, "a perfect Aladdin" (in reality, the son of a dentist), dances with the five-year-old Lorchen. In the casual atmosphere, with girls dancing with girls, boys with boys, this coupling goes unremarked. But when Lorchen is called to bed, she becomes hysterical over the prospect of leaving her glamorous partner. Cornelius is distraught that she must learn so early the torments of love.

He is as impotent as any father when it comes to protecting his child. Seldom has Mann treated so universal a complaint. But he does it his way; the professor's historical perspective turns a domestic drama into a social critique. More than that, the details of youthful androgyny make the story a surprising complement to Klaus's *Pious Dance*. The characters are drawn from life: Bert and Ingrid are obviously Klaus and Erika; the Manns' chauffeur, Ludwig, is reborn as Xaver Kleinsgutl ("little fortune"—a harsh, South German name in the "Klöterjahn" tradition). Cornelius is a historian, not a novelist, but he specializes in lost causes. He writes about Philip II, the Spanish ruler during the Counter Reformation: a "belated" figure, operating "against the whole trend of history—against the new, kingdom-disrupting power and Germanic idea of freedom and individual liberty." This sounds perilously close to Thomas Mann in the last stages of his

Reflections, fighting an intellectual Masada against the coming victory of democracy.

Though he composed the story in 1925, it takes place during the 1923 inflation, "these desolate, distracted times." With their worn and shabby clothes, the parents barely represent their class; meanwhile their children belong to the "villa proletariat." Among the servants, Fräulein Cecelia has fallen from middle to working class. Refusing to wear "a cap or other badge of servitude . . . she passes the dishes with averted face and elevated gaze." One evening Abel and Lorchen observe her suffering, and "both with one accord burst into tears." She is someone Mann could have described in *Buddenbrooks*, with all the class confusions of Aunt Tony—or of Julia Löhr.

Changes in wardrobe and physical manner obfuscate all distinctions, sexual or economic. Boys wear rouge, girls wear pants; the household prince Bert wants to be "a dancer, a cabaret actor—or a waiter." Xaver, the chauffeur, is his mirror image, a late-rising fop who deigns to work when he feels like it—Mann would shortly lament the disappearance of reliable servants. Xaver and Bert sport the same long hair, "give their heads the same characteristic toss to throw it off the forehead," wear the same blouses "rakishly girt with a leather strap." In another setting, it's easy to imagine the two dancing together; though, as the professor observes, all the physical grace belongs to the chauffeur.

Who before Mann had so described a character like Xaver, this working-class, bohemian Bolshevik, master of the harmonica, the shimmy, and the fox-trot?

> With his whole soul he loves the cinema; after an evening spent there he inclines to melancholy and yearning and talking to himself. Vague hopes stir in him that some day he may make his fortune in that gay world and belong to it by rights—hopes based on his shock of hair and his physical agility and daring. He likes to climb the ash tree in the front garden . . . once there he lights a cigarette and smokes it as he sways to and fro, keeping a lookout for a cinema director who might chance to come along and engage him.

Xaver could be any pretty boy Klaus might ogle in an after-hours club. For Mann, who shared Klaus's susceptibility, this parody of self-representation is rich. The excruciating tactics of Thomas Buddenbrook are hilariously reincarnated in the lazy, self-infatuated Xaver, posed for an audition. The image of Buddenbrook on a podium fades into Xaver waiting for his closeup.

All these observations are *echt* Mannian. And who else would be so struck by the decline of etiquette? Nobody has manners anymore; everyone addresses each other by first name (Peeperkorn's "Sie" and "Du" games become as anachronistic as his imitations of Tolstoy). It is popular culture —and its emphasis on androgyny and bisexuality—that prompts the change. Without stressing the point, Mann suggests that political and sexual liberation are indivisible, and, given the economic conditions, ineluctable, whatever the professors think.

The professor himself is a pretty queer fellow. Perhaps no writer before Mann had so captured the obsessive nature of parental love. Cornelius adores Lorchen as intensely as Aschenbach loves Tadzio. His feelings are not quite without calculation. He has been "preparing for it . . . been prepared for it." A sense of duty and obligation have finally paid off: as Mann wrote, Elisabeth was the first child he spontaneously loved. His "conservative instinct" finds an eternal image in "father love and a little child on its mother's breast." But this affirmation of "family values" is a rear-guard strategy. "There is something ulterior about it, in the nature of it; that something is hostility, hostility against the history of today, which is still in the making and thus not history at all, in behalf of the genuine history that has already happened—that is to say, death."

We remember that this story is composed in the present tense, unlike *The Magic Mountain*, with its counterpoint of historically ripened moments. Sure enough, Mann observes that Cornelius's devotion has "something to do with death, it clings to death as against life, and that is neither right nor beautiful—in a sense." Paternal love becomes a political statement! In Cornelius's ideology, the nuclear family symbolizes death; and the post-heterosexual choreography, its living—and terrifying—alternative.

The youngsters jabber away while Cornelius retires in gloom. Anything can set him off: the cigarette smoke becomes "particularly poignant to those whose youth—like the professor's own—has been oversensitive." (There may be an echo of Mann's early tales of tobacco-induced highs.) He chooses Philip II because he exemplifies "things steeped in melancholy and penetratingly just." Therefore, while "it behooves one to display the scientific spirit, to exhibit the principles of enlightenment," simply not to offend anyone's political sensibility, he can't quite manage this epistemological pluralism (a reflection of the "Neue Sachlichkeit"—New Objectivity—that supposedly characterized the 1920s). Justice has a "secret affinity with the lost cause," even if his children tell him that "taking sides is unhistoric now."

Only one of the young guests shares his feelings. The actor Herzl (Gründgens?) is a "revolutionary artist" with a bad conscience. He wears rouge but is "exaggeratedly polite" to "mitigate its effect." Cornelius wonders, "How can a melancholy man rouge?" Coming from a Mann brother, Heinrich or Thomas, this qualifies as a rhetorical question.

The essayistic musings on history are interrupted by word that Lorchen has become hysterical. But Max comes to the rescue; the idea is Xaver's. He kisses Lorchen's forehead, begs her not to dream of him—"not at your age"—and leaves her to sleep away her troubles. The professor's response is ambivalent. In the great tradition of Tonio Kröger, he feels "thankfulness, embarrassment and hatred." Attraction, too, we can guess.

The happy ending self-destructs. Cornelius thinks of a tale in which a dying child asks to see a clown "he had once, with unforgettable ecstasy, beheld in a circus." The clown appears, and the child dies contented; even Cornelius finds this analogy morbid. But he's not only grieving for his child. Mann/Cornelius brings his own years of rejection to the "big folks' " dance. His own chance had passed, had he ever possessed the will to grab it, and now the child of his heart would live again the Mannian cycle of unrequited love.

Even without this highly biographical reading, "Early Sorrow" marks a transition in Mann's career, quite literally from offspring to parent. In his earlier works the sons had caught out the fathers—whether it was Hanno seeing through his father's disguise, or Felix Krull reporting on the "poison" his father bottled as wine—and helped to bury them. Likewise, sexual precocity was experienced by the youthful subjects, even that delayed adolescent Hans Castorp. But starting with this story, Mann's focus switches. Now it's the father who sees desire manifest itself, virtually in the cradle. The romance of Jacob and Joseph may then be read as Mann's only successful attempt to know both lovers from within!

By June 1925, the month the story appeared, Mann had decided that his next project would be a triptych of novellas, based on the lives of three historical figures: the Old Testament Joseph, the Renaissance humanist Erasmus, and Professor Cornelius's hero, Philip II. He had been thinking of them for years—a portrait of Erasmus had graced his first chambers, and, according to *Tonio Kröger*, the weeping Spanish king had enthralled him since his adolescence. The interest in Joseph was more recent. It is usually traced to December 1923, when Hermann Ebers, a Munich artist and friend of Katia's, "showed me a portfolio of illustrations of his, depicting quite prettily the story of Joseph the son of Jacob."

In retrospect, we can guess why this project attracted him as a successor to *The Magic Mountain*. Philip II stood for his devotion to lost causes, the atmosphere of the *Reflections*, while Erasmus symbolized his more recent politics, as expressed in "Goethe and Tolstoy" or "The German Republic." Yet of the three, only Joseph would receive a complete fictional account, perhaps because, as a beautiful youth, he offered the most appealing image.

Mann's next story, "Mario and the Magician" (1929), was also drawn from his experiences as a doting father. The occasion was a vacation trip to Forte dei Marmi during the summer of 1926. The first half of the story recalls the domestic tone of "Early Sorrow." A couple of German tourists allow their little girl to run nude along the beach. But fascism has made the Italians prudish (a surprising addendum to the Mann brothers' arguments over lascivious Rome). Controverting *Death in Venice*, they regard the northerners as orgiastic interlopers. The second half of the story involves a display of the magician Cipolla's powers.

The latter's downfall occurs when he hypnotizes the handsome young waiter Mario into believing that the magician—ugly, humpbacked—is really his girlfriend. Brought to his senses, Mario shoots and kills him. This atypically melodramatic ending was suggested by Erika; equally atypical was Mann's editorializing conclusion: the death was a "liberation." (See the upcoming chapter 7, "A Political Light.") Yet consider that "Magician" was his children's nickname for Mann, or that for every Hermes in his work, there's a Michelangelo or an Aschenbach, an artist deploying the tricks of his trade to win an impossible prize.

These two stories give both sides of Thomas Mann: the Magician and the magician, the paterfamilias, guilty at worst of loving his child too much, and the lover of young men, who must rely on artful imprecations. (In 1950, a Hollywood movie adaptation was planned. The screenplay introduced the possibility of an affair between Mario and the narrator's wife!)

I n these domestic sketches the wife seldom plays a role. "Early Sorrow" describes her as "languid . . . broken and worn" by the household responsibilities. In the children's memoirs she appears as a resourceful manager, slightly giddy, unlike their abstract, abstracted father.

Where Thomas "never seemed to remember exactly with whom [Klaus] lived," Katia noticed everything but may have avoided the sexual implications. Consider this episode when Mann asked his son his recent whereabouts.

> My mother [was] very much accustomed to act as mediator between
> him and a world whose extraneous details constantly evaded his mind.
> . . . "But, darling, didn't I tell you only yesterday that Klaus has had
> a very interesting time in Paris with his friend Crevel? But you know
> Crevel—the nice one, with the bushy hair and beautiful eyes. Of
> course, you know him quite well: we met him at this ghastly party at

Katia Mann and her favorite son, Klaus, 1927

your publisher's house, when we were in Paris, last spring. He talked so rapidly, you couldn't understand him at all. . . ." And then, my father would say something about René, which proved that he knew much more about him than I had expected.

To be sure.

Thirty years later, the American writer Frederic Morton noticed a similar quality. Morton, himself an émigré, was alert to the family's bourgeois decorum. Herr Mann looked like a prosperous Swiss businessman, while Frau Mann seemed positively dapper, a vivacious woman quite proud to serve as her husband's publicist. At one point, describing his recently completed *Felix Krull*, Mann said that he wished to incorporate "matrimonial and penitentiary episodes." Katia responded, "Please don't make them sound so synonymous."

Katia Mann was clearly very smart and ferociously loyal to her family. During the 1920s, she had not merely to contend with the universal domestic complaints: food was scarce, the children frequently sick. Periodically her consumption flared up. In addition, there were constant worries over Klaus, his failures in school, his flights to Berlin, his erratic disposition. Her beloved Erika's marriage to Gustaf Gründgens was, to say the least, questionable, and didn't last. Her flighty sister-in-law Lula was another burden; and Heinrich remained "the strangest man I ever met." Meanwhile, her own family was not peaceful. The Pringsheim fortune was greatly reduced. (Happily, *The Magic Mountain* obviated the need for gifts to the Manns. Now the generosity went in the other direction.) Her mother continued to lament Pringsheim's very public infidelities. The scandal of her brother Erik, murdered in South America by a cuckolded husband, balanced the Mann history of suicides and mental collapse.

That she kept the family going, establishing the "parental home" about which Mann boasted to Adorno, makes her the heroic figure of Thomas Mann's life. Yet he fails to create any female character who reflects her intellectual and moral strengths. Rachel, Jacob's wife and Joseph's mother, is a charming figure, and her death in childbirth—its grueling details drawn from Katia's pregnancy—brought the whole family to tears when Mann read it to them. But Katia was too feisty for pathos. We know that she missed very little. Thomas informed her in 1950 of his love for the waiter Franzl. As for *Death in Venice*, she tells her children in *Unwritten Memories* that he was "infatuated" with the Polish boy, "although he didn't pursue him." To the American publisher William Koshland she was even franker. Tired of the endless inquiries, she exclaimed, "Can't you see he was in love?"

There are hints of an amiable marital arrangement. On November 18, 1933, Thomas wrote Heinrich that Katia was suffering from "a female ailment, non-threatening, but probably a signal for reduced future activity." Five months later, on April 23, 1934, Mann acquires a young fan, Hans Rascher, to whom he offers a complimentary ticket for that night's lecture. "I seem to have made a conquest there, or so Katia thinks." The boy was about Tadzio's age, "his delicately modeled face . . . disfigured by scars. But his eyes are still beautiful, or rather gentle."

Two days later, another youth caught his eye.

Passing the plant nursery I was pleasantly smitten by the sight of a young fellow working there, a brown-haired type with a small cap on his head, very handsome, and bare to the waist. The rapture I felt at the sight of such common, everyday and natural "beauty," the contours of his chest, the swell of his biceps, made me reflect afterward on the unreal, illusionary, and aesthetic nature of such an inclination, the goal of which, it would appear, is realized in gazing and "admiring." Although erotic, it requires no fulfillment at all, neither intellectually nor physically. This is likely thanks to the influence of the reality principle on the imagination; it allows the rapture but limits it to just looking.

A Katia might allow this obsession with young men when it was so definitively circumscribed. Yet, since Mann saw fit to employ analytic jargon, one might note a charged error he had recently made. On February 25, preparing for a new section of *Joseph in Egypt*, he "studied up on the sex of trees" and was struck by "the mystical motif of bisexuality." This reminded him of Platen, his favorite poet, and he proceeded to quote lines filled with "enormous . . . spiritual fervor, their mythical roots far deeper than I had previously realized":

> I am as wife to man, as man to wife to you
> I am as body to spirit, as spirit to body to you.

In fact, he had transposed the lines, thereby emphasizing the physical and erotic union before the spiritual. This Freudian slip was no less revealing than his adherence to the "reality principle."

Following the line of 1933, he wrote in 1935 that at sixty he lacked the enthusiasm ("always girls") Goethe displayed in his seventies. But whenever Thomas Mann grew smug, life tended to surprise him. At seventy-five he would lament as yet again "the loins sprang up." For once he allowed that he would enjoy tender embraces with Franzl, though it's not clear whether this restraint expressed his weakened condition, his fear that greater intimacies would be rejected, or his limited erotic repertory. However, he enjoys figures of speech for sexual intercourse, particularly in *The Holy Sinner* with its neologisms like *"Fickfackerei."* (His insistence that adoration was enough, that he sought no other fulfillment, was echoed almost fifty years later by Roland Barthes: "Mere eye contact and an exchange of words eroticizes me." Like Mann, Barthes would find this a temporary consolation.)

In America Katia exhibited the familiar resources of émigré wives. As always, she had to manage the house, drive the car, communicate with the servants.* Klaus continued to perplex her. In 1941, after yet another botched suicide attempt by her eldest son, she asked Elisabeth, "If you

* When he was seventy-seven, Mann described Katia's role as the family administrator: "She sits and types my dictated letters, records, publishing payments. She works out the tax declarations, and writes long, motherly letters of advice."

want to kill yourself, can't you be more efficient?" That's the irreverent tone, the *Berliner Schnauze*, of her grandmother Hedwig Dohm, the gallows humor that émigrés came to regard as common sense, the exile's natural idiom.

The Mann family specialized in Gippern. In "Early Sorrow," the oldest children develop a telephone language, all code and private metaphor. There seems to have been a great deal of talk about psychoanalysis, Erika being particularly attuned to every new trend. One California neighbor, Yalta Menuhin, complained to her son that the Manns only discussed homosexuality. (She much preferred the less graphic language of her favorite writer, Willa Cather, perhaps not realizing that Cather was a lesbian or that she had been deeply impressed by Mann's Joseph tetralogy.)

But this talk may have simply been gauged to Mann's needs. In 1949 he writes that Erika has determined that Frido, Michael's son, then all of nine years old, would make a perfect homosexual. Mann didn't approve, and in fact she was wrong. But couldn't she have said it because Mann worshiped his grandson, calling him his "last love"? Similarly she mocked Thomas's crush on Franzl but insisted that he retain Felix Krull's flirtation with the old Scottish lord, a replay of the Zurich encounter. Tact was a sign of fidelity. In 1933, when Mann asked Golo to transport his diaries out of Germany, he requested that they be left unread. Golo obliged, thus sparing himself the revelations that his father also loved men, and that even there he preferred Klaus as an object of his incestuous desires.

The diaries indicate Mann's loyalty to Katia. She was the enduring center of his life. Even when he describes the latest Hermes, Katia remains a presence. For example, on November 29, 1950, he could write that Gore Vidal's homosexual novel *The City and the Pillar* had stimulated and inspired him, and in the same entry observe that "Katia and Erika [still mourning Klaus] cling even less to life than I do." Which is to say that he juggled two realities: "young men are my suffering and my delight," and he was the husband of a magnificent woman and the father of six complicated children.

Under these circumstances marriage became his breastplate buckle, his invisible shield, the "abstract institution" that ordered his life. This becomes evident in the essay on marriage he contributed to a 1925 anthology on the subject. It is a peculiar piece, a limp apology for heterosexual love. Mann's essay was designed to counter André Gide, who a year earlier had published his autobiography, discussing both his sexless marriage and his promiscuous homosexuality. After finishing the essay in August 1925, he wrote Erika that it was "a rather comprehensive document, highly moral, and includes an objective account of homoeroticism. . . ." It seems that the only alternative to marriage he could imagine was love of boys. Once again, as if by design, he gave himself away.

Mann treats marriage as a historical phenomenon, lately imperiled by the twin forces of feminism and "boy love." He admits that the past cannot be recaptured; his tone is generally liberal, and he opposes any "obscurantist" flight into outmoded historical forms. In modern society the "domestic sphere," as Kant knew it, has vanished. Simply expressed, this means that "domestic service" no longer exists.

The feminist movement, Mann says, was once "ridiculous and childish" (fortunately Hedwig Dohm did not live to read these words). But today it is absolutely natural for the sexes to dress alike, to meet as equals in education, sports, or politics. He sketches the traits of an emancipated woman, "bike-riding, driving, studying, masculine intelligence" (all of them exemplified by Katia Mann). But concomitant with the strong woman is a feminized male. Gallantry has gone the way of household help. The young man today sees himself as "beautiful," and "in human terms" this means something other than "male."

The phenomenon of male narcissism leads, inevitably, to homosexuality. Mann cites Gide's "passionate dialectical apology." He offers his own, but the dialectics are questionable and the passion invisible. As he presents it, "boy love" is the equivalent of art for art's sake, amoral and antinatural. It should not be censured—Greek states thrived under it—but it shouldn't be overvalued, either. Simply put, it is "immoral, unfaithful, unproductive"; it counterposes a "sterile libidinage" to "foundation" and "generativity." In other words, gay men don't make babies.

Mann realizes this is a skimpy argument. He confesses his love for Platen, the great poet of a doomed and transient beauty, the master of a homoerotic aesthetic, alienated from nature and life, though not from art. He contends that artists must be "ironic mediators" between the two forms of love. Like Hans Castorp, they are life's problem children, consigned to moral purity and goodness. At twenty-four he knew the other side: "I could tell" and show the lure of "individual metaphysics" to the wearied and distracted Thomas Buddenbrook. He admits the affinity between Buddenbrook and Aschenbach. There but for marriage might Thomas Mann have gone as well. But there is a "way of the spirit," lately endorsed by Hans Castorp, and it delivered Mann from his characters' fate.

Barely two years earlier Mann had found in Whitman's tribe of loving comrades the origins of democracy. Now he gleans another "sexual community," built on a "sacramental and spiritual foundation," offering the comforts of "institutional stability." He allows that women can no longer be dominated. In this post-patriarchal era, marriage must be reconceived, but spirit and good faith will renew it.

Marriage is moral, politically justified, a social necessity. But Mann never suggests that it's fun. He allows that it often survives the decline of sexual interest. Together with his tribute to the smart, bike-riding modern wife, this may be addressed to Katia. The gentle jeremiad against Gide was probably meant for Klaus. But it all rings hollow. In 1928 Mann complained that his editorials in support of democracy were artistically inferior to his reactionary *Reflections*. Not always, we might argue, especially in the liveliest passages of "The German Republic." But he writes better under than outside Platen's shadow. He would later incorporate some of the marriage essay in a tribute to the poet, this time without any of the gratuitous censure. In the interim his other life caught up with him, making the marriage essay seem quaint, if not downright hypocritical. Yet, as usual, Mann gives good value; his tough-thinking bicyclist and new-breed dandy survive the sloppy dialectics.

Gustav von Aschenbach was the moral arbiter of his generation until a glimpse of Tadzio made him break his own rules. It was thus a Mannian form of poetic justice that an encounter with a youth would make a sham of his marriage essay. In August 1927 Mann took a vacation at Kampen on the northern island of Sylt, together with Katia, Monika, Elisabeth, and Michael. There he met the art historian Werner Heuser and fell in love with his seventeen-year-old son, Klaus. Two months later, Mann invited the boy to Munich. During his fortnight visit, Klaus H. met Klaus M. Obviously coupling with a twenty-one-year-old made more sense than with a fifty-two-year-old. Thomas implies as much in an astonishing letter he wrote Klaus and Erika, dated October 19.

> Yesterday I wrote a detailed letter to Kläuschen Hauser who left here eight days ago. This Klaus, as distinguished from Eissi [Klaus Mann], is as a fact probably overestimated. I call him *Du*, and he consented to my embracing him on my breast. Eissi is herewith asked to voluntarily withdraw and not to invade my circle. I am already old and famous, and why should you be the only ones who constantly sin, because of that? I have it in writing that these two weeks were the most beautiful of his life, and that it has been difficult to return home. I believe that, and the sobriety of his expression must be taken into consideration, for here he was overwhelmed with amusements. And

better still, in a little climax, I read in the theater at the Kleist Festival, in his presence, from my analysis of *Amphitryon*, on which "he," if one may say so, was not without influence. The secret and almost silent adventures in life are the finest.

Circuitous, dense with qualifying asides, this remains a frank confession of intent, and a direct request that Klaus keep his hands off. "Secret and almost silent" no more, Thomas Mann informs his children not merely that he shares their predilection, but that a beloved youth could serve as his muse.

On October 10, in the Munich Schauspielhaus, Mann had indeed lectured on Heinrich von Kleist's *Amphitryon*. Nearly thirty years earlier, when he wrote Otto Grautoff that he wished to display his literary power before Paul Ehrenberg, he had dreamed of such a courtship. Whether Klaus Heuser understood that the lecture doubled as a lover's valediction is not known; this bliss most likely was Mann's alone, and, within his life, unique.

In Kleist's retelling of the myth, Jupiter visits Amphitryon's wife, disguised as her husband. Once the god puts on mortality, he becomes all too human; despising his power, he wishes to be loved for himself. This situation does not appear to be an exact parable of Mann's love for Klaus. Yet there are passages scattered throughout the essay that bespeak erotic liberation, as Mann understood it. He begins by rejecting a century of scholarship: "I mean to talk about [the play] as though it were new, as though I were the only person who had ever read it or talked about it." Hooray for the culture in which falling in love allows one to read better.

In Kleist's drama, the hub of action is nonverbal: "It is all expressed in the [smile,] where the unsearchable heights meet the unsearchable depths of the heart. The idea gleams through of election, of godlike arbitrary favor and the elevation of the unworthy." One smile from Tadzio's lips and Aschenbach becomes a new creature. But the drama of his situation is reconceived here as pure delight. Moreover, as in the introduction to *Joseph and His Brothers*, Mann reduces the sky above and the depths below to the dimensions of one man's heart, even as the universe descended into Hans Castorp's lap.

Two months later Mann visited the Heuser family in Düsseldorf. The actual romance may have ended then, but it continued to haunt him. In the early years of exile he thought back on the episode as "a late surprise, with a quality of benign fulfillment about it but already lacking the youthful intensity of feeling, the wild surges of exultation and deep despair" that ravaged him during the Paul Ehrenberg years. "This is doubtless the normal course of human affections," desire dwindling with the years, "and owing to this normality I can feel more strongly that my life conforms to the scheme of things than I do by virtue of marriage and children."

The brief affair was "more mature, more controlled, happier" than the one with Ehrenberg. In September 1935, after his children remembered how handsome Klaus had been, he thought back to "that time and its passion, the last variation of a love that probably will not flare up again. Strange, the happy and fulfilled man of fifty [*sic*]—and then *finis*." A week later he encountered Heuser at a hotel on Lake Lucerne. "Unchanged, or little changed, slim, still boyish at twenty-four, [*sic*] the eyes the same. Kept looking into his face and saying 'My God!' . . . He expected me to kiss him, but I did not do so. I did manage to say something loving to him before he left, however. It was all over in a moment as he had to leave almost at once."

Klaus lived on in his memories, and in the pages of his diary. On February 20, 1942, he writes, "Read a long time in the old diaries from the Klaus Heuser time when I was a happy lover. Most beautiful and touching, our farewell in Munich when I took for the first time, 'the leap into dream,' and rested his temple against mine. Well, I have lived and loved. Black eyes filled with tears over me. Lips which I kissed. It was there I also had it. I will be able to say that, when I die."

On May 6, 1943, in a letter to Bruno Walter he describes Frido, "grown much prettier than last time . . . my daily delight." The child has a "clumsy tongue" that speaks heart's truth. "When he has had enough of anything, or wants to console himself because there is no more of it, he says: *'habt'* ['had']. I find that perfect. When I am dying, I too shall say, *'habt.'* " He described both Klaus Heuser and Frido as his last love, the first in private, the second before the world. How better to express his memories of love, the moments that "conformed to the scheme of things," than using the most elementary language, a child's solecism? It remained a family affair.

During his last years, Mann's predilection became an open subject of conversation. When he was seventy-nine and living in Switzerland he met with Klaus Heuser's mother and learned that her son had spent eighteen years in China and had never married. Mann remembered that he had immortalized their love in the opening lines of an essay. As for Klaus's devotion? Erika observed, "If he couldn't have the Magician, he preferred to remain alone." Neither father nor daughter elaborated on the implications for the Magician himself.

6

"THE UNLOVED ONE"

I

In 1950 Hans Mayer described Thomas Mann as a friendless regent, presiding in isolation over German letters. Mann was appalled. He responded, "I was not, am not, and don't want to be unloved. I deny it, I won't have it. . . . I am a 'loving' person. I don't want to be thought of as 'unloved.'"

It was the old family problem, convincing the world that a formal manner disguised a loving heart. He was not persuasive; many reminiscences complained that he was a dull conversationalist, plodding and humorless. ("He never says anything profound" was how Golo's friends put it.) There is even a report that his American publisher, Alfred A. Knopf, referred to him as "that old bore." Knopf, who pooh-poohed his political engagement ("You're a Dichter, so dicht!"), was apparently no more sensitive to the real Mann than any of those who, as Mann had written Paul Ehrenberg, "respect my talent and find the actual man disgusting."

Representation exacted yet another price. In a lifetime that included 670 interviews, Mann wound up talking in private as if he were facing a microphone. His long-winded, excruciatingly well-considered "sound bites" would have impeded any chance of relaxed communication even if he weren't shy and self-conscious. (During Mann's early lecture tours of America, Rabbi Joachim Prinz used to preside over the question-and-answer periods when Erika was absent. One time, trying to make small talk, he congratulated the author on a new translation by H. T. Lowe-Porter. "Yes," Mann acknowledged, "greatness will come through.") To paraphrase Yeats, he made rhetoric out of social intercourse, art out of his secret life.

He had professionally correct relations with his fellow novelists, but a competitive note often intruded. Robert Musil courted his patronage, as we saw, and then proceeded to bad-mouth him shamelessly. In September 1938 Mann and Katia visited the Musils in Zurich. He offered to expedite Musil's immigration to America, where he was then in the catbird seat thanks to the publication of *Joseph in Egypt*. Martha Musil later reported that "Joe's father" (her idea of humor, or her husband's?) looked elegant and relaxed, but he remained "dry and dull," while the vivacious Katia resembled a prettier version of the Witch in "Hansel and Gretel."

A German-Austrian rivalry may have underlined such petty remarks. Mann was not immune. In private the Manns condescended to gossip, speculating about the Hofmannsthals and the Schnitzlers. There were also tragic parallels between these literary dynasties. In 1928 Schnitzler's nineteen-year-old daughter, Lili, committed suicide, as did Hofmannsthal's eldest son a year later.

Among his fellow Germans, Mann's allies were men he knew to be his inferiors—Bruno Frank, Alfred Neumann, and (this friendship is disputable) Lion Feuchtwanger. Inge Jens depicts him as "always the star," outshining his satellites, and she implies that they were chosen for the dim light they cast.

Meanwhile, his old enemy remained afoot. Alfred Kerr might contend that he was maintaining standards, but it didn't help that he had courted Katia at the same time as Mann. She claims that his response upon learning of her engagement was to pull his beard and swear, "I can only become a drunk, kill myself, or both." Instead, he applied his violent tendencies in print.

Kerr's critique of *Fiorenza* had enraged Mann with its "murderous nature." The Berliner had more in store for the Uncle Bräsig of modern letters. In 1925, after *The Magic Mountain*'s publication, Kerr published a sixty-stanza satirical poem about Thomas Bodenbruch (literally "Groundbreak"):

> As a boy I was already ossified,
> Catty, because my talents were so small.
> Then I rampaged through literature
> With a bourgeois, patrician folly.
> I always discuss in detail my parents' bankruptcy.

Kerr didn't grant Mann any creative advantage; he called him a "phony patient," incapable of rendering the invalid's condition—so much for Hans Castorp's years on the mountain. Kerr concludes:

What a consolation, I excel everyone in thoroughness and dullness.
I remain the treasure of educated families.
They appreciate and never contradict Thomas Bodenbruch
I am in short the pride of the middle class.

Kerr jabbed Mann to the quick; Mann might represent himself as a "doubtful charlatan" or a "vain puppy," but "middlebrow" was unforgivable. At one point Kerr has the unfortunate Bodenbruch say, "I've been cursed by a piston-nose," an ironic payback for the anti-Semitism of his early years—a Jew making fun of "die alte Familien Nase"!

In 1925 there were friendlier outpourings. Upon Mann's fiftieth birthday, congratulations arrived from several writers. Among the well-wishers, Jakob Wassermann applauded "the dialectical voices of his orchestra," Musil declared his symphonic novel a great work of conscience, and Max Brod recollected Franz Kafka's admiration of the early stories. Hauptmann and Mann had reconciled. Was he not entitled to boast, as he would twenty-five years later, of his literary friendships?

Hardly. As we saw, Musil never stopped regarding Mann as a dangerous middlebrow, diverting attention from his superiors. Brod had employed the birthday occasion to promote Kafka, his lifetime project. Hauptmann was a dubious ally, not a little cracked, as became terribly clear in his later career as a Nazi. Though Mann shared the first years of exile with Wassermann, and sympathized with the Jewish despair, he also confided in his diary that Wassermann's technique no longer interested him.

Most troubling was a similarity of ambitions with other authors. On March 9, 1944, after reading Hesse's *Magister Ludi*, Mann became disturbed by the parallels with *Doctor Faustus*, a novel he had yet to complete. "Frightening. Same idea of fictional biography. The reminder that one is not alone in the world is always unpleasant."

There had been a time when Mann did not stand alone, when all his works were compared, ipso facto, with another's. The looming presence had been Heinrich. But by 1944, that competition was irrelevant.* In 1918 Thomas had prophesied that neither he nor Heinrich would survive the war

---

* Though their letters were uniformly conciliatory, at least once in his journal (August 2, 1937), Thomas described Heinrich's latest, filled with praise of the Soviet Union, as "one-sided, naïve, and, as always, unjust in his sense of his own importance."

with their reputations intact. He lived to see half of his prophecy realized. The career of Heinrich—his mirror, his brother—lay in ruins.

A photo from the 1920s shows the two brothers together, smiling in their self-contained fashion, standing on a brick sidewalk, city lights behind them. Both are models of elegance: each sports a homburg; Heinrich wears a tuxedo and a bow tie; Thomas, spats. Heinrich's goatee is neatly trimmed, as is Thomas's mustache. If any unrest is apparent, it may be in Heinrich's tightly gripped hands; Thomas, either more relaxed or more secretive, keeps his in his pockets. The photo whispers politely that these men have won.

In fact, their reconciliation had worked only in Thomas's favor. A socialist perspective had enriched and deepened his art, but it was less happy an influence on Heinrich's career. He made *Der Untertan* the first part of a trilogy, *Das Kaiserreich*, which was supposed to examine all the classes. The second volume, *Die Armen* (*The Poor*, 1917), revolves around Balrich, an employee of the monstrous Diederich Hessling. From an enraged activist he develops into a "son of the spirit" and winds up a lawyer, buying into the system to fight its exploiters. The vanguard shoots itself in the foot. In the third novel of the trilogy, *Der Kopf* (*The Chief*, 1925), two largely impotent intellectuals take on the Establishment. Their peregrinations across the ideological landscape only confuse the reader; politics seem reduced to a metaphor for literary *Geist*. In another 1925 work, the novella *Kobes*, the title figure is a profiteer—two years earlier, during the inflation, Heinrich had observed that "the wealthiest people" had conquered the country without a putsch. Kobes's only enemy is an employee of his Propaganda Department, Cabaret Division, who hopes to kill his boss with comedy. It is typical that Heinrich conceives political dissent as a nightclub routine, a tendency realized with great success by his niece Erika in her 1930s traveling revue, *The Pepper Mill*. (George Grosz contributed sketches to the book's first edition, indicating a congruent assessment of the Berlin robber barons.) But the efforts fail, the satire is misunderstood, and the intellectual commits suicide.

Heinrich wrote tributes to youth and the working class, aware that for neither was he a convincing spokesman. His books stopped selling, and he wound up doing free-lance work—newspaper articles, radio lectures, even an appearance at a Berlin department store. His writings of the 1920s support a bewildering range of positions, from the acutely critical to the amorphously spiritual. He attempted a series of entertainments, trying to compete with movies and potboilers, only to be outdone by *The Blue Angel*.

His always brilliant literary essays began to discover the origins of modern politics: in an essay on Stendhal he discerned the "fascists of capitalism" gathering their strengths even before the French Revolution. This certainly sounds like dialectical materialism. Yet he so despised the agitprop Marxism of his day that he began to extol "spirit" in whatever form he found it. The lifelong agnostic suddenly praised the church as "the only form in which the West has seen the spirit triumphant over nonspiritual powers. . . ." Later he said, "We must found our church"—shortly before he found his haven in a heartless world: Stalinism.

This brief homage to religion suffused his worst novel, *Mutter Marie* (1927), in which a reckless woman and her spoiled protégé are spiritually transformed—she, quite literally, when she regains her childhood faith in Jesus. Like Diederich Hessling, she vanishes as the novel ends, but if he retires to his banal hell, the whore-saint flies to heaven. The novel appeared in America translated by Whittaker Chambers. In Heinrich's career, it was yet another blow that his translator would later inform on his comrades.

Heinrich divorced Mimi Kanová in 1930. He had long exhibited a weakness for soubrettes. In 1928 he took up with Trude Hesterburg, a Berlin actress. When Josef von Sternberg purchased Heinrich's novel *Professor Unrat* for the movies, Hesterburg expected to play Rosa. She lost out to a younger performer, Marlene Dietrich. Rosa became Lola; Dietrich became a star; and Heinrich would be left to complain that his reputation depended on Hitler's book-burning and Marlene's legs: had they only been Trude's!

By the late 1920s Thomas's victory in the fraternal conflict was self-evident. On August 27, 1927, Heinrich wrote: "You know as well as I do myself that your honors and successes do not bother me. Sometimes a few crumbs are even tossed my way," and he proceeded to quote a published remark that the Mann family were the absolute rulers of German literature.

But the poor quality and commercial failure of Heinrich's novels distressed them both. Even as Thomas continued to promote his brother, integrity—and perhaps a residual fit of competition—obliged him to qualify his praise. In 1930 he reviewed *The Big Deal*, Heinrich's satire of postwar capitalism. He found the novel overloaded with "stimuli," a less-than-artful blend of "sloppiness and brilliance, contemporary slang and intellectual drama."

In a left-handed compliment he compared Heinrich to such radical modernists as Hamsun, Döblin, and Hemingway (one of his first citations of an American writer) and concluded that Heinrich surpassed them all in single-minded nihilism. No reactionary, he said, could have waged so merciless an attack on German democracy. Heinrich seemed to value almost nothing—and this was one of Thomas's affirmative periods. Tellingly, he finds a lack of "epic" humanity and good nature: obviously the brothers' literary ambitions still did not converge.

But he did applaud one breakthrough in the novel. Any hope for politics came in a sexual guise. "Social spirit is an erotic spirit," Mann explains. ". . . Spirit with sex, phallic spirit, spirit infusing the artist." This restates his own paean to democracy. And immediately he adds that erotic sensibility is not "narrow." At "a wild business conference," a young man flirts with his boss—Thomas alludes to an encounter he had imagined more than once. As the youth summons him with a charming smile, the boss begins to contemplate "a new turn to his emotional life. . . ." Mann applauds this adumbration of his own affectional preference: "Excellent." Not since the homoerotic story "Abdankung" had he expressed such a full-throated identification. The "new turn" possibly reminded him of the way Klaus Heuser had transformed his life.

Ultimately Heinrich would acknowledge most of Thomas's criticisms. In 1934, absorbed in the second part of his masterpiece, *Henry, King of France*, he dismissed his social novels as "oldish." It had been a doomed, quixotic task to celebrate the republic while it was collapsing before his eyes. A decade later he admitted that he had not sufficiently resisted temptation in life—or in art: "The two are the same." His father's practice should have been his model, since "there is no genius outside of business hours."

Although Erika and Katia played strong roles in his life, Mann had few women friends. He wrote admiring essays about the novelist Ida Boy-Ed and the historian Ricarda Huch. Annette Kolb remained a chum for years, until his unflattering depiction of her in *Doctor Faustus*. He met the Nuremberg bookseller Ida Herz in 1925 and maintained a lifelong friendship with her. It was motored largely by her phenomenal devotion. Once again life imitated his fiction; the stumbling wallflower of *Tonio Kröger* had become his archivist.

He was not always grateful for Herz's attention. In March 1934, while in Switzerland, he describes her "as something of a burden to have around." On September 21, 1935, the day he was briefly reconciled with Klaus Heuser, Mann took a walk in the woods with Hans Reisiger—to discuss Heuser?—interrupted, "unfortunately," by lunch with Herz. Elsewhere he calls her an importunate "spinster." Even when she was imprisoned for anti-Nazi actions, he patronized her as "that poor creature Ida Herz." For her part, she admitted that Mann could be curt and condescending; one simply learned not to take offense. She eventually saw him as a dear friend, and his last diaries are free of the earlier criticism. After his death Herz

Heinrich Mann,
"the Hindenburg of
the Left," 1930

claimed that it had come to him unaware; he was too kind to otherwise abandon those who loved him.

His relations with Lowe-Porter were cordially distant. During the 1920s he wrote Alfred A. Knopf, questioning whether any woman could translate *Zauberberg*, particularly since her version of *Buddenbrooks*, which appeared in 1924, had been criticized. On November 24, 1933, he noted in his diary a negative review in the New York *Herald Tribune* of his Wagner essay. "It seemed to have been very badly translated." Since it had been the proximate cause of his exile, a superior representation was essential.

He didn't make things easier for her. Each novel grew more abstruse and allusive, filled with echoes of German verse, modern and archaic, not to mention several forms of dialect and a narrative style that could be solemn, whimsical, ironic, and sensual, all within the course of sentences of a Jamesian length and Talmudic complexity. Virtually any translation would be inadequate; and Lowe-Porter's errors, mercilessly itemized by critics, did not improve matters.

Usually Mann affirmed his female mediator. But during the 1940s when attacks grew vehement (she referred to "my bad press"), he seemed to abandon her. As she wrote Knopf: "He always acts as though I were not there, unless I am called to his attention—a fine masculine attitude, for which, I dare say, I am partly to blame." (On May 1, 1945, Mann wrote Kahler that "I don't regard Lowe-Porter as a reader; she is a mute instrument, never lets out a peep.") Perhaps he wasn't gallant; yet too often she did him a disservice, making him seem arch and pompous. By slighting the homosexual aspects of his prose, she nearly denatured him. Finally his translator was overprotective of his *Haltung*. She considered him "a great as well as a good man," and may have honored him too much. Her own modest assessment was that "his books would not have made money in English translation if they had not—out of my profound respect for the English tongue—been 'easily readable.' I will not claim more for them than that, because it is enough."

In later years Mann's best American friend would be Agnes Meyer, wife of Eugene Meyer, the publisher of the *Washington Post*. She offered a hospitality commensurate with her wealth; and secured his appointment as consultant to the Library of Congress. But she also assumed an interest in his life and work—and those of Klaus and Erika—that he found intrusive. Their letters bespeak devotion—he claims to worry about her children as if they were his own—but in his diary he complains about her "depressing fixation on my person." Their relation grew "stupid and humiliating"; even her gifts seemed like "secondhand goods." Finally, on May 26, 1943, an attack by Meyer on his children's left-wing politics led him to terminate their friendship. He described himself as someone "agitated by everything, who needs quiet and peace as I do my daily bread, who can neither accomplish anything nor even merely live in the midst of bickering and quarrels, but instantly go to pieces. . . . You did not have the humor, or the respect, or the discretion, to take me as I am, even though, at the age of nearly seventy, my life was . . . thoroughly formed and fixed."

They were reunited within a week but after 1945 they continued to have fierce arguments about America's move to the right. During this time Mann was gratified by Lowe-Porter's support; she shared his political fears. For the moment her deficiencies as a translator were forgotten.

Meyer was very impressed by Erich Heller's critique of Mann. But Mann despised Heller's attempts to saddle him with a "conservative imagination," thereby overlooking his political and intellectual development since 1923, or, worse, patronizing it as aesthetically inconsequential. Indeed, he thought such efforts furthered the cause of "Catholic fascism" (Diary, January 26, 1951). Heller's disparagement echoed the nationalistic Germans of the 1920s. It also found favor with editors of the CIA-funded magazine

Encounter, among them Stephen Spender. Even if Meyer and Heller loved their Thomas Mann, the author deplored their attempts to rewrite him.

Yet no matter what he sometimes thought of her, his salutations escalated from "Dear Friend" to "Dear Princess and friend" (an echo, perhaps, of *Royal Highness*) and he told Erich von Kahler that she was "my Diotima [and] by no means unintelligent." He wrote her letters filled with self-revelation: the admission that he falls to pieces easily had previously been reserved for the likes of Heinrich or Ernst Bertram. (Though, by 1945, he was telling Bruno Walter that he was a "nervous old man.") To the end of his life, he was unashamed to solicit her gifts even if he pronounced her taste cheap and provincial. Upon his death, she was one of the chief mourners.

In his last years he became very excited by a woman novelist. But Marguerite Yourcenar was an extremely Mannian writer, and her masterpiece, *Memoirs of Hadrian*, is homoerotic and male-bonded in the extreme; it required no sympathetic reach—he could have composed it himself. Paradoxically, the rarity of such an expression of admiration for a female intellectual indicates that his deepest responses continued to be inspired by men.

However, her example led him to imagine writing about women. In February 1955 he wrote a fan letter in German: "Surely you can read German. I trust you for that. In truth, I would trust you for anything ever since the *Memoirs of Hadrian*, and since your *Elektra* still more." In that drama he was most impressed by a confrontation between the heroine and her mother, the murderous Klytemnestra. "It struck me what a range of mythological traditions surrounds that scene of impassioned strife between the two women." A tradition stretching from the *Nibelungenlied* to Schiller's *Mary Stuart* and Wagner's *Lohengrin* has achieved its "modern psychological peak." Only a recent viral infection prevented his composing an essay on this theme.

So, in his last months, he might finally have considered the question of female passion. The subject was new but the slant was old: the relations would be monosexual, as if these remained more provocative than the heterosexual kind. According to this view, women, like men, contend most vigorously with each other.

When he was smitten with Franzl, Mann wrote that "even a girl" excited him. Coming after the great essay about Schiller's pursuit of Goethe, the Yourcenar tribute would have allowed his imagination to roam, but not far. (It would also have constituted a seminal text for lesbian theorists. By this light, *Royal Highness*, with its depiction of a paranoid lesbian, composed three years *before* Freud's famous analysis of Daniel Paul Schreber's homosexual paranoia, had been a most precocious development.)

II

Yet, *pace* Meyer, Mann did have some rich and lasting friendships with men of letters. The most significant may have been with Hermann Hesse and Erich Kahler. Meanwhile Klaus's friend André Gide would play a unique role in his development, as perhaps the only contemporary author from whom Mann actually expected to learn.

The first relation began when the sightly younger Hesse praised *Buddenbrooks*. It was tested when he panned *Royal Highness* and intimated that Mann was too much of a thinker to be an artist; and was reactivated during the Nazi era. In 1931 Hesse, who had been a Swiss citizen since 1923, resigned from the Prussian Academy of Arts, predicting that its members would be as politically misguided as the intellectuals who had supported the war in 1914.

A year later, Mann reassured Hesse that he was unmoved by the Nazis. For him "to side unequivocally with the maternal and the 'Queen of the Night' "—a reference to the Bachhofen / Bäumler / Klages tributes to irrationalism and the Great Mother—would be "a kind of snobbery." Instead he would pursue "the lesser evil and incur a reputation for dry humanitarian rationalism." Of course, this pursuit is just what Hesse had condemned in 1909, and what he observed in Thomas of Trave, the character patterned on Mann in *Magister Ludi* or in "another world-famous author . . . who signed more than two hundred appeals to reason, which is probably more than he had actually read."

Whether or not he so intended, Mann was telling Hesse that they exemplified very different forms of intellectual resistance, and that his rationalism immunized him from sentimentality and political kitsch. This became clearer when the Swabian confessed to being moved by the "blue-eyed enthusiasm" of some young Germans and the Nazis' "spirit of self-sacrifice." Mann had long said good-bye to all that.

In 1935, Hesse sought to defend Mann against young people who found him "too intellectual, too reasonable, and too ironic," and so missed "how much he has in him of the heroism and also of the demonism of those who are possessed by their work and sacrifice themselves to it." This sounds like a rebuttal of his own critique. Yet the demonic sense of vocation meant little to his constituency. They wanted a prophet, and Hesse gave them a technician. In *Magister Ludi*, Thomas of Trave, while a master of construction, lacks enthusiasm and avoids "grand and exciting themes." His "friendly and ironic glance" induces an "anxious, constricting sensation."

During Mann's years in Switzerland, the two corresponded regularly, and upon Hesse's sixtieth birthday in 1937, Mann wrote: "I long ago chose him as the member of my literary generation closest and dearest to me," excluding Gide perhaps because he was French and six years older. He asserted that *Steppenwolf* was as radically experimental as *Ulysses*, a remark that he probably doubted, and saluted Hesse's tireless promotion of "the Prague Jew Franz Kafka" as a secret king of German prose: a very generous statement from Mann, as well as a political assault on Nazis who would never grant a Jew such prominence. (All the same, two months later he informed Hans Reisiger that his friendship with Hesse had been sidetracked. "Talk about Hesse, my courting of him and his resistance, his preferring not to hear anything about me, and of uneasiness, possibly envy.")

Other than praising Kafka, sheltering recent émigrés from Hitler, and remaining with his Jewish wife, Hesse's response to the Nazis was to drop out of public life. He advised Mann to do the same. Mann couldn't oblige, and eventually left Switzerland (writing Hesse in 1941 that the country hadn't been "so very nice to exiles like us").

Three of Germany's
most famous novelists,
Saint Moritz, 1931.
LEFT TO RIGHT:
Herman Hesse, age fifty-four;
Mann, age fifty-six;
Jakob Wasserman,
age fifty-eight

They resumed correspondence after the war. Unknown to Hesse, Mann did not welcome the appearance of *Magister Ludi*, initially fearing that it would threaten the reception for *Doctor Faustus*. *Magister Ludi* was half-*summa*, half-parody, pretty much what Mann intended *Faustus* to be. To his relief, its vision of an artistic and scholarly Utopia did not impinge on his dystopian reading of German history. As he wrote Klaus, it pleased him to see that "the hero finally dies while swimming after a boy in too cold water. Just as I expected." He didn't remark that Hesse's treatment of Magister Ludi Joseph Knecht and the boy Tino was filled with homages to Mann himself. Tino performs a dance to the sun, much as Mann's Joseph had danced to the moon. He beckons Knecht into the water, a fatal journey that recalls Aschenbach's final pursuit of Tadzio. After all these years was Hesse engaged in an intertextual courtship? If so, it was as one-sided as Schiller's of Goethe.

However, when his friendly rival was accused of having been insufficiently anti-Nazi, Mann leapt to his defense . . . although his words of February 8, 1947, can be read two ways: "There must be a good deal of quiet satisfaction and gratitude for a successful life that a merciful fate has always excluded from the horrors of the times."

Mann wasn't the only reader to perceive Hesse's limitations. On March 19, 1947, he wrote Klaus, quoting *Time*'s negative review of *Steppenwolf*, complete with an invidious reference: "It stands in fiction deep in the shadow of *The Magic Mountain*." By then he was so attuned to the shifts in public taste that he saw himself potentially threatened: if, as *Time* said, *Steppenwolf* was "a repellent example of that beery old thing, German Romanticism . . . tinged with Lutheran, Nietzschean, and Freudian influence," wait till they got their hands on *Doctor Faustus*!

Nine months later, an émigré similarly used Mann to bring Hesse down to size. Erich Kahler, grumbling that modern German literature was a wasteland, called Hesse an "oversweetened, flavored pudding. . . . That *Steppenwolf*—what a sentimental, self-pitying pulp, without structure, without character, without shape. . . . All this symbolism, this romantic nonsense, how insipid, how thin and pasted on, and how foolish. And *that* twenty-five years after Tonio Kröger!" Mann answered that Kahler was largely correct about German fiction, but that he had done Hesse an "injustice." He admitted to not having looked at *Steppenwolf* lately, but *Narcissus and Goldmund* was a fine book and the homoerotic *Demian* "also had something that hit a nerve." He even praised the "dreamy boldness" of *Magister Ludi*, adding, "a highly conservative boldness, granted." Since, in the same letter, he called *Doctor Faustus* his " 'wildest' book," Hesse's daring seems passé. He liked best Hesse's "beneficently non-German Germanness"—meaning perhaps romanticism without any of the Nazi filigree. Because of that, "he has something I feel to be *distantly* fraternal" [italics mine].

In terms of Mann's psychic and artistic development, André Gide was far more influential than Hesse. He admired Gide's political engagement, his love of Goethe, Nietzsche, Whitman, and Dostoyevsky, his devotion to reason, and—above all—his militant homosexuality. Moreover he could share Gide with Klaus, who wrote a book-length study of his hero. In a letter praising that work, Mann called Gide the most remarkable union of educator and seducer "since—since Socrates": a typical exchange between a father and son equally drawn to pantheons filled with their homosexual heroes.

In 1925, as we saw, Mann had been cooler to Gide's published statements, and the marriage essay had characterized homosexuality as socially useless. But four years later, inspired no doubt by his love for Klaus Heuser, he was more sympathetic. In December 1929 he reviewed Gide's memoir, *If It Die*, thereby making literary the political identification evident in his public statements about sexual freedom (see next chapter). Mann recognized in his French colleague a Mannian blend of "conservatism and daring." He was a Protestant in a Catholic country, reminding Mann that the Protestant-biblical element is strong enough in Goethe to justify his paradoxical *selige Sehnsucht* (literally, longing of the soul). Noteworthy, considering Mann's forthcoming work on Goethe, is that he shows Gide's homosexuality to be rooted in the Protestant tradition of moral independence.

Yet Gide, Mann wrote, is more Rousseauan than Goethe and less censored. His honesty is too much for bourgeois Germans; out of "good taste" his translators have expunged his erotic adventures in Algeria. Demonstrating that he's another kind of German, Mann poses some frank questions. How could a man with Gide's nature get married? Does he separate his erotic attraction to boys from his emotional need for women? (Briefly applying Freud to Gide, Mann wonders if a childhood episode in which Gide bit a female cousin and drew blood left him too scared to hurt women with his body.) Was he afraid to burn his bridges back to "normality"? All these questions could be asked, as well, of Thomas Mann. He was either indulging in spectacular bad faith or, as so often, partially disclosing himself.

Alluding to the political battles over sexual identity, he adds, "Nowadays some observers . . . still think, as strange as it may sound, that real, inherent [self-rooted] homosexuality doesn't even exist." Gide seems to have "divorced" his sexuality "from soulful tenderness" and directed it toward "same-sexual acts." Where in 1919, Mann, following Hans Blüher, distinguished a homoerotic public world from heterosexual privacy, in 1929 he makes a more visceral distinction between "a higher spirituality" and lust.

He recognizes temperamental affinities with Gide: the latter's epigram, "In spite of every attempt at honesty, once you describe your own life, you can only utter half-truths," or his warning to writers, "If you knew what you were getting into, you'd never start," could have been written by Mann. Therefore he presumes to ask questions, ostensibly about literary technique, implicitly about sexual preference. Reversing his customary relation with his readers, Thomas Mann now depends on another writer to show him "how to live."

Why, in *The Immoralist*, when the hero first sleeps with a boy, isn't Gide's narrative technique more "epic"? There has been no preparation for so life-changing an event: "The reader must place it retroactively in the novel and feels dumb, like someone who must admit, 'I would never have guessed.' " Gide is capable of epic strengths; when he mourns for his dead mother he renders "the typical and eternally human . . . unique. This mother and this son are always and everywhere and these are the tears which we all share in the most sacred and bitter hour of our life." (In 1951, Mann wrote Erich Kahler that his mother's death had been "a unique shock and wrench.") Excepting Kafka, Mann never claimed such a kinship with a contemporary; the image of tears comes out of *The Magic Mountain*, the demand for an epic overview out of *Joseph*.

Gide thanked the recent Nobel laureate for his friendly words. On January 20, 1930, Mann replied, immediately indulging in shop talk. He longed for a French translation of *The Magic Mountain*; despite what Gide might have heard, the narrative elements balanced the critical, and at once apologized, "I am talking too much about myself." But then he came to his most personal admission, "Your autobiography made a profound impression upon me, both for what you set out to do and for the way your intention was realized, and I think that this impression will one day prove fruitful in my own life. A certain type of writer is, in the long run, not content with the stylized and symbolically clothed confession, and since reading your book I dream more distinctly than I did before of an autobiographical account of my own."

We don't know if Gide understood the subtext of Mann's agenda, or knew how much the two married homosexuals resembled each other. Soon after, Mann wrote an autobiographical sketch that failed to meet Gidean standards. To paraphrase Tonio Kröger, for Mann there was no clear way to truth; it would have to be "symbolically" or epically "stylized." *Young Joseph*, the most overtly homoerotic novel of this epic tetralogy and the one most evocative of Klaus Heuser, was probably completed in 1930, as were his essays on Platen and on Paragraph 175. These must stand in for the autobiography Mann promised Gide and himself.

Twenty-one years later, following Gide's death, Mann drew further parallels between them. A critic had called Gide " 'a cautious radical and a daring conservative'—and precisely this mixture makes me confess to brotherly feelings." He was equally describing himself when he wrote that Gide had "won out over guilt and neuroses through the discipline of his art; . . . language and style." Or when he found in Gide "a rejuvenation and renascence through strong and demonic energies, imported from without," considering that these forces were embodied in Conrad, Dostoyevsky, Whitman, and Melville.

M ann told Erich Kahler that his relations with Hesse were "distantly fraternal." This would not define his friendship with Kahler, which was relaxed, warm, and intimate. Born in Prague, educated in Vienna, Kahler was one of several Jewish members of the George-Kreis, under whose auspices he met Mann in 1930. Both went into exile in 1933, both spent several years in Switzerland. They would be reunited in Princeton, where Mann lived between 1938 and 1941, before moving to California, and Kahler remained until his death.

Kahler became something of Mann's resident Lukács, the interpreter whose advice and affirmation meant the most—particularly when academics like Jacques Barzun, Leslie Fiedler, and Harry Levin turned against him. (Shades of old Germany, Jews were still among his most loyal supporters and his toughest critics.) When these Americans attacked him, Mann would assume a magisterial distance, more bemused than hurt—at least with other Americans. But with Kahler he could speak plainly, as he did in 1944, saying of the critics who "disparaged" *Joseph the Provider*, "a humorous book in a totally popular vein," as "a monstrosity . . . full of Olympian attitudinizing," that they were "idiots."

Like so many of his literary friends, Kahler was Mann's conduit to another writer, in this case, Hermann Broch (1886–1951). Despite his hugely ambitious *Death of Virgil* (1945) and a vast array of philosophical interests, Broch remained dependent on academic fellowships. His loyalists considered Mann the villain, hogging the spotlight from the more deserving and affable Broch. Mann praised the *Virgil* even though, he said, most readers found it "abstruse and sophistical . . . almost impossible to read." He considered it, along with his *Faustus* and Heinrich's last novel, *Der Atem*, the product of a wiser, more profound generation, born before 1900. Upon learning that Broch, who was then very frail, had surmised that Mann would never support his candidacy for the Nobel Prize, Mann wrote Alvin Johnson, "What hypochondria! Good heaven, I am sure I need his 'backing' more than he does mine. He belongs with those minds upon whose good opinion we base our belief in ourselves and in the benign support of posterity." Though, he reminded Johnson, neither Joyce nor Kafka had received the Nobel Prize, Mann agreed to support Broch. Alas, within six weeks, Broch was dead. He had been reduced to living in New Haven student digs, and he succumbed after lugging a heavy suitcase upstairs, despite a severe coronary condition. It was easy to see his death as a suicidal gesture, and this exacerbated his friends' contempt for that child of fortune, Thomas Mann.

For Kahler it was a particularly grim time, since his mother, with whom he had still been living, had died shortly before Broch. Yet his affection for Mann remained undisturbed. He didn't sentimentalize the novelist, regarding him as "both conservative and radical, thoroughly proper and deeply demonic, even diabolical at times." He perceived the literary adventurer disguised behind a bourgeois facade, capable of "the most daring things presented in a faultless form." He was equally proud of his friend's secular humanism. Contrasting Mann with Heidegger—how that must have offended Hannah Arendt!—he said that Mann alone among the century's great minds had articulated "clearly defined values." To the end, Mann's most devoted ally would be a Jewish refugee.

III

It is possible that German grammar impeded Mann's chances of friendship. In 1946, he addressed Bruno Walter on his seventieth birthday: "Dear Friend, it is very annoying. After a rigorous test period of thirty-four years, we have just agreed to say 'du' to each other henceforth, and now I have to write you a birthday letter in which this handsome innovation won't count at all, since in this damnably overcivilized English one addresses even one's dog as 'you.' " This kind of formality, second-nature to Germans of his generation—remember that Heinrich never employed "Du" with Katia—would seem culturally, if not emotionally, pathological in America.

Isolation has been further imposed posthumously by critics who exaggerate Mann's estrangement. They contend that he was sui generis and figuratively without issue. According to Marcel Reich-Ranicki, he left no descendants and never contended with the significant figures or literary movements of his time. Other critics note his promiscuous endorsements of virtually any émigré writer: praise so universally distributed had no value. They see Mann as hermetically sealed in the nineteenth century.

They are wrong. As we know, he responded to contemporary phenomena, from movies to phonograph records, with an acuity that matches the insights of Benjamin or Adorno, while contributing a quality of sensuous participation absent in their neoacademic work.

He also finally addressed the phenomenon of psychoanalysis. In 1925, Mann told an Italian journalist that Freud had influenced his work for years, beginning with *Death in Venice*. "Without Freud I would never have thought of treating this erotic motif; or I would certainly have treated it differently" (assertions one might question). He admitted feeling intimidated by Freud's "X-ray" invasion of the artist's soul. Once everything is known, "the secret of creativity" fritters away. So even as he learned from Freud, he conceived means of challenging him. A master stroke was to make Freud his peer, recommending him for the Nobel Prize in *literature*.

In 1929 he saluted Freud's attempt to create a countermyth to fascism. Freud responded with gratitude. Mann, assuming a faux-naïf guise, apologized for coming so late to psychoanalysis: "I am altogether, and in all respects, *slow* by nature." Freud had mentioned his interest in literature. "You love the poets? But chiefly, I suppose, as objects for your investigations; with a few boring exceptions we are all born to that use—myself in the vanguard I would say, if it did not sound conceited."

Was he inviting a Freudian interpretation? It is hardly likely; as we saw, he denied Freud's therapeutic goals. Masochism, which Freud considers a "plainly feminine trait" in men, was the operative mode of all his heroic invalids, from Schiller and Platen to Dostoyevsky and Kafka. Moreover, as Mann wrote in 1950, he considered psychoanalytic interpretations of homosexuality, foregrounding the mother, as "learned nonsense." As an object he didn't require the analyst's investigation.

He spoke with significantly less ambivalence about other writers. Of course these remarks tended to elaborate his vast and great confession, but the revelations only enhance the charm of his commentary. At such times he enjoys *not* being alone in the universe.

Mann liked his English novels socially and discursively complex. Among nineteenth-century novels, he favored *Vanity Fair*. Thackeray's Becky Sharp exhibits the same entrepreneurial knack for flirtation as Felix Krull, as well as a similar elusiveness—one never knows whether to trust them—and a comparable trajectory from petit bourgeois to lower aristocrat. His other favorite was George Meredith's *The Egoist*, a novel in which relations between the sexes are problematic and marriage a less-than-happy ending. Among twentieth-century novelists writing in English, his favorite was Joseph Conrad.

He came late to Conrad, largely because German translations were not available until 1920. The similarities are remarkable. Both considered themselves outsiders: Conrad as a Polish émigré writing in a second language, Mann as both the offspring of a "mixed" marriage and the belated student of his father's culture. Conrad famously proposed "fidelity" as his moral touchstone; Mann liked to call himself "the Good Tin Soldier." Neither can be pinned down politically. Both write about monstrous figures, Conrad's Professor or Mann's Naphta, who are similarly described as walking epidemics and human time bombs. Both are singularly gifted at capturing "the horror" that suffuses modern life, whether it is the doomed Mr. Kurtz or Thomas Buddenbrook stricken in the snow, or Dr. Faustus himself, immobilized by his guilt; whatever they perceive turns them to stone. Conrad's inspired notion of secret agents abroad in the land could be a Mannian concept. Who better than he knew how to juggle moral authority and subversion?

In early 1926 he finally got to write about Conrad, in an introduction to *The Secret Agent*. His analysis is appropriately political. Although the book was published in 1906, Conrad's Polish animus against Russian villains transforms it into a work of anti-Soviet propaganda. For, as Mann sees it, the novel exhibits an "unequivocal, even tendentious western bias."

Conrad dramatizes the misuses of scientific methodology, and the false dichotomy set up between masculine rigor and feminine emotion. In his novel political terrorists attempt to justify their brutal actions in terms that evoke the laboratory; indeed, the murderous Professor becomes a forerunner of Dr. Strangelove, exploding the world to save it. Like their opposite numbers in the police, these men exhibit a "disregard for art . . . combined with a boundless credulity and reverence for totalitarian science." Cops and crooks alike think emotional response is women's stuff. Both sides are foiled by a woman, Mrs. Winnie Verloc. Upon learning that her double-agent husband has unwittingly caused her brother's death, she murders him.

This ironic dénouement has political ramifications. At this time Mann was trying to reconcile socialist principles with traditional culture. Therefore, when he updates Conrad by noting that "Bolshevism" is yet another "sternly scientific conception of the world," he may be setting an agenda for his own fiction, informed by and yet distrustful of scientific practice and political ideology. Not surprisingly he is drawn to Conrad's most apolitical character, Stevie, the mentally retarded brother, the novel's holy fool. He calls him "the finest type in the book," or at least the most lovable.

Conrad's "modern power of seeing both sides" allows him to virtually "canonize the clinically deficient" Stevie while "never belittling the pathological or romantically closing his eyes to it." Has any other critic, Marxist or not, spotted the ways objectivity and bias overlap to a narrative's *advantage?* The artist always evades his critic, who can never predict which of his multiple selves and tones will be deployed next. Only someone who understood that irony can coexist with unabashed emotion would emphasize both Conrad's attacks on pseudo-science and his scientifically informed depiction of the retarded youth. In the midst of spies and counterspies the novel's solid rock is Winnie Verloc's love for her brother. This union of irony and fidelity, so crucial to Mann's approach to narrative, makes Conrad his soul mate. As late as April 26, 1949, he would comment, "Strange, how long Conrad has been my favorite reading."

In 1952, he told Irita van Doren that Conrad, not he, was "the foremost novelist of the age." "I could never have written *Nostromo*, nor the magnificent *Lord Jim*, and if he in turn could not have written *The Magic Mountain* or *Doctor Faustus*, the account balances out very much in his favor."

He saw in Conrad an Anglicized version of Dostoyevsky's interest in political action and psychological motive. Conrad attracted him, but apparently Henry James did not (although several critics feel that Mann's rambling periods find their English analogue in James). In fact, after praising Gide for his promotion of Dostoyevsky, Mann adds, "When he found Henry James too artificial, too rational, too French," he took up his cudgels for Conrad, Melville, and Whitman. Mann's preference for Conrad over James bespeaks his interest in politics, as well as his concern with the passionate and outspoken, even his instinct for melodrama.

For D. H. Lawrence there was no such affection. Yet throughout the 1920s, Mann included books by Lawrence in his lists of the year's best works. Mann and Lawrence were unlikely cohorts. Lawrence had written an early, hostile review of *Death in Venice*, acknowledging the narrative skill but adding wickedly that "Thomas Mann is old and we are young." Their disputes were cross-cultural. During the years when Lawrence lived with Frieda in Munich, he gravitated to the circles of Otto Gross and Ludwig Klages. It was a milieu pledged to blood brotherhood, matriarchal rituals, and vituperative antirationalism. Not surprisingly it considered itself above mere politics and despised Jews as uncreative, aphysical, rootless skeptics. Along with the Stefan George circle, these bohemian-aesthetes condemned the "Jewish sciences." Martin Green has demonstrated the proto-fascist elements in their makeup.

Lawrence echoed their party line. As early as 1920 he wrote, "You can't save mankind by politics," while Thomas Mann was coming to the recognition that nothing else could save Germany. In the 1920s, in his half-inspired, half-demented writings on sexuality, Lawrence heaped abominations on Marx, Freud, and Einstein, hyperintellectual killers of the spirit. Lawrence tried to demote intelligence from the brain to the solar plexus. Mann didn't appreciate the attempt. In 1934, he responded to a query about Lawrence from Karl Kerényi, a Jungian critic with all the anti-Freudian bias that such an identity suggests.

The Englishman had been on his mind lately. In April 1933 he noted in his journal, "Interesting piece (for my *Faust*) by Huxley about Lawrence and his letters." Whether he saw Lawrence as a literary exponent of Munich's fanaticism, or saw another parallel between the Englishman and his hero is fascinating to speculate.

Mann allowed that Lawrence was "no doubt a significant phenomenon and characteristic of our time, but [his] fevered sensuality has little appeal to me." He belonged, said Mann, to the sphere of those who display "a kind of rancor against the development of the human cerebrum, a rancor which has always struck me as a snobbish and ridiculous form of self-negation." Mann catches these snobs out—"snob" had also been his epithet for Oswald Spengler—in the volumes they compose in praise of silence.

He adds, "I am no friend of the anti-intellectual movement . . . in Germany. I feared and fought it early, because I saw through all its brutally anti-human consequences before they became apparent." This may be the first time that he boasted about his prescient awareness of intellectual folly. Lawrence's "hectic, fevered sensuality" and its "anti-human consequences" make for a terrifying combination from Mann's exiled perspective.

And yet, and yet, Lawrence and Mann still resemble each other, and not merely to Vladimir Nabokov, who dismissed them both as bourgeois Philistines, overpraised second-raters. Both men are always alert to a denial of logic arising out of jumbled emotions—witness Lawrence's condemnation of Gerald Crich in *Women in Love*: "Without bothering to *think* to a conclusion, Gerald jumped to a conclusion." The indictment would serve for Joachim as well.

Moreover, if *Death in Venice* is Europe's first great homosexual story, Lawrence's "Prussian Officer," composed a few months after his review of Mann's novella, is its second. Both novelists can't help exposing themselves: Mann in the numerous passages we have observed; Lawrence perhaps most completely in the preface to *Women in Love*, where he admits that Birkin adored men's bodies and women's clothes. (In a recently discovered draft of *Sons and Lovers*, Paul Morel puts on his mistress's stockings.)

Not surprisingly Lawrence and Mann also shared literary enthusiasms, Nietzsche and Whitman. In the early 1920s, Lawrence's critique of American literature found in Whitman a cultural breakthrough: he particularly cites Whitman's "sympathy, a great new doctrine of life, feeling with people as they feel with themselves." His words could be a paraphrase of Mann's argument that Whitmanesque sensuality has become a political metaphor. At least Mann doesn't use Whitman to defend marriage. But Lawrence is guileful in the extreme when he cites Whitmanesque "sympathy" to justify the hero's heterosexual affair in *Mr. Noon*.

While they attempt to disguise their own tendencies, both authors seem compelled to find them elsewhere. Mann specializes in deferred romances (Goethe and Schiller; Chamisso and the native guide). He also goes beyond Germany's borders; he becomes the tourist who spots his kind in foreign cities. How different was Lawrence? His attraction to American literature remains predicated on authors like Melville and Whitman. Either his "American soul" is isolate and a killer or it swims in Melville's ambergris, a homoerotic orgy of mythic proportions.

Similarly the wily duo convert their obsessions into "metaphors" or "symptoms" by projecting them on the world. Mann understood that his Magic Mountain, honeycombed with dangerous fools and sexy knaves, overlooked all of Europe. And Lawrence could make English history culminate in Sherwood Forest, when Birkin initiates Ursula into a night of buggery.

No author has final say about his image: a detail Mann pondered to the end of his days. Lawrence and Mann would both suffer the misinterpretations of their most devoted advocates, F. R. Leavis and Lukács, respectively, in part because these critics had so much else to consider. Lukács might have been sympathetic to Mann's erotic nature, yet where Lawrence and Mann are most alike, in their desires for men or in their acknowledgment of the appeals of unreason, they elude the moralistic strictures of mid-century British criticism. The Lawrence who resembles Mann is the Lawrence whom Leavis hates to think about. Perhaps for this reason Mann wrote Ida Herz in 1949, "Strangely I have no luck in England, just not there": he discounted the honorary doctorates from both Oxford and Cambridge. And just then, when Leavis commanded his Lawrentian troops, he might have had a chance. Only recently has A. S. Byatt claimed that Mann (with Proust)—and not yesterday's hero Lawrence—is the proper heir of George Eliot. Of course, some of Mann's best readers are English academics—T. J. Reed and David Luke.

Mann and Lawrence seem at once complementary and antipodal figures. Mann was far more sympathetic to Franz Kafka. Indeed, if he left a literary trace, it lies in Kafka's treatment of Mannian themes.

He was introduced to Kafka's work shortly after the war, and by 1925 had become its most famous advocate. Hermann Hesse and Mann helped turn an avant-garde eccentric into the exemplary modern voice. We know that Kafka worshiped Mann. He used a most telling verb to describe his affection: "I *hunger* for Thomas Mann [italics mine]," the word of choice for two men so perpetually unsatisfied. Both Mann and Kafka grasp the procedural core of the other's work. Kafka cites *Tonio Kröger's* "particularly profitable love of contradictions," and Mann applauds Kafka's tonal resilience. They share an unsurpassed ability to make gallows humor side-splittingly funny. Take, appropriately, Kafka's Hunger Artist, a figure worth placing beside Mann's performers. This hero becomes a circus star, enthralling audiences with his ability to go without food. Even when the public wearies of his singular talent, he persists. But he declines to see his career as a parable of artistic devotion. When at last he dies, he admits that he would gladly have eaten if he had only found something he liked. This is the kind of joke, doubtless to be recited with a Yiddish comedian's shrug, that Mann relished.

There was another similarity. The unexpurgated diaries of Kafka reveal homoerotic tendencies expressed with astonishing vigor, particularly from a writer so associated with repression and impotence. During his teens, Kafka had devastating crushes on his fellow students. Biographers like Ernst Pawel dismiss these episodes as adolescent and nonsexual. But ten years later he exhibited the same inclination.

Kafka may resemble the Mann who declared that looking was good enough for him. But if so, his attentions were more hot-blooded. During a train trip in January 1911, he noticed a young salesman whose "well-rounded penis" made his pants swell, perhaps in response to Kafka's glances. In July 1912, Kafka took one of many health cures, this time in a nudist male spa. He was struck by "handsome young Swedes with long legs, so well-formed and taut that one could gladly lick them": a response more ardent than Mann's when he beheld the legs of his Argentinean Hermes.

Kafka was a close friend of Franz Werfel, another Prague Jew. In November 1917, he writes Max Brod: "If I go on to say that in a recent dream of mine I gave Werfel a kiss, I stumble right into the midst of Blüher's book." Like Mann, Kafka found himself reflected in Blüher's homo-eroticism—but only to a point. "The book upset me; I had to lay it aside for two days. However it shares the quality of other psychoanalytic works that in the first moment its thesis seems remarkably satisfying, but very soon after one feels the same old hunger." He knows that this hunger can be explained away "psychoanalytically: instant Repression." But like Mann he didn't find the method useful in explicating his desires.

Kafka shares another enthusiasm with Mann, Hans Pfitzner's opera, *Palestrina*. More important, the two both worship at the shrine of Saint Sebastian. Their martyred saint is an obvious symbol of masochism and self-pity: for centuries he has served as the homosexual's Saint Jude. One need not argue that homoeroticism pervades Kafka's fiction to the same extent as Mann's. But surely the masochistic pleasure Kafka's heroes take in their humiliation, the protracted denial of their wishes, and the superior forces of powerful men, have a certain erotic basis. In "The Penal Colony," a prisoner chooses his fate: he will have the words "Honor Thy Superiors" inscribed on his flesh. The torture he endures bears a resemblance to sado-masochistic ritual. (In 1952 Erika suggested a possible homosexual inter-pretation of *Amerika*. Mann preferred to see the novel as an expression of "Jewish chastity.")

For both Mann and Kafka, there is no place scarier than home. When Thomas Buddenbrook demands that Hanno perform before an audience of relatives, the boy's disgrace is quite as terrible as Gregor Samsa's meta-morphosis: indeed, Kafka literalizes Hanno's feelings of absolute worthless-ness. Kafka's miserable relations with his archetypically bourgeois father are well known. To find a parental figure as wayward and capricious as Kafka's tormentors, one must turn to Mann's "God," the deity of *Joseph and His Brothers*, who punishes his worshipers by killing their loved ones.

Of course terror had been integral to Mann's work, from the fear and panic that united Thomas and Hanno Buddenbrook to the emotion which Naphta invoked as the true longing of modern man. (As late as 1950 Mann speculated whether his contemporaries preferred terror to freedom.) In Kaf-ka's hands terror became abstract and ubiquitous, a distillation of psycho-logical and political anxiety, yet more than either. To that degree, as in his eroticizing of male power, Kafka is the next step after Thomas Mann.

In 1903, the year of Mann's great stories "The Hunger" and *Tonio Kröger*—both of them inspired by his love for Paul Ehrenberg—Kafka, in a letter, used virtually the same formulations of anomie and despair that Mann employs in these tales.

> We are forsaken like children lost in the woods. When you stand before me and look at me, what do you know of my sufferings and what do I know of yours? And if I fell at your feet and cried and told you, would you know any more about me than you know about hell when they say it is hot and sets one shivering? Therefore we men should stand before each other with as much awe, thoughtfulness, and love as before the gates of hell.

In a similarly physical/metaphysical rush, Mann's Detlef pleads, "Love one another, little children."

Though he alluded to Kafka throughout the 1920s, Mann's fullest statement appeared in a 1940 introduction to *The Castle*. This provides a rare instance of a literary father defining his son's work. Mann even boasts that Kafka loved *Tonio Kröger* and yearned as hopelessly as Tonio does for the "bliss of the commonplace." Thus he merges the North German Tonio Kröger with his *Ostjuden* readers, a salute to all the cosmopolitan Jews from Kafka to Bruno Schulz who found themselves trapped between two worlds.

Mann begins with a photo of Kafka, his "eyes, at once dreamy and penetrating." The latter trait prevents Kafka from becoming a "romantic." He stands outside the tradition of Wagner or Novalis—Mann's own. Like Mann, the belated student, Kafka becomes a "late and doubting and most desperately complicated representative of German letters." As a token of respect Mann now invokes Goethe, the subject of his latest novel, and applies to Kafka qualities—"ironic, parodistic, yet charming to laughter" —that he holds supreme.

Mann understands the implications of Kafka's novel. He calls Kafka a "religious humorist" of an unparalleled audacity: the word he needs—but doesn't use—is "chutzpah."

> And never has the divine, the superhuman, been observed, experienced, characterized with stranger, more daring, more comic expedients, with more inexhaustible psychological riches, both sacrilegious and devout, than in this story of an incorrigible believer, so needing grace, so wrestling for it, so passionately and recklessly yearning for it that he even tries to encompass it by stratagems and wiles.

In Mann's enthusiasm he begins to conflate Joseph K. with Felix Krull, or his own "heavenly confidence man," Joseph. After the years he had spent on the *Joseph* novels, for Mann to give Kafka the praise that he sought for his own work—a cornucopia of irreverent "comic expedients"—is an act of generosity. It could not have escaped Mann's attention that his own syntax, dense with clauses and qualifications, tends not to resemble Kafka's lucid economy. It was as if Faulkner were to argue Hemingway's superiority. (To extend this parallel, Mann, in 1955, compared Faulkner's attempt at metaphysics, *A Fable*, unfavorably with Kafka and his "religious dream-vagueness, comedy, unpredictability, and profundity.")

Far more tentative were his comments on Proust and Joyce, the authors to whom he was most frequently compared. He had shared many interests with Proust, indeed anticipated more than a few, but only in the depiction of Mut's love for Joseph did he discern a Proustian element. (And even then, his real inspiration was Paul Ehrenberg.) Similarly Joyce's verbal innovations were beyond him, though he welcomed any suggestions that he and Joyce were instinctive and incorrigible parodists.

On March 1, 1945, he wrote Bruno Walter about a crisis in literature and music: for writers like Mann steeped in the past, Joyce was "quite as outrageous to the classical, romantic, realistic traditions as Schönberg and his followers." He added that he couldn't read Joyce because one has to be "born into English culture to do so." (See Katia's remark to Charles Jackson that non-Germans couldn't understand her husband.) Since music was the international language as well as the form in which Germans excelled—and Thomas Mann felt most comfortable—was *Doctor Faustus*'s treatment of avant-garde music a cipher for his engagement with Joyce? In *The Holy Sinner*, the novel after *Doctor Faustus*, he indulges in Joycean wordplay, puns, and solecisms in a homemade Anglo-German, inflected with American slang.

Proust and Joyce were familiar threats. But to Mann's astonishment, Kafka, his literary offspring, would gradually assume the posthumous—and surely unsought—mantle of a parricide. Mann's demotion came with the imprimatur of an American university. Initially, the Halls of Ivy had welcomed him. In 1935 he and Einstein received honorary doctorates from Harvard. Four years later he spent some time in Princeton, where he gave the previously cited lecture on *The Magic Mountain*, an earnest attempt to connect with American students; later both Yale and Princeton established archives of his work.

But in 1949 Harry Levin wrote a highly negative critique of *Doctor Faustus* in *The New York Times Book Review*; the daily *Times* had printed another pan, by Orville Prescott. Mann wrote his publisher that Prescott was not to be taken seriously, but he was astonished by Levin's response. It was particularly galling because Levin had previously intuited the value Mann placed on publicity. In a witty analysis of *Joseph the Provider*, Levin discovered analogies between Joseph's "gliding" through the Egyptian court and Mann's sojourn in "the sphere of publishing and reviewing."

Worse yet, he learned that Levin had changed the title of his famous Harvard course, "Proust, Joyce, and Mann," to "Proust, Joyce, and Kafka"! No wonder he took special pleasure that year in Lukács's latest analysis of his work. He began to call Lukács the greatest living critic, perhaps to shore up his image against the Anglo-American readers who had begun to abandon him. In 1950 he wrote Klaus Jonas that the latest word on him was *"major but not that major."*

In his last years, Mann returned to the note of his fiftieth birthday address. In a preface to Jonas's massive *Fifty Years of Thomas Mann Studies*, he revived Shakespeare's "Thou com'st in such a questionable shape." Downplaying his Olympian reputation, he claimed "a certain winking allusion to the great." But he added that—unlike, say, Wagner—he was better as an admirer than as the subject of admiration. This was a charming restatement of Aschenbach's discovery that God dwells in the lover.

Two years earlier, in 1951, Mann informed Irita van Doren, the literary editor of the New York *Herald Tribune*, that adjectives like "Olympian," "pompous," and "ponderous" left him speechless. "My friends know that I have not a trace of Olympian airs, that all solemnity, affectation, exaltation, and prophetic and arrogant pretensions are wholly alien to my nature and my taste—and that 'ponderousness' is an adjective which, if it were apt, would signify the failure of all my efforts. My ambition is to make the difficult easy; my ideal is clarity." He also insisted, "Never in my life have I lifted a finger to 'advance my cause,' to invite honors, or to promote the publication of books concerning me." (The last clause may have been true; the first two strictly weren't—as Mann had agitated for his work as early as 1899 with Otto Grautoff, as late as 1943, when he asked Frederic Prokosch whether Clifton Fadiman was favorably disposed to his work. Considering that at twenty-four he was an unknown novelist, and at sixty-eight the financial support of his wife, children, and brother, his behavior requires no defense.)

He considered himself primarily a humorist, specializing in "a not cynical but affectionate parody of tradition." Since 1925 he had moderated—and Americanized—his project to the point that humor was its preferred vehicle of "fellow-feeling": even *Doctor Faustus* employed "humor" as its principal means. (Few readers saw this.)

Mann's enemies drove him to insist that "if modesty in praising oneself did not cease to be modesty, I would call myself a modest person." Not so, perhaps—but surely no less so than for Brecht, Döblin, or Hermann Broch. All these writers had the confidence of great work, and the doubt instilled by exile and a fickle public. Mann's frankest admission to Van Doren was "I regard my work as an extremely personal and very precarious coming to terms with art."

He ended with an overview of his career: "Individually, [the books] often are unreadable and it is not this or that book which has produced the success, but the whole. A long life, filled with work, has gradually made a certain impression."

Once English-speaking audiences turned to Kafka, Mann found himself oddly grateful to the Germans. "Only they understood me." Now he began complaining about the "denatured" English of Lowe-Porter's translation. He had become "a great unloved name. I don't know whether I may add unloved because unknown."

7

A POLITICAL LIGHT

I

While *The Magic Mountain* secured Mann's international reputation, it also earned him a battalion of new foes on the home front. Beginning in 1925, and for the last three decades of his life, he wasted huge amounts of time calculating the effects of his fame on those who wished him ill. Although he never made friends easily, he also went out of his way not to offend. Yet the very thought of Thomas Mann outraged some authors. As he observed in 1952, he had become "the envy of the gods and even more so of men." At twenty, at fifty, even at eighty, he was obliged to frame himself for public display.

On January 16, 1952, after reading a snide attack by Stephen Spender, Mann wondered to himself, "From where and why this hatred and contempt? How did I provoke it?" The answer was simple. The provocation was political, and he had been inciting his enemies for over thirty years. Between 1922 and 1925 Mann made his boldest foray into the political arena. From then on his image would remain that of a committed activist.

(As early as 1922 German liberals were proposing Heinrich for the presidency. In 1923 he made his first postwar visit to Paris, before an audience of fifty thousand gathered to honor the memory of Victor Hugo, three years before Thomas risked a visit to his nation's enemy.)

He would not have predicted this after completing *The Magic Mountain*, when he still believed that an artist should avoid politics. In May 1925, he wrote Ernst Fischer, a twenty-seven-year-old Austrian socialist, that he was not quite as engagé as *The Magic Mountain* might suggest. True, there were "moral repudiations" of "prewar capitalism," but any claims for his prowess as a social critic, he said, rang false. "In the final analysis, the novel is not historical, but I myself am." His roots were romantic, bourgeois, Goethean, and Wagnerian. His great link to modernity was "my experience of romanticism's self-transcendence in Nietzsche." What Fischer found provocative or "fascinating (in the bad sense)" was the irony of "parodistic conservatism by means of which I as an artist hold myself suspended between eras." An artist's "vocation, his nature, consists not in teaching, judging, and pointing directions, but in being, doing, expressing stages of the soul."

He could have written these words in 1918. But they were belied by the public role he had assumed since *The German Republic.*

A month later he delivered a commemorative essay on Lübeck's seven hundredth birthday. As he had done ten years earlier in the *Reflections*, he wrote himself into history, insisting on his representative status. In 1916 his identification had been shrill and reactionary; this time his was a command performance, and, following upon *The Magic Mountain* and his political essays, he appeared as a confidently didactic liberal.

Beginning on a personal note, he presents himself as his father's son. "How often in life have I confirmed with a smile, caught myself frankly in the act, that it is still actually my dead father's personality that, as a secret model, determines my conduct." (At one point, Heinrich, the favored child, might have questioned that.) True to his father's class, Mann declares that he has always had one story to tell, the transformation of the burgherly spirit into the artistic. Not, he adds, into the bourgeois capitalist or the Marxist, but into the "irony and freedom of art poised to wander and escape."

"Irony" for Mann is a term saturated with desire and contempt, but he saved that message for another day. Now he posited the *bürgerliche* qualities of moderation and humor as the virtues that would rescue Germany. Everything became an adjudication between sides: Marxist and capitalist, East and West, artist and bourgeois.

At forty, Mann had used German politics to illuminate his career. At fifty, it was the other way around.

Some readers understood his novel as a political apology. Walter Benjamin had detested Mann for his "Thoughts on War," but he was enthralled by the novel, which he considered a reversal of the essay. Benjamin accepted Mann's argument that left-wing politics had liberated his art.

Within six months of its publication, *The Magic Mountain* became a source of political metaphor. Mann viewed the 1925 candidacy of Field Marshal Hindenburg as " 'Der Lindenbaum'—to put it mildly," romantic nostalgia turned rancid. He trusted that his countrymen had learned their lesson; as he boasted to Julius Bab, "Little Hans has come that far." He began to conceive of Germany as a nation of Hans Castorps. Less than a year later he described the ways spiritual confusion had made his country-men "problem children of life," as if Hans's complaint had grown epidemic.

Fiction rendered him a national spokesman, invited to represent Germany at international peace conferences. These efforts boomeranged at home. Right-wing journalists deplored his trips abroad. When he attended the Carnegie conference in Paris, the German press "spoke in big letters of my scandalous kowtowing." Frequently quoting his own words against him, they contended that he had sold out both his nation and himself. In 1927, when he spoke out in favor of improved Franco-German relations, the *Berliner Nachtausgabe* ridiculed "the man who speaks on behalf of traitors to the fatherland and defames his people." Mann replied in the *Literarische Welt* that such "megaphoning" gave patriotism a bad name. (A month later he spelled out his views in an essay baldly titled "Culture and Socialism.")

In 1948 Mann recalled the period:

> Whatever I did from then on: my defense of that poor creature of defeat, the universally sabotaged republic, my opposition to rising nationalism and to all the philosophical endeavors and maneuvers that accompanied it . . . all these were received at best with a dubious shrug, perhaps accompanied by the puzzled question—"Why does he do these things? Is he angling for a cabinet office?" For the most part, however, my attitude was interpreted as treason and apostasy from a Germany that I saw reeling toward a barbaric dictatorship.

He had spent the 1920s, he wrote, "under the pressure . . . of national odium." Official recognition didn't help: "It only imposed on me the obligation of making all sorts of academic addresses and politically adjuring statements."

In an era divided between *Neue Sachlichkeit* and old illusions, the number of bamboozled intellectuals was high. (It included the psychoanalyst Carl Jung, the zoologist Ernst Haeckel, and numerous men of letters whose ethos had attracted Mann up to the early 1920s.) The various combinations of pagan ritual, lyric poetry, and bad science reminded Mann of the lunatic excesses of 1890s Munich. What made the kitsch incendiary was its explicit racism and xenophobia. What made it ubiquitous was the triumph of mass communications, the radio broadcasts of Hitler's message, and the Nazis' stunning use of visual imagery in newspapers and films.

Mann dreamed of a more progressive alternative; that's why he initially called the movies "a democratic power." Similarly, photomontagists like

John Heartfield tried to combat the Nazis' agitprop with a counterimagery of the left. But, alas, the ultramodern and the reactionary fed off each other. Scientific miracles facilitated the transmission of Wagnerian myths: much as television satellites would later broadcast the messages of right-wing evangelists. From one perspective, then, Mann's attempt to outargue the enemy was not a diversion from traditional culture, but a dying gasp of that culture, a deployment of language and reason in the age of what he called "mechanical mysticism" and "technological romanticism."

He lacked comrades. Perhaps it was a question of style. Conservatives complained that his progressive speeches lacked the *Reflections'* poetic flair. Meanwhile, left-wingers found his deliberations cautious to a fault. George Grosz remembered attending a dinner at Samuel Fischer's "beautifully appointed villa in Grunewald near Berlin," some time after 1929. All eyes were drawn to the honored guest, Thomas Mann, "secretly envied as a winner of the Nobel Prize in literature . . . the highest honor that a German writer could be awarded, since titles could no longer be conferred by a republican Germany." Grosz claimed to admire Mann's "ability, seemingly, to say yes and no at the same time, all with an air of cool grace." But Grosz reports that the smart young leftists "were not satisfied until they could tag a man with a definite party affiliation." Mann wouldn't oblige them: "He stood aside and a bit above all parties. . . . Like all really great writers and deep thinkers, he observed mankind with the eye of a skeptic." This is not intended as praise: Grosz portrays Mann as someone too rarefied to see clearly. Sharpening his critique, he reports that the next time he encountered Mann, in 1934—in New York at a luncheon in Reuben's restaurant—both Mann and Katia still believed that Hitler was a temporary phenomenon: Katia declared Grosz "quite a horrible person" to think otherwise.

As Grosz's unfriendly remarks suggest, Mann was a halfhearted party man. Ironically it was only in America in the 1940s that he actually stumped for a candidate, Franklin Delano Roosevelt. Meanwhile, unknown to him, FDR considered appointing Mann the leader of postwar Germany. Given the number of enemies he had acquired, his tenure would have made Václav Havel's in the Czech Republic seem a joyride. If the apparatchiks didn't assassinate him, the *nomenklatura* would have.

One of the earliest anti-Mannians was the formerly obsequious Josef Ponten. In an essay commemorating the sixtieth birthday of the liberal writer Ricarda Huch, Mann had chastised the "hostile idiots" who, "ostrich-like," maintain the "dreary, rotten distinction between the German poet (*Dichter*) and un-German man of letters (*Schriftsteller*)." The distinction, misguided in 1900, now seemed a mark of political reaction, part of a nationalist conception of culture that Nietzsche had dismissed fifty years earlier. Ponten's response was an open letter in a Berlin newspaper: his attempt to counter Mann's earlier appeal to that city's youth. It was unclear whom he despised more, Mann the democrat or Mann the *Schriftsteller.* (Mann didn't see himself as a journalist; he boasted that even the political passages of *The Magic Mountain* revealed "a touch of the poet.")

Like a scorned lover, Ponten humiliated himself with each attempt to capture his master's attention. On January 21, 1925, Mann replied that he could no longer disregard "the picturesque breach which you have evidently had an irresistible compulsion to open up publicly between us." He continued that he hardly needed Ponten to bring him to his senses. He understood the allure of reactionary art better than anyone else in Germany.

> Anyone acquainted with the musical dialectic of *The Magic Mountain* likewise knows that, and also knows that I would be quite capable of answering you. Every sensible person understands why today it seems right to me—to keep to the terminology that you have taken over from our conversations—to come down on the side of "intelligence" —without at all worrying that "nature" in our Germany can ever be so overbalanced that it will go flying off into the blue sky.

Germans can never become *too* rational; they remain a tribe of poets and madmen. Ponten may have "mobilized the nationalistic youth against me" with his *dichterliche* mumbo-jumbo, but I can summon my own troops: "a good many young hearts" have been lifted by the novel.

Because German culture has not changed greatly, Mann employs a century-old argument to clinch his case. In a personal letter Goethe states that his fellow Germans are "three steps from barbarism." As a result, said Mann, Goethe conceived his task, his national calling, as essentially a civilizing one; therein lay the deepest and most German meaning of his "renunciation": a rejection of atavistic tendencies he had experienced himself. Just as Mann would renounce a lifetime of bohemian pleasure, he imagined Goethe as filled with "potentialities for a more savage, more rank, more dangerous, more 'natural' greatness which was only reined in by his instinct for self-restraint." Defying his own nature—ruthless, egomaniacal, all-too-German—Goethe advanced an "ethical culture," a term so rank with philistine piety, with the atmosphere of a ceremonial banquet, that Ponten, the nationalist-cum-aesthete, probably wanted to squeal with rage: I cry for Wagner, and you give me Bertha von Suttner!

Ponten counseled the public to see through Mann's pompous effusions.

Mann viewed that public with equanimity; sometimes they loved him, he told Ponten, sometimes they didn't: "I am so used to being seen in a bad light, the illumination that falls upon me has already changed so frequently, that I have renounced the thankless and scarcely dignified nuisance of self-defense and self-justification. I am resolved to leave everything to time and to whatever slow, continuous influence my character may exert." Three months later he wrote again to Ponten, revealing an expert awareness of his shifting position. He joked that very few people considered his celebrated irony "destructive, nihilistic, and diabolic." If anything, "my literary antagonists tend to see it as the expression of a mild and unradical bourgeois temper, and those who take a more affirmative attitude toward me customarily speak of kindness."

This is justly stated. Mann's enemies from left (Brecht) to right (Nabokov) saw him as a bourgeois milquetoast, a middlebrow passing himself off as deep, while his champions rallied to his ideas of "ethical culture." Very likely the real Mann resided elsewhere, in a domain of "forbidden love," renounced only in the flesh. But neither side wanted that Mann. Much like the Christian devotees of Wittgenstein when they learned of his homosexuality, those who admire Mann the humanist were stunned, if not demoralized, by evidence that *Death in Venice* was not simply a metaphor.

Mann realized that he had become a public object, about whom no word is final. Therefore let the antagonists contend. "I do not know who is right; I don't see myself, no one does." Replying to Ponten's "pathological" jealousy forces Mann to generalize about his fame. In so doing he discovers in himself a nature so protean that each critic finds himself reflected in it. By now Mann knows that whatever he does will serve as an incitement, a bad light will always turn him into somebody's devil. A combination of paranoia and discretion would henceforth characterize his public statements about himself. What some readers take as vain or arch is more often the calibrated declaration of someone who expects to be misunderstood.

That Mann's friendship with Ponten survived his forthright commentary indicates the latter's inability to relinquish the proximity to fame. On August 29, 1927, Thomas informed Heinrich that Ponten was campaigning for Mann's appointment to the presidency of the Prussian Academy of Arts, although the idea of Thomas Mann in an administrative position was risible. He confided that Ponten was a "follower who is perpetually troubled by my literary existence and overcompensates by a blindly zealous friendship." (Mann was willing to consider Ponten's proposal, he declared, only to be agreeable. It was a "ticklish" matter keeping what Heinrich once called his cast of extras satisfied; essentially he considered the apparent devotion of "these fellows" fraudulent: he quipped that "hypochondria"—apparently his synonym for paranoia—was a great eye-opener.)

Though Ponten became a Nazi supporter, as late as 1938 he could write that his correspondence with Mann documented one of the great literary relations of the century. This was a courageous boast in Hitler's Germany, but it vastly overrated his significance to Mann.

P olitics intruded into Mann's only substantial friendships. Ernst Bertram and Hans Reisiger were his soul mates, both gay, both steeped in literary culture. At one time Bertram had been the closer, evoking Mann's Nietzschean tendencies. Whatever confidences they shared is not reported, but in 1949 Mann wrote Bertram, "I believe you know me as one who never loses anything."

Events began to turn sour during the late 1920s. The friendship floundered over Bertram's "enthusiastic faith in the rising Third Reich. . . . How many conversations I remember! He saw roses and marble where I saw nothing but diabolic filth, a poisonous intoxicant for the populace, innate murderousness, and certain ruin for Germany and Europe. Communication between us ceased to be possible."

All the same, in 1948 he told a young German that Bertram had been "for many years, my and my family's best friend." It would be an everlasting shame that his best friend and favorite Nietzschean had wound up a Nazi.

I n April 1925, after *The Magic Mountain*'s publication, Mann told Julius Bab that he lacked an aptitude for politics: "metaphysics" and psychology were his provinces. Instead, in a series of groundbreaking essays he investigated popular culture, employing a not-quite-political approach to issues that only appeared extrapolitical. Mann was convinced that his fellow Germans were unprepared for political responsibility, a lack that made them vulnerable to the worst demagogic appeals. By examining the individual pastimes—if you will, the "metaphysics" of fads and hobbies—that served in lieu of politics; he anticipated the reign of unreason that swept his country.

A month later a Berlin paper sought his opinion of "the Cosmopolitan idea." He responded with an essay poised between autobiography and prescription. He had become a cosmopolitan by default, he now realized, simply by loving to read. He admitted his provincial origins: "I am no man of the world, anything but polyglot"; when he heard that Gide learned

English simply to read Conrad, he felt ashamed. But at that moment, cosmopolitanism was suspect: "ethnic obscurantists," he said, wished to ban all foreign invaders. They wouldn't succeed, because "the enemy is in our midst." Our greatest writers—Goethe, Schopenhauer, Nietzsche—exemplify "European prose," even in the "original German." (He could have added that Nietzsche wanted his readers to "de-Germanize" themselves.) The genius of narrative is inherently international.

As the essay continues, Mann personalizes the dialectic. A writer can be simultaneously representative and eccentric, internationalist and a homebody: both a world-class figure and a plodding craftsman, dismissed by his neighbors as a dull mediocrity. (All this from a man who lamented that he was singularly without personality.) The local becomes the global: "A writer can become more German, while simultaneously changing the face of his nation to the eyes of the world." That writer is obviously someone serving elsewhere as *The Dial*'s correspondent.

Confounding his right-wing admirers, this position was not a temporary phase. As late as 1952, it struck him that Goethe had fought the same battle. When he took on the fads of medieval Catholicism, "poetic Tartufferie and refined obscurantism," the motive was political—even if he didn't realize it—since these movements would coalesce into the counter-revolution.

Mann had fought a similar war in the 1920s, when he attacked the various tendencies—from anti-Semitism to mother worship—that won the approval of fascists. Some of his fellow members of the Prussian Academy were *völkische* nationalists. Their kitsch radicalized him; as he later said, "fascism pushed me to the left." This animus reverberates throughout his 1927 essay, "Munich as a Cultural Center." He opens by remembering when Munich seemed preferable to Berlin, more humane and tolerant, even more democratic than its Prussian counterpart. But the city has become a "haven of reaction, poisoned by anti-Semitic nationalism." He examines the old cliché about northern "brains" and southern "soul." But Munich sentiment is now unmediated by thought. Feeling is not enough; feeling characterized the assassins of Walther Rathenau; if Europe commits collective suicide, it will do so "with the deepest feeling." Unfortunately "anyone who shows traces of intellect is considered a Jew and that finishes him."

Mann heartily deplores the kind of Munich smugness latent in a dialect idiom, "Mir san Gesund." ("We're healthy," as in the British "I'm all right, Jack," or the French "Je m'en fiche.") No, you're not healthy, Mann asserts, recalling the period thirty years earlier when he had told Grautoff "how I hate healthy men."

Much like the *Reflections*, these essays constituted a last-ditch effort to salvage the past. But that same year he wrote "Culture and Socialism," in which he proclaimed the battle lost. ("Cosmopolitan" later became a Stalinist indictment, usually reserved for Jews, a turn of events that would not have surprised Mann.) None of his idols—Goethe, Schopenhauer, or Nietzsche—were democrats, though he continued to insist that they weren't proto-Nazis, either. All cultural questions had been politicized, either a siding with the nation (ipso facto, the national became international; its culture, civilization) or a retreat into the dark night of *völkische Kultur* (heavy stress on the "K," he added). With a kind of logical inevitability, he concluded "that what we are really dealing with is socialism." And, alas, none of Germany's great men offered "the social, the socialistic ingredient."

He seemed to be calling for a left-wing Nietzsche, and every sign indicated that he himself fit the bill. But while he announced himself a socialist, he realized that further identification with the proletariat was inappropriate for the very symbol of bourgeois culture. He also sensed that "faith in the saving grace . . . of the proletariat" was kitsch on the order of religious fundamentalism or *Kultur* itself. As he had advocated since 1922, Germany, the great land of the middle, would henceforth fulfill its geographical destiny as the midpoint between Athens and Moscow. Marx would read Hölderlin—assuming that the exchange was not "one-sided" —and all would be well.

"Culture and Socialism" was prompted by an attack composed by a right-wing journalist, Arthur Hübscher, writing in a "Naziclub" magazine (actually, the *Süddeutsche Monatshefte*). Hübscher accused Mann of revising the newest edition of the *Reflections* in order to dilute its conservative message. In fact, he had only condensed the anti-Heinrich material; none of the wartime polemic was lost. Mann had even admitted that his conservative prose was more artful than his recent propaganda for the Weimar Republic.

Personal and political became as tenuously separated as essay and fiction. Two months after "Culture and Socialism" appeared, an editor whose magazine he had boycotted over a purely literary dispute (the editorship of a series of novels) retaliated by publishing letters between Hübscher and Mann. In one, dated June 27, Mann had ridiculed Munich's obsession with two pilots who had made the first flight across the Atlantic. "The nationalist headstands . . . our misguided city is performing in honor of the two flying dunces" struck him as worse nonsense than *Johnny spielt auf*, a popular jazz opera by Ernst Krenek. With these impious words he became non grata twice over, as both a socialist and a slayer of sacred cows.

Describing the resulting brouhaha, Mann wrote Willy Hass on March 11, 1928, that it was all a case of "pure, dynamistic romanticism, pure glorification of catastrophe for its own sake. Basically it is popular culture and this is the sort of thing that an organ of the revived bourgeoisie presents to its readers nowadays as entertainment. These are curious times."*

About this time the Nazis invented a new term, "die Thomasmänner," to describe the socialist humanists who shared Mann's perspective. The pun, translatable as "Mann Men" or "Mannians," turned him into the personification of what later conservatives dubbed "trendy liberalism" or "radical chic."

The cultural essays reveal Mann as Cassandra, a role he kept playing after 1925. To deepen the parallel, cultural politics became entwined with sexual liberation. A question of "family values" would also disturb his peace. Then as now, some patriots discovered treason in the bedroom. Foreshadowing the religious right, German nationalists took special aim at "red queers." Among their first targets were Mann's children Klaus and Erika.

Klaus's play *Anya and Esther* opened in the fall of 1925 to mostly negative reviews. One Munich critic, Tim Klein, who judged a play by whether "it strengthens youth for the coming war of *revanche*," found this bisexual version of musical chairs unconducive to a warrior spirit. (Contradicting Hans Blüher or Mann's recent works, "forbidden love" had become a political liability.) On November 6, Mann wrote Erika a birthday note, citing the neanderthals in the press and adding that "I too . . . have been thoroughly belabored, in print as well as in rough and incredible anonymous letters. But these don't bother me in the least." He was both tactful—implying gently that the play was awful: "by no means as bad as people pretend"—and protective, since negative criticism always disturbed him.

This was yet another development Mann had predicted: popular culture came in many forms, including scandal sheets. Yet for the virtual embodiment of *Haltung*, it remained a terrible situation, the modern Goethe and his family ending up in the German equivalent of the *National Enquirer*. In 1930, when Katia joined some friends in a pacifist organization, the Nazi press decried these impertinent "wealthy Jewesses," including "Frau Thomas Mann." A year later it turned on the more militant Erika, deploring her mannish outfit, and dubbing her a "Bolshevik Fury." Right-wing tabloids continued to stalk the Manns, particularly Erika and Klaus, after World War II. In the 1960s, when the German press spread new rumors about an incestuous relation between the siblings, Erika pursued a libel case and won. (The ultimate tabloid exposé appeared in 1991. After the

---

* Paul Nikolaus Cossmann, editor of the *Süddeutsche Monatshefte*, was yet another right-wing Jew; for all the good his chauvinism did him, he died at seventy-three in Theresienstadt.

publication of Mann's diaries involving Franz Westermeier, a German weekly did a feature on "The Coming Out [in English] of Thomas Mann.")

II

Goebbels's famous remark "When I hear the word 'culture' I reach for my gun" may have been a response to Thomas Mann. From 1929 to 1932 Mann argued that since cultural questions were inherently political, the proper thrust of German culture should be left-leaning, antifascist, indeed socialist. "Culture," then, became as much his code as the Nazis'.

There were other alternatives he disdained, namely those represented by "Moscow" (Bolshevism) or "Rome" (Italian fascism). He considered the Fascists mystifiers and the Communists dullards. One side offered a caricature of spirituality, the other of materialism. Yet he had affinities with both groups: the Fascist love of spectacle and its cadre of gleaming warriors appealed to elements in his personality he had grown to mistrust; while the Communists' revelation of class interests coincided with his own irreverent take on capitalist society.

(At least once he defended a Communist who faced execution for his political activities. In 1927, Lukács asked him to intercede with Admiral Horthy, regent of Hungary, on behalf of Zoltán Szántó, a member of the illegal Hungarian Communist Party, who was about to go on trial in Budapest. Mann replied, as he had to Ernst Fischer, that the writer's role was to avoid the "political arena." Lukács replied that he was a "high-minded liar." Shamed by his admirer, Mann sent a telegram within a few days, stating "I have sent a cable to Admiral Horthy." Lukács informed Judith Marcus that he subsequently destroyed the correspondence so that Mann's gesture would seem altruistic, and not Communist-inspired. Twenty years later, Mann needed no such encouragement to defend left-wing radicals.)

Like Brecht, Mann re-examined his tradition to find ethical and political models. In January 1929 he gave a lecture on Gotthold Lessing (1729–81), the Berlin-based playwright and critic, author of the philo-Semitic play Nathan the Wise, and the German voice of enlightenment. Echoing the diction of his Joseph novel, he made Lessing the master of a "timeless" myth recurring in a "perpetual present." As if to stress the contemporary relevance, he recorded his lecture on film, an early use of the medium for didactic purposes.

The brief was self-exculpatory. He too, much like Lessing, was a "controversialist," attacked for confusing literary art and propaganda by nationalists posing as formalists. Lessing was a deist, exhibiting a theological seriousness worthy of Martin Luther, although he detested Luther's textual fetish: "The letter killeth the spirit." The faith he articulated was rational, tolerant, and modern, but it failed to please either Lutherans or Catholics —as Mann offended radicals and conservatives alike.

During the war, Mann had praised Luther's self-obsession as the German alternative to Western politics. But Settembrini finds in Luther's "cranial formation" and "quiescent beatitude" the marks of Asia. Germany, standing at the center of Europe, must reject Luther, must finally and definitively ally itself with the West, with reason and politics. Mann deftly placed Settembrini's remarks in the chapter "A Soldier Good and Brave," in which Joachim dies, thus making the noble warrior appear as reactionary as the egregious theologian.

Alas, in 1929 Luther's intolerance is flourishing, while Lessing's "Enlightenment . . . is intellectually out-of-date." It seems vapid beside the roaring appeals of competing creeds, namely the brownshirts marching through the streets of Munich. Everywhere its enemies attack reason as a bourgeois ploy, a Jewish scheme, or a case of repression. The nation hungers for a new myth. But the pendulum shift from rationalism to anti-intellectualism needs correction. "We are so far gone in the irrational . . . to the joy of all the baser enemies of light." The "chthonic crew" must be dispatched back to their murky grotto.

This obliges Mann to quote a more appealing figure than Luther— Nietzsche, whose words had so frequently validated his thoughts. Until now: for in the "perpetual present," he sees with horror that one side of Nietzsche's "mind-drunken prophecy," turning on itself, condemned both rationalism and idealism. In this anachronistic battle of Germany's soul, fought with words, not bullets, Lessing became the anti-Luther and the counter-Nietzsche. In his name and spirit, Mann imagined "a union of blood and reason which alone merits the name of complete humanity."

This new humanism had become the agenda of his *Joseph* project as well. Conservatives were right: his fiction had been politicized. So it was of a piece that shortly after the Lessing essay he composed "Mario and the Magician," the tale inspired by the Mann family's vacation in Fascist Italy, something he claimed to have written off the top of his head. As mentioned earlier, the magician Cipolla shares many traits with Mann, including a bad case of artistic insecurity and a hopeless love of young men. A less biographical reading simply depicts him as a proto-Fascist, combining artistic formulas with demagogic references to *il Duce*. Mann welcomed this interpretation as further evidence of his prophetic talent.

The magician is a spellbinder, manipulating his audience with the finesse of an American evangelist. Indeed, at one point, a woman starts to dance in the aisles like a member of a revivalist church. (Klaus Mann believed that Hitler's microphone technique had but one antecedent, that of the California faith healer Aimee Semple McPherson.) A year later, Mann described Nazi rallies in terms that fit evangelistic services: "political scenes in the grotesque style, with Salvation Army methods, hallelujahs and bell-ringing and dervishlike repetition of monstrous catchwords, until everyone foams at the mouth"—a Nazi glossolalia.

Mann regarded this secular Pentecostalism as "epileptic ecstasy" and, rewriting Marx, discerned the transformation of politics into "an opiate for the masses." (He would have been ready for talk radio.) A mix of sweat, noise, and blood sealed the triumph of all the "priests of a dynamic or-gasm," from Cipolla to Hitler. But where, amidst such lunacy, was room for Thomas Mann?

He received more prosaic evidence that his star had passed. In October 1929 the Buddenbrook bookstore in Lübeck went out of business. The avant-garde found his work old-fashioned; radicals despised his politics.

But on November 12 he was awarded the Nobel Prize for literature, the first such award to a German since before World War I. On the Berlin radio Heinrich saluted Thomas's journey from right to left, as if the 200,000-mark prize were his reward for time on the mountain. Apparently the Nobel committee was less impressed by this turn: Mann learned that one judge, "the Stockholm critic and professor of literature [Martin Fridrik] Boök, who usually has a decisive influence upon the choice of the Nobel Prize winner, publicly proclaimed *The Magic Mountain* a monstrosity and said I was receiving the prize exclusively, or at any rate chiefly, for my early novel *Buddenbrooks*." He got around Boök by using his acceptance speech to acknowledge Germany's political development; he made it clear that the days of *Buddenbrooks* were past and gone.

Within months of the award, he had already turned it into a mythic comedy, the kind of honor a Joseph would understand as more—or less—than personal.

The famous award of the Swedish Academy, which once more, after a space of seventeen years, fell to Germany's lot, had, I knew, hovered over me more than once before and found me not unprepared. It lay, I suppose, upon my path in life—I say this without presumption, with calm if not uninterested insight into the character of my destiny, of my "role" on this earth which has now been gilded with the equivocal brilliance of success; and which I regard entirely in a human spirit, without any great mental excitement. And just so, in such a spirit of reflective and receptive calm, I have accepted as my lot in life the resounding episode, with all its festal and friendly accompaniments, and gone through it with the best grace I could muster—even inwardly, which is a harder matter.

On December 10, in a formal ceremony, he received the award from King Gustav V. He accepted "the prize, which more or less accidentally bears my name," in the name of "my country and my people." He could speak with a certain pride as their representative: "Those of my ilk feel more closely bound to the German soul" as it has grown more democratic. With these words he challenged the people who denied the value of his cultural politics.

Singlehanded, he had worked Germany's artistic redemption. The voice counseling reason and tolerance, cosmopolitanism and socialism had drowned out the Wagnerian chorale. Or so it seemed.

A month later, on December 20, he spoke on German radio about the prize and its meaning for a social democracy. Underlying his affiliation, that evening he read from *The Tales of Jacob* at a benefit dance for the Jewish Care for the Aged.

From February to April 1930, Thomas and Katia toured Egypt and Palestine as he soaked in the atmosphere experienced by his wandering Jew; both husband and wife spent time as patients in a local hospital, recovering from dysentery. By then, he had finished *The Tales of Jacob*.

The next summer he purchased a beach house at Nidden on the Kurisch coast, a Baltic region which was later the setting of Günter Grass's *The Tin Drum*. Here, amidst "the fantastic world of sandy dunes mile on mile, the birch and pine groves full of elk," he continued to work on *Young Joseph*. He was too absorbed in his novel to accept Fischer's request for an essay on Goethe: "My books come about freely, from necessity and amusement." For the moment, he needed to tell Joseph's story. Joseph had been drawn at least partially from Klaus Heuser. During that affair three years earlier, one poet had been his troubadour. So it was apt that he now made his boldest statement about politics and homosexuality in a lecture on Platen.

In the 1930s, Mann would put these words in Goethe's mouth: "Ours is a time that casts a sharp and ruthless light which brings out the political element inherent in everything, in all beauty, all humanity." This perhaps was the "light, more light" that Nietzsche believed would dispel Wagnerian heat; it was also the "light, more light" that had been Goethe's dying request. A political light forced him to re-examine whatever he loved most about his culture. In 1945, he even warned American GIs not to be fooled by the Germans' "cleanliness, orderliness, politeness," astonishing advice from the always impeccable Mann, whose sartorial reflex rivaled Thomas Buddenbrook's. (In 1925, he wrote, "If someone puts on his best coat, such good manners deserve honor.")

His political courage appears all the more remarkable when contrasted with the tepid performance of his literary peers. James Joyce refused to publish an essay in *Mass und Wert* because it had published Mann's ground-breaking reply to the dean of Bonn. (Guilt by association might threaten *Ulysses'* publication in Germany.) Yeats spent his last years flirting with fascism. Gide's voice was muted after his trip to the Soviet Union, and stilled during his North African exile. Robert Musil sulked in Switzerland, possibly more angry at Mann and Stefan Zweig than at Hitler.

Mann knew that of all his forms and masks, that of the political ad-vocate was the strangest. "An itinerant preacher of democracy [was] a role whose comic element was always evident." When in 1951 Philip Toynbee called his image, "Almost too-good-to-be-true," he half-agreed. "It is slightly questionable [a lagniappe of Fontane], all my . . . optimism . . . humanitarianism . . . even my 'world-citizenship,' since my books remain desperately German." Yet, to paraphrase the story of Joseph, it was this highly questionable candidate whom fate chose to become the literary voice of anti-Fascism—official, no less: vetted by the White House. "I am he": his surprise was greater than Joseph's.

Mann's dream of a Marxist romanticism signified a "conservative imag-ination," rooted in the not-so-distant past, though Erich Heller might object to seeing his term so employed. The attempts in *Doctor Faustus* to find a cultural explanation for Nazism were anticipated in these essays. Then, as later, Mann bewildered historians who found more obvious causes than a misreading of poetry.

Yet he was right. Culture had become explicitly political. In 1933 the Nazis' first holocaust was cultural: a massive book-burning (including the works of Klaus Mann). Afterward Mann decided that culture had become a killing ground for dictators. "Never before did men of power speak ex cathedra about culture." Napoleon or Bismarck had ignored culture; they were unembarrassed Philistines. But Hitler, who had once sought employ-ment as Lion Feuchtwanger's set designer, considered himself culturally advanced. His devotion to Wagner and Nietzsche was legendary; both would suffer a retroactive guilt for *his* misinterpretation. Mann couldn't rescue Wagner; he tried gamely with Nietzsche.

Although in 1933 Mann didn't know that cultural abuses in the name of politics were also rampant in the Soviet Union, the idea of a Cultural Commissar would not have shocked Naphta's creator. Today, when Pentecostal pit bulls like Pat Robertson attack the specter of "secular humanism," they behave exactly the way Mann anticipated. A political invasion of culture, whether in the name of socialist realism, the Third Reich, or family values, has been an enduring phenomenon of the century, and Mann was among its earliest prophets.

Twice he specifically linked cultural and sexual politics. The first time was 1922, when his discovery of Whitman coalesced with the Weimar Republic. The second derived from a comparable source. On October 4, 1930, he gave a lecture on Platen (later published in *Essays of Three Decades*) to a group of scholars in Platen's birthplace, Ansbach. In it he merges critical analysis with personal confession; subtly, and perhaps for his pleasure alone, he yokes erotic memory to political manifesto.

Like Mann, Platen had enemies everywhere. The right considered him a turncoat, while the left dismissed him as "a Junker and a count." Liberals like Heine distrusted him because he was not merely an aristocrat but a homosexual, dabbling in "an aristocratic vice." About this tendency Mann speaks as freely as he had in 1922: "Literary history, out of lack of knowledge, and with a reserve *today out of date* [italics mine], has spoken with foolish circumlocution about the decisive fact in Platen's life: his exclusively homosexual constitution." Mann had first defended Heine when he was eighteen—and had put himself on the line for his socialist convictions—but his greater loyalty was to Platen. In a few years Maxim Gorky would declare that the way to stamp out fascism was to end homosexuality: a contention that infuriated Klaus Mann. In the Platen essay Thomas defends Klaus's case before the fact, exhorting leftists to accept homosexuals as their natural allies.

Not since *Death in Venice* has Mann dramatized so vividly the bonding of language and Eros. (Considering that Platen's verse saturates the novella, the essay seems two decades overdue. But then Mann always needed time.) A new "frankness of speech" enables him to crack Platen's code. The poet's abstractions, his refusal to identify the object of his desires, disguise "a spirit-whisper of nameless love." Improving on Oscar Wilde, Mann shows that Platen, not free to name his love, chose the forms most often adopted by homosexual poets. In his 1920 letter to Carl Maria Weber, he offered a roll call of virile homosexuals; now, a decade later, he lists the forms—

"Persian ghazel, Renaissance sonnet, Pindaric ode"—that homosexual poets have found amenable. He jokes about the outlandishly "forced accents" that result from Platen's linguistic experiments. Subjecting the language to foreign influences, Platen alternately "expanded and tortured it." But it wasn't simply an instance of arriviste gaucherie. "The strictly formal and form-plastic character had an aesthetic and psychological affinity with his Eros." Mann supports this argument with a quotation from Nietzsche: "The degree and kind of a man's sexuality permeate the very loftiest heights of his intellect."

The philosopher understood as well that one gains "the loftiest heights" by conquering his "lower drives"; he virtually introduced the word *sublimieren*. As so often, Nietzsche was Mann's prophet. A highly conscious sublimation was the way Mann dealt with the loss of erotic happiness. Unable to love men in the flesh, he chose to pursue them in literary forms. His celebrated "irony" was the equivalent of Platen's odes; to paraphrase his remark at twenty, the Form was the Mask.

Similarities between the two men leap off the page. A "passionate but reckless quixotry" disposed Platen to seek fame in ways both anachronistic and fustian. He cherished "pathetic, out-of-date notions about laurel wreaths" and wished to be remembered for having won "second prize for odes." Mann finds himself in an awkward position, considering that he had been a recipient of such a wreath five years earlier. He admits that Platen preens with a high-toned flamboyance—one literary peacock disputing the other's tail. Yet, he adds, the affectation was joyless; his "nature" was "austere melancholy," a characteristic with which Mann's readers have grown familiar.

Heine and his friends, Mann says, tried to "conventionalize" Platen without seeing that he shared their "scorn for the petty, middle-class meanness of life." (It didn't help that, as Mann doesn't mention, Platen had made snobbish, anti-Semitic remarks about Heine's "garlic breath.") Such an indictment has not escaped Mann's lips before, but love of Platen—and Klaus Heuser—drives him to new heights of rhetorical outrage. He makes Platen's radicalism a function of his love of beauty, thereby placing him less in Heine's camp than in Whitman's.

> Beauty, which he worshipped, and has certainly every reason to worship, is indeed the anti-useful and thus the anti-moral principle, since the moral is nothing but what is useful to life. The poet-immorality with which it plays is in reality radical anti-morality, a deep bond with the beautiful, even contrary to the interests of nature. . . . The

moral libertinage of his Eros unites all free and hyper-useless elements in a bond against the mean, ordinary, anxious ones of life.

These words completely undermine the marriage essay of 1925. The "anti-useful" means both the unproductive (ergo homosexual) and the "anti-bourgeois"; the bohemians have invaded Professor Cornelius's library. Fifty years earlier Nietzsche granted his readers license to behave like libertines as a means of self-conquest. But Mann goes a step further, making the "anti-moral" serve not an *übermenschliches* enterprise but the needs of social democracy. "The beautiful is now simply the humanly decent, in contrast to all mental obfuscation, all slavish pettiness and dishonor born of tyranny. It becomes the source of humanism, which, as it were circumventing nature, brings [Platen] into enthusiastic contact with the idea of the human." In 1925 Mann had declared that homosexuals "circumvented nature" with their barren fruitless love. But in the new dispensation, those who maneuver "contrary to the interests of nature" fabricate an ethical system all the more humane for its artifice. In an essay filled with astonishing turns, Mann homosexualizes the romantics' debate between spirit and nature.

That's not all. He socializes the question of sexual freedom, thus providing the intimate subtext previously missing from his cultural essays. "Did Platen perhaps hope that the socialization, the politicizing of the beautiful into the humanly worthy would raise him above himself, that his own love of freedom would end by freeing himself?" Platen, and Mann speaking through him, becomes an avatar of gay liberation, a phrase that might have sprung from Mann's critical vocabulary. But the poet dreamt "in vain." Anger and struggle that "exalted" others left him embittered and longing for death. Mann sketches a tale that would have made one of his saddest fictions, a poignant coda to *Death in Venice*. It may profitably be compared to the "not there, not then" which separates the two friends, Indian and English, at the end of *A Passage to India*, or with Birkin's failure to save Gerald Crich in *Women in Love*.

Surveying Platen's grandiose passion, Mann can't help smiling. All that fervor devoted to such callow types, "quite ordinary and average." The love objects welcomed their anonymity: instead of gratitude for his lyrical effusions, they felt "middle-class relief" that nobody caught on. Platen exhausted himself defending "a love like anybody else's"—Mann's line presumes a vaster tolerance than obtained in 1930. But there's a proviso: "like anybody else's, only—at least in his time—with smaller prospects of happiness." In that parenthesis lurks the memory of Klaus Heuser's embrace.

Platen's critics notwithstanding, he achieved the only wisdom Mann considers heroic, that "loving abnegation raises one above the beloved." This defense of Platen becomes a class action, enfolding all those who follow the poet's commandments. Aschenbach is more than absolved.*

Never again would Mann write so confidently about the "nameless love." Yet if, as he says, each moment of a story contains its own truth and casts its own "light," then the Platen essay demonstrates that he could envision the very happiness he felt obliged to renounce. He would come to share Platen's melancholy, taking for granted that the Franzls were his Sancho Panzas, out for a buck and not for glory. His "smaller prospects of happiness" dwindled with the years.

Platen died at thirty-nine, his final disease (a "vague typhus") a mere pretext for hastening an end he had long sought. What kept Mann from a similarly premature fate? Perhaps the work habits of a medieval craftsman; perhaps the demands of political commitment.

Throughout his life Mann found humor redemptive. Shortly after his arrival in America, he wrote, apropos of Kafka, that "laughter . . . is perhaps the best thing left to us." Indeed he finds Platen wanting in only one area: "the joyless crusader of an order devoted to death and love" had no sense of humor. "Truth, Beauty's earthly sister . . . a child of life, can see also the funny side of things." In his relentless morbidity, Platen became as "touching and absurd" as Don Quixote. This explained why his appeal remained limited to the cognoscenti, even among Germans. It also recalled Mann's admonition to himself while planning *Die Geliebten*—a work as homosexually driven as anything by Platen—not to forget "the humor." Without it, he ran the risks of Platen, being patronized and pitied. Even with it, his story was sad enough.

The political ramifications of his Platen essay were clear. As we saw, Mann's political radicalization was coextensive with, if not derived from, his interest in sexual liberation. Nineteen twenty-two, the year of "The German Republic," was also the first year he signed a petition condemning Paragraph 175. Before that, his tribune had been Hans Blüher, exponent of "manly," uniquely German pederasty, and not Magnus Hirschfeld, the

---

* Platen's most famous poem, the one beginning "He who ever gazed upon true beauty / Is already into death's hand given," bears the title "Tristan." "How strange!" Mann comments. "It must have been in some peculiarly abstracted and sleep-walking state . . . that his hand traced this title above the lines. . . . 'Significant, almost clairvoyant,' " Bertram had called it in his study of Nietzsche, considering that Wagner's *"Liebestod"* wasn't composed until twenty-two years after Platen's death.

effeminate Jewish socialist. But by 1928 he would dedicate a short tribute to Hirschfeld on his sixtieth birthday; thanking him for showing "that certain laws are no longer in accordance with our present knowledge of body and soul." (Other contributors to the festschrift included Freud, the Marxist Karl Kautsky, Heinrich Mann, Jacob Wassermann, Stefan Zweig, Ernst Toller, Alfred Kubin, who had illustrated *Tristan*, Mann's friend from the Paris Conference, Richard Coudenhove-Kalergi, and two of his greatest enemies, Theodor Lessing and Alfred Kerr.)

Despite the support of such prominent—and largely Jewish—intellectuals, homosexuality was strongly condemned by right-wing parties and some Christians, who felt that 175 didn't go far enough. As the Reichstag elections of 1930 approached, Mann composed an essay attacking that position. It appeared in a special edition of *Der Eigene*, the premier homosexual journal. While probably composed in late 1929, the essay appeared sometime between July 18, 1930, when the Reichstag was disbanded, and September 14, when new elections were held. At roughly the same time that he argued Platen's case in literary circles, he made this explicitly political defense of homosexual love.

As if he were predicting American politics of the 1990s, Mann discerned a link between those who honor both "the holiness of property" and traditional morality. But what do they consider immoral? "Sexual tenderness between two grown men, based on a feeling that is as old as mankind"; powerful words from someone currently absorbed in the Old Testament.

Great art, he said, has been inspired by such love: the tomb of the Medicis, Platen's Venetian sonnets, the Symphony *Pathétique*, "heaven knows what else," the latter comment a private joke. Paragraph 175 is grounded in "out-of-date popular ideals," yet another indictment of a benighted populism. Meanwhile a large number of men will have to be locked up, "if you want to obey the law thoroughly" (Hitler's projected policy). In fact, the authorities tend to be tolerant. It's only the reactionaries who cry for homosexual blood—and the extortionists.

Public decorum, he grants, must be maintained. But are homosexuals less "inclined to public decency than normal people (who are often in their desires and practices even more perverse)?" This remarkable statement endorses one of the chief arguments of homosexual propaganda, questioning the very category of "normal." If that weren't enough, he adds a virtual defense of male prostitution. While minors ought to be protected, if a "young hustler" sells his services, he has no right to blackmail his "frightened lover." The man should go free; the boy should have "his ears boxed."

What's needed is a little more "humor, reason, and humanity." Athens declined not "because of boy love" but because it lacked political will, a deficiency that could yet prove to be Germany's downfall. These arguments taken with his "Appeal to Reason" make homophobia the concomitant of political reaction.

On another front he played no games and disguised no tendencies. Throughout the 1920s, Mann held firm against the Nazis, increasing the attacks he had begun in 1921 and broadcast to America two years later. His friendship with Bertram reached a crisis. After a meeting in late September 1930, the latter complained that Mann had exhibited "a terrible rage against Hitler." On October 17, 1930—thirteen days after the Platen lecture—Mann made an impassioned "Appeal to Reason" from one of Berlin's largest concert stages, the Beethoven Hall, the site in 1922 of his defense of the republic. Speaking with the confidence that all good Germans would stand together against the Nazis, he distributed praise equally between the Marxist Social Democrats and Gustav Stresemann, the former businessman who had steered Germany back into the family of nations. (He was a more enlightened, though no less conservative, Konrad Adenauer.) While he spoke, a crowd of Nazis took over the balcony, led by Brecht's old friend the playwright Arnolt Bronnen, "rendered partly unrecognizable by dark glasses," whom Mann had introduced to readers of *The Dial* as a nihilistic homosexual.

Bronnen had spent the 1920s flitting between the Nazis and the Communists. The Nazis had finally claimed him, though only after he had demonstrated to his friend Goebbels's satisfaction that the Jew whose name he bore was not really his father. He was still Brecht's friend, if no longer his lover, and his attack may have been a payback for Mann's earlier descriptions of the two playwrights as gay. Mann had long detected a homosexual element in the Nazis, an ugly version of tendencies he had observed in Blüher and Wagner. On a theoretical level, his dream of a homoerotic democracy had been killed by homoerotic fascists. Brecht would have laughed.

The Bronnen gang tried to shout Mann down. When the audience swiveled in their seats to signal their displeasure, a crony of Bronnen's photographed them from above, and the next issue of the Nazi rag *Völkischer Beobachter* (*The People's Watch*) printed it above the caption "Audience Turns Their Back on Thomas Mann." Years later, Bronnen, rehabilitated in the East, declared that it had been an impromptu episode, a case of bohemian hijinks. (Would Brecht have enjoyed the game, Nazi or not, at Mann's expense?)

It is wonderful to contemplate Mann standing before his enemies, pronouncing his uttermost scorn while his publisher's wife keeps pleading, "Stop as soon as you can!" He outraged the Nazis as much with cultural critique as with political. It was bad enough when he endorsed the Social Democrats (while denying any Marxist elements in their platform other than a commitment to peace, democracy, and workers' rights). But he cut to the quick when he aligned against them, Goethe, Schopenhauer, Nietzsche, and the composer of *Tristan*. With that opera's "noble malady" in their blood, Germans would never conform to "a primitive, pure-blooded simplicity, artless in mind and art, that smiles and submits and claps its heels together." In fact, he placed too much faith in Wagnerians.

The evening ended abruptly, without questions from the audience. Bruno Walter led Mann through the Beethoven catacombs to a getaway car he had parked next door. Each step must have shown Mann that the "humanly decent" had become a fragile prop against the barbarians now vandalizing his culture.

8

EXILE

I

"After the age of fifty," says Jorge Luis Borges, "all change becomes a hateful symbol of the passage of time." Not for Thomas Mann. His life after fifty involved a new series of astonishments: exile from Germany, American citizenship, and a final return to Europe; a new career as a political orator; and several big books—some more "skyscrapers" to succeed the two that soared over his first half-century.

In 1930, having won the Nobel Prize, he published *A Sketch of My Life* (*Lebensabriss*). "Sketch" was *le mot juste*. Much was hinted, little revealed, as if telling just this amount obviated further disclosure. It is surprising that someone who specialized in microscopic examination of motive should depict himself as an untroubled type, gratuitously smiled upon by fortune. He glided over his life's worst moments: Carla's suicide; the conflict with Heinrich; even his love for Paul Ehrenberg, disingenuously presented as a "happier" version of his infatuation with Armin Martens.

He concluded by noting with satisfaction the "mathematical clarity" that gave his story its shape. He remained a man of the center, born at midday (this wasn't really true) in the middle of a decade. He rounded out each development: *Buddenbrooks* in 1900; marriage in 1905; *The Magic Mountain* in 1925 (it was actually completed earlier). It pleased him that his children had arrived "in rhymed couples: girl / boy / boy / girl / girl / boy." He even anticipated dying mid-decade, at seventy, like his mother. He concluded with a glancing advertisement for his novel: he and Katia would soon embark for Egypt and Palestine, where he expected to find "the sky above and much of the earth beneath unchanged after 3,500 years."

Modest tone notwithstanding, this placed his oeuvre within the rock of ages.*

Heinrich and Thomas shared a need to see life as a story. This tendency coincided with a kind of ritual celebration of each other's existence, complete with valedictory homages of a largely symbolic nature. It began in 1925 with Thomas's fiftieth birthday. In 1931 Heinrich's sixtieth birthday was similarly honored. At the Prussian Academy of Art in Berlin, Thomas recalled their provincial youths when later successes were simply not imaginable—not for sons of their class. Mann called these public ceremonies "Childlike Big Moments," occasions to dress up and act, not like adults—he wasn't that self-parodying—but like men of prominence, a dreamlike state: "Who would have thought it?" In the Manns' hands these moments became moral events with the ramifications of a national myth.

During the early 1930s, when they were stellar members of the Academy, Heinrich observed that, for the first time, Germany could boast of three "great old men": the composer Richard Strauss, the playwright Gerhart Hauptmann, and the painter Max Liebermann. Liebermann would die in 1935, aged eighty-seven, and avoid the fate of his fellow Jews. Both Strauss and Hauptmann would be condemned for remaining in Nazi Germany. The Goethean old age that the Mann brothers tried to live was more than self-promotion: it was an attempt to declare what portion of German culture was worth saving.

The audience dwindled; the ambition remained constant. In 1931 the "Childlike Big Moment" occurred in a Berlin hall before a large crowd. In 1941 it was held at the Hollywood home of Salka Viertel, an émigré screen writer, before no more than twenty guests. In Christopher Hampton's uninformed drama *Tales of Hollywood*, Thomas's speech is made to appear ponderously old-fashioned. Actually it was a heroic attempt to sustain the tradition by honoring its most farsighted representative; the equivalent of an émigré's "Next year in Jerusalem." Except that Thomas understood there would be no return.

In his tribute, Mann said that opposition to Hitler had changed all their work. Once they could indulge in fashionable distinctions between "bad" and "evil." No more: "Nietzsche's distinction between evil and bad has nothing more to say to us: the bad is the evil, it is the most evil of all, and evil is the worst that can be—thus we have experienced it, and in

* On that trip to Palestine, he met Judah Magnes, the great Jewish educator. From that visit may date his Zionism; by 1932, he recognized a "present crisis" that made emigration inevitable. During the next fifteen years he wrote often about the destruction of European Jewry. Whether this was a spillover from his epic, or a response to the times, is unimportant.

a way so thoroughly without irony that a while ago we would not have regarded it as worthy of intellectual contemplation." Forecasting Hannah Arendt, Mann cited the "banal expression" with which Nietzsche asserted his fundamental decency. Ever since the late 1920s, when conservatives ridiculed his newfound socialism as prosaic, Mann had known that a humanistic devotion to the "good" could make one intellectually déclassé. Employing every stylistic resource—including "irony"—in defense of the good, he had been punished with the worst.

Thomas had the early 1930s in mind when he spoke of events that had once seemed unworthy of contemplation. In retrospect, his last years in Germany acquired a narrative inevitability. Every advance was checked, every progressive cry drowned out by the Nazi hordes.

On July 8, 1931, he had joined a group of artists and intellectuals converging in Geneva as the Comité Permanent des Lettres et des Arts: the adjective was premature. His fellows included Paul Valéry, John Masefield, Béla Bartók, and Karel Čapek. Effectively they represented the non-Communist opposition. In his inaugural address, Valéry discerned an advancement of intellectual relations through new means of communication, what Mann lamented in Germany as "technological romanticism," but with a positive outcome. Speaking of the group, Mann later said that each participant, "emerging from his productive loneliness," had joined "in sociable discussion."

Two months later, a less happy event took place. Since 1922, Mann had tried to lead young Germans out of the wilderness. While at first they had interrupted his lectures with stamping feet, by 1929 they were applauding his Freud lecture with its appeal to democracy. But that September, when he spoke at his former high school, the Katharineum in Lübeck, the response was worse than 1922 Berlin. Once he began attacking the Nazis, loud demurrals arose from the students. After that, young people became suspect. In June 1932 he wrote Walter Perl that their ingenuous enthusiasm no longer impressed him: "To be good-hearted and promising is not enough." They had been seduced, along with their professors, by a "reactionary patriotism."*

There was always an alternative possibility for youth. In January 1932, while contemplating *Young Joseph*, he anticipated "a turning away from all extremes, experiments, sensational and exotic materials," by which he

---

* In his 1929 essay on Freud, he regretted the sight of young men goose-stepping and lifting their arms up to Hitler, thereby "lending their biological charm" to the advancement of evil.

meant any diversion from the Judeo-Christian heritage, whether it issued from Moscow, Rome, or Munich. The times wanted something simpler: "back to the original and simply human matter." (He cited the phenomenologist Max Scheler, who had conceived a "new anthropology" founded on communal love and religious faith.) In short, the Old Testament, not the *Nibelungenlied.* He denied that this "link between [my] conception and the general tendencies" was self-serving: "The artist is much less of an individual than he hoped or feared to be." He had merely grabbed hold of the *Zeitgeist,* once more expressing the true longing of the German people. He still believed that humanism could sway the masses, that the *Thomasmänner* were not a dying breed.

He went back on the road, hoping to find them.

In March 1932, interviewed after a lecture in Vienna, he attacked Hitler yet again. Seven months later, he returned to address a group of workers. "I, a writer born of the middle class, am standing for the first time before a socialist group of workers. . . . [This is] symptomatic of the times . . . and decisive for my personal life and intellectual development." (Such boldness alarmed Ida Herz. He brushed aside her qualms, momentarily buoyed by a whole new public.)

It was remarkable that in Vienna, a city of Nazi lovers—as well as the home of Karl Kraus and Robert Musil—a Lübeck boy should sound the alarm while Kraus and Musil kept still. But in the intervening months, Mann had drawn confidence from the support in other German-speaking cities for his magisterial remarks about the sage of Weimar, Goethe.

Nineteen thirty-two was the centenary of Goethe's death, and Mann, the Nazis' sworn enemy, delivered two commemorative lectures that drew large crowds in Frankfurt, Weimar, Munich, and Berlin. Exquisitely separating the fissures in his own persona, he called them "Goethe as a Representative of the Bourgeois Age" and "Goethe's Career as a Man of Letters."

These charged essays were at once a summation of Goethe's literary and social importance, an incitement to further analysis by Mann himself, an occasion for political propaganda, and a chance at self-justification. In the most public forum of his career, Mann defined his own Great Confession. This allusiveness was part of the game—Goethean, he might contend. (In July 1932 he told a Frankfurt paper that "the emergence of self-consciousness," usually identified with Goethe, "is needed by a people who have suffered like the Germans." Narcissism became democracy's handmaiden.)

Goethe defies category. He is poet and scientist, bureaucrat and scholar, a sacerdotal libertine balancing in equal measure "dignity and sensuality." A radical in sexual matters, he gravitated toward wealth and power, serving for ten years as Weimar's minister of state. At least nominally, he was a political conservative, one time signing the death warrant for a young girl charged with murdering her child. Mann found this decision by the creator of Gretchen "almost as shattering as the whole of *Faust*."

The Goethe he depicts is "ironic and bizarre," defiantly not good-natured. Whenever someone grows impassioned, he always has "a cold douche on tap." One time he offers a boulevardier's whimsy, "Every poem is a sort of kiss given to the world." Then he adds the deflating caveat, "But kisses don't make babies." He specifically disdains the pleasures of the masses. While his neighbors heatedly sway to *"Du, du liegst mir im Herzen,"* he slights "the folkish, barbaric and ethnic." His answer to populism: "the public is led by its nose."

The young Thomas Mann, a Schopenhauerian pessimist, lacking "a vocation for ordinary life," found this sangfroid inhuman. In "Goethe and Tolstoy," he makes the health and longevity of "nature's privileged ones" verge on the brutish. He's more comfortable representing Goethe's chronic ambivalence. This, Mann observed, was the misanthrope who said that "the mere sight of a human face could cure his melancholy"; the renaissance man who admitted, "I never was happy." He incarnates the bourgeois life force, and then accedes to an unproductive and *echt Deutsch* concern with disease. But it is this morbidity that makes him the exemplary man of letters. For, as Hans Castorp discovered, a poet who lacks "sympathy with death" cannot steer his fellow Germans toward life—just as only the man who personified German letters could have invented the concept of "world literature" and devised its name.

Despite Goethe's fealty to the Establishment, Mann insists that he was not a reactionary. "He expressly objected to being called a conservative, since the word might mean that he desired to uphold everything that was—even social evils." Jumping to the present, Mann sees the bourgeois age that Goethe inaugurated as *kaputt*, replaced by an egregious, cutthroat capitalism. The bourgeoisie was once consecrated to individual dignity and communal service. That dignity has worn thin, the suit unraveled by sensual indulgence and reactionary politics: for the past thirty years, Mann has witnessed that disrobing.

But some form of the bourgeois spirit can survive, "by virtue of technological and national utopianism." With a "sober enthusiasm" the new bourgeois will march—"if one takes the word broadly enough and is willing to understand it undogmatically—into the communistic."

Demonstrating a Goethean reasonableness, Mann argues that there is no alternative. Once the bourgeoisie might have endured by dint of its aptitude for "practical matters." (He praises the commercial realpolitik that led old Goethe to value the Panama Canal over all poetry.) But in 1932 Germany has become fatally impractical. He delivers a Goethean indictment: "a suffocating soulfulness," "a decadent and provincial soulfulness" has driven us mad. Later that year, after the Nazis had rioted in Königsberg, he deplored "this sickness of the people, this mishmash of hysteria and outmoded Romanticism. . . . Even the pastors, professors, teachers, and men of letters follow chatteringly along after it."

Only socialism remains to salvage the bourgeois ideal. Mann's careful insistence "Consider it undogmatically" would become his trademark. As Goethe counseled, the word must be tested in living use. Otherwise it becomes a tribal fetish, what he later called a "spook word."

For the rest of his life Mann would intertwine socialism and humanism. Yet he was not prepared to lose his conservative readers, providing they were not fascists. In 1943 he wrote his former secretary Konrad Kellen that a forthcoming speech for the Library of Congress included some "alarmingly 'leftish' things, but I hope to protect myself from any scandalous effect by sprinkling it all with rather a lot of conservative and traditional powdered sugar." These words revealed a performer's savvy. On April 23, 1934, he noted with equanimity that the "communistic" passage of the Goethe essay had enthralled his listeners, although he was always more of a socialist than a Communist, and on November 24, 1933, had discerned "[a] closeness, [a] kinship, yes, even [an] identity [between] National Socialism and Communism." The solution may be to take him at his word: the "communism" he derived from Goethe was simply the Judeo-Christian idea of economic justice. It was no more theoretical than that: in 1930, he had written that he could not separate economic and intellectual spheres into structure and super-structure.

Mann offered Goethe's ethos as an alternative to fascism. But integrity demanded that he acknowledge a psychological crisis for both Goethe and himself that qualified the prospects of any political solution. Unlike Schiller, whose grandiose hopes were invariably dashed, leading him to despair of mankind, Goethe had no hopes and therefore no illusions. There was in him "a peculiar coolness, ill will . . . an inhuman, elfish irresponsibility— which one cannot indulge, but must love along with him if one loves him."

Simply put, children of Nature, like Goethe—or Thomas Mann?— believe in nothing, while ideologues like Schiller or Heinrich Mann achieve clarity, decisiveness, *lux* and *telos*, "much more easily." The others learn that "nature does not confer peace of mind, simplicity, single-mindedness; she is a questionable element, she is a contradiction, denial, thorough-going

doubt. She endows with no benevolence, not being benevolent herself."
And therefore, Goethe's bouts of misanthropy and maladjustment exhibit
"a profound, uncanny link to his mistrust of ideas."

These lines echo Mann's letter to Heinrich questioning "freedom," and
his Great War denunciation of political dogma. Coming after *The Magic
Mountain*, they suggest a darker interpretation of that novel's vision. *All*
ideologues, Naphta and Settembrini alike, are whistling in the dark, and
the tune is "Der Lindenbaum."

Even so, he ends "Goethe as a Representative of the Bourgeois Age"
trusting that "democracy, whatever her power-hungry foes pretend to be
able to do, *can do it too*; namely, lead forward into the new and the future"
[italics in text]. These ringing words were often echoed, during the Nazi
era, or when the Marshall Plan challenged the Communists' appeal. The
question is whether he believed them, in those Goethean states when all
theories seemed naïve.

Perhaps because the Goethe lectures were Mann's swan song, the last
time Germany acknowledged his preeminence, he took Goethe into exile
as virtually his property, to be guarded from the Nazis. Upon first visiting
Goethe's Frankfurt home, he had seen a resemblance to his father's house
in Lübeck. A year into exile, he was reminded that Gottfried Benn had
once said, " 'Do you know Thomas Mann's house in Munich? There is
something Goethean about it.' The fact that I was drawn away from that
existence is a serious flaw in the destined pattern of my life . . . and it
gnaws at my heart."

Beyond the rhetorical advantage it offered, Goethe's protean character
was an ideal subject for Mann's inspection, and he drew implicit parallels between them. Like Mann, Goethe suffers from a precocious fortune:
"It is dangerous to have the world embrace you" reads like a parody of
Heinrich ridiculing Thomas. Goethe is not so much the artist that he lacks
"an eye for his own [economic] advantage." Throughout the exile years,
Mann would bombard his German publisher, Bermann-Fischer, with financial demands, and he would amaze his American publisher, Alfred A.
Knopf, with a detailed knowledge of his royalties, their rise and fall. Not
incidentally, aesthetes like Novalis considered Goethe a boringly "practical"
poet.

In this game of representation, who is Mann's subject? "In him the
tendency to autobiography, confession and self-portrayal, becomes imper-
sonal, turns outward, and becomes socialized, even statesmanly. . . ." These
words appear in both Goethe essays: "the working-up and working-out of

ideas, going back to his young days, which he carried about through the decades and filled with all the richness of his life so that they accumulated breadth and originality." A lifetime of justifying himself had led Mann to the point where Goethe became his alter ego.

Mann confesses. "It was always the personal and the intimate that made Goethe produce"; his lack of ideology would allow no other impetus. Moreover, "in no other poet can we so well and rewardingly study the personal mystery of conception." Tonio Kröger returns; a work of art resembles a crime, it stems from a "priceless and guilty secret."

Mann had embedded his intimacies within a political summons. The essays caused a sensation. In June he delivered the second lecture in Munich. The city may have been crawling with SA men, but sixteen hundred people attended. He wrote Bertram, "The people, many of them young, appeared to be strongly moved. One may say of Germany what one will; my sort will never be alone."

That sort was formed in the image of Mann's erotic democracy. An echo of "The German Republic" would appear in the Goethe novel when the poet offers himself as Germany's "image and pattern. . . . I am . . . the productive male-female force, conceiving and procreating, susceptible to the highest degree." He identifies himself as womb and seed, the personification of "androgynous art." In other words, Germany's proper position toward the world is that of a bisexual lover.

The Goethe Mann re-creates in his novel is halfway modeled on himself. The two embark on similar projects; and while Goethe's imaginings tend to be happier—and more sexually explicit—Mann's achievement glows with the warmth of his predecessor's humor. Goethe's soliloquies bear a close resemblance to the self-indicting, self-delighting narrative voice in the *Joseph* novels. The most blatantly sexual portion is lost in translation; as Mann complained, Lowe-Porter's version "woefully corrupts it . . . necessarily eliminating all the small pleasures and subtleties of the language." For example, Goethe's monologue in Chapter 7 begins with the poet awakening from an erotic dream of Venus and Adonis. He looks down, congratulating himself on an erection: "Good show, old fellow!" This conveys the "selfishness and sensuality" of his power over people and events. It relates also to Mann, who on several occasions notes his own morning erection, implying there's life in him yet. (February 27, 1947: "Strong sexual potency, and not just of late. It never ends, and flatters one's vanity.") The first paragraph of the monologue ends in praise of administering one's "very own secrets," a matter of artfully deferred pleasure.

Goethe reincarnates Mann's ambivalence: "his attitude is one of all-embracing irony"; his motto, "Culture is parody." He demonstrates "the gaze of absolute art, which is at once absolute love and absolute nihilism and indifference and inspires that horrifying approach to the godlike-diabolic which we call genius." This also characterizes Adrian Leverkühn, or, for that matter, Cipolla (with a quick bow to our old friend Tonio Kröger). Like Mann's ill-fated heroes, Goethe suffers for his intransigence. At the novel's end, speaking of those he has exploited for art's sake, he confesses, "You are all in my love—and in my guilt."

Following the laws of Mannian discourse, a Goethean confession lies within these allusive pages. Goethe remembers the beauty of his son, August at thirteen, Klaus's age when Mann became infatuated with him. We also learn that "to be the son of a great man . . . is an oppressive burden, a permanent derogation of one's own ego," a thought Mann would echo when explaining Klaus's inability to escape his shadow. Indeed, after Klaus's suicide, Mann informed Heinrich that "the absence of my son" troubled him: words Goethe had used following August's death.

Another Klaus left his impression. Goethe makes huge claims for growing old: "Mind and power are products of age. Love too comes only then; what is any youthful love beside the spiritual and intellectual strength of love in age? . . . the head-turning flattery paid to lovely adolescence singled out by maturity and greatness—its tenderness exalted and adorned by the force of his mighty emotions!" Already this constitutes a brief for Aschenbach. But then Mann adds, "What beside the glowing bliss of age when the love of youth confers on it the boon of a new life": a close paraphrase of his tribute to Klaus Heuser! So, if we accept the essayist Mann's advice, the "psychological" source of that brilliant old age he reserved for Heinrich and himself had a name and a face, Klaus Heuser's, a date and location, the summer of 1927 on the Baltic coast.

II

During those months Mann seemed to have the Establishment behind him. In May he attended a performance of Wagner's *Siegfried* with his youngest children, Michael and Elisabeth. The conductor Hans Knappertsbusch's baton flew out of his hands and landed between the children's legs. Later "Knappi" presented it to them as a memento. In July Mann complimented Count Hermann Keyserling for attacking "the detestable Spengler." Back in 1920 he and Keyserling had agreed with Richard Wagner that "the German is a conservative," but now they preferred to honor "balance and tolerance"—in a word, democracy. To paraphrase his 1922 manifesto, that word was theirs before they knew it.

But it wasn't 1922. After Goethe, it was determined—by fate or history or simply the antipodes of his nature—that Mann consider an opposing titan, Richard Wagner, the poet of reaction and "sympathy with death." This time it wasn't so easy. If Germans could allow a "communistic" Goethe, they couldn't abide a leftist Wagner. Confirming his observation that every cultural question was now political, the Wagner essay precipitated Mann's exile.

In January 1933, he could still declare himself a socialist and a democrat in an essay that the Nazis called a "Socialist Confession." His timing was very bad. On January 30, 1933, Hitler became Chancellor of the Reich. Barely a week later, on February 4, Mann wrote Kurt Schlesinger, "Certainly the moment may come when there is nothing else to do but throw everything aside and put oneself on the barricades. But at the moment, one keeps praying, 'Take thou this cup from me.'"

On February 10, he delivered a commemorative lecture, "The Sorrows and Grandeur of Richard Wagner," at the University of Munich, where some years earlier he had lamented the assassination of Walther Rathenau. The Nazis, led by Hitler, prided themselves on their love of German culture, and Wagner was their particular idol, an inexhaustible source of melody and metaphor. Thomas Mann presumed to correct them. His dazzling essay snatched Wagner from the reactionaries while transforming him into an avatar of Thomas Mann himself.

Mann loves Wagner's "art-idiom" but despises his "theory." As he had done with Freud, he diminishes Wagner—at least in the eyes of his admirers—by claiming him for literature. The composer's achievement comprehends "psychology, symbolism, mythology, emphasizing everything"—all the attributes of a great novelist—but it is simply not "music in the pure and uncontaminated sense." His most haunting refrain, Mann's particular favorite, "the ever-yearning chromaticism of the *Liebestod* is a literary idea": a kind of pornographic program music. Accordingly Mann summons Freud to illuminate *Parsifal* and contends that Kundry, that great earth mother, is Wagner's most powerful creation, a remark guaranteed to offend the chauvinists who recognized a line from Siegfried to Hitler. Mann applauds *Parsifal*'s conjunction of sex and religion, alluding perhaps to his similar attempt in *The Tales of Jacob*.

For those who considered Wagner's oeuvre holy text, Mann revives the strictures of *Death in Venice*. No matter how deep—nay, life-shattering— his work, an artist is "yet *not quite*—and therefore, not at all"—serious: a man to be loved, honored, even pitied, but not to be trusted. He knows that his art springs from muddied sources. Wagner, above all, the artist who craved both the intellectuals and the "dummies too," employed dubious, shabby means; showmanship was his "stock-in-trade." Therefore he is nobody to emulate: "This man knows as little as do any of us the right way to live": Mann himself had once been less modest. Instead an artist is "lived through," life extracting from his work what it requires, his intentions be damned.

A note of implicit autobiography is sounded. Like Mann, Wagner considered his reading of Schopenhauer *the* great" formative "event." Like Mann, he feared extinction at forty, and would compose for decades after. Like Mann, he exhibits a "bourgeois fastidiousness." He suffers in comfort, languishing in satin bathrobes, quite unlike poor Schiller, who toiled in the fume of rotten apples. Mann accepts most of Nietzsche's arguments against Wagner, but not his priggish refusal to decode the "word" that hovers unsaid in *Tristan*. At twenty-five, Mann admits, he was more scrupulous; but now he announces unashamedly that the point is "sensuality, unbounded, saturated with spirituality," portrayed naturalistically but insatiable by conventional means. Such a cosmic account is both noble and funny. Funnier yet is Nietzsche's averted glance, revealing the preacher's son hidden within the nihilist. (These remarks also provide an addendum to Mann's story "Tristan," where the music's programmatic thrust goes strenuously unsaid.)

In passing Mann subjects Schopenhauer to a drastic rereading. He becomes the "capitalist philosopher," a fundamentally erotic writer despite his attacks on the rampantly devouring Will. Max Weber may have found capitalism's sources in prayer and meditation; Mann juxtaposes them to the stirrings of the id. Moreover, we live in the "last stages of capitalism." Ignoring all Wagner's reactionary statements, particularly his anti-Semitism, Mann stresses his radical history. Like an earlier Thomas Mann, Wagner realized that culture and politics are inseparable. George Bernard Shaw famously compared him to the anarchist Bakunin. Mann calls him a democrat, virtually a populist, a "cultural Bolshevik" by 1933 standards. To a Nazi audience those were fighting words.

On February 10, after the first Wagner lecture in Munich, Thomas and Katia began a vacation tour. Within the next week he would repeat the lecture in Amsterdam, Brussels, and Paris. Foreign audiences were delighted; at home the response was shock and fury. Mann discovered that his cultural provocation had endangered his safety. On March 13, he wrote Lavinia Mazzucchetti, his Italian translator, that matters were grim. The

Nazis' electoral triumph in Bavaria "affected us like a senseless natural disaster." There was now a "reign of terror"; he was on the list of "those who have committed . . . 'intellectual high treason.' "

He doubted whether "the likes of me" would find breathing room in the new Germany. "At the age of fifty-seven such a loss of settled life and livelihood, to which I had become adjusted and in which I was already growing a little stiff, is no small matter. But I think my being an artist has kept me elastic enough for such a new beginning on an entirely different footing, and as long as I have my brave wife by my side, I am afraid of nothing."

There was plenty to fear. In April a Munich newspaper printed "A Protest from Richard Wagner's City of Munich," signed by forty-five musical notables, including Hans Pfitzner, Hans Knappertsbusch, and Richard Strauss. It contained an intelligent explication of Mann's essay, stressing his citation of Freud. It chastised his recent politics, his "unfortunate" exchange of nationalism for "cosmopolitan-democratic views." Instead of "a modest and decent reticence," the impudent Mann dares call *Wagner* "philistine." This is the same slippery fellow who reprinted his political reflections "in such a way that the meaning of the key passages was completely reversed." He is "completely unreliable and unknowledgeable." Wagner is "the musical-dramatic embodiment of the deepest German sensibilities," and the snide chatter of this self-proclaimed internationalist is simply "insufferable."

Within days Mann replied in print that he was the victim of a "gross misunderstanding," and that his "loyalty to German culture and tradition," and to those "who look with quiet favor on my work," was absolute and unquestionable. In July he wrote a long letter to Pfitzner, not published until 1974, in which he questioned whether his enemies would allow him "to finish his life and work in the manner in which he began." He saw himself "getting older," his cultural liberalism "superseded" by "a humanity 'après nous,' " with which he could no longer identify.

Skirting apology, he advised Pfitzner of his willingness to serve this new age, despite the disagreement, since he had "tentatively anticipated" some of its elements, particularly the Nazis' opposition to "the enfeebling and life-abasing obsession with psychology." These words hark back to the old conflicts with Heinrich, the resistance to Kerr and Theodor Lessing, and, indeed, the Great War reflections. Once again he contended that Aschenbach's failure to vanquish the indecent psychologists did not mean he was wrong to try. But rescuing himself from the appearance of collaboration, Mann refused to let Aschenbach's hard-won truths be vulgarized into "mass slogans." A Nazi had recently applauded the triumph of metaphysical Germany over "materialistic hair-splitting analysis." But Mann insisted on the need for more, and yet more hair-splitting. Humanity might be "having a hard time" at present, but "its democratic spirit" would survive. This was not what the Wagnerians cared to hear.

He had been the victim of a critical ambush. "Did none of them feel strong enough to tackle me alone, man to man?" he asks Pfitzner. "Was it really necessary to assemble so many big guns in order to overpower me?" They were avenging a decade of provocative statements, and, not incidentally, reviving the old distinctions between poet and writer. In December 1933, he noted "their historical jabs," quoting, "Th. Mann was only the top-ranking writer of his time, not the top-ranking poet." Such "twaddle" reminded him of nonpoets like Dickens, Dostoyevsky, Tolstoy, Balzac, Proust, and Maupassant. United against his Munich critics, these novelists joined him behind the barricade.

The literary battle over politics evolved into a political battle over literature. On May 16, 1934, Mann congratulated his friend René Schickele: "Excellent—your observation on the novel as the total work of art! It's something I've always thought myself. Wagner's notion of it was ludicrously mechanical. . . ." Perhaps he would have reached this conclusion on his own, but the strident attacks by the Wagnerians undoubtedly strengthened his determination. At least since 1927, Mann had argued that literature, not music, had become the necessary art. Thus, if *Parsifal* coupled music and myth, sex and religion, the Joseph novel would outdo its achievement. Like a Wagner opera, it would transpire in a mythic synchronicity, a timeless era. But it would subject that era to a critique informed by political and psychological understanding, a modern consciousness, and a postmodern critique of its own procedure. That would be a *total* work of art, incorporating even the weak, fallible artist so that he too would be lost in an endless time, subject at once to spiritual sensuality and "materialistic hair-splitting analysis." The furor over the Wagner essay had served a literary function. He had never been so ambitious.

Or threatened. The Nazis now fought culture with guns and torches. His books were not among the first ones burned by Hitler, as were those of both Heinrich and Klaus. But the Munich Protest was virtually a death sentence, prompted equally by his irreverence and his party affiliation. The repercussions were immense, carrying him into a lifelong exile from his native land.

Besides the immediate consequences, Mann anticipated an enigma that would baffle postwar intellectuals. How could men love Beethoven—or Wagner—and still administer the death camps?

Mann may have been the first to raise the issue. As early as 1939 he told American audiences that Germany's music had not saved her from a bloody "farce," thus articulating the link between grandeur and barbarism. Or, more recently, how could rock-and-rollers vote for Reagan, protect their investments, and utter racist diatribes? The assumption had been that a love of music is good for the soul.

Thomas Mann knew better. He concluded that beneath the shade of that linden tree, outside the city walls, a dreamer may lose sight of life itself. He never sacrificed his love of music; instead he argued that Wagner's oeuvre remains unfinished, not ideologically settled, for all Cosima Wagner's love of Hitler. How could he think otherwise? As he left questions of literary reputation, particularly his own, to history, music would have to be subject to perpetual reappraisal, a permanent revolution in taste.

Among those discomfited by his approach was Theodor Adorno, his musical adviser during the mid-1940s. Adorno's cultural views were unmitigatedly dour. Loathing the idea of art as consolation, he begged Mann *not* to offer any prospect of aesthetic transcendence, no matter how small, in the compositions of Adrian Leverkühn: art could only be about itself. Adorno famously declared that after Auschwitz, it was unthinkable to write poetry. This most un-Mannian statement presumed that poetry was exclusively a matter of form, and Mann preferred to see art in ethical, historical and psychological terms. Adorno, at least figuratively, shut down the house of many mansions when new rooms were most urgently needed. That artists had failed constituted a fresh subject for art—perhaps the most challenging and debilitating: Mann admitted that writing *Doctor Faustus* nearly killed him. In that novel, artists are complicit in the German disaster. He would have seconded J. Robert Oppenheimer's words that scientists had known evil. But science couldn't stop with this guilty knowledge. Nor, for Mann, could art.

(In 1936 he wrote that unlike poetry, "the novel, because of its analytical spirit, its consciousness, its innate critical attitude" could not remain "undisturbed and sweetly oblivious of the world." Finally settling the *Dichter* versus *Schriftsteller* argument, he declared that "these very prosaic qualities of consciousness and critical attitude" made the novel "in our stage of history, the representative and dominant form of literature.")

In 1930, Mann had predicted Adorno's dilemma. Young people had asked how one could write during so intense a class struggle, especially when a new war appeared "inevitable." His reply held in 1944: "We believe in the seriousness of play and its dignity. We believe in secrets, in the human secret of art." *Doctor Faustus* was most serious play—even if Mann lamented the universal failure to notice its humor; it was also crammed with secrets, particularly his love for Paul Ehrenberg. "Serious play"—or some variation thereof—would remain his singular defense of art in bad times.*

Mann deeply vexed Wagnerians by stressing their hero's compromised position between high and mid-culture, "I want the dummies too." Wagner became for him the emblem of proto-fascistic kitsch. In October 1937, when Mann visited Triebschen, the composer's Swiss home, he found bad taste regnant: "Dreadful oil paintings, utterly Hitler. One absolutely revolting gigolo of a Siegfried." As usual he was alert to the sexual undercurrent: "Elements of a frighteningly Hitleresque quality plainly discernible, even though only latent and anticipatory, ranging from the over-blown kitsch to the Germanic fondness for boys."

The latter tendency remained with Mann, but no longer in a militaristic guise. Earlier that year he and Katia had attended a screening of *Lives of a Bengal Lancer*. Contrary to the Wagnerian in his soul, he felt "a curious feeling of shame in the face of this virility." Like most war movies, the film indulged in "the sentimentality of primitive masculinity by the admission of patriotism ('England, England, all for England!')." Echoing "The German Republic," Mann finds the cinematic propaganda "unpleasant to me, for it is specious, and basically detracts from the pure manliness." That year he found new inspirations, not from British soldiers but from Indian dancers, whose ravishing bodies would appear in *The Transposed Heads*, the novella that interrupted his tale about the beautiful Hebrew.

A few years later, in *The Beloved Returns*, a connection between militarism and homosexuality would be made by an intellectual spinster. "The warlike national spirit is connected with an increased enthusiasm of man for his own sex," she says. "The phenomenon is an inheritance from the customs of the ancient Spartans. It has a strange, harsh flavor not very acceptable to us women." In a novel overflowing with parody, was Mann alluding to 1917, when he imagined German wives competing with their husbands' fellow soldiers? His women characters are often sexual isolates or, like the circus acrobat in *Felix Krull*, heroic androgynes. So the remarkable point is not that a woman sees the link between sex and violence but that she is as erotically disenfranchised as Mann himself!

* For that matter, he even anticipated Adorno's dissection of "the authoritarian personality." In 1940, he called anti-Semitism, "the mob's form of nobility," a witty complement of August Bebel's definition of "the socialism of fools." During the war years, he decried a certain kind of bigot, who reveled in his superiority to Negroes and Jews.

III

The first months of exile were spent in Switzerland. Mann was enjoying a rest cure in Arosa, following his Wagner tour, when he received a call from his children in Munich, warning about "bad weather." Three days later, on March 15, 1933, he wrote in his diary that

> a morbid dread has oppressed me for hours on end these last ten days, during which my nerves have been strained and exhausted. It is a sort of fear-ridden, intense melancholy such as I have previously experienced to a milder degree, when parting from material things. Recently this feeling reached a crisis one night when I had taken refuge with Katia. From the character of this crisis it is clear that what is involved is the pain of leaving a long-familiar situation, the awareness that an era in my life has come to an end, and the recognition that I must find a new basis for my existence. Despite the *rigidly set ways of my fifty-eight years* [italics mine], I view this necessity as spiritually beneficial and I affirm it.

Even as he confessed his terror, he gave himself a rhetorical boost.

March 15 was also the day Hitler proclaimed the Third Reich. That day Mann resigned from the Munich branch of the Writers' League. When the composer Max von Schillings, president of the Prussian Academy, submitted a declaration to him (drafted by Gottfried Benn): "Are you willing to continue to be identified with the Prussian Academy of Arts in light of the changed historical situation? A positive response to this question will prohibit you from any public activity against the government and commit you to loyal collaboration in the national cultural tasks—recognizing the changed historical situation—falling by statute to the Academy." Mann replied: "I cannot give the desired response to the declaration placed before me. I have not the least intention of working against the government, and as far as German culture is concerned I believe I have always served its cause and will try to do so in the future. But I have come to the decision to disengage myself from all official duties that I have accumulated over the years and to pursue from now on my private concerns in complete retirement." Therewith he resigned from the Academy. In his diary he was more belligerent: "I refuse to apply the term 'historical' as Schillings used it in his Academy declaration, in reference to this monstrous phenomenon, the frenzied consumption of a counterrevolution we have been caught up in for the past fourteen years."

He felt isolated. There were no political ground rules: the Nazis acted worse than "Bolshevists"; in fact, he saw little difference between the groups. Count Arco, the right-wing student who had assassinated Kurt Eisner, now confessed that he had planned to kill Hitler. As confirmation of Mann's fears about "technological romanticism," he reported the triumph of the Nazis' "brazenly sadistic propaganda plans . . . the boldly modern, fast-moving futuristic approach put to the service of an antifuture, a philosophy devoid of all ideas, a mammoth advertising campaign for nothingness."

Three days later, after a car trip over "spectacular stretches of highway," the Manns were ensconced in a small house, "not without charm were we in better shape psychologically, beautiful landscape with half-frozen lake." That night, he awoke at half past five. "Horrible sense of frenzy, helplessness, twitching muscles, almost a shivering fit, and feared losing my rational faculties." He required Katia's comfort for the next hours, as well as the barbiturate Luminal.

It was the worst of times. Alluding to Germany's 1918 defeat, he called "the domestic Versailles . . . more horrible than the outside one." Like right-wing patriots of the 1990s, the Nazis wanted "to annul not only the domestic consequences of the defeat, that is to say all progressive, socialist measures, but also to establish a new state of mind, as though the war had been won rather than lost."

On March 28, he reports letters from Golo and Frau Pringsheim warning against Katia's "ever visiting Munich," though, on the same day, Ludwig Fulda, a Jewish émigré writer, declared that the Germans would never lay a finger on Thomas Mann. (Fulda eventually returned to Berlin, out of homesickness, and committed suicide there in 1939.) On March 29 an article in the Basel *National Zeitung* made "the point that if I were in Germany, I would be in the Dachau concentration camp." Even if his life weren't endangered, his books would be. The Jewish-owned Ullstein Publishing Company had "stopped the sale of Feuchtwanger's *Josephus* because of the author's alleged involvement in the dissemination of stories of anti-Jewish atrocities in Germany. How long before censorship is directed against books? Doubtful whether Fischer who has published Trotsky will be able to continue his business in Berlin."

That would be very bad but he was most alarmed by the prospect of his diaries being discovered. On April 20, he wrote, "My fears now revolve first and foremost almost exclusively about this threat to my life's secrets. They are deeply serious. The consequences could be terrible, even fatal." Very likely he feared the homosexual revelations. Once again he was prophetic; the first book the Nazis burned was by Magnus Hirschfeld.

*Thomas, Katia, and Elisabeth with the elderly Pringsheims
at the summer house in Nidden, circa 1929*

In May Klaus and Erika returned to Munich from a tour of her musical revue, *The Pepper Mill* (Mann had thought up the name). They arrived in time to see "the triumphant entrance of General Franz Xaver von Epp, Hitler's Gauleiter and representative in the Bavarian province," whom they remembered as the head of the White Army in 1919. They were met at the train station by Hans, their chauffeur, who warned them both, "but especially Fräulein Erika," that the Nazis were after them. Later they learned that "he had been a Nazi spy throughout the four or five years he lived in our family." (When in America Erika accused Golo of bringing CIA agents into their home, her suspicions were informed by memories of "our Hans.") While Klaus and Erika remained in Munich, he continued to serve them. After he drove Klaus to the station for his trip out of Germany, he sued for mercy. "You must understand my position, Herr Klaus. A fellow's got to live, after all. No hard feelings, I hope?" This "good-natured scoundrel and twofold double-crosser was the last person [Klaus] talked with in Germany."

Mann's diary and the *Joseph* manuscript were shipped to him that

spring. Further items were delivered on November 1 (Lenbach's portrait of
Katia as a girl, a Venetian lion, a cobra candlestick, the old Joseph pictures,
a Chinese ashtray) and November 25 (the picture of swimming youths by
Ludwig von Hofmann and a childhood portrait of Elisabeth). Mann saw in
those beloved objects a material confirmation of exile. "The arrival of the
furniture has affected me strongly, so that I am left with a headache and
great fatigue."

He had become disgusted with his best friend: "Bertram's little book
of poems, loftily depressing, decent yet revolting." On April 2 he described
Bertram's assurance of his future safety, should he return to Munich, as
"foolish and frivolous." That same day he determined on "a cautious, somewhat shamefaced silence." But while the world speculated, he let Bertram
know that his position had not changed. On January 9, 1934, he wrote
that their "old friendship" ran so deep that further arguments would only
"cause more sadness." But don't fool yourself; my "attitude or verdict are
[not] determined by the spirit of other exiles. I stand for myself and have
no contact at all with the German emigration scattered over the world."
Your "new Germany" is not new; it's the same force that has threatened
me for years. "I see it as I am accustomed to see things, with my own
eyes." But do you see it? By now, have you begun to feel *shame*?

Initially Mann was demoralized to the point of apathy. On June 12, 1933,
he wrote a Swiss friend that for the moment he was as quiet as old Gerhart
Hauptmann. "Why talk himself out of all his possessions and his country
as well?" Speaking up had lost Mann everything; for the moment his situation was bitter and any decision "perilous to life itself."

Actually he was furious at Hauptmann, who had shown him exactly
not the path to take. His May 9 diary contains the toughest indictment of
another writer he ever composed:

> this man of the Republic, friend of Ebert and Rathenau, who owes his
> stature and his greatness to Jews. On the "Day of Labor," he allowed
> the swastika flag to be flown from his house. Perhaps he thinks himself
> Goethean in his firm opposition to everything common. . . . I hate
> this idol whom I helped to magnify, and who magnificently rejects a
> martyrdom that I also feel I was not born for, but which I am driven
> to embrace for the sake of intellectual integrity.

On July 26 he noted, "My staying out of Germany speaks eloquently
enough." That same day he wrote Hesse, "I've had a struggle and now it's

over. True, there are still times when I ask myself: Why? Other people manage to live in Germany—Hauptmann, Ricarda Huch, Hans Carossa, for instance. But the temptation is short-lived. I couldn't do it. I'd suffocate and waste away. And it is impossible for purely human reasons as well, because of my family. One of these days I shall have to say this publicly." For his family, that day couldn't come soon enough. His silence infuriated Erika, and within months Katia too expressed a wish that he would broadcast the "horror, contempt, and revulsion" that he privately admitted to Hesse.

He was given opportunities. Klaus's friend, the publisher Fritz Landshoff, had emigrated to Amsterdam, where he had started Querido Verlag. He offered to publish *Joseph*. While this would have established the house and confirmed Mann's anti-Nazi credentials, it would have ruined his chances of publication in Germany. Gottfried Bermann-Fischer, as cautious as the Ullsteins, didn't want to risk that. In June, Bermann-Fischer tried to convince him that "Hitler-Goebbels-Goering [were] the 'moderates.' "*

Erika was bolder than her father. In January 1933, *The Pepper Mill* had opened and quickly closed in Munich. Once the city had been famous for political comedy, but the mood had changed. The fearless Erika took her creation abroad. In European cities she tried to laugh the Nazis out of existence.

Mann applauded this mode of cultural protest. On January 9, 1934, in a generally anguished letter to Bertram, he mentions her success in Bern, Basel, and other Swiss towns. It pleases him more than "the applause that *Joseph and His Brothers* has received. That is the imperceptible and painless creeping abdication of advancing age in favor of the young folks."

He was less supportive of Klaus's project, *Die Sammlung* (*The Collection*), the first émigré journal of antifascism. The premier issue included blazing attacks on the Nazis from both Klaus and Heinrich. In fact Klaus had misled his father and the possible ramifications terrified Mann. Hearing that his name was connected with a baldly anti-Nazi magazine, "I had an attack of anxiety." Klaus's homosexual reputation may have contributed to that anxiety. Gottfried Bermann-Fischer, determined to continue publishing Thomas Mann in Germany, advised him to withdraw from Klaus's editorial board. He did so, and his telegram, "CAN ONLY STATE THAT CHARACTER OF FIRST NUMBER SAMMLUNG DOES NOT BEAR OUT ITS ORIGINAL AIMS," was much quoted. Mann knew that it would "arouse bitter disappointment in émigré circles."

This was an understatement. Other famous writers had withdrawn, among them Alfred Döblin and Stefan Zweig, but Mann's action was seen

* During the early 1940s, Landshoff and Bermann-Fischer cofounded the L. B. Fischer Verlag in New York, which published Klaus's autobiography, signifying a reconciliation between the latter and Bermann-Fischer.

as the real scandal. A Viennese newspaper that had applauded him a year before proclaimed this latest action a "Betrayal of the Intellect," a phrase drawn from Heinrich's *Geist und Tat*. Émigré Communists were beside themselves. Several had fled to Moscow, and they sent an emissary to Heinrich asking him to denounce his brother. For decades after, they would not forgive Thomas Mann. Curiously Döblin, a convert to Catholicism, was later welcomed back into the tribe, while Zweig was always seen as a hopeless bourgeois, particularly after his suicide in 1942. But with an unseemly smugness, people who overlooked the faults of Joseph Stalin would not absolve Mann for a reticence initiated by his Jewish publisher. (Bermann's father-in-law, old Samuel Fischer, was less accommodating. On May 2 he told Mann that he distrusted Bermann. As he saw it, all their writers should simply get out of Germany.)

Erika and Klaus were outraged. Mann's disloyalty was further proof of his lack of respect for Klaus. They never took back their anger, and Mann later admitted they were right. But in August 1933 he wrote Bermann, boasting that *The Tales of Jacob* would enrich them all: "Even the dreaded 'essayistic' prelude is not so bad, in its fashion," and the rest pure pleasure. He suggested printing the names of Jacob and Joseph in Hebrew script. That would make a striking cover—he had momentarily forgotten the reigning anti-Semitism—unless readers mistook it for a kosher restaurant.

When the book appeared three months later, Heinrich supported its publication. Unlike his niece and nephew, he welcomed the continued presence of Mann thought and language in the German marketplace. Within two months nearly twenty-five thousand copies were sold, apparently vindicating Bermann-Fischer. As Mann wrote Alfred A. Knopf, given the financial depression and the attacks on his politics, these sales were "fantastic." On January 1, 1934, Mann wrote that the times were " 'irrational' or 'irnational,' as a typographical error in a German newspaper recently had it." The Nazis had confiscated his property but had stopped blocking his royalties. He had submitted his application to the Berlin compulsory organization of writers, in order to keep publishing, but refused to sign any pledge of loyalty. "I assume that I shall continue to be regarded as a member of the German literary profession, and that further formalities are unnecessary."

In the confusion of exile, others lost sight of their political goals. Brecht was no shining example. Until his last months in Germany, he maintained friendship with his Nazi pals. Each New Year's Eve, he gave a stag party, and in 1932 it was attended by Arnolt Bronnen and his guest, Ernst von

Salamon, a conspirator in the death of Walther Rathenau, another one of the bourgeois—and homosexual—fathers whom Brecht despised. In the first months of exile, Brecht refused to allow a benefit performance of his plays by the Committee of Jews Driven Out of Germany. After Mann and Döblin withdrew from the board of *Die Sammlung*, a German Communist, Alfred Kurella, denounced them both in a scurrilous poem. Everything would change; everything would stay the same. In Hollywood, Brecht, who enjoyed attacking Mann's mythopoetic *Joseph*, overlooked Döblin's piety and befriended him. Dictators came and went, but these deep thinkers always had Thomas Mann to kick around.

Though he derided "culinary" bourgeoisie, Brecht shared with Mann an abiding concern with his material welfare. Mann didn't want to lose his goods, much less his reputation, or worse, should his "life's secrets" be published. Meanwhile he was busy figuring out the enemy. Two weeks after the Night of the Long Knives (July 20, 1934), when the SA leader Ernst Roehm and his followers were murdered, Mann wrote that the Nazis denied the obvious, their intrinsic homosexuality.

In a grotesque elaboration he next found a Nazi-gay connection almost within his home. His former son-in-law, Gustav Gründgens, had become the top theater man in Germany. "Hitler's interest in him is interpreted as erotic." Mann doesn't specify whether this is received wisdom or Erika's insight. The significant detail is his profoundly erotic—and intimate—vision of politics.

Hermann Weigand's analysis of *The Magic Mountain* cheered the gloomy author, particularly its comparison of Mann and Goethe with their common deployment of "irony." On October 29, 1933, Mann wrote, "Here is a genuine case of imitation in the mythical sense, and of discipleship"— mythical because unwilled and unwitting. Like Joseph, Mann needed outside intervention to learn that he was the one.

Such a happy use of myth was rare. More common was a kind of mythic insanity, as if too much Wagner had lobotomized the Germans. Myth had become a political weapon, regularly invoked by the dictators who now commanded the culture, along with the economy and the Reichstag. Jews alone were immune to the national psychosis.

Compulsively alert to historical parallels, he read Stefan Zweig's biography *Erasmus of Rotterdam* with fascinated horror. Erasmus, the archetypal symbol of secular humanism and tolerance, had been defeated by Luther. "The terrible chaos," Mann wrote,

> had to come because of his unshakable conviction and his powerful imagery, the Brute of Wittenberg desired it, and at bottom, mankind

desires it as well, for mankind has no use for rational, decent order or tolerance, no yearning for "happiness" at all, but prefers recurrent tragedy and untrammelled, destructive adventure. *Habeat.*

This proved to be a crucial text for Mann. Erasmus, symbolizing humanistic values, never married, though Mann doesn't mention this, and was perhaps homosexual, unlike the famously married—albeit misogynistic—Luther. Mann's critical ear discerned the power of Luther's "imagery," much as he spotted the Nazis' sensational mastery of radio and film. As Nietzsche had instructed him, Luther represented Protestant zealotry, a smug conviction that the Holy Spirit dwelled within, thereby insulating the believer from the snares and delusions of Greece and Rome. Mann linked Nazi terror with Lutheran intolerance, as if Naphta's Jewish-Catholic vision of a strategic terror had met its ecumenical prophet in the ur-Protestant.

Mann had chanced upon a key metaphor of his last years. He didn't retire from politics but found himself, like Erasmus, battered on all sides. In America he fought against "Catholic fascism"—namely, figures like Francis Cardinal Spellman, whose modern versions would be Pentecostals like Pat Robertson, Oliver North, and Randall Terry. Yet he frequently offended Stalinists; for example, in 1936, after Zenzl Mühsam, a German exile in the Soviet Union, was arrested, he complained to Alexei Vasilievich Koltsov, the chairman of the League of Russian Writers, that his country was turning into a vast "prison cell."

Depending on his mood, Nietzsche's "eternal recurrence" became either a sign of hope or of despair. For the rest of his life he would find himself echoing the formulations of those early days of exile. In 1951, after a series of vicious attacks on his putative fellow-traveling, he wrote, "I will not return to America"; *mutatis mutandis*, he had used similar words to disown Germany in 1933.

In June 1933, the Manns had joined the exile colony in Sanary-sur-Mer, outside of Nice, at the invitation of René Schickele, the editor of *Die Weissen Blätter*, who had moved there in 1932 for health reasons. Their neighbors included Arnold Zweig, Feuchtwanger, Toller, Brecht, Erwin Piscator, Hermann Kesten, Werfel, and Wilhelm Herzog. As a group they were either Jews, radicals, or both. Mann felt alienated from them all. He had more in common with the art historian Julius Meier-Graefe. (Despite his death in 1935, Meier-Graefe would influence American criticism through his self-appointed disciple, Clement Greenberg.)

Sanary, the summer of 1933. LEFT TO RIGHT: *Golo, Mrs. René Schickele, Mrs. Julius Meier-Graefe, Mann, Meier-Grafe, Katia, her cousin Ilse Dernberg, and Erika. Erika had recently been touring in her anti-Nazi musical,* THE PEPPER MILL.

By September he and Katia had moved to Küsnacht, a town near Zurich. His living arrangements had changed. From now on, excepting periods when he was the guest of wealthy patrons, he would live in houses that resembled each other more than the luxurious homes in Lübeck and Munich: according to Golo, it was "always the same modest villa near a town, the same desk with the same photographs and statuettes." By the fall of 1933, Elisabeth and Michael were attending Swiss schools, having found their Munich Gymnasium overrun with Nazis.

Despite everything, Mann's circumstances were not unbearable. A quiet life, a friendly public, and, perhaps best of all, a spoken German unsullied by Nazi distortions. The latter was crucial. On December 23 he wrote Meier-Graefe, "At bottom I am aware that my books were not written for Prague and New York, but for Germans." (Of course he would become a citizen of Czechoslovakia and later describe that country's betrayal as the worst event of his life. It would be associated with the name Munich, yet another accident of history he could take personally.)

He added a note of chauvinism. "The rest of the world has always been an 'extra,' and I still don't see how I can manage with it alone."

The decision was no longer his: the modern Goethe would have to settle for World Literature. Six months later he made his first trip to America.

It was an irony painfully apparent that he shared his exile with his Jewish enemies. In the first months his diaries expressed some ambivalence. Any suppression of Alfred Kerr's "brazen and poisonous Jewish-style imitation of Nietzsche," he wrote in April, suited him fine. Likewise he noted that some Jews, like Oskar Goldberg, had exhibited fascistic tendencies.

On July 12, 1934, he wrote in his diary, "The Jews who are now deprived of their rights and driven out of Germany are not only such dyed-in-the-wool and naïve German patriots that they are called in Paris *les Bei-uns* [lit. "our house" or "back home"], but they also shared in the development of those intellectual currents which raise their ugly heads in the present political system—albeit in an extremely contorted way. They have helped pave the way for antiliberalism not only as members of the George-Kreis. . . . The inner attitude of these Jewish writers to the new state must create a real conflict for them; the state rides roughshod over them and all the while they must theoretically approve what it does." These are strong words, and Mann knew that there were many Jews on the left, some having directed the Munich revolution. When Hannah Arendt made similar observations, about the passivity of the Jewish establishment, she drew down tremendous wrath from her coreligionists.*

Again in April 1933, he wrote, "I could have a certain amount of understanding for the rebellion against the Jewish element were it not that the Jewish spirit exercises a necessary control over the German element." Mann particularly deplored attacks on Freud's supposed "soul-destroying overvaluation of drives," when the Nazis exemplified the triumph of "precisely such drives." Or after Hitler informed Max Planck that he was no anti-Semite, there were simply too many Marxist Jews, Mann observed, "He has a different lie for everyone."

When Albert Einstein wrote a letter applauding the Wagner essay. Mann declared it "the greatest honor that has come my way . . . but it praises me for conduct that was natural to me and therefore scarcely calls for praise." Using words he later employed in his letter to Pfitzner, he admitted that he was too formed by the Goethean tradition to feel "destined for martyrdom." Yet to have warned early and vehemently about the Nazi

---

* Once more he was prescient. Fifty years later, conservative American Jews rallied to the defense of Pat Robertson, despite his deployment of anti-Semitic texts; as students of religion they should have known that his Pentecostalism acknowledged only one way to be saved. They assented "theoretically" to the evangelist's politics even as his theology doomed them to hell.

threat would "someday certainly accrue to the honor of all of us, although we may possibly be destroyed in the process."

Equally prophetic was a letter to Bertram in late 1934, when he prayed for a World Spirit to "liberate this nation from political life, to dissolve it and disperse it into a new world like the Jews, with whom so much kindred tragic destiny links it." Years before he put the same words in Goethe's mouth, Mann predicted that Germans and Jews would be bound forever.

The first victim in Mann's set was his old friend Jakob Wassermann. At twenty-one, he had admitted to a "dastardly plagiarism" of Wassermann's work, simply because "his influence is generally in the air." (Wassermann was then twenty-three.) By 1933 he had begun to detect "a certain empty pomp and solemn verbosity in his works," while granting that he "as a fashioner of plots [is] far greater than I am": for Mann, who felt art was not about inventing, this was an easy concession. Nonetheless, Wassermann's death on January 1, 1934, greatly upset him: "No need to note the fact that the death of this good friend and contemporary raises with particular vividness the question of how much longer I myself will live."

Four days later he observed that the German newspapers dismissed Wassermann as "one of the most highly regarded writers of November [1918] Germany. He had almost nothing to do with German literature. Is that my obituary too?" The Nazis were punishing the Bolsheviks of Munich, and apparently they included him in the ranks. He would maintain his silence until 1936, when he replied to a Swiss critic, Eduard Korrodi, who had described a Jewish "internationalization" of the German novel, achieved by the likes of Wassermann. Mann contended that he and his brother had also contributed, "and we are not Jews. Perhaps it was the drop of Latin blood (and Swiss blood from our grandmother), which enabled us to do that. The 'international' qualities of Jews are nothing more nor less than their Mediterranean European qualities. And these are at the same time *German*; without them, Germanism would not be Germanism, but a totally useless sluggishness."*

He was touching on both his life and his work. That work was presently about religion, and he boldly defined the Nazis' anti-Semitism as directed against "the Christian and classical foundations" of humanism. (Actually, Hitler was a professed Christian.) He could offer no higher praise of Jews,

---

* At times, an oversensitive Mann discerned a Jewish cabal waged against him. In May 1937 when Hermann Kesten praised Döblin's "mythical epic" without mentioning *Joseph*, Mann wrote his—Jewish—friend Bruno Frank that "a fellow Jew" had been elevated "over me, the dumb goy." Overwrought, no doubt. But we know that Kesten's view of Mann was ambivalent—he preferred Heinrich—and Döblin was Mann's sworn enemy. To paraphrase the suppressed ending of "The Blood of the Walsungs," the goy felt "begoniffed."

who had awakened Western and vitalized German culture. The lifelong identification with outsiders was now complete, and, with an autobiographical specificity that takes the breath away, Mann concluded his letter to Korrodi with a quote ("Far wiser to renounce the Fatherland") from "a truly noble German poet." (He had quoted this passage in his diary as early as October 1933.) That poet was, inevitably, Platen, who, like Mann, might have faced the Final Solution in a land that killed both Jews and homosexuals.

Even before he could attack the Nazis openly, Mann found an outlet for his revulsion. *"Achtung! Europa"* (1935) was intended for delivery at a meeting of the League of Nations in Nice. He was unable to appear, but the speech, translated into French, was read in his absence and provoked violent dissent, except in a few percipient souls like Gide.

Instead of the Nazis, Mann's theme was the degeneration of popular culture, a topic that had disturbed him at least since the Flying Dunces made fools of Munich. This new "collectivist age" sought only immediate gratification. Once a form of religious enthusiasm, "intoxication" had descended to the level of falling-down drunk: "another instance of the vulgarization of great and venerated European ideas by the commercialization of the masses."

Reviving his 1918 critique, but from the left, he said mass democracy catered to the lowest common denominator. Where nineteenth-century socialists had sought to educate the masses, contemporary demagogues exploited their most primitive needs, drugging them with "the pennydreadful and sensational films." Similarly, romanticism had been reduced to a "jargon" of faux-populism and hysterical chauvinism. Casting off the self-control inculcated by "nineteenth-century humanism," the masses had fallen prey to "bogus sciences and charlatanisms, strange sects and foolish backstairs religions, gross humbug, and every kind of superstition." He had the Nazis in mind, but in an era of New Age channeling, of UFOs, and of Pentecostals laughing and vomiting in the spirit, his analysis has not dated. Technology and Marx spelled revolution, said Lenin; in Mann's version, technology and irrationalism equal fascism. He would see a group of computerized bigots gathering on-line as more of the same.

"Achtung!" became a wake-up call for a new "militant humanism" devoted to "the principles of freedom, tolerance, and honest doubt." Something, though, was missing: the enemy's name. But not for long.

On December 19, 1936, his honorary doctorate from the University of Bonn was revoked. He closed the year with a letter to Karl Justus Obenauer, dean of Bonn's philosophy faculty, in which he singled out, among many atrocities, the Nazis' poisoning of the German language. Within weeks, thanks to a donation from Alice Mayrisch de Saint-Hubert, the widow of a Luxemburg steel magnate, he had cofounded *Mass und Wert* (*Measure and Value*), a journal of emigration distinguished by its adherence to a left-wing humanism: i.e., its ideology left room for "honest doubt." Its subtitle was "A Bimonthly for Free German Culture." Mann gave the magazine a tone of "conservative revolution," by which he meant a restoration of the principles he ascribed to Goethe and Nietzsche.

In his preface to the first issue, he wrote that he considered himself a socialist because he refused to rank the political-social sphere lower than the inner life: *Innerlichkeit* required a political prop, just as revolutionary politics needed an infusion of humanism. This was an echo of "Culture and Socialism" (there were other echoes, favorite quotations from Goethe, as well as the French bon mot that "When a German tries to be graceful he jumps out of the window that he shared with Grautoff when he was a teenager"). Appropriately the issue contained excerpts from *The Beloved Returns*.

In these political times, he wrote, art seems to have "declined into a false and fatuous aestheticism," at least according to the Communists and Fascists. He disagreed. Art could recapture "the pattern of the human," a kind of anti-fascism which avoided agitprop or Socialist Realism by virtue of "its membership in two worlds, that of the spirit and that of nature." Therefore, following Goethe's example, his magazine would regard "sentimentality and false piety" as political crimes, the left's version of grade-B movies.

(This part was non-negotiable. In 1950, fighting new enemies, American congressmen, he was obliged to confirm that he was not a communist to the extent that he opposed "power and illegality, concentration camps, total management of culture, and its level determined from below to the taste of the little people." The significant detail was his disavowal of populism. As in 1935, he refused to see a link between defending the lower classes and accepting their bad taste.)

The journal's editors knew how to hate; Goethe had boasted, "I rejoice in feeling that there are things which I hate." But their animus would not be crass, and if the very name, *Mass und Wert*, struck some readers— Brecht?—as too "highbrow" and "polite," its discretion was substantive. Only by distinguishing itself from the fanaticism and hysteria of populist discourse could humanist culture win out. The *Thomasmänner* were not defeated yet.

9

A MYTH FOR OUR TIME

E verything Mann wrote acquired a political subtext. In 1925, although
he could hardly anticipate what lay ahead, he began to conceive a myth
adequate to an era poised on the lip of an abyss. In his imagination
he fled the mountain for the delta, replacing moisture and darkness with
"dry air and a bright sky."

Mann's projects tended toward the inflationary. He had conceived *The
Magic Mountain* as a novella-sized comedy and ended with a thousand-page
epic. Similarly he now planned a novella about Joseph as an expansion of
the Bible story, a project once contemplated by Goethe. Almost two decades
later he would have a fifteen-hundred-page tetralogy. This time his comic
intentions were clearer, and he later called the work a "light opera" by
comparison with his subsequent novel, *Doctor Faustus*.

The Magic Mountain had excavated the roots of modern life. Since he
didn't wish to repeat himself—as he often said, he could have grown fat
writing sequels to *Buddenbrooks*—he could surpass himself only by looking
elsewhere, to the Eastern origins of Western civilization. He composed a
kind of epistemological thriller in which his characters learn how to think
and to reflect, to make sense of their feelings, to proceed from intuition to
induction, from the local to the general. They begin as priests and end as
historians. The origins of mental life are encapsulated in one generation,
that of Joseph and his brothers.

Where Spengler perceived the decline of the West, Mann envisioned
something happier in its Judeo-Christian heritage. Another element was
involved, closer to his heart, and proceeding inevitably from his decision

to plant his characters in the East. The slant first became evident in 1926, when Mann attended an international peace conference in Paris. His journal of this visit, "Parisian Reckoning," includes a most audacious passage masquerading as a journalistic aside. Parisian life has changed, Mann says, since his last visit. He sits in a café beside a square formerly inhabited by street-walkers. The prostitutes remain, only now they're men. The habit formerly associated with "Orientals, Southern Europeans, Anglo-Saxons, and Germans" crosses borders. Mann discerns a new form of internationalism aptly located in Paris, the home of "Proust and Gide, that friend of Oscar Wilde." This newest import will shake up French theorists; their "classical psychology" will have to reckon with "Oriental psychoanalysis"—by which he means the "pansexuality" of the famously "Jewish science."

It is most telling that he celebrates this internationalization of homosexuality right after he condemns the Nazi Baümler's attempt to link Nietzsche with Bachofen, the mythographer of matriarchy. In fact, Baümler's edition of Bachofen's *The Myth of Orient and Occident* was among his sources for *The Tales of Jacob*. But his annotations expressed severe displeasure: "The whole thing smacks of cultism; it is tendentious and repellent. In a time like this, to give the Germans such nonsense is abominable." His very citation of the Jewish—and eminently patriarchal—Freud underlined his opposition to the matriarchal anti-Semites. (In 1929, he added his old enemy Ludwig Klages—who had rediscovered Bachofen—and the "snob" Spengler to the reactionary obfuscators Freud had supplanted.)

As a locale, Venice had offered five centuries of vice and sexual experiment. The East was even more generous, offering cultures ruled by androgynous deities and rife with homosexual encounters. Among these no society was as male-bonded, no patriarchy as riddled with sexual tensions, as the Hebrew. Carrying his fellow Westerners to their spiritual birthplace, Mann discovered a familiar territory. In the season of Klaus Heuser, another seventeen-year-old, Joseph, became the fictional object of his attention.

His research was prodigious. Twice he visited the locale of his story. In March 1925, he first saw Port Said, Cairo, Luxor, Karnak, and the "timeless" desert. He traveled by Pullman; obviously he didn't seek to duplicate Joseph's nomadic woes. In the journal of his tour, *Unterwegs*, the temporary bachelor observed that women seemed absent from the Egyptian bazaars, a possible inducement to place his hero there. An all-male "festival" would have been unimaginable in Europe.

In addition he needed a point of view, not the easiest acquisition for a man of little faith. Mann's decision to retell the Old Testament was manifestly philo-Semitic. German nationalists were horrified that the author of the *Reflections* should devote so much time and space to the Jews. He chose

Jewish tutelary spirits, but they were peculiarly matched: a revisionist reactionary scholar, Oskar Goldberg, and Sigmund Freud, the virtual founder
of "Oriental psychoanalysis."

Oskar Goldberg was a Berlin Jew, born in 1885, who emigrated to
America in 1941 and died there in 1952. His book *The World of the Flesh*
continued the tradition of Jewish anti-Semitism popularized by Otto Weininger. He agreed with Weininger that modern Jews were effeminate weak-
lings, but his ideal comparison was not their Christian neighbors but their
Hebrew ancestors. He envisioned a cloistered, chthonic mystery-world, now
corrupted by intellectualism. In his view, as long as the Jews had maintained a visceral, organic bond with Jahweh, they knew glory on earth, but
effectively things went bad after Solomon built the temple. Goldberg attacked the philosopher Moses Maimonedes for reading Aristotle. What price
sophistication? Who needed the Greeks when their forefathers had walked
with God?

Goldberg had his admirers, like Walter Benjamin, and detractors, like
Benjamin's friend the historian Gershon Scholem, who saw him as yet another ugly, imperious Jew, sharing the temperament, if not the ideology,
of Lukács or Alfred Kerr. In this unappealing form he would show up as
Breisacher, the right-wing Jew in *Doctor Faustus*, a character who offended
Katia and Erika, not to mention the Jewish readers who had suffered from
gentile fascists.

Mann eagerly relied on Goldberg's interpretation of early Jewish culture. Five years earlier he had discovered homoerotic communities while
reading Hans Blüher and the histories of medieval Russia; and now, thanks
to Goldberg, he found a group exhibiting the same tendencies thousands
of years before the Christian era. In *The Tales of Jacob*, the tetralogy's first
volume, God is nearly as unreflective as his worshipers, a jealous patriarch
demanding perpetual adoration, and—according to Mann—virtual emas-
culation in the form of circumcision. To walk with God means to be ravished by him. Mann took Goldberg's interpretation and made it bluntly
sexual.

Therefore his attraction to Freud was not, as it may seem, merely an
antidote to Goldberg, but an extension. In a 1929 essay he placed Freud
in the romantic tradition of Novalis and Hölderlin—and, implicitly,
Platen—wrenching him *into* the culture, even as he had previously found
room for Marx and Whitman. "When Freud speaks of a narcissistic libido
of the ego and derives it from the products of the libido which hold the
body cells together, the idea is such a romantic-biologic speculation that
its absence from the writings of Novalis would seem to be due to mere
chance." (Alert readers know of its presence in *The Magic Mountain*.)

There follows rapprochement impossible to imagine coming from anyone but Mann. "What has been falsely called Freud's pansexualism, his theory of the libido, is, to put it briefly, nothing but natural science divested of mysticism and becoming romanticism." Moreover, it is a romanticism in which mind and soul combine; according to Mann, the "intellectual ingredient in Freud's theory" (what German anti-Semites might call the Jewish need to systematize) distinguishes psychoanalysis from "the anti-rationalist scientific movement of today."

While one Jew, Oskar Goldberg, allowed Mann to conceive ancient history as a homoerotic romance, another Jew, Sigmund Freud, assured him that an approach that cut to the erotic quick of all relations was scientifically correct. Like some new convert, Mann insisted on the therapeutic values of psychoanalysis. But, as in the politics he affirmed, he chose only the passages where Freud's theory acknowledged his own desires. Thanks to Freud, Mann could eroticize practice and praxis.

Once he understood it, he particularly relished Freud's "revolutionary affront to . . . all philosophical habits of thought." At times Mann would coyly allow that he had anticipated Freud without any training, when he almost imputes the Viennese Jew's achievement to himself. One can joke that if Freud hadn't existed, Mann would have invented him. Don't episodes in Freud's life resemble Mann's fiction? Consider the relation with Wilhelm Fliess. Freud's passionate folly as revealed when a letter from Fliess made him faint; his betrayal of medical standards—and a patient's safety—to advance his idol's theories; even his pompous assertion, after the fact, that in transcending his "homosexual cathexis," he had grown in wisdom: all of these read like incidents imagined by Thomas Mann. (Not least would be the apparent avoidance of sexual union, although the nature of the relation is never doubted by its supremely reflective actors.)

A political bias characterizes Mann's interpretation of Freud. He first gave his lecture "Freud's Position in the History of Modern Thought" in Munich—Hitler's turf—before an audience of left-wing students. Freud was not only anti-Hitler, he was anti-Jung (though once, much like the characters in Schnitzler or in Mann's "Blood of the Walsungs," he had courted Jung precisely for his Aryan qualities). Mann's affirmation of Freud is significant given the fact that Jungian scholars like Karl Kerényi were among his sources for later volumes of the *Joseph* books. In March 1935 Mann reports on Jung's "revolting conduct." He cannot deny the man's intelligence; he particularly likes his recognition that neuroses can be "a precious part of the soul"—something like the wound he never hopes to heal. But he despises Jung's "total rejection of rationalism, when the moment has long come for us to fight for rationality with every ounce of strength we have." To whom is Jung useful? Mann has no doubts: "His thought and his utterances tend to glorify Nazism."* (Similarly, in 1940, he condemned a young American Jungian, Joseph Campbell, for insisting that art be divorced from politics. Such quietism could only please the enemy.)

Politics informed Mann's retelling of Scripture. *Joseph and His Brothers* was seen by readers like F. O. Matthiessen as a bible of secular humanism, tolerance, and—in Mann's words—"good will." In the last novel, *Joseph the Provider*, Mann imagined him as a biblical FDR, a leader removed by class and education from those he governs. By some lights, this final Joseph is a class traitor. "Read between the lines," and he pursues an "astonishing mixture of socialization and freehold occupancy." Mann even sneaks in a whiff of Brecht. When the hero is reconciled with his brothers, he insists upon being fed: "Bread comes first, before any hallelujahs." Of course, this defeats the notion of table blessing; it also paraphrases *Mahagonny*.

In 1942, while composing these pages, Mann gave a lecture, "How to Win the Peace": "We feel today that in the relation of freedom and equality the center of gravity has moved toward the side of equality and economic justice, away from the individual and toward the social. Social democracy is now the order of the day." For almost fifteen years he had depicted the dissolving of an individual will into the general, transforming his Joseph from narcissist to public servant.

Myth is a tricky figure in politics. Jungians like Joseph Campbell employed their mythic understanding to counsel political reaction, while Freudians have used their patented myth any which way. Mann was alone in imagining a providential role for so whimsical a hero, and in combining "Oriental psychoanalysis" and left-wing politics. *Joseph the Provider* revealed the paradoxical identity of his later years, as the onetime emissary between life and death became a courtier-socialist.

O f all Mann's big novels, *Joseph* was furthest from his experience. His chosen hero became the archetypal exile shortly before Mann's own flight from Germany; and he found himself sharing Joseph's task, singing the Lord's song in a new land. In April 1938, while visiting Beverly Hills, he recalled the "provisional" nature of his past life, of a home conventionally

---

* In 1938, in an admittedly "ironic jest," he suggests that since the Nazis fight reason as if it were a nation state, "the élan of their March on Vienna had a secret spring." It was directed at Freud, the "great disillusioner," whose disciples never foamed at the mouth, unlike Hitler's pentecostal hordes.

measured by goods and property. "But what is it to be without a home? In the works which I write is my home. Engrossed in them I feel all the familiarity of being at home. These works are language, German language and thought form, my personal development of the tradition of my land and my people. Where I am is Germany." A year later, in *The Beloved Returns*, Goethe says of his benighted countrymen, "They think they're Germany, but I am."

These oft-quoted words bespoke a grand confidence: like Joseph, "I am he," come to renew the tradition. He wasn't always so game; he speaks elsewhere of "the heartache of exile, the uprooting, the chill of homelessness." But in this moment he articulated the deepest conviction of Hitler's émigrés. Germany could survive *only* in exile, her spirit rescued from contaminated soil.

Klaus Mann once lamented that exile began in the passage from infantile bliss to early childhood. Paradise is, by definition, perfect, a gratuitous gift extended to Joseph by his father, God, and his mother, the moon. Utopia is an equivalent dream, with the exception that it is manmade and unfulfilled. Paradise came before: Utopia is yet to be. Joseph is exiled from paradise to Utopia, from sensation to thought, from adolescent eros to adult vision, from tribal chaos to bureaucratic order. The knowledge he acquires in barnyards, jails, and palaces came to Mann in an equivalent variety of settings, from Swiss hotels to Hollywood studios and the White House.

Mann made an ancient text conform to his desires. He frequently observed that he sought to renew myth with "jests and allusions." This chimed with his conviction that parody was the only form appropriate for latecomers like himself.

The first volume, *The Tales of Jacob*, retells the stories of Joseph's ancestors. The characters are almost all male; Dinah appears, but she exists mainly to incite a display of masculine violence by her brothers. Mann follows the Old Testament by downplaying the role of women. Those critics who discern a Jungian air to his tetralogy hope for a reconciliation of opposing forces, in the mode of Jung or Bachofen. But Mann's binoculars remain shortsighted. He imagines some women: e.g., the noble Rachel, who dies in childbirth, in a scene drawn from Katia's near-fatal pregnancy; but she exists mostly as a visual trace. Jacob adores Joseph because he resembles Rachel as a young girl; we saw the origins of this construct in Mann's own desires for his son, who supposedly resembled him as a boy. Mut, the wife of Potiphar, the pharaoh's steward, vivifies *Joseph in Egypt*. Her mad infatuation with Joseph is often cited as Mann's rare depiction of heterosexual lust. In his diaries he admits that she's his stand-in, and that he based her passions on his own for Paul Ehrenberg. Of Joseph's wife we learn almost nothing. The reconciliation between sky and earth is not intersexual, but all within one man's heart.

Franz Werfel made his *Song of Bernadette* a hagiography. But his years with God left Mann a doubter. In 1931, after two volumes of *Joseph*, he wrote, "Belief? Unbelief? I hardly know one from the other. I really couldn't say if I consider myself a believer or unbeliever. I have the deepest doubt or skepticism toward both positions." (Twenty-three years later he circulated a joke in which a man says of his friend, " 'Jödl really believes there is no God. I don't even believe that.' Perfect!") God, as a concept, left him unimpressed. "One work, one world . . . I can do that too. That is no art. Rather, it is nothing but art, and no reason to bang one's head on the ground for." Two novels later, he was still impious. Congratulating Klaus for the Olympian galaxy in *The Turning Point*, he wrote, "One is tempted to suspect that you willfully selected only those gods who have quirks. But if one tries to name some who haven't, one discovers there are none who fill the bill." Including Klaus's king of kings, Jesus.

Following the Old Testament, Mann sees the relations of God and the Jews as symbiotic. In *Young Joseph* he asserts that Abraham is God's father. By recognizing Him, then speaking about Him, he makes Him real: his thought and language give God life. In *Joseph the Provider*, God creates a mirror in man precisely to know himself. Once Joseph begins his travels, he will encounter gods more androgynous and civilized than the primitive, phallic deity he left behind in Canaan.

God can't excel Himself, can't move any higher. So Mann ascribes to him "an ambition to mingle, a craving to be like the rest, a desire to stop being unusual." This means, literally, getting down with the people: "Add the spice of sense to His existence. To exchange a lofty but somewhat anemic spiritual all-sufficiency for the full-blooded fleshly existence of a corporeal folk-god; to be just like the other gods." To a reader of Mann's fiction, God sounds like all the princes whose "melancholy sensuality" longs for the commonplace.*

In *The Tales of Jacob* he skirts blasphemy; at the very least he allows his characters a Pirandelloan attack on their creator's design. In *The Magic Mountain* he had described a moribund girl whose legs twitch angrily, a physical rejection of her fate that contrasted with the general acceptance of death. When Jacob loses Rachel, he brings forth a stream of invective

---

* Jack Myles's recent study, *God, A Biography*, follows a similar line: God as an evolving literary subject.

against God. It matters not that he later regains his faith. The cry registers as authentic, much as Satan remains the persuasive figure in Milton's epic.*

He injects another note, fully of this century. As in the Bible, Jacob tricks his father, Isaac, into giving him Esau's inheritance. Thereby he advances God's plan for the Hebrews, but leaves his victim bereft and impoverished. Esau's rage is equal to his loss. It's not hard to see in him all those unchosen people, racial inferiors like Esau, "the red one," and Ham, effectively written out of history.

Esau's outburst—"Curse it! Betrayed, betrayed betrayed!"—reads like a collaboration of Shakespeare's Caliban and Frantz Fanon. The chosen one, embarrassed by his brother's righteous despair, slips away. In their conflict Mann anticipated a rage that swept the postwar world. Since he had first broached the subject of miscegenation—and universal brotherhood—in his 1921 essay on the Jews, this forecast can be read as more than accidental.

The beneficiaries of Jacob's crime are depicted as unreflective, deeply passionate, and frequently bloodthirsty men who slaughter their enemies (as in the story of Dinah, their sister, whose rape is avenged in a virtual genocide). Their God is scarcely more evolved, intolerant and capricious. He resembles an oppressive lover, forever escalating his demands, expecting operatic and frequently gruesome pledges of devotion. His lovers must place Him before women; their foreskins become tokens of praise. Reading the Old Testament in the same way that he does Michelangelo's poetry, Mann homosexualizes God. (He later said that he visualized the deity as the thickly muscled giant presiding over the Sistine Chapel.)

Rewriting the Bible let Mann play with form. *The Tales of Jacob* includes his most experimental prose to date and, in a kind of proto-postmodernism, advertises his daring. The bravado was inherent in the project. Like a jazz saxophonist performing a standard, Mann must tell a familiar story as if it were brand-new. Like that same musician, he cannot pretend naïveté. Artistic integrity demands that the saxophonist perform as brilliantly whether it's the blues or a ballad. Just so, Mann brings to Joseph's story all his narrative resources, including the self-conscious examination of his own style. He infuses a personal, even autobiographical, voice into a nar-

---

* The agnostic Mann despised the customary bromides usually employed to alleviate grief. In 1934, when Bertram's lover, Ernst Glöckner, died, he wrote a letter of condolence without consolation: "In the spirit of that brave nineteenth-century pessimism which I have always prized, I hold with Storm's 'Then you will never be again / Just as you never were before.' "

rative conventionally told as if the speaker were divinely inspired. With his voice he deconstructs the tabernacle.*

The tetralogy begins with a two-sentence paragraph. "Very deep is the well of the past. Should we not call it bottomless?" This auto-critique constitutes a less-than-welcoming overture, plunging the reader into Mann's interrogation of the narrator's role, something usually reserved for a private journal. It seems quixotic to begin an epic on such a note. Why, readers might inquire, continue? If it can't be done, why try it? (In 1931 Mann wrote a friend that his "biblical-mythological tale" was "a highly capricious undertaking for me and perhaps too much an experiment for me to have invested so much time and energy in it.")

Mann makes the act of literary composition seem kingdom-challenging and life-threatening. In "Descent into Hell," the prelude to *The Tales of Jacob*, the narrator confesses fear and excitement, an incorporation of Eros and Thanatos, underlined by his claim that "to die means to lose sight of time," and yet "I now shudderingly descend" into a past consecrated to death. He reminds us and himself that "the essence of life is presentness," to know yourself in time. Like the ignorant Hebrews, he must enter a sphere which it is impossible to know.

His solution comes in a flash.

> For it *is*, always *is*, however much we may say it was. Thus speaks the myth, which is only the garment of the mystery. But the holiday garment of the mystery is the feast, the recurrent feast, which bestrides the tenses and makes the has-been and the to-be present to the popular sense. . . . Feast of storytelling, thou art the festal garment of life's mystery, for thou conjure up timelessness in the mind of the folk, and invoke the myth that it may be relieved in the world of the present.

---

* *The Tables of the Law* (1943), a novella composed in the afterglow of *Joseph the Provider*, is about Moses, who becomes grander than God as he becomes literary: "[Before] he had thought only of 'writing'—not at all of the fact that one could just not 'write.' " With an influx of talent, he acquires horns "out of sheer pride of his god-invention." His head on fire, he composes a universal text. Later, in anger with the orgiastic Jews, he smashes the tablets. In a cooler moment, he welcomes the chance to rewrite: "There were a few bad letters in them, I will confess to You now, that I thought of it when I smashed them." Moses, as introduced, is a Mannian type: "His birth was irregular, hence he loved order. . . . His senses were hot, so he craved the spiritual." And when Moses lists the acts forbidden his sacrilegious brethren, the penultimate is "What are you thinking of, to sleep with a boy as with a woman?" Three sentences later: "At first, [the Jews] had the feeling that if one obeyed at all, life would not be worth living."

Alas, Thomas Mann's solutions always turn in on themselves. "It always is" denies the revisionary power of consciousness, under whose auspices everything changes, much as his narrative itself rewrites the past. More relevant than this Jungian apothegm is Mann's tribute to the festival, the garment (recalling the one ripped from Joseph that leaves him naked), and "the popular sense," the customers and bazaar keepers who accompany Joseph through the fleshpots of Egypt.

Mann speculates about the nature of time, and, as with Proust, the question invokes both human suffering and literary technique. Proust could have written this analysis of the process of expectation:

> A half-hour of pure and mere waiting is more frightful and a crueler test of patience than a waiting that is put into a life of seven years. What we await close at hand affects us, precisely because of its nearness, as a much keener and more immediate stimulus than if it were far off, it transforms our patience into nerve- and muscle-consuming impatience, it makes us morbid, we literally do not know what to do with our limbs, while a long-term waiting leaves us in peace; it not only permits, but forces us to think of other things, and do other things, for we must live.

In such passages can be detected the writer whose soul was torn between desire and renunciation. In one uniquely Mannian paragraph, he goes from physical torment to an almost biblical serenity, "for we must live."

Unlike Proust, Mann is most concerned with how time advances, not how it retreats into the portals of memory. He presents each moment as so full, each stage of the story so complete, that one can hardly take it in; the allotted time is never enough. At one point, while depicting Esau, who has yet to be despoiled of his treasure, Mann suggests that we should *not* extend irony to his delusion; i.e., we shouldn't interject our knowledge of the future. In a magnificent aside, he adds:

> Events do not happen all at once, they happen point for point, they develop according to pattern, and it would be false to call a narrative entirely sad because the end is so. A tale with a lamentable close has yet its stages and times of honor, and it is right to regard those not from the point of view of the end, but rather in their own light, for while they are the present they have equal strength with the present-ness of the conclusion.

These words summon up a range of responses from the naïve—"Tell me the good parts again," says the child, requesting a beloved story—to the advanced—Mann anticipates the possibilities of "hypertext," the infinitely flexible, computer-generated narrative. Seeing each stage of the tale "in its own light" is perhaps Mann's only dream of paradise, his deliverance from closure. He shares Proust's optimism on this point.

In his previous novel Mann had counterpointed mountain- and land-time, rounding off a lyric with a march. A greater discrepancy obtains in *Joseph*, between a time where "presentness" is all and an era that can pick which presentness to light upon. Mann comments, "These mysteries deal very freely with the tenses." The Hebrews regard their ancestors as coevals, and every moment as charged with its past: they display "a method of thought which quite simply recognized a deluge in every visitation by nature." They are narcissists and zealots obsessed with "names" and "blessings." They assume the improbable task of inventing simultaneously their history, culture, and language.

But, *mutatis mutandis*, "It always is"; each generation replicates the process, albeit with less symphonic refinement. Mann assures us that the past is foreign but not strange. The prelude ends in "a country such as we have often seen . . . not [quite] like home but certainly not fantastic, and above it move the familiar stars." Having defined the nature of presentness, he plunges us into it with the first words of chapter 1: "A spring evening so brightly moonlit that one could have seen to read." (The difference between the prelude's end and the novel's beginning is that between essay and fiction . . . or still photo and movie.) Familiar stuff indeed, taking us back to the night when Hans Castorp rows on a lake momentarily lit by sun and moon, a blinding image of the dualities battling for his soul. He weighs and ponders until "the balance finally settled in favor of the night and the moon." Joseph, Castorp's successor—and ancestor—exhibits no such ambivalence; he already considers himself as a "consecrate" of the moon and her mysteries.

Joseph's dance leads to a disrobing, a striptease performed for the delectation of two voyeurs, the moon and his father, Jacob. He possesses "a rather full and heavy torso" (perhaps inspired by a young Spanish classmate of Monika and Golo's) in contrast to his pretty, girlish features. His whole body seems alive, universally receptive. His beauty is of an order that inspires worship, "an act of piety," although the faith Mann invokes is more Greek than Hebrew.

His few blemishes—mostly baby fat—enhance the impression, granting him "the attractiveness of the incomplete." We've been here before. Joseph is a healthier specimen of the Tadzio line. He's also a stronger version of Hanno Buddenbrook; like that unhappy youth, "Joseph well knew that his father had not always played the dignified and heroic role in life." It's a sign of his superior power that he, not his father, has the gift of representation, carrying himself with an intense "feeling for pure effect." Jacob understands his son. Observing the "somewhat decadent ritual of wooing" that constitutes Joseph's dance, he commands him to "cover thy nakedness." He's adoring but "ever-anxious," troubled by what Joseph's coquetry foretells, and even more by the way it stimulates him.

A few pages earlier, Joseph had cast himself as God's bride, a Babylonian fancy that anticipates the notion of the church as the bride of Christ. As Mann tells it in his prelude, Joseph shares with female votaries of the goddess Ishtar "a sense of consecration, an austere bond, and with it a flow of fantasy." Felix Krull had a similar gift, ushering in the Great Joy of his solitary pleasure. The narrator's apology disappears into the maw of a present now past, and we see Joseph, tempting the moon, his father, God himself, and perhaps a writer scribbling the morning away in Munich.

Joseph becomes a consummate flirt whose "emasculated" penis makes him a pansexual creature of pleasure: Mann interjects explanations—Joseph is drawn to the moon "through his horoscope and by all sorts of intuitions and imaginings"—that simply appear fanciful. Inasmuch as the moon represents beauty, Joseph is feminized by worshiping her. His love of beauty is really self-love.

He has shown off his altered condition in an overheated gesture calmed by the "cool brightness" of evening. There follows a passage that turns piety into a form of homosexual flirtation.

> We must remember that the rite of circumcision, taken over as an outward practice from the Egyptians, had in Joseph's family and tribe long ago acquired a peculiar mystic significance. It was the marriage commanded and appointed by God between man and the deity, performed upon that part of the flesh which seemed to form the focus of his being, and upon which every physical vow was taken. Many a man bore the name of God on his organ of generation, or wrote it there before he possessed a woman. The bond of God was sexual in nature, and thus, contracted with a jealous creator and lord, insistent upon sole possession, it inflicted upon the human male a kind of civilizing weakness into the female [alternative translations: "that verged on the female," "akin to a female's"]. The bloody sacrifice of circumcision had more than a physical connection with emasculation. The sanctifying of the flesh signified both being made chaste and the offering up of chastity as a sacrifice, in other words, a female significance.

These words are explicit enough, but Mann proceeds to underline their significance for Joseph. His effeminacy is not simply the outcome of Jewish ritual; it draws on pagan ceremony and vanity:

> Joseph . . . as he knew himself, and as everybody told him, was both beautiful and well-favored—a condition which certainly embraces a consciousness of femininity, and "beautiful" was an adjective always and by everybody used to describe the moon . . . so that in Joseph's mind the idea beautiful and the idea nude flowed together and were interchangeable almost at will, and it seemed to be the part both of vision and of piety to respond to the unshrouded loveliness of the planet with his own.

In his marriage essay Mann says that men today are as obsessed with their own beauty as women, and therefore not quite male. A biographer might remember the adoring look Mann had bestowed on the adolescent Klaus Mann or the teenager Klaus Heuser. Mann's literary game-playing reached its height in this scene with its combination of dialectical finesse and pornographic detail.

Another prelude might have been composed by Klaus Mann. We know that Thomas was sexually aroused by his adolescent son, consoling Klaus with "tendernesses" in an attempt to prop up his "uncertain manliness." There is no evidence that Klaus registered this attraction, but in 1924, aged seventeen, he wrote "The Father Laughs," a story in which a pompous civil servant, Hoffmann, flirts with his daughter Cunegonde. Very probably a surrogate for Klaus, she is described as "boyish," "unfeminine," "manly." A subtler code may obtain: Hoffmann admires her as a charming "Marquis," a medieval knight, a "Grand Inquisitor." These are all images of male beauty found in Mann's diaries of 1918–21. The father scolds Cunegonde for her wayward behavior, and she retaliates, "Who are you to reproach me?"—a reply Klaus may have wished to make even if he never did.

Finally, in a hotel room, she teases him—"Would you like it if I danced with you?" He recoils in horror, but, "unperturbed," she sways closer: "her pert and charming mouth met his." When he resists, she woos him with "her soft, metallic voice, so coquettish that the blood froze in his veins." Her mouth "sucks his with a sharp bite," and he rips the clothes from her body. The melody changes to "a duet where she set the tone." They spend the night together, and in the morning she finds him "naked." The story ends with them rolling about, laughing ecstatically.

We don't know whether Mann found this story an affront or a provocation. But some years after, he imagined a scene in which a similarly androgynous child performs a similarly coquettish dance. This time, however, it's the father who observes his child's nudity.

D uring the late 1920s, traces of Mann's love for the two Klauses appeared throughout his work. Although his Platen lecture was delivered to a scholarly conference, its subtext was more intimate than academic; as he later remembered, Platen's lyrics had "entered into my heart when I was in love." An echo of that period occurs in another essay, composed two months before the Platen lecture. Writing about Theodor Storm, Mann celebrates the novelist's sexual vigor, "a strongly sensual, passionate nature" that reawakened in his fifties. Mann's comment "the gratitude of the aging man for a last, late visitation of joyous intoxication" is paraphrased in his diary whenever he mentions Heuser.

Like Joseph, Mann teases the reader with a naked display of his affections. This occurs in the first paragraphs of *Young Joseph*, the second part of the tetralogy, composed quite obviously in the shadow of Klaus Heuser. This section deserves comparison with Proust's *Cities of the Plain* as a statement of the splendors and miseries of homosexual love. Surprisingly, Mann's view is less clandestine or surreptitious. Rather than imagine a world of disguises, he opens his heart to the world. He deploys the same tone as before, writing as if he's still simply retelling what everyone knows. Received wisdom in this case is a testament to pederasty.

Mann repeats his marriage essay's warnings against a barren, fruitless beauty: "impractical" is his bourgeois formulation. But then he reverses himself. Exceptions occur, "and," he adds ingenuously, "can be proved." The magic ingredient is "youth," a state that "affects the beholder as beauty, and is even so affected itself, as its smile unmistakably betrays." The coquette delights himself with a charm that falls "between the masculine and the feminine." The preferred age is seventeen—the age of Klaus Heuser in 1927—for then "a youth . . . is not beautiful in the sense of perfect masculinity. Nor yet in the sense of fruitless femininity—that would be worst of all. But so much we must admit: that beauty in the guise of youth must always seem inwardly and outwardly to incline toward the feminine."

Amid the attendant dangers, Mann maintains his magisterial confi-

dence. He writes as if all the world agreed that a young boy is the most
perfect instance of human beauty. He chastises Joseph for considering himself unique,

> since there were and are hosts of his like. Since the time when man
> no longer lived in the deep or crawled on his belly, but had travelled
> some way toward the bodily image of God, many a youth of seventeen
> has displayed to admiring eyes quite as slender legs and narrow hips,
> quite such a well-shaped throat and golden-brown skin. Many a youth
> has seemed neither too tall nor too short, but precisely the right height;
> many have known how to stand and to walk in a way that is half
> divine, many have found the exquisite mean between delicacy and
> strength of form . . . smiling to boot with a smile that is half divine.
> That happens every day.

Even as we read, some golden youth is breaking an older man's heart.

Mann explores two kinds of narcissism. The first one, exemplified by
Jacob adoring in his son images of a bloody past and transcendent future,
partakes of the social, erotic, and mythic. (The absence of such parental
narcissism, or of any erotic interplay, doomed the relation of Thomas and
Hanno Buddenbrook.) The other form is masturbatory. By exaggerating
Joseph's self-adoration, Mann can participate in it. Joseph has enough vanity
to spare.

From childhood, he is acclaimed as an interpreter of dreams. (A nod to
Freud, or a rebuke? In *Joseph in Egypt*: "It is false to regard dream as a free
and savage domain . . . what the waking state doesn't know is shut off
from the dream"—i.e., we only dream what we already know—sounds like
a denial of the repression theory.) His older brothers detest his analytic
bent. But Jacob loves it, as does Benjamin, his younger brother, who sits
enthralled as he recounts his dream visions. One includes a flight to heaven,
in which he is scooped up by an eagle, like a Hebrew Ganymede. The
dream is filled with images of muscular angels naked to the waist and of
God Himself, looking like Jacob, his father / lover. Joseph's language culminates in an ecstatic climax: "While the Lord so singled me out for joy,
my flesh was on fire, my veins glowed brightly, my bones were like a fire
of juniper wood, the casting up of my lashes like a lightning flash, my
eyeballs rolled like balls of fire, the hair of my head was a lambent flame,
my limbs were fiery pinions, and I awaked." This is closer to Felix Krull's
Great Joy than the joy that supposedly cometh in the morning. No wonder
Joseph tells it to Benjamin, and not to his father.

Despite his rich dream life, Joseph remains a callow youth until he

acquires imagination, which Mann defines as sympathy, "divining the emotional life of another." Until then he doesn't recognize that his words can
wound; his spirit is inventive rather than imaginative. Because they're sick
of his endless self-referential talk, his brothers punish Joseph by throwing
him down a pit. As he falls, direr thoughts await him about jealousy,
conspiracy, a human world that doesn't center around him: "Lower down
were others yet more real, like their undertones and ground-basses, so that
the whole was like a moving musical, perpendicularly composed, which his
spirit was occupied in conducting on all three levels." This visceral epiphany is among Mann's greatest achievements.

It leads to a discussion of the unspeakable. "We are easily persuaded
to call a situation unbearable. The sympathetic friend's relation to this
reality, which is, of course, not his own, is an unreal and *sentimental* one.
He commits an error of the *imagination*, for the sufferer, thanks to his
suffering, is in a different category. What do we really mean by the unbearable, when there is nothing to be done but bear it, so long as we are
in our senses [italics mine]?*

Young Joseph ends in a reversal of its opening pages. There a vain adolescent, enjoying his temporary charms, aspires to godhead. In the last
chapter, after the boy's apparent death, his father's despair reduces him
from man to "mere creature," reverting from "allegory" to the "crude thing
itself and to the horrible reality." In the crucible of suffering he becomes
indistinguishable from a bereaved animal. Continuing the parallel and sym-
metry, where Joseph exhibited the boy/girl qualities of youth, old age leaves
Jacob a hideous caricature of his son's androgyny: "nerveless arms, spent
thighs, womanish breasts."

Mann analyzes Jacob's "double-sexed yearning": the "double-love" of a
"double-object," by means of which, since Rachel's death, he has been
Joseph's father and mother, loving Rachel-in-Joseph as a man, loving
Joseph-in-lieu-of-Rachel as a woman. Age reverses the sexes. "Women get

---

* Mann extended these ideas in his description of Hell in *Doctor Faustus*—a scene which drew
on his knowledge of "Gestapo cellars." There the noise of Joseph's grief is amplified ad infinitum:
in "rocking ecstasies of anguish no man can hear his tune, for that it is smothered in the general,
in the thick-clotted diapason of trills and chirps lured from the everlasting dispensation of the
unbelievable combined with the irresponsible." But, as Mann goes on, the noise degenerates
into a "shameful pleasure," a soundtrack to "the lusts of hell," and there may be too much
diabolical pleasure on the author's part. The simpler description of suffering as another category
of sensuous life is more persuasive, and also more attuned to his interrogations of verbally
intractable experience. (It is also close to the contentions of Jean Améry or Primo Levi that the
death camps were beyond description, although not beyond living through.)

beards, men get bosoms. . . . I will be his mother." Because he has his son's "tendency to deal freely with sex," he views his effeminized body as a sign that he can become Demeter, searching underground for her lost child.

Thus Mann balances the mindless exhilaration of youth with the shriveled wisdom of age. More subtly, he shifts the focus from Joseph to his lovers. This becomes clearer in *Joseph in Egypt*, when he analyzes Mut's love for Joseph. Mut sees along with the narrator of *Young Joseph* that Joseph's strength is "but average"; there are thousands like him. As Jacob became Joseph's mother, love masculinizes Mut. Her breasts, "once so tender and maidenly," become asymmetrically abundant, her thighs develop "illicitly," becoming vigorous enough to grip a broomstick between them. She resembles an obscene caricature of two stereotypes, Madonna and whore. While this may betray Mann's misogyny, it may also recall Jacob's spent flesh and wasted thighs. It is also a parody of the Great Mother of Bachofen's anthropology. Attempting to seduce Joseph, Mut says, "With his mother each man sleeps—the woman is the mother of the world, her son is her husband, and every man begets upon his mother. . . . Isis am I, the Great Mother." Since this makes heterosexuality tantamount to incest, the visions of Jacob and God that rescue Joseph provide a homosexual alternative. Mann's answer to Bachofen or Freud recognizes the Great Mother but prefers the Father.

His treatment of Mut goes completely against tradition. In most other versions of the story—including recent movies starring Richard Gere and Ben Kingsley—she is a nameless shrew, tempting the virtuous Joseph with the devil's own wiles. Having given her a name and a heart, Mann won't "disgrace her in public"; she may cry, "I have seen his strength," but we can't. Instead Mann shows us Joseph the half-witting tempter, and makes her "God-intoxication" more vivid than his. The idiosyncratic rewriting of Scripture has reached its zenith.

While Mann's interest in the Jews was bound to offend nationalistic Germans, his hero's career is itself a rebuttal of Jewish claims of exceptionalism. Left-wingers had their own objections. By 1943 Bertolt Brecht, when he wasn't accusing Mann of either starving his brother or salivating like a "reptile" over the prospect of a million dead Germans, was dismissing him as a "clerico-fascist," using *Joseph* to make his case. In *The Beloved Returns* Mann anticipates this attack. There Goethe defines "religious symbolism" as "a cultural treasure-house, wherein we have a perfect right to dip when we need to use the familiar image to make visible and tangible some general aspect of spirit."

Joseph is closer to Nietzsche's idealized pan-European Jew. He survives by assimilating; observing the commandment against worshiping other gods doesn't prevent his enjoying pagan ritual. It was singularly audacious—and, as so often, virtually unnoticed—for Mann to balance the overly virile Hebrew God with the double-sexed Egyptians. (By comparison, Klaus Mann gravitated to the Catholic church for its theatrical ceremony and loving mother—a simpler faith, entirely.)

Although Joseph is reconciled with his aged father, he does not inherit Jacob's blessing; this failure makes him a tangent—a "nervous exception" —to the royal line of Jewish history. The chosen heir is his elder brother Judah. Brash and unworldly, Judah seems an unlikely candidate. But he is also impassioned, lust-driven, both hotheaded and kindhearted: in short, Mann's notion of a virile warrior, a healthier Joachim, a more soulful Hans Hansen.

Where Joseph has spent his lifetime impervious to temptation, Judah remains at seventy-five a "slave" to desire. But as Jacob pours out his blessing in the form of holy oil—Judah is literally soaked—the son realizes, "Well, well, in spite of everything! Then it was not so bad after all— maybe the purity I craved is not so indispensable to salvation; maybe it is all taken in together, even hell itself is taken in."

Mann believed that the brothers expressed two "aspects of experience, the playful and the serious." But seriousness wins out—Judah's final epiphany, "The oil is pouring over me, I did not waste my life," is far more stirring than the mature Joseph's relentlessly ironic aphorisms. The narrator agrees: "I confess that I have found it more enjoyable to talk about the charming seventeen-year-old lad." Mann finds a way to recapture the early world of circumambient Eros, of sensual delights whispering to Joseph from his moon mother and every flowering tree.

Joseph is reunited with his brother Benjamin. We forget that the elder is fifty-five, exhibiting a theatrical interest in his "toilet" reminiscent of Thomas Buddenbrook; the younger, fifty-three. Instead we re-enter a sphere of Proustian synesthesia shared by these two alone: "And Benjamin was pervaded by an old, familiar childhood air: pungent, sun-warmed, spicy, the essential aroma of all the love and trust, security and admiration, all the childlike bewildered sympathy, intuition and self-knowledge Benona had ever known."

Is there a similar literary yoking of polymorphous pleasure and infantile love? Arrayed with Judah's lusty pronouncements, it restores the wordless sensuality that charges Mann's best writing.* For a moment, all his youthful loves are contained in the figures of two middle-aged brothers: "Writing *Joseph* is so much pleasure for me that I can hardly wait until the next morning."

On December 25, 1933, Heinrich wrote Thomas, full of praise for *The Tales of Jacob*. "Rich poetry, probably your richest, and the most magical thing about it is precisely its derivation from a 'known' background, although everyone learns through you that what he knew was in fact nothing and that man's past, when made contemporary, is even more of a fairytale than even he himself can have wished it." Heinrich remained his brother's most attentive reader: he added that Thomas had achieved a mysticism indivisible from thought.

Mann does more than elaborate a familiar story. He surrounds each incident with so much commentary, so many parodistic devices and atemporal allusions, that he virtually pre-empts criticism. Yet he also renews forms of response that he had apparently parodied out of existence. By the time Joseph and Jacob finally reconcile, "the painfully beautiful motif of reunion" is as poignant as ever, the suspense as great.

"At the climactic moment of the Joseph story," Bruno Walter observed, "the poet bids music to lead the son, believed to be dead, into his father's arms . . . the supreme pathos of an incomparable human event is dissolved in the lovely song of the child Serach." Yes, and it's also Mann's attempt at the novel as total work of art, embracing song, the aural in lieu of the visual; he always felt most at home in the acoustic sphere. This reunion of an old man and his son, inspired so many years earlier by his love for the two Klauses, Mann and Heuser, became his challenge to *Tristan and Isolde*!

II

There were influences from abroad. They happened to be French ones— a nice critical joke on the Mann who had previously disdained French psychology, but who since at least 1925 had seen France as the homeland of Gide and Proust. In 1936, Gide visited Mann in Switzerland, and was reportedly enthralled by the newest sections of *Joseph*, as well as by the

---

* Typically Mann spoofs: "Naturally Benjamin's heart throbs. . . . Since there must always be some humor in the telling, I explain the state of his soul as indescribable, but then go on to describe it."

Hofmann painting of young swimmers. A year earlier, Mann admitted to a friend something about Potiphar's wife. "At the moment the poor lady has a great deal to suffer; psychologically she seems to be slightly influenced by Proust, whom I find suddenly fascinating. He has a fantastic leisureliness that disconcerts and attracts me."

The narrative of Mut's passion is Proustian in its slow-paced itinerary of desire, and its attention to the manic phases, excess that Mann had previously denied his German lovers. In 1939, when *Life* magazine ran a story on "Germany's foremost literary exile," the critic Marquis Childs called Mut's "anguished and frustrated love . . . one of the most superb accounts of passion in all literature."

As we saw, Mann had a more personal relation with Gide. During the 1930s the two novelists were equally ardent antifascists. Gide was briefly attracted to the Soviet Union, though after observing Stalinism up close, he wrote *Back from the U.S.S.R.* (1937), saying, among other things, that Trotsky was a more reliable anti-Nazi than Stalin. After that he became persona non grata on the left, but Thomas and Klaus Mann remained loyal to him.

Mann's identification with Gide became clearest after the latter's death. On March 12, 1951, he was outraged to read in *The Nation* an obituary that called Gide "the dirty old man" of French letters. Mann saw this as a Stalinist form of homophobia: "obviously a Communist [trick]." Shades of his defense of Platen against Heine, he continued to find left and right equally benighted on the subject of homosexuality. His rallying to Gide's defense suggests that, Erasmus-like, he would remain "battered on all sides," precisely because of his sexual nature.

Meanwhile he feared that *Felix Krull* was *too* similar to Gide's *The Immoralist* and privately chastised Gide for announcing his desires. Mann could not imagine flirting with a young man; the outcome being foredoomed, he preferred to keep "his dignity and honor" rather than destroy a "beloved youth's admiration" through such "unthinkable baseness."

These were the words of a sad old man who had rarely known erotic bliss. While he could not imagine a youth's returning his love, his spirits were lifted whenever he found his desires reflected in other men's work. He applauded Balzac's description of Vautrin's passion for the youth Rudempré in *Les Illusions Perdues*. Vautrin exemplified the kind of man too virile for women, a type he had praised as early as 1920. A few months later he was struck by the attraction of Leo Tolstoy, "this most manly of men," to handsome young Cossacks.

Sexual response became an explicit criterion. In his memorial to Bernard Shaw, he found much to commend, particularly the habits which steered the playwright away from intoxication and vice. Like a German Mann, Shaw worked a daily routine between breakfast and lunch. Yet there was no "sensual abandon" in his art. He would never have echoed Michelangelo's "Como paò asser ch'io non sia piu mio"—words Mann had quoted during the summer of Franzl. Conversely, Michelangelo resembled Mann on a level that went beyond hard work to serious play. Clinching his position in the pantheon, he demonstrated an "exile's grudge" of a sort very familiar to the battered refugee Thomas Mann.

The later Mann became homosexually alert to all forms of art. Listening to Tchaikovsky's *Pathétique* Symphony, he intuited the "depression of a boy-lover." It was not a virile work, "inclining to the overly sweet," until an "astonishing" end that foreshadowed the composer's death. (Mann prefigures the recent tendency to hear gender preference in musical composition. Fortunately he didn't settle for the banal equation of homosexual and epicene famously made by Charles Ives. Instead he demonstrated that homosexual expression was dialectical: for instance, there's nothing "sweet" about Leverkühn's music.)

He remained a glutton for visual stimulation. It is not surprising that he found a postcard reproduction of Praxiteles' Hermes "adorable." But he also responded to more robust frames. The movie *A Streetcar Named Desire* was embarrassingly overwrought: "The audience laughs though it is a tragedy." But Marlon Brando's "gorgeous naked torso" exhibited a "terrific sex appeal." The movies had long supplied him with images of hyperbolic virility, abundant thighs and "primitive" chests.

He also found in the movies, as he did in Michelangelo's sonnets, a model of age's love for youth. On June 7, 1952, he notes with pleasure David Lean's film of Dickens's *Oliver Twist*. "The little boy pretty and seen with a specific English boy-love. The rich grandfather sympathetic. Thought of Frido." Once again, art showed him his true self. While he often referred to his love for Frido, analogizing that love to pedophilia was something new—although for the man who had found desiring his son "quite natural," it might have been another case of the eternal recurrence!

The particular sympathy between Mann and those like him continued in America. In 1950, Mann guessed that "the world knows more about me than it will admit." Those in the know were his homosexual brothers. Thus, while Harry Levin excoriated *Doctor Faustus*, another Harvard professor, F. O. Matthiessen, found in *Joseph and His Brothers* themes celebrated in American romanticism by Melville and Whitman. (Matthiessen was, like Klaus Mann, a left-wing homosexual, demoralized by the same phenomena; they committed suicide within a year of each other.) Glenway Wescott, a gay novelist, proved to be one of Mann's best critics, perhaps because his

approach strayed from the academic. His essay first given in a commemoration organized by Caroline Newton provides an oddly Mannian slant. For
example, he notices that Hans Castorp is "slightly homosexual" and that
the flirtation between Hans and Clavdia Chauchat resembles homosexual
courtship, heavily emphasizing the visual cruise. Outside of *Buddenbrooks*,
he prefers Mann the miniaturist. This is not Matthiessen's conclusion, but
it shows how gay readers of their generation divided Mann's oeuvre between
them, recognizing themselves in all its forms.

America had influenced Mann long before he arrived here. Whitman's
poetry inspired his politics during the early 1920s. Almost three decades
later, a more personal transformation occurred that would reflect on all his
fictional Hermeses from Felix Krull and Tadzio to young Joseph. In the
fall of 1950, while he was still pining after Franzl, Mann read "The Hitchhiker," Donald Windham's story about a gay pickup. The tale charmed
him. As mentioned earlier, he praised the ways this "surprising little story
poeticizes with serene composure the naïveté of the flesh and its warmth."
Later, although Mann objected to the promiscuity described in Gore Vidal's
The City and the Pillar, he derived great pleasure from its hero's first embrace
of another boy: "The love play between Jim and Bob is glorious." Here,
unbeknownst to him, was a marriage of true minds. Vidal idolized Mann,
and had based a long dialogue in his novel on the philosophical debates
between Naphta and Settembrini; he also shared Mann's distaste for the
"fairy-bar."

The young American writers Vidal and Windham inspired Mann as
surely as had Whitman. For while that poet hastened his political conversion, the novelists fomented a literary passion: encouraged by their example,
he resumed *Felix Krull*. That most European of con men steps back on the
scene, trailing a new breed of Jims and Bobs.

It was this other example of American freedom, sexual rather than political, that accompanied Mann on his return to Europe in 1952. In 1954
he condemned "the overcrowded, overburdened, dragging and thoroughly
opaque periods" of William Faulkner, to whom he had often been compared: his own sentences were "graceful toe-dancing" by comparison. His
encomiums for the gay tyros Vidal, Windham, and Charles Jackson indicate
that their subject matter was far more compelling than anything he could
derive from a recognized master like Faulkner. A year later, just before he
exhibited the signs of coronary thrombosis that would prove fatal, he
composed—on a Dutch beach, surrounded by youthful Hermeses—a tribute to "the most beautiful story in the world." F. O. Matthiessen would
have been pleased: it was *Billy Budd*.

In a final act of erotic sympathy, Mann stated his preference for the

American sailor over Shakespeare's Desdemona. After quoting from Melville's text, he evoked the crew who all love their Billy: "die alle ihren Billy lieben." With this description of homosexual love Mann would end his career.

There was another more ironic consummation for a man who had renounced intimacy and loved music. Benjamin Britten's operatic version of *Death in Venice* (1973) dramatized a frankly sexual interpretation that Mann might evade but could not in good faith deny. In Britten's *Billy Budd* (1951), the eponymous sailor joins Tadzio as a homoerotic icon. Thus, in the highly stylized imagery of ballet and opera, Mann survives as a mythographer of homosexual desire. The Englishman Britten—who had shared a house in Brooklyn with Golo Mann, Auden, and several other notable intellectuals—recognized a link between the German writer and Americans like Melville and Whitman that neatly defines the second half of Thomas Mann's life.

August 6, 1950, was a particularly bitter day for Mann. His love for Franzl served to remind him of his lifelong *Sehnsucht* ("the temptation of manly youth . . . cannot be surpassed in the world") and its eternal frustration ("impossible to attain . . . there can be no *promesse de bonheur*"). He remained enough of a bourgeois to find it "incomprehensible" that something so tawdry should provide "the foundation of artistic endeavor." Still, he found amusement rereading the opening paragraphs of *Young Joseph*, where he had "joked about the dearest thing to me." Thinking of Joseph —and Franzl—he quoted Michelangelo's vow "Your breath" inspires "my word." How much he had parodied his feelings became clear in the entry for August 28. After writing that he desired "godlike youths" far more than women, he added, "Franzl was no young god, simply lovable."

During the 1930s, Mann had taken a vacation from the *Joseph* project and composed *The Beloved Returns*. On January 17, 1940, Heinrich sent his congratulations: he found it particularly heartfelt. On March 3, 1940, Thomas replied, "I don't know whether it is my most beautiful work, but it is dearest to me, because it contains the most about love and erotic union, despite all the mocking and ironic verisimilitude which enshrouds this love."

As we saw, the Goethe novel contained a quiet trace of his love for Klaus Heuser, that rejuvenating "boon of new life." But this was a fleeting allusion, legible only to the reader of Mann's diary. Ten years later he acknowledged that *Young Joseph*, with its unabashed focus on male beauty, contained his deepest feelings about "erotic union." The glimpse of sexual freedom offered by Americans from Whitman and Melville to Windham and Vidal let him see what indeed was "dearest" to his heart. Therefore, *Felix Krull*, while it was composed in Zurich, where he spent his last years, may be his most complete literary response to America, and his last working out of the mythic possibility of transcendence.

Still he lacked a more intimate pretext, until one came in a dream. On March 6, 1951, Mann lamented that he could no longer masturbate while erect: "it seems that the end of my physical sexual life has come." But he remembered one youth who had inspired earlier masturbatory fantasies. "In half-sleep I dreamt that with a kiss I took leave of Franzl, the last loved one, as a representative of the whole adored genre."

Two weeks later the dream was transformed. On March 22, he wrote, "The present erotic chapter apotheosizing the young man occupies me powerfully and urges me on." In this chapter a French novelist, Diane Philibert, aka Madame Houpflé, invites Krull to her room. They make ecstatic love —for the first time Mann describes an orgasm. She also relishes the "perversion" of her love for young men—the more insignificant, the better. Tonio Kröger returns: "The intellect longs for the delights of the non-intellect . . . in love with the beautiful and the divinely stupid." He lets Diane beg to be degraded—"Call me whore . . . *J'adore d'être humiliée*"— and shiver at the prospects of Krull's robbing her, as if an infatuation with the mud has to end in crime.

Comedy facilitates Mann's confession. Diane adores Krull, but almost as an abstract principle. "You, you young, very young men with Hermes legs . . . would you believe, beloved, that I have loved only you, always only you since I was able to feel?" (On June 8, 1950, Mann had called Franzl the "divine boy," and then added—echoing Mut, predicting Diane—"by which I do not mean this particular one.") And so, approaching his eightieth birthday, Thomas Mann finally confessed. "I live in my so-called perversion," Diane says, "in the love of my life that lies at the bottom of everything I am . . . I live in my love for all of you, you, you image of desire, whose beauty I kiss in complete abnegation of spirit." The linguistic games continue, the "Du" is really "Sie"—the countless Hermeses from Armin and Willri and Paul and Klaus and Franzl to the anonymous waiters and gardeners, the images of desire that offered Mann life's greatest joy: in Diane's words, "The idea of you, the lovely instant you incarnate . . . nothing, nothing in the whole visible world equals the enchantment of the youthful male." To the end, recycling and parodying his deepest emotions, he lets Diane rephrase in aphoristic French Michelangelo's promise of aesthetic redemption: *"Tu vivras dans mes vers et dans mes beaux romans."*

As for all the rest—the world of representations, the "sexual community" that sheltered Mann in his marriage essay—it has nothing to do with Diane's love. Her passion is shamelessly sterile, she says, "inadmissible, not practical, not for life, not for marriage. . . . It's a matter of indifference to me—this whole world of men and women and marriage. . . ." Mann's son-in-law Auden once declared that the god of language forgives all crimes. As if in agreement, Mann sequestered his confession in a comic novel.

He did more than confess. For an affectionate reader, *Felix Krull* marks several forms of erotic advance for the old writer. Diane's penchant for having young men bind and rob her is sadomasochistic. Such activity seems brilliantly appropriate to Thomas Mann. The Mannian lover is torn between desire and contempt. From the unhappy voyeurs of his early tales all the way to Aschenbach, Mut, and Diane, the lover's intellectual and verbal skills avail them naught: unless in the blatantly sadistic actions of the magician Cipolla or Adrian Leverkühn, they lead to murder. More often, intellectual mastery and erotic slavery are the norm. In Diane's affection for bondage Mann found a physical correlative. For isn't sadomasochism a perfected form of the sexual dialectics he once called "erotic irony"?

Since 1909 Felix Krull had allowed Mann the chance to impersonate the object of his desires. All during the 1930s, Joseph had let him simultaneously adore and analyze—indeed, meta-psychoanalyze—the hero. But in his last novel, the literary finesse with which he had once dominated his beloved enemies, shown them his "power," was employed against him. The hero parodies Mann's words in order to reject his advances. For example, Krull, while employed as a waiter, is wooed by a middle-aged Scot, Nectar Lord Strathbogie, who looks and sounds like Mann:

> His lordship was a man of obvious distinction, about fifty years of age, of moderate height, slender, elegantly dressed, his still thick, carefully brushed hair was iron grey, like the clipped moustache which did not conceal the almost feminine delicacy of his lips. There was nothing delicate or aristocratic about the cut of his too large, almost blocklike nose, which jutted straight out of his face to form a high rise, between the somewhat slanting brows beetling above the green-grey eyes. These eyes seemed to meet one as though with a great effort of self-discipline.

The merciless author co-opts the physical details cartoonists had relied on, all of them represented as comically—if not grotesquely—unattractive. Lord Strathbogie exhibits other traits of the author, observed with a very cold eye: "There was always a kind of embarrassment in his way of entering the dining-hall . . . completely compensated for by his extreme dignity, and it simply led one to imagine there was something remarkable about him and that he therefore felt himself singled out and observed." Mann doesn't spare himself. Lord Strathbogie has the soft Mannian voice, his tone "friendly but tinged with melancholy." He also exhibits the furtive glance with which Mann observed his young Hermeses, possibly including Franzl serving dinner in Zurich.

Lord Strathbogie invites Felix to move to Scotland with him. Felix rejects the offer. To the reader he explains his decision in an echo of Mann's reservations about sexual union: "A confident instinct within me rebelled against a form of reality that was simply handed to me and was in addition sloppy—rebelled in favor of free play and dreams, self-created and self-sufficient, dependent, that is, only on imagination." Autobiographical parallels are underlined: "When as a child I had waked up determined to be an eighteen-year-old prince named Karl . . . that had been the right thing for me. . . ." The clandestine prince, like the Good Tin Soldier—or Adrian Leverkühn—will not marry.

He speaks kindly to the older man. But his words echo both Diane and Thomas Mann himself: "Please—I don't want to wound you or minimize the honor you have paid me, but if someone precisely like me occurs only once—each of us, of course, occurs only once—there are nevertheless millions of young men of my age and general physique, and except for the tiny bit of uniqueness, one is made very much like another. I know a woman who declared that she was interested in the whole genre without exception—it must be essentially that way with you, too. The genre is present always and everywhere."

In 1950, Mann expressed amazement that a similar disclaimer by *Young Joseph*'s narrator mocked "the dearest thing to me." Now, the last Hermes addresses his words, not to Mann's amused readers, but to the author himself, or at least his fictional counterpart. Yet there is nothing meanspirited about Felix's rejection. Tact, discretion, all the rhetorical advantages of an ironic—Mannian—style, serve to lessen the pain. Dignifying Strathbogie may have allowed Mann to forgive himself for an act so uncouth, so Gidean as a proposition. Felix feels "sympathy," and after Lord Strathbogie gives him "a very handsome emerald," commends the man's behavior—as if Tadzio were complimenting Aschenbach for being such a gentleman!

Diane's verse had been "kissed by the lips of all of you": an echo of Goethe's remark that each poem was a kiss. Goethe added that kisses don't make babies; but in the self-referential design of Mann's confession, frustration becomes the progenitor of art.

And if this seems too abstract, Mann finally describes a physical union of artist and model. Diane's verbal seduction does the trick. Felix allows that "so much praise and adoration, finally even expressed in poetry, had greatly excited me." There are many erotic failures in Mann's work, but at least this time, "your breath inspires my verse," and my verse arouses your desire. Almost eighty, Mann granted himself the kindness of a one-night stand.

He had not died sexually. On September 5, he reported "a full erection and strange, hopeful feeling of love." A month later, he admitted that *Krull* was his confession: "Beginning to feel courageous about the memoirs— which is how I prefer to describe them, since their only charm lies in the way I use my life, as I did in *Faustus.*" But even now a vast contradiction lay between Diane's admission "Mes beaux romans, every one of them— never breathe this to the world—has been kissed by your lips," and his own privately expressed wish "The world should know me."

Mann was immensely satisfied with the Diane chapter. On December 31, 1951, the last day of a year plagued by political attacks in the American press and the apparent disloyalty of his closest American friends, he drew comfort from his work. "A marvelous piece," he wrote, adding in English, "Doesn't resemble at all any other novel of our time."

E motional need can reverberate throughout a career, determining tone and content, as well as the subtlest verbal detail. Young or old, Goethe returned to Faustus. Mann's abiding subject was Felix Krull, the adorable poseur of his mid-thirties, reincarnated as Joseph, "the heavenly confidence man" of his middle years, and as the *picaro* of his last novel. On March 11, 1951, he wrote a friend, "Excuse me if I fall into Krull's style. His is now once again my language (how many others' languages have I spoken!), and every morning I seek distraction in this merriment."

His daily returns to Hans or Joseph or Felix verged on a lover's trysts. The Eros would be apparent, he thought, to anyone who shared the "feel-ing." While it saturated his work, it was most evident in the stories, wherein Katia, for one, found him most artful. Or else in those episodes within the great books that, aspiring to the condition of novella, virtually undermined the grandiose structures: the ill-fated loves of Hans for Clavdia and Joachim; Jacob, Benjamin, and Mut, all for Joseph; Leverkühn for Rudi Schwerdtfeger; and finally, in an apotheosis of self-parody, Lord Strathbogie for Felix. Mann never forgot that *Tonio Kröger* and *Death in Venice* were his most popular works, along with *Buddenbrooks*, that anthology of wonderful tales.

Naturally he deplored it when readers skipped the talk for the story. And yet wasn't there often a silent compact between him and his readers, that if they only trudged through the abstruse passages with Teutonic application, they'd be rewarded with Gallic escapades? Occasionally he regretted that his last novel was a frivolous descent from the metaphysics of *Doctor Faustus*; but as an old man he lacked the strength for work of that scope, the requisite study and intense contemplation. Yet the comic novel retraced the same ground as the tragic, and drew equally on the Munich period of fifty years earlier, the time of Paul Ehrenberg. To paraphrase Nietzsche, this was his Eternal Recurrence: with fewer distractions, the same old story.

Had Paul Ehrenberg returned his love, Mann might never have spent seven years on the mountain, or fifteen years in Egypt. In a 1954 essay on Chekhov, he admitted that he may have wasted his days building these monuments. Reading Chekhov let him see that "genius can be bounded in a nutshell and yet embrace the whole fullness of life by virtue of a brevity and terseness deserving of the highest admiration."

He had recognized this at least twice before. Fifteen years earlier, he had Goethe announce that "the last and highest effect of art is charm. No scowling sublimity." The deeper, more revealing passages ought to be implicit: "For the people, gay pictures; for the cognoscenti, the mystery behind." Five years before that, momentarily stymied by the vast apparatus of *Joseph in Egypt*, he considered "something quite different—perhaps less than a novel, much lighter and dreamier."

He also recognized more passionate alternatives. In a tribute to Heinrich von Kleist, composed in May 1954, a month after he had completed the Strathbogie episode, he saluted "something pre-Olympian" in Kleist, "something ecstatic and enthusiastic, generating excesses of expression." Fifty years earlier, he had accused his brother of neglecting the "uncanny" overflow of passion; this time, siding with Kleist obliged him to temporarily condemn Goethe, who had found Kleist undisciplined. (It also may have summoned memories of Klaus Heuser to whom he had once directed his essay on Kleist's *Amphitryon*.)

The "nutshell" for Mann contained the love dramatized in *Young Joseph* and *Felix Krull*. The sadness attending that love was the price he paid for being "human," the singular access of this devoted husband and father to the "fullness of life" that he hoped to discover in art. Epic ambitions had been brilliant diversionary tactics. Old age returned him to Yeats's rag-and-bone shop of the heart. His lament for loves unexperienced was of a piece with his regret for a "brevity and terseness" sacrificed at the altar of representation.

Did Mann ever believe that the power of his work could win a young man's heart? García Lorca told a friend that he wrote so people would love him, a fantasy shared, no doubt, with Walt Whitman. Mann, unlike Proust, whose involuntary flights carry him deeper into the past, or unlike those poets who transform literature into a refined act of flirtation, followed Goethe's command: "There is no past that one is allowed to long for. There is only the eternally new, growing from the enlarged elements of the past; and genuine longing always must be productive, must create something new and better." It had to be that way. For, as he recognized at seventy-seven, his past contained "too many unpleasant memories and only intermittent satisfactions."

"It always is": the enduring story Mann told himself was not about marriage and family, nor did it express his prophetic understanding of modern politics—or his belief that life was "a cultural product, a series of mythic clichés." Its theme was simpler, embedded in the act of composition, the myth of love for a "genre present always and everywhere." The image of some new Hermes led him from the beaches of Travemünde, where Hans Hansen (or Armin Martens? or Armin Martens / Hans Hansen?) blithely withheld his affection, to Venice, where he first spied Tadzio, to Kampen and the summer of Klaus Heuser, back to the North Sea resort where Billy Budd became the divine summoner. He had even forecast that moment, letting Diane say, "This intoxication will never end. I shall die of it, but my spirit will woo you forever with its wiles."

Mann composed what others experienced and, more profoundly, the failure to experience—an overpowering dramatization of impotence and self-denial. "In your breath is my word" signified the mitigation of a lifetime's torments. The redemption of fruitless beauty was an endless flow of narrative. Right before their farewell Charlotte tells Goethe, "Your reality looks different; not like renunciation, or unfaithfulness but like a purer fulfillment and a higher faith. It is so imposing no one dares even inquire after the might-have-been." Vindication for the author; cold comfort for the man. That a lifetime of magnificent achievement, of a political courage that shames his peers, was motored by unmet erotic need may be the reason he wished the world "to know me and forgive me." From his earliest years he believed that some hungry children would never be well fed.

There would be a sequel once the world found out. After the 1950 diary was published Franz Westermeier became a famous man, at least in Europe. By then he was living in Forest Hills, New York, and working at the St. Regis Hotel. He and his Berlin-born wife were invited to appear on German television. She remembers that "the smallest paper in the smallest town" ran a story on her husband.

When he first courted Brigitte Kath, Franz tried to impress her with the celebrities he had served: Elizabeth Taylor, Frank Lloyd Wright, Thomas Mann. That name alone brought her short. Having loved Mann's "wonderful language" since childhood, she could not imagine an encounter between her Bavarian hotelier and the great author. After the news broke, Franz went through *Felix Krull* to see just what he had inspired, shades of Charlotte reading *Werther*. But, as Mann had foreseen, the Hans Hansens were not meant to read him. "I put it down six or seven times. It was so hard." However, suggesting that Mann had underestimated Life Itself, Franz enjoyed *Buddenbrooks*: "Now that was beautifully written."

While he was complimented by Mann's attention—though "shocked" to learn that Mann has masturbated to his image—his wife was moved. "When I read *Felix Krull*, I was so touched, because I also love Franz. I could really feel with him. In our lives, we don't change so much, and he always had to hide his feelings." This episode contained a Mannian fulfillment. Literature had rendered the chance of happiness impossible, even had Franz been so disposed. Instead, empathy had come from another lover. That she was a Berliner was all to the good. In 1909 he had said they alone knew how to read.

POSTSCRIPT

"I think it's important to always fall upstairs," Mann wrote Kahler in 1938. That's where he had found himself. Excepting Einstein and Marlene Dietrich, no other émigré succeeded as well in transporting his fame from Europe to America. He first visited New York in 1934. On his fifty-ninth birthday he had lunch with the editors of the *New York Times*, and in the evening was the recipient of a testimonial dinner at the Plaza Hotel, attended by three hundred guests, among them Mayor Fiorello La Guardia, Willa Cather, Sinclair Lewis, and Dorothy Thompson. His address was not significantly different from his fiftieth birthday speech in Munich. ("The man who addresses you, ladies and gentlemen, is one who depends on solitude and seclusion. . . . For that reason, however, he loves people and knows, too, or rather hopes, to ally himself to them by means of the quietest and most personal pursuit of his calling.") The low-keyed but delighted author blew out fifty-nine candles with one breath.

He returned to Europe, hoping to pursue a Goethean old age despite Hitler. This proved impossible, and over the next three years he found himself back in the United States three times: in 1935, when he received an honorary doctorate from Harvard, along with Einstein, and had a private meeting with President Roosevelt at the White House; in 1937 for a lecture tour; and then again in 1938 for a tour that coincided with the publication of *The Coming Victory of Democracy*. Following the Anschluss, which occurred during his tour in March 1938, Thomas and Katia Mann "truly believed we would never see Europe again." First they felt stranded. Then, on May 5, they immigrated officially. On May 27 he accepted a job at Princeton

University, beginning a new academic career at sixty-three. He enjoyed the fresh-faced male students, as well as the elegant home provided by a wealthy patron, Caroline Newton, but he never took to the milieu. "Forever being with the same professors . . . began to feel constricted to me," he wrote Kahler.

The Manns continued to visit Europe during the summer. In September 1939, they were flying from Sweden via Holland to England, shortly after Germany had invaded Poland. Having heard that Luftwaffe pilots had been flying close enough to examine the passengers, Katia demanded that Thomas exchange window seats with her. A few days later, the brother-in-law of the publisher Benjamin Huebsch was shot through the same window. Erika was convinced "that they got the wrong man and were really gunning for T.M."

The Nazis knew their enemy: the Manns had become the First Family of Antifascism. In 1939 Elisabeth had married Giuseppe Antonio Borgese (1882–1952), a historian and literary scholar, only slightly younger than her father though far more ebullient: an articulate Hauptmann. Borgese was quite as militant as Mann, who dubbed him "the antipapist." Elisabeth remembers the two arguing over who hated the fascists more. Mann noticed that the couple only spoke English with each other, boycotting their native languages as a gesture of political opposition. (According to Golo, at the Thomas Manns one only spoke German.)

Erika and Klaus were living in New York. Janet Flanner wrote that newly arrived émigrés needed to be vetted by the illustrious siblings, and their antifascist credentials confirmed. After *The Pepper Mill* flopped in New York, Erika became a lecturer. Klaus quoted her agents, "She has a message! She has a personality!" He attempted to follow her, lecturing on such topics as "The Two Germanies" and "My Father and His Work." Thomas Mann's sold-out lectures were vastly more successful. (According to Golo, "the influence of America made my father more at ease in his public appearance and in his general behavior.") In 1939, *Life* reported that *The Coming Victory of Democracy* had sold more copies in bookstores than had *Joseph in Egypt*. Finally reaping the rewards of his move into politics, he was doubly honored as novelist and prophet. Erika became his interpreter. She also wrote publicity for him, including the highly dubious suggestion that he had become a fan of the Princeton football team. Whether Klaus enjoyed appearing in his father's behalf is another question.

Compared with most émigré intellectuals, Mann was sitting high. *Life* reported that his royalties for 1938 were $20,000. For the moment he was in a strong position, able to make provocative statements and get paid for them. Not only was he agitating for a war against Germany—Agnes Meyer,

The Manns at Princeton, 1939. LEFT TO RIGHT: *Christopher Isherwood;*
his friend W. H. Auden, Erika's husband; Erika, Mann, Katia, and Elisabeth,
still the images of each other; and Klaus

as mentioned before, even called him a warmonger—but he was finally able
to confront the phenomenon of Hitler directly in an article daringly entitled
"This Man Is My Brother," which appeared in the March 1938 issue of
Esquire. In no way did Mann defend Hitler; he called him an unmitigated
"catastrophe," but also felt obligated to call him a "brother," a fellow artist
inasmuch as he displayed the artist's vanity, self-doubt, and permanent
dissatisfaction. Many readers missed the irony, or the implicit manifesto
that ended the piece: in the future, art would transcend "brainlessly irresponsible instinct." Once Mann's kind of socialist humanism prevailed, resemblances with Hitler would no longer apply.

(In the article Mann anticipated the debate that arose sixty years later
among biographers like Sir Hugh Trevor-Roper and Alan Bullock over
Hitler's state of mind. The former considered him a sincere monster. The
second initially saw him as a charlatan, but came to believe that he mes-
merized himself along with his public. Mann offered a subtler interpretation. Hitler, he said, was a "successful hysteric," fueled by an "insatiable
craving for compensation" and obsessed with acutely remembered insults.

A never-ending sense of personal injury, projected on the nation, kept him in a state of permanent arousal: a "sleepless compulsion" drove him "to take the world's breath away." Such a man could not be appeased.)

While Mann was attacking German politicians, he felt obliged to defend German culture. In November 1938, when New York's Hunter College threatened to cut off funding for its German department, he opposed the decision: it was imperative that German "values be kept alive in America." Three years later he entertained Berkeley students with the conceit that Nietzsche, were he still alive, would be another exile in California.

He became a tireless advocate of émigré writers stranded in Europe (though he privately questioned their foresight), among them Heinrich and Golo, who had succeeded him as editor of *Mass und Wert*. (These two made a celebrated escape together over the Pyrenees in 1940, along with Franz Werfel and his wife Alma Mahler Werfel.) Once this last group of émigrés was settled in California, several of them received temporary sinecures in the movie studios. None did well. Viewing Heinrich's disastrous luck, Thomas quipped that the devil's mercies were more reliable than the whims of Hollywood. Another instance reminded him of the difficulties faced by old men in a new world. Ludwig Hardt, the monologuist, from whose lips he had first heard Kafka's words, had also fled the Nazis. His métier was almost laughably un-American, but he had hopes. One night he invited Mann and the novelist Scholem Asch, among others, to a public audition for American agents. Hardt delivered his routines in a virtually incomprehensible English. "It was," Mann later wrote, "the saddest evening I have ever experienced."

When Hitler finally declared war on America, Mann and his six children were all safe. Monika had been the last to escape. She and her husband Jenö Lanyí were aboard a British evacuation ship, *City of Benares*, that was sunk by a German U-boat. Lanyí drowned while Monika clung to the boat for twenty hours and survived. (Katia's father died in Switzerland in 1941; his wife a year later.) By the end of 1940 Mann had two American grandchildren, Michael's son Fridolin ("Frido"), born in Carmel, California, on July 31; and Elisabeth's daughter, Angelica, born in Chicago on November 30. (Michael's second son, Anthony, was born on July 20, 1942; Elisabeth's second daughter, Dominica, was born on March 6, 1944.)

Mann later defined the war years as both grueling and "morally good," and like most émigrés he adored the Roosevelts to the point of idolatry, even re-creating Joseph in FDR's image. And yet, up to 1941 he suspected everyone of being insufficiently antifascist: the duplicitous imperialists in England; the "childish," ahistorical Americans; and the Soviet Union after what he and Klaus considered its treasonous 1939 nonaggression pact with

Pacific Palisades, 1944. LEFT TO RIGHT: *Frido, "my last love," age four;*
Katia; Toni, age three; and a very satisfied grandfather, Thomas Mann

Hitler. By 1942, sounding like a Trotskyist, he felt that the Allies were
more concerned with protecting their empires than with fighting Hitler.

That year, when his political essays were collected in *Order of the Day*,
the flyleaf contained a message from "Dr. Mann," whose "reputation as one
of the truly great minds of our time rests not only on his novels and stories,
but also on what he has written concerning the crucial political issues in a
world at war with fascism." In this message he asked his readers to buy
War Savings Bonds. Having seen how profligate spending led to the
German inflation, he trusted that Americans would curtail their domestic
purchases and invest in the state. Unlike Germans threatened by the Gestapo and the concentration camp, he said, "democratic and disciplined
citizens" would make voluntary sacrifices on their own. After all, defeating
the Nazis was "more important than dollars and cars." The refugee Mann
was preaching democracy to the natives. But he frequently suspected that
Americans valued their system less than he did. What did they prefer? (In
1943, he got word of Paul Claudel's collaboration with the German occu-

pying forces in Paris, and, in a letter to Agnes Meyer, he lamented that "Catholic fascism" would rule the postwar world, a combination of religious fundamentalism and conservative economics.)

É migrés like Brecht and Paul Tillich, joined by the American theologian Reinhold Niebuhr, despised Mann for continuing to hold the German people responsible along with their leaders. While, as he wrote Brecht, he had, in an address to the Library of Congress, quite nervily declared anti-Communism a folly, he refused to countenance Brecht's Stalinism. (Assistant Secretary of State Adolph Berle advised him not to participate in the Free Germany movement, lest he jeopardize his chances for citizenship.)

Nineteen forty-four brought him the greatest financial success in years. *Joseph the Provider* was selected by the Book-of-the-Month Club. He was now doing conspicuously better than most émigrés, though not nearly as well as Lion Feuchtwanger, who lived in palatial splendor, but whose neo-Stalinism Mann's enemies found sympathetic.

June 6, 1944, his birthday, fell on D day, when the Allies landed in Normandy. For anyone with a tendency to grandiose analogies, it was the birthday gift of a lifetime. (A few years later when asked for a list of his favorite recordings, he included Roosevelt's D-day message, the only non-musical selection.) Seventeen days later he became an American citizen. When the judge asked his witness, Max Horkheimer, whether Mann would make a good American, Horkheimer replied, "You bet!"

Yet even as he rejoiced over the Nazis' imminent defeat, and refused to sign the manifesto to the Council for a Democratic Germany, he was attacked as being too soft on his former homeland. Following the appearance in the *Atlantic Monthly* of his essay, "What Is German?," in which he argued that the good and bad Germany were inseparable, particularly in himself, Henri Peyre of Yale wrote in the *Atlantic* that Mann was reverting to *Betrachtungen* days. An extremely subtle and scrupulously honest discrimination—Heinrich felt it was enough to justify a lifetime of letters—was read as special pleading. Mann was obliged to answer Peyre in the same magazine, even though he noticed with his sensitivity to shifts in the critical wind that some Americans had tired of his paeans to democracy. About the time of Peyre's article, Agnes Meyer wrote that she had fallen in love with the *Betrachtungen*. He replied that the book was still "secretly dear to me" and "surprisingly witty out of sheer agony." Indeed, "American intellectuals may be 'ripe' for it; they are tired of my democratic Sunday sermons." He saw that left-wing intellectuals were on the verge of moving right. (The occasion was a negative review of *Joseph the Provider* by William

Mann at Princeton, 1938, one of his most relaxed photos

Phillips, a dean of neoconservatism.) Give the future conservatives some of my Great War complaints and "I would make more of a literary splash."

The rate of suicides among émigrés grew epidemic. Mann had observed the phenomenon for years, intimately in the cases of his sisters or of Klaus's friend and schoolboy lover Ricki Hallgarten. In 1939, Ernst Toller, the Student Prince of the Munich Revolution, committed suicide in New York's Hotel Mayflower. Shortly afterward the great Austrian writer Joseph Roth drank himself to death. (A Trotskyist, Jewish-Catholic, Hapsburg-monarch-lover, Roth was more protean than Naphta.) Mann recorded that émigrés considered Roth's death a response to Toller's. In 1942, Stefan Zweig and his second wife, miserably exiled in Brazil, committed suicide.

The only émigré writer whose popularity matched Mann's or Feuchtwanger's, Zweig had persuaded him that Erasmus was as much his alter ego as Goethe. He wrote Zweig's first wife, Friederike, "could he concede the enemy such a triumph?"

Two years later there was a family suicide: Heinrich's wife, Nelly Kröger (1898–1944). She was almost thirty years his junior; a pretty, animated ex-barmaid, originally from Lübeck, she had met him in Berlin, where she succeeded Trude Hesterberg as his companion. He had found the real thing; not "Lola," but Lola in the flesh. Nelly left Germany a few months after he did and joined him in France where they married in 1939. During their years in Hollywood she was famous for making trouble: opening the front door in the nude; complaining her man was an old bore. In 1944, after several unsuccessful attempts, she took a fatal overdose. Though Heinrich was devastated, Thomas and Katia were relieved. Unlike the more celebrated suicides, there was nothing allegorical about poor Nelly's death. It was simply another instance of the Manns' bad luck in love.

Roosevelt's death on April 12, 1945, did leave Mann in despair. He felt "orphaned and abandoned," he wrote Kahler on May 1. Already he discerned a flight to the right, with the Nazis not yet defeated: "This is no longer the country to which we came."

In the war's aftermath, he learned how many old friends had either been complicit with the Nazis or had lived among them in equanimity. His younger brother had probably been in the party; two of his nieces had lost their husbands fighting for Hitler. Bertram's affinities had long been acknowledged, and as he confided to Kahler, Hans Reisiger was not spotless; though never a Nazi, he was guilty of sloth and disloyalty for remaining in Germany after Mann had found a teaching job for him in Berkeley. (The two men would reunite; Reisiger forgiving Mann for depicting him in *Doctor Faustus*, Mann forgiving Reisiger for not leaving Germany. After they reconciled, Mann wrote sadly about what might have been: "We could have laughed together and worried together. We could have borne fate together. Instead you used your best years in fear and silence in that rotten atmosphere.") Kurt Martens had moved from Munich to Dresden, where, following the Allied bombing in 1945 of the city, he took his life. The news that Carl and Paul Ehrenberg had been Nazis was a bitter disappointment.

Both Klaus and Erika revisited Munich, discovering how intimately their fortunes were bound up with their enemies'. In May 1946, Klaus wrote that their Poschingerstrasse house had been converted to a home for unwed mothers birthing future warriors for Hitler, while Göring had commandeered the Nidden summer house.

Erika became the only woman reporter to cover the Nuremberg trials. She also happened to wander into a prison cell containing Julius Streicher, former editor of the grotesquely anti-Semitic *Der Stürmer*. Typically she wore a men's shirt, tie, and slacks. Her appearance was a kind of feminist triumph over the Nazi publicist who had once mocked her lesbian attire. "Ah, you've come to see the animals in the zoo," he said, and dropped his pants. Unimpressed, she walked out. Klaus, as a correspondent for *Stars and Stripes*, interviewed the English-born Winifred Wagner, and found her an unregenerate admirer of Hitler. She remembered him, years later, as a refugee who insisted on speaking English with an atrocious German accent. Gustav Gründgens, the Nazis' favorite actor, outlived his sponsors. After a brief sabbatical, he returned to the German stage. His first postwar appearance was a huge success, unapplauded by only one member of the audience, Klaus Mann.

In 1945, Thomas Mann was operated on for cancer, and seven ribs were removed. While he was unconscious, he apparently said, "I suffered so much," though he had no memory of what pain—physical or emotional— prompted the remark. In the Bible, Hezekiah receives sixteen years of grace; Mann got ten. Though his diaries are filled with reports of physical complaints, he never quit working. Indeed he boasted to Kerényi that a thirty-year-old couldn't have recovered as fast. "Well, of course, if one were a squealing child one couldn't have achieved what is, after all, there, and will not be blown away so uneasily." Unlike Zweig, he wouldn't let the enemy grab him.

Also, perhaps, he saw the physical test as a requisite purgatory. On July 18, 1947, concerning his reworking of the past in *Doctor Faustus*: "Each 'murder' I have paid for with my lung operation, which was undoubtedly connected to the novel."

(After his seventy-first birthday, a smart-alecky reporter from *Time*, remembering that he had anticipated dying at the age of seventy, asked Mann how prophetic he was feeling these days. He replied that, in fact, he had been "gravely ill," which showed that prophecy could be "fulfilled in part.")

A weaker person might not have withstood the blows. Four months after Germany's surrender, he wrote an essay, "Why I Won't Return to Germany," explaining that his fellow writers, by remaining, had been guilty of the ultimate *trahison des clercs*. Immediately a literary cohort, dubbing themselves the Inner Emigration, began attacking him for jumping ship. He spent the better portion of the next year denying reports that during the early years he had sued for peace in order to return to Munich. These proved completely unfounded. Meanwhile he was horrified to see, at least in the American, British, and French zones, the resumption of power by Nazi dignitaries, civil servants, and industrialists who had been enriched by slave labor.

As the Cold War began, he became convinced that America would have preferred to fight on Germany's side against the Russians. While his diaries display great skepticism toward the Soviet Union, the fact that it had lost 21 million victims to the war against Hitler—the United States had lost nearly 300,000—made him less eager to criticize it. Also, since he had never been a Communist, he didn't experience the severe withdrawal symptoms of "The God That Failed" group (Arthur Koestler was one of Mann's critics). The main enemy was always fascism, and he had reached the conclusion that the West had picked up where Hitler left off. He ended 1945 despairing that fascism had not been beaten. "Instead it is enjoying a steady growth. In Europe, here, everywhere. The change of mood is pro-German and hence anti-exile. . . . What a good period the war was. Deceptively good."

Mann's extreme pessimism has been adduced as evidence that he didn't understand America, the swings and cycles from right to left that have long characterized the country's politics. He would reply that each postwar cycle left the country further to the right, and that the left-liberalism he supported—as well as the American version of *Thomasmänner*—was never as strong again.

He knew America more than well enough, particularly its popular culture. His diaries contain references to Miss America contests, the gossip columnist Walter Winchell, mass-circulation magazines and best-sellers. He even knew about Superman from Frido's unfortunate preference for comics. He often found American high culture naïve; that William Saroyan would title a novella *The Human Comedy* was prototypical. Yet he enjoyed many movies, was thrilled by the more explicit treatment of homosexuality in the work of young American novelists, and positively reveled in Jack Benny's humor. In 1949, one of his saddest years, the diary contains twenty-nine references to Benny's Sunday broadcast. The comedian's persona of a sexually repressed martinet who neither displays nor evokes warmth and affection would seem closely attuned to Mann's sense of himself.

His knowledge informed his vigilance. Together with Einstein and Linus Pauling, he became the leading critic of the red-baiting phenomenon known as McCarthyism. The 1947 HUAC hearings began with the film industry, and the first witnesses called on October 4 were the sister and brother of his friend Hanns Eisler. The day before, Mann described the American regime as "fascistic," and a day later he imagined an investigation of the investigators: "What oath would Congressman Rankin or Thomas take if forced to swear that they hated fascism as much as Communism?" Later that day he decided to write a Zola-like "J'accuse" defending Eisler against the threat of deportation—a stunning instance of his progress since 1918, when Heinrich's "Zola" had inspired a book-length rebuttal. However, Adorno advised him not to get involved. As the dominant intellectual of the Frankfurt School, Adorno is usually identified with sustained critical resistance. But it was Mann who took up the challenge. On October 30, he prepared a statement for the group Hollywood Fights Back. He was an old movie fan and not unsubtle, he wrote, but if there was any red propaganda in Hollywood films, it had escaped him. Such jokes didn't help any more than they had twenty years earlier in Munich.

As the red-baiting grew more strident, he sensed that history was repeating itself. The same targets (left-wing radicals) and the same establishment (right-wing clergy, "bankers and generals," industrialists like IG Farben and their international brigade of legal advisers, including the future Secretary of State John Foster Dulles.) On September 18, 1948, as if predicting the Republican congress of 1995, he forecast that the New Deal would soon be regarded as an "un-American activity." On October 31, 1948, Mann's statement defending the Hollywood Ten was read at the First Unitarian Church of Los Angeles: "As an American citizen of German birth and one who has been through it all [how durable that formula had proved!], I deem it not only my right but my solemn duty to state: We —the America of the Un-American Activities Committee; the America of the so-called loyalty checks . . . are well on our way towards the fascist police state and—hence—well on our way towards war."

Other émigrés were more circumspect, though no less alarmed. Heinrich, who was now saying that Thomas had grown more radical than he, was too exhausted; and who would have paid him attention? Another writer on politics, Hannah Arendt, was unusually quiet during the McCarthy years. She wrote essays carefully distinguishing between "former Communists" like, though she didn't mention him, her husband Heinrich Blücher, and ex-Communists like Whittaker Chambers, who had made careers out of unmasking their former comrades. Not unintelligent, Mann might have said, but irrelevant to the "order of the day." In 1950, he was upset that Arendt's *The Origins of Totalitarianism* cited only his right-wing propaganda for World War I, a highly selective reading of his career. Arendt avoided placing blame on traditional German culture, precisely the target of Mann's most devastating attack. She also managed to overlook the Nazi past of Martin Heidegger, her former professor and lover, though she could argue that Brecht had paid for his Stalinism with the loss of his talent. By comparison, Mann did not absolve his dearest friend, Ernst Bertram. (In 1948, when asked his opinion of Bertram, he said, "I am against Bertram's being recalled to an academic teaching position. . . . But I am decidedly for his being granted a decent retirement salary and the right to determine his own rules for his creative work.")*

In Germany, ex-Nazi journalists targeted Mann through Klaus and Erika. Everywhere he detected a "gutter press" controlled by financial interests. By the late 1940s, his critical reputation in America had fallen dramatically. In the *New York Times*, Harry Levin blasted *Doctor Faustus*, as did the daily reviewer, Orville Prescott. (When Prescott reviewed Mann's *Collected Essays* he stated that Mann had joined the anti-Nazi fight very late—a falsehood that remains in circulation. In a letter to the paper Mann demanded a retraction, recalling his vocal opposition since 1922.) Leslie Fiedler wrote an "impudent" review of the essays, saying that Mann was writing only about himself. In fact, he wrote about himself and others; the tributes to Platen or, for that matter, Goethe and Wagner were of the highest quality. Another academic, Jacques Barzun, detected "elaborate flabbiness of mind, akin to indolent caprice" in Mann's free play with his categories. Mann took none of this lightly (Barzun was "vile and ignorant"), and saw it as an offshoot of the critics' right-wing politics. Especially when left-wingers like Matthiessen or Kahler found the same essays exhilarating.

In the midst of all this, he learned of the death of his old enemy Alfred Kerr, who had spent his last years in England. To his surprise, Kerr had reviewed *Doctor Faustus* "very positively." Once that critical about-face would have been of the utmost importance; now it was merely an echo of the old battles.

If sniping from the right troubled his days, he got worse treatment from the left. Alfred Döblin, after a series of failures in California, returned to the French-occupied zone of Germany and began to edit one of the first postwar journals of German literature. He told contributors that he wanted no references to Mann except negative ones, even printing an essay, "Döblin oder Thomas Mann," that gave him the advantage. Mann found this spectacle "echt Deutsch," harkening back to the "H. oder T.M." sibling rivalry set up by contending political groups.

Another left-wing émigré had a more devilish amusement. Brecht was interviewed by HUAC, and through a masterly performance—he claimed that his agitprop had been mistranslated—he escaped their clutches. Safely back in Switzerland, he wrote a couple of poems under Mann's name and privately circulated them.

---

* In the 1950s, Bertram and Mann met again for a couple of occasions that Katia found dull.

ON SEDUCING ANGELS

Angels aren't for ravishing—unless it's quick.
Just drag him straight into the entrance hall
Shove your tongue right down his throat and stick
Your finger up him, turn him to the wall
   And when he's good and moist, lift up his gown
   And fuck him. Should he groan as if in pain
   Hold him hard, bring him on; once, and again—
   That way he'll lack the strength to strike you down.

Remind him that he has to move his butt
And tell him he can go ahead and touch
Your balls, that he must just let go and come
While earth and sky are slipping from his clutch—
But while you're fucking don't look on his face
And see his wings unruffled stay in place.

                    —"Thomas Mann"

Besides vulgarizing his image as a chicken hawk—derived perhaps from
Death in Venice—this failed to reflect the sober, long-winded Mann whom
Brecht knew and hated. A quick assignation would have been out of character for someone moved to languid flirtation. Brecht's other "Mann" poem
is a better satire of the "author" 's bourgeois obsession with cleanliness.
(Brecht's own inattention to questions of hygiene was legendary.) It begins,
"First you fuck, then you bathe," goes on to depict a healthy thrashing
with balsamic branches, and ends with the subject having carefully washed
"the fuck out of your bones." Dodging scurrilous attacks from the right-
wing press and obscene poems from the left, Mann was slandered by both
sides.

During 1948, Jewish magazines like *Commentary* began to publish criticism of his satirical portraits of Jews in *Doctor Faustus*; and, to be sure,
between the fascistic Breisacher and the flamboyant agent Fitelberg (who
seeks to "represent" the German Leverkühn to "the world"), he made a
skimpy survey of Jewish types. Even so, he devoted much time that year
to pleading Israel's case. When, in March, the United States withdrew its
approval of the establishment of a Jewish state in Palestine, he acted as if
it were the 1938 abandonment of Czechoslovakia: "Why are we cursed to
support everywhere the evil, the filthy reaction that is hated by the
people—in this case the feudalism of the Arabian oil magnates—and to
destroy democracy when we pretend to defend it?" A week later his old

acquaintance Judah Magnes argued that a Jewish state would exacerbate tensions with its Arab neighbors. Mann replied that the big powers— namely the United States—could end the fighting with a "firm word" to the British and Arab princes: "The Arab League . . . is a creature of the British." He added, "Please keep in mind, dear Dr. Magnes, that we liberals are living here under circumstances where we are being decried as Communists and that we are fighting a difficult struggle against tendencies which we fear might morally and physically ruin this intrinsically decent country." After so many years of mixed sympathy, he had now identified his interests with Jewry.

It had long struck him that Germans should be scattered throughout Europe, like the ancient Greeks—or Jews. Yet with an astonishing sense of fairness, in October 1948 he used the royalties from his German publications to establish a foundation for preserving the Lübeck altar by Memling and for the rebuilding of St. Mary's Church. He also tried to help those few "nonaligned" German intellectuals, "neither fascist nor Communist," who remained in deplorable conditions. That same month he wrote to Walter Lippman, hoping the journalist would intervene in their behalf, recognizing that a word from Mann would be taken amiss from those even less forgiving than he.

Nineteen forty-nine was perhaps the worst year. In April he was one of the endorsers of a World Peace dinner held at New York's Waldorf-Astoria Hotel, the last big gathering of the Popular Front. When former attorney general Francis Biddle wrote to condemn his association with Communists, Mann replied on April 14, "I am neither a dupe nor a fellow traveler and by no means an admirer of the quite malicious present phase of the Russian revolution." All the same, he realized that a withdrawal from the Cold War would precipitate an economic crisis, leaving as the only possible solution "actual warfare." He gathered that the speakers had distributed blame equally between both sides; and "what is wrong with treating the guests from that great, uncanny country" in a friendly manner?

A week later, his youngest brother died. They had established a friendly correspondence; in a plaintive letter of January 1948, Victor had wondered why *Faustus* treated their family so badly, abandoning them after Clarissa / Carla's suicide. He proceeded to write a sweetly anecdotal—and unreliable—memoir, *Wir waren Fünf*, which Mann joked had succeeded in making their family seem *gemütlich*.

On May 10, Mann, Katia, and Erika flew to London. He had agreed to give a lecture, "Goethe and Democracy," honoring the poet's two hundredth birthday, in several cities beginning with Oxford. It promised to be a triumphant addendum to his 1932 speeches honoring the hundredth anniversary of Goethe's death. To make it more inclusive, he decided to give his speech in both West and East, Allied and Soviet, zones of Germany, having little respect for either occupying force. (On November 10, 1948, after reading German-language magazines produced by both sides—*Soviet Literature* and *Der Monat*, the latter edited by Melvin Laski—he pronounced their quality "equally awful" and one-sided.)

On May 21, he received the news that Klaus had finally succeeded in killing himself. Shocked and grieving perhaps more for Katia and Erika than for his son, he decided, with their encouragement, to complete his schedule. This seems heartless, and, perhaps, can be explained by the facts that Klaus's drug addiction and continual cries for help had exhausted his family, or that his highly "theatrical" gesture (the adjective he used to describe Carla's suicide) demanded an equally public act of defiance. Whatever his motivation, three days later Mann delivered "Goethe and Democracy" in Stockholm.

From July 23 to August 8, he toured through Germany. On July 24 in Frankfurt, he declared, "I recognize no zones. My visit is to Germany itself, Germany as a whole, and to no occupied zone." There was a fierce outcry about his decision to speak in Soviet-occupied Weimar. While there, he agreed not to visit Buchenwald, which now held many Soviet political prisoners, some of them leftists. He did criticize the Soviet forces, saying that czarist repression had returned, uniting autocracy and revolution, which they found unforgivable. Introducing himself in Weimar, he declared that he was both Faust and Mephistopheles, his very words when he was twenty.

As he wrote Kahler after his return, both sides left him unmoved. Quoting Fontane, "I can't take anything seriously. That's over forever." Shades of *Royal Highness*: "It is really curious to see to what regal situations such a life of play and dreams finally leads when you keep up long enough. In Germany, it is true, the 'royal' aspect consisted chiefly of a Soviet police escort." Yet he appreciated the fact that he heard no "screeching" criticism in Weimar, no attacks on his children, no denunciations of his disloyalty to the homeland. The Eastern Zone was governed by intellectuals, some of them like Johannes Becher, old friends of Heinrich's, or Walter Benjamin's sister, Hilde Benjamin, while the West's bankers and generals were more concerned with industrial recovery. A paradox of Communism was its cultural conservatism and respect for tradition. As has been frequently observed since 1989, "dead white European males" and their descendants still lived in the East. Mann had more in common with these intellectuals than with the fast-talking, Americanized anti-Communists. Naturally he reserved such remarks for Kahler.

A month earlier, however, he had replied to an Open Letter from Paul

Olberg, a German Social Democrat living in Sweden, who had questioned his tour of the East. In his own letter he repeated his attack on the autocratic revolutionaries in Russia but added that the political liberties of the West had been put to "outrageous use." At least, in "the authoritarian people's state . . . stupidity and baseness must hold their peace." Was this due to "the threat of Buchenwald" or to "a kind of popular education which, more thoroughly than in the West, instills respect for a stand such as I have taken"? The East was so respectful of literary talent that it issued stamps with Hauptmann's portrait, forgiving his acquiescence to the Nazis out of gratitude for his earlier dramas of working-class life. The Communist functionaries included some "despots" but also many who exhibited an "ascetic seriousness" and "austere calm" (again the language of *Royal Highness*). As for Buchenwald, "concentration camps" were "a terrible educational method. . . . But attempts to bring about Socialism without violence, such as [Edvard] Beneš [the Czech leader overthrown in 1948 by Communists in league with Slovak ex-Nazis] made, have also failed." Dismissing the scholar-politicians out of hand would be "self-interest" covered with "cant." This was a risky letter in 1949. Olberg had it published and Mann was greeted with denunciations upon his return to California.

While in Munich he had met with Walter Opitz and Carl Ehrenberg, but Paul had not shown up—perhaps, Mann surmised, because he still owed him money from 1933. On November 22, 1949, he learned that Paul had died a month earlier from an embolism following a stomach operation; the announcement was signed by Carl and by Paul's son, Wolfgang, of whose existence he had not known. After his political adventures, and the deaths of Victor and Klaus, this was a very private grief, but he found himself "stirred" by old memories.

He ended the year trying to pacify Schönberg, who had been profoundly insulted by *Doctor Faustus*'s use (or misuse) of his work. Schönberg felt Mann had virtually plagiarized his *Harmonielehre*. On December 19, Mann replied that he had confused a loan with a gift, "perhaps because in a higher sense it had really become a possession to me." He had made a similar defense in 1925 when Hauptmann objected to his fictional representation as Peeperkorn. Mann begged Schönberg's pardon: "However you insist on being my enemy, you will not manage to make me yours." Subsequent editions of the novel acknowledged his theoretical debt to Schönberg: "I have transferred this technique in a certain ideational context to the fictious figure of a musician, the tragic hero of my novel." Words like "I," "my" and "tragic hero" nicely co-opted Schönberg's complaint. Even so, it was more nuisance than two men in their mid-seventies needed.

On March 14, 1950, Heinrich died. He had been about to return to East Germany, which regarded him as a prime literary catch, evidence of how much the authorities respected culture—and of how much they dwelled in the past. As Mann wrote to Maximilian Brantl, their old friend, Heinrich had "wanted to [go] and did not want to." It was Thomas's fourth loss in a year.

Two weeks later he wrote a memorial tribute to Klaus, calling him perhaps the most gifted member of his generation, but someone squeezed to death, like his last hero, between Wall Street and the Kremlin. As if to confirm his words, a month later the Library of Congress canceled his scheduled address, "The Years of My Life," on the ground that he had become persona non grata. (In January the Beverly Wilshire Hotel had temporarily canceled a lecture by "the Communist Dr. Mann.") He gave the lecture in New York instead, at the YMHA auditorium, sponsored by the German Jewish periodical *Aufbau*. Increasingly that weekly became his sole outlet in a country whose president had once considered naming him the head of postwar Germany. That summer he went to Switzerland, and it was in Zurich that he encountered Franz Westermeier. When he wrote, "Here is something for the heart," he may not have understood that this late burst of sexual desire would be the closest thing to happiness he would know for the next two years.

In January 1950, he had written Adorno that he still loved America— "although the political atmosphere is becoming *more and more unbreathable*," the language of 1933; he also complained that he would have to pay $16,000 in taxes for the Cold War. But after his return from Switzerland, his mood changed to unrelieved pessimism. In January 1951, he was one of several co-signers, along with Paul Robeson, Linus Pauling, and W. E. B. Du Bois, of a statement by the American Peace Crusade that called for a cease-fire in Korea, negotiations with the Soviet Union, and the admission of China to the United Nations. On February 1, 1951, the *New York Times* published an article, "Robeson, Mann Join New 'Peace Crusade.' " (In the February 12 issue of *Time*, printed earlier, Mann's participation was reported in an article titled "The Way of the Dupe," that gloated over Erika's "voluble explanation" that her father hadn't known of Communist participation in the conference: Mann, "in a time when every man must keep his wits about him, had not been paying strict attention." Did Whittaker Chambers write this?) The next day, Alfred A. Knopf wrote Mann that he was "enormously disturbed" by the article. He granted that Mann was "free, white, and twenty-one" but he ought to have avoided anything "which involves even the *name* of Paul Robeson as you would . . . the Bubonic Plague."

Though Mann wrote a letter to the *Times* defending his position, Knopf and Agnes Meyer used their connections to squelch its publication. Mann considered Knopf's intervention patronizing, and found Meyer typically hysterical. He wrote to Knopf: "She threatened me with the loss of my citizenship; accused me of being a traitor to my country; predicted that I would plunge both myself and all those near me into disaster and perdition; and wound up by offering to save my soul. You, at least, refrained from doing any such thing. Thanks." (This colloquial tone suggests Erika's co-operation in drafting the letter.)* Nevertheless, the same day, he informed the United Press that any further appearance of his name on any public statement, "unless I were the sole signer," should be adjudged a forgery. Regretfully he told Philip Morrison, a nuclear physicist and the conference's organizer, that the peace movement risked being co-opted by the Communists. Of course, as he wrote an American pacifist, Allan M. Butler, on March 18, "The concept of communism has come to be extremely flexible. . . . Liberalism, free-thinking and feeling—one doesn't get away with that sort of thing any longer."

For the first time, he compared the present era to "the inevitable 'Either/ Or' of the sixteenth century, the riotous time of the Reformation, Luther's time, when Erasmus wrote, 'For the rest, I see that it is my fate to be stoned by both sides while striving to serve the whole.' " On March 29, he repeated this comparison in an interview with a Los Angeles journalist. He added that he "would refuse to let 'this kind of pressure' force him to make a denunciation of something which he had never embraced." On April 4, the Un-American committee read the names of notables affiliated with various peace organizations or Communist fronts, including Mann, Einstein, Marlon Brando, Norman Mailer, Artur Schnabel, Frank Lloyd Wright, and Mark van Doren. " 'Listed' [in English]," Mann wrote in his diary that day. "Ridiculous."

He was terrified. On April 23, 1951, he wrote Kahler, "I myself am nothing but nerves, trembling at every thought and word. Only yesterday I let myself break down and weep listening to the *Lohengrin* prelude." The émigrés kept their spirits up with new installments of gallows humor. One popular joke, he quoted, had two friends spying each other on boats sailing to and from Europe, crying out simultaneously, "Are you crazy?" This time, however, the endlessly deliberating Mann didn't equivocate; the man sailing westward was "just a trace crazier."

---

* In 1953 he was pleased to note that the staunchly Republican Meyer had spoken out publicly against McCarthy.

(Not that he didn't remain aware of the horrors still being perpetrated in the East. Sometime in 1951, he wrote Walter Ulbricht, deputy prime minister of East Germany, seeking mercy for former Nazis and so-called spies jailed in that country's prisons. He had no sympathy for "these miserable human vermin," but, in truth, they shared their guilt with "more or less . . . the whole German people." This was the letter his critics had expected him to write in 1949. That he didn't publicize it now indicates his greater concern with the safety of Ulbricht's prisoners.

In a 1952 lecture for the BBC but not for American radio [though it might have done him some good at *Time*], he observed that "my writing is filled with Communist bugaboos—Formalism, Psychology, Skepticism." Most incorrect of all were "my humor and weakness for truth, a particular weakness in the eyes of unconditional partisans." After all, "I don't have much faith or faith in faith," parodying a cliché of the period.)

On April 24, 1951, he sent a sixtieth birthday greeting to Johannes R. Becher. The East German published the letter, which prompted a round of attacks by Eugene Tillinger, an émigré ex-Communist who had gone after Mann since 1949. On June 18, an essay by Tillinger appeared in *The New Leader*: "Thomas Mann and the Commissar." That same day, Mann's local representative, Congressman Donald L. Jackson, placed Tillinger's article in the *Congressional Record*, and advised Mann that ingrates are seldom invited back to dine. On June 22, the *Pacific Palisades Post* reported Mann's troubles in an article beginning "Pacific Palisades novelist Thomas Mann was attacked for his alleged sympathies with Red Communism this week." (For the second Goethe to be known simply as "Pacific Palisades novelist" might once have given the Manns a good laugh.) The comments by writers like Alfred Kazin that Mann exaggerated his difficulties can be dismissed. His local representative *and* neighborhood paper had branded him a Red. His anguish was appropriate.

Though he had once seen Eisenhower as a liberal alternative to Truman, the general's presidential campaign of 1952 horrified Mann, largely because of Ike's running mate. As a Californian, and a supporter of Helen Gahagan Douglas, he had disliked Nixon since the late 1940s. He described the Checkers speech as a "television comedy," and called its author the "Hiss murderer." (He was so preoccupied with the Hiss case that he named his poodle Alger. Later he would publicly denounce the execution of the Rosenbergs.)

On February 22, 1952, in a memorial essay on the tenth anniversary of Stefan Zweig's suicide, he wrote that the option no longer appeared indefensible. In June he and Katia returned to Switzerland. In December they rented a house in Erlenbach, near Zurich. "We are again taking up the form of life from 1933–1938, which during the fifteen American years I have actually always wished for." In his application for resettlement, he gave as his purpose, " 'to spend the evening of my life and to write.' That is nice, isn't it?"

Later that month, he felt obliged to hold a press conference in which he proclaimed his continued loyalty "to the great cultural heritage of the west. Can anyone who has really read one of my books deny that terror, force, lies, and injustice are to me a horror?" He scolded the reporters. "Does one speak . . . to grown, democratically educated men, or is one dealing with over-excited boys?"—the heirs of those rambunctious students who had stamped their disapproval in 1922 Berlin and 1931 Lübeck. He ended by comparing himself to Erasmus. "In our bloody world, broken into two, no end is to be seen of misunderstanding, prying, suspicions, and denunciation, and I shall thus not rest until the end of my days." Out of all his public representations, this was the most bitter, the least conciliatory, no longer advertising a need for the world's affection but a plea that it leave him alone.

During the last two and a half years of his life, he still made occasional statements hoping for German unification, and warning against German rearmament. Up to the last week of his life, he supervised the circulation of a peace motion; he had received promises of support from E. M. Forster and Bertrand Russell. His Cassandra days never ended. In retrospect, his prophecies had been accurate enough to justify his fame on that count alone. He foresaw the conflicting uses of popular culture; the emergence of a religious right specializing in attacks on secular humanism; the question of a Europeanized Germany versus a Germanized Europe; the relation between homosexual emancipation and politics, whether the virile patriotism of Hans Blüher or the democratic eros of Walt Whitman.*

Well into his old age, Mann remained alert to cultural change. In his commentary he resembled Adorno without the overdependence on theoret-

---

* Prophecy seemed to be a family talent. Between 1940 and 1942, Klaus edited *Decision: A Review of Free Culture*; the echo of *Mass und Wert: A Bimonthly of Free German Culture* was deliberate. Besides offering a forum to émigré talents from Brecht to Werfel, Klaus published several essays that still resonate. Golo used a review of New School economics as a pivot for an attack on Marxism, and dismissed the terms "capitalist," "socialist," and "revolutionary" as being obsolete, while paying homage to the "permanent revolution" of America. This predicted his later turn to the right (in Germany, during the 1970s, he supported Franz Josef Strauss, the epitome of Bavarian conservatism) as well as the postwar politics of many conservative émigrés. In the final issue of *Decision*, a Trinidadian analyzed the potential for black fascism and pointed out that the separatist Marcus Garvey had negotiated with the Ku Klux Klan. To the extent that Thomas Mann read such articles, he remained apprised of the complexities of American politics.

ical abstractions, or Walter Benjamin without the vague religiosity and unstable Marxist categories. (Of course, some readers think Benjamin's metaphysics convey profundity, and Adorno's conceptualizing a kind of discursive high adventure.) But Mann never fixated on cultural history, perhaps because he was so active a participant. No matter what movie he saw the night before, no matter what attack awaited in the morning newspaper, he kept writing.

During the early 1950s, he worked on *The Holy Sinner*, *The Black Swan*, *Felix Krull*, numerous reviews and essays, and, increasingly, tributes to dead friends. On March 20, 1952, he wrote Kerényi: "I would not lack ideas, even if I reached 120." One would have been a study of Erasmus, symbolic of his lifelong battle with the sons of Luther. (On December 23, 1954, came his last attack on "the healthy men," in this case the "bourgeois sporting rabble" who were robbing the Alps of "their quiet menace.") He also considered a novel about Achilles. The warrior with a vulnerable heel is first discovered by Odysseus disguised as a girl, a bit like Eichendorff's Good-for-Nothing, who had amused Mann almost forty years earlier. Achilles loves both women and men, dying while he avenges Patroclus. "Who else is capable of such a project?" Mann asked Kerényi, who replied perspicaciously that Tonio Kröger and Young Joseph would find a brother.

Mann continued to read in public. After one particularly successful evening, Erika suggested that they tour as a father-and-daughter team. He was momentarily amused, but it was a sign of her diminished expectations. Brutalized by a series of FBI interviews, she had felt her career destroyed in America. Once something of a star, reigning at the height of international bohemia, she had become too much his satellite. Elisabeth says that her sister was "a good anti–" and was inhibited from fighting back where it counted. Her conflicts with Golo accelerated; she suspected, correctly, that his friends like Melvin Lasky were American agents. In 1943, Mann had described Golo as "perhaps our most devoted child." Whether he detected that Golo's arguments with Erika concealed his ambivalence toward Mann himself is not clear from the diaries. But they show him finding Erika petulant, Golo sniping, Michael a philanderer, and Monika hysterical. Only Elisabeth, who had been widowed in 1952, did not seem to disappoint him.

(The filial revenge of his two surviving sons would be slow paced. Neither left the family circle; and when Mann died, Michael wept "buckets of tears," according to Golo, who became so distraught he required morphine. After that, Golo became the clan's Tin Soldier. Only when he was seventy-one did "an elderly gentleman [himself] say farewell to an old, old lady [Katia] from whom he had never really been able to part, for better

Thomas Mann in Princeton, 1938, with his standard desk arrangement

or worse." Perhaps the latter, since, even after Klaus's death, he remained her favorite son. While she was living, Golo contributed an intelligent and sweet-natured memoir of his father. But after her death, he composed *Reminiscences and Reflections*, in which Mann is blamed for the sins committed sixty years earlier. In Golo's old age, he became a vocal opponent of his family's brand of democratic socialism. In a television interview, he blamed it all on Erika's pernicious influence, but he was really settling scores with his father.

Michael's story was more complex. As a young man, he became an alcoholic and frequently crashed the family car—as if he were perpetuating the damage he had unwittingly caused as a child. He became a professional violinist and toured, for some years, with Yalta Menuhin, the sister of Yehudi Menuhin, and the Manns' neighbor. They began an affair, to the chagrin of their separate mates. Thomas and Katia had grown very fond of Gret, Michael's wife, and they took her side against him, especially when Yalta's husband accused Michael of beating *her.*

After Mann's death, Michael became a literary scholar—and the family's literary executor. Unlike Golo, he applauded Thomas's turn to the left. The only heterosexual male in the family, he was not perturbed by the sexual revelations in the diaries, having been the first to recognize Strathbogie's resemblance to his father, and demanded a high price for their American publication. (Old friend Fritz Landshoff would publish them.) After Michael received his Ph.D., he gave a lecture on Mann at Rutgers University. Forewarned that he was tracing his father's footsteps, Mann having lectured there previously, he quipped, "He's dead now, what can he do to me?" He then proceeded to trip off the podium and break his leg. On January 1, 1977, Michael greeted the new year with a fatal combination of alcohol and barbiturates. His death may have been a suicide, though Elisabeth has said that it may also have been a cry for help gone wrong. His last gifts to her, a copy of *Faust* and a compass, can be read either way: they also seem like proper symbols for a son of Thomas Mann's.

As for Monika, like the ill-fated Lula, she became the family embarrassment. Elisabeth used to tell her daughters: "Don't be a Tante Moni.")

As Mann's career drew to a close, he began to acknowledge its idiosyncrasies. On January 8, 1953, he wrote Hesse, "I can never quite bring myself to put my own work in [your] class. It always strikes me as too personal, too much of an ad hoc arrangement with art to allow of being mentioned in one breath with 'the real thing.' I have simply tried to get by. But in the end even that is honorable enough." He might also have been the last artist who could confess in that ingenuous/disingenuous way that art had been his means of survival. The letter to Hesse doesn't say he's given up. Following the celebration of his eightieth birthday, he wrote Hesse, "But when will I start to emulate my models in earnest?"

While he was writing *The Holy Sinner*, the idea of grace became very appealing to him. "Isn't it pure grace," he wrote Kahler, "that after the consuming *Faustus*, I was able to bring off this little book of God-sent jests and diversions?" The novel's hero, Pope Gregorius, marries his mother, who is also his father's sister. (Parodying what could have been a Christian version of the Oedipus tragedy, the hero and his wife/mother/aunt reveal at the novel's end that they always guessed they were related; and simply wanted to give the gods some amusement.) For many years, Gregorius is chained to a "savage stone," and survives off milk secreted by the rock. Mann told Adorno that he was drawing on Roman ideas of the earth's nourishing breast, though he understood that milk from the rock was a rather desperate ploy or "shift."

This jeu d'esprit was also his most linguistically experimental work: "It is after all a supernatural medieval world of my own whimsical invention, and I simply could not conceive it except as linguistically dappled." The narrative, crammed with solecisms and Anglo-German compounds, is variously devout and ribald. On May 30, 1951, he wrote Julius Bab, his critic friend from Berlin, whom exile had carried to Roslyn Heights, Long Island, filled with pride over this latest invention. "I have done all my things only once and there is no reason to leap to the conclusion that every experiment is a 'blind alley' in which the author will now be stuck for all eternity. Basically every one of my books has been a blind alley from which it was impossible to go any further in that particular direction, yet each time I emerged to go onto new things." Thus was grace manifested in the artist's life, a fleet-footed escape from entrapment in subject matter or narrative technique. He could have echoed the African-American gospel song, "I've come so far, I believe I can run on some more." The enemies might have driven Einstein to his death, or so he contended when the scientist expired on April 18, 1955 (since Einstein was four years his junior, he considered the death premature). But he remained to find them out.

E ven so, the Tin Soldier had begun to weaken. Mann sometimes felt that he was written out, that the literary games were an unseemly climax to a decade that began with *Doctor Faustus*. Meanwhile the survival into old age of sexual desire was both a source of amusement and a reminder of a lifetime's frustration. His resilience had become a mixed blessing. On February 7, 1953, he wrote Kerényi, "I am often sick of [the world] though healthy enough to make any death wish comical. Also a dilemma."

Erika reports that in his last year he often quoted Prospero's lament, "In my ending is despair," and, according to Golo, once after an unpleasant encounter with a customs official, he said, "It is loathsome to live amongst people." (Golo adds that this wasn't his "last word," that there was no "last word.") On April 15, 1954, he made his last move, to a new home in Kilchberg, another solid bourgeois residence with a view of Lake Zurich, and room for "my California sofa . . . in the corner of which I wrote large portions of *Doctor Faustus* and *The Holy Sinner*." The paraphernalia of work had acquired the status of totems, the carefully ordered desk, the neatly arranged pens, the fresh paper, the sofa and chairs.

On February 11, 1955, the Manns celebrated their golden anniversary. He wrote Agnes Meyer that he wouldn't want to live it all again, but then, recovering within the space of a paragraph, he granted her one more revelation—"I have always liked Andersen's fairy tale of the Steadfast Tin Soldier. Fundamentally it is the symbol of my life," as well as his dream of an emerald stone for his birthday. "I reveled in it like a child—like the child I am, to the extent that I top it off by confessing the dream to you." She didn't take the hint, but his children gave him a green stone, a tourmaline.

On May 8, six years after his commemoration of Goethe, he gave his great Schiller lecture, having in his old age, after years of exile, returned to praise Germany's most famous writers. A week earlier, he had written a letter to Guido Devescovi, an Italian scholar, discussing questions of literary paternity and fraternity. He told Devescovi that a young German scholar, Hans Egon Holthusen, had viciously attacked *Doctor Faustus*. Mann claimed not to have read the essay but he reported Holthusen's excuse, "Something had to be done. He was crushing us all, you know." After living through the enmity of his contemporaries, he had the chance, granted only to the very old, to see what lay ahead for his imperiled reputation.

More gratifying had been Devescovi's attempt to revive interest in Heinrich. For the last time, Thomas spoke of the boy who had once been his greatest rival, and who had known him longer and more intimately than anyone else. He was proud that they two had Europeanized the German novel, but his way had been more "traditionally German and closer to music, including a more ironic note than [Heinrich's]," a "dubious" but "real advantage" for the German and the Italian public. Nonetheless, compared with Heinrich's "intellectually formidable work," he always felt like "the little brother looking up to his elder."

"I feel quite sure," he concluded, "that posterity will establish justice insofar as the hierarchy of this *family* is concerned. But it was an indescribable shock to me, and seemed like a dream, when shortly before his death, Heinrich dedicated one of his books to me with the words, 'To my great brother, who wrote *Doctor Faustus*.' What? How? He had always been the great brother [a pun on "great" as well as "big"]. And I puffed out my chest and thought of Goethe's remark about the Germans' silly bickering over which was greater, he or Schiller. 'They ought to be glad that they have two such boys.' " If Mann still played the game of mythic identification, he was ready to share the spotlight with his brother.

This was his final gesture of loyalty to Heinrich. Three weeks later, he was back in Lübeck as the recipient of an honorary citizenship, reading at the Stadttheater three passages from *Tonio Kröger*, "The Coat of Many Colors" from *Young Joseph*, and the circus chapter of *Felix Krull*, representative works from 1903, 1930, and 1953, all of them instances of the forms and masks with which he had moved among men.

His eightieth birthday brought honors and greetings from around the world; he had become literature's elder statesman. Festivities lasted for three days. Among his gifts were a twelve-volume edition of his works published by the East German Aufbau Verlag; a donation by West Germany of fifty thousand marks to the Thomas Mann Fund for the support of sick and indigent writers; a specially printed *Hommage de la France*, with tributes from Camus, Malraux, Picasso, and Yourcenar as well as Mauriac's resplendent words, "He has preserved the honor of Germany."

During his last vacation he wrote the tribute to *Billy Budd* that crystallized his debt to a New World vision of homosexual love that had constituted his Goethean rejuvenation by American energy. In late July he entered the Zurich Canton Hospital for what were to be his last days. It turned out that his doctor was an admirer, particularly of Hanno's death scene in *Buddenbrooks*, yet another literary echo and omen.

On August 8 he wrote a letter to Kahler that included a final sketch, this time of the excessively optimistic chief resident, and one last mythical identification, this time with Mozart. Reading Alfred Einstein's biography of the composer, he learned that "Mozart did not want to see anything at all, and repeatedly drew his inspiration from music alone—a kind of filtering and aristocratic in-breeding, anti-popular like Goethe." (Or like Mann himself: to the end a socialist-humanist but never a populist.) Mozart's visual incapacity linked Mann to another of his gods. A few months earlier he had compared himself to Schiller: "The world of the eyes is not my world, either, and at heart, I want to see nothing, just like him."

Demonstrating that he remained a writer to the end, the next day, August 9, he improved on his description. In a letter to his musician son Michael, he added that Mozart's "whole life long he suffered from his physical smallness and unprepossessing appearance. He really must have looked like nothing at all." On his deathbed, Mann came up with a last elegant formulation: "Mozart made music out of music, as it were, a kind of artistic inbreeding and filtered production." A Mozart biography joins *Die Geliebten* and *Maja* among the masterpieces he didn't write.

On August 10, he received the highest German honor, "Pour le mérite," but the next day he told a Parisian publisher that news of a French festschrift pleased him more. The last words he spoke to his physicians that evening were a combination of French and English, exile's dialect from the representative German. He died the following day.

Felix Krull contains his final joke about the vocation that he had embraced for sixty years. "Writing is not a conversation with oneself," the narrator insists. But for Thomas Mann, it had rarely been anything else.

NOTES
SELECTED BIBLIOGRAPHY
INDEX

NOTES

Frequently cited works by Thomas Mann include:

Altes und Neues: Kleine Prosa aus Fünf Jahrzehnten. Berlin, 1956.
Aufsätze, Reden, Essays: 1893–1913, 1914–1918, 1919–1925, 3 vols., edited by Harry Matter. Berlin, 1983–86.
Briefe 1889–1955 und Nachlese, 3 vols., edited by Erika Mann. Frankfurt am Main, 1961–65.
The Correspondence of Heinrich Mann and Thomas Mann, edited by Hans Wysling, translated by Donald Renau. Berkeley and Los Angeles, forthcoming.
Diaries 1918–1939, edited by Hermann Kesten, translated by Richard Winston and Clara Winston. New York, 1982.
Ein Appell an die Vernunft 1926–1933, edited by Hermann Kurzke and Stephan Stachorski. Frankfurt, 1994.
Für das neue Deutschland 1919–1925, edited by Hermann Kurzke and Stephan Stachorski. Frankfurt, 1993.
Gesammelte Werke, 13 vols., edited by Hans Bürgin and Peter de Mendelssohn. Frankfurt, 1990. Henceforth referred to as *GW.*
Letters of Thomas Mann 1889–1955, 2 vols., translated by Richard Winston and Clara Winston. New York, 1971.
Notizbücher 1–6 and *7–12,* edited by Hans Wysling and Yvonne Schmidlin. Frankfurt, 1991–92.
Tagebücher 1937–39, 1940–43, 2 vols., edited by Peter de Mendelssohn. Frankfurt, 1980, 1982.
Tagebücher 1944–46, 1946–48, 1949–50, 1951–52, 4 vols., edited by Inge Jens. Frankfurt, 1986–93.

Unless otherwise noted, all translations from the German are by this author.

PART I : A PRODIGAL SON OF HIS CLASS

CHAPTER 1 : SENATOR MANN'S SON

Mann describes his birth in *Lebenslauf* (1936), in *GW*, volume 11; his parents, his father's death, Lübeck, and Travemünde in *A Sketch of My Life*; the "noble pirates of Lübeck" in "Lübeck as a Way of Life and Thought," trans. by Richard and Clara Winston, in *Buddenbrooks*, trans. by H. T. Lowe-Porter; the continuity of history, the watchword of "safety," and the English influence in "The Years of My Life," translated by Heinz and Ruth Norden, *Harper's*, October 1950. His letter about Armin Martens, dated March 19, 1955, appears in *Briefe*, volume 3. His mother's devotion is described in a letter to Agnes E. Meyer, *Briefe*, volume 2. His letter about "Abdication" appears in *The Correspondence of Heinrich Mann and Thomas Mann*; his discussion of the Jews, in *"Zur jüdischen Frage"* (1921), in *GW*, volume 13; his description of clumsy Germans, in a letter to Otto Grautoff, February 20, 1901, in *Briefe an Otto Grautoff und Ida Boy-Ed*, edited by Peter de Mendelssohn; his remarks about Lübeck as his Faubourg St. Germain in a letter to Boy-Ed in the same volume. His remarks about German in a letter to Peter Pringsheim, October 10, 1916, are included in *Letters of Thomas Mann, 1889–1955*. His mother's coldness is discussed on April 19, 1935, in *Diaries 1918–1939*; also cited is *Tagebücher 1949–50*, for entries of March 12, 1950 (family's sexual problems), and August 28, 1950 (Mann's love of young men). He calls Thomas Buddenbrook his "double" in *Reflections of an Unpolitical Man*. He discusses his first love in *"Meine erste Liebe"* (1931) in *Ein Appell an die Vernunft*.

Also cited are Heinrich Mann, *Briefe an Ludwig Ewers* (Berlin and Weimar, 1980); Hermann Kesten, *Der Geist der Unruhe*; Golo Mann, *Reminiscences and Reflections: A Youth in Germany*; Katia Mann, *Unwritten Memories*, edited by Elisabeth Plessen and Michael Mann, translated by Hunter Hannum and Hildegarde Hannum (New York, 1975); Peter de Mendelssohn, *Der Zauberer: Das Leben des deutschen Schriftstellers Thomas Mann*, volume 1, 1875–1918 (Frankfurt, 1975); Klaus Mann, *The Turning Point*; interview with Elisabeth Mann Borgese.

CHAPTER 2 : A PRINCE IN DISGUISE

Mann's 1931 letter to Heinrich is contained in *The Correspondence of Heinrich Mann and Thomas Mann*. Mann's letters to Frieda Hartenstein (October 14, 1889), to Erika Mann about his need for work (December 23, 1926), and to Ida Herz about Aldous Huxley (March 21, 1954) are found in *Letters 1889–1955*; his letter about "healthy men," in *Briefe an Otto Grautoff und Ida Boy-Ed*. His description of "another Gypsydom" in "The Years of My Life." Essays cited include *"Süsser Schlaf"* (1904) and *"Kinderspiele,"* both in *GW*, volume 11; *"Vom schönen Zimmer"* (1929) in *Die Forderung des Tages* (Frankfurt, 1986); "The Fall of European Jewry" (1943) and "An Enduring People" (1944) in *An die gesittete Welt* (Frankfurt, 1986); and *Listen, Germany: Twenty-five Radio Messages to the German People over BBC* (New York, 1943).

Also cited are Klaus Mann, *The Turning Point*; Walter Benjamin, *Reflections: Essays, Aphorisms, Autobiographical Writings*, edited and with an introduction by Peter Demetz, translated by Edmund Jephcott (New York, 1978); and Arthur Schnitzler, *The Road into the Open*, introduction by Russell Berman, translated by Robert Byers (Berkeley, 1992).

CHAPTER 3 : A SELECTIVE EDUCATION

Mann discusses his first reading of Schiller, Schopenhauer, and Nietzsche in *A Sketch of My Life*; his sense of authorial freedom in *"Bilse und ich"* (1906), in *GW*, volume 10. For a similar argument see his letter to Theodor W. Adorno, December 30, 1945, in *Letters 1889–1955*. His relation to his ancestors is discussed in "Lübeck as a Way of Life and Thought"; his bad memories of school in *"Pariser Rechenschaft," GW*, volume 11. His letters to Carl Maria Weber, July 4, 1920 (about homosexuality); to Alexander M. Frey on November 10, 1936 (about literature as "a track of my life"); and to Emil Preetorius on October 20, 1949 (about not living in the past) appear in *Letters 1889–1955*. His letter to Heinrich about his talent (December 29, 1900) and his "falling to pieces" (January 8, 1904) in *The Correspondence of Heinrich Mann and Thomas Mann*. *Diaries 1918–1939* contains his April 25, 1934, description of his sexual desires; *Tagebücher 1944–46* contains his July 20, 1945, dream of Cynthia Sperry; *Tagebücher 1949–50* contains his comments on Gérard Philipe (October 17, 1949); on his need for the world to know him (August 27, 1950); and on his trust in those with a "feeling" (October 23, 1950). *Tagebücher 1951–52* contains his comments on Marlon Brando (November 14, 1951). Also cited are *"Die deutsche Stunde"* (1917) in *Die Forderung des Tages*; *"Erinnerungen aus Lübecker Stadttheater"* (1930), in *GW*, volume 11; "Platen" (1930) from *Essays of Three Decades*; *"Versuch über Schiller,"* and its translation as "On Schiller" by Richard and Clara Winston in *Last Essays*; and "Bernard Shaw" in *The Listener* (London), January 18, 1951.

Also cited are Hanns Eisler, *Gespräche mit Hans Burge* (Leipzig, 1975); Marcel Reich-Ranicki, *Thomas Mann and His Family*, translated by Ralph Manheim; and "The Circus Animals' Desertion" and "Politics," in William Butler Yeats, *Collected Poems* (New York, 1956). The March 1, 1954, diary quotation is from Ronald Hayman, *Thomas Mann: A Biography* (New York, 1994).

PART II : AN ARTIST WITH A BAD CONSCIENCE

CHAPTER 1 : A COLD LOOK

Mann's letters to Heinrich Mann (March 7, 1901) and Hermann Hesse (April 8, 1945) are found in *Letters 1889–1945*. His description of life outside school is from *A Sketch of My Life*; and of his father's death is from *"Fragment über das Religiöse"* (1931) in *Ein Appell an die Vernunft*. *Diaries 1918–1939* contains his May 25, 1919, description of Heinrich's behavior following their father's death, the 1934 depiction of "calisthenics," and the July 15, 1935, discussion of Otto Grautoff's death. *Tagebücher 1949–50* contains his description of "Timpe's shavings"; *Tagebücher 1953–55* contains his comments on "eternal love of boys." Also cited are letters contained in *Briefe an Otto Grautoff und Ida Boy-Ed*; and *"Frühlingssturm"* (1893) and *"Heinrich Heine der Gute"* (1893), both in *GW*, volume 11.

Senator Mann's will is quoted in Ulrich Dietzel, editor, *"Dokumente zur Geschichte der Familie Mann," Sinn und Form: Sonderheft Thomas Mann* (Berlin, 1965).

Also cited are Erika Mann, "Letter to My Father," in *The Achievement of Thomas Mann*, edited by Charles Neider (New York, 1947); and *The Last Year of Thomas Mann*, translated by Richard Graves (Freeport, N.Y., 1970); Klaus Mann, *The Turning Point*; Victor Mann, *Wir Waren Fünf* (Konstanz, 1949); Heinrich Mann, *Ein Zeitalter wird besichtigt* (Stockholm, 1945); George Grosz, *A Little Yes and a Big No*, translated by Lola Sachs Dorn (New York, 1946); Frederic Prokosch, *Voices: A Memoir* (New York, 1983). The quotations from Kurt Martens and Carl Zuckmayer are included in Richard Winston, *Thomas Mann: The Making of an Artist, 1875–1911* (New York, 1981). Also cited is an interview with Edith Jonas by the author.

CHAPTER 2 : "THE BEST 'MÜNCHEN' THERE EVER WAS"

Mann's descriptions of his education, office experience, life in Munich, and the early response to his work are contained in *A Sketch of My Life*. Other descriptions of Munich can be found in *Reflections of an Unpolitical Man*. His letters to Grautoff about Gippern, "healthy men," Alfred Kerr, poetry, his poverty, his ambitions, and Jewish journalists are included in *Briefe an Otto Grautoff und Ida Boy-Ed*. His August 15, 1919, description of Stefan George is in *Diaries 1918–1939*; his citation of Paul Bourget (1894) in *Notizbücher 1–6*. The December 30, 1946, letter to Emil Preetorius concerning Schopenhauer and his August 5, 1949, letter to Ludwig Kunz about older writers are included in *Letters 1889–1955*. He discusses literary decadence in "The Years of My Life." Also cited are *"Ostmarklärung"* (1895) and *" 'Das Liebeskonzil' von Oskar Panizza"* (1895) in *GW*, volume 13; and "Schopenhauer" in *Essays of Three Decades*. His contribution to Ilse Martens's keepsake album is in Peter Robert Franke, *Der Tod des Hans Hansen: Unbekannte Dokumente aus der Jugend von Thomas Mann* (Lubeck, 1991). The letter to Ernst Bertram is found in *Briefe*.

   Also cited are Heinrich Mann, "My Brother," in *The Stature of Thomas Mann*; and Martin Green, *The Von Richthofen Sisters: The Triumphant and the Tragic Modes of Love* (Albuquerque, 1974).

CHAPTER 3 : NOBODY LIKES THEM, NOT EVEN THEIR DOGS

All the translations quoted are by H. T. Lowe-Porter, amended by the author. Mann's letter to Grautoff is from *Briefe an Otto Grautoff und Ida Boy-Ed*. *Letters 1889–1955* contains his November 9, 1894, letter to Richard Dehmel about the "misera plebs."

   Also cited are Theodor W. Adorno, "Notes on Kafka," in *Prisms*, translated by Samuel and Shierry Weber (London, 1967); and Glenway Wescott, *Images of Truth* (New York, 1962).

CHAPTER 4 : DREAMS OF LAUREL WREATHS

Mann's description of his first apartment and bicycle are from *A Sketch of My Life*. His letters to Grautoff are in *Briefe an Otto Grautoff und Ida Boy-Ed*. *Letters 1889–1955* contains his June 29, 1900, letter to Paul Ehrenberg and his April 27, 1912, letter to Heinrich concerning his military service. All other letters to Heinrich are quoted in *The Correspondence of Heinrich Mann and Thomas Mann*. Also cited are "The Years of My Life"; and *"Bilse und ich"* and *"Im Spiegel"* (1907) in *GW*, volume 11. Ilse Martens's recollections are quoted in *Thomas Mann: Ein Leben in Bildern*, edited by Hans Wysling and Yvonne Schmidlin (Zurich, 1994).

   Also cited is Heinrich Mann, "My Brother," in *The Stature of Thomas Mann*.

CHAPTER 5 : BUDDENBROOKS

Although the translation is by H. T. Lowe-Porter, a newer translation of the novel by John E. Woods (New York, 1993) is livelier, less redolent of nineteenth-century British fiction, and therefore, perhaps, more accessible to modern readers.

Also cited are "The Years of My Life," *Reflections of a Non-political Man*, and *The Correspondence of Heinrich Mann and Thomas Mann*.

CHAPTER 6 : THE RIVALS

Mann's December 29, 1900, letter to Heinrich about his "church mouse" condition is included in *The Correspondence of Heinrich Mann and Thomas Mann*. Other letters to Heinrich—January 8, 1901, on hard times, and January 3, 1918, on helping others to live—are in *Letters 1889–1955*. Mann's description of burning himself is quoted in Richard Winston, *Thomas Mann: The Making of an Artist*.

Also cited are Thomas Mann, *Briefwechsel mit seinem Verleger Gottfried Bermann-Fischer, 1932–1955*, edited by Peter de Mendelssohn (Frankfurt, 1973); and Hermann Kesten, *Der Geist der Unruhe*. Kurt Martens's review is quoted in *Thomas Mann im Urteil seiner Zeit: Dokumente, 1891–1955* (Hamburg, 1969). Rilke's review is included in *Thomas Mann: A Collection of Critical Essays*, edited by Henry Hatfield (Englewood Cliffs, 1964).

For a further discussion of Heinrich Mann's early fiction, see Anthony Heilbut, "Heinrich Mann," in *European Writers: The Twentieth Century*, edited by George Stade (New York, 1989).

CHAPTER 7 : "THAT CENTRAL EXPERIENCE OF MY HEART"

Mann's January 28, 1902, letter to Paul Ehrenberg is included in *Briefe*, volume 1. *Letters 1889–1955* contains his June 29, 1900, letter to Ehrenberg; his January 8, February 13, March 7, and April 1, 1901, letters to Heinrich; his March 14, 1902, letter to Hilde Distel; and his November 6, 1948, letter to Erika Mann concerning *Doctor Faustus*'s "allegory." *The Correspondence of Heinrich Mann and Thomas Mann* contains his May 17, 1901, letter concerning Mary Smith. All the letters to Otto Grautoff are in *Briefe an Otto Grautoff und Ida Boy-Ed. Briefe*, volume 3, contains his letter to Charles Jackson. His 1899 poem was published in the newspaper *Die Gesellschaft* and is quoted in *Thomas Mann, Sehr Menschlich*, edited by Richard Carstensen (Lübeck / Zurich, n.d.). The story *Gerächt* is included in Thomas Mann, *Sämtliche Erzählungen* (Frankfurt, 1963). His 1950 reply to Henry Hatfield is found in the Harvard University Archives. *Diaries 1918–1939* contains his May 6, 1934, description of his affair with Ehrenberg. *Tagebücher 1946–48* contains his correspondence with Walter Opitz about the Ehrenburg brothers' discussion with him about homosexual passages in *Doctor Faustus*. *Tagebücher 1951–52* contains his October 9, 1951, reference to *Doctor Faustus* as a "memoir." All passages from his notebooks and plans for *Die Geliebten* are from *Notizbücher 7–12*. His description of the affair as a "bourgeois experience" is from *A Sketch of My Life*. The 1903 poem to Ehrenberg is translated by Richard Winston in *Thomas Mann: The Making of an Artist*. Also cited is *The Story of a Novel: The Genesis of "Doctor Faustus"* (1949), translated by Richard and Clara Winston (New York, 1961). He describes Gide's career in "Gide's Unending Search for Harmony," a review of Albert J. Guérard, *Andre Gide*, in *The New York Times* (August 19, 1951).

CHAPTER 8 : HYSTERICAL RENAISSANCE AND INFANT PRODIGIES

All translations of the stories are by Lowe-Porter, amended by the author. *The Correspondence of Heinrich Mann and Thomas Mann* contains Mann's letters of January 21, 1901; December 5, 1903; and January 8, 1904. *Diaries 1918–1939* contains his December 6, 1919, reference to the completion of *Fiorenza*. Also cited is *"Über Fiorenza"* (1908) in *GW*, volume 11; *"Das Ewig*

Weibliche" (1903) in *GW*, volume 13; and "Pablo Casals" (1954) in *Die Forderung des Tages.*

The Schaukal and Kerr reviews are quoted in Klaus Schröter, *Thomas Mann im Urteil seiner Zeit: Dokumente, 1891–1955.* Also cited are Katia Mann, *Unwritten Memories*; and author's interview with Elisabeth Mann Borgese.

CHAPTER 9: "HOW CAN YOU SEE IT AND NOT PLAY IT?"

Both translations are by Lowe-Porter, amended by the author. Mann's descriptions of Kubin's art and of the composition of *Tonio Kröger* is from *A Sketch of My Life. Letters 1889–1955* contains his October 29, 1903, letter to S. Fischer concerning Gerhart Hauptmann. *Tagebücher 1949–50* contains the July 13, 1950, entry. *Notizbücher 7–12* contains his comment about *Tonio Kröger* and himself. Also cited is *Order of the Day: Political Essays and Speeches of Two Decades,* translated by H. T. Lowe-Porter, Agnes Meyer, and Eric Sutton (New York, 1942).

Also cited are Klaus Mann, *The Turning Point,* and Jens Peter Jacobsen, *Niels Lyhne,* translated by Tina Nunnally (Seattle, 1990), which quotes Mann's praise of the novel.

CHAPTER 10: MARRIAGE! HAPPINESS!

Mann's letter to the Ehrenberg brothers is included in *Briefe,* volume 3. Erika's description of her grandfather is quoted in Hans Bürgin and Hans-Otto Mayer, *Thomas Mann: A Chronicle of His Life,* translated by Eugene Dobson (Alabama, 1969). Mann's marriage plans are discussed in *A Sketch of My Life.* His description of Katia and her "equally pretty" brother is from *"Katia Mann zum siebzigsten Geburtsage"* (1953) in *GW*, volume 11. His remark about the "Jew-girl" is quoted in *Der Zauberer;* and about her unflattering hat is in *Notizbücher 7–12,* which also contains the description of Hedwig Dohm and his plans for *Maya.* His December 1903 letter to Grautoff is quoted in *Briefe an Otto Grautoff und Ida Boy-Ed. The Correspondence of Heinrich Mann and Thomas Mann* contains all the letters to Heinrich and Julia Mann's letter to Heinrich describing the wedding. *Letters 1889–1955* contains all the letters to Katia, the three letters to Kurt Martens, and the October 29, 1904, letter to Philipp Witkop.

Also cited is Klaus H. Pringsheim, "Thomas Mann in Exile: Roosevelt, McCarthy, Goethe and Democracy," in *Thomas Mann: Ein Kolloquium,* edited by Hans H. Schulte and Gerald Chappie (Bonn, 1978).

PART III: RENUNCIATION AND EROS

CHAPTER 1: MAKING SENTENCES OUT OF THINGS

Letters 1889–1955 contains Mann's letters of March 28, 1906, and November 1906 to Martens. His November 18, 1906, letter is quoted in Richard Winston, *Thomas Mann: The Making of an Artist. The Correspondence of Heinrich Mann and Thomas Mann* contains all the letters to Heinrich as well as Mann's "Anti-Heinrich" and Heinrich's letter to Ines Schmied. The description of the Villa Rosenberg is from *Briefe an Otto Grautoff und Ida Boy-Ed.* Also cited are *"Bilse und ich," "Die Lösung der Judenfrage"* (1907) in *GW*, volume 13; *"Im Spiegel," "Versach über das Theater"* (1908) in *GW*, volume 10; *"Mitteilung an die literarhistorisches Gesellschaft in Bonn"* (1906) in *GW*, volume 11; *"Zur jüdischen Frage"* in *GW*, volume 13; "Fantasy on Goethe" (1948) translated by Richard and Clara Winston in *Last Essays.*

Also cited are Katia Mann, *Unwritten Memories*; Shelley L. Frisch, *Erika Mann* (New York, forthcoming). Schaukal's review is quoted in Schröter, *Thomas Mann im Urteil seiner Zeit*. Hedwig Pringsheim's remarks about her sissy ("Pimperling") son-in-law is in Thomas Manns *Schwiegermutter erzählt: Lebendige Briefe aus grossbürgerlichen Hause*, edited by Hans-Rudolf Wiedemann (Lübeck, 1985). Mann's letter to Ilse Martens is quoted in *Thomas Mann: Ein Leben in Bildern*.

CHAPTER 2 : THE LEFT-HANDED PRINCE

The Correspondence of Heinrich Mann and Thomas Mann contains Mann's February 6, 1908, letter about the Harden trial. *Briefe*, volume 1, contains his August 26, 1909, letter to Walter Opitz. *Tagebücher 1946–1948* contains his July 24, 1938, letter to Dr. Harry F. Young about Maximilian Harden. Also cited are Mann's 1939 preface, translated by H. T. Lowe-Porter, to *Royal Highness*, translated by A. Cecil Curtiss (New York, 1983). The Wagner passages are from *Thomas Mann: Pro and Contra Wagner*, edited by Patrick Carnegy, translated by Allan Blunden, with an introduction by Erich Heller (Chicago, 1985). Also cited is *"Über Fiorenza."* All passages from "Mind and Art" are translated by T. J. Reed in *Thomas Mann: The Uses of Tradition* (Oxford, 1974).

CHAPTER 3 : THE EDUCATION OF A CONFIDENCE MAN

Letters 1889–1955 contains Mann's 1910 letters to Kurt Martens and to Paul Ehrenberg. His June 7, 1910, depiction of Lübeck as his Faubourg is from *Briefe an Otto Grautoff und Ida Boy-Ed*. *The Correspondence of Heinrich Mann and Thomas Mann* contains all his letters to Heinrich, and Ines's letter to Heinrich. His letter to Hesse is included in *The Hesse-Mann Letters: The Correspondence of Hermann Hesse and Thomas Mann, 1910–1955*, edited by Anni Carlsson and Volker Michels, translated by Ralph Manheim (New York, 1975). Carla's suicide is described by Thomas in *A Sketch of My Life* and by Heinrich in *Ein Zeitalter wird besichtigt*. Mann's letters to Bertram are included in *Thomas Mann an Ernst Bertram: Briefe aus den Jahren 1910–1955*, edited by Inge Jens (Pfullingen, 1960). Also cited are *"Der Doktor Lessing"* (1910) in *GW*, volume 11; "On Pornography" (1911); "The Old Fontane," (1912) and "Chamisso" (1913) in *Essays of Three Decades*; and *"Gedenken an Liebermann"* (1944) in *Tagebücher, 1944–46*.

Also cited are Klaus Mann, *The Turning Point*; Katia Mann, *Unwritten Memories*; T. J. Reed, *Thomas Mann: The Uses of Tradition*; Hans Wysling and Yvonne Schmidlin, *Bild und Text bei Thomas Mann: Eine Dokumentation* (Bern, 1989).

CHAPTER 4 : DEATH IN VENICE

The translation is by Lowe-Porter, considerably amended by the author. Also quoted are the critical comments of David Luke in *Death in Venice and Other Stories* (New York, 1988). Mann describes "a quick improvisation" in *A Sketch of My Life*. He discusses his influence on Lukács in *Reflections of an Unpolitical Man*. His descriptions of 1909 Bayreuth are included in *Thomas Mann: Pro and Contra Wagner*. *The Correspondence of Thomas Mann and Heinrich Mann* contains his December 1911 letter to Heinrich; Heinrich's review; and Mann's March 3, 1940, letter about *The Beloved Returns*. *Briefe an Otto und Ida Grautoff Boy-Ed* contains his letter to Boy-Ed. Mann's work notes are quoted in Judith Marcus, *Georg Lukács and Thomas Mann: A Study in the Sociology of Literature* (Amherst, 1987), translation slightly amended by this author. *Tagebücher 1951–52* contains his January 26, 1951, comment on Erich Heller and his March 3, 1951, comments on the homosexual subtext of his fiction. Mann's April 9, 1950, letter to Donald Windham is quoted in *Tagebücher 1949–50*. Also cited are *"Die Erotik Michelangelos"* in *Altes und Neues: Kleine Prose aus fünf Jahrzehnten* (Berlin, 1956); *"Gesang von Kindchen"* (1919) in *Sämtliche Erzählungen*; and Mann's *Letters to Paul Amann*, edited by Herbert Wegener, translated by Richard and Clara Winston (Middletown, 1960).

Also cited are Katia Mann, *Unwritten Memories*; Erich Heller, *Thomas Mann: The Ironic German* (South Bend, 1979); Harvey Goldman, *Max Weber and Thomas Mann: Calling and the Shaping of the Self* (Berkeley, 1991); Harry Slochower, "Thomas Mann's *Death in Venice*," *American Imago* 26 (1969); and interview with William Koshland by the author.

CHAPTER 5 : MAKE WAR, NOT LOVE

Letters 1889–1955 contains Mann's letters of December 7, 1912, to Frank Wedekind; of April 30, 1913, to the Royal Bavarian Commissioner of Police; of May 28, 1913, to Kurt Martens; of May 29, 1913, to Wedekind; of August 7, 1914, to Heinrich Mann; of November 11, 1914, to Philipp Witkop; of December 14, 1914, to Richard Dehmel; of August 28, 1916, to Ernst Bertram; of October 10, 1916, to Peter Pringsheim; of November 25, 1916, to Bertram; and of May 25, 1932, to Erika and Klaus Mann. *Briefe* contains August 31, 1913, letter to Julius Bab.

All other letters to Heinrich Mann and the letter to Maximilian Brantl are included in *The Correspondence of Heinrich Mann and Thomas Mann*.

Also cited are Mann's *"Vorwort zu dem Roman einer Jungverstörben"* (1913) in *Aufsätze*, volume 1; *"Gedanken im Kriege"* and the *Svenska Dagbladet* letter in *Von deutschen Republik* (Frankfurt, 1984); "Frederick and the Great Coalition" (1915), translated by H. T. Lowe-Porter in *Three Essays* (New York, 1929); "I Stand with the Spanish People" (1936), in *Order of the Day; Reflections of a Nonpolitical Man* (1918), translated and with an introduction by Walter D. Norris (New York, 1983); and Mann's *Letters to Paul Amann*, edited by Herbert Wegener, translated by Richard Winston and Clara Winston (Middletown, 1960).

Also cited are Golo Mann, *Reminiscences and Reflections*; and Bruno Walter, "Recollections of Thomas Mann," in *The Stature of Thomas Mann*.

CHAPTER 6 : THE POLITICS OF A NERVOUS EXCEPTION

Mann's August 28, 1916, letter to Ernst Bertram; his January 3, 1918, letter to Heinrich; and his November 6, 1948, letter to Erika are quoted in *Letters 1889–1955*. Heinrich's unmailed response is quoted in *The Correspondence of Heinrich Mann and Thomas Mann*.

Also cited are *Reflections of a Nonpolitical Man* and *A Sketch of My Life*. Mann described his reading of Burke and de Maître in *"Der Künstler und die Gesellschaft"* (1952), in *Altes und Neues*.

For a different slant on Mann's wartime conservatism, see Erich Heller, "The Conservative Imagination," in *The Ironic German* (Cleveland, 1965); and Irvin Stock, "Reflections of a Non-Political Man" in *Ironic out of Love: The Novels of Thomas Mann* (Jefferson, N.C., 1994).

PART IV : PARODYING NATURE

CHAPTER 1 : BEGINNING THE WORLD AGAIN

Letters 1889–1955 contains Mann's letter of April 18, 1919, to Karl Strecker; of June 26, 1919, to Kurt Martens; and of October 7, 1941, containing his comments to Rilke, to Agnes E. Meyer. All diary passages are from *Diaries 1918–1939*.

Also quoted are Mann's *"Gesang vom Kindchen"* and *Letters to Paul Amann*.

Also quoted are Heinrich Mann, *Der Untertan* (1918; privately published in 1916), translated as *Man of Straw*, no translator cited (New York, 1984); Elisabeth Mann Borgese, *Ascent of Woman* (New York, 1963); Golo Mann, *Reminiscences and Reflections*; Klaus Mann, *The Turning Point*; Ernst Bertram, *Nietzsche* (Berlin, 1918); and Richard Exner, " 'The Secrets of My Life' or 'Holding On to the Fleeting Day': Thomas Mann's Diaries, 1933–1936" in *World Literature Today* (Spring 1979).

CHAPTER 2 : THE MUNICH REVOLUTION

Letters 1889–1955 contains Mann's May 23, 1918, letter to Philipp Witkop.

All diary passages are from *Diaries 1918–1939*, except for November 19, 1918, in *Tagebücher 1918–21*, edited by Peter de Mendelssohn (Frankfurt, 1977).

Also cited are Mann's story about Hedwig Dohm, "Little Grandma," in *The Nassau Lit* (Princeton, 1942); and Klaus Mann, *The Turning Point*.

CHAPTER 3 : MANN ONSTAGE

Mann's letter to Josef Ponten is quoted in *Briefe*, volume 1. All diary references are from *Diaries 1918–1939*. Brecht's review of Mann is quoted in Hans Bürgin and Hans-Otto Mayer, *Thomas Mann: A Chronicle of His Life*, translated by Eugene Dobson.

CHAPTER 4 : A FAMILY MAN

Letters 1918–1939 contains Mann's letter of July 4, 1920, to Carl Maria Weber; and of August 18, 1920, to Paul Steegemann concerning Dostoyevsky.

All diary passages are from *Diaries 1918–1939* except for Erika's description of James Agee, May 2, 1945, in *Tagebücher 1944–46*.

Also cited are Thomas Mann, *"Knaben und Mörder"* (1921), in *Die Forderung des Tages*, and *"Gesang vom Kindchen."*

Also cited are Klaus Mann, *The Turning Point*; Katia Mann, *Unwritten Memories*; Monika Mann, *Past and Present*, translated by Frances F. Reid and Ruth Hein (New York, 1960), and "Papa," in *The Stature of Thomas Mann*; Golo Mann, *Reminiscences and Reflections*; Erika and Klaus Mann, "Portrait of Our Father" in *The Stature of Thomas Mann*; interviews by the author with Elisabeth Mann Borgese, Christiane Zimmer, and Fritz Landshoff; and Curt Riess, *Das war ein Leben* (Munich, 1986).

PART V : IMPERIAL PASTIMES AND DEMOCRATIC VISTAS

CHAPTER I : THE BLACK SHEEP'S TRIUMPH

Letters 1889–1955 contains Mann's letter of February 2, 1922, to Ernst Bertram; of February 17, 1923, to Heinrich Mann; and of March 1, 1923, to Felix Bertaux.

Briefe contains his April 4, 1921, letter to Ludwig Ewers. *Thomas Mann an Ernst Bertram* contains the letter about his mother's death.

Diaries 1918–1939 contains his 1937 comments about Heinrich. *Tagebücher 1951–52* contains his June 21, 1952, comments on Heinrich; see also July 19, 1952. Also cited is *"Fragment über Zola"* (1952), in *Die Forderung des Tages.*

The decline of Julia Mann Löhr is described in Golo Mann, *Reminiscences and Reflections.*

CHAPTER 2 : "DO WE LIVE IF OTHERS LIVE?"

Letters 1889–1955 contains Mann's letter of January 4, 1924, and of September 27, 1925, to Karl Bohm; of September 12, 1924, to Josef Ponten; of April 21, 1925, to Gerhart Hauptmann. Mann's letter about Lukács (1923) and comments about him (1949) are quoted in Judith Marcus, *Georg Lukács and Thomas Mann.* The depiction of Count Richard Coudenhove-Kalergi is from *"Pariser Rechenschaft."*

Also quoted are *Diaries 1918–1939; "Ein Schriftsteller leben,"* in *Neu Zürcher Zeitung,* November 30, 1921; "Goethe and Tolstoy" (1921), translated by H. T. Lowe-Porter, in *Essays of Three Decades;* and *"Verjüngende Bücher"* (1927) in *Die Forderung des Tages.*

CHAPTER 3 : EROS AND THE REPUBLIC : DEMOCRATIC VISTAS

Letters 1889–1955 contains Mann's letters of September 4, 1922, to Arthur Schnitzler; October 20, 1922, and February 17, 1923, to Heinrich Mann; and December 5, 1922, to Ida Boy-Ed. His November 1922 letter is quoted in Bürgin and Mayer, *Thomas Mann: A Chronicle of His Life.*

Also cited are Thomas Mann, "The German Inflation" (1942) in *Über mich selbst* (Frankfurt, 1983); *"Zur jüdischen Frage"; "Von deutscher Republik"* (1922) in *GW,* volume 13, and translated by H. T. Lowe-Porter in *Order of the Day; "Goethe und Tolstoi"* in *Für das neue Deutschland; Geist und Wesen der deutschen Republik, dem Gedächtnis Walther Rathenaus"* (1923), "Five Years of Democracy in Germany" (1923), and *"Tischrede in Amsterdam"* (1924), all three in *Aufsätze,* volume 3; and "Pariser Rechenschaft."

Also cited is H. M. Peters, *Zarathustra's Sister* (New York, 1986). Frederick A. Lubich, "Thomas Mann's Sexual Politics: Lost in Translation" in *Comparative Literature Studies* no. 2 (University Park, Pa., 1994), is a valuable essay on this chapter's topic.

CHAPTER 4 : IMPERIAL PASTIMES

Letters 1889–1915 contains Mann's letter of January 21, 1922, to André Gide, and of March 1, 1923, to Felix Bertaux. *The Correspondence of Heinrich Mann and Thomas Mann* contains his sixtieth-birthday address to Heinrich.

Also cited are *Diaries 1918–1939; "Die demokratische Macht"* (1923) in *Aufsätze,* volume 3;

"Über den Film" (1928) in *Die Forderung des Tages*; "An Experience in the Occult" (1924) in *Three Essays*; "Nietzsche and Music" (1924) in *Past Masters and Other Papers*; the screenplay of *Tristan and Isolde* (1923) in *Pro and Contra Wagner*. Mann's letters to *The Dial* appeared in November 1922, May 1923, September 1923, April 1924, and September 1925.

Also cited is John Fuegi, *Brecht and Company: Sex, Politics, and the Making of the Modern Drama* (New York, 1994).

PART VI : THE MAGICIAN

CHAPTERS 1–4 : THE MAGIC MOUNTAIN

The translation cited is by H. T. Lowe-Porter. John E. Wood's new translation will be published in 1996: sections read by this author have been most promising.

Letters 1889–1955 contains Mann's letter of January 6, 1925, to Herbert Eulenberg; of February 5, 1925, to Josef Ponten; of February 22, 1925, to Julius Bab; and of January 3, 1930, to Sigmund Freud; and of March 30, 1945, to Upton Sinclair. Also cited are *Briefe an Otto Grautoff und Ida Boy-Ed* and *Letters to Paul Amann*.

Mann's description of Ludwig von Hoffmann's work is found in *Tagebücher 1918–21*. All other diary passages are from *Tagebücher 1949–50*.

Also cited are *"Über den Film"*; *The Genesis of a Novel*; "Dostoyevsky—in Moderation," foreword to *The Portable Dostoyevsky* (New York, 1946); "In Memoriam Hugo von Hofmannsthal" (1929) in *Rede und Antwort* (Frankfurt, 1948); "Vorwort zu einem Gedächtnisbuch für Klaus Mann" (1950) in *Altes und Neues*; and *The Black Swan* (1953), translated by Willard R. Trask (New York, 1954).

Also cited are Hermann J. Weigand, *The Magic Mountain: A Study of Thomas Mann's Novel "Der Zauberberg"* (Chapel Hill, 1965); Carlos Fuentes, "The Discovery of Mexico" in *Granta* 22 (Autumn 1987); author's interview with Richard Exner; and letter from Konrad Bloch to author.

CHAPTER 5 : DISORDER IN THE FAMILY

Letters 1889–1955 contains Mann's letter of January 6, 1925, to Herbert Eulenberg; of May 7, 1925, to Erika Mann; of July 12, 1948, to Theodor W. Adorno; of July 22, 1939, and of November 12, 1948, with a reference to Christopher Isherwood, to Klaus Mann. *Briefe* contains the August 1925 letter about the marriage essay and the October 19, 1927, letter about Klaus Heuser. Other correspondence is quoted from *Thomas Mann an Ernst Bertram* and *The Correspondence of Thomas Mann*.

Also quoted are *Diaries 1918–1939; Tagebücher 1940–43; Tagebücher 1949–50*; and *Tagebücher 1953–55*.

Also cited are Thomas Mann, "Kleist's *Amphitryon*" (1926), in *Essays of Three Decades*; "Über die Ehe" (1925) in *Rede und Antwort*; "Unterwegs" (1925) in *Über mich selbst*; and "A Brother" (1938) in *Order of the Day*.

Also cited are Katia Mann, *Unwritten Memories*; Klaus Mann, *The Turning Point* and *The Pious Dance* (1925), translated by Laurence Senelick (New York, 1987); and "Kindernovelle" (1926) in *Maskenscherz*, edited by Uwe Naumann (Munich, 1990); interviews with Thomas and Klaus Mann in *Uhu: Das Magazin der 20er Jahre*, edited by Christopher Ferber (Berlin, 1979); Michael Mann, "Truth and Poetry in Thomas Mann's Works," included in *Thomas Mann: Ein Kolloquium*, edited by Hans H. Schulte and Gerald Chapple (Bonn, 1978); and Golo Mann, *Reminiscences and Reflections*.

Also cited are Marianne Krüll, *Im Netz der Zauberer: Eine andere Geschichte der Familie Mann* (Frankfurt, 1990); Glenway Wescott, *Continual Lessons* (New York, 1990); Roland Barthes, *Incidents*, translated by Richard Howard (Berkeley, 1992); Lionel M. Rolfe, *The Menuhins: A Family Odyssey* (North Hollywood, 1978); Frederic Morton, "Interview with Thomas and Katia Mann," the *New York Times* (June 1955); and interviews with Elisabeth Mann Borgese, Fritz Landshoff, William Koshland, Richard Plant, Helen Wolff, and Christiane Zimmer by the author.

CHAPTER 6 : "THE UNLOVED ONE"

Letters 1889–1955 contains Mann's letter of January 6, 1925, to Herbert Eulenburg, citing Wassermann's praise; of January 20, 1930, to André Gide; of February 20, 1934, to Karl Kerényi; of March 9, 1943, to Klaus Mann, concerning Gide; of May 26, 1943, to Agnes Meyer; of June 25, 1944, to Klaus Mann, concerning Hesse; of March 1, 1945, to Bruno Walter, concerning James Joyce; of October 8, 1950, to Klaus W. Jonas, concerning his literary status; of April 18, 1951, to Alvin Johnson, concerning Hermann Broch; of August 28, 1951, to Irita van Doren; and of January 19, 1952, to A. M. Frey, concerning himself as "a great unloved name."

Diaries 1918–1939 contains the April 6, 1933 comment on D. H. Lawrence; the September 21, 1935 remarks about Ida Herz; and the September 15, 1937 comments about Hesse. Also cited are *Tagebücher 1944–46* for the March 9, 1944 discussion of Hesse. *Tagebücher 1949–50* includes his tribute to Joseph Conrad; his August 8, 1950, attraction to "even a girl"; and his criticisms of Agnes E. Meyer. *Tagebücher 1951–52* contains his January 26, 1951, comments on "Catholic fascism."

Mann's letter to Alfred A. Knopf and H. T. Lowe-Porter's letter to Knopf are both contained in the Knopf archives. His letter to Marguerite Yourcenar is contained in the Harvard University Mann Archive. His letter to Bruno Walter on Walter's seventieth birthday (1946) is included in *Altes und Neues*. His letters to Hermann Hesse in *The Hesse-Mann Letters*; and to Erich Kahler in *An Exceptional Friendship, the Correspondence of Thomas Mann and Erich Kahler*, trans. Richard and Clara Winston (Ithaca, 1975).

Also cited are Thomas Mann, "Joseph Conrad's *The Secret Agent*" (1926), in *Past Masters and Other Papers*; "Homage" (1940), in *The Castle*, translated by Willa and Edwin Muir with additional materials translated by Eithne Wilkins and Ernst Kaiser (New York, 1964); "Gide's Unending Search for Harmony"; "*Ein Wort hierzu*" (foreword to Klaus W. Jonas, *Fifty Years of Thomas Mann Studies*) (1953), in *Die Forderung des Tages*; and "*Tischrede bei der Feier des fünfzigsten Geburtstheft*" (1925), in *Altes und Neues*. Mann's review of Heinrich Mann's *The Big Deal* is included in *The Correspondence of Heinrich Mann*; his review of André Gide's *Si le grain ne meurt* in *Ein Appell an die Vernunft*.

Also cited are Hans Mayer, *Thomas Mann: Werk und Entwicklung* (Berlin, 1950); Martha Musil, quoted in Karl Corino, *Robert Musil: Leben und Werk in Bildern und Texten* (Hamburg, 1988); Hermann Hesse, *Das Glasperlenspiel* (Zurich, 1943); Inge Jens, "*Es kenne mich die Welt, auf dass sie mir verzeihe*": Thomas Mann in Seinen Tagebüchern* (Frankfurt, n.d.); Katia Mann, *Unwritten Memories*; Alfred Kerr, quoted in *Thomas Mann, Sehr Menschlich*; Heinrich Mann, "My Brother," and Harry Levin, "Joseph the Provider," both in *The Stature of Thomas Mann*; Marcel Reich-Ranicki, *Thomas Mann and His Family*; Mann's interview about Freud, quoted in Wolfgang Michael, "*Thomas Mann auf dem Wege zu Freud*," *MLN* 45 (1950); D. H. Lawrence, "German Books: Thomas Mann," in *Phoenix: The Posthumous Papers of D. H. Lawrence*, edited and with an introduction by Edward D. McDonald (London, 1961), and "Herman Melville's *Moby Dick*" and

"Whitman," in *Studies in Classic American Literature* (New York, 1971); see on the subject of Lawrence and Whitman Anthony Heilbut, "All Mixed Up," in *The Nation* (February 9, 1985); Franz Kafka, *Letters to Friends, Family, and Editors*, edited by Max Brod, translated by Richard and Clara Winston (New York, 1977), and *Tagebücher* (Frankfurt, 1992); Ernst Pawel, *The Nightmare of Reason: A Life of Franz Kafka* (New York, 1984); and Martin Green, *The von Richthofen Sisters.*

CHAPTER 7 : A POLITICAL LIGHT

Letters 1889–1955, contains Mann's letter of January 21, 1925, to Josef Ponten; of February 22, 1925, to Julius Bab; of November 6, 1925, to Erika Mann; of May 25, 1926, to Ernst Fischer; of March 11, 1928, to Willy Haas; of January 20, 1930, to André Gide.

The Correspondence of Heinrich Mann and Thomas Mann contains Heinrich's 1927 letter to Thomas and the 1938 reference to Ponten. *Diaries 1918–1939*, contains the April 21, 1933, reference to Erasmus and the September 8, 1933, reference to Nazi culture.

Tagebücher 1949–50 contains several references to American popular culture; there are twenty-two citations of Jack Benny in 1949 alone. *Tagebücher 1951–52* contains the January 16, 1952, reference to Stephen Spender. (Queried in 1994 over the WNYC-AM radio program *New York and Company*, Spender said he had no memory of attacking Mann, but that he would have had Mann been a Communist.)

Also cited are Thomas Mann, *"Zum 60. Geburtstag Ricarda Huchs"* (1924), in *Altes und Neues*; "Cosmopolitanism" (1926) and "Culture and Socialism" (1928), in *Past Masters and Other Papers*; "Mario and the Magician" (1930) in *Stories of Three Decades*; "Lessing" (1929) and "Platen" (1930) in *Essays of Three Decades*; "Lübeck as a Way of Life and Thought"; "An Appeal to Reason" (1930) in *Order of the Day*; *"München als Kulturzentrum"* (1927) and *"Der Künstler und die Gesellschaft"* (1952) in *Altes und Neues*; "Mein Sommerhaus" (1931) and "Rede in Stockholm" (1929), both in *Über mich selbst*; and foreword to the 1948 edition of *Joseph and His Brothers* (New York, 1978). *"Pariser Rechenschaft,"* in *Über mich selbst*, contains the remark that sartorial elegance should be praised. His depictions of "mechanical mysticism" and "technological romanticism" are from "An Address on America's Entry into the War" (1941) in *An die gesittete Welt*. His 1928 tribute to Magnus Hirschfeld and 1930 protest against Paragraph 175 are in *Ein Appell an die Vernunft*.

Ernst Bertram's comment about Mann's antifascism is quoted in Bürgin and Mayer, *Thomas Mann: A Chronicle of His Life.*

Also cited are *The Correspondence of Walter Benjamin*, edited and annotated by Gershom Scholem and Theodor W. Adorno, translated by Manfred R. Jacobson and Evelyn M. Jacobson (Chicago, 1994); George Grosz, *A Little Yes and a Big No*; Klaus Mann, *The Turning Point*; Bruno Walter, "Recollections of Thomas Mann," in *The Stature of Thomas Mann*; and Arnolt Bronnen, *Arnolt Bronnen gibt zu Protokoll* (Hamburg, 1954); Judith Marcus, *Georg Lukács and Thomas Mann*; and *"Die Enthüllung des Jahres: Thomas Mann und der Kellner,"* *Bunte* (December 21, 1991).

CHAPTER 8 : EXILE

Letters 1889–1955 contains Mann's letter of November 6, 1896, concerning his "plagiarism" of Jakob Wassermann to Korfiz Holm; of January 8, 1932, concerning new literary prospects, to "Unknown"; of June 22, 1932, concerning right-wing youth, to Walter Perl; of July 30, 1932, to Count Hermann Keyserling; of March 13, 1933, to Lavinia Mazzucchetti; of May 17, 1933, to Albert Einstein; of June 12, 1933, concerning Hauptmann's silence, to Alexander M. Frey;

of August 19, 1933, to Gottfried Bermann-Fischer; of December 23, 1933, concerning "the world as an 'extra,' " to Julius Meier-Graefe; of January 1, 1934, concerning "irnational" politics, to Alexander M. Frey; of January 9, 1934, and July 20, 1934, to Ernst Bertram; of January 20, 1934, to Alfred A. Knopf; of May 16, 1934, concerning the supremacy of fiction over music, to René Schickele (a similar point is made in *"München als Kulturzentrum"*); of February 3, 1936, to Eduard Korrodi; and of August 1, 1936, to Alexei Vasilievich Koltsov; and of August 19, 1943, to Konrad Kellen. Mann's July 1933 letter to Hans Pfitzner is quoted in *Pro and Contra Wagner*.

The Correspondence of Heinrich Mann and Thomas Mann contains Thomas's addresses on Heinrich's sixtieth and seventieth birthdays.

Diaries 1918–1939 contains all journal notes of 1933 and 1934. *Tagebücher 1933–1934* contains his comments on right-wing Jews. *Tagebücher 1937–39* contains the October 13, 1937, attack on a Jewish cabal. *Tagebücher 1951–52* contains his June 6, 1952, remark about Erika's fear of the FBI.

Mann's comment about the Geneva conference is quoted in Bürgin and Mayer, *Thomas Mann: A Chronicle of His Life*.

Also quoted are Thomas Mann, "Freud's Position in the History of Modern Thought" (1929), in *Past Masters*; "Goethe's Career as a Man of Letters" (1932), "Goethe as Representative of the Bourgeois Age" (1932), and "Sufferings and Greatness of Richard Wagner" (1933), all three in *Essays of Three Decades*; *"Die geistige Situation des Schriftstellers in unserer Zeit"* (1930), in *The Living Age* 339 (1930); *"Rede vor Arbeiten in Wien"* (1932), in *GW*, volume 11; "Europe Beware" (*"Achtung! Europa"*) (1935) and *"Mass und Wert"* (1937) in *Order of the Day*; "The Dangers Facing Democracy" (1940), in *An die gesittete Welt; Lotte in Weimar* (1939), translated by H. T. Lowe-Porter as *The Beloved Returns* (1940).

Also cited are "A Protest from Richard Wagner's Own City of Munich," in *Pro and Contra Wagner*; Salka Viertel, *The Kindness of Strangers* (New York, 1969); and Bertolt Brecht, *Journals 1934–1956*, translated by Hugh Rorrison, edited by John Willett, with its June 8, 1942, reference to "the circle around Thomas Mann" (New York, 1993).

CHAPTER 9 : A MYTH FOR OUR TIME

Letters 1889–1955 contains Mann's letter of May 23, 1935, comparing Joseph to Hanno Buddenbrook, to Louise Servicen, his French translator; of October 31, 1935, concerning Proust, to René Schickele; of December 30, 1945, concerning "mythic clichés," to Theodor W. Adorno; of May 30, 1951, to Julius Bab; of August 28, 1951, to Irita van Doren; and of August 22, 1954, concerning Faulkner, to Agnes E. Meyer.

Briefe, volume 2, contains his letter of May 5, 1942, concerning the reunion of Joseph and Benjamin, and of May 14, 1942, concerning his pleasure writing the novel, both to Agnes E. Meyer. *Briefe*, volume 3, contains his letter of March 11, 1951, concerning Felix Krull's language, to Alfred Neumann. *The Correspondence of Heinrich Mann and Thomas Mann* contains their letters about *Lotte in Weimar*.

All diary references are from *Tagebücher 1949–50*, and *Tagebücher 1951–52*.

Also cited are *"Pariser Rechenschaft"* and "A Living and Human Reality" (1932) in *An die gesittete Welt; Joseph and His Brothers*, comprising *The Tales of Jacob* (1933), *Young Joseph* (1934), *Joseph in Egypt* (1936), and *Joseph the Provider* (1943); *The Tables of the Law* (1945); "Theodor Storm" (1930), in *Essays of Three Decades*; "Bernard Shaw"; "How to Win the Peace" (1942), in *Atlantic Monthly*, February 1942; *Confessions of Felix Krull, Confidence Man: The Early Years* (1954), translated by Denver Lindley (New York, 1954); foreword (1954) to Heinrich von Kleist, *"The Marquise of O" and Other Stories*, translated by Martin Greenberg (New York, 1962); "Chekhov"

(1954), translated by Tania and James Stern, in *Last Essays*; foreword to *Die schönsten Erzählungen der Welt* (1955) in *Die Forderung des Tages*. Mann's annotation of Alfred Bäumler is quoted in T. J. Reed, *The Uses of Tradition*, translation by this author.

The April 1938 remarks "Where I am is Germany" etc. are quoted in Herbert Lehnert, "Thomas Mann in Exile, 1933–1938," in *Germanic Review* (New York), November 1963.

Also cited are Brecht, *Journals 1934–1955*; Klaus Mann, "Der Vater lacht" (1925) in *Maskenscherz*; Marquis Childs, "Thomas Mann: Germany's Foremost Literary Exile Speaks Now for Freedom and Democracy in America," *Life*, April 17, 1939; Bruno Walter, "Recollections of Thomas Mann"; Glenway Wescott, *Images of Truth*; F. O. Matthiessen, *From the Heart of Europe* (New York, 1948); and interviews with Gore Vidal and Brigitte and Franz Westermeier by author.

POSTSCRIPT

Letters 1889–1955 contains Mann's letter of November 30, 1938, to Anna Jacobson; of September 15, 1942, to Friedericke Zweig; of July 30, 1948, to Werner Schmitz, concerning Ernst Bertram; of September 7, 1948, and February 9, 1955, to Agnes E. Meyer; of August 27, 1949, to Paul Olberg; of January 9, 1950, to Adorno; of March 19, 1950, to Maximilian Brantl; of May 1, 1955, to Guido Devescovi, concerning Heinrich; and of August 9, 1955, to the Michael Mann family.

His letters to Kahler are included in *An Exceptional Friendship*; and to Karl Kerényi in *Myth and Humanism*. His letter to Walter Ulbricht is quoted in Henry Hatfield, *From the Magic Mountain: Mann's Later Masterpieces* (Ithaca, 1979).

All diary passages are from *Tagebücher 1946–1948*, perhaps the richest volume, which also contains a list of his favorite recordings, his memories of Ludwig Hardt, his correspondence with Walter Lippmann, and his first speeches attacking HUAC; *Tagebücher 1949–1950*; and *Tagebücher 1951–1952*, which contains his correspondence with Alfred A. Knopf.

Also cited are "A Brother" (1938) in *Order of the Day*; his description of his operation in *The Story of a Novel*; "The War and the Future" (1943) and "Germany and the Germans" (1945) in *Literary Lectures Presented at the Library of Congress* (Washington, 1973); "Stefan Zweig zum zehnten Todestag" (1952), "Vorwort zu einem Gedächtnisbuch fur Klaus Mann" (1950), "Der Künstler und die Gesellschaft" (1952) in *Altes und Neues*; and "Zum Tode von Albert Einstein" (1955) in *Rede und Antwort* (Frankfurt, 1987).

Also cited are Golo Mann, "Memories of My Father," and *Reminiscences and Reflections*; Erika Mann, *The Last Year of Thomas Mann*, trans. Richard Graves (Freeport, 1970); Bertolt Brecht, "Über die Verführung von Engeln," translated by Michael Morley, and "Sauna und Beischlaf," translated by the author, in *Gesammelte Werke*, Supplement II (Berlin, 1982); "Mann Declares He's Still 'Loyal Son of the West,' " New York *Herald Tribune*, December 31, 1952.

SELECTED BIBLIOGRAPHY

BY THOMAS MANN

Aufsätze, Reden, Essays 1893–1913, 1914–1918, 1919–1925, 3 vols., edited by Harry Matter. Berlin, 1983–86.

Frage und Antwort. Interviews mit Thomas Mann 1909–1955, edited by Volkmar Hansen and Gert Heine. Hamburg, 1983.

Gesammelte Werke, 13 vols., edited by Hans Bürgin and Peter de Mendelssohn. Frankfurt, 1990.

Gesammelte Werke in Einzelbände. Frankfurter Ausgabe der Werke Thomas Manns, edited by Peter de Mendelssohn. Frankfurt, 1980.

Notizbücher 1–6 and 7–12, 2 vols., edited by Hans Wysling and Yvonne Schmidlin. Frankfurt, 1991–92.

Tagebücher, 1918–21, 1933–34, 1935–36, 1937–39, 1940–43, edited by Peter de Mendelssohn. Frankfurt, 1979–82.

Tagebücher, 1944–46, 1946–48, 1949–50, 1951–52, 1953–55, edited by Inge Jens. Frankfurt, 1986–95.

Werke, paperback edition in 12 vols. Frankfurt, 1967; new edition, 1975.

CORRESPONDENCE

Briefe 1889–1955 und Nachlese, 3 vols., edited by Erika Mann. Frankfurt, 1961–65.

Briefe an Otto Grautoff und Ida Boy-Ed, edited by Peter de Mendelssohn. Frankfurt, 1975.

Briefwechsel mit Autoren, edited by Hans Wysling. Frankfurt, 1988.

Briefwechsel mit seinen Verleger Gottfried Bermann Fischer 1932–1955, edited by Peter de Mendelssohn. Frankfurt, 1973.

Die Briefe Thomas Manns. Regesten und Register, 5 vols., edited by Hans Bürgin, Hans-Otto Mayer, Gert Heine, and Yvonne Schmidlin. Frankfurt, 1973.

Thomas Mann an Ernst Bertram. Briefe aus den Jahren 1919–1955, edited by Inge Jens. Pfullingen, 1960.

Thomas Mann–Agnes E. Meyer Briefwechsel, edited by Hans Rudolf Vaget. Hamburg, 1986.
Thomas Mann–Heinrich Mann Briefwechsel 1900–1949, edited by Hans Wysling. Frankfurt, 1968.
Thomas Mann–Heinrich Mann Briefwechsel. Frankfurt, 1975; new edition, 1984.

IN ENGLISH

All published in New York and, unless otherwise stated, translated by Helen T. Lowe-Porter.

Royal Highness, translated by A. Cecil Curtiss, 1916, 1939. Preface to 1939 edition translated by H. T. Lowe-Porter.
Buddenbrooks, 1924. New translation by John E. Woods, 1993.
Death in Venice and Other Stories, 1925.
The Magic Mountain, 1927. New translation by John E. Woods, 1996.
Children and Fools, 1928.
Three Essays, 1929.
Mario and the Magician, 1931.
Joseph and His Brothers, 1933–44; in one edition with preface by Thomas Mann, 1948.
The Tales of Jacob (published under the title *Joseph and His Brothers*), 1934.
Young Joseph, 1935.
Joseph in Egypt, in two vols., 1938.
Joseph the Provider, 1944.
Stories of Three Decades, with preface by Thomas Mann, 1936.
Freud, Goethe, Wagner, 1937.
An Exchange of Letters, 1937.
This Peace: A Lecture, 1938.
The Coming Victory of Democracy: A Lecture, translated by Agnes E. Meyer, 1938.
This War: A Lecture, translated by Eric Sutton, 1940.
The Beloved Returns, 1940.
The Transposed Heads, 1941.
Order of the Day, essays with new preface by Thomas Mann, 1942.
Listen, Germany! Short-Wave Broadcasts to Germany, 1943.
The Tables of the Law, 1945.
Essays of Three Decades, 1947.
Doctor Faustus, 1948.
The Holy Sinner, 1951.
The Black Swan, translated by Willard R. Trask, 1954.
Confessions of Felix Krull, Confidence Man: The Early Years, translated by Denver Linley, 1955.
Last Essays, translated by Richard and Clara Winston and Tania and James Stern, 1959.
A Sketch of My Life, 1960.
Letters to Paul Amann, edited by Herbert Wegener, translated by Richard Winston and Clara Winston. Middletown, 1960.
The Story of a Novel, translated by Richard and Clara Winston. 1961.
Letters of Thomas Mann 1889–1955, 2 vols., selected and translated by Richard and Clara Winston. 1971.
An Exceptional Friendship: The Correspondence of Thomas Mann and Erich Kahler, translated by Richard and Clara Winston. Ithaca, 1975.
Mythology and Humanism: The Correspondence of Thomas Mann and Karl Kerényi, translated by Alexander Gelley. Ithaca, 1975.

The Hesse–Mann Letters, edited by Anni Carlsson and Volker Michels, translated by Ralph Manheim, with a foreword by Theodore Ziolkowski. New York, 1976.

Diaries 1918–39, edited by Hermann Kesten, translated by Richard and Clara Winston. 1982.

Reflections of a Nonpolitical Man, translated by Walter D. Morris. 1983.

Death in Venice and Other Stories, translated by David Luke. 1988.

The Correspondence of Heinrich Mann and Thomas Mann, translated by Donald Renau. Berkeley, forthcoming.

Pro and Contra Wagner (edited by Patrick Carnegy), translated by Allen Blunden, with an introduction by Erich Heller. Chicago, 1985.

BY OTHER MEMBERS OF THE MANN FAMILY

ERIKA MANN

Briefe und Antworten, 1922–1950, 1951–1969, 2 vols., edited by Anna Zanco Prestel. Munich, 1988.

The Last Year of Thomas Mann, translated by Richard Graves. Freeport, 1970.

GOLO MANN

"Memories of My Father." *Universitas* 11 (1969).

Reminiscences and Reflections: Growing Up in Germany, translated by Krishna Winston, introduction by Peter Demetz. New York, 1991.

HEINRICH MANN

The Blue Angel (Professor Unrat), no translator cited. New York, 1979.

Ein Zeitalter wird besichtigt. Stockholm, 1946.

Gesammelte Werke, 24 vols. Berlin and Weimar, 1965–73.

Man of Straw (Der Untertan), no translator cited. New York, 1984.

Young Henry of Navarre, translated by Eric Sutton. New York, 1979.

JULIA MANN

Aus Dodos Kindheit. Konstanz, 1903.

KATIA MANN

Unwritten Memories, edited by Elisabeth Plessen and Michael Mann, translated by Hunter Hannum and Hildegarde Hannum. New York, 1975.

KLAUS MANN

Abenteuer des Brautpaars (stories), edited by Martin Gregor-Dellin. Munich, 1976.
Briefe und Antworten 1922–1949, edited by Martin Gregor-Dellin. Munich, 1987.
Mephisto, translated by Robin Smith. New York, 1977.
The Pious Dance, translated by Laurence Senelick. New York, 1987.
The Turning Point: Thirty-Five Years in This Century, with a foreword by Shelley L. Frisch. New York, 1984.

MICHAEL MANN

"Thomas Mann and the United States of America: A Twenty-Year Relationship," in *Perspectives and Personalities: Studies in Modern German Literature Honoring Claude Hill*, edited by Ralph Ley et al. Heidelberg, 1978.

MONIKA MANN

Past and Present, translated by Frances F. Reid and Ruth Hein. New York, 1960.

VICTOR MANN

Wir Waren Fünf: Bildnis der Familie Mann. Konstanz, 1949.

BOOKS AND ARTICLES ABOUT THOMAS MANN
(A VERY SELECTIVE LIST)

Amery, Jean. "Venezianische Zaubereien: Luchino Visconti und sein *Der Tod in Venedig.*" *Merkur* 25 (1971).
Baer, Lydia. *The Concept and Function of Death in the Works of Thomas Mann.* Freiburg, 1932.
Barnouw, Dagmar. *Weimar Intellectuals and the Threat of Modernity.* Bloomington, 1988.
Baron, Frank. "Sensuality and Morality in Thomas Mann's *Tod in Venedig.*" *Germanic Review* 45 (1970).
Basilius, H. A. "Thomas Mann's Use of Musical Structure and Techniques in Tonio Kröger." *Germanic Review* 19 (1944).
Baumgart, Reinhard. *Das Ironische und die Ironie in den Werken Thomas Manns.* Munich, 1964.
Berendsohn, Walter A. *Thomas Mann: Artist and Partisan in Troubled Times*, translated by George C. Buck. University, Alabama, 1975.
———. *Thomas Mann und die Seinen: Portrait einer literarischen Familie.* Bern, 1973.
Berlin, Jeffrey B., editor, *Approaches to Teaching Mann's "Death in Venice" and Other Short Fiction.* New York, 1992.
Bermann-Fischer, Gottfried, and Brigitte Bermann-Fischer. *Briefwechsel mit Autoren*, edited by Reiner Stach. Frankfurt, 1990.

Bernini, Cornelia, et al., editors. *Internationales Thomas Mann–Kolloquium 1986 in Lübeck*. Bern, 1987.

Blissett, William. "Thomas Mann: The Last Wagnerite." *Germanic Review* 35 (1960).

Bloom, Harold, editor. *Thomas Mann*. New York, 1986.

Böhm, Karl Werner. *Zwischen Selbstzucht und Verlangen: Thomas Mann und das Stigma Homosexualität*. Würzburg, 1991.

Bolduc, Stevie Anne. "A Study of Intertexuality: Thomas Mann's 'Tristan' and Richard Wagner's Tristan und Isolde." *Rocky Mountain Review of Language and Literature* 37 (1983).

Brennan, Joseph G. *Thomas Mann's World*. New York, 1962.

Bürgin, Hans. *Das Werk Thomas Manns: Eine Bibliographie*. Frankfurt, 1989.

Bürgin, Hans, and Hans-Otto Mayer. *Thomas Mann: A Chronicle of His Life*, translated by Eugene Dobson. University, Alabama, 1969.

Busch, Frank. *August Graf von Platen–Thomas Mann: Zeichen und Gefühle*. Munich, 1987.

Carstensen, Richard. *Thomas Mann, sehr menschlich: Streiflichter-Schlaglichter*. 2nd edition. Lübeck, 1975.

Cerf, Steven R. "Mann and Myth. The Author's Response to the *Ring*." *Opera News* 54 (1990).

Corngold, Stanley. *The Fate of the Self: German Writers and French Theory*. New York, 1986.

Corngold, Stanley, Victor Lange, and Theodore Ziolkowski, editors. *Thomas Mann, 1875–1955*. Princeton, 1975.

Craig, Gordon A. *The Germans*. New York, 1982.

Crick, Joyce. "Thomas Mann and Psycho-analysis: The Turning Point." *Literature and Psychology* 10 (1960).

DelCaro, Adrian. "The Political Apprentice: Thomas Mann's Reception of Nietzsche." *Studies in the Humanities* 12 (1985).

Eloesser, Arthur. *Thomas Mann: Sein Leben und Werk*. Berlin, 1925.

Exner, Richard. " 'The Secrets of My Life' or 'Holding On to the Fleeting Day': Thomas Mann's Diaries, 1933–1936." *World Literature Today* (Spring 1979).

Ezergailis, Inta M., editor. *Critical Essays on Thomas Mann*. Boston, 1988.

———. *Male and Female: An Approach to Thomas Mann's Dialectic*. The Hague, 1975.

Fetzer, John Francis. *Music, Love, Death, and Mann's "Doctor Faustus."* Columbia, 1990.

Feuerlicht, Ignace. *Thomas Mann*. New York, 1968.

———. "Thomas Mann and Homoeroticism." *Germanic Review* 57 (1982).

Fischer, Samuel, and Hedwig Fischer. *Briefwechsel mit Autoren*, edited by Dierk Rodewald and Corinna Fiedler. Frankfurt, 1990.

Flanner, Janet. "Goethe in Hollywood." *New Yorker* (December 13 and 20, 1941).

Franke, Peter Robert. *Der Tod des Hans Hansens: Unbekannte Dokumente aus der Jugend von Thomas Mann*. Lübeck, 1991.

Garland, Mary. *The Oxford Companion to German Literature*, 2nd edition. Oxford, 1986.

Gay, Peter. *Weimar Culture: The Outsider as Insider*. New York, 1968.

Gillespie, Gerald. "The Ways of Hermes in the Works of Thomas Mann." *Sinn und Symbol: Festschrift für Joseph P. Strelka zum 60. Geburtstag*, edited by Karl Konrad Pohlheim. Bern, 1987.

Goldman, Harvey. *Max Weber and Thomas Mann: Calling and the Shaping of the Self*. Berkeley, 1988.

———. *Politics, Death, and the Devil: Self and Power in Max Weber and Thomas Mann*. Berkeley, 1992.

Gray, Ronald. *The German Tradition in Literature, 1871–1945*. Cambridge, 1965.

Gronicka, André von. *Thomas Mann: Profile and Perspectives*. New York, 1970.

Grosz, George. *A Little Yes and a Big No*. Translated by Lola Sachs Dorin. New York, 1945.

Hage, Volker. *Eine Liebe fürs Leben. Thomas Mann und Travemünde.* Hamburg, 1993.

Hamburger, Michael. *Contraries: Studies in German Literature.* New York, 1970.

Hamilton, Nigel. *The Brothers Mann: The Lives of Heinrich and Thomas Mann, 1871–1950 and 1875–1955.* New York, 1979.

Hansen, Volkar. *Thomas Manns Heine-Rezeption.* Hamburg, 1983.

Hatfield, Henry. *From "The Magic Mountain": Mann's Later Masterpieces.* Ithaca, 1979.

———. *Thomas Mann.* New York, 1962.

———, editor. *Thomas Mann: A Collection of Critical Essays.* Englewood Cliffs, 1964.

———. "Thomas Mann and America," in *The Legacy of the German Refugee Intellectuals*, edited by Robert Boyers. New York, 1972.

Hayes, Tom, and Lee Quinby. "The Aporia of Bourgeois Art: Desire in Thomas Mann's *Death in Venice.*" *Criticism* 31 (1990).

Hayman, Ronald. *Thomas Mann: A Biography.* New York, 1995.

Heilbut, Anthony. *Exiled in Paradise: German Refugee Artists and Intellectuals in America from the 1930s to the Present.* New York, 1984.

Hollingdale, R. J. *Thomas Mann: A Critical Study.* Lewisburg, 1971.

Hughes, H. Stuart. *Consciousness and Society: The Reconstruction of European Social Thought, 1890–1930.* New York, 1958.

Hughes, Kenneth, editor. *Thomas Mann in Context: Papers of the Clark University Centennial Colloquium.* Worcester, 1978.

Jens, Inge. "Es kenne mich, die Welt, auf dass sie mir verzeihe." *Thomas Mann in Seiner Tagebüchern.* Frankfurt, 1989.

Jonas, Ilsedore B. *Thomas Mann and Italy*, translated by Betty Crouse. University, Alabama, 1969.

Jonas, Klaus W. "The Making of a Thomas Mann Bibliography (1949–1989)." *Deutsche Vierteljahrsschrift für Literaturwissenschaft und Geistesgeschichte* 64 (1990).

———. *Die Thomas Mann–Literatur: Bibliographie der Kritik*, 1896–1955, 1956–75, 2 vols. Berlin, 1972, 1979.

Kaes, Anton, Martin Jay, and Edward Dimendberg, editors. *The Weimar Republic Sourcebook.* Berkeley, 1992.

Kahler, Erich. *The Orbit of Thomas Mann.* Princeton, 1969.

Karst, Roman. *Thomas Mann: Der Deutsche Zwiespalt.* Munich, 1987.

Kaufmann, Fritz. *Thomas Mann: The World as Will and Representation.* Boston, 1957.

Kesten, Hermann. *Der Geist der Unruhe.* Cologne, 1959.

Koch-Emmery, E. "Thomas Mann in English Translation." *German Life and Letters* 6 (1953).

Kohut, Heinz. "*Death in Venice* by Thomas Mann: A Story About the Disintegration of Artistic Sublimation," in Ruitenbeck, Hendrik M., editor, *Psychoanalysis and Literature.* New York, 1964.

Koestler, Arthur. *Arrow in the Blue.* New York, 1952.

Koopmann, Helmut. " 'German Culture Is Where I Am': Thomas Mann in Exile." *Studies in Twentieth Century Literature* 7 (1982).

———, editor. *Thomas Mann–Handbuch.* Stuttgart, 1990.

———. *Thomas Mann: Konstanten seines Literarischen Werks.* Göttingen, 1975.

Kroll, Fredric, and Klaus Täubert. *Sammlung der Kräfte: Klaus Mann–Biographie (1933–1934)*, vol. 1. Wiesbaden, 1992.

Krüll, Marianne. *Im Netz der Zauberer: Eine andere Geschichte der Familie Mann.* Zurich, 1991.

Lehnert, Herbert. "Thomas Mann in Exile, 1933–1938." *Germanic Review* 38 (1963).

———. "Thomas Mann in Princeton." *Germanic Review* 39 (1964).

———. "Thomas Mann und Schiller." Rice Institute Pamphlet: *Studies in Modern Languages* 47 (1960).

Lehnert, Herbert, and Peter C. Pfeiffer, editors. *Thomas Mann's "Doctor Faustus": A Novel at the Margin of Modernism*. Columbia, 1991.

Leser, Esther H. *Thomas Mann's Short Fiction: An Intellectual Biography*. Rutherford, 1989.

Lichtheim, George. *Europe in the Twentieth Century*. New York, 1972.

Linn, Rolf N. *Heinrich Mann*. New York, 1967.

Lubich, Frederick A. "Die Entfaltung der Dialektik von Logos und Eros in Thomas Manns *Tod in Venedig.*" *Colloquia Germanica* 18 (1985).

————. "Thomas Mann's Sexual Politics: Lost in Translation." Comparative Literature Studies 31, no. 2 (1994).

Lublinski, Samuel. *Der Ausgang der Moderne*. Edited by Gotthart Wunberg. Tübingen, 1976.

Lukács, Georg. *Thomas Mann*. Berlin, 1957.

Marcus, Judith. *Georg Lukács and Thomas Mann: A Study in the Sociology of Literature*. Amherst, 1987.

Martin, Robert K. "Walt Whitman and Thomas Mann." *Walt Whitman Quarterly Review* 4 (1987).

Matter, Harry. *Die Literatur über Thomas Mann: Eine Bibliographie, 1898–1969*, 2 vols. Berlin, 1972.

Mayer, Hans. *Outsiders: A Study in Life and Letters*, translated by D. Sweet. Cambridge, 1982.

————. *Thomas Mann*. Frankfurt, 1984.

McWilliams, James R. "The Failure of a Repression: Thomas Mann's *Tod in Venedig.*" *German Life and Letters* 20 (1967).

Mendelssohn Peter de. *Der Zauberer: Das Leben des deutschen Schriftstellers Thomas Mann*. Part 1. 1875–1918. Frankfurt, 1975.

————. *Der Zauberer: Das Leben des deutschen Schriftstellers Thomas Mann*. Jahre der Schwebe: 1919 und 1933. Nachgelassene Kapitel. Gesamtregister, edited by Albert von Schirnding. Frankfurt, 1992.

Meyer, Agnes E. *Out of These Roots: The Autobiography of an American Woman*. Boston, 1953.

Mosse, George L. *Nationalism and Sexuality: Respectability and Abnormal Sexuality in Modern Europe*. New York, 1985.

Neider, Charles, editor. *The Stature of Thomas Mann*. Freeport, 1968.

Newton, Caroline. "Thomas Mann and Sigmund Freud." *Princeton University Library Chronicle* 24 (1963).

Pike, Burton. "Thomas Mann and the Problematic Self." *Publications of the English Goethe Society* 37 (1966–67).

Prater, Donald. *Thomas Mann: A Life*. New York, 1995.

Prokosch, Frederic. *Voices: A Memoir*. New York, 1983.

Reed, T. J. "Text and History: *Tonio Kröger* and the Politics of Four Decades." *Publications of the English Goethe Society* 57 (1987).

————. "Thomas Mann, Heine, Schiller: The Mechanics of Self-Interpretation." *Neophilologus* 47 (1963).

————. *Thomas Mann: The Uses of Tradition*. Oxford, 1974.

————. "Thomas Mann: The Writer as Historian of His Time." *Modern Language Review* 71 (1976).

Reich-Ranicki, Marcel. *Thomas Mann and His Family*, translated by Ralph Manheim. London, 1990.

Scher, Steven Paul. *Verbal Music in German Literature*. New York, 1968.

Scherrer, Paul, and Hans Wysling, editors. *Quellenkritische Studien zum Werk Thomas Manns*. Bern, 1967.

Schröter, Klaus. "Literatur zu Thomas Mann um 1975." *Monatshefte* 69 (1977).

————. *Thomas Mann im Urteil seiner Zeit: Dokumente 1891 bis 1955*. Hamburg, 1969.

————. *Thomas Mann in Selbstzeugnissen und Bilddokumenten.* Reinbeck, 1975.

Schulte, Hans H., and Gerald Chapple, editors. *Thomas Mann: Ein Kolloquium.* Bonn, 1978.

Slochower, Harry. "Thomas Mann's *Death in Venice.*" *American Imago* 26 (1969).

Spalek, John, and Joseph Strelka, editors. *Deutsche Exilliteratur seit 1933,* vol. 1. Bern, 1976.

Spangenberg, Eberhard. *Karriere eines Romans: "Mephisto," Klaus Mann und Gustaf Gründgens.* 2nd ed. Munich, 1984.

Stevenhagen, Lee. "The Name Tadzio in *Der Tod in Venedig.*" *German Quarterly* 35 (1961).

Steakley, James D. *The Homosexual Emancipation Movement in Germany.* New York, 1975.

Stern, Fritz. *The Politics of Cultural Despair.* Berkeley, 1974.

Stock, Irvin. *Ironic out of Love: The Novels of Thomas Mann.* Jefferson, N. C., 1994.

Swales, Martin. "In Defense of Weimar: Thomas Mann and the Politics of Republicanism," in *Weimar Germany: Writers and Politics,* edited by Alan F. Bance. Edinburgh, 1982.

————. *Thomas Mann: A Study.* London, 1980.

Thirlwall, John C. *In Another Language: A Record of the Thirty-Year Relationship Between Thomas Mann and His American Translator, Helen Tracy Lowe-Porter.* New York, 1966.

Vaget, Hans Rudolf. *Thomas Mann: Kommentar zu Sämtlichen Erzählungen.* Munich, 1984.

Vaget, Hans Rudolf, and Dagmar Karnouw, eds. *Thomas Mann: Studien zu Fragen der Rezeption.* Bern, 1975.

Weigand, Hermann J. *The Magic Mountain: A Study of Thomas Mann's Novel "Der Zauberberg."* Chapel Hill, 1965.

Weiner, Marc A. "Silence, Sound and Song in *Der Tod in Venedig*: A Study in Psycho-social Repression." *Seminar* 23 (1987).

Wescott, Glenway. *Images of Truth.* New York, 1962.

White, Andrew. *Thomas Mann.* New York, 1965.

Winston, Richard. *Thomas Mann: The Making of an Artist, 1875–1911,* with an afterword by Clara Winston. New York, 1982.

Witte, Karsten. " 'Das ist echt! Eine Burleske!' Zur 'Tristan'-Novelle von Thomas Mann." *German Quarterly* 41 (1968).

Wysling, Hans. "Aschenbachs Werke: Archivalische Untersuchungen an einem Thomas Mann Satz." *Euphorion* 50 (1965).

————. *Narzissmus und illusionäre Existenzform: Zu den "Bekenntnissen des Hochstaplers Felix Krull."* Bern, 1982.

————. "Thomas Mann: Der Unpolitische in der Politik." *Neue Rundschau* 91 (1980).

Wysling, Hans, and Cornelia Bernini, editors. *Jahre des Unmuts: Thomas Manns Briefwechsel mit René Schickele, 1930–40.* Bern, 1992.

Wysling, Hans, and Yvonne Schmidlin. *Bild und Text bei Thomas Mann: Eine Dokumentation.* Bern, 1989.

————, eds. *Thomas Mann: Ern Leben in Bildern.* Zurich, 1994.

Yourcenar, Marguerite. "The Humanism of Thomas Mann." *Partisan Review*, Spring 1956.

INDEX

Page numbers in *italics* refer to illustrations.

PERMISSIONS ACKNOWLEDGMENTS

Grateful acknowledgment is made to the following for permission to reprint previously published and unpublished material:

Harry N. Abrams, Inc.: Excerpts from the *Thomas Mann Diaries*, copyright © 1977, 1978, 1979, 1980 by S. Fischer Verlag GmbH, Frankfurt am Main, West Germany; English translation copyright © 1982 by Harry N. Abrams, Inc. Reprinted by permission of Harry N. Abrams, Inc.

Stefan Brecht: The poem "On Seducing Angels" by Bertolt Brecht, copyright © 1990 by Stefan Brecht. Reprinted by permission of Stefan Brecht, administered by Jerry Couture, Esq., Fietelson, Lasky and Aslan.

S. Fischer Verlag GmbH: Excerpts from *Tagebucher 1949–1950*; *Tagebucher 1951–1952*; *Briefe*; *Correspondence with Otto Grautoff and Ida Boy*; excerpts from "Pariser Rechenschaft," "Bilse und Ich," "Michelangelo," "Friedrich," "Review of André Gide's 'Si le Grain Ne Meurt,'" "Attack on Paragraph 175," "Zur Judischen Frage," "Von Deutscher Republik" from *Notizbucher* by Thomas Mann. Reprinted by permission of S. Fischer Verlag GmbH, Frankfurt am Main.

Alfred A. Knopf, Inc. and S. Fischer Verlag GmbH: Excerpts from *Order of the Day: Political Essays and Speeches* by Thomas Mann, translated by H. T. Lowe-Porter, copyright © 1937, 1938, 1939, 1940, 1941, 1942 by Alfred A. Knopf, Inc. Rights in the United Kingdom administered by S. Fischer Verlag GmbH, Frankfurt am Main. Reprinted by permission of Alfred A. Knopf, Inc., and S. Fischer Verlag GmbH.

Alfred A. Knopf, Inc. and Secker & Warburg Ltd.: Excerpts from *Letters of Thomas Mann 1889–1955* by Thomas Mann, translated by Richard and Clara Winston, copyright © 1970 by Alfred A. Knopf, Inc.; excerpts from *Stories of Three Decades* by Thomas Mann, translated by H. T. Lowe-Porter, copyright © 1930, 1931, 1934, 1935, 1936 by Alfred A. Knopf, Inc.; excerpts from *A Sketch of My Life* by Thomas Mann, translated by H. T. Lowe-Porter, published in 1960 by Alfred A. Knopf, Inc., all rights reserved; excerpts from *Joseph and His Brothers* by Thomas Mann, translated by H. T. Lowe-Porter, copyright © 1934, 1935, 1938, 1944, 1948 by Alfred A. Knopf, Inc.; excerpts from *Doctor Faustus* by Thomas Mann, translated by H. T. Lowe-Porter, copyright © 1948 by Alfred A. Knopf, Inc.; excerpts from *The Beloved Returns* by Thomas Mann, translated by H. T. Lowe-Porter, copyright © 1940 (copyright renewed 1968) by Alfred A. Knopf, Inc.; excerpts from *The Magic Mountain* by Thomas Mann, translated by H. T. Lowe-Porter, copyright © 1927 (copyright renewed 1955) by Alfred A. Knopf, Inc., copyright © 1952 by Thomas Mann; excerpts from *Buddenbrooks* by Thomas Mann, translated by H. T. Lowe-Porter, copyright © 1924 (copyright renewed 1952) by Alfred A. Knopf, Inc.; excerpts from *Essays of Three Decades* by Thomas Mann, translated by H. T. Lowe-Porter, copyright © 1929, 1933, 1937, 1947 by Alfred A. Knopf, Inc.; excerpts from *Confessions of Felix Krull, Confidence Man* by Thomas Mann, translated by Denver Lindley, copyright © 1955 by Alfred A. Knopf, Inc. Rights in the United Kingdom administered by Secker & Warburg Ltd., London. Reprinted by permission of Alfred A. Knopf, Inc., and Secker & Warburg Ltd., an imprint of Reed Consumer Books Ltd.

ILLUSTRATION CREDITS

A NOTE ON THE TYPE

The text of this book is set in Garamond No. 3. It is not a true copy
of any of the designs of Claude Garamond (1480–1561), but an adaptation of his types, which set the European standard for two centuries.
It probably owes as much to the designs of Jean Jannon, a Protestant
printer working in Sedan in the early seventeenth century, who had
worked with Garamond's romans earlier, in Paris, and who was denied
their use because of the Catholic censorship. Jannon's matrices came
into the possession of the Imprimerie Nationale, where they were
thought to be by Garamond himself, and so described when the Imprimerie revived the type in 1900. This particular version is based on
an adaptation by Morris Fuller Benton.

Composed by PennSet, Inc., Bloomsburg, Pennsylvania
Printed and bound by Quebecor Martinsburg,
Martinsburg, West Virginia
Designed by Dorothy S. Baker